But if in your fear you would seek only love's peace and love's pleasure,

Then it is better for you that you cover your nakedness
and pass out of love's threshing-floor,

Into the seasonless world where you shall laugh, but not all of
your laughter, and weep, but not all of your tears…

Love has no other desire but to fulfill itself.

But if you love and must needs have desires, let these be your desires:

To melt and be like a running brook that sings its melody to the night.

To know the pain of too much tenderness.

To be wounded by your own understanding of love;

And to bleed willingly and joyfully.

To wake at dawn with a winged heart and give thanks
for another day of loving;

To rest at the noon hour and meditate love's ecstasy;

To return home at eventide with gratitude;

And then to sleep with a prayer for the beloved in your heart
and a song of praise upon your lips.

— Kahlil Gibran, The Prophet, 1923

ISBN 978-1-943951-25-3 (eBook)
ISBN 978-1-943951-26-0 (pbk)

Living Dreams Press
Santa Barbara, CA USA
www.livingdreamspress.com

Printed in the United States of America

FOREWORD

Dear Readers,

I am absolutely thrilled to be able to offer *The Complete Clairvoyant* Book Set!

Many things have changed in my own life since first embarking on the writing of the first book, *You Are Psychic*. For example, my son is no longer a baby, in fact at the age of 21 he just had a baby boy of his own! I no longer live in Sedona, rather I'm living on a river that flows into the sea, off the coast of Oregon. I'm no longer a single mom but have been in a loving relationship for almost 18 years now, and boy has that been one big adventure! I'm also finishing up a Ph.D. in Psychology, which I embarked on mostly because I found myself doing remote viewing research related projects and really wanted to polish up my formal research skills. Like everyone else in the world right now, I'm also living in the middle of a pandemic and in the midst of uncertain times, even for a psychic. Still, I find every day I am able to make healthy choices (except for the chocolate cake), keep myself and my family safe, and have endless ways to help others precisely because I continue to apply the information in these books.

Not much has changed as far as the techniques, lessons, methods, approaches, and ideas expressed in these books. They are as relevant today as they ever were. I've come a long way in my personal practice as a clairvoyant reader and healer, medium, and remote viewer, and I've now witnessed literally thousands of students develop from having no idea of how to control or direct their intuitive abilities to the point it's just second nature. This doesn't mean it's always easy, but they have the tools and wherewithal to deal with much of what may come their way. Many readers of these books, and students of my classes, have gone onto start or enhance their own professional practices, while others have gone onto to simply make use of their blossoming psychic skills in creative and meaningful ways.

As always, life can be a roller coaster. These exercises can't stop or prevent the ups or downs, but they sure can even things out – helping you to cope with more ease, grace and peace then you otherwise might have had. Of course, as with any natural human skill, the more you practice and integrate the techniques and lessons offered in each of the three books, the more results you will see and the sooner you will experience them.

Finally, I'd like to thank you from the bottom of my heart for having faith in myself and these books. Please know that every moment I wrote these words, I did so with the hope and prayer they would be a blessing to you in your life.

Wishing you the greatest joy in all of your endeavors,

XOXOXOXO (fully masked!)

Debra (http://www.debrakatz.com/)

YOU ARE
PSYCHIC

The Art of Clairvoyant
Reading and Healing

DEBRA LYNNE KATZ

Living Dreams Press
livingdreamspress.com

Editor's Note and Invocation

The first edition of *You are Psychic: The Art of Clairvoyant Reading and Healing* was published by Llewelyn Worldwide in 2004. It was received with extraordinary acclaim and sold tens of thousands of copies across the globe. This second edition by Living Dreams Press has been updated to reflect the changing times of doing business in a more technologically advanced world and to incorporate new insights of the author, who has been conducting clairvoyant readings, trainings and mentoring sessions for thousands of clients and budding psychics for two decades.

Since the original publication of this book, Debra Lynne Katz has founded the International School of Clairvoyance: www.urpsychic.com, and created a popular online community: www.seventhsight.org. She has also collaborated with the top psychic researchers and remote viewers to conduct scientific studies, serving both as scientist and subject. In this edition, she fine-tunes techniques based upon those endeavors.

While everyone has natural psychic ability, there are few people who have been as committed and productive in pursuing their visions as Katz. Her mission in life is to help everyone become aware of their God-given sixth sense (or seventh or eighth) and to guide those seeking mastery in these realms to actualize their full potential. As she often says, "The secret isn't becoming psychic, it's realizing you already are." This book is a gift that holds nothing back; it makes arcane knowledge common knowledge.

One of the greatest values this book has is its normalizing and comforting effect: by sharing intimate details of her own readings, along with step-by-step techniques, she catalyzes "breakthrough" experiences that change lives for the better and show readers that clairvoyance is fun, numinous and enlightening.

Perhaps, most importantly, those who experiment with the material in this book will gain immediate awareness of the profound connection all beings have with each other. May these pages open up such pathways to deeper, more meaningful relationships between you and others, and within you. May this book be a bridge to more awareness, more empowerment, more peace, more prosperity and more love. As this second edition is a further flowering of the author's path, may you, dear reader, harvest the wisdom herein and also blossom and grow.

— Editor, Living Dreams Press

CONTENTS

Extraordinary Psychic

Free the Genie Within

Prologue

Within the first week of moving to Sedona, Arizona, and beginning my new career as a professional psychic at the Center for the New Age, I was blessed to find a wonderful woman named Sharon to babysit my infant son. Each morning, I would drop little Manny off at Sharon's home and say hello to her husband, Brian, who was usually slouched over a copy of the Red Rock News, gulping down a cup of coffee at the kitchen table. He was always courteous, but distant. One afternoon, Sharon confided in me that her husband did not believe in psychic phenomena and was convinced that all psychics were frauds. "Please give him a reading to show him that what you do is legitimate," she implored. I replied with a resounding "No."

I explained that the most unpleasant and difficult people to read are skeptics because no matter what you say, they will find a way to discount it, putting up a wall that takes tremendous effort to penetrate. "It's certainly not impossible to read a non-believer, but why should I waste my time on someone who really has a lot invested in maintaining a limited paradigm of himself and the world?" I wondered aloud. "It's a fact of life that there will always be people who have no belief or understanding of what I do and that is something I just have to live with if I want to be of service to those who really are open to receiving my help." Sharon pretended to agree with me.

The following Monday, I was greeted by Sharon's husband at the door. He advised me that his wife had run out to the store, and that I should wait for her in the den, where he was sorting through some paperwork. After a few minutes of silence, he muttered,

"So how's business?"

"Fine," I answered cheerfully.

A few more minutes of silence elapsed, and then he said,

"So, you don't really believe in this psychic stuff, do you?"

I tried not to feel insulted. "Do you actually think I would be going to work day after day, working forty-plus hours a week, spending all this time away from my son, just to do something I don't believe in? Do you really think I would engage in a career that is based on lying to people?" I asked him, sounding a bit hurt, in spite of myself.

"Well, I believe that you think what you are doing is real, but I just don't see how it can be," he replied.

At this point I had two options. One was to remain silent, and the other was to tell him some stories. Since the first one has always been difficult for me, I opted for the latter.

"When I was living in the Philippines, a businesswoman came to me for a reading. In broken English, she stated that she wanted to know about the future of her business. I did not know anything about her or the nature of her work and was a bit nervous about reading someone from such a different culture. The first image I saw was that of her looking around herself and then just focusing on a single point. This meant that she needed to focus her attention on one task.

"That is what I am struggling with," the woman complained. "Many opportunities have recently been presented to me. What should I focus on?"

"Well, I see you standing at a blackboard doing some kind of teaching or demonstrating. This seems to be related to providing jobs for people," I advised.

"Yes, that is true," confirmed the woman. "I hire and train sales people to sell products door to door. But I really am not sure which product to sell." I then focused my attention on her products.

"I see a person rubbing something under her arms. It's a pink bottle, possibly deodorant, but I've never seen anyone in the Philippines use deodorant."

"Oh yes," said the woman. "I used to sell women's deodorant to the high-society women, but that was many years ago."

"Well, I also see a woman wearing an apron. No, it's not quite an apron. There is a woman's butt sticking out and someone is tying some strings around her waist very tightly. I think it's a girdle. I also see women putting on makeup."

"Yes, but that does not really help," the woman responded in frustration. "I used to sell girdles and now I am selling makeup. But my salespeople owe me thousands of dollars in products I fronted, and it has taken me years to get out of debt. I want to prevent this from happening again."

I looked to see what the problem was and saw an effeminate-looking man making fun of her, as if he did not respect her. I saw a heavyset woman with long hair go to one house and then leave in frustration, returning to her apartment where she sat down in front of the television.

"First of all," I began advising the woman, "you need to get a much bigger backbone. Your employees know they can walk all over you and you won't do anything about it, so they don't respect you. I see that if you write a new policy and contract clearly outlining your expectations, and then authoritatively verbalize the repercussions of breaking the contract, you will initially lose some potential applicants, but the ones you hire will be more dependable.

"I also see you with a tough-looking man with big muscles who is knocking on some doors. It appears that hiring a man like this to help with collections will be helpful because even if you make progress with your weak demeanor, this man will instill more fear in your debtors than you ever will. It's also clear that some of your sales people get easily discouraged, so they tell you they have been working all day when in fact they went only to one or two houses and then gave up and went home. So you need to train them not just in your office, but also in the field. Your problem is not your products, it's your management of your employees."

My readee acknowledged that she had a hard time asking people for the money they owed because she did not want them to dislike her. She confirmed that she was in the process of drawing up a new employee manual and that the tough-looking man I had seen was her cousin, whom she had recently hired as a debt collector. The effeminate man and the heavyset woman were both prior employees.

"You saw all that?" Sharon's husband still eyed me suspiciously. "How is that possible?" I ignored his question and continued my discourse, enjoying this opportunity to talk about my work.

"Yesterday a woman came into my office. I knew nothing about her except her name. She looked like any other middle-aged tourist who visits Sedona. Her only question was, "Will my financial situation improve?" I closed my eyes and began talking about the images flashing in my mind. I saw her with a tall, mustached man. She was leaning on his arm and he was taking money out of his wallet. I saw a flash of a whiskey bottle and then he hit her. In another image, she was washing the floor under his feet (a common image for me that indicates an imbalance in power).

This man seemed like someone with whom she had recently been involved.

I sensed that she had been relying on him for money. At this point in the reading, the woman acknowledged that this totally described her boyfriend, whom she had broken up with last week. He had helped support her, but had been abusive.

I directed my attention to see what type of work she did and saw an image of her stripping off her clothes, exposing some sleazy lingerie. She threw herself on top of a man who was fully dressed except for his trousers. The realization came into my head that she had engaged in prostitution. Afraid of insulting her, I timidly asked if she had ever been a dancer.

"Yes," she added just as meekly.

"Umm, were you ever a prostitute?"

"Yes," she answered reluctantly, "but I don't do that anymore." I then directed my attention to see what kind of work she would really like to be doing. However, nothing was coming to me. I had the realization that she really did not have any career goals; her focus was solely on finding a man who would take care of her. She again confirmed that this was correct.

I looked into the future and saw that she really was not going to be successful if she continued on the path of seeking "easy money" and that it was likely she would revert to her former profession of prostitution unless she made some changes in her attitude.

At this point I saw an image of her shooting a needle into her arm and advised her that she would find more answers by seeking out the assistance of a drug or alcohol counselor rather than that of a psychic. She was clearly irritated by my comments, but acknowledged that she was still struggling with a drug problem."

"Hmm," Sharon's husband made no other comment, but his ears were perked up like a dog who hears his master approaching.

"Then there was the woman whose head was sticking out of the ceiling…"

"What!?!" Sharon's husband leaned forward in his chair. I laughed and continued my story.

"Well, not really, but that was the image I saw when she asked if she was going to get a raise. She gave me no information about herself prior to the reading. However, I immediately saw her head sticking out of the ceiling and the walls squeezing in on her, which clearly indicated that she had outgrown her job. I was then surprised to see an overweight, balding man wearing a white jacket. He opened her blouse and was staring unabashedly at her breasts. He then passed through a door into what looked like a waiting room and, using a magnifying glass, examined the large breasts of several other blond women.

At this point I really didn't know what any of this meant, but I got the feeling that my readee was very disgusted with this man. Fearful that I sounded crazy, I stole a peek at my readee and found her enthusiastically nodding her head.

"That is my boss!" She exclaimed. "He is a plastic surgeon and most of his clients are women desiring breast enlargements. But I often get the feeling that he is being unprofessional by making sexual comments to me about his clients. I feel like he does not respect women and that he does not trust me enough to give me more challenging tasks, so the only way I'll stay there is if I get a big raise."

"So did you see her getting a raise?" Sharon's husband seemed to appreciate that story. I shook my head.

"I did not even look at her future because it was clear that she already knew she was going to leave this job and that remaining there would be counterproductive. The reason she came to me in the first place was not really to learn if she would get a raise but rather to have someone else confirm what she was experiencing in the present and, in a way, give her permission to leave."

"Hmm," Sharon's husband pondered. "From all those advertisements on TV about psychic telephone hotlines where you see a big-haired broad wearing lots of mascara telling some other dopey-looking woman that she is going to meet Prince Charming and have lots of brilliant children and a big house, I always thought psychics concentrated on the future, which really is not verifiable until the victim has shelled out some big bucks and the psychic has left town."

"Sure, there are frauds out there," I agreed. "But that has nothing to do with what I or so many other legitimate psychics are doing. Anyway, the future can be changed depending on a person's actions in the present. If you just look to the future without connecting it to the present or the past, it really does not help the person other than to alleviate some worries or to cause a lot more. But even lots of my first-time clients have the same misconceptions, so they will ask about one thing when they really are wondering about something else. Part of my job is to search for the 'right question' and answer that one. But I must be boring you."

"Oh, no, please continue."

"Well, there was the couple I read just yesterday. The woman's only question was, "Do you see any upcoming career changes?"

I immediately saw the image of her being buried under a stack of papers and tearing out clumps of her hair. This showed me that she was obviously overburdened and stressed at her current job. Next, I saw her absent-mindedly kicking around a can and then watering some flowers in a garden. This told me that she was going to be retiring soon. She was worried about having too much time on her hands, but she would eventually adjust and find solace in hobbies such as gardening. I sensed that she was worn out from work and that her and her husband's financial situation was secure enough that she really did not need to work anymore. She confirmed that this was all true.

Suddenly, the wrinkled face of a white-haired woman intruded on my train of thought. The method of intrusion was similar to those of deceased people who had appeared uninvited in past readings.

"Did your mother or grandmother recently pass away?" I asked the woman.

Not wanting to disrupt my trance state by opening my eyes, I took her startled gasp as an acknowledgment that I was on to something. Suddenly I felt an intense wave of pain pass through my head, which told me that whomever I was looking at seemed to have suffered from some kind of head pain. Next, a strong wave of grief passed through me, causing tears to gush from my still-closed eyes. I felt the sadness coming more from my readee than from this deceased spirit.

"She says that you did everything you could have done and that you need to stop punishing yourself for not getting there soon enough. She also wants you to know that she is very proud of you—she always has been, but just was never able to express that properly."

My readee began sobbing loudly. I took a few minutes to do some healing work on the deceased spirit by visualizing her surrounded by the light of God. I also asked one of my healing spirits to act as her guide from this world to the next.

"If you'd like, I can do some healing work to help you make some separations from your mother so that she will be freer to move on and you will be able to get on with your life."

I opened my eyes. The woman was shaking her head.

"No," she said. "I still need her with me. I'm not ready to let her go yet." She then turned to her husband and, wiping her eyes, scolded him. "See, this is why I did not want to ask her about my mother. How can we go out for dinner with mascara all over my face?!"

Her husband then confirmed that his mother-in-law had died from a mysterious head injury. They found her alive, collapsed and bloody on the floor, but by the time they reached the hospital, she had passed away. Part of the woman's grief was that she had always longed for her mother to tell her that she was proud of her, but until this moment her mother had kept those feelings to herself."

"Wow!" Sharon's husband exclaimed. "You really got all that from a reading? Okay, so let's say you are somehow able to pick up that information, although I really don't understand how that is possible. What is that healing work you talked about?"

"When I am performing a clairvoyant reading, what I am really doing is looking at energy," I explained. "This energy comes in the form of images, thoughts, sounds, feelings, etc. As soon as I start to look at the energy or image, it begins to change. When the woman began sobbing, this was not just an emotional release, but an energetic one. So if I wish to perform a healing on someone, say to help them release pent-up sadness or the energy of a deceased relative, all I need to do is manipulate the image through visualizing the release of whatever no longer serves my client, and then I watch the desired outcome take place. That is what is referred to as a 'clairvoyant healing.' Oftentimes, people can even physically feel what I am envisioning."

I then told him another story as an example:

"A young woman came to me for a reading, desiring to know where she should live. I saw her carrying a stack of books and wearing a graduate's cap. I then saw a map of the United States, and northern California or Washington seemed to spring out of the map. I then saw an image of a black-haired woman angrily scrubbing some dishes. There was something strange about her mouth, like it was moving very fast. There was a harshness about her that made it unpleasant to be around her, even clairvoyantly! I sensed that this angry woman was very jealous of her daughter. I suddenly felt a sharp pain in my throat and realized that this woman had said many discouraging and hurtful things to her daughter throughout her life, and was now trying to get in the way of her daughter fulfilling her dreams by going to graduate school out-of-state. My stunned readee voluntarily acknowledged that everything I said was 100 percent correct.

My clairvoyant gaze then zoomed to my readee's throat, where I immediately saw a deep, dark-red slash going through it. I sensed that if she made one wrong move, her head would fall off! Feeling an urgency to help this bright young woman and sensing that she would be open to some healing work, I visualized (imaged) that this foreign red energy was effortlessly pouring out of her throat, and that the space was filling up with her own energy, which I saw as a lighter shade of pink.

I did not tell her what I was doing, but suddenly she yelled out,

"Oh my gosh, something is happening in my throat! It feels like someone's hands are inside my throat yanking out something awful!"

I admitted that I was in the middle of performing a healing on her throat, and she became very excited, saying she had been suffering from repetitive ailments like laryngitis and tonsillitis for much of her life and somehow had always sensed that this pain was related to the demeaning words of her mother.

Sharon's husband had now risen from his chair. "Well, I don't know if I really buy this healing work. It just does not make sense. But if you really are doing what you say, why is it that you can do these things that are impossible for everyone else? I mean, no offense, but what makes you so special?"

"That's my whole point. I am not so special!" I was happy to tell him.

"Everyone has these abilities, even you! You just need to develop them."

"Oh, come on now."

"Yes," I persisted, totally forgetting about my earlier commitment not to try to convince him of anything. "I always had an interest in psychic phenomena and occasionally had spontaneous psychic experiences that I did not understand while growing up, but I never had the slightest inkling that someday I would be able to do what I do today. That all changed five years ago when I took a meditation class from a teacher who offered a free reading as part of the class. She not only was able to see intimate details of my past, but also effortlessly peered into my imagination and told me what my very own visualizations looked like. I asked her how I could learn to do the same thing, and one week later I was performing my first clairvoyant reading and learning how to control my God-given abilities to an extent I never dreamed was possible."

"So how did you learn?" he asked.

"The same way you learned your profession. I went to school. There are many schools in California and in the United States, even around the world, that can teach you how to develop your clairvoyance. I was able to start picking up information the very first time I attempted to do a reading, and I myself have seen close to a hundred other students go from having no idea what they were doing to giving me and others incredibly accurate and helpful clairvoyant readings in just a few months. Someday I intend to write a book so everyone will have access to this knowledge."

At this point, Sharon entered the room and, glancing from me to her bewildered husband (who was now pacing back and forth across the room, biting his knuckles), mischievously exclaimed, "Oh, I see you had some time to chat."

"Yes," I smiled. "We were just talking about boring things like work."

I handed her my napping baby and made a quick escape.

PART I

An Introduction to Your Psychic Abilities and Energy

CHAPTER 1

Introduction

One night as I was doing some last-minute Christmas shopping, I heard a group of excited teenagers discussing the blockbuster film Harry Potter and the Sorcerer's Stone and the series of books by J. K. Rowling that have made her the second wealthiest woman in England. They were saying how cool it would be to attend the fictional Hogwart's School of Witchcraft and Wizardry, where Harry Potter discovers that he has extraordinary abilities that he never imagined existed but that occasionally exhibited themselves in startling and detrimental ways until he was taught to control these talents.

I smiled to myself as I thought about the esoteric school of clairvoyance that I attended, and the one I later established in Sedona, where every day, every minute, was a new adventure, filled with discovery, drama, mystery, and challenges unheard of by most living beings. It still amazes and saddens me that I lived twenty-seven years of my life without the slightest inkling that I possessed clairvoyant abilities, and that there were schools that could teach me things that were not supposed to even be possible.

It's my dream that someday there will be no need for clairvoyant training schools because clairvoyant reading will be understood, encouraged, and taught by parents, as well as teachers throughout our educational institutions. Unfortunately, we are not there yet. I hope this book will provide the initial wake-up call for the slumbering adults in the United States who are still oblivious to their own clairvoyant abilities and talents and are therefore unaware of their own true potential and that of their children. If I could send everyone to a clairvoyant training school, I would, but that is neither feasible nor really necessary. Instead, I am bringing clairvoyant school to you, in this book, which I am dedicating to the thousands of clairvoyant students and teachers out there who can attest to the validity and usefulness of the information and guidance you are about to receive.

This is the only book of its kind devoted to the specific psychic ability of clairvoyance, although the techniques presented herein will aid in the development and attainment of other spiritual/extrasensory abilities as well. This book is based on the truism that every person is a natural-born clairvoyant and healer, and with training, practice, and faith, anyone can learn to perform detailed and accurate readings. The simple techniques described here are guaranteed to lead to immediate results, provided that you, the reader, do your homework.

This book will travel with you on your path of psychic and spiritual development: from learning basic techniques, to coping with the challenges of being psychic in mainstream society, to braving the business world of professional reading. Most importantly, this book will help you recognize how you naturally and constantly employ your psychic abilities (clairaudience, telepathy, transmediumship, and clairsentience) and will help you understand how these abilities may be enhancing or hindering your life

This material will provide you with invaluable, empowering tools that you can use in your everyday life, for the rest of your life, for guidance, healing, protection, manifestation, and creativity. This book will answer many questions and bring hope to those of you who have been experiencing problems for which there are no "logical" solutions.

About the Author and Creation of this Book

I began my clairvoyant training in 1994 at the Berkeley Psychic Institute in Berkeley, California, where I underwent an intensive thirteen-month clairvoyant training program. Within one week of my training, which required us to attend class three hours a week and perform readings two to three times a week, I was accessing my clairvoyance for the first time in my twenty-seven years of existence in this lifetime. I was actually performing accurate and helpful readings, which was not uncommon for beginning students. Upon graduation, I went on to take classes and work with beginning clairvoyant students at the Aesclepion Healing Center in Marin County, California.

The Berkeley Psychic Institute was founded by a brilliant psychic healer and spiritual teacher named Lewis Bostwick. Lewis recognized that people were suffering from pain and distress as a result of their lack of awareness of themselves as Spirit. He traveled throughout the world studying and practicing a variety of religions and disciplines, such as Catholicism, Scientology, the Rosicrucian Order, and Philippine faith healing, all of which strongly influenced the development of his clairvoyant reading and healing techniques. He designed and perfected specific techniques that have served the thousands of students who practiced them, as well as the hundreds of thousands of people who have received psychic readings from these students. Lewis Bostwick "fathered" generations of clairvoyant teachers, many of whom went on to establish their own clairvoyant and healing institutes and training programs.

I began my clairvoyant training about two months after Lewis' death, and many of the techniques in this book were taught to me by his talented students. Robert Skillman, David Pierce (founder of Intuitive Way, a psychic training school), John Fulton (founder of the Aesclepion Healing Center), and Chris Murphy were a few of my most influential teachers.

Lewis Bostwick believed in an oral tradition of teaching. While his school published its own magazine with articles presenting simple techniques and concepts, he never published a comprehensive manuscript on clairvoyant training such as I am doing here. I never received any written materials during my clairvoyant training and have none to refer to as I write this book. Lewis felt that whoever really needed the information supplied by his school would find their way there.

In the late 1990s, I left my job as a federal probation officer in Oakland, California, and moved to the Philippines for nine months, where I studied with the faith healers and psychic surgeons and eventually met Manuel, the father of my son. Manuel was a self-taught acupuncturist and together we traveled to remote regions and villages, healing and giving clairvoyant readings to the indigenous people who had no other access to medical care or counseling.

After the birth of our son in Las Vegas, where I began my teaching career doing workshops through a local spiritual organization called Spiritual Endeavors, I found my way to Sedona, Arizona, where I embarked on a career as a professional psychic and went on to establish the Sedona Psychic Training Center out of my home. The Sedona Psychic Training Center has never had an affiliation with the Berkeley Psychic Institute, although its curriculum was partially based on my own course of training from BPI and from the Aesclepion Healing Center, which was founded by one of Lewis' most talented students, John Fulton.

The Sedona Psychic Training Center offered intensive month-long training programs in order to fit the schedules and lifestyles of Sedona's transient population, unlike its predecessors, which offered a lengthy course of study of at least one year for students under the age of thirty six and two years for older students (many older students require longer periods of study because they have more pictures, resistances, programming, etc., to work through, although this is not nearly as true today as it was twenty years ago when BPI was established).

My own thirteen-month course of clairvoyant training was a sacred experience of which I would not trade a single minute. It was perfect for who I was, where I was, and what I needed to achieve at the time; however, I began to realize that not everyone desired, could manage, or even needed such an intensive and demanding commitment.

Most of my classmates at Berkeley had no prior psychic training; in fact, many had never had an identifiable clairvoyant experience in their life. However, in Sedona, Arizona, many of my friends and students had been exploring their spiritual paths for decades. They already had attained a certain level of intuitive development. These were people who would never have found their way into a year-long clairvoyant training program because they were not beginning students and would not tolerate being related to as such.

Three months after my arrival in Sedona, I created a television program called The Psychic Explorer: Adventures of the Spirit, which aired on channel 17, Geronimo Communications, and later channel 18, the Arizona Channel. I was the host, producer, and director. Channel 17 was only equipped to produce and air four hours of programming at a time, so there were weeks where my half-hour to an hour program ran every four hours, all day and all night long. Whether or not anyone intended to watch my show, if they owned a TV in Sedona, there was no way they could avoid it!

On the show, I would teach clairvoyant reading and healing techniques and interview a variety of metaphysically-oriented guests, several of whom were graduates of various clairvoyant training programs throughout the country.

Sedona is a small town and I was constantly being approached on the street, in the grocery store, the video store, and even on hiking trails by people who expressed gratitude and a burning interest in learning more about their clairvoyance. At the same time, during reading sessions, client after client would ask me questions about how to protect themselves, how to break agreements with ex-lovers, how to overcome their blocks to manifest or get more in touch with their own energies, how to communicate with their spirit guides, and how to develop their clairvoyance.

Occasionally I would intuit that a year-long clairvoyant training program was appropriate for a particular client, but more frequently I would find that teaching these clients a few specific techniques was all they really needed. It became more and more apparent that trying to teach these techniques in the course of ten minutes at the end of a reading was not going to cut it. Many clients asked for books on the techniques that I knew to be effective from direct personal experience and observation of classmates and, later, my own students.

I felt helpless and discouraged that I could not refer them to such a book because to my knowledge a book of this kind did not exist. I realized that the only way I could provide these hungry people with the information they needed in a simple, concise, and practical manner was to write a book myself.

As I began work on the book you are now reading, my work with my clients became more pleasurable and less stressful because I knew that soon I would have a means to continue to help them long after our session together had ended. Soon I would have a way to help masses of people help themselves, which is really the key to long-term healing. Before I had even finished writing the second chapter of this book, I already had a long list of clients waiting for its publication.

In this book I will present the techniques that I learned through the various clairvoyant training schools and workshops I have attended and that I have found to work for myself, my classmates, and my students. There is not one word herein that does not represent my own truth based on time-tested personal experience.

The process I have undergone during the past 17 years of my own spiritual and clairvoyant development has been extremely challenging and, at times, stressful and painful. After only one month of my own clairvoyant training, I knew I would someday teach clairvoyance and healing, and I have approached every single reading and personal experience from the perspective that whatever I was learning was not just for myself, but for my future students. You, the reader of this book, are as much my student as those I have met face-to-face, and I am honored to share with you keys to knowing yourself and the universe in ways you may have never imagined.

Who Should Read This Book?

Whether you have a casual interest in psychic phenomena or a burning desire to develop your abilities, there is something for everyone in this book. The entertaining real-life stories, thought-provoking discussions, and easy-to-follow techniques will appeal to novices and gurus alike. The techniques are simple yet extremely powerful. In my workshops and classes, I have witnessed beginning students accessing their clairvoyance within a matter of minutes. Many professional psychics that I encountered and taught in Sedona who had been reading for decades were surprised and delighted to discover new methods of clairvoyant development and healing techniques that profoundly enhanced their work and particularly their own health and wellness.

This book offers explanations and insights into the energetic dynamics of relationships, communication, and physical and mental health that you may not find in any other manuscript. It is an eye-opening resource for anyone in a helping profession, such as therapists, counselors, social workers, nurses, psychologists, and even elementary school teachers. Not only will it give you insights into many of your clients' problems, it will also help you avoid and overcome burnout. What's more, it will provide you with techniques you can put into practice and share with your clients.

How to Utilize This Book

First I implore you to read this book with an open mind. This is not a research paper. There are no statistics and no reports of scientifically controlled experiments, although it could easily be the impetus for numerous experiments, and I encourage all readers to explore the plethora of psychic research that has been written about in journals and other books. (Visit my website www.urpsychic.com to read about the Remote Viewing research I have been involved in for the last several years.) The techniques presented here have been proven to work by thousands of students who have performed countless hours of readings over the past few decades. My purpose in presenting real-life examples is not to convince you of anything, but to illustrate certain ideas and concepts that I and many of my students have found to be true for ourselves.

If you read this book with an open mind, it will increase your awareness of yourself as a spirit and of the unseen forces around you that affect you, whether or not you choose to diligently practice the exercises. If you do practice the clairvoyant techniques, you will discover your clairvoyance. It is my belief that learning through experience is the only way to know truth. This book is designed to create a safe and effective learning environment so that you may have your own experiences leading to truth and greater enlightenment.

For those of you who are natural-born skeptics, I ask you to exercise patience, not just with this book, but with yourself. While skepticism is healthy and necessary in moderation, an unwillingness to even consider that there is more to life than what your eyes see can be detrimental to your health, relationships, and life in general, as I will illustrate in later chapters.

Fanatical skepticism, atheism, doubt, and negativity are dense energies in the form of programmed thoughts and emotional pain that block your abilities and prevent positive, nurturing experiences from gracing your life. The only way to work through these blocks is to ask the universe to bring you experiences that will open your mind, and then be patient and permit the answers to arrive in unexpected ways. I realize that asking the faithless to have faith is an oxymoron, but it is not impossible.

If you cannot suspend your judgment long enough to attempt to have an experience that might teach you something, then ask yourself what emotion (probably fear) is behind this resistance. Ironically, every single skeptic I have met that had such a vengeful resistance to the possibility of extrasensory perception was actually more sensitive and more naturally intuitive that the average human being. A quotation I read years ago in a book about past lives has always stuck with me: "It is no more amazing to have lived many lives than to live even one life" (author unknown). The fact that we humans exist at all is so mind-boggling and wondrous that to question the possibility of anything in this world is a wonder to me. What a miracle we all are, regardless of our psychic abilities! If you so sincerely doubt the possibility that you are psychic, how can you even believe in your own existence?

For believers and skeptics alike, I suggest that you first read the book from cover-to-cover and then go back and practice the exercises. Many of the chapters build upon the preceding one, so reading them in chronological order will enhance your comprehension of the material. Of course, as with anything, there are no rules that apply to everyone. Some of you may be drawn to the book because of a single sentence; intuitively opening the book to a particular page where a much-needed message is waiting may be all you ever need from it.

I recommend practicing the clairvoyant exercises and psychic tools as they are prescribed, since every step of each exercise is presented for a specific reason. However, if you feel uncomfortable with a particular exercise or are not getting results with continued practice, go within yourself and see what modifications you can come up with that will work better for your particular needs.

Common Questions

What is clairvoyance?

Clairvoyance means seeing clearly. It is the ability to access and decipher visual information through extrasensory means in the form of images or pictures. It does not involve the eyes, but rather the infinite universe behind the eyes. When you access your clairvoyance, you are using the same mechanics and parts of your brain that are active when you dream or use your imagination to visualize. If you have the ability to visualize anything, even something as simple as a circle, then you have clairvoyant ability. When you perform a clairvoyant reading, you relax your logical mind and let information in the form of images appear to you. Often you will obtain information that you could not possibly have obtained through logical or physical means.

Why would I want to learn how to do clairvoyant readings?

First and foremost, the reason to do clairvoyant readings is because they are fun! It is like sitting back and watching a movie unfold before your eyes, or dreaming while you are awake. You get to see all kinds of fascinating things, and access information firsthand about other people and yourself that you would otherwise never get to experience. Clairvoyant reading is like embarking on a great adventure: you are often surprised by the images that appear, and like a detective you work your way through clues in the form of pictures, sounds, colors, and feelings until you solve the mystery of what these images mean for the person you are reading.

Clairvoyance enables you to know your fellow men and women on an extremely intimate level. It enables you to tap into the deepest realms of the subconscious mind of yourself or of any creature, including your pets. It automatically turns you into the master of all time travelers: with your spirit as captain and your clairvoyance as your time machine, you can easily zoom from the past to the future (which you are really doing all the time anyway, just without awareness), enabling you to bring back immeasurable treasures of insight to your present body. Also, when you "read" energy, you can alter it, so having clairvoyant ability not only makes it possible to pick up information about people that they themselves aren't even privy to, it also makes it possible to help them heal, change, and grow.

A clairvoyant reading can be extremely beneficial for both the person receiving the reading (the readee) and the person performing the reading (the reader). Clairvoyant reading is a form of meditation. More than any other mental exercise, it forces you to concentrate, since the second that your attention wanders, you will stop accessing information and this will be immediately apparent to the reader and readee. Clairvoyant reading brings you into a state of relaxation and makes it impossible for you to continue to focus on your own worries.

When you clairvoyantly read other people, you naturally heal yourself. By the end of a session, you are often in a completely different frame of mind and emotional state than you were at the beginning. Disciplined use of your clairvoyance will send you sailing through vast oceans of perceptions, paradigms, experiences, challenges, and opportunities that were previously nonexistent, or at best were only murky shadows in your logical mind. Through doing clairvoyant readings you will process energy, break patterns and programming, and heal wounds and heartbreaks for yourself and the person you are reading faster and more easily than you ever would doing anything else in your life! Reading other people helps you gain insights into your own situation because you will be drawn to read people who are mirrors for yourself.

While reading yourself may be a bit trickier than reading other people (since it is harder to concentrate and you have more biases to work through), you'll find it very valuable when you need clarification about a relationship in your life or are wondering about an upcoming event, like the result of a job interview.

Through developing your clairvoyance, you will access your power in ways you never imagined. I use the term power in the sense of personal power, power over oneself. While clairvoyance can give you power over other people as well, as in some forms of black magic or voodoo, that is not a path I chose to pursue and one that will not be addressed in this book. Control over others is always fleeting and self-defeating because what you are usually trying to get from someone else is what is missing in yourself, or is based on uncomfortable emotions within your own body from which you are trying to escape. It is only when you find your own inner power and peace that you can be truly satisfied.

If people are not doing what you want them to do or are not giving you what you desire, go inward and ask yourself how you can change your own thoughts and actions in order to obtain the joy you seek. Otherwise, you are going to waste a lot of your own vital energy, hurt other people, probably incur some nasty karma, and in the end be no further from where you began. (Think about a time in your life when you tried to change someone's mind about something they felt strongly about, or when you manipulated them into doing something against their will. Is that person still in your life? Were the consequences lasting and fulfilling? Probably not!) Along with increasing your personal power and confidence, clairvoyant development will help you access a higher form of learning: you will learn through direct experience rather than through regurgitation of someone else's information. You will be better able to discern fact from fiction, truth from lies. Clairvoyance can also be utilized to help access creative energies and ideas that can greatly enhance creative projects and artistic endeavors.

What is the difference between clairvoyant reading and spiritual counseling?

A clairvoyant reading is one of the most effective and easiest forms of therapy/counseling because the clairvoyant can immediately identify the client's core issues; uncover unconscious motivations, desires, dreams, and fears; and actually witness and thus validate the client's past and present external and internal experiences. An experienced clairvoyant can identify and bypass a client's defense mechanisms within a single session. He or she can see through the most convincing persona and reveal the true face behind the most deceptive mask.

Because information is accessed through extrasensory means, the usual pitfalls of traditional psychotherapy can be minimized or even avoided during a clairvoyant reading, provided the clairvoyant understands these may be present and is open to receiving and committed to sharing whatever information emerges. Some of these pitfalls include faulty or deceptive self-reporting by clients; a client's inability to communicate (due to age, interpersonal skills, or disability); erroneous identification of the problem or issue by the client and therapist; and the time-consuming and difficult task of establishing trust.

A doctor deals with the physical body. A psychotherapist deals with the psychological, cognitive, and emotional functioning of the individual. A social worker may deal with the psychological as well as social, family, political, economic, and community factors. A clairvoyant deals with all of these plus one additional and essential element: the spirit. A clairvoyant can see the spirits of humans, both living and deceased. Clairvoyants can see the spirits of animals, plants, and alien life forms. A clairvoyant can even see ascended beings such as Jesus and Buddha and, of course, the greatest spirit of them all, God (see chapter 21).

It is not only unfortunate but downright tragic that so many people (spirits) live their whole lives having no knowledge that they are something other than a physical body and mind. These people can never fully know their true self or who they really are because they are not in touch with their true essence. People who have no concept of their own spirit often suffer from depression and feelings of hopelessness and frustration, and their lives as well as the process of their death are riddled with pain and fear.

In order for a person to thrive, that person's spirit must be nurtured through recognition and validation. Clairvoyance is actually an ability of the spirit. A clairvoyant accesses information by connecting with a readee's spirit or the Universal Spirit and then brings this information into the physical and mental realms.

For many people, the first time they feel as if they have truly been "seen," recognized, understood, and respected for who they really are is during a clairvoyant reading. To give this gift to a fellow human being is one of the most rewarding aspects of performing a reading.

A clairvoyant reading is a powerful catalyst for self-awareness and growth not just because it has a psychological effect on a person but because it actually has an effect on one's energetic and psychical body. It can elicit an instantaneous change in perception for both the client and the clairvoyant. When a clairvoyant looks at energy, that energy responds with movement. So emotions and pain, which are energy, may instantaneously be released. When a clairvoyant focuses on those energies and wills them to behave in a certain way, a "clairvoyant healing" is being performed.

Why would anyone want to receive a clairvoyant reading?

People have a lot of misconceptions about what clairvoyant/psychic readings are all about. While they can be used to access information about the future, a good clairvoyant reading will also focus on you in present time and see what is working for you or what changes need to be made in order for you to create the type of future you would like to have. Readings can help clarify your feelings and experiences and dispel confusion. While they can tell you things you didn't know, more importantly they will often uncover thoughts and feelings that you were afraid to admit to yourself. Sometimes when a relationship is headed in the wrong direction, such as in a violent or abusive marriage, we need an objective witness who can say, "This is what's going on and it's not conducive to your well-being." When a psychic you have never met tells you the details of your life and how remaining in your current situation is detrimental to your self-respect and physical health, you really can't remain in a state of denial. Hearing the truth from someone who does not know you or your situation makes a much greater impact than hearing the same thing from your family and friends who may be biased and too emotionally involved in your situation.

Readings can be performed on couples and families as well as individuals. They can serve as an extremely powerful form of marriage or relationship counseling since the reader does not need to rely on self-reports of who is to blame. The reader can look at agreements and past lives between the couple and see what is working for them as well as what's not. He or she can communicate thoughts and feelings that one partner may have been unable to adequately and neutrally voice. A clairvoyant reader/counselor can also look to see where the masculine and feminine dynamics of each partner are in conflict or harmony.

Why would I want to do clairvoyant healings?

Whether you are aware of it or not, you already are healing people around you. Whenever you sympathize with someone, whenever you wish you could help or change or transform someone's pain and suffering, you are healing that person. Most people have never thought of themselves as a healer or sought this out as a profession, but we all (with the exception of sociopaths) have experienced a desire to help. When we have that desire, when we feel someone else's pain as our own, when we attempt to give them advice, when we pray for them or try to change them, when we become frustrated with them for being stuck in their lives, we are calling forth our healing energy.

This has both positive and detrimental effects on that person and on ourselves, as we will discuss in the next few chapters. When you understand the dynamics and effects of your own healing energy and abilities, you will be better equipped to make the conscious choice of what you would like to do with your energy (which dictates your mental and physical health). You can decide whether or not you want to share someone else's suffering and whether or not you want to take on or interfere with their karma and spiritual path. Instead of feeling helpless or drained and transmitting negative energy (in the form of worry or judgment), you can actually learn to consciously employ simple techniques that will likely have a useful effect on a person you care about. The purpose of learning how to heal is not just to help others, but to avoid healing in ways that are inadvertently dangerous to yourself and to those around you.

If I am so psychic, why don't I know it?

I still marvel at the fact that I could have lived most of my life without knowing I had any clairvoyant ability, or even knowing what clairvoyance is. Most people don't believe me when I tell them that they have the same ability that I and many of the best psychics out there have, because they mistakenly believe that if they did have that ability, they would surely know it. Well, how do you know if you have any ability? The only way is by attempting it. If you never attempted to sing, you would not know that you had a beautiful voice. If you never attempted to play the piano, you would not know that you have the ability, with training and practice, to play the piano. The same is true with clairvoyance. With knowledge of some simple techniques and a moderate dose of patience, practice, and discipline, anyone can access their clairvoyance.

Thanks to religious influences dating back to the time of the Inquisition, mainstream society has done its best to squelch any sign of psychic abilities and gifts in children (and its adult members) through techniques ranging from ridiculing and ignoring signs that a child is communicating through extrasensory means, to punishing and forbidding the child to ever speak of such matters. Between being burned at the stake in past lives and being laughed at by the people we love and depend on in this lifetime, it is no wonder that we have turned off our natural abilities to the point that we forget we even have them!

Even in today's modern world, many of the psychics I know feel they must remain "in the closet." Much like gay and lesbian people, many talented psychic readers and healers hide their activities, abilities, and true selves from their families, coworkers, and neighbors out of fear of being ridiculed, misunderstood, labeled, ostracized, and discriminated against. These closet psychics are some of the most dedicated, honest, loving, and concerned citizens on this planet, and it is a travesty that they feel they have to hide their good deeds in order to maintain their jobs or relationships with people who reject and fear their own spiritual abilities. I know many of these psychics. I was one of them.

Of course, there are some psychics and spiritual leaders out there who would rather maintain the illusion that they somehow have been given special gifts that set them above the average person. This is done by some to maintain power, prestige, and wealth, and by others out of ignorance. Also, many "followers" of psychic gurus prefer to believe that their designated human "God" is more powerful than they are and will do whatever they can to maintain this illusion in order to avoid taking responsibility for their own lives. Ironically (since they will tell you they are following a guru in order to reach enlightenment), this act of dependence can block them from reaching their fullest potential.

People often turn to gurus because to go it alone is sometimes a difficult, lonely, and uncertain path. Many people want to believe that a guru or specific religion has all the answers because the truth that no one really knows for sure what the heck is going on out there can be really scary. Gurus and spiritual teachers can be very helpful and sometimes essential to personal growth, provided the relationship between student and teacher is balanced and healthy.

Many spiritual groups throughout the ages have sought to control information similar to that shared in this book because they feared that people would not use it ethically or responsibly. It's my belief that people are already doing so much harm by using their abilities without awareness that far more people will benefit from understanding the information presented in this book than will misuse it. There are so many books in existence that directly address the subject of black magic, available to those with ill intentions, that there is no reason for anyone to bother trying to extract information for evil purposes from a text such as this one that is intended only to enhance people's lives.

The greatest enemy of awareness is fear. Many people have so much fear about what is behind the door to their own personal power and freedom that they choose to remain in the dark. The path of clairvoyance is a path of personal transformation, and transformation is not always easy, as you surely know. When you begin to open up to your clairvoyance, it is like bringing a bright lantern into an ancient cave. You may or may not like what you see. There may be breathtaking crystal formations or perfectly preserved hieroglyphics, or decaying mummies guarded by drooling, man-eating tigers! While you can dim the light or even turn it off, you can never totally forget what you saw during the period of illumination, or how it felt to see so clearly. This is one of the major reasons people shy away from exploring their psychic abilities.

Sometimes during my workshops I'll ask the audience, "If there were a stranger hiding in your house, would you want to know about it or would you rather he just stay hidden away so you wouldn't have to deal with him and feel the fear and anxiety that might arise from the awareness that he is there?" Most people respond that of course they would want to know about this stranger so that they could protect themselves and get rid of him. I wonder how many people feel the same way about all the "strangers" in the form of spirits or foreign energies that are lurking in their auras and chakras, playing havoc with their relationships and communication with others as well as their inner selves?

I choose to know what is really going on, no matter how ugly "it" is, so that I can choose whether or not I wish to keep "it" in my life. In this book you will learn how to turn on the light and then deal with or conquer anything you don't wish to have in your personal space. By using the techniques presented here, your fear will diminish because you will know that you really can handle just about anything lurking in the dark.

The path of clairvoyance is one that must be undertaken by choice and free will. Undoubtedly many readers are still questioning whether they have psychic abilities, or if they have them to the extent that I suggest. The only way I can convince you of this truth is to share the techniques that have not only been proven effective by myself, but by thousands of others. You must do the rest.

I'm not good at visualization. Is it possible it's just not for me?

In my 15 years of teaching, I've encountered hundreds of students who seriously doubted they would be successful developing their clairvoyant abilities because they thought they weren't good at visualizing. While some did feel like they could visualize, once classes started their confidence faltered and they felt like their classmates were experiencing clear visions but they weren't. The problem isn't lack of innate ability, it's in their expectations of what visualization is all about. Many people simply have no idea that they are doing it when they think about something to visualize, because visualizing is just so incredibly natural and undramatic most of the time.

Relax and do the following exercise: Think back to the most beautiful looking person you've ever seen. What features made him or her seem appealing? What did his or her face, hair, eyes and body look like? Now think back to what your bedroom looked like when you were a teenager. Come back to the present and think about what your car looks like today. What color is it? Is the body in perfect condition or are there some minor, even major imperfections? If you remembered or pictured colors, or shapes, or patterns, or dimensions you were visualizing. Plain and simple. Now you may say, well that's just my memory or imagination. What I'd say to that is...exactly!

I don't know where anyone got the idea that visualizing was anything other than using one's imagination, because it's not. When we use our clairvoyance we are doing the same thing. We are just imagining or remembering other people's experiences (that we weren't involved in) instead of our own. It is also possible that we may be remembering our own experience, but one that hasn't happened yet in time. Just because one thought might produce a sharper, clearer or longer lasting image than another that is fleeting and barely discernable doesn't make it any more or less valid. Of course, memories are not only visually based; many involve a sense of scent and touch. Or a sound. When you observe your own memories, you'll find that there is often some sort of visual that accompanies them, even if it's a quick, almost indiscernable flash.

Many people who will read this book are aware that they often spontaneously pick up information on a feeling level, through their clairsentient or empathic abilities. There are countless psychics who consciously utilize psychometry to access and trigger the flow of information, which is as simple as touching an object like a set of keys or a piece of jewelry. It's the sense of touch that may stimulate the flow, but within the flow are visuals and instant knowings.

Many people think that because they naturally pick up feelings, or because they have a more kinesthetic orientation towards learning, that they aren't or can't be visual. This is not true at all, it just means they may need to literally lift themselves out of their comfort zones, (the chakras below the 6th) and allow themselves to try a new way of perceiving information. Feeling energy (clairsentience) can be a fantastic launching point, and is a first step in becoming aware that the readee or client is experiencing a certain emotion or physical sensation. In fact, these will significantly increase with the practice of the techniques in this book. However, accessing information on a feeling level is seriously limited as far as the level of detail it can provide. Clairvoyance, in conjunction with instant knowing and augmented by feeling, is limitless.

Bottom line: if you think you can't visualize or you can't be clairvoyant, it's simply because you haven't put enough attention on these aspects of yourself, and you don't understand just how subtle and fleeting the majority of clairvoyant images are. You just don't yet know how to access these and make use of them. Don't worry, you've come to the right place! It's the goal of this book to help you turn that around as quickly and dramatically as possible.

How much work is this going to take?

Rome wasn't built in a day. Neither were you. Well, at least the "you" that is reading this and hopefully comprehending what you can at this time. Yes, you will see some immediate results if you practice the techniques in this book on people and subjects/objects/targets outside yourself, but the truth is, psychic development is a life-long practice and in order to perceive information clearly you need to be clear. Your progress is dependent on five major factors:

1. Learning the techniques to help you call forth information and share it in a comprehensible manner.
2. Your own level of clarity, focus and ability to manage your emotions, as well as your level of self-discipline to get through challenges.
3. Your willingness to see life and yourself as they are and not how you think or wish them to be.
4. Your ability to speak your truth, even if others don't like it. If you can't do this then you won't be able to even access information that makes you feel uncomfortable sharing.
5. Your ability to accept change in your life. If you can't handle change, you can't grow and you can't heal. If you can't grow and you can't heal and you can't change, then you will naturally be forced (by your own mind) to block out perceiving any information that would force you to replace your current paradigms and behaviors with new ones. Why? Because these new thoughts will ultimately make you feel dissatisfied with certain things in your life, thus requiring you to take new actions or to suffer. So if you don't want your interests, your relationships, your work habits—all the things that make you feel safe in this world—to change in any way, you will only be able to perceive a very narrow spectrum of information when reading people. Hence, learn to embrace change in your life or your readings will suffer.

From the above, you can see there was no mention about intrinsic psychic "gifts." It's about your personality, and whether you are willing to put in at least a bit of time (actually a ton of time if you are going to surpass the abilities of most humans and even other accomplished psychics) and face the changes that will surely come your way when you embark or move further down on the path of psychic and spiritual development.

At the time of writing this revised edition, I've now been doing this work consistently for about 18 years. In the past six months alone, I took three psychic related classes totaling 70 hours, valued at $4000. I also attended three related conferences consisting of 15 days and costing me about $3000, including travel expenses. I do about 20 to 30 hours of clairvoyant readings and remote viewing sessions every week (my second book, Extraordinary Psychic covers the topic of remote viewing). I'm starting to see progress like never before, and I've been doing pretty well at all of this for some time.

Psychic development is a life-long practice if you are going to work out all the kinks. That being said, if you practice the techniques within this book, even just a little (which is the goal I suggest for most readers to start off with) and work your way up, without placing huge demands on yourself, you will see results.

My readers who don't see results are almost always the ones who aren't practicing. It's like reading a book about music theory and playing piano without ever attempting to play because you are afraid of making some noise. How many times does one mess up before the song starts sounding like something? If you can't deal with noise, with messing up, with starting over and over again, with people laughing at you or telling you to be quiet, then you just won't progress very far. I wish that were not the case, but it is. That's life. Also, practicing on others outside yourself is going to be essential for those of you who are having trouble staying focused on yourself or who feel like your own expectations and hopes are getting in your own way. Doing both readings on yourself and others is highly recommended.

What kind of impact will this book have on my life?

Beware: this book is likely to bring about change in your life! Just as energy is moved and altered when a clairvoyant sees it during a reading, energy is also altered when you read books like this one. When energy moves, perceptions and beliefs begin to get shaken up. It's like an inner earthquake of the mind and emotional body. My teachers refer to this phenomenon as a "growth period." A growth period is actually a very exciting thing because it will turn you into more of who you really are and want to be and can get you back on your spiritual path.

However, while undergoing a growth period, you may experience extreme emotions (such as sadness, fear, or anxiety) and sometimes a short period of turbulence in various aspects of your life. This is because we live in the illusion that our thoughts are the truth. The more we believe in our convictions, the more secure we feel. As we release and move energy, our convictions may suddenly crumble—our security blanket may be snatched out from underneath us with little warning (consider this to be your warning!).

As our convictions metamorphose into newer and more productive ways of thinking about ourselves and the world around us, our behavior may change, which will elicit change and reactions in those around us. As energy moves, either from reading a book or giving or receiving clairvoyant readings and healings, many of the emotions and pain we have ignored and suppressed from birth (and sometimes even before birth) may surface so they can be released, assimilated, and processed in a healthier way. As this energy in the form of physical and emotional pain is released, we may experience it in the present and misinterpret it as having to do with something happening in the present. This is known in psychological terms as transference.

If your reaction to a present situation is more extreme than the situation logically warrants, this is a sign that your present situation is merely triggering emotions that you did not adequately deal with in the past. The best way to handle a challenging growth period is to recognize when you are in one, to stop resisting it, and then to enjoy the ride.

If you find yourself in a particularly difficult growth period and would like communication from professionals who understand what you are experiencing, there are numerous clairvoyant training centers with a caring staff and enthusiastic students throughout the United States that will be happy to discuss your situation for free or give you a reading or healing, in person or long-distance, for a very modest price (see chapters 24 and 25).

CHAPTER 2

You Are Already Using
Your Psychic Abilities

I'm always amazed and saddened when someone tells me they have never had a psychic experience. We are all actually having psychic experiences every moment of our lives; we just don't realize that is what's happening. So many of our thoughts, feelings, bodily sensations, dreams, fantasies, anxieties, etc., are coming from sources outside ourselves, but we mistakenly believe that they are being generated from our own mind and body.

For many of you, it's only when you have a psychic experience that is obvious and clear-cut that you will consider the possibility that you are psychic. For example, you are thinking of a friend whom you have not heard from in years and a moment later she telephones you; you have a dream about a male relative meeting some ill fate and the next morning you find out that he passed away during the night; you ignore your "irrational" mother when she tells you she feels anxious about you leaving the house on a particular evening, and then you total your car in a strange accident that night.

Some people only consider the possibility that they are psychic when they have an extreme out-of-body experience, like where they see things in a room that they could only observe from the ceiling, or they undergo a miraculous healing from a fatal illness without having a clue that throughout the day their spirit is entering and leaving their body a thousand times, or that every week they are undergoing healings that have saved them from death on countless occasions.

If you gain nothing else from this book, I hope you will at least begin to consider the possibility that you are psychic, not just on rare occasions but all the time. Psychic abilities are spiritual abilities. As a spirit, you possess the same qualities often attributed to God. Spirits are creative; they are omniscient (all knowing) and omnipresent (everywhere at once). Your spirit has these abilities even when it is attached to a living body—your body. Some of these psychic/spiritual abilities can be classified as clairaudience, transmediumship, telepathy and clairsentience, all of which will be illustrated in this chapter.

Clairaudience is the ability to hear the thoughts of other spirits, both with and without bodies.

Transmediumship is the ability of your spirit/energy to leave your body and to bring other spirits/energies into your body. Telepathy is the ability to send and receive thoughts through extrasensory means. Clairsentience is the ability to feel the emotions of others. When used consciously, these psychic abilities can assist you in understanding and healing yourself and others. When used unconsciously, as is so often the case, they may be the cause of much unnecessary confusion, pain, and suffering.

As identical twins, my sister Amy and I were constantly asked what we thought to be a very silly question: "If one of you is in pain, does the other one feel it?" We always answered this with an exasperated "No!" But almost twenty years later, I realized that not only was I feeling Amy's pain and emotions, I was feeling the pain and emotions of everyone around me. This concept was never introduced into our frame of reference because it was foreign to our parents, teachers, and the society we grew up in. The ability for one person to experience the feelings of another was possible only in the realm of fantasy, or mythical stories and dreams. According to our close-minded society, if you feel pain, there can be only one explanation for it: there must be something wrong within your own body. And, of course, we were taught that the only acceptable ways to get rid of pain are to wait and see if it disappears, go to the doctor and take medication, or undergo some kind of operation.

I began to understand the limitations and dangers of this paradigm soon after embarking on my clairvoyant training. Because clairvoyance does not involve the intellect, the only way to develop it is though direct practice. So I was thrown immediately into readings without having any preconceived notion of what would happen. For the first few months of my training program, I usually read with other students (see chapter 17). This is an excellent way to build your confidence as a psychic, because as a beginning clairvoyant student, you have very little trust in what you are looking at, and even less courage to speak up about it. This is true even though you may be seeing the same thing that the more advanced students are viewing. Inevitably, someone else in the reading will talk about the same thing you have been silently looking at or sensing, and this of course will increase your confidence and let you know that you are really psychic and not "just using your imagination."

Much to my surprise, I soon began to notice that not only was I seeing the same images as my fellow psychics, I was also feeling the same sensations in my body. For example, during one reading I began to feel a strong pressure on top of my head, as if someone were sitting on it. I was also experiencing some intense pain in my upper back and a constriction in my throat. As I was wondering what was wrong with me and trying to figure out if my health insurance would cover a doctor's visit for these ailments, the other students doing the reading began voicing similar complaints. Much to our relief, one of our teachers finally entered the room and stated: "You all might want to say hello to those religious family spirits that are pounding you over your heads. Also don't be surprised if you are having difficulty reading because there are a lot of energies in the room that don't want you to talk about what you are seeing. And by the way (addressing the readee), have you had some back problems lately because I can feel that is some pretty intense pain you are in!" As soon as the reading was over, all of my pain and discomfort vanished.

A few minutes before another reading, I suddenly felt a strange tingling in my gums. Again I wondered what was wrong with me. When the readee entered the room, she apologized, saying, "Forgive me if I look funny. I just had a root canal and the Novocain has not yet worn off." From these experiences, I began to understand that these bodily sensations were not really mine; rather, I was channeling them.

Clairaudience, Transmediumship, and Telepathy

Most people assume that every thought in their mind is their own, but sometimes this could not be further from the truth. Have you ever been struggling with some nagging problem or question, and just when you were about to give up all hope, a brilliant answer just seemed to land in your mind? Where do you think this came from? Sometimes we really give ourselves too much credit! Albert Einstein and many other brilliant scientists, artists, writers, inventors, etc., were never so vain as to think that they alone were responsible for the monumental ideas that often came to them in their dreams or upon awakening. I believe that these thoughts come from other spirits and people.

You probably have noticed that people to whom you are very closely "connected," such as a sibling, best friend, or your husband or wife, etc., will finish your sentence or ask a question that you were about to ask. Sure, sometimes this might just be because of the similarities between the two of you, but many times it has more to do with your psychic abilities.

My first conscious lesson in clairaudience, transmediumship, and telepathy occurred a few weeks into my clairvoyant training. Instead of feeling excited like I usually did before a reading, on this particular occasion I felt a strange sort of dread as I drove to the Berkeley Psychic Institute. Several times I came close to turning my car around and going home. I told myself that if I couldn't find a parking space immediately in front of the door, I would do just that. I felt nauseated as I parked a few feet from the entrance, and meandered inside.

I had already been sitting in front of our readee for about fifteen minutes and the only thing I could see was darkness. My usual cheerful mood was replaced with feelings of worthlessness and self-ridicule. "What am I doing here?" I chastised myself. "This is all a big joke. I don't really have any psychic ability. This is a waste of time!" On and on the conversation droned in my head until finally I heard the words, "You are a f***ing, stupid bitch." This surprising profanity was music to my ears, because I had the instant realization that the words somehow did not belong to me! While I do have a tendency to criticize myself, I never use this language (well, only if I'm stuck in traffic!).

Intuitively, I knew these harsh words were somehow coming from somewhere else. Since trying to "look" at the readee was not working, I redirected my attention to whatever it was that was sending me these thoughts. I immediately saw an image of two glowing, slanted eyes, and then suddenly my entire body was pierced with a bolt of electricity and I was thrown back in my chair.

This "lightning bolt" did not hurt as much as startle me, but again I was filled with excitement because it only further confirmed my suspicions. Spontaneously, I knew that whatever this energy or spirit was, it had been having an effect on the readee. Without waiting for my fellow student to finish whatever he was saying, I blurted out to the woman, "You have been struggling with self-esteem issues for a long time, and I think you probably have some very self-punishing thoughts on a regular basis."

For the first time she excitedly spoke up, "Yes, yes, that is the whole reason I came in for this reading. Sometimes I even hear voices telling me to hurt myself and I really think they might be spirits rather than the hallucinations my therapist thinks they are."

This early experience was very significant because it prompted me to pay attention to the source of my thoughts and bodily sensations, not just in my readings, but in my everyday life.

As these examples demonstrate, your self-esteem can be influenced by the way other people think and feel about you, or even how these other people think about themselves. For example, imagine you are sitting in a classroom. You are confident with the course material and things are going well for you in life in general. Suddenly a woman sits down next to you who is very worried about getting a good grade and is feeling very unattractive or unintelligent. Within seconds, you could easily absorb or match her energy and your own self-esteem could plummet dramatically, regardless of whether you even speak to her or notice her at all.

Most of you have had at least some experience with public speaking, even if it was just during a speech class in school. If you think back to it, your success or failure may have been directly proportional to the receptivity and accompanying energy of your audience, in that they may have healed you or psychically attacked you. The energy of nervousness and anxiety is not only contagious, it also has a snowball effect, so that you may actually be a confident public speaker but when surrounded by others experiencing stage fright, you might match their fear and have a much harder time delivering your speech.

The energy generated by angry groups of people, such as neo-Nazis, white supremacists, protesters, drunken fraternity students, etc., can be quite contagious and seductive. This accounts for how some individuals can commit heinous acts when in a group, but would never even think of engaging in such behavior on their own. History has shown that many individuals who have surrendered to a poisonous groupthink are so mortified by their own actions that they cannot bear to live with themselves afterward, and end up suffering from posttraumatic stress disorder or trying to commit suicide, as in the case of many Vietnam veterans.

In part 2 of this book, you will learn techniques to help you make a separation from other people's fear, anger, and negativity. These tools will help you maintain your composure and confidence during public speaking or in any challenging situation, and make it easier for you to understand when you are being influenced by sources outside yourself.

Clairsentience

While undergoing my clairvoyant training in the evenings, I was working full-time as a federal probation officer. One day as I was walking down the hall, I felt a peculiar sensation in the back of my first chakra, the energy center located at the base of the spine. It felt kind of like a burning pain, but not exactly. I wondered what was wrong with me. A minute later, I was approached by an enraged attorney clenching my sentencing recommendation in his upraised fist. The closer he moved to me, the more severe the sensation in my lower back became. I realized that the two were related.

The next day I felt a similar sensation, only this time in front of my fourth chakra, or chest. A few minutes later I was approached by a hysterical woman who begged me to do something about her youngest son, who had just been sentenced to several years in prison. The longer I was in her presence, the more intense the burning in my chest became, until it was difficult to breathe. During both occasions, these sensations completely subsided as soon as my companions departed. Luckily, I realized that I was being affected by my psychic ability of clairsentience rather than by health problems in need of medication.

Soon I was able to predict with great accuracy the mood of the person I was about to encounter or the type of interaction we would have by paying attention to unexpected bodily sensations. I also began using this as a diagnostic tool in my healing work. However, this type of clairsentient precognition had its limitations since I still did not know the content of our future contact, or whom I would be encountering (for that kind of detailed information, I would need to sit down and do a clairvoyant reading). The most helpful aspect of my new awareness was that rather than be a victim to whatever sensations I was having, I now had the ability to sort out which feelings were mine and which belonged to other people. Then, by employing some of the techniques I will share later in this book, I was able to alleviate the unpleasant sensations in a timely and effective manner.

At the same time that I was becoming aware of being affected by other peoples' emotions and thoughts, I also seemed to be getting more sensitive to them. I wondered how many times in the past I had felt pain or emotions and had assumed that they were my own, when they were not. I started investigating the complaints of my friends, family, and coworkers to determine whether or not they too might unwittingly be picking up foreign sensations (using their clairsentient abilities). I was surprised to discover how often this was in fact the case.

On one occasion, I was sitting next to my mother in the waiting room of a hospital while we waited for my cancer-stricken grandfather to undergo some tests. I was feeling stressed so I began to meditate and give my fifth chakra (the energy center in the throat) a healing. After several minutes I had the realization that my mother, who was silent beside me, was "matching" me. I knew she was literally feeling the pain that was coming out of my throat by sensing it in her own throat. I considered whether to mention this to her, but decided not to disrupt my meditation.

A minute later my mother loudly cleared her throat and exclaimed, "Damn it, I must be coming down with another cold. My throat is killing me." I then attempted to explain to her what was really happening, but alas, the concept was too foreign to her and she left for the pharmacy in search of medication to alleviate her pain. I felt very saddened by this because I wondered how many times she and hundreds of thousands of other people had taken unnecessary medications or had even undergone surgery for mysterious pain they had truly experienced but falsely assumed was their own.

Unfortunately, most other people in my "everyday life" also refused to even consider my assertions, even when I was able to present a clear and logical argument by demonstrating the true source of their discomfort. Luckily, I found comfort in my fellow clairvoyant students, who were making similar discoveries in their own personal lives as well as in our readings together.

Clairsentience is not just limited to pain, but to many other energies, including emotions, obsessions, and sexual arousal. Oftentimes in my readings, I will see that a person is experiencing an intense emotion, such as depression, anger, or anxiety, and then trace this emotion to the person's spouse or parent, who may be alive or deceased.

During another reading, I saw that my client was obsessed with losing his money, even though it seemed his financial situation was better than that of most people. This was affecting his relationship with his wife and his enjoyment of life. I traced this obsession to his deceased father, who had committed suicide at the time of the Great Depression. His father and some other punishing spirits were plugged into his third chakra, which caused him a lot of stomach pain. He acknowledged that he had suffered from intense pain in his abdomen for years, but the doctors had never been able to determine the source. He felt as if he were being punched in the stomach. I performed some simple healing work to help him release this foreign energy. One month later he called to tell me that for the first time in twenty years, the pain was gone and he was getting much more enjoyment from spending his money.

My students often ask me, "How can we tell if an emotion is our own or is originating in another person?" A sign that the emotion is not really yours is when it feels totally out of control, as if no matter what you do, you cannot change your mood. The depression or sadness you feel may seem so intense and agonizing that the only recourse seems to be death, even though logically you know you have many reasons to live. Another sign that the emotion is coming from an outside source is when there is no logical cause for this emotion. Confusion, disorientation, or the inability to think are also signs that someone else's considerations are in your head.

From readings and my own personal experience, I am certain that what psychologists term "free-floating anxiety" is just that: anxiety that is flowing freely from an outside source to an unsuspecting recipient. I have found that by searching for the creator of the anxiety (which can be done through simple inquiry or observation of your companions), the feeling will quickly dissipate and will have little effect on you. Unfortunately, many people do just the opposite: they become anxious about feeling anxious, and before you know it, they are off to the psychiatrist for a prescription of anti-anxiety medication.

Another sign that you are "channeling" someone else's emotion is if you find yourself getting angry for no discernible reason only when you are in that person's presence. For example, have you ever been in a perfectly happy mood, feeling great about yourself and looking forward to seeing someone, but then soon after spending time with that person, you suddenly felt irritated or even enraged, for no apparent reason? This may have happened on a number of occasions, with the same person. While there could be a number of reasons for this, one possibility is that you were picking up on that other person's unexpressed anger and actually channeling it through your own body.

From the plethora of clairvoyant readings I have done for couples, I have ascertained that this transfer of emotions occurs commonly in relationships involving a partner, often the male, who has difficulty expressing emotions such as depression or anger. The partner who gives herself greater permission to express emotions will inadvertently begin to channel and eventually outwardly express this repressed emotion of her partner. Since it doesn't really belong to her, she cannot deal with the emotion as effectively as she can with her own and may become quite unbalanced, even hysterical.

This common male/female dynamic has been utilized for centuries by emotionally repressed men in order to justify their superiority over the women they label as "irrational" or "overemotional." Ironically, if and when this type of person (again, often male) begins to take responsibility for the proper expression of his feelings and re-own them, his partner will consequently be freed from feeling the effect of his emotional energy, and both partners, along with the relationship, will reach a more harmonious state of equilibrium. As noted earlier, emotions are most often overwhelming when they are not our own.

Sexual feelings and emotions of joy and excitement are energies that can also be absorbed and transferred from one person to another. When two people are attracted to each other, they are often unconsciously exchanging sexual energies. Oftentimes they are not aware of the actual energy exchange; they merely feel aroused and conclude that there is something they like about the other person that is making their own body respond. Think back to a time when you felt aroused around a person with whom you had nothing in common and did not particularly like or find attractive. It is very possible that they were running their sexual energy through you and you interpreted it as your own. This likely led to feelings of confusion and perhaps to behavior that you later regretted.

From the numerous readings I have participated in, it is clear that sexual fantasies are an extremely potent energy force and can affect either the person being fantasized about or someone in close proximity to the fantasizes, as if the fantasy were actually occurring to them. Many times I have read someone who I saw had all the symptoms of a victim of sexual abuse or who appeared to be a victim of incest. When I described what the abuser looked like and when the abuse occurred, the readee immediately knew who and what I was talking about, only they insisted that the abuse had never actually physically occurred.

For example, one woman, whom I'll call Alice, had a father who was a subscriber to several pornographic magazines. He spent several hours each day locked in the family bathroom with these magazines while his wife was busy with the household chores. He carefully kept these magazines out of sight from his family, so his daughter never saw one until she was an adult. When she would inquire why her father was locked in the bathroom, her mother explained that he was having stomach problems. However, beginning at the age of seven, whenever she walked into that bathroom, she would have extremely explicit sexual fantasies about acts she had never witnessed or even heard about. These led to confusing but strong feelings of arousal, which then prompted intense feelings of shame and self-disgust. It was clear from my reading and her subsequent confirmations that she had been absorbing the sexual images and feelings that had been generated in the bathroom.

This story demonstrates the need for what I call responsible fantasizing. Sexual fantasies are natural and at times desirable, but they need to be monitored and controlled so that we do not accidentally influence other people, particularly our children.

CHAPTER 3

Energy and Your Body

As discussed in the previous chapter, we are constantly picking up information about our universe and other people through extrasensory perception. We do this by transmitting and absorbing information (in the form of pictures, images, emotions, and pain) through our physical bodies and various energy systems that correspond to our physical anatomy. Two of these energy systems are the aura and the chakras. While an in-depth discussion of these complex energy systems is beyond the scope of this book, having a basic understanding of their function and major attributes can help us understand how we process foreign energies, how we are influenced by them, and how we can have more control over them. When doing clairvoyant readings, it is helpful to be aware of these energy systems and of some simple characteristics of energy so that we can better navigate our way through a reading. Understanding various energy systems as they correspond to the physical body makes it easier to locate problem areas on a client's body, thus facilitating the process of clairvoyant healing.

Your Aura

Read any spiritual text from the Hindu, Buddhist, Sufi, and Cabalistic traditions and you will find universal agreement that human beings are much more than a physical body. Our physical body is really only a very small percentage of who and what we are. Our spirit is housed inside our body, but it flows far beyond the tenuous walls of our flesh. The part of our spirit that surrounds the outside of our body is an energetic field that is often referred to as an aura.

This aura actually registers on physical instruments and its colors can be seen through Kirlian photography. Your aura reflects everything about your personality and experiences in this lifetime and in other incarnations. Clairvoyants can see the information in this energy field in the form of colors and images. The aura consists of layers, or spiritual bodies. Throughout the ages, there have been a number of spiritual disciplines and religions that describe the aura in a very similar fashion. Typically it is thought that the aura has seven main layers, or bodies. In Kirlian photography, these layers are not very distinct; the colors blend together, sometimes completely covering up the subject of the photograph. The colors of the aura or other energies often unexpectedly show themselves in regular photography as well.

For the purpose of doing a clairvoyant reading, it is helpful to distinguish between the layers of the aura, imagining that each layer is separate and unique from the others. This makes it easier to navigate your way through the complex system of information contained in your readee's energetic field (see chapter 16).

In my experience, the first layer (the first auric body) often contains information about the physical body since it is closest to the body. The second layer corresponds to emotions and sexual energies. The third layer often has information in it about power, control, and self-esteem. The fourth layer seems to contain information about matters of the heart and relationships. The fifth layer concerns communication. The sixth layer contains information about how a person perceives himself or herself. Finally, the seventh layer, farthest from the body but closest to the outside world, often holds information about other people's perceptions as well as foreign energies that are entering and leaving the aura. There may be additional layers that I have not experienced due to my training and preconceived notions about the aura.

Your aura contains your own energy and energy from other people and the environment. Everything about you—everything you have ever been, ever thought, dreamed, experienced, felt, desired, as well as every relationship you have ever had—is recorded, stored, and transmitted through the aura. I hesitate to describe the aura in any detail because the best way to learn about it, as with anything, is through your own clairvoyant observation, experimentation, and experience.

Color

Clairvoyants see energy as color. Since the energy that makes up a person and their aura is constantly changing, the colors of the aura are always in flux. One day the first layer of the aura may be predominantly blue. The next day it may be green, depending on the person's emotions, actions, and the foreign energies affecting them.

There are numerous books on the aura that attempt to define the meaning of every color. I shy away from this because colors are symbolic representations and the meanings of symbols are derived from personal as well as universal experiences (the same could be said about dream interpretation). Two clairvoyants may see the same energy as the same color, as different shades of the same color, or as two completely different colors, depending on their life experiences. All information is filtered through the reader's life experiences, emotions, personality, biases, and MEI pictures (see chapter 4). This is true in every aspect of life, not just when performing a reading.

When communicating about energy, clairvoyants will discuss similar information but provide different perspectives. Clairvoyant #1 might see yellow in the first layer of the aura and see this as the readee's mother's energy, while Clairvoyant #2 may have a clear sense that he is looking at the readee's mother's energy, but to him it looks blue. Further probing or questioning of the colors may lead Clairvoyant #1 to say, "The yellow energy tells me that your mother is praying for you constantly and that she really cares about you," while Clairvoyant #2 might say, "The blue energy I am looking at tells me that your mother is worried about you and is trying to protect you, but this protection is blocking you." Clairvoyant #1 is unconsciously focusing on the energy of prayer because he and his own mother pray a lot. Clairvoyant #2 is picking up the energy of worry because he is presently working on moving his own mother's concerns out of his own aura so he does not have to be afraid to take certain steps in his life. Both clairvoyants are accurately picking up information that is useful for the readee to hear.

Sometimes I will see red in the first layer of a client's aura and I discover that it represents my client's anger. In another reading I will see red in the seventh layer and it represents a creative energy being generated from a love interest. I may never know why both appeared as red, but for the purpose of performing clairvoyant readings, the answer is completely inconsequential. When performing a reading, you must turn down and get out of your analytical/logical mind in order to see what is in front of you. If you see a particular color, the last thing you want to do is impose a preconceived interpretation on it. Instead, ask the color to show you an image of what it means. Then ask that image to tell you what it means. This process is fully described in chapters 13 and 14.

After performing several clairvoyant readings, you might begin to build a vocabulary of images and colors, but these are only springboards for further clairvoyant investigation. When I see white in someone's aura, it often represents transmedium energy or energy from disembodied spirits. Cancer also seems to resonate as a white color. When I see black in an aura, it often represents a lower vibration, one of interference or disease. However, both these colors can have infinite meanings and it would be irresponsible and negligent to make loose assumptions about them when performing a reading.

Characteristics of an Aura

The aura is stretchable. Sometimes it is only a few inches from the body, while other times it spans hundreds of miles. Each individual has a different way of carrying his or her auric field. Some people are more comfortable having it close to their physical body, but in certain situations will expand it, and vice versa. People who are more reserved and introverted tend to keep their auric field closer to their body than people who are outgoing. When your aura is out very far, you can be affected and effect the people who are sharing physical space with you. It is often helpful to call your aura more closely around you when you feel overstimulated, such as when you are stuck in traffic or in a crowd of people. It is possible to expand or contract the aura simply by visualizing this and stating your intent.

One of my clairvoyant friends spent a couple months living with me when she was in between apartments. She had a tendency to walk into a room and spread out her aura so that she could feel secure. Her aura would actually meld into the walls. This was highly irritating to me because she was taking over the space that I was already occupying. It felt as if I were being swallowed up by her thoughts and emotions so that I could not think of anything else but her. The first time I mentioned this to her, she admitted that her former psychic roommates had complained about this as well. With a gentle reminder, she could call her aura closer to her body through visualization.

I encourage you to play around with your aura in a variety of situations to see what feels most comfortable to you (and to your housemates!) and to help you become aware of your aura as well as to strengthen it. Flexing and contracting your aura is much like exercising the muscles of your body. As you exercise your aura through visualization, it will grow stronger and you will gain more control over your energy field as well as your clairvoyance.

Chakras

Within the aura are concentrated centers of energy that correspond to the body. These energy centers are known as chakras. Chakra is a Sanskrit word for "wheel" or "centers of radiating force." There are also several of these main energy centers that rise above the head into the aura, as well as in the hands and feet. Chakras appear to be strong connection points where the spirit and physical body meet, and like the aura, they contain a plethora of information.

My clairvoyant and healing experiences confirm that all illnesses actually start in the chakras, and if the chakras are not functioning properly, the corresponding organs within the body will be adversely affected. Many psychics, including myself, see these energy centers as very small spinning disks. When they are not spinning, this means there is an imbalance in the chakra or the energy flow of the body.

Personally, I do not usually see chakras in great detail. I don't have a technical/mathematical orientation or inclination and am more interested in the information stored in the chakra than its structure. You may be able to see chakras in richer detail and complexity. As you develop your clairvoyant abilities, I encourage you to look at chakras and every other energy system of the body and spirit for yourself.

The first chakra is located at the base of the spine and in women at the base of the cervix. It has to do with issues concerning survival of the body and connections to society. There is usually a first chakra connection or cord running between a mother and her baby. When my infant son is not feeling well, I will feel an intense pain in my first chakra.

According to Ruth and Gary Marchak, the founders of the Seven Centers School of Yoga Arts in Sedona, Arizona, when the first chakra is malfunctioning, a person will have difficulty manifesting money and other things in life that they desire and need, whether it be fulfilling work, cash, or healthy relationships. In chakra yoga, which is a form of kundalini yoga, there are specific postures and movements that influence a particular chakra. Oftentimes, all it takes to rebalance the first chakra and begin to create abundance in one's life is to perform a series of exercises (physical or mental) on a consistent basis for about a week.

The second chakra contains information about emotions, power, and sex. It corresponds with the reproductive organs. When you are tuned in to your clairsentient abilities and you meet someone to whom you are physically attracted, or when being physically intimate, you can actually feel narrow cords of energy, like needles, going into your second chakra. The second chakra also corresponds to the psychic ability of clairsentience. Again, there are particular yogic movements as well as visualizations that can be used to increase the energy flow through this chakra.

In my readings, I have observed that prostate cancer is often a result of a loss of power and energy flow through the second chakra. Caroline Myss has a wonderful series of audiotapes called Three Levels of Power and How to Use Them, which I highly recommend. She explains that men who retire from lifelong careers seem to develop prostate cancer more frequently than those who continue to work. Men who retire suddenly are disconnected from the source of energy that fueled their sense of personal power and self-worth, which was their job. When they lose this power, their energy bleeds from their second chakra, thus causing physical problems.

Women who suffered from sexual abuse at an early age, as well as those who have experienced neglect, abuse, or extreme disappointment in intimate relationships or who have remained in an unhappy situation against the wishes of their heart, often develop ovarian cancer or some other disorder of the female reproductive system.

The third chakra has to do with issues of control and self-esteem. People who are "Type

A" personalities or "control freaks" tend to have stomach problems such as ulcers because their third chakra is in overdrive. Because the third chakra is responsible for energy distribution of the entire body, this is a very powerful chakra. When someone has their third chakra reved all the way up, it is like a stereo blasting music at a deafening volume, so that everyone in the vicinity is affected by it.

On the other hand, if this chakra is shut down or depleted of energy, a person will be lethargic and their very life may be in jeopardy. They will also be extremely needy of other people's energy. People need energy in order to thrive and function. When someone's third chakra is not generating enough of its own energy, it will seek out that energy in others, like a magnet. Some of the most powerful people in the world operate this way, including spiritual gurus, religious and cult leaders, politicians, movie stars, and corporate leaders. Because they either lack their own energy or are performing monumental tasks that require an exorbitant amount of energy, they must rely on and be sustained by the help and energy of devotees, followers, fans, or a large staff.

Our energy systems can replenish themselves but we have a limited amount of energy at any given time. That is why we need to eat and sleep and relax. There are only so many creative projects, relationships, responsibilities and problems we can handle before our systems start to malfunction through physical, mental or emotional illness.

For a period of time, I was performing an unusually high number of clairvoyant readings on women who were trying to do too much in their lives (undoubtedly because that was one of my own issues). In every case the message was clear: we all needed to stop trying to do everything; rather, we needed to narrow our focus to the things in our lives that were in the greatest alignment with our life goals. This meant eliminating projects, jobs, activities, and relationships that were not directly helping us achieve these goals. It didn't matter whether these goals were general, such as having peace, or if they were as specific as publishing a book. When we try to do more than we have energy for, the energy gets so watered down that none of our relationships or projects receive the energy they need in order to be successful and enjoyable.

The third chakra distributes energy and is connected to the other chakras. Since developing my psychic abilities, I have noticed that when I hurt any part of my body, whether I stub my toe or slam my finger in a drawer, I can feel a tightening or aching in my third chakra. John Fulton, the director of the Aesclepion Healing Institute in San Rafael, California, suggests that if you are ever in a position to assist someone who is suffering from injury and potential shock, you should place your hand on their third chakra (solar plexus area) and gently tell the injured person to focus all of their attention on their body beneath your hand. What this will do is redistribute the energy that accumulated in the injured area and that is producing the pain and shock. As the person shifts their attention from the injured area to their third chakra, the pain will decrease. Focusing on the third chakra will also help the person's spirit (energy) reenter the body in the event that it got knocked out of it at the moment the injury occurred. The person will need as much energy as possible in order to heal. I've discovered that this technique works well with young children and even infants.

Some faith healers and psychic surgeons in the Philippines work solely on the patient's third chakra, regardless of the type or location of their ailment. They postulate, demand, visualize, and pray that all of the illness in the body collects in the third chakra, and then employ a variety of techniques to extract the illness or foreign energy from that chakra.

The fourth chakra corresponds with the heart and is concerned with affinity for oneself and others. People with disappointments over relationships, or who are perfectionists and tend to be very hard on themselves, often will have heart attacks because of the malfunctioning of energy in the fourth chakra. I have clairvoyantly observed that women who suffer from breast cancer often have felt stifled or disappointed in relationships, and may not have had permission to even acknowledge this to themselves. Women who have a martyr complex also seem vulnerable to breast cancer.

The fifth chakra corresponds with the throat and is involved in communication, both on physical levels and on telepathic levels. When people channel the voice or thoughts of other spirits (as in clairaudience), this is often the chakra that the spirit will plug into. Sore throats, laryngitis, neck pain, and headaches are often related to a disruption in the flow of energy to the fifth chakra. People who have difficulty communicating their feelings often exhibit these symptoms, and their fifth chakra is usually too closed or clogged.

Sometimes years of withholding communication will cause damage to the fifth chakra, while other times the communication problem is a result of a damaged chakra. Most damaged throat chakras contain foreign energies from a family member or significant other who had an interest in keeping this person quiet or who desires to control their communication. Well-intentioned parents often insert a sort of energetic dam into their baby's fifth chakra in order to quiet them down. Whether the energy is in the form of a verbal reprimand or a telepathic one, the child will receive the message that "expressing yourself is undesirable, irritating to others, or shameful," and as a result the fifth chakra will contract.

Setting limits for children is necessary, and an occasional reprimand is not going to do much damage, but parents can help maintain the integrity of their children's chakras by being aware of their own energies and making sure they do not use their energy to overwhelm the sensitive and unprotected chakras of their children. By creating a safe environment where children are encouraged to appropriately express their feelings (including anger at their parents), children will maintain healthy chakras and be less vulnerable to physical ailments throughout their lives. They will also become more competent and confident communicators and public speakers.

People who are unable to verbalize their emotions and communicate feelings of anger, disappointment, or frustration to others can never truly be in their own power, so the fifth chakra also has to do with issues of personal power.

The sixth chakra, also known as the third eye, is the center of clairvoyance. It is located in the center of the head, slightly above the eyes. When someone is curious about what you are thinking or doing or doesn't want you to see them, they will unconsciously plug into your sixth chakra. As with the fifth chakra, the sixth chakra is very sensitive to foreign energies. Children often learn to turn down their sixth chakras, and essentially turn off their clairvoyance at an early age, in order to avoid seeing what their parents don't want them to see.

Fortunately, it is fairly easy to clear out foreign energies, either through energetic healing work or by activating the sixth chakra through intent and use. I have witnessed numerous beginning clairvoyant students who could not "see" a thing due to a clogged sixth chakra turn into amazing psychics within a matter of weeks just by showing up for readings and attempting to use their clairvoyance. There have been a handful of students whom I personally read before they ever had an inkling that they possessed clairvoyant abilities (and would be using them someday soon), usually because no one had given them permission to use their sixth chakra to its full capacity. Less than a year later, after learning the techniques discussed in this book, each of these students gave me a phenomenal reading that exceeded even my own expectations.

The seventh chakra is located in the top of the head. It is the seat of the soul, with the bottom half of the spirit running from the top of the head down to the feet and the upper half of the spirit running from the feet to the head. The energy continues up to God or the part of ourselves that can be called our God self. The crown chakra is where you access spiritual information through "spontaneous knowing," and where your spirit exits and other spirits enter. This is the chakra that your guru, spiritual teacher, or people who want to have power over you will plug into. The seventh chakra is often depicted as a golden halo above the heads of figures like Christ and other saints and angels. When I am under surveillance, either by a policeman's radar or a video camera, I will feel pressure on my crown chakra, which lets me know I'd better slow down and behave myself!

In this book, you will learn to bring in your cosmic energy and your own energy through the seventh chakra. You will learn how to set and maintain your crown chakra at a vibration that is comfortable and pleasant so that you do not inadvertently "match" lower vibrations (see chapter 9). You will also learn how to tune in to the seventh chakra of your readee (which essentially is tuning in to their spirit and unique energy vibration/essence) so that you can effectively perform a clairvoyant reading (see chapter 14).

Did you ever play the game "Light as a feather, stiff as a board" when you were a child? In this game, one child pretends they are dead and imagines that they are as light as a feather and as stiff as a board. At least two children kneel beside the "dead" person, and each one gently places two fingers of each hand beneath the body. One child sits at the crown chakra and places two fingers behind the head and makes up a story about how the person died. Then everyone repeats the words "light as a feather, stiff as a board," and at the count of three they attempt to lift the person off the floor, using only their two fingers.

I played this game countless times at slumber parties. On one occasion, my sister and I shocked and frightened ourselves by actually raising an extremely chunky fellow third grader above our heads, until we lost our concentration and dropped her. To this day I don't know if she ever forgave us!

I once attended a lecture by a healer who revealed the secret of this game. He told us that it has to do with tuning in to and aligning with the subject's crown chakra. He demonstrated this by inviting a few people to stack their right hands over one man's crown chakra. The man must have weighed at least 180 pounds and was sitting upright in a chair. The three people were instructed to visualize the same color for about thirty seconds. Then they each placed two fingers under the man's chair and effortlessly lifted the chair several feet. The healer informed us that this process would work even if the three people had aligned themselves with the crown chakra of someone other than the man they were lifting. Somehow, aligning with the powerful energy of a fellow human's crown chakra gives the other participants the energy, power, and strength to do extraordinary feats. This would make a very interesting research project for any of you scientists out there!

The hand chakras are associated with healing and are located on the inside palm of each hand (also the feet). The Taoist and other Chinese energy healers call these points "bubbling wells." After several years of doing psychic readings and healings and undergoing numerous psychic surgeries on my hand chakras in the Philippines, I can easily feel other people's pain through my hand chakras. This is helpful when it comes to identifying problem areas, and is particularly useful with babies and people who cannot easily communicate. The downside is that sometimes the pain is as strong and unpleasant as if it were my own. Luckily, some of the techniques suggested in this book, such as grounding, offer instant relief (see chapters 7-12).

The feet chakras are connected with the earth. A variety of energies enter and exit through the feet. One of my favorite faith healers in the Philippines, David Oligoni (aka "The Exorcist"), works primarily with the feet. I have received several healings from him and observed him heal at least sixty other people. During a healing, he invites you to lie on a table. He then gently touches your big toe with one or two fingers and then commands the demons in your body to exit. At first this seems ludicrous, until the most agonizing pain starts releasing out of your big toe! This pain usually lasts about a minute, but seems like a lifetime. It is just as intense as labor pains, if not worse! Supposedly, not only is a "demon" being excised, but you are being cleared of all the pain that the unfortunate spirit was plugged into.

During my first healing with David Oligoni, I became furious because I thought he must be using some sharp object to pierce my toe. I thought, "I did not come all this way to the Philippines just to be prodded mercilessly by this witch doctor!" The only thing restraining me from kicking him in the face was fear that the other onlookers would accuse me of being possessed! However, a year later, he picked me out of another group of students and invited me to assist him in a healing. He directed me to gently place my finger on the healee's toe while he clasped his fingers around mine. Soon the healee was not only screaming out in pain, but was muttering strange sounds and convulsing on the table. Since the healee was a trusted friend of mine, I knew this was no act.

A few weeks later, upon my return home, I was performing a simple aura healing on a clairvoyant friend (working around the third chakra) when I heard myself silently muttering the same words the exorcist had muttered to our helpless feet: "Get out, you demon, get out!" I wondered, could I actually be performing an exorcism? Then suddenly my friend screamed out in agony, "Oh my gosh, my toe! There is a horrible pain leaking from my toe!"

You can focus on the aura and the chakras during a reading to learn about a person or to heal that person (see chapter 16). Although there are plenty of books that have been written on these energy systems (a few of these are recommended in the bibliography), as I've already mentioned, the best way to learn about them is through your own direct perception, in readings and in meditation.

Out-of-Body Travel

Our spirit is constantly in flux. When a clairvoyant performs a reading on a client, she is reading a person's spirit. When the spirit is out of the body, the clairvoyant will not be able to adequately perform a reading unless she calls the spirit back into the body, or travels to wherever that spirit is located. Most of the time when I have difficulty focusing on a client at the beginning of a reading, or I find that my attention is wandering, it is because the client's spirit is out of the body or has wandered out of it during the course of the reading. This exodus usually occurs when the client is hitting pain levels as a result of the communication they are receiving. Beginning clairvoyant students will save themselves a lot of frustration if they can be aware of this energy dynamic. Calling someone's spirit or energy back into the body can be as simple as letting the person know they have wandered, touching them on the shoulders, or visualizing their spirit's return to the body.

On the other hand, when performing certain kinds of healings, it may be desirable to bring the client's spirit out of the body so the healer can clear the negative energy that is clogging up the communication between the spirit and the body. Imagine that you are cleaning your car and the floor mats; in order to get both of these clean you need to separate them for a while. During times of intense stress and pain, the last place our spirit wants to be is in the body (where the pain is being experienced), so the spirit will leave the body and travel to another person, place, or time. Usually it will eventually return to the body, but not always.

It is for this reason that sleep is so important. A person who is not feeling well will need, or desire, more sleep. During sleep, our spirit is particularly free to leave our body and reunite with its source to be replenished. At the same time, our body can release tension, pain, and foreign energies so that upon awakening, both body and spirit are reenergized and ready to deal with each other again. It has been well documented that people who go for periods of time, even as little as three days, with no sleep will hallucinate and have psychotic reactions. Some people with sleep disorders who could not sleep for several months have actually died from lack of sleep. In these rare cases, the body was a prison from which the spirit could not escape, and in a sense, the spirit starved to death because it could no longer sustain itself.

Our spirit can leave our body not just in sleep, but at any time. Many people are familiar with the term out-of-body experience (OBE). This usually refers to an intense experience that occurs when you are awake but your spirit leaves your body and you become aware of this process. During this type of conscious OBE, a person will feel himself floating above his body and often realize that he is looking at his body from above.

Caroline Myss, in her outstanding audiotape series Why People Don't Heal and How They Can, tells an extraordinary story about a woman who was in a car accident. She was seriously injured and felt herself rise above her body until she was looking down at the accident scene. Suddenly she became aware of a passenger in a nearby car. The passenger was reverently praying for her. She noticed the license plate of the car, from her vantage point outside her body, and memorized it. Weeks later, after she was released from the hospital, she managed to trace the license plate and contact the passenger to thank her. The stunned passenger acknowledged that she had in fact witnessed the accident and prayed for the victims.

People are constantly having out-of-body experiences, they just are not aware of this fact. Even you, at this very moment, may be more out of your body than in it.

When you daydream or feel "spacey," you are traveling out of your body. Maybe you have been trying to solve a problem or have been rehearsing for an upcoming presentation. Maybe you were thinking about an attractive man or woman, or worrying about paying your bills, and before you realize it, hours have passed, you can't find your hairbrush or your car keys, and you have worn out the carpet from pacing back and forth.

Have you ever driven somewhere and upon arrival were shocked to realize that you could not really remember most of the drive? Or perhaps you intended to take a five-minute shower, but thirty minutes later you still have not even washed the shampoo out of your hair? Luckily, lots of us can at least function adequately enough when our spirit is busy elsewhere, but not always. Have you ever sat through a class and walked out without the slightest inkling of what was discussed? Wherever you were traveling to was much more interesting than what was happening in the classroom.

Every person has a different way of operating their body. Artists and writers tend to spend more time out of their body because this is where they have greater access to creative ideas. People who choose careers as policemen, firemen, surgeons, or accountants tend to spend more time in their body because they must constantly be focused on what is happening in their environment in the present moment. While these two types of people can complement each other's deficiencies, oftentimes their coupling is disastrous because they have a hard time understanding each other. Those of us lost in space (who can't get ourselves out of the house before noon) can be pretty maddening to deal with. However, those of you who try to cut in on our space travel time by imposing your rigid schedule and rules of organization can be equally annoying.

In cases of child abuse and neglect, it is common for the child's spirit to escape far from the body and to let other energies or spirits come in to operate the body. This is why there is a high correlation between child abuse and dissociative disorders such as multiple personality disorder. Epilepsy, catatonic schizophrenia, autism, senility, and many other disorders are related to the spirit's precarious relationship with the body. The fact that there are also biochemical or physical manifestations of these conditions in no way undermines the validity of this spiritual separation theory; unfortunately, modern medicine tends only to focus on the biological. While medications can placate parts of the brain enough to coax the spirit to integrate better with the body, taking pills without addressing the spirit's needs is like putting bandaids on an amputated limb.

A sign that part of your spirit has vacated the premises of your body is when you feel constant boredom or sadness, or like something is missing from your life but you can't figure out what it is. What is missing may be you!

Moving your spirit in and out of your body can be very simple. Oftentimes, all that is necessary is for you to focus on wherever you want your spirit to be, and then imagine and/or postulate that it is going to that desired location. Play around with this and notice the difference. Also, throughout the day, before you make an adjustment, close your eyes and ask yourself, "Where am I?" You are sure to get some amusing answers!

Healers of all traditions, from Native American shamans to East Indian gurus, have known about soul travel since the beginning of time. When I first met healer Manuel Lukingan at his acupuncture clinic in Baguio City, Philippines, he asked me to read some papers he had written in order to correct his English. I was surprised to find an essay entitled "Paypay," which translates in his dialect as "Calling for the Spirit Left Behind." I include it here with Manuel's permission because it corresponds so closely to the clairvoyant information I accumulated during readings prior to my arrival in the Philippines and demonstrates the universality of some of the concepts just mentioned regarding soul travel. This essay is based on stories told to Manuel by his "tribal elders" from Data, in the Mountain Province, where people still live in grass huts with no running water or electricity. He wrote:

Paypay: most victims of this strange illness are young children at an age where the emotional, mental and spiritual being is not formidable enough to protect itself. The victim's soul is said to have been left behind somewhere, sometimes in a physical location he previously occupied. Only a few people who are revered as psychic could see or understand the circumstances of how, when and where this occurred. Sometimes, the spirit of those victims is cordially invited or attracted by other spirits in other places as a result of being hurt by accident or cruelty, and the spirit is left behind. In these cases, the child will exhibit a depressed demeanor, engage in unusual crying, unusual sensitivity but zero communication, and suffer from standing body hair, and sleep and eating disorders. In these cases a healer, often an old woman, along with the parents, will return to the area where the child's spirit left, such as the seashore, and call it back by telling it how much it has been missed and promising it food and nurturance. Unfortunately this primitive practice that has helped so many people has been discarded by modern allopathic doctors who have no understanding of the spirit.

Retrieving your spirit, or energy, is often as simple as willing it so. Chapter 8 is devoted to techniques that can help you with this process. In some instances, help from a healer or spiritualistic therapist is needed, particularly when intense trauma resulted in the spirit's longterm departure, or when another spirit has taken over the body (see chapters 22-25).

Exchanging Energies

Clairvoyantly, I have seen that there are minute threads of energy, in the form of light, connecting everybody and everything together. Without these minute connections, we could not exist or communicate. The more intimate we are with a particular person, or the stronger our spiritual agreement, the larger or more dense these connections or cords of energy become.

Your energy has the ability to be immediately transported through space or time. When you have a thought, that thought is made of energy. Your thoughts are not just mental processes, but energetic ones. When you think of someone else, it is because that person's energy has entered or is remaining in your own energetic field, or because your energy has just traveled over to that person, or has been there for a while. In a similar manner, when you think of your work at the end of the day, when you think about a project, when you remember the past or worry about the future, your energy has traveled and is engaging with these things. If we could be paid for all the hours that our energy and not just our physical body was at work, we would surely be wealthy! Your emotions and your pain are also energies that can travel outside of your body, sometimes even faster than you can experience them. These examples demonstrate how psychic abilities such as clairsentience, clairaudience, and clairvoyance are possible.

In order to be influenced by someone else's energy, or vice versa, it is not at all necessary that either the recipient or sender be aware of the energy exchange or its effects. Sometimes one or both parties will even consciously intend the opposite reaction, as is often the case when the energy of protection is involved. Many times I have read a person who was suffering from confusion, self-doubt, and anxiety about a course of action that they had previously felt very enthusiastic about. It soon became apparent that the source of these nagging emotions was nothing more than their silently nagging mother or sibling!

These relatives had perfectly honorable intentions and were attempting to "protect" their loved ones through prayer, visualization, or just their "love." But what was really happening was that the worries and fear behind the prayers and protection were what was being transmitted, so that my clients were suffering far more from this energy than from whatever misfortune their relatives were hoping to protect them from. In many cases, the relatives outwardly gave their blessings and said nothing to indicate that they were worried. This made it especially difficult for my clients to recognize and understand what was happening. Usually, the most difficult energies to deal with are the ones that come from family members and close friends who "love" us. Because we care about them and their opinions, we are much more vulnerable to their energy than even to some stranger who is consciously using his energy to harm us.

The point of being able to recognize when you are being affected by someone else's energy is not so you can then confront them or blame them or avoid them (although in some cases confrontation or avoidance may be the most advantageous course of action), but rather so you can do whatever is necessary to release the energy. Frequently, the moment I look at or point out the foreign energy in someone's aura, they will release it, provided they are no longer in agreement to having it there. This is basically what a clairvoyant healing is about (see chapter 21). However, sometimes people want to keep foreign energy in their body and energy field, despite the consequences, because it has been there for a long time or it is giving them the energy they personally lack. They are comfortable with the energy and think they need it. This is what happens in codependent relationships.

In light of all of this, it is clear that sometimes the best thing you can do for someone you care about is to not even think about them, especially if you have an opposing opinion about the course of action they are taking. When you worry about what someone is doing (such as their choice of boyfriend) or try to convince them that they are wrong, what you are essentially doing is questioning God or the God within them. You are preventing them from learning the life lessons they may really need to learn. You may be pulling them off their true path. Even though you have the best intentions, you may be committing some major spiritual no-noes, and in the end this may severely backfire on you.

This is not to say that you should not pray for people. Prayer can be extremely helpful if done properly. It's essential that you choose not only your words, but your thoughts and intentions behind your prayer wisely. Rather than praying for the specific effect you want for the person (or even what you are certain the person wants), pray instead that God or the universe will help the person on their spiritual path, whatever that is. Sometimes a spirit wants to have a particular unpleasant experience, even though their ego may be in total resistance. Sometimes a person is meant to become injured or even die, and the most loving thing you can possibly do is to allow this to happen with grace.

Your Energy Versus Someone Else's Energy

Your spirit is made up purely of energy, while your body is made up of energy and matter corresponding to physical laws. The energy of your spirit and body is the part of you that survives after you die and that is busy while you are sleeping. It is the part of you that is engaged when you are meditating or using your psychic abilities.

Your energy is analogous to your DNA. Every living creature on the planet is made up of the same materials or stuff, but the way it is organized or coded makes it unique to you. It is for this reason that the energy that works best for you in your body is not that of your mother (unless you are a fetus), or your lover (unless you are in the middle of sexual intercourse!), or your guru, or even your favorite ascended master. The best energy, or fuel, for your body is your own. If you don't believe this, then take a look at the physical health of the many psychics, healers, and channelers who don't make a point of clearing out the foreign energies after completing their work. These people are usually overweight and suffer from a variety of physical and even emotional problems.

It amuses and disturbs me when people involved in the "New Age" movement declare, "I'll give you some energy" or "I got so much energy from being around those people!" Yes, sometimes when another person is happy, excited, and enthusiastic, you can absorb this energy and feel great yourself. But often you don't just get a single dose of foreign energy, but the establishment of a lasting link via an energetic cord, so that when your companion's jovial mood eventually sours (most people are not in a state of bliss twenty-four hours a day), the nature of the energy you were so greedily sucking into your heart chakra won't seem so appetizing! Even worse, if you are feeding off someone else's energy, they may start to lose so much of their own that they feel depleted and exhausted. You may also inadvertently send over some of your own pain and grief through the energy cord you unintentionally created.

I have clairvoyantly observed the detrimental effects of foreign energies on hundreds of people. Sometimes these people are my clients, or readees, and sometimes these people are the unwitting recipients of the energy of my clients. This foreign energy can cause confusion, exhaustion, sadness, discomfort, pain, illness, and even death. It can keep people from loving themselves and others. It can keep them not only from achieving their dreams, but from even recognizing them.

As mentioned earlier, we are all energetically connected; if we were not, we would not be able to communicate and probably could not exist. So the exchange of energy is natural and desirable. What I am talking about here is when the amount of energy, or the force behind the energy exchange, is extreme or unbalanced. When performing readings, we always want to be aware of how we are exchanging energies with our clients in order to protect both parties.

Absorbing the Energy of Others

People who are particularly vulnerable to this type of extreme energy exchange are those who are "natural healers." These natural healers are people who care deeply about other people and do whatever they can to ease the suffering of others, sometimes to the detriment of their own well-being. These caring people often take on the professional roles of psychics, social workers, nurses, therapists, etc.

There are some very powerful spiritual healers, such as Native American shamans and East Indian yogis, who purposefully take on the disease or illness of another person in order to heal them. Sometimes these healers are then immediately able to release this illness from their own body, but not always. Sometimes these healers actually choose to suffer from someone else's illness on a long-term basis or even die from it because they have some spiritual agreement to absorb the karma of those they help. People who are natural healers (yourself, for example) also do the same thing, only unconsciously.

From my own personal experience as a healer by nature and study and profession, I have both consciously and unconsciously performed this method of healing. I can say with certainty that for myself and most people, taking on the suffering of your clients is not a prerequisite for being a good healer! Also, most of you have enough of your own karma to work through without the additional burden of anyone else's. So I don't advise trying this at home.

On a few occasions when my baby, Manny, was suffering from intense stomach pains and screaming out in agony, I prayed out of desperation that his pain would be transferred to me. Of course there were other healing techniques I could have employed, but they required more patience and rationality. My prayers were granted, and my son seemed to have immediate relief; however, I was then stuck with some hardcore pain that was so bad I almost wished that it would return to him! I was in so much pain I could barely care for Manny and feared I was going to have to call the paramedics. It was clear to me that if I chose to continue this type of healing, my profession would be short-lived and so would I. Fortunately, there are many other healing methods that are highly effective and do not require the healer to take on the suffering of clients. These are the techniques that will be focused on in this book.

Taking on Other People's Problems

A few years ago, I had a frightening experience with this type of unintentional "natural healing." I was leaving a party one Saturday night in Berkeley, California. I had not had any alcohol to drink. On the way to the car, we encountered a woman who appeared to be mentally ill. Her hair was a mess and she was wailing, "Someone help me! I can't find my home." I was mortified at her predicament and wanted to do something to help her, but my companion insisted that she was merely intoxicated and hurried me along.

Once in my car, I felt remorse about not assisting the poor woman, but I put in one of my favorite CDs and by the time I reached my apartment complex, I had forgotten her. I drove into the underground parking garage, parked my car, and entered the elevator. I exited onto the second floor and abruptly halted in confusion. I did not know which way to go and I could not remember my apartment number, even though I had lived in the same apartment for more than two years. I was completely disoriented; every door looked the same. I meandered from one door to the next, desperate for some sign that this was where I lived, becoming more and more confused and frightened. I wondered if I was having a stroke or if someone had slipped some LSD into my drink! Finally I let out a yelp of relief when I saw my companion (a fellow clairvoyant student) standing in the door of apartment number 212. I tearfully described my perplexing loss of memory and he laughed. "You were healing that woman. You took on her confusion. Just ground yourself and you will be fine."

"How do you know?" I implored.

He explained, "Don't you remember what she was muttering: 'Help me! I am lost. I can't find my home.' That's why you suddenly could not find yours!" Hmm, I hated to admit it, but he was right.

So how do you know if you are taking on the suffering of your clients, friends, family, and even street people? A common sign that you are taking on their problem as your own is if you are talking to one of them or thinking about them and suddenly you start to feel that their situation is hopeless, as if there is no solution. Another sign is when you feel a tremendous urgency to act immediately, or if you can't stop thinking about them and feel stressed by their situation. While this may fit your definition of "caring," any experienced social worker or therapist will also recognize this as a certain road to burnout.

On an emotional level, when you take on someone else's problem, then you can no longer really objectively help them, especially when this occurs during a reading or a healing. It's like attempting to save a drowning person when you are drowning yourself. Also, as already noted, you may be encroaching on another's spiritual path, which is presenting a difficult life lesson for the person to learn. When you take on someone else's energy or problem and try to solve it as your own, you are in a sense taking on some of their karma that they themselves need to work through.

This in no way means that you should not continue to help others or be supportive or care about them deeply. It is really just a matter of pulling back your energy, understanding that you are trying to solve a problem that is not truly your own, and getting some emotional distance so you can view their situation more objectively and effectively. Sometimes the simplest method of achieving this is to quietly state to yourself, "This is not my problem," even while you are in the process of healing them through doing a reading, spiritual healing, counseling session, making a donation, etc.

CHAPTER 4

MEI Pictures and Matching Pictures

Mental/Emotional Image (MEI) pictures are concentrated pockets of emotional energy and corresponding thoughts/ideas/beliefs that have accumulated in a certain location of our body. These pockets of energy are formed over time and are records of our experiences with corresponding feelings and thoughts about the experiences. They are frames of reference that motivate and control human perception; they dictate the manner in which people interpret and react to every aspect of life. Clairvoyants see this coagulated grouping of thoughtforms, emotions, and memories in the form of images or pictures, thus the term Mental/Emotional Image picture.

Some MEI pictures are born from an initial emotionally charged or traumatic experience. Oftentimes they were created centuries ago during a person's former incarnation (past life). This experience forms a core of energy that acts like a magnet for similar experiences and energies. Over time, this collection of experiences can have a snowball effect. They can become extremely emotionally charged and have quite a strong influence on one's perceptions, attitude, and lifestyle. Some people believe that when we were initially created as spirits, we were essentially a "clean slate." We did not have any of these pictures. Over time we become polluted, clouded, and dimmed by the accumulation of these emotional and mental energies.

A core MEI picture is one that is developed early and, over time, attracts similar but less emotionally charged pictures. Many of our core MEI pictures were given to us by other people, early in our lives. They might have been handed over quite blatantly, as when a parent or teacher verbally tells us that we are defective in some way, or the picture could have been sent over energetically through telepathic thoughtforms.

As we move through everyday life, we are constantly being bombarded by other people's thoughtforms. Our self-esteem is very closely tied to how other people perceive us or how we think they perceive us, as well as the energy that they send (and that we accept). You may have noticed that when involved in certain intimate relationships, your self-esteem either rises or declines. This is largely because you are reading and to some extent buying in to the pictures that your significant other has of you, which may be totally unrelated to who you really are, but resonate with energy already in your aura.

MEI pictures can block our energy flow in a particular part of our body or energy field. They also create pockets of vulnerability. When a spirit or person wants something from us, they will usually plug into an MEI picture. During a clairvoyant reading/healing, it is helpful not only to uncover foreign energies in the chakras and aura, but also to look at what pictures these energies are attached to and then to describe these pictures. Otherwise, the foreign energy or similar energies may reattach themselves.

Not only do these pictures or pockets of energy attract similar experiences, they attract people into our lives who join us in playing out these experiences and who possess similar pictures, which are referred to as matching pictures. When someone has a matching picture with us, they have usually gone through similar life experiences. The people who are closest to us often have many matching pictures with us. Usually people who come to us for readings or healings have matching pictures with us, or one major core picture, which we are both working on at the time of the reading. Initially, this may be difficult to identify because their personalities and lives may seem quite different from our own.

In order to effect change in a person, these pictures need to be de-energized, illuminated, destroyed, or replaced. Just as accumulating these pictures is a natural process, so is discarding them. That is why we attract people in our lives with matching pictures. Every experience, event, person, etc., that we meet provides the opportunity to work through our MEI pictures so that these pictures need not control us. As already mentioned, oftentimes the energy from these experiences will glob onto the core pocket of energy to give it even more power. Just as frequently, these experiences or people will "light up" or activate the emotional energy from the picture so that we can re-experience it, release it, and move on.

Psychologists have observed for a long time that people exhibit patterns in their life that pertain to their experiences and relationships. You yourself have probably noticed how you tend to attract the same sort of love interest in your life or the same conflicts at work. When you send the intention out into the universe (through determination) that you plan to break this pattern and not repeat past mistakes, this sets a healing process in motion. The universe's response will be to send a person or experience into your life that will stimulate the core energies so you can eventually release this type of programming. In some cases you may encounter a string of unbelievably similar people within a frightfully short period of time, especially if you live in high-energy places like Sedona, Arizona, where I live, or when your determination to heal yourself is relentless.

I believe that when yogis or Buddhists talk about attaining "enlightenment" and "nonattachment," they are in a sense referring to eliminating these pictures. Since we can see these pictures during a clairvoyant reading, it is possible to work with them through clairvoyant healing by deenergizing the pictures so they have less power over our clients.

As healers, we do have the ability to actually remove a picture from the readee's energy field. But caution and discretion is advised in this area, since we may then be tampering with Mother Nature and our client's spiritual blueprint. Some spirits have worked very hard to accumulate their experiences and don't want some meddlesome psychic taking them away! Also, people ground through pictures in order to feel secure. If the MEI picture is ripped away from them too suddenly, the client may not be able to cope. What is more advisable is to identify these pictures and describe them to the client and let them know when they have "fallen into a picture" or are "stuck in a picture."

When someone is trapped inside an MEI picture, they are drowning inside a concept and emotion; they can't see the forest for the trees. This MEI picture will totally color their world. It is as if they had a paper bag over their head. Inside the bag are old snapshots of past situations and limited statements about life. The problem is not that they are trapped inside a paper bag, but that they don't know they are. The most helpful thing a psychic can do is remind the person that they are trapped within the confines of the MEI picture so they can calm down and become more of a neutral observer to their process. Oftentimes this reminder is all they need so they can begin to climb out of the picture where they can see things from a more balanced and realistic viewpoint, which will have a calming effect on their emotional state. They can then decide whether they wish to hold on to this picture or begin to establish a plan to work through the picture.

Sometimes a client will have been working on a picture for quite some time and is looking for the final catalyst to help them discard or "blow" the picture (a term used in clairvoyant training circles because you can visualize the picture exploding), which is the clairvoyant reading. However, some people are so deeply embedded in the MEI picture and controlled by it that if you try to make them aware of this fact, they will become very angry and accuse you of being insensitive.

When a psychic encounters a highly charged mental image picture and has a matching picture of their own, it may be difficult to read this picture or to talk about it. Imagine trying to read a book in the middle of a cyclone! The charge can be lessened by visually draining the emotional energy off the picture, while leaving the picture intact (see chapter 13). Since energy moves when it is observed, a psychic helps people to blow their pictures even when neither of them have an intellectual understanding or awareness of this process.

I make a point of getting at least a couple intensive readings a year from reliable clairvoyants in order to discover where I have fallen into a rut (picture) in my thinking and actions. Often a reading will set the stage for a paradigm shift, which makes room for a whole new set of experiences to enter into my life. Sometimes a client will come for a reading who may not be ready for lifetimes to work through certain pictures, but has been sent by God or the universe to the clairvoyant because the clairvoyant is ready to discard the matching picture. This is one of the main benefits of performing a reading and why it's a good idea for students to perform readings on a frequent and consistent basis. Reading helps move and release energy for both the readee and the reader.

Working Through MEI Pictures in Your Readings

The old adage "can't see the forest for the trees" can be applied aptly to MEI pictures: you don't see them when you are in the midst of them. During a clairvoyant reading, there are a few telltale signs you can watch for that will let you know when you have a matching MEI pictures with your readee. The more you have in common with your readee, the more matching pictures you have. Your readee might be so similar to you in terms of age, life experiences, issues, problems, and even appearance that there will be no doubt that this person has been sent to you to help you work through your pictures.

When you encounter several people who could be your twin in a short period of time, you will know that you are getting close to working through a huge core picture, and your awe for the perfection of the universe and the divine order of things will really grow. Initially, you may be sent a readee who seems extremely different from you, but as your reading progresses, you will discover that you do share a similar issue and thus a matching picture.

Sometimes you will have nothing in common with the readee, but they might be very similar to a person in your life who was responsible for the formation of a picture, such as a parent or spouse. In this case, you may feel a strong aversion to reading this person, even before you begin the reading, and strong emotions during the reading (often anger or fear) will emerge.

As a clairvoyant reader, any time you discover that you are experiencing an emotion, it is helpful to acknowledge to yourself that you are experiencing the emotion, to get into the center of your head (see chapter 9), and then ask God or your higher self to help you understand why you are feeling this emotion. The answer will come when the time is right. In following these steps, you will become more of an observer to your emotional state and less of a victim to it. Other indicators that you have a matching picture with your client or are on the verge of "blowing" a core picture are when you are reading along and suddenly become highly emotional or can no longer access your clairvoyance.

MEI pictures affect clairvoyants not only during readings, but in their everyday lives. Any strong judgment or idea about how things should be or must be is really just an MEI picture. One way to tell that you are trapped in an MEI picture is when you are resisting a certain situation or convinced that there is only one way to deal with a situation, but that way is not working. We are most likely trapped in an MEI picture when we are in competition with God (for example, making statements such as "my life is not supposed to be like this"); when we are resisting the hand that God or the universe has dealt us (resisting is different than trying to make positive changes; there is no grace in resistance); or when we are certain of how things are supposed to be, despite the fact they are not that way. These are the pictures that create our pain.

In addition to giving and receiving readings, watching movies can also help with the process of moving through and freeing ourselves of pictures that do not serve us. Just as with any experience in life, there is a spiritual reason why we see a particular movie at a particular time. Since movies consist of a string of millions of mental image pictures derived from the screenwriters, directors, and actors, they will certainly light up our own pictures. The more a person performs clairvoyant readings, the more adept they will become at moving though energy and pictures. I actually start to feel sluggish if I have stopped giving readings for a while, and often will start to watch a ridiculous number of movies until I resume a heavier reading schedule. Books can also have a similar cathartic effect. People who do not perform readings or watch movies are still naturally working through MEI pictures every time they converse with people or encounter new situations, only their process may be much slower and more painful if done unconsciously.

Conversely, there are many healers and psychics who get stuck in their pictures instead of working through them, and suffer more than the average person who is not doing any kind of energy work. These "sick" psychics and healers become drained and even traumatized because they don't know how to recognize and work with their matching pictures and are not using the tools presented in this book or elsewhere for releasing energy and revitalizing their own energy source (see chapters 7-12).

Upon blowing or working through a core picture, there is going to be a period of adjustment, referred to as a growth period. During this period, all kinds of emotions—possibly conflicting ones—may arise, and it can feel very unsettling because you will have just discarded what you previously thought was you, but was really just a bunch of past time perceptions, ideas, and emotions. For a while you may find yourself hanging in midair, not knowing where you will land or even who you are. You may also experience grief for all the time you wasted being caught up in those silly pictures. Just remember to go easy on yourself; you were exactly where you needed to be when you were there, just as you are perfect as you are now.

Clairvoyant Images

Clairvoyant images are essentially made up of the same stuff as dream images and visual pictures evoked through memory, imagination and visualization. Within our minds we have what my teachers called, for lack of a better term, "the picture-making apparatus or machine." This energetic apparatus seems to be located within the area of the sixth chakra, behind the physical forehead area. Many people refer to this as the third eye. Clairvoyant images are derived from the brain as well as from a universal source. They can be sent through both verbal and telepathic communication to other individuals or through visualization and prayer out into the universe where they can create and manifest physical representations (see chapter 12).

Clairvoyant and dream images can have both literal and symbolic connotations. For example, during several readings I have clearly seen the image of a person wearing a nurse's uniform. Sometimes I subsequently discovered that my readee was actually employed as a nurse. At other times it was clear that my client did not work as a nurse, but possessed a nurse's caring and healing nature, which was symbolized by nurse's attire.

One of the most difficult aspects of performing a clairvoyant reading is knowing when an image is intended as literal or symbolic. Obviously, if one misinterprets a symbolic image as a literal one, it will not only decrease the accuracy of the reading, but may cause the readee distress. For example, if you see an image of your readee stretched out in a coffin beneath a tombstone, this could literally mean that your readee is going to physically die. However, it may also symbolize dramatic change, as in a spiritual death.

There are several ways to deal with the problem of how to interpret a clairvoyant image. Oftentimes, along with a clairvoyant image you will receive a bonus from your intuition or knowingness (the psychic ability located in your seventh chakra), which gives you instant awareness of what it is you are looking at. Unfortunately this is not always the case, especially for beginning clairvoyant students. So first, I recommend that if you are confused as to whether an image should be interpreted symbolically or literally, you ask the image to show you another image that will provide more clarity. With patience and perseverance, your request will be granted more often than not.

During one reading, I saw the image of a heart that looked all black and that seemed to be struggling to continue beating. Unsure of the meaning of this image, I further probed the image by visualizing the weak heart and directing it to reveal more details. This time I saw an image of my client lying in a hospital bed with an IV in his arm, which told me I was looking at a literal image.

When further prompting of a questionable image fails to produce useful clues, you can tell your client, "I am seeing this image, but I don't know what it means." Of course discretion must be used when the literal interpretation points to something serious, like a death or severe illness or injury. It gets tricky when seeing information regarding the physical body because sometimes an illness may not yet be visual or noticeable to the readee but will already be having an effect on the energetic body. In the above-mentioned reading, I gently "tested the waters" with my client with the question, "Have you been experiencing any health problems lately?" My readee confirmed that he had recently had open-heart surgery, which helped me know that I was on the right track and further confirmed that the image did have a literal meaning.

During another reading on a female client, I again saw an image of a heart. It appeared to be bleeding and looked mutilated or crushed. This time further clairvoyant questioning of the image displayed pictures of an angry man jumping on her chest. Because it was unlikely that a man had literally been jumping on her heart, I was fairly certain I was dealing with symbolism. My intuition/knowingness and logical understanding of the effects of emotional trauma on the physical body told me that if my client did not release the pain that was associated with the man in the image, she could be vulnerable to a physical heart attack. As in most readings of this type, I described the symbolic images but also recommended that she follow up with a medical examination just in case the image also had a literal meaning. She later revealed that her husband of twenty-five years had betrayed her, and that she had undergone heart surgery a year before.

When training beginning clairvoyant students, I advise against asking the readee too many questions, since this pulls the students from their reading space and tempts them to rely on a source other than their own clairvoyance. Also, the readee may give an incorrect response (sometimes intentionally, sometimes inadvertently), which will confuse and negatively impact the certainty of the fledgling student. It also puts pressure on the readee to communicate and validate the student, which is not the readee's responsibility since they are there to receive.

When doing a clairvoyant reading, I suggest that you get out of your logical mind and resist the urge to interpret everything you see. If the clairvoyant image is not accompanied by a clear knowing, then simply describe the image precisely as you see it. Whenever I have been wrong about information in a reading, it was due to my logical interpretation and not to the image itself. Clairvoyant images are almost always pure and do not lie. There is always a reason a particular image is being generated. You don't always need to know the reason or the meaning for every image. You'll be surprised at how often your client knows exactly what is meant by the imagery you have described. Sometimes your client will not want you to know the meaning, and that is why you aren't getting the information.

Clairvoyant images are generated by the mind of the clairvoyant, by the mind of the person receiving the reading, or from a third party such as another spirit or one of the subjects of the reading. Clairvoyant images also come from what is sometimes referred to as the universal mind or the collective unconscious (a term coined by Carl Jung).

Sometimes your readee will understand the meaning of the images you are looking at before you do because the images have been borrowed from their personal library rather than yours. Sometimes you won't be able to interpret an image because you are stuck inside an MEI picture (see chapter 4).

During a reading with a client named Sarah, I saw an image of a glowing golden heart that seemed to have been carefully placed in the back seat of a black limousine. I had absolutely no idea what this meant, and further probing did not help. I almost disregarded this image because it did not make sense to me, but fortunately I obeyed my intuition and communicated the vision to Sarah. She immediately burst into tears and explained that her father used to be a limousine driver and had given her a small golden locket in the shape of a heart a few days before he died. I felt that this image was generated by both her and her deceased father. The image really had no personal meaning for me.

During another reading, I was asked by a mother and daughter to explain the questionable death of young man who had been a close friend of the family. I immediately saw an image of a man lying on his side, his head casually propped up by one arm. He was smiling. Because it was uncommon for me to notice the position in which someone is lying during a reading, I suspected that this must be significant, although I had no idea why. I described the image, which prompted the mother to yank out her wallet and thrust a photograph into my hands. The photograph was of a young man lying in that exact position, with a huge grin on his face. I felt that this image was generated by either the man who had died or the women I was reading. These woman later revealed that they initially had doubts as to the authenticity of my reading abilities. Unbeknownst to me, I had participated in a demonstration that won their confidence so that they were able to trust the subsequent information I revealed regarding this man's mysterious death.

While I vehemently avoid the game of "prove it" or "test the psychic," I began making it a general practice at the beginning of a reading to ask my clairvoyance to give me a symbol related to the person in question so that my client and I would both know that I was tuned in to the correct person. This request has become so automatic that I no longer consciously have to voice or think about it; oftentimes the first image that comes to me in a reading is this telltale symbol.

After many years of doing readings, I have found that there is a direct correlation between the clarity of my images and the clairvoyant ability and permissiveness of my readee. When my clairvoyance is operating at full force, it is usually because my readee is naturally very open to their own clairvoyance. When I can't see anything, it is because this person does not have permission (their own or from others) to use their clairvoyance. When I see very amusing images, it is usually because my readee has a good sense of humor, just as dramatic images seem to come from dramatic clients. When I see images depicting one problem after another, it is usually because my readee is focused on problems. When I see lots of sexual images...well, you guessed it!

Usually, a symbol becomes a symbol because a person or entire culture had an experience with an object and then later the object was used to represent that experience. The swastika was used by the Nazi Germans, so now when most people encounter this symbol, they think of hatred and intolerance, although that was not its original meaning. As a child, I had an extreme fear of bugs, so when I see images of bugs surrounding a person, these bugs symbolize some kind of fear-producing agent in the readee's life (this has been confirmed on numerous occasions by my clients).

In the psychic realms, since there really is no time or space, the usual sequential process of symbolism can be reversed, so that the clairvoyant or readee encounters a seemingly meaningless and unfamiliar object during a reading and only later do they have a personal experience with this object that gives the object significance.

Clairvoyant images are almost like living entities. They have a life of their own, and they reveal themselves in mysterious ways. As a beginning clairvoyant student, it is easy to become frustrated with the mischievous elusiveness of these enigmas. I encourage you to treat these visions as your personal teacher or guru. At times your teacher will give you an immediate response and tell you exactly what you want to know in very straightforward terms. At other times they will send you blindfolded and stumbling into the forest so that you discover your answers through direct experience. Some of the most helpful traits a clairvoyant can have are patience, determination, and the ability to apply these simultaneously, with grace.

Library of Symbols

Over the years, I have built up a collection of symbolic images that help me pick up and interpret information more quickly and efficiently during a reading. I did not create them with my logical mind; rather they spontaneously and repeatedly appeared to me in my readings and later in dreams as well. On many occasions, these particular symbols appeared to other psychics when they were reading me. These particular symbols are shortcuts and signposts that provide information to me in a concise and easily identifiable manner. These images are animated; they move. They interact with other images to tell a particular story about the person I am reading. Their relationship to other images provides even more information than the image itself.

Clairvoyant symbols operate in the same way as symbols in real life. When you drive down the street, you will often see a stop sign. A stop sign is an easily identified and understood symbol that communicates the message that you need to stop. In order to fully understand its meaning, you need to look at its relationship to its location and to other cars and people, including yourself. A stop sign will always mean stop, but it may not be telling you to stop if it is positioned across the street or if it is turned away from you. In the same way, when a stop sign appears to me in a clairvoyant reading, I understand that someone is saying stop, but I need to look further to find out who is holding the stop sign, who is reading it, and why they are saying stop.

Some of the images I have accumulated in my personal clairvoyant library are those of a window, an apple, a tree, champagne glasses, a piano, a ceiling, a staircase, a mirror, a playground swing, a sun, and a stop sign. In chapter 16, I offer suggestions on how you can utilize some of these symbols to help you navigate your way through a reading. Over time, you as a clairvoyant will develop your own library of symbolic images. The more you work with them, the richer they will become and the more they will appear in your dreams and other aspects of your waking life.

PART II

The Psychic Tools

CHAPTER 6

Introduction to
the Psychic Tools

The psychic tools are visualization techniques that can be utilized throughout a psychic reading as well as in your daily life. When performed in solitude, they also form a simple yet powerful method of meditation. These clairvoyant tools can help you prepare to do readings and healings on other people by strengthening your visualization abilities. They will protect and energize you, help you maintain boundaries, aid in the release of foreign or unwanted energies, help you be in present time, facilitate a sense of calmness and neutrality, and strengthen the communication between you and your innermost self. In other words, these are self-healing techniques. They are also methods that can later be used in the healing of others. In the following chapters, I will explain the purpose and value of each tool and then provide a step-by-step description of how to use each one.

When you are visualizing something, you are not "just using your imagination," a popular expression that implies you are merely playing around with some mental processes that go no further than your mind. As I already described in previous chapters, your thoughts consist of energy. This energy can be propelled outward into the universe to elicit a response. Likewise, when you form a mental image in your mind, you are actually organizing energy into a powerful form that may influence other energies in yourself (mind, spirit, and body) and in other people. Therefore, when you are visualizing or utilizing the "psychic tools," you will actually be manipulating, moving, and changing energy. Sometimes this will be accompanied by an obvious corresponding physical sensation or emotional response. For example, when you ground, you may feel pain pumping out of your foot; when you call back your energy, you may feel a tingling or pulsating sensation in your head.

Other people can also feel the effects of your visualizations. At the beginning of the reading, while my client is sitting across from me, I prepare for the reading by running through my repertoire of psychic tools. On several occasions, my more sensitive clients (usually other professional psychics who are unaware of these tools, but are in desperate need of them) have suspiciously asked, "What are you doing to me? I can feel all kinds of things happening with my energy." Surprised, I assured them, "I was not doing anything to you. I was totally focused on myself. In fact, for a few moments there I was not even conscious of you being in the room. I was grounding myself and running my earth and cosmic energies. Your body was just matching my own."

Beware of Expectations

In addition to reaping the benefits of the psychic tools that will be presented in subsequent chapters, sometimes it is the corresponding physical sensations that propel the novice clairvoyant from a state of faith to one of certainty. However, I must caution that the most certain road to failure and frustration is the one laden with expectations.

You will experience the psychic tools in your own unique way. Some of you will be blown away by your first visualization attempt and others will not feel a single thing. Some of you will find using the psychic tools to be fun, easy, and gratifying, while others will initially be frustrated and may call it quits before realizing the benefits. Some of you who have already been using similar techniques for years will appreciate the reminder that there are many paths to the same kingdom, while others will think that their techniques are superior and feel irritated by my suggestions. The important thing is to do what works for you. Sometimes, before you know what works, you need to have faith and experiment a bit. Some miracles occur instantaneously, while others take time and perseverance.

CHAPTER 7

Psychic Tool 1: Grounding

Webster's Vest Pocket Dictionary defines grounding as "a conductor that makes electrical connection with the earth or a framework." For animate and inanimate physical objects, grounding is achieved through the law of gravity. Gravity is defined in the same dictionary as "attraction of bodies towards the center of the earth." Without gravity, we would be plummeted into space and would not be able to exist on earth. We would be unstable, like a feather caught in a cyclone.

To some extent, our physical bodies are always grounded or connected to the earth (even when flying in an airplane, we are still connected to the earth's atmosphere by the gravitational pull, therefore we can walk down the aisle of the plane without floating away). But what about our energetic or spiritual bodies? Some people are more grounded than others, and our grounding, our connection with the earth, can change drastically from minute to minute. Oftentimes, when a person is experiencing stress, nervousness, pain, or extreme emotions, their spiritual body becomes ungrounded. When a person is ungrounded, even though their physical body is still attached to the earth, the rest of their energy may be all over the place. It might be soaring above their head, searching for a kinder and gentler abode; or it might be racing through whatever unfortunate person happens to be in their path.

People who lose things frequently, who become hysterical or "hyper," who are spacey, who have trouble following directions, or who are not conscious of what they are doing or feeling are often ungrounded (don't feel bad, most of those adjectives describe myself as well!). When you are ungrounded, you are much more vulnerable to becoming the effect of whatever or whoever is around you, and other people may find it difficult or annoying to be in your presence.

For example, if you are ungrounded and visit a friend who is also ungrounded and in a lousy mood, within minutes your original cheerful disposition may be replaced by your friend's grouchiness. Or if you are ungrounded and driving, not only might you become lost, you might also become as irritable as all the other drivers who are in a hurry, even though you have plenty of time to reach your destination (road rage would probably not occur if everyone were well grounded). In the same respect, if you are ungrounded during a psychic reading, you will be more likely to match whatever negative energies are in the room.

The grounding of our spirit and even our physical body can be strengthened through the use of a grounding cord. This energetic vehicle will harness your energy so that you can focus and remain calm and strong even in the face of adversity.

Picture a thousand-year-old redwood tree with enormous roots going a half mile or more deep into the earth. Do you think a strong gust of wind or an overly enthusiastic lumberjack could knock over this tree? Not likely! Could this wind capsize a ship secured into the depths of the ocean by a rope as thick as a man and an iron anchor as large as the Empire State Building? Probably not! In the same way, if your body and spirit are connected into the earth by a strong energetic cord (achieved through visualization), then when your boss unexpectedly reprimands or fires you, when a mugger jumps out at you from the bushes, or when the person you are clairvoyantly reading suddenly leaps from their chair and starts barking like a dog, you will be able to retain your calm composure and respond rather than react. If this does not seem likely, then you are probablyjust not used to being grounded!

In addition to securing you to the earth and harnessing your energy, grounding is a very powerful and effective means of releasing negative energy or energy that is no longer serving you, as in the case of pain, anxiety, stress, unwanted thoughts, etc. Gravity not only pulls you toward the earth, but also everything in and around you. So your grounding cord can ground out everything and everyone that is in your body or energetic field that no longer serves you. Any worries, any emotion, any thoughts, any image, any pain, any problem, or anyone else's energy can be immediately released through your connection to the earth.

A grounding cord can be visualized as any object. A strong rope, a column of light, a string of flowers or stars, a waterfall, a tree, an extension of your legs, a hollow pipe, a hearty string of pearls, or a fluffy pink boa (for formal occasions!) are just a few possibilities. The grounding cord should be plugged into your first chakra (spinning energy center), located at the base of your spine. It extends and connects you to the center of the planet. In the realm of spirit, there is no time or space, so your grounding cord can instantaneously reach the center of the earth, and of course it can pass through whatever happens to be beneath you. You can ground anywhere, even from an airplane. However, grounding outside, with your feet touching the earth, is often the easiest.

While you can ground from any part of your body, I suggest grounding from your first chakra because this is the energy center that actually regulates the functioning of your lower body and its connection to the physical world. It is important to realize that even though this is where the connection point is located, you can easily release energy from any point of your body or energetic field, even from the top of your head. Just imagine whatever you wish to release within yourself dislodging itself effortlessly from wherever it is located, and immediately passing through your first chakra (as if that were a drain) and falling down your grounding cord until it is released into the center of the earth. Thanks to the gravitational pull of the earth, you don't really need to exert any effort. Just let gravity suck whatever you wish to release (you don't need to know what that is) down your cord.

Once whatever you are releasing reaches the center of the earth (which is scalding hot), it dissipates and returns to its original source, so you are not polluting or hurting the earth in any way. When you release another person from your energy field, you are actually freeing their energy so it can be returned to them. You are not hurting them in any way. You may experience feelings of guilt or fear when you imagine a loved one falling down your grounding cord. These feelings have to do with breaking your former agreement to heal, carry, support, and feed that person your energy, and with that person's resistance to detaching from your field. If you do feel guilty when you release someone down your cord, then ask yourself what color might represent that feeling and visualize the color releasing down your cord as well. Also remember that a person has no more right to be in your field than they do to touch your physical body or enter your home without your permission.

The following example will illustrate how to release a person from your energy field with the use of your grounding cord. Let's say that you keep thinking about your boss, who is worried about meeting some deadlines. You realize that you can't stop thinking about your boss because his energy is inside your head. Imagine that there are some trap doors at the bottom of your head. Then visualize your boss and his energy (ask yourself what color represents your boss' energy or assign it a color, and see that color releasing so that next time you see that color, you will know whose energy it is) falling through these doors and being sucked into your grounding cord, where he continues to fall until he reaches the center of the earth. Then see his image exploding or dissipating. If you become worried that you are hurting or irritating your boss by sending him into the fires of the earth, then visualize a color that represents the worried feeling and send it down your cord as well. Then imagine that his energy is being cleansed in the hot earth, and in your imagination watch it as it returns to his body, which you can postulate is growing happier and healthier as it fills up with his own essence.

Once you have grounded your body, it is important to make sure that your aura, or the energy field surrounding your body, is tucked into your grounding cord so that you can release whatever stubborn foreign energy may be trapped inside. This is easily accomplished by willfully tucking or inserting the entire circumference of your aura into your cord below your feet. Remember that your aura surrounds your entire body, including your head and feet. Even though the bottom of your aura is what is tucked into the cord, anything lodged in the top of your aura will be sucked downward by the gravitational pull. This is done through your imagination and intent. The more clearly you can visualize this, the more effective it will be.

You can practice grounding anytime, anywhere. I recommend practicing grounding when you are alone in meditation so you can really focus, as well as in public places so you can experience the difference. I suggest playing around with your grounding in a variety of situations, such as when dealing with a stressful family event, when attending a staff meeting, when running or doing aerobic exercise, when you are lost, and even when you are intoxicated!

When performing grounding the first few times, you may want to do it alone in a quiet place so you can feel free to release any emotions that may come up. Some people like to ground themselves in their car. While it is very helpful to be grounded when driving, you should be cautious because visualizing any of your psychic tools does take some concentration that will pull your attention away from anything else you are doing at that moment, which obviously can be dangerous when driving. Also, sometimes grounding may cause you to feel sleepy due to the various energies you are releasing, and this could cause further problems when driving.

Grounding can be done when you are standing or sitting. In order to prepare yourself to perform clairvoyant readings, I suggest that you ground yourself while sitting in a chair, versus the floor, since you will usually read other people from a chair and what you do in your meditation space will create an automatic response in your reading space.

Some yogic postures and dance practices naturally ground a person, while others have the opposite effect. It is always good to ground yourself when beginning and ending any activity. If you engage in any type of spiritual/psychic practice that facilitates the release of your spirit or traveling of your energetic bodies, I highly advise that you ground yourself and call your energy back to your body at the completion of the session. Otherwise you may have a difficult time driving home or functioning in your daily life.

When you visualize your grounding or any other psychic tool, it is helpful to see it in as much detail as possible. With your grounding cord, you should occasionally check the connection points to make sure it is secure (one end connected to your first chakra, the other at the center of the earth). Sometimes you will have to willfully create the details of your cord, while at other times your cord will show itself to you in a form that appears spontaneously, without your conscious manipulation. When this happens, you are apt to be surprised and even impressed with the imagery that came from somewhere other than your logical mind. The important thing is to really see the cord in your imagination rather than just intellectually postulate that it is there. This attention to detail demands some discipline, but the results will be more fruitful.

If at any time you notice that your grounding cord has changed in a way you do not desire, or you feel uncomfortable with its appearance, or it appears damaged, or you see the image of someone you know in it, then it is a good idea to destroy this grounding cord and create a new one, preferably one that is in some way slightly different from the last. The reason for this is because your grounding may get polluted with the energies you have been trying to release, or may become the target of energies that wish to influence or control you. When you change your cord, those energies have a harder time locating you again.

If you are having difficulty visualizing a certain part of your cord, or you find it very difficult to concentrate when you attempt to create one, you are probably being affected by some foreign energy. This is similar to what happens with a clogged vacuum cleaner, a malfunctioning garbage disposal, the rusty pipes connected to your kitchen sink, or even your own intestines.

Destroying Your Grounding Cord

If there is foreign energy affecting your grounding, there is an easy solution: get rid of it! All you need to do is will that energy to go down your cord, or destroy it along with the cord and continue to create and destroy new ones until you are no longer experiencing any difficulty. Destroying your grounding cord is very simple to do. Just imagine that you are rolling it up into a little ball, and then see that ball exploding or dissipating into nothingness. (If you are having any difficulties with destroying, read chapter 12.) There are also preventative measures you can take against attack of your grounding by postulating and imagining that your cord is impenetrable. You can even give it a protective shield similar to the one that protects the Starship Enterprise on Star Trek! Even if you have complete faith in the cleanliness of your grounding, it is still helpful to occasionally destroy and re-create it (even though it may seem easier to just keep the old one—sure, you'd also save time if you never took a bath or changed your clothes!).

Just like your energy and your mind, your grounding cord can easily get stuck in past time. The type, size, and nature of your grounding cord will change from day to day or even minute to minute. Sometimes a thin and light cord is sufficient, while during stressful times a super heavy-duty cord is in order.

One way to make sure that your cord is in present time is to create a new one in your imagination and write the date and time on it. You can also write your name on it with the same color as the clothes you are presently wearing. Then postulate that you are bringing your grounding cord into present time, in sync with where your body currently is, which is, and can only ever be, in the present. If you take a vacation, move to a new apartment, spend the night with a friend, etc., you should make sure that your grounding cord is connected to the earth below your present location and not where you were previously located. Jet lag and culture shock could be minimized and even prevented if most people understood the concept of grounding in present time.

Grounding Yourself

The following exercise can be performed in a number of ways. I suggest that you read the exercise through a few times and then attempt it. If you have difficulty recalling each step, you can attempt the exercise as you read along. Another effective method would be to dictate the words into a tape recorder and then play it back. You could also practice with a friend, taking turns reading the exercise to each other.

After performing this grounding exercise a few times, it will become natural, and you can then play around with creating your own grounding methods and individualized grounding cord. Give yourself at least ten minutes to perform the following exercise. The more time you spend grounding, the greater the benefits.

Close your eyes, sit in a chair with your feet touching the ground, and relax. Imagine that there is a very heavy and strong rope, weighing hundreds of tons, sitting under your chair. Picture this rope and all the details. Examine the fibers. How thick are they? In what way do they twist? What is the color of the rope? Is the rope consistent all the way down in terms of shape, color, and size? How long it is? How thick is it? Does the thickness change from top to bottom? Smell the rope. Taste it (oops, you may need to pull out some of the prickly fibers from your tongue!). Notice that the rope is hollow inside, and this hollow is lined with very strong and slippery metal. See both ends of the rope and notice if the rope is frayed at all or if there is a neat knot on each end. You are free to change anything about the rope that makes you doubt its strength or makes you uncomfortable.

Now, physically, pantomime picking up part of the rope. As you reach down under your chair, see yourself picking up one end. Next, bring the end of the rope up to your first chakra, at the base of your spine. With your left hand (remember, you are holding the rope in your right hand), feel the base of your spine. See your first chakra at the base of your spine spinning like a washing machine.

Now you are going to insert one end of the rope into this spinning center. The knot on the rope is bigger than the chakra, so once it is in there, it will not fall out. See it in there. Tug on it. If it comes out, make the knot bigger, then try again until it is secure. You can always use some hearty glue to stick it in there and hold it in place, glue that cannot fail unless you wish it to come loose.

Now reach under your chair again and take hold of the other end of the rope. Also under your chair is a very heavy, very large cement brick. Loop the rope around the brick. Now, at the count of three, you are going to drop this rope into the earth. It is the kind of rope that can expand as long as it wants, even millions of miles. There are no time or spatial limitations when dealing with energy and your imagination, so it only takes a a millisecond to reach the center of the planet. This rope can penetrate any kind of physical matter, so even if you are at the top of a twenty-story apartment building or flying in an airplane, you will be able to ground.

Now see the rope in the center of the planet. What does the center of the planet look like? Is there molten lava? What color is it? If you are having any difficulty, you can even draw a circle around the brick and write "center of the planet" with your magic crayon. You may try tugging on the rope to see what happens to the brick. If it rises up a bit, you may want to secure it more firmly into the center of the planet. Congratulations, you have formed your grounding cord!

Now just watch this cord for a few minutes. Look at it from the top to the bottom. Notice how your body feels. Now that your cord is secure, it is time to release out of it. Since the gravity of the earth is naturally sucking all the foreign/negative energies out of you, your aura, and your cord, you don't have to exert any effort. Just relax and watch to see what is being released. If you feel yourself making an effort, then release this down your cord. If you are becoming distracted by thoughts about other people, your work, or various problems in your life, know this is the energy that you are releasing. Visualize these distractions in the form of an image or symbol and see them falling down your cord into the center of the planet.

At this time, it may be a good idea to ground your aura. Imagine that the part of your aura around your feet is melting into your grounding cord (which in this exercise is in the form of a rope). You may need to first expand the circumference of your rope so that all of your aura can be tucked into the rope. Now postulate that all foreign energies in your aura, even from the very top of it, are effortlessly falling down through your grounding cord into the center of the planet. When you are finished, you can thank your cord for its good work and then see the cord exploding into a million pieces. Once it is fully destroyed, create a new grounding cord. Introduce yourself to this new cord and ask it to keep you secure and help you release, throughout your day.

Now that you have released all the unwanted energies, it's important to fill yourself up with your own energy, which you will learn how to do in the next chapter.

Grounding Your Surroundings

Once you have mastered the concept of grounding yourself, it is important to ground your surroundings. Otherwise, the gravitational pull of your powerful grounding cord will inadvertently suck up whatever energies surround you, and these energies may overwhelm you. This is similar to what happens when you are vacuuming the floor and the nearby rug gets sucked into the vacuum cleaner as well, making it difficult to clean the portion of the floor you were concerned with. Sometimes the rug may even damage or break the vacuum cleaner. If your grounding cord sucks up all the energies in the room, then you will likely experience those energies, which would defeat the purpose of your grounding. The solution here is to give your surroundings (that is, the room you are sitting in) a grounding cord of their own. This will help cleanse the room, strengthen the power of your own grounding cord, and allow your cord to work just for you.

Visualize the room you are occupying. Imagine that you are drawing a column of golden light in each corner of the room. It is a column or pillar, much like in the Greek Coliseum or outside the typical white house. It is very wide and sturdy even though it is made of light. Each column runs from the ceiling of the room (it could extend upward to the roof) down to the floor. Once it reaches the floor it continues to extend below the floor, past the foundation of the house, down through the mud and rocks and water until it reaches into the center of the earth. Once you have at least one column in each corner of the room (some rooms have more then four corners so you could do a column for the other corner, but this is not essential), then make a column that is twice as thick in the center of the room, extending this one down ward to the center of the earth. Next, connect each column in the corners to the one in the center of the room with lines of golden light. By the time you are finished, you will have what looks like a may pole.

Now you can command all the energy in the room that is not in alignment with you and your goals to leave the room through these columns of light. Imagine that the earth is effortlessly pulling down deep into its center the energy from people, spirits, or other entities; extraneous emotional energy; any energy that is getting in the way of your serenity, happiness, ability to accomplish your tasks, etc. As the energy releases, you can look to see what colors are falling down the columns, or you can just know that they are being released. As you do this, be aware of any physical sensations you may be feeling.

Once you have grounded the room, it's time to own it. Imagine that you are writing your name, in a color of your choice, across at least four of the walls. See your picture hanging on the wall as well.

Once you have finished grounding and owning the room, you can go on to ground your entire house, office, etc. You can repeat this procedure for each room, or you can imagine that the entire building is surrounded by a golden ball of light. Imagine that the ball of light has an absolutely enormous grounding cord that secures it firmly into the center of the planet. Imagine all extraneous energy releasing down through this grounding cord. Next, you can go on to ground the entire street, then the neighborhood, city, state, country, or even the universe!

Benefits of Grounding and Owning the Room

Grounding and owning the room not only protects you and keeps your own grounding cord intact, it actually allows you to heal a room. When I conduct house healings, 95 percent of my technique is the one just described. Once you have grounded a room or house, you will find that it is either much easier to be in it, to keep it clean and organized, or to move away from it if that is what is in your best interest.

Grounding a room or building can be done while you are in it or from a remote location. When you ground and own a location, you are actually making it safe for yourself. If you ground a location before a job interview, a party, a confrontational meeting, a court proceeding, or even a visit to the grocery store, it is much more likely that you will arrive at your location feeling comfortable and that things will either work out in your favor or they will at least flow in a much more pleasant and peaceful manner.

Grounding a Lost Object

You can use the technique of grounding to help find any lost object or person. All you need to do is ground yourself first, and then ground the object with a grounding cord of the same color. Visualize and feel yourself being happy as you find the object, and then start wandering aimlessly around the location where you believe you lost it. If the object is somewhere else, you may suddenly feel inspired to go to that location, or the object will turn up sometime in the near future.

This process doesn't have anything to do with thinking or clairvoyant reading. I have greater success with grounding an object as opposed to clairvoyantly reading the location of the object, because my logical mind usually gets in the way with thoughts about where the object should logically be. Personally, I have a 99 percent success rate with finding lost objects through the use of grounding. However, I do know other psychics who are quite adept at finding objects clairvoyantly, so I encourage you to try finding them through reading as well as through grounding.

Grounding an object seems to work in a few different ways. For objects that are hidden right under your nose, grounding the object removes whatever energy may be concealing the object from you, while grounding yourself removes the energy from your aura that is blocking you from seeing the object. This process also helps remove blockages from your memory. Grounding yourself and the object with a grounding cord of the same color creates a magnetic attraction on the physical plane between these two cords that helps you find the object. Since thoughts and emotions create reality, visualizing yourself finding the object while feeling happy naturally draws the lost object to you.

CHAPTER 8

Psychic Tool 2: Self-Energizing Technique

As discussed in chapter 3, your energy has the ability to leave your body and aura and travel anywhere. Oftentimes it is hanging out in places like your workplace, in any project you have been focused on, in your spouse's aura, or even in your computer! Most people have a large amount of energy in the future or the past, which makes it difficult to appreciate and make the most of the present moment. Since your energy is where your thoughts are, if you are worrying about where you should live in six months or about a rude comment your coworker made several weeks ago, then your energy is out of present time and plugged into the source of your worries.

The most extreme example of a spirit's energy being separated from the body is in death. When a person is sick or has organ failure, it is usually because their own energy is not running through that part of their body, either because their energy is somewhere else, or because someone else's energy is in that part, obstructing the flow.

Our energy often goes to our relationships and the people we are in relationship with. When this happens, it is harder to think and act for ourselves, to focus on ourselves or creative projects, and to maintain our emotional, mental, and physical health. When our energy is engaged in an unhappy or abusive relationship with a negative thinking or behaving person, we are particularly vulnerable to illness and exhaustion. However, even if we have a perfect relationship, when too much of our energy is going to that relationship or person, we can still become unbalanced. Anytime a person suffers from an addiction, whether to a substance, to their job, or to another person, they are experiencing a problem with their own energy flow. One way to solve this problem is by using techniques that aid you in calling back your own energy.

If you spend most of your time thinking about your lover, spouse, child, friend, or whoever, you are most likely giving them too much of their energy, or their energy is occupying too much of your energetic field. Anytime you decide you don't want to think about someone or something anymore but can't stop yourself from having obsessive thoughts, then this is a sure sign that you need to call back your energy. Calling back your energy will not only help stop unwanted thoughts, it will also decrease confusion and increase your ability to communicate with your inner voice. It will also help you feel more alive, peppy, motivated, and enthusiastic about your life.

Just be aware that other people can very strongly feel when you are extracting your energy from them, or when you are shifting it away from a project that they are invested in as well, and you are likely to get a strong reaction from those people. In the case of calling your energy back from your boyfriend, you could get any number of reactions. He may suddenly begin to feel insecure and call you to find out why it's been three full hours since you last talked! Or he may welcome his newfound sense of space and autonomy, which will make him feel so happy and appreciative of you that he buys you a gift or even proposes. On the other hand, he may finally have enough distance from you that he can do what he has been unable to do for months-break up with you! (Oops, did I say something wrong?) The only sure thing will be that he and the universe will notice your shift in energy and respond in an appropriate manner for your ultimate good. However, your ultimate good is not always what you desire in the moment. You may or may not be emotionally ready for the response you get when you call back your energy.

People who are involved in creative projects such as artists, writers, filmmakers, etc., will really benefit from the tool of calling back their energy because part of the creative process has to do with leaving one's body and entering into the project at hand.

While I first began writing this book, I spent about four hours a day typing ferociously at the computer, unaware of anything besides the words pouring out on the page, and not even really aware that I was moving my hands over the keyboard. This worked well during the writing process, but once I was finished for the day, it was very annoying because I found I could think of nothing else. Not only was I losing sleep, but I was walking around like a zombie, totally absorbed in my book. Several times a day my son's father would ask me if I was all right and even my baby would be looking at me quizzically, like "Where are you, Mommy?" The problem was that so much of my energy was merged with this book. Oftentimes the only way I could rectify the situation was by calling back my energy during a meditation session.

I have found that oftentimes the creative process requires us to leave our bodies and go elsewhere so that we can be free to explore new avenues and be totally immersed in our projects. This is fine until it is necessary to come back down to earth and accomplish the more mundane tasks of life, like driving to work or paying our bills. Then we need to have a way to get more fully back into our bodies and into the present moment.

The psychic tool of calling back your energy will help tremendously with this necessity. During a clairvoyant reading or healing, it is particularly important to call your energy back both during the reading and upon completion of it because it is so easy for your energy to enter the other person's energetic field as you are wandering around in there.

One of the difficulties I have had as a psychic is that during particularly challenging readings I will sometimes go too deeply into a person because I will be trying so hard to look at the source of their difficulty, while they are not really open to knowing it. So rather than back off, I go deeper and deeper until I find the answer. When this happens, essentially what I am doing is merging my energy with theirs, and by the end of the reading not only do I feel depleted, but I may not be able to stop thinking about the person (a sure sign that this has happened is when I start having nightmares about the person!). The only way I have found to rectify this situation is to consciously call my energy back when I notice that I am doing or have done this.

During a clairvoyant reading, you will be releasing lots of energy as you read, particularly when you use a grounding cord. If you don't fill yourself up throughout the reading, you will not only become exhausted, but you will be more vulnerable to bringing in undesirable foreign energies. Anytime you use the powerful release tool of grounding, it's important that you call back your own energy. As my teachers used to say, "Nature abhors a vacuum." If you don't fill yourself up with your own energy after you have grounded, then something else will (possibly the energy you just released!). There's a pleasant thought!

Calling Back Your Energy

Visualize a big golden shimmering sun. Its rays are molten hot and so bright that you must squint when you look at it. See it levitating a few inches above your head. Now pretend that you are taking a magic marker and writing your name in the middle of this sun. Just beneath your name, see a strong shiny magnet. This is one of the most powerful magnets in the world, but the only thing that it will attract is your own energy. Now you are ready to call back your energy.

Postulate that wherever your energy is, no matter how far away, within a few moments at the most it is going to return to you in your golden sun. Call back your energy from your relationships, from your job, from your goals, your projects, your family, your pets, your possessions, your past, and your future. All of this energy is going to collect up inside your golden sun first, where it can be cleansed and revitalized. Know that any foreign energy that is attached to your energy will not be able to withstand the heat of your golden sun. See the sun getting bigger and bigger until it is ready to burst.

Now using your physical fingers, touch the top of your head. Pretend you are poking a hole in your crown chakra, or the top of your head. Now physically take your finger and poke a hole in the bottom of your golden sun. (Note that by physically going through these actions, you are helping your spirit and imagination to more fully accept and integrate these actions.) Once you have done this, you can relax your hands.

Now imagine that all of your revitalized energy that has collected up in your golden sun is effortlessly pouring from the bottom of the sun into the top of your head. It instantaneously falls to the tip of your toes and fills up your feet, ankles, calves, thighs, torso, chest, shoulders, and neck. It spills into your arms and hands, filling them up until your energy flows through and out of the little spinning chakras in your hands and into your aura. Your own energy continues to fill up your neck, face, and head, spilling back out of the hole in the top of your head and into your aura.

Know that your body and aura are getting filled so full with your own energy, your own life force, that the energy overflows from your eyes, mouth, ears, and nose. It continues to fill up your organs, such as your heart and lungs, and you even see it flow through your veins and cells. See the energy flow through your chakras so strongly that it causes them to spin. See a little bit of your energy as it runs down your grounding cord, strengthening it and helping you own it. Once you are certain that you have completely filled up your entire body and being, imagine that you are sealing off the hole that you created in the top of your head. Thank your golden sun for working for you and then visualize it floating off into the atmosphere until it's time to call upon it again.

CHAPTER 9

Psychic Tool 3:
Neutrality

A psychic's best friend is her neutrality. A psychic's worst enemy is her emotional response as well as expectations and attachment to outcome. When you are neutral, you are calm and collected. You are like a conscientious captain, navigating his ship safely through stormy seas, which may require changing the ship's original course. When you are caught up in the whirlwind of your emotions and expectations, you are like a desperate captain who is so intent on reaching the desired destination that he forces his ship into the eye of the storm, becoming lost at sea and causing his crew to declare mutiny. During a clairvoyant reading, the psychic must navigate her way through emotions and energies as tumultuous as any hurricane and address problems of tidalwave proportion. If you don't know how to swim well, you are likely to sink, no matter how clearly you can see images or pick up extrasensory information.

Many of your clients will be in pain, in fear, in doubt, and in trouble. Many people who come to you for a reading are not just coming for a reading. They are coming to be healed, to have all their pain eliminated, all their problems solved, all their worries banished—instantaneously. If they don't leave the reading feeling better (even though you just gave them important or even life-saving information, but information they did not want to hear), there is one person they will blame...YOU.

Some people will ask a question, but will then do everything possible to block you from seeing the true answer. Some will demand that you tell them everything while revealing nothing, greedily guarding their secrets with every ounce of their being, erecting fortresses around their quivering souls faster than you can burrow through their walls of defense. Some will lie. Some people will worship you, some will lust after you, some will compete with you, and still others will hate you, being unable to be okay with themselves until they have turned you to mush. On very rare occasions a client could actually become violent.

In your readings you will see people who are hapless victims of insidious abuse and who are molesters of children. You will read thieves, liars, drug addicts, and adulterers. People's problems will range from being unable to find their favorite toothbrush, to losing custody of their children, to losing their own mind. Some people will be hysterical, and some will be speaking in tongues. Some will be suicidal, some will be dying, and some will seem already dead. During a reading you will find that people are unwilling or unable to make the changes that you know are necessary for growth. You will trace the path they are now on as it meanders into their bleak future and you will see loneliness, despair, and death. Sounds like fun, huh?

Actually, this may sound crazy, but some of the most fun, exciting, interesting, and inspiring readings I have done included many of these elements. When you are reading from neutrality, it is like watching a scary movie or an emotional drama. You will view all kinds of interesting life experiences, to which you ordinarily would have no access, in the safety and comfort of your own mind. You can be totally absorbed in what you are watching, and even experience a variety of emotions (without becoming the emotion). You might have some level of expectation or hope for the end of the movie, but know that there is nothing you can do to change the characters or to rewrite the script. You may go home pondering the moral of the story or recalling some climactic moment, but you likely will not lose any sleep over them.

On the other hand, if you lost your neutrality during the reading, it will be a lot more difficult to deal with these challenges. You will have a hard time maintaining your focus, and you will be inclined to give advice based on your own limited information rather than wait for the infinite wisdom of your clairvoyance to reveal itself. If you lose your neutrality, you may lose your temper and lose your ability to communicate effectively and honestly. So, with all of that said, how does one accomplish neutrality?

Reading From the Center of Your Head

Just as your spirit is free to leave your body and travel anywhere, it can travel anywhere within your body as well. While some of your energy is distributed throughout your entire body at all times, there is a part of you as a spirit that tends to center itself in a specific place. Many men (but certainly not all) are either located in their second chakra (sexual center) or in the analytical part of their brain. Many healers and therapists tend to be in their heart chakra.

The location of your spirit naturally changes throughout the day, from situation to situation. When you are playing with your children, you might be in your heart chakra. When you are arguing with your spouse about finances, you might be in your third chakra. When you are having sex (good sex), you will be in your second chakra. When doing a clairvoyant reading, oftentimes your energy will naturally go to your sixth chakra (corresponding to the third eye), since this is where your clairvoyant abilities lie. However, as the reading continues, you will be vulnerable to matching whatever chakra your client is operating from, or falling into your own matching pictures.

When you read from a chakra other than your sixth chakra, the reading will tend to take on the energy of that chakra. Since your lower chakras have more to do with emotions, you will read through the filters of these feelings and be more vulnerable to their influence. When you remain in your sixth chakra, or the center of your head, you can maintain a certain degree of neutrality there that you cannot maintain in the lower chakras. (Note that being in the center of the head is not the same as being in your analytic mind, whose location is also in the head.)

Many psychics perform readings because they are natural healers. They care about people and want to help them. Unfortunately, the majority of psychics out there aren't aware of the difference between the center of their head and their fourth chakra. This is fine until they encounter a difficult person to read and then lose their ability to objectively see information and communicate it, or they weaken their own system by taking in too much of the readee's energy because of their emotional involvement.

I always know that I have dropped down to my heart chakra during a reading when I begin to cry or feel so hopeless or angry that I can barely remain in my seat. Sometimes I become so wrapped up in saving the person that several minutes will pass before I realize I have stopped reading and am just spewing advice that is not helping anyone. Eventually I realize that I have lost my neutrality and within a minute of performing the neutrality technique described in the next section, I'm back on track, providing clairvoyant information that contains far more wisdom than my logical mind or my heart are able to provide.

Obviously, it is not necessary or desirable to be in the center of your head, or sixth chakra, all the time. Some of the greatest joys in life are when you feel intense love in your heart chakra, when you have a sexual experience in your second chakra, or when your spirit flies off into daydream land somewhere high above your seventh chakra. There is a proper time and place for objectivity just as there is for reckless abandon. You must remain objective during a clairvoyant reading. Your effectiveness and well-being depend on your ability to do so.

Neutrality Technique

First, sit down in a comfortable position and close your eyes. Bring your attention inward. Take your physical hand and place a finger on your third eye, which is slightly above and directly between your eyebrows, and press gently with your finger. Now postulate that you are bringing your awareness and your spirit about two inches from your finger, in the center of your head. Once you are there, take a step or two back. Ask yourself where you just came from. Did it seem like you were down lower and now you are higher, or were you above your head and now you are in a lower position? You may or may not be able to discern your previous location at first, and that is fine. I suggest that you do this merely for your own awareness of where you tend to center yourself.

Now that you are in the center of your head, imagine that you are looking out of your third eye, as if it were a window in your forehead, right where your finger is touching the skin. (You can keep your finger there or remove it at any time during the exercise. If at any point you are no longer certain that you are in the center of your head, bring your finger back to your forehead and repeat the procedure just described.) Pretend that you can actually look out this window and that you are looking at what is really in the room. For a second you can open your physical eyes to remind yourself what the room looks like, then close your eyes and pretend that you are seeing what you just saw with your eyes. Since the window of your third eye is slightly above your physical eyes, you may want to imagine what the room looks like from a slightly elevated position. Now call any of your energy from your lower body or chakras, as well as any of your energy that may be floating above your head, and tell it to come to that point in the center of your head, a couple inches behind your third eye.

Now we are going to create a special place for you in the center of your head. See it as a single room. Put a comfortable chair or sofa in the center of that room with your imagination. See the color of the upholstery. Sit down in the chair and notice how it feels. Is it soft like a pillow or hard like metal? Imagine that you are taking a magic marker or some paint and then paint your name on the four walls of the room. As you do this, know that you are owning this room, which is a representation of the center of your head.

Next, give this room, the center of your head, a grounding cord. You can ground this room in the same way that you would actually ground a room in a house (see chapter 7). Put columns of golden light in each corner and connect these to a large column in the center. Then command any foreign energies that may want to keep you out of the center of your head, or that have been occupying that space, to go down your grounding cord. Watch this energy as it leaves the center of your head. Notice how this feels on a physical level.

As a final step, visualize yourself sitting in the chair in the center of your head. Then stand up and run around this chair. With your imaginary hands, touch all the walls, the floor, and the ceiling of this room in the center of your head. Dress up in your favorite dance costume and celebrate being in the center of your head by dancing the silliest dance you can think of. Congratulations, you have just claimed the home of your neutrality!

CHAPTER 10

Psychic Tool 4: Running
Your Earth and Cosmic Energies

Your physical body is in a state of health when your energy is flowing through it. When the flow of energy has completely stopped, you will be dead. When the flow is sluggish, you will feel sluggish and your immune system will be compromised. When energy is stuck or has ceased to flow in a specific area of the body or energetic counterpart (i.e., in the chakras or aura), you will often experience pain, numbness, or disease in that location.

When energy is flowing through your body, it not only reflects a state of health, it also protects the body from invasion by foreign energies and entities. Most people have either learned or intuitively discovered that a good way to protect the body from harm or evil is to visualize light around the body. What they don't realize is that this light should be flowing. After all, a moving target is much harder to shoot than a stationary one. If you don't want someone to find you or glob on to you, then moving often or quickly will be your best strategy. Think of the vitality and power generated by Niagara Falls or the rapids of the gushing Colorado River compared to the stagnancy of the stale, flea-infested, and oftentimes putrid waters of the Great Salt Lake in Utah or the lethargic swamp lands of the South teeming with all kinds of mischievous varmints.

There are many ways to increase the energy flow through your body and aura. Acupuncture, massage, physical exercise, energetic healing, dancing, singing, painting, and even showering increase the flow of energy and therefore relieve pain and discomfort.

Exercise is one of the easiest and most natural ways of increasing the flow of energy in the body. When you are engaged in aerobic exercise, such as jogging, walking briskly, rollerblading, playing basketball, etc., you are obviously moving your body, which causes your energy to move within your body. When you are sedentary for a long time, the energy in your body slows down. Breathing also circulates energy through the body. The ancient art of yoga uses exercise and breathing to consciously propel energy throughout the body to attain optimal health, peace, and even euphoria. Another easy way to circulate energy throughout the body is through visualization.

During a clairvoyant reading, your body remains sedentary. Because your attention is so focused on whatever it is you are clairvoyantly viewing, your breathing and autonomic nervous system will often significantly diminish to match that of a person in a deep state of sleep. While it is helpful to remind yourself to breathe whenever possible, it is not really practical or possible to perform structured breathing exercises at the same time that you are clairvoyantly reading another person. And I have yet to see anyone jog around the room at the same time that they were doing a clairvoyant reading.

Earth and Cosmic Energies

Both your body and the earth consist of the same energy, called earth energy. When you are outside in nature, you naturally run more earth energy than when you are inside a building made out of synthetic materials. I began to see the value of running earth energy when I moved to Sedona, Arizona. The difference between a person who has spent a few hours trekking through the meandering canyons of Oak Creek or climbing the stunning red rocks, compared to someone who has just flown in from a city like New Jersey and has been away from nature for months, if not years, is phenomenal. Those who had spent even a couple hours outdoors had vibrant auras, spinning chakras, and appeared far healthier and more attractive. Oftentimes I would feel the tingling of earth energy in my feet as soon as a person who had recently been hiking entered my office. This would remind me of the importance of taking some time out from my readings to go take a walk, since I was looking more like a depleted city dweller than a resident of one of the most beautiful natural spots on earth.

Earth energy enters the body through the feet chakras. It is a somewhat heavy or coarse energy, but can be adjusted to your own comfort level through visualization and intent. While earth energy can run through any area of your body, your upper body and chakras are more delicate and do not need as heavy a dose as your lower body and chakras. Your upper chakras are better designed for the processing of what are commonly referred to as cosmic energies, energy gained from the air and from the source of your spirit.

In acupuncture, the earth and cosmic energies are referred to as the yin and yang, and much attention is paid to the balancing of these energies for the relief of pain and disorders such as arthritis, carpal tunnel syndrome, diabetes, epilepsy, paralysis, etc. In his enthralling book Autobiography of a Yogi, Paramhansa Yogananda attributes cosmic energy to the acquisition of miraculous powers. Yogananda describes his meetings with two women from India who never ate. He explains that one of these women, Girl Bala, did not eat any food for over fifty-six years, yet she remained in a state of maximum health. At the age of twelve, she had pleaded with God to help her control her insatiable appetite for food. Her prayers were answered in a vision where a guru appeared and taught her a secret yoga technique that allowed her to recharge her body with cosmic energy from the ether, sun, and air. (Yogananda, p. 536). Her case was rigorously investigated by several reputable Indian scientists and found to be authentic.

The other woman, Therese Newman, had not consumed any food or drink in over twelve years. Upon praying to Saint Teresa in 1923, she was miraculously healed of blindness and paralysis. Soon after, every Friday, she would fall into a deep trance in which she would relive the crucifixion of Christ. The stigmata (sacred bleeding wounds of Christ) would appear on her head, breast, hands, and feet, and blood would pour from her eyes. She stopped eating soon after her healing, knowing that she would be sustained by the grace of God and the cosmic energies of the universe. Her case was authenticated by the Catholic Church, who oversaw the rest of her life and monitored her activities and associations. (Yogananda, p. 537).

I must admit that although I frequently run my cosmic energies, I still have an enormous appetite for edible food and am not yet ready to totally replace my passion for chocolate chip cookies and french fries with a diet of cosmic ether! However, in the several years that I have used visualization to consciously replenish my cosmic energies (sometimes accompanied by exercise and breathing), I have been able to eliminate pain within my own body and other people's bodies and to revitalize myself when feeling tired and stressed. I have also observed many students and classmates undergo remarkable changes in their mental, emotional, and physical health as the cosmic and earth energies helped release generations of programming, MEI pictures, and foreign energies.

During a clairvoyant reading, the simplest and most effective way to make sure that energy is circulating adequately throughout your body is through visualization. The following techniques will teach you how to tune in to your cosmic and earth energies and circulate these throughout your body and energetic fields. These techniques can be used during a clairvoyant reading, as well as during any other activity, whether you are simply sitting in meditation, working at your desk, or running a marathon.

Running Your Earth Energy

Find a comfortable chair to sit in. Close your eyes and turn inward. Destroy your current grounding cord and create a new one. Let your attention drop down to your feet. Imagine that you can see your little feet chakras spinning around.

Postulate that they are going to open up as wide as possible. Notice how this feels. Now close them down as far as possible. Repeat these steps several times and then postulate that you are opening your feet chakras up to 80 percent.

Now visualize a spot deep in the earth directly beneath you where the energy of the earth lies waiting for your call. Find the cleanest spot, where there are no toxins or chemicals. See a color for this earth energy and bring it up through the ground, through the grass or floorboards, and up into your feet chakras. Let the earth energy circulate through your feet chakras, cleaning them out. Imagine that your feet chakras look like miniature washing machines where you can see into the circular doors. The earth energy is washing out foreign, stuck energy from your feet chakras.

After a few moments, let the earth energy effortlessly rise up your legs, running through the bones, muscles, skin, and veins of your ankles and calves up to your knees, where they circulate through and cleanse your little spinning knee chakras. After a few moments the earth energy will rise up through every cell of your thighs, buttocks, and genitals until it reaches your first chakra (root chakra), located at the base of your spine, or at the opening of your cervix if you are a woman. Let the powerful flow of earth energy circulate through your root chakra until that chakra is spinning and glowing brightly. Then watch as gravity sucks 80 percent of the earth energy back down your grounding cord and into the center of the planet. Take the other 20 percent of earth energy that is flowing freely through your first chakra and bring this up through your body. As it rises, let it circulate through each of your major chakras as well as through your muscles, bones, and skin, until it rises up and out of your crown chakra, spilling out into your aura. Let the earth energy fall to the bottom of your aura around your feet and rise up again until it reaches the top of your aura.

Continue to watch this energy pattern for several minutes. You can visualize your body as it is sitting there and watch the circulation process. In addition to using your visualization, notice how the flow of energy feels throughout your body. Do you feel any peculiar or unexpected bodily sensations?

If you are having trouble with this exercise, you may need to adjust the flow in terms of the strength or amount of energy coming in. Play around with these. If that still doesn't help, then try finding another spot within the earth and adjust the color of the earth energy (avoid very dark or muddy colors or colors you dislike) and see if that makes a difference.

I recommend practicing this technique as a meditation exercise in itself for at least twenty minutes a day for a week before running your cosmic energy. If possible, keep a journal and record your experiences related to the exercise. Record any unusual occurrences that begin to happen in your body or in your life. This will help you realize the benefits of running earth energy as opposed to the benefits of running cosmic energy.

Integrating Your Cosmic Energy With Your Earth Energy

Check in with your grounding cord and create a new one if necessary. Run your earth energy for a few minutes, as directed in the last section. Next, visualize a point way up in the sky. This point will be what we call the cosmos, where cosmic energy comes from. You can think of and visualize the cosmos as being above the sun or way out in the universe, or see it as a place in heaven, somewhere over the rainbow, or even located in the hands of God. I like to think of my cosmic energy as coming from whatever source created me.

Next, imagine that there is a bright golden energy effortlessly pouring from the sky. This energy is totally neutral; it contains no foreign energy. See it fall or pull it down into the top of your head, or crown chakra. See it spinning around your crown chakra, cleansing and activating that chakra and all of its abilities. After a few moments, watch as it pours down the back of your head through two channels on either side of the sixth chakra. These channels run all the way down your back along the spine. Watch as the spinning of the sixth chakra causes the cosmic energies to flow down through all of your upper chakras. Watch as the cosmic energy flows down through the vertebrae of the neck, all the way down the spine. The cosmic energy races down the back channels until it lands in the first chakra, where the earth energy is already circulating. Watch as 20 percent of your cosmic energy continues to flow downward through your legs, out the feet, down into the center of the planet, as well as down your grounding cord.

Next, bring your attention back up to your spinning root chakra. Watch as the cosmic energy joins with the earth energy. See these two colors and watch them intermingle until they form a new color. Then take this new color (which will be a combination of 80 percent cosmic energy and 20 percent earth energy) and watch as it flows up the trunk of your body, out the top of your head. These channels run alongside the front of your major chakras. Watch as the energy flows freely through every muscle, bone, and vein of the front of your body and anywhere it has not yet had a chance to flow.

When the mixture of energy reaches your throat chakra, watch as some of it breaks off and travels to each shoulder and down each arm, racing to your hand chakras, where it circulates around and around until the chakras become full and the mixture of earth and cosmic energies overflows out into the aura surrounding your hands. See the rest of the energy mixture as it flows up through your face and head and fountains out of your crown chakra, spilling into your aura.

Watch as your entire aura from the bottom of your feet to the top of your head swells with this radiant energy. Watch this pattern of energy flow for at least ten minutes a day for a week as a meditation, and notice what thoughts, feelings, and sensations occur.

Helpful Tips

When running your earth and cosmic energies, there are a few important factors to keep in mind. The first is that you don't have to do any work or put any effort into making the energy flow; you are merely inviting it in, directing it, and watching it flow. If you find yourself making any effort, then choose a color for that effort and watch it release down your grounding cord.

Also, understand that this energy is neutral. As long as you call the energy from a fresh, clean source, it will be clean. Proclaim that no other energies can interfere or combine with your earth and cosmic energies without your conscious permission, and this will be so.

Keep in mind that running your earth and cosmic energies is not just a visualization exercise. The energy flow is causing all kinds of changes to occur in your body, and as we have discussed in other chapters, sometimes when you release pain or emotions, you will feel these as they release. So if you feel any unpleasant sensation, know that this is temporary and not due to the earth and cosmic energies themselves, but rather to whatever materials the earth and cosmic energies are helping you release. This is a very powerful exercise, and therefore it is best to perform it in a safe, comfortable, and private environment for a while before attempting to do it when you are driving your vehicle or interacting with a lot of people in a professional setting.

The pattern of energy flow described here is one that seems to work, but it doesn't have to be set in stone. If you are having difficulty with it, I suggest that for a few weeks on a regular basis you continue to follow the pattern, because difficulty with it could indicate places where you have energy blockages or MEI pictures. However, I do encourage you to experiment with running your earth and cosmic energies however you see fit. Some people prefer less structure, and in that case they may choose to let the energy flow more freely.

CHAPTER 11

Psychic Tool 5: Creating and Maintaining Boundaries

Often when I am performing a psychic reading, my readee will be so interested in what I am saying that she will expand her aura until it encompasses me. This if more likely to happen if my readee closes her eyes and falls into a deep state of relaxation. When my client's aura intermingles with my own, or vice versa (it is much easier to blame everyone else for encroaching upon your space than it is to acknowledge that you are invading theirs!), this not only feels uncomfortable to my body, but makes it more difficult to clairvoyantly read the client.

If you try to look at an object by putting it right up to your nose, you will not be able to see it clearly or see the whole thing, because it is too close. This concept also applies to psychically viewing a person's aura. This is why I usually have at least a few feet of physical distance between me and my readee, even though my eyes are closed. Sometimes I find it helpful to ask the readee to sit back in her chair and call her aura closer to her body. However, this request sometimes confuses or invalidates the readee. Therefore I often opt to take matters into my own "psychic hands" by visualizing an object at the end of my aura and postulating that my client's energy is receding to the opposite side of this separation object.

A separation object is valuable because it helps you create an energetic boundary between yourself and others, and in turn helps strengthen psychological boundaries, which may be weak (a separation object is a necessity for people who struggle with issues of codependency). A separation object reminds your body and your energy what is yours and what is not yours. It also serves as a method of protection. However, I prefer to refer to this tool as a separation object rather than a protection object because when your focus is on protection, you may inadvertently attract that which you are trying to avoid (through your resistance).

This technique can come in handy in everyday life, as I discovered one afternoon several years ago when I attended a fascinating lecture on crop circles given by the pioneering and inexhaustible researcher Colin Andrews. The lecture hall was packed and I took the only remaining chair. A woman with a child strolled into the room, and a generous man gave her his seat and walked to the back of the room, where I was seated. The lights were dimmed as Andrews began his slide show of the exquisitely complex crop circles. I have no idea how much time had passed until suddenly I was overwhelmed by a heavy wave of exhaustion.

"Oh my gosh, what is wrong with me?!" I wondered. A minute before I had been feeling great, but now I felt that if I did not lie down, I would pass out. Thankfully, I became aware of the gentleman who had earlier relinquished his seat. He was standing next to me only a couple feet away. I tore my eyes from the slides to glance at him and noticed that he was uncomfortably shifting his weight from foot to foot. "Hmm," I wondered. "Could I be matching this man's state of exhaustion? After all, he has been standing all this time."

I quickly imagined that there was a bright red daisy circulating around the edge of my aura. I visualized his energy as a bluish color leaving my aura and returning to his body. I then called back my own energy to my body. As I did this, the man looked at me as if on some level he knew I was doing something, and then walked to the other side of the room.

I instantaneously felt better and returned my attention to the lecture. However, about twenty minutes later I again felt that same wave of exhaustion. "Maybe I was mistaken," I said to myself. "Maybe I am just getting sick and it had nothing to do with that guy." The lecture ended and as I stood up to leave, I stumbled into the same man who at some point, without my knowledge, had inconspicuously taken a position right behind me. I extracted myself from the room, rechecked my separation object, and once again felt like my normal self.

A separation object can be visualized as any object: a flower, a tree, a fence, a mirror, a hundred dollar bill (to remind you of your abundance), etc. It is helpful to use the same type of object over a period of time, because you can take a clairvoyant look at the object from time to time to see if it has changed due to the energy it may have absorbed or been affected by. As with a grounding cord, you should frequently destroy the separation object and create a new one to make sure it is working for you in present time.

Also, different situations may call for different sizes, strengths, and qualities of an object. If I encounter a hostile person who is actually wishing me harm, I will sometimes imagine a mirror or a fan that is flinging back whatever energy is coming at me. At other times I will visualize a giant heart with a Smiley face on it to remind myself (and maybe that hostile person) that love is stronger than hatred. I might even visualize something really funny or ridiculous to change the negative vibrations around me, since amusement is a much higher vibration than anger or fear.

Your separation object should be at the edge of your aura. If it is only at the edge of your body, or somewhere within your aura, then whatever you need separation from will still have access to your aura and will affect you as if it were in your body. You can visualize a single object that rotates around your aura, or you can use several objects. Beginning students who have less trust in their separation object tend to want to create more of them, to cover every inch of their aura. However, one object will work just fine.

You can postulate that even though the object is located at a single spot on the edge of your aura, it has the ability to protect your entire aura and body. You can see the separation object as being stationary or as orbiting around your aura, since moving energy is more powerful than stagnant energy, as mentioned earlier. You can use your other tools, such as running energy and grounding, in conjunction with your separation object to further increase its effectiveness.

A separation object is a highly effective tool, so you have to be careful not to create such a strong fortress around yourself that you become invisible or isolated. This is usually not a problem until you have been practicing the technique for a long period of time.

CHAPTER 12

Psychic Tool 6:
Creating and Destroying

The process of clairvoyant reading and healing requires you to be able to create certain images and then destroy them. You must be able to consciously create a reading screen and a viewing receptacle in order to have a place where your clairvoyant information can present itself. You must then be able to destroy these images so they don't have a negative impact on your health, and so new information will have a place to display itself.

The techniques presented in this chapter and book, when practiced over time, will dramatically increase your ability to create visual images and destroy them. Your ability to create and destroy visualizations may be directly related to your ability to create and destroy many other things in your life, and it will be important for you to be aware of this when you find yourself struggling with a certain technique. When you create and destroy an object in your mind, you are moving energy and impacting everything around you.

There are many people who have no inkling of their tremendous creative potential. You hear them say, "I don't have a creative bone in my body." These very people have jobs, children, houses, and bank accounts. Who created these things in their lives, if they did not? Our lives are a continual cycle of creation and destruction. From birth to death, from preschool to high school graduation, from marriage to divorce, from beginning a new job to resigning from it, from purchasing a new dress to donating it to a used clothing store, from earning a nice fat paycheck to spending every penny of it, these are our creations and destructions.

During every moment of our lives, we are creating and we are destroying. When I am thirsty, I go to the kitchen and pour a glass of milk, and I have just created a glass of milk. Of course I did not make the glass or milk the cow, but ultimately I formed an idea of a desire in my mind and took the necessary actions to create a glass of milk for myself. I then consume the glass of milk. The milk that I consume no longer exists. Essentially, I have destroyed the milk.

I get in my car and see I am low on gas. I know I need more gas. I have a mental image picture in my mind of what I will do to get more gas. I drive to the gas station and fill my car up with gas. I did not drill in the ground for the gas, and I did not haul it over to the gas station, but I did drive there and pump the gas into my car. Essentially, my thoughtforms helped me create the gasoline that I desired for my car. I then drive my car for a week, and suddenly the car has consumed the gas. The gas I had created is no longer there. The gas has been destroyed. I have destroyed it.

I believe that everyone has equal abilities when it comes to creating and destroying. However, people differ drastically in terms of their issues and MEI pictures surrounding these two activities. There are all kinds of emotions and thoughtforms that affect a person's ability to create or destroy. Some people feel guilty when they create something for themselves, or even think about creating something, while others feel guilty when they release or destroy something, such as a relationship with a romantic partner, a job, etc.

Many people have a lack of understanding of how the physical laws of creation work. Others have fears, insecurities, anxieties, family programming, and mental blocks that get in their way. Actually, most people don't have a problem creating (although they'd tell you otherwise), it's just that they are too busy creating other things that don't allow time or space for their new creations.

One reason it's important to meditate before performing a clairvoyant reading is that when your head is so full of thoughts and any number of foreign energies, there is no place for the clairvoyant information to go where you could possibly distinguish it from the rest of the traffic in there. Once you make the decision to only focus on the clairvoyant information, or certain visual images, then you will have to find a way to get rid of or destroy all the other thoughtforms in your head. This is done through meditation and practice of the psychic tools presented in chapters 6-12. If you have trouble letting go of all the garbage in your head, you may also have trouble letting go of all the garbage in other areas of your body and life, or vice versa.

As we have discussed in other chapters, clairvoyant reading and healing speeds up the process in which thoughtforms, emotions, and foreign energies become stimulated and are then released, both for the person giving the reading/healing and the one receiving it. Anyone who embarks on a path of clairvoyant reading and healing needs to be comfortable with this process of release and destruction.

Release and destruction involve change. If you cannot tolerate change in your own life, then you will have a problem with destroying. If you have a problem with destroying, then you and your life are going to become overwhelmed with your creations to the point that you become ill, can no longer create what it is you really want, and eventually have some kind of breakdown, which will cause you to have to make changes in your life anyway. If you cannot tolerate change in your own life, then seeing it or initiating it in your readee's or healee's life is going to be too painful for you. During your readings, you will therefore block yourself from seeing images that have to do with change and will be unable to effectively communicate messages regarding change. You will only be able to read people who are as stuck as you are!

Now, after reading the preceding paragraph, you may be thinking, "Well, I don't like change, and I don't feel particularly creative, and I know I hate to let go of anything, whether a possession or a relationship. So maybe I'd better stop reading this book and let go of any further silly ideas I might have about learning how to do clairvoyant readings." Well, stop that thought immediately! Sure, doing clairvoyant readings is going to speed up the release and transformation process, which will force you to deal with your resistance to destroying on a more intense level. But eventually you are going to have to deal with these things anyway if you hope to achieve your dreams and have a truly fulfilling life. It's up to you whether you want to do it now or thirty years from now.

If your life is not going the way you want it to, or things are working out just fine but you are constantly plagued with anxiety and the fear that at any moment your life might change, then you have a problem with creating and destroying, and the only way you are going to learn how to cope with your life and find more peace and happiness is to deal with these gifts that God gave you more effectively and gracefully. Clairvoyant reading and/or practicing the techniques presented in this chapter and book will help empower you to consciously create and destroy so that you can become a better reader, a better healer, and at the very least, a more peaceful and confident human being.

If you have a strong interest in doing clairvoyant readings, then you are meant to do them. Don't ever let your fear of not being good enough stop you from learning what it takes to become good enough!

The "D" Word

One day I casually mentioned to a close friend that I was writing a chapter on the subject of creating and destroying. He emphatically insisted, "I wouldn't use the word destroy if I were you. That's too strong a word. It might make people uncomfortable."

I responded, "What's wrong with that? Destruction is a part of everyday life and if it makes people uncomfortable, then isn't it better to help them learn how to become comfortable with it than to just not bring it up? I know a lot of things I say in this book are going to make my readers uncomfortable and that is okay, because the purpose of this book is to provide techniques, tools, and methods for coping with whatever makes them uncomfortable. Maybe they weren't brave or strong enough to face these topics in the past because they didn't know that there were solutions. This book is about solutions.

I became aware of the importance of the ability to destroy after doing several readings in which my readees asked me to look at why they were having problems with creating and manifesting in their lives. One of my very first readings involved a woman named Sarah. Sarah was longing to create a new relationship. She had not dated anyone for three years, since her divorce, and she was feeling very lonely and frustrated. When I put up a viewing receptacle and asked it to show me some information regarding who her next boyfriend would be, I immediately saw an image of her opening her closet door and being buried under an avalanche of clothing, boxes, and miscellaneous junk. She thought this was funny and admitted that this was pretty much what happened whenever she opened her closet doors. (I will explain how to create a viewing receptacle in the next chapter.)

"But what does that have to do with a relationship?" Sarah asked. I didn't have the foggiest idea, so I asked that image to show me another image. The next image I had was of furniture. I saw a big green sofa that looked very comfortable, but was very worn and old. I asked this image what it meant, and I saw a man reclining on the sofa. He had a bald spot and a big tummy. He was watching a wrestling match on TV. I hesitantly described this man to her, thinking this was probably not the kind of boyfriend she would want to hear about! However, I was relieved when she said, "That perfectly describes my ex-husband, and our sofa. He gave me all the furniture when we divorced." I continued the reading, trying to ignore all these elements, since I was only interested in learning about her future boyfriend.

I destroyed the images and viewing receptacles that I was looking at and created a new viewing receptacle in the form of a rose. I saw a faint image of a man holding a bouquet of flowers, knocking on the front door. When my readee opened the door, a flood of water pushed him down the hallway. I focused on the water and saw images of kids, furniture, and, once again, the readee's husband. He started to strangle the guy with the flowers, who then ran down the stairs and out of the apartment building.

The whole story was becoming clear. Sarah was having trouble creating a relationship, not because there were no interested men around, but because there was no room in her house or her life for a new relationship. She had been divorced for three years, but her husband's energy was so present that he might as well have been sitting on the sofa in the middle of her living room right then. I intuitively realized that the very first thing Sarah needed to do was physically clear out her closets, which could symbolize the areas in her life where she was unconsciously holding on to the past. Next, she needed to get rid of her sofa and any other furniture that her former husband had been grounded into. Most importantly, she needed to release her husband's energy, which occupied several areas of her body.

Sarah at first adamantly refused to get rid of the sofa, citing all kinds of reasons why this was impossible. When I suggested that perhaps she was not ready to let go of her husband's energy, she admitted that she was still having a hard time with the divorce and talked to her ex-husband frequently. She had thought that if she found another man, it would be easier to let go of the past, but was beginning to realize that the opposite was true. She also told me that every time she attempted to throw something away, she would become confused as to whether to put it in the garbage, give it to charity, etc., and then she would just stuff it away in the closet.

While I was looking to see what might help Sarah with all of this, I saw an image of her looking in front of the mirror, examining her rear end, with a frown on her face. It seemed like her inability to let go of things, or in a sense to destroy them, was also making it difficult for her to let go of excess weight on her body, which made her feel less attractive and therefore made her less attractive to potential suitors. (Most people I know who are overweight have problems with destroying in terms of letting go of unhealthy relationships from the past and letting go of possessions. Some of them actually eat more than they need because there is an unconscious fear that they might not be able to create more food when they need it in the future.)

In order for Sarah to create a new relationship, she needed to bring her agreement with her husband into present time. They had gone through a legal divorce, but not an energetic one. Spiritually she had not been ready to break off the relationship, so she didn't. When I asked her if she'd like me to help her with this, she said, "No, I'm not ready to let go." I told her that this was okay, and that the important thing was that she realized this. Eventually she would need to either physically reunite with her ex-husband or energetically break their agreement. Until she did so, it was unlikely that she would create a relationship with another man.

To close the reading, I clairvoyantly looked for one action she could take that would not overwhelm her. I saw her having a party where her friends came over and helped her clean out her closets. They would not have the same attachments and resistances to getting rid of things, and they looked like they were having fun. She thought this was a great idea and knew exactly who she'd ask for help.

The elements of this session repeated themselves time and time again in reading after reading, and taught me about why we must be able to let go of things in order to create our present dreams and desires. They also showed me how resistant people are to change. I learned that doing something as simple as cleaning your house, or donating a box of old clothes, can be an enormous first step to clearing out all kinds of other stubborn energies in your life. I learned how to monitor where I am in my own life by paying attention to when my home, car, purse, or wallet becomes disorganized and overflowing with items I haven't used in months or even years. I now know that if my outer life is messy, my inner life is even messier!

The Importance of Faith

We all want to feel secure, to know that if we leave a relationship or job, if we sell a house or a car, that there will be an even better one right there for us so we won't have to feel any anxiety, loneliness, stress, or uncertainty. How many times have you said to yourself, "I can't leave my job until I find another one," or "I can't let this relationship go (even though my boyfriend broke up with me two months ago) because what if I never meet anyone as handsome or funny or compatible?"

The truth is, many times (but not all) you won't create what you ultimately crave in your heart until you make a leap of faith and destroy what is no longer serving you so that something that will serve you can move in. Life actually may work this way because you are meant to learn about having faith—faith in God, faith in your ability to create, and faith in your ability to handle any situation for a temporary period of time. If you have no faith, if you can't deal with uncertainty or loneliness or even poverty, then you will always be a prisoner to what seem to be your needs but are really your desires. You can always handle so much more than you think you can. You are so much more powerful than you could ever imagine!

The good news is that when you jump into life, perhaps blindfolded but with both feet first, you usually don't have to deal with the things you fear the most for too long, because life does want to reward you for putting your dreams over your fears.

Creating and Destroying Simple Images

The following technique will help you exercise your visualization muscle and will help you practice creating and destroying images. It will also act as a powerful meditation in which all other thoughts in your mind will dissipate. Because it requires you to be so active, you will be less likely to be distracted by extraneous thoughts. If you find that you do get distracted or get very sleepy, as soon as you notice that you have gotten off track, go back to the last number or letter you were working on before you lost awareness of it.

Begin by giving yourself a grounding cord (see chapter 7). Imagine that you are standing in front of a blackboard, holding a bright red piece of chalk in your right hand. Draw the number one on the blackboard. Once you are finished, study the number to see how it looks. Is it a straight line or kind of wiggly? How big is it? Is it very bright on the blackboard or kind of faint? Now imagine that you are holding an eraser in your hand and watch as your hand completely erases the number one. Check your grounding cord and invite any energy that has been stimulated to release down this cord, into the center of the planet.

Next, repeat this exercise by going through all the numbers until you reach number twenty. Then repeat this exercise by going though all the letters of the alphabet.

Creating and Destroying Objects

When you visualize an object in your imagination, you are actually creating the object on an energetic level. This object will actually possess properties that can have an effect on the physical plane. When you imagine that you are destroying the object, you are actually moving and changing the molecules that make up this energy form. When you create and destroy an object, an energy force is set in motion that affects all other energies surrounding it. Therefore, you can utilize this process to move and release unwanted energies.

Creating and destroying objects is a simple yet extremely powerful healing method. Practicing this tool on a frequent basis not only will keep your energy moving, but will also help you exercise your visualization and concentration muscles. I recommend that you try creating and destroying objects when meditating and reading, as well as when you are at work, walking your dog, swimming, watching movies, etc. Practice this technique for varying periods of time and notice how you feel after you have been creating and destroying objects for several minutes as opposed to a few seconds.

This technique has become such an ingrained practice for me that often I will realize that I am in the process of creating and destroying an object (usually a rose because that was the only object my clairvoyant school utilized) without willfully attempting to do so. I will discover that there is actually a negative energy near me that needed to be cleared out or dealt with. My subconscious somehow sensed this and went to work way before my much slower conscious mind became aware of the situation or could respond.

In order to create and destroy objects, you will first need to learn how to create a reading screen. This is described in detail in the next chapter, so I recommend that you read chapter 13 now and then come back and read the rest of this chapter.

The first step in creating and destroying objects is to quickly create a red flower on your reading screen. See all of its petals, its stem, and its leaves, and then destroy it. Next, create a blue flower, observe it, and then destroy it. Now create a yellow flower, observe it, and destroy it. Next, create a black flower, observe it, and destroy it. See how quickly and for how many minutes you can continue to create and destroy these flowers.

Then try another category of objects. In your imagination, visualize a car. See the color, the shape, and the size of the car, observe the interior and the exterior, and then destroy it. You can explode it, erase it, see it crash and blow up in flames, watch it melt away, or simply watch as it disappears. Next, create an airplane. Observe it and then destroy it. Do the same with a boat, a train, a bicycle, of a pair of roller skates.

Next, check in with your grounding cord to make sure it is connected into your first chakra as well as the center of the planet. Create an image of a person who, to your knowledge, does not exist. Observe that person's features. Then destroy that image of the person. Next, create an image of a person you used to know but haven't seen in years. Observe the person's features, and then destroy that image. Know that you are not destroying them, but that this process may remove any of their energy from your body and aura.

As a final step, visualize a person who is currently in your life, someone you love. Observe their features, their clothes, the look on their face. Then destroy this image. Again, remember that you are not hurting them or doing anything malicious. You are merely moving energy associated with their image. They may actually feel this energy movement or spontaneously think of you as you do this exercise. Don't be surprised if they call you or come over for a visit soon after you create and destroy an image of them.

Cleaning Your Reading Screen

The following techniques can be used to clear off any stuck or foreign energies from your reading screen that may be getting in the way of your clairvoyance. They can also be used very effectively to clear off your chakras, a particular body part, or an area of your aura, and to practice your creating/destroying skills.

On the upperhand left corner of your reading screen, visualize a little red footprint. Observe the footprint, and then destroy it. Directly next to it, create another footprint in a different color. Observe the footprint, and then destroy it. Moving from left to right, continue creating footprints as if you were walking across your reading screen. When you get to the far right side of the screen, go back to the far left side, immediately under the row that you just walked, and continue to create and destroy these colored footprints. Continue the exercise until you have created and destroyed a footprint on every part of the screen. You can substitute any image for the footprint, such as a hand, a flower, a sun, or the moon. Every time you create and destroy the footprint, you are releasing energy from your screen that may be hindering your clairvoyance.

Another way to clean off your reading screen is to imagine that you are plugging the cord of a vacuum cleaner in to an outlet on the side of your reading screen. Change the vacuum cleaner bag and destroy the old one before turning on the vacuum, and then proceed to vacuum every square inch of your reading screen. When you are finished, destroy the vacuum cleaner.

Manifesting a Desire

Through use of visualization and clairvoyance, anyone can learn to create and manifest their desires, dreams, and wishes, no matter how big or small these are. With all the literature published on the subject, most people have at least heard of, if not directly experimented with, the concept that thought creates one's physical reality. There are so many great books currently available that teach people the universal laws governing manifestation through thought that it would be redundant (as well as impractical, given how much other information needs to be covered) to go into much detail here. In addition to using the clairvoyant technique for manifestation that I am about to describe, I also recommend the following books on the subject: The Power of Your Subconscious Mind by Joseph Murphy, Your Heart's Desire by Sonia Choquette, You'll See It When You Believe It by Wayne Dyer, Your Life: Why It Is the Way It Is, and What You Can Do About It by Bruce McArthur, Creative Visualization and Living in the Light by Shakti Gawain, and any book by Marianne Williamson.

Begin by giving yourself a grounding cord. Then create a reading screen (see chapter 13). On the viewing or reading screen, create an image of a crystal lotus flower. Notice the number of petals, how open the bud is, how long the stem is, etc., and then ground the stem into the center of the planet. Then visualize yourself standing inside the lotus, receiving your desire. See yourself at the moment when you realize that you have been granted this desire. See yourself looking jubilant, ecstatic. You are so excited that you are jumping up and down, with tears pouring forth from your eyes, and you fall to your knees in gratitude, thanking everyone from God to your mother who brought you into this wonderful life where your dreams would be realized as they are now.

Next, look for a color of any energy that might be blocking you or has been trying to block you from having this desire in your life. This energy could belong to you or to someone else.

Once you see this color, you can either conduct a mini reading on it, or help the color release down the stem of the lotus into the center of the planet.

Now choose a brilliant color that represents your desire and let it circulate through the lotus. See it grow bigger and bigger until it expands outside the lotus and outside your reading screen, until it is filling up your entire body and aura and filling up the entire room, then the neighborhood, then the entire city, state, country, and universe. As you do this, continue to feel gratitude and happiness for achieving your goal.

As a final step, imagine that you are cutting the lotus from the ground, and watch it float off into the universe to begin creating for you. Or you can hand it up to an image of God that you have created. See it floating into God's hands and see God blessing this creation. You can also imagine that you are planting the lotus in a lovely garden. Every few days you can check on the lotus to see if it is growing or if it is in need of attention. Water it with love and excitement, using the color of the desire's energy whenever you take a peek at it.

PART III

CLAIRVOYANT READING

CHAPTER 13

Learning to Read Yourself

In this chapter, you will learn the clairvoyant reading techniques that are the foundation of this book. These simple techniques can be learned by almost anyone for the purpose of accessing information. You can use them when reading yourself or other people, animals, energies, etc. This particular chapter provides exercises for reading and healing yourself. In the following chapter, you will learn how to apply these techniques during readings on other people.

As a beginning clairvoyant student, it is best to perform the following exercises when you are alone. If you are indoors, it is essential to secure yourself in a room where no one else is present or will be coming in. If you are outside, then find an area where you are the least likely to be disturbed.

The ideal time to practice these techniques is when no one else will be in the house. As you practice your psychic tools and perform clairvoyant readings, your energy will change and whoever is around will unconsciously sense this and become very curious about what you are doing. Therefore, they will likely come up with a very good excuse to disturb you, whether that means knocking on your door or energetically joining you, which may make it more difficult for you to concentrate. Unplugging the phone is also essential, since this is usually the time when your relatives will call. If you feel you are being distracted by other people, then invite their energy to go into a glass bubble, look to see what color their energy might look like, and visualize the bubble floating back to them.

Make sure you turn off any music within hearing distance and especially the television set. Music may be relaxing for some forms of meditation, but it can be very distracting when reading. If you clairvoyantly read in a room (or house) where a television set is turned on, you will likely start picking up images from the television, which will interfere with the images of the energies you are intending to read.

Informing the Universe of Your Intention to Read

The time you spend doing a clairvoyant reading is unique from the rest of your day. You are accessing a part of yourself that has different intentions, concerns, energies, and relationships. Therefore it is helpful to make it clear to your body, mind, and spirit that you are embarking on a special project that requires a shift. This can be done by establishing a routine that you go through prior to every reading. As part of this routine, and to help your body make this transition, it is helpful to put your body into a position that will give it the signal that it is time to perform a reading (the same is true for meditation or even writing). Designate a room, a part of a room, or a chair that is intended only for clairvoyant reading. At the very least, find a cushion to place on your chair, or a cozy blanket to drape over your shoulders, or some warm slippers for your feet that you will use only when you read.

Sit in the same position every time you read. I recommend sitting upright with your feet on the floor since this will facilitate your grounding and make it easier to stay awake (since we always or usually sleep in a reclining position, our bodies are programmed to fall asleep when placed in a reclining position). This is also the position you will be most likely to sit in when reading another person. Placing your hands on your lap with your palms facing upward will facilitate the flow of your energy and will also serve as a cue in future reading sessions that you are intending to perform a reading. Close your eyes and keep them closed until you are finished with your session and ready to shift back into your other daily activities.

Whatever you do to set yourself up for a reading, it is important to do it in a way that is as nurturing as possible, as with meditation. This is your special time to go inward, to shower yourself with the personal attention, respect, and love that you deserve and need in order to lead a happy, stable life. When you give to yourself in this way, you send a message out into the universe that you are worthy and open to receiving respect and love in general, and you will begin to attract other people who reflect these qualities back to you (see chapter 22).

Accessing your clairvoyance will be easier if you meditate beforehand. If you have followed the steps given thus far in this chapter, you will find that you are now in an ideal situation/position for meditation as well as for clairvoyant reading. Meditation helps you focus and empties out the extraneous thoughts cluttering your mind. It also helps you relax your body. Clairvoyant reading can be done anywhere, at any time, regardless of how you have prepared yourself. Reading in itself is a type of meditation, since it requires complete concentration and focus. If you read for fifteen minutes or longer, you will discover that your consciousness and brain waves have shifted. However, it is much easier and safer to access your psychic abilities when your mind is clear. If you begin to read without first meditating, you will find that the first several minutes (if not longer) of your reading time will be spent releasing those pesky thoughtforms that have nothing to do with the reading, particularly if you are new to psychic reading.

To prepare yourself for a reading, I recommend that you take about twenty minutes to run through the psychic tools presented in chapters 6-12 before attempting to access your clairvoyance. If you have other meditation styles or techniques that you prefer, then meditate in any way you'd like and complete the last five or ten minutes of your meditation with a run-through of the psychic tools. The psychic tools are not only meant to protect and heal you during your clairvoyant reading, they are also warm-up exercises for utilizing your visualization clairvoyance. Once you feel grounded, centered, energized, and protected (using the psychic tools or whatever methods you'd like), you are ready to begin reading.

Prayer

Beginning your reading/meditation with a prayer will help you set the energy of your session and connect with the source of your energy and information, and will serve as a further cue to let your spirit know that it is time to access your clairvoyance. It will also serve as protection. Any prayer that you like will work. Some people prefer a structured prayer, while others may say a mantra or some simple words of gratitude. I usually start a reading with words of gratitude regarding the reading, such as this: "Thank you, God, for the gift of my clairvoyance. Thank you for helping bring forth the most helpful information at this time. I thank you for your protection, your wisdom, and your assistance as well as the assistance of the universe and all of my guides."

The energy of gratitude is one of the highest forms of energy that exists. Within gratitude there is joy, acceptance, love, and forgiveness. When you pray by expressing your gratitude, either for what has already occurred or for what you hope to manifest, you are bringing these healing energies into your reading space as well as into your life. Structured prayers such as the Lord's Prayer are beneficial to recite when dealing with negative energies, because they are highly energized by the masses of people who have recited them throughout history.

The words of your prayer are, for the most part, insignificant compared to the zeal with which you pray. Whether you are making up your own words or reciting a well-known prayer, your prayers will be much more effective if you are focused and aware of every single word, and you say each word not just with your mouth or brain but with every ounce of your being. This is true whether you pray to God, to Jesus Christ, to Muhammad, to your Creator (whoever that is), to the universe, or to a particular saint, ascended master, spirit, etc.

Clairvoyant Reading Technique

The preliminary steps just described are highly recommended to help you prepare to access your clairvoyance. However, the following three steps are the meat and potatoes of a clairvoyant reading: creating a reading screen, creating a viewing receptacle, and calling energy into your viewing receptacle. If you perform nothing else in this book except the following three fundamental steps, you at the very least will know how to access your clairvoyance.

Creating a Reading Screen

If you are going to access psychic information through clairvoyance, you must have a place where this information can be displayed. Just like you need a television screen in order to watch a television program, or a monitor in order to view information on your computer, you will need a reading screen in order to view your clairvoyant images. From the center of the inside of your head, with your eyes closed, image that you are looking out through your third eye (located at the middle of your forehead, in between and slightly above your physical eyes) at a screen that is placed a few inches out from your forehead. Notice or decide what this screen looks like. It can be the size of a small television screen or as big as a movie screen in an extravagant theater. Notice if the screen has a border and what that border looks like. Notice if the border or the sides of the screen are straight or bent or symmetrical to each other. Notice or decide on the color for the border of your screen as well as for the inside of the screen. Notice if there is anything that you would consider unusual about this screen.

Whenever you create an image, such as your reading screen, it is a good idea to ask your mind to first just notice what it looks like before attempting to consciously create it. After a reasonable period of time, if you don't get an impression of how it looks, then make a decision to design it a certain way. Sometimes your screen or another object you are attempting to visualize already exists, and the way it appears has to do with the type of energies that are affecting it and you. If you don't like what you see, then simply imagine that you are grounding out the part that you don't like, or imagine that the entire screen is being destroyed, and then consciously decide how you would like to recreate your screen. Next, observe the appearance of this new screen. Patiently continue watching this screen for a minute or two to see if any aspect of it changes. Any change that does occur (without your conscious manipulation) will be a result of the energy that is affecting it.

Grounding Your Reading Screen

You can release any mischievous energy from your reading screen (including energy that might be getting in the way of you focusing or visualizing your screen) by giving your reading screen a grounding cord. In chapter 7 you learned how to create a grounding cord by connecting your body to the center of the earth. In the same way, for the same reasons, you can give your reading screen its own grounding cord. Just imagine that you are connecting your screen with a column of energy into the center of the planet. You can imagine that the grounding cord for your screen looks like anything, such as a strong metal pole, an anchor, a tree trunk, etc. Once your reading screen is secured into the center of the planet, invite whatever foreign energy that might be affecting it or blocking it from your vision to be released from the screen's grounding cord. Watch or imagine that a particular color is effortlessly being sucked down the cord by the gravitational pull of the planet and imagine it being absorbed into the earth. Now look at your reading screen again and notice if it has changed.

Additional tips to working with your screen and other visual tools.

It's always helpful to start every reading by bringing yourself behind the third eye located in the center of your head (between your eyes) and beginning to visualize your reading screen in front of you. These actions help you to orient yourself to your body and ensure that you aren't floating out of your body and over to your client (where things can get energetically and emotionally messy for you). As you can see, your screen has many functions. It is an orientation tool, an activation tool and a reading preparation device that, when activated, is waiting to receive your images. When you bring your attention to your screen, you are activating the frontal lobes of your brain, including the amygdala, and the pituitary and pineal glands that early theosophists, healers and many neuroscientists found to correspond with increased psychic ability. (Slade, Neil. "The Frontal Lobes Supercharge; Slade Publishing, 1998).

You can further activate your screen by imagining a dial or a switch on one part of it so that when you are ready for your clairvoyance to be turned up high you can turn the "lights" up to 100 percent. Conversely, if you are ready to be in another mode, perhaps to go to sleep or turn down the psychic noise around you (if things get too intense), you can turn the dial down. In this way you get more control over your psychic input.

You always have the option of visualizing yourself by imagining your body directly, or by seeing it as if you were looking in a mirror. Most students find it easier to start off looking directly at their body when they are visualizing a grounding cord or seeing their cosmic and earth energy running. Once you get that down, go ahead and practice seeing yourself as you are physically on your screen, but then adding in your psychic tools. You can imagine that you are looking at your aura, your chakras, etc., on your screen. Practice moving your attention back and forth between viewing your body directly and seeing yourself on your screen, or at least in the middle of where the screen is.

The following is extremely important to keep in mind: Like all of your psychic tools, there is a time and a place for the screen. If there is one thing that readers of the earlier editions of this book have gotten confused about more than anything else, it's that they think they have to be trying to maintain the frame of the screen throughout the entire process. Once you have checked in with your screen and are ready to proceed to read, you can really forget about it until you need it again. Instead, turn your focus to the next visualizations we will discuss, or to whatever shows up.

If information is flowing in the form of visuals, messages and instant knowing, then don't bog that down with the idea that you have to use any of the tools in this book. Just let the input of information flow and don't ever stop the flow because you feel like you aren't following instructions properly. The screen and viewing receptacle tools (which we will discuss next) are primarily there to help you start the flow of information, or restart it if it stops coming. Just to reiterate, there is no reason for you to keep the image of the screen up when you are focusing on the other visuals, unless you have a personal desire or other reason to do so.

If any of this seems too complicated or you find yourself getting frustrated with the process, then just take a moment to check in with yourself and see if you have a picture of "how" you think you need to do this process or if you feel you need to do it in a certain way. If so, release this picture. Most likely, it isn't based on my picture as your instructor of how things have to be, but rather an expectation you are manufacturing in yourself.

To help you release this, imagine a symbol for the expectation or a color for the energy of frustration. Ask yourself where this feeling or thoughtform "that you aren't doing things right" exists in your body. Visualize the symbol or color in your body, and then see these flowing downwards and releasing down your grounding cord. Yes, you are being given tools and techniques to help you so that you always have something to focus on, but these are to be used interchangeably, when needed. Don't become dogmatic with the tools. Think of them like a hammer or a screwdriver or a saw. You might use both of these tools in your work on a constant basis, but certain situations call for a hammer and certain ones call for a screwdriver and you aren't doing the job wrong if you don't always use every single one, nor are you doing the job wrong if you come up with your own creative uses for these, or brand new tools no one else has thought of. One of the greatest uses of your psychic abilities is to come up with new techniques, or at least alternatives, that will be useful to yourself and to others. Those offered in this book are just a launching pad to get you started.

Creating a Viewing Receptacle

Once you have created a reading screen where you can focus your attention, you then need to create a viewing receptacle that you can place on the screen. Within this receptacle will appear the energy/information that you wish to read in the form of color and images. A reading screen is like a dining room table. You sit yourself down at the table and on it you place a receptacle, like a bowl, which will hold your soup. If you poured your soup directly onto the table, your soup would spill all over. It would not only be difficult to eat your soup, but there would be a big mess that would require a lot of effort to clean up. A viewing receptacle placed on your screen is like a disposable bowl placed on a table. It contains the energy and information so it that it can be digested as easily as it can be disposed of. The viewing receptacle not only receives information/energy in the form of images and colors, but will be directly affected by energy so that its appearance will be altered. You will read the energy initially by watching to see how the receptacle is affected.

The viewing receptacle can be visualized as any neutral object, such as a bubble, balloon, or flower. Most of the clairvoyant training programs throughout the country suggest using the image of a rose as the receptacle. A rose is a good image to work with because it can be visualized in a very simple manner, such as in outline form, or in all of the complexity of a real rose with its numerous petals, leaves, and thorns. Roses come in all different colors, shapes, and sizes, they can be open or closed in a variety of positions, and they can be destroyed easily by plucking away their petals. Also, because a rose has a stem that grows from the ground, it has its own naturally built-in grounding cord. The image of the rose was always used as the viewing receptacle in my own clairvoyant training and is therefore the one I am most comfortable with. I will use the word rose interchangeably with the term viewing receptacle throughout this book.

Since a rose can be visually complex, it is helpful to place a real living rose or a picture of a rose in front of you and closely observe it before trying to visualize one. Over time it will become easier to create this image in your imagination. If you feel that the image of a rose is too complex, I suggest just starting off with the image of a glass soap bubble and gradually working your way up to that of a rose.

Grounding Your Viewing Receptacle

Visualize or imagine that you are looking at your reading screen. Now imagine that you are placing a clear, neutral crystal rose onto your reading screen. This rose is transparent, so you can see inside it. The rose is neutral—it has no charge or meaning at this point. It is a blank canvas. Notice how it looks. See the size and the shape. You have just created a viewing receptacle! If you are having difficulty visualizing the rose or whatever image you are using, then give the receptacle a grounding cord. Connect the stem of your rose into the center of the planet, and postulate that the gravity of the earth is effortlessly sucking up any energies that may be interfering with your visualization.

If you notice that your receptacle is doing something unusual or taking on a life of its own, don't be alarmed! Your rose is being affected by some kind of energy and you are already performing a reading by seeing the effects of this energy! Whenever something unusual happens with an image that you are visualizing, there is a reason for it, and it's up to you to use your clairvoyance to explore the reason for that behavior. If it wasn't important for you to see, you wouldn't notice it!

Calling Energy Into Your Viewing Receptacle

The purpose of performing a reading is to gain access to information from a source other than our logical mind. In order to do this, we need to have a question or a goal in mind that will then direct the information into our viewing receptacle. This question or goal can be very simple or very complex; it can concern yourself or someone else. For example, you might wonder what your creative energy looks like. You might wonder why you are feeling sad. You might wonder if your psychic protection is working for you. You might wonder whether or not you should marry your fiance. You might want to know why your boss is mad at you, why you procrastinate, what the pain in your stomach is trying to tell you, what energies are affecting your third chakra, whether you are going to get the job you applied for, etc.

The answer to whatever question you ask will come in the form of energy. A clairvoyant reading is as simple as inviting this energy into your viewing receptacle and then asking your viewing receptacle to show you the answer in the form of colors and images. Here are three methods for doing this. I recommend that you do all three exercises, although this is not essential.

Exercise 1
On your reading screen, create an image of a neutral clear glass rose. Study the shape of the rose and the petals. Next, imagine that the rose you have created is traveling to the outermost layer of your aura. Take a few moments to see what happens to your rose. Did the appearance of your rose change? If you notice anything unusual or different about the rose, ask whatever change has occurred in the rose to give you another color, image, or message about the meaning of what you are looking at in the rose. Then destroy this rose by imagining that is it exploding into a million pieces.

Exercise 2
On your reading screen, with your imagination, create an image of a rose. See the color, shape, and size. Study this rose for a few moments. Now postulate that the stem of the rose is a grounding cord. Ground the rose deeply into the center of the planet. Postulate that the rose represents yourself and that the stem/grounding cord is going to release any foreign energies that you are now ready to release. Watch the rose and its grounding cord and notice if anything changes about the rose. You can end the exercise as soon as you see a change occur, or you can continue with a more in-depth reading by investigating the meaning of these changes. Further investigation involves asking the rose more questions and then waiting for further changes in the rose or for images to appear. Remember to destroy the rose when you are finished. You can see it exploding, or imagine that you are erasing it with a colorful eraser, or pretend that it's dissolving in a brilliant fire.

Exercise 3

On your reading screen, create another image of a neutral transparent rose made of glass. Postulate that the rose represents something in your life that you would like to create, such as a job, a lover, money, happiness, etc. Before consciously manipulating the rose in any way, just watch the clear rose and notice what happens to it. Does the color change? How open is the rose? What is its posture like (standing erect or wilting)? Is there a particular color coming into the rose? How many petals are there? Are there leaves or thorns on the stem? After watching the rose for a few minutes, you will most likely notice something happening that you did not intend to happen. You will probably be curious about at least one aspect of the rose. So continue with your reading by asking the rose to tell you the meaning of that aspect.

For example, let's say your rose turns purple and pink, there are only a few petals on the bud, and the whole flower is drooping to the left. There are so many aspects to explore! In this example you could first ask the purple to tell you what it represents. Once you pose a question to it, just relax and watch. You should not be trying to figure anything out because this process has nothing to do with your logical mind. Just wait and literally see what happens. (For many clairvoyants, students and experts alike, the hardest part of reading is being patient and letting go of the need to control.)

Next, you can ground the stem of the rose into the center of the planet and watch these aspects to see if they remain constant or if they change or leave the rose. Since this rose represents something you would like to create in your life, you can play around with it in a variety of ways. You can imagine that you are giving the rose to God and then watch the rose to see what happens. Or you can imagine that you are showing the rose to a particular person in your life (like your spouse or your mother) and again watch the rose to see what happens to it. When you are completely finished with this exercise and satisfied that your rose represents only you and the vibration you would like to create it in (for example, enthusiasm versus fear), then imagine that you are sending it off to God or the universe to help with your creation.

Troubleshooting

I am not a visually oriented person. I am having trouble visualizing my screen and my viewing receptacle. What can I do?

For some people, visualization takes practice. Start with a simple visualization exercise, focusing on just one aspect of a simple object. For example, hold a piece of fruit in your hand, like an apple. Study it for a few minutes and then close your eyes and imagine that you are looking at the same apple. Some people become overwhelmed by their expectations of how their visualizations or clairvoyant images are supposed to look. Sometimes I can visualize an object as vividly as if I were seeing it with my physical eyes, while at other times, I can just see enough of an object to know it is there. If all you can muster up is the outline of an object, then that is completely acceptable. If you are unable to do even that, then just postulate that you are visualizing the object.

When I call the energy I want to see into my viewing receptacle, nothing happens. All I see is black.

Congratulations! You are seeing something black! There is a reason for everything you see and everything you don't see! If you draw a blank or just blackness, there are a couple things you can do. First, be patient. Continue to watch the black (or nothingness) for a few minutes and see what happens. Then ask the black (or nothingness) to show you an image of what it represents and continue to observe. If nothing happens, then try grounding your reading screen and the viewing receptacle to release any energy that is blocking the information. The best advice I can give is to be patient and calmly relentless in your intent to get an answer!

I have been known to sit for half an hour in total silence in front of a client until the elusive information to an important question finally appeared (the client is usually more willing to let the question go than I am!). Any time information is not easily accessible, there is a reason for it and that reason may be what is blocking you or your readee or both from being where you would like to be in your life. Pursuing the answer, no matter how much work it takes on your part, is what will make your readings effective and valuable. There are plenty of capable but lazy psychics out there who will give up immediately if the information is not made available. This serves no one, especially the psychic. When information you are seeking resides in your or your readee's unconscious mind, when there have been years, if not decades, of psychological defense mechanisms and other energies repressing this information, you will find that it is much harder to see. Sometimes you may not be ready emotionally or psychologically to deal with the answer that comes to you. If this is the case, you will probably get distracted, fall asleep, or naturally give up (which may be what is supposed to happen; our defense mechanisms are there to help us, even through they block us at the same time).

Another reason you may not get a response when posing a question to your viewing receptacle is that you may be asking the wrong question. Early in my clairvoyant training, I read a client who asked the question, "Should I marry my fiance?" I put up a clear glass image of a rose on my reading screen and posed the same question to the rose. I got absolutely no response. After about fifteen minutes of trying all of the above suggestions, the answer finally came to me, which was that in the realm of spirit, there is no should or should not! There was no answer to that particular question. I refrained the question to the rose and asked, "Would my client be fulfilled and happy in her life if she married her fiance?" The response was immediate—an image of her crying. I have had this same experience so many times that without a doubt I can advise that you should never use "should" in your questions!

Whenever I attempt to do the exercises in this chapter I fall asleep.

There are a few reasons why you might fall asleep during clairvoyant reading and meditation. The most obvious reason is that you are tired! I used to pride myself on the number of hours I could sit in meditation on a daily basis, being totally alert and focused. That was until the birth of my bouncing baby boy, when I became a single mother who worked three different jobs (not including writing this book) and went to filmmaking school full-time. Now I am lucky if I can meditate in an upright position for two minutes before falling asleep.

If at all possible, try getting a good night's sleep and then change your routine. Try practicing your clairvoyant exercises earlier in the day, after you have had a chance to digest your food but before you are hungry again. Drinking one small cup of coffee or black tea before attempting these exercises might help as well (not that I want to advocate the use of caffeine; I have seen the negative impact of too much caffeine on the throat and the fifth chakra in several readings).

You might also try reading in a different location. If possible, avoid reading and meditating in a place where you usually sleep, whether that is in your bedroom or on the sofa in front of the TV, since your body is programmed to sleep in these situations. Make sure to practice these exercises in an upright position; reclining or lying down will cause most people to fall asleep. Experiment with reading and meditating after you have engaged in some physical exercise. Physical exercise naturally gets your energy flowing and might help you focus, although it could have the opposite effect on some people.

When we do this work, we are altering our brain wave patterns from our normal waking state. Sometimes we move into the Theta brain wave level which borders on a sleep state, so if we go too deep we are likely to fall asleep. Riding the edge of this state takes a lot of practice, but it can pay off in the long run as it's felt by many researchers that being in Theta facilitates some of the most vivid and lucid visual experiences. It's kind of like walking a tightrope where we are constantly falling off on either side. One side pulls us back to a state of overanalyzing, the other side pulls us into slumber. (For more about these states I highly recommend researching the work being done by The Monroe Institute in Virginia).

Following the above suggestions, including making sure you have light in your room and an environment that is stimulating but in a relaxing way, should help you avoid constantly falling off the edge into slumber. Most times, merely giving yourself the command that you aren't allowed to go too deep, and standing up and/or stretching when you do start to feel yourself nod off, can help. Sometimes there is just no avoiding it. If you fall asleep, so be it.

When I read myself, I don't know if I am getting accurate information or if I am being biased by what I want to see.

Reading objectively is a challenge and one reason why I personally find it much easier to read people I don't know than myself. If you are having this problem, try the following exercise.

Visualize a rose and postulate that this rose will contain the accurate and unbiased answer or information to your question. Then create another rose and postulate that it contains the energy of the answer you would like to hear. Ask the first rose to show you a color, and then ask the second rose to do the same. Notice whether the colors are the same or different. Ask each color to show you what it represents.

For example, let's say you have just met a good-looking guy and you are hoping he will ask you out. Waiting to see if he does is, of course, too agonizing, so you decide to do a little clairvoyant reading for yourself. When you pose this question to your viewing receptacle rose, you see an image of him calling you on the telephone, but you are not sure if you are just making this up. So you destroy that rose and create two new ones. The first rose, which represents the true answer, is blue. The second rose, representing your desires, is green. When you ask the blue to show you what it means, you see the good-looking guy sitting in an office buried in papers; he seems stressed out. When you ask the green to show you what it means, you see the two of you smooching! The fact that the two colors and images are different probably indicates that your exact desire may not manifest. However, now you have a better idea of why he has not called. It's not that you are unworthy of his attention, but that he is distracted by his work.

This exercise will help you explore your biases, but will not eliminate them. As long as you realize when reading yourself that you are not neutral and that your information could be heavily biased, you will not get into trouble. (The problem of personal bias is significantly reduced when you know nothing about the person you are reading.) Over time, you will be better able to distinguish between psychic information that is coming from your ego versus information that is coming from a higher source. Don't let the fear of confusing the two get in the way of practicing and enjoying your readings.

I enjoy reading other people, but when I try to use my clairvoyance on myself, I get too distracted and give up before getting any results.

It is a lot harder for most people to read themselves than it is for them to read other people. When reading yourself, you are susceptible to the same distractions that make it difficult for so many people to meditate (or even get to the point of attempting to meditate). It is very easy to get lost in all the energy in the form of thoughts that are swimming around in your mind and aura. Foreign energies can easily distract you. One solution is to use a tape recorder. As you do the exercises in this chapter, give a detailed account of everything you are doing, seeing, and experiencing. Another solution is to do the exercises with a partner who can verbally guide you with questions and listen to your responses.

It is in no way mandatory that you first read yourself before reading other people, and if you are having too much difficulty reading yourself, or it's not fun, then by all means move on to reading someone else, which will be covered in the following chapter. When you read another person, you have no choice but to focus on that person's energy. The moment your thoughts wander, you will no longer be reading the person (who is sitting there, excitedly waiting for your communication), and you will momentarily realize this and come back to the reading (which is not usually the case when you are reading yourself).

Many people think that they can only read another person once they have perfected their clairvoyance. That is the one of biggest mistakes you can make! The only way to develop your clairvoyant abilities, or any ability, is to practice and to take risks. The more you practice, the more you will realize what you can do. As long as you begin by reading receptive, supportive people who understand that you are just learning, you will be fine! (I don't recommend accepting money for readings until you are confident and have a number of readings under your belt—see chapter 23).

There is value both in reading yourself and in reading others. Continue to try both of these experiences and over time you will find that they get easier. Many of the difficulties you run into when you are first beginning to develop your clairvoyance will soon become obsolete as you grow and heal yourself through reading and using your psychic tools. Who you are now is not who you will be later. The path of clairvoyance is a path of growth, and there is richness and meaning in every difficulty you encounter in your meditation and readings and everyday life. This book would not exist if it were not for the challenges I have faced during my own readings.

CHAPTER 14

How to Read Another Person

In this chapter, you will learn everything you need to know in order to effectively perform a clairvoyant reading on another person.

Reading Over the Phone Versus In Person

There is no time or space when it comes to psychic information. This means that readings over the phone are as easy (and accurate) between two people who are at opposite ends of the world, as they are between two people sitting a foot apart from one another. The only difference is that the emotional and empathic connection may be lessened slightly when reading over the phone, but not always. In fact, being separated can actually be helpful to some readers as the "in person" connection can be so strong it is distracting. In fact, emotions and energy are often felt strongly over the phone as well and as we will discuss throughout this book, the ability to feel other people is helpful only to a certain extent. Once you know someone feels sad or is in pain, you need to move away from that to higher levels of information so you can help that person understand it more or overcome it. Wallowing in their intense emotions, while dramatic, is only going to be a distracter. This is more likely to happen in an in-person reading. Still, this in no way means you shouldn't do in-person readings.

I highly recommend giving yourself a broad range of experiences that include both reading people in-person and over the phone, and revisiting both from time to time, just to be able to experience each one and compare them for yourself. Until you do both, you just won't know. Since every reading is different, you'll probably want to do several of each before deciding which you prefer.

Communicating Expectations

Expectations for the reading should be discussed before both parties agree to participate in the reading and preferably before the client arrives for the reading. These expectations include the length of the reading, whether compensation is expected, the general format of the reading, whether the future will be addressed, and whether the client will have an opportunity to ask questions. Most people feel some level of anxiety prior to a reading because they don't know what to expect or whether their expectations will be met. If they have no idea how much you will charge them or whether there will be an opportunity for them to ask you a pressing question, then their attention will be focused on their anxieties and on the future. Since as a reader your attention will tend to go to where the readee's attention is, you will have a harder time concentrating in the present moment, which is where your clairvoyant images are located. You will also sense your readee's anxiety, which will decrease your enjoyment of the reading.

Discussing expectations is an ethically sound practice, particularly when financial compensation is involved. The more you are in integrity, the less energy you will expend. Communicating expectations minimizes future ethical dilemmas and arguments, and decreases the possibility of disappointment and resentment for both parties. Most importantly, when both parties understand the expectations upfront, they can make the most conscious and informed decision about whether or not to proceed with the reading.

That being said, once expectations have been communicated, they should not be set in stone, because after all, you can never know (even if you are psychic) how either of you will feel once the reading has begun. The readee may be really happy with the reading and request that the time of the reading be extended. You may agree to look at the future, but when the time comes you may only receive information about the present. The format of the reading could change depending on the particular issues of your client.

At any point, either you or your readee may decide that the reading is not going well and choose to terminate it. Of course, if this happens, the agreed-upon compensation may need to be reconsidered. As a reader you are never obligated to complete a reading or give a reading, and one of your most challenging but rewarding lessons will occur when you are faced with the dilemma of whether or not to prematurely end a reading if something about it does not seem conducive to your well-being. The more money you stand to make from a reading, the more difficult this dilemma will be. For more discussion on this issue, see chapter 23.

Location

Prior to the reading, you will need to find the right location for the reading. This is true whether you are reading people in-person or over the phone. Ideally this location will be a quiet one with minimal distractions, where you can feel safe sitting across from a stranger. That being said, the truth of the matter is that you can do a clairvoyant reading anytime, anywhere. I have performed readings on crowded airplanes, at raucous parties, in moving vehicles, on mountaintops in the rain, in an agent's office at the Federal Bureau of Investigation, and at psychic fairs where I and thirty other psychics were doing readings so close to each other that the hairs on our arms were touching. A reading can be performed under any circumstances. However, for the purposes of learning how to do readings and feeling grounded and comfortable, ideally you will want to make arrangements so that you and your readee can sit in two comfortable upright chairs, in a well-grounded, peaceful environment. As you become more experienced, you will want to practice reading in more distracting and uncomfortable places so you can realize that you too can read under any circumstance.

Timekeeping

During a reading, it is helpful to have a clock or timer nearby so you know when your time is up. Some people are fine with the sound of a timer, though personally I find it too jolting. I prefer to have a large clock placed on the wall behind my readee at my eye level, so I can effortlessly open my eyes and glance at the clock without breaking my concentration. Oftentimes I have an inner alarm clock that tells me when we are nearing the end of the reading. You may have experienced a similar phenomenon when waking up on the morning of an important event. You may set your alarm clock, but then find that you wake up a couple minutes before the clock is supposed to go off. This is because there is a part of you that is awake and aware of everything going on around you at all times.

However, when you first begin doing readings, you will have greater difficulty judging the passage of time and will be more inclined to get drawn into reading longer than you intended by the desires of your overzealous readee ("Please, just one more quick question!"), and by your own compulsion to heal every problem your readee has ever had! A clock or timer will not only help you judge the passage of time, but you may actually need to show it to your readee in order to bring them back to "reality" and help them understand that the reading is really over.

Pre-Reading Meditation

I recommend meditating for at least twenty minutes before embarking on a reading. This meditation should include psychic tools such as grounding yourself and the room, centering yourself, running your energy, creating and destroying objects, clearing your chakras, etc. Meditation will help flush out all the rambling thoughts of the day so information of a more subtle nature can be grasped. If you don't spend some time meditating or working on your tools prior to the reading, the first several minutes of the reading will be more of a struggle and the clairvoyant information may not initially be as vivid or accessible. You will also be less vulnerable to negative energies at the onset of the reading if you take the time to secure yourself to the earth and have your energy running before your readee enters the room.

Setting an Intention

At the start of a reading, it is also a good practice to pick one or two things that you are going to work on or intend to accomplish during the reading for yourself. This could be anything from postulating that you are going to work on your grounding tools to kicking out a former girlfriend's (or boyfriend's) energy from your aura. Setting an intention will serve to remind you that you are equally as important as your readee and that reading is a healing and personal growth process for you as a reader. Also, when you are using your clairvoyant abilities, you are accessing the spiritual realms where time and space and physical limits do not exist. It is here where intentions, dreams, and wishes can manifest much more quickly and with less effort (see chapter 12).

Setting Boundaries

You will often sense the readee's energy coming toward you before you actually attempt to tune in to that person. This might happen before the readee arrives or as soon as they enter the door. You will know this is happening if you spontaneously think about them or if you begin to pick up clairvoyant information before you have officially "tuned in" to them. Sometimes you may feel nervous and therefore be drawn to take a peek at the readee before you start. Some readers will actually do a reading before the readee arrives so they feel less pressure during the reading, a practice I discourage. A reading is not a performance and it does not need to appear flawless.

I personally set strong limits for myself (and for my students) in that I am only allowed to read that person when they are in front of me and when I have officially begun the reading. If I find myself thinking about the readee before or after the reading, then I know there is an energy exchange going on that could become messy very quickly. It is for this reason that I generally do not ask the readee what their questions are before I officially am ready to start the reading, and once the reading is over, I cease to discuss their issues. Otherwise the reading could continue on a telepathic level for days, years, or even an entire lifetime!

It's important to understand that if a woman approaches you on a Saturday and schedules a reading for the following Tuesday, you could potentially end up reading her for the next seventy-two hours if you aren't careful. Your aura could become merged with hers and then you will begin to feel and live all of her pain, problems, anxieties, etc., without even being aware that this is happening. The way to avoid this is first to make the commitment to yourself that you will not permit an energetic connection to form until you consciously will this connection to form, and then to establish a routine that lets your body and spirit know when the reading is beginning and when it is ending. Using your psychic tools on a regular basis will also help you with this.

Don't Allow Anyone in the Room or on the Phone Except the Readee

Invariably, a client will arrive for a reading and they or their companion, whether it be their husband, mother, or friend, will ask if it's alright if the companion stays in the room. Ninety-nine percent of the time I say no, unless the readee is a child (see chapter 19) or the questions pertain to a couple's joint goals, such as when they are buying a house together. There are a few reasons for this. First of all, the energy of the readee's companion could easily interfere with the reading and you may inadvertently start reading that person without being aware of this. Furthermore, clairvoyant readings tend to be very personal, and you don't want to be inhibited in any way from sharing information of a personal nature.

On many occasions when I had to put my foot down and asked the readee's companion to wait outside or return in an hour, it actually turned out that the readee had questions about their relationship with that person and never would have felt comfortable asking or talking about those issues in the companion's presence. Sometimes clients just don't know how to speak up and set boundaries for themselves, so you will need to do this for them. Remember, during a reading you are in control.

Most clients understand when you explain that another person's presence will interfere with your reading, and they really appreciate that you are trying to give them the best experience possible. Occasionally the readee will explain that they are in an intimate relationship with their companion and are working on similar goals and this is why they want to both be present for the reading. In that case, you can ask them if they are seeking a relationship reading and read them as a couple, as discussed in chapter 18.

Reading Routine

I have fallen into a particular routine that assists me in maintaining boundaries. This routine also helps keep the various steps of the reading organized and signals my subconscious as to when the actual reading is going to begin.

For in-person readings: Begin by greeting your readee. Introduce yourself. Show your readee where to sit. I like to read directly across from my readee, with a few feet of space in between us so our auras are not totally enmeshed, but close enough so we can speak on intimate terms and hear each other well. Both parties should be sitting upright in comfortable chairs or sofas.

Eliminate distracting sounds and music. Whether the readee comes to you or you go to them, it is important for you to take control of the environment before the reading begins. If you cannot assert yourself enough to ask to rearrange some furniture or turn down the music, energetically you won't be able to assert yourself enough to get past the readee's resistances or to keep the readee out of your energy field. Music or noise from a television set often will pull you out of your body and out of the reading.

For readings done over the phone or via Skype: Make sure the readee can hear you clearly. Make sure you explain to them that they can and should feel free to interrupt you at any time if they can't hear you. Many people will sit through an entire phone reading struggling to hear and missing a good portion of it because they were afraid to interrupt you. This seems ludicrous, but I can't tell you how many times this has happened to me. At the end of the reading the person will admit, "Well, I didn't hear half of it but what I did hear made sense!" Also let the person know what to do if the call is dropped—whether they should call you back or you should call them back.

Once you are both situated with the technology aspects out of the way, explain to your readee what a clairvoyant reading entails. This is what I usually say to new clients: "So what I will be doing today is a clairvoyant reading, where I will be looking at different images that come up. Some of these will be symbolic, while others will have literal interpretations. As I talk, some things will make sense while other things may not make any sense at all. Eventually things will become clear."

Highlighting the General Order of Activities

Next, I explain that I will first go into a light trance and ground myself. This trance is nothing deeper than a relaxed state of awareness. I mention that I will now close my eyes and have them closed for the entire reading. I let the readee know that this will take a few minutes and I won't charge them for this time.

I then explain that after I go into my trance, I will ask my readee to state their name a few times in order to tune in to their vibration, and that throughout the reading I may ask them to restate their name if I feel I need to strengthen or reestablish my connection with them.

I explain that after I am tuned in to their vibration, the readee will have an opportunity to ask questions or discuss their issues, or at that point we will discuss the format of the reading.

Next, I reassure the readee that I will walk them through the process and that there is nothing they need to do now except to keep their feet flat on the floor (to keep them grounded) and to remain in an alert state of consciousness with their eyes open. Many clients automatically match me as I go into a trance, and then I have more difficulty reading them, so I do what I can to keep them awake. However, some people just cannot help but close their eyes, and to force them to keep their eyes open would make them too uncomfortable. For these people, I just gently remind them from time to time to come back to their body, and I ask them to repeat their name more often than those people who naturally stay alert.

Running Through Your Psychic Tools in the Presence of the Readee

When I first began doing readings, I felt awkward taking the time to run through my psychic tools while sitting across from another person. I felt self-conscious, as if they were staring at me, judging my appearance, my clothes, and the way my eyes fluttered. I felt like they were thinking about the money they were paying for every second I sat there in self-absorbed silence. Over time I realized that yes, some people were doing these things. But many others were sitting there worrying about their own behavior and appearance, while the majority were very happy to give me whatever time I needed to get ready to give them the best reading of their life.

Years later I still take a few minutes at the start of every single reading to run through my psychic tools (I do this even if I already sat in meditation for an hour before their arrival—something I'd like to do all the time but don't!), and I'm at the point now where I really couldn't care less about what anyone is doing or thinking during that time. In fact, lots of times I completely forget that there is anyone sitting less than two feet away and staring at me. I am only reminded of their presence when they sneeze or move their chair.

Taking this time for yourself in the presence of the readee is vital to your well-being and it serves your readee in a number of ways. Even if you just spent two hours meditating before they arrived, it's necessary to check your psychic tools to make sure they are still working in the presence of your readee. Your readee's energy will have an effect on your grounding cord, your ability to stay in the center of your head, and on your tools such as running your earth and cosmic energies. So you want to double-check that these are still working for you after your readee has arrived.

Furthermore, meditating in the presence of your readee makes the statement to yourself and to your readee that you are important and that you have a right to take care of yourself at all times. As you take care of yourself in the presence and under the scrutiny of another person, you are modeling this behavior for your readee. Some readers start picking up information about their readee during this time. As mentioned earlier, I try to push away this information until I have made sure that I have sufficiently prepared and cared for myself.

Running through your psychic tools at the start of every reading will also serve as a signal to your body and your psychic faculties that you are about to begin a clairvoyant reading, so that when you actually attempt to access the clairvoyant information, it will flow more easily. I tend to not officially start the time for the reading until after I have gone into a trance and run through my tools, although some people feel strongly that this is time spent on the reading and they should be compensated for it.

Furthermore, during a reading, you should periodically take short breaks from reading to run through your psychic tools to make sure you are still reading from a grounded place of neutrality, releasing whatever needs to be released, and energizing yourself. This again is good modeling behavior. In professional readings, I tend to worry that my readee will feel cheated from their time, but I know that taking these breaks makes me a better and clearer reader, and people usually appreciate this.

Redistributing Your Energy

As part of your pre-reading meditation, you will want to redistribute your energy from your lower three chakras to your upper chakras. As you go through your everyday life, there are lots of times when it is necessary and desirable to have your energy running though your lower chakras, particularly when you need to use your body for physical activity. However, during a reading, your body really doesn't have to do anything beyond maintaining its minimal automatic functions. Instead, your psychic and cognitive abilities will be needed in full force, and therefore the chakras that house these abilities will be in greater need of your energy. By redistributing your energy from your lower chakras to your upper chakras, you will call forth the inherent spiritual abilities of the fifth, sixth, and seventh chakras, while inhibiting the energies of survival, control, and emotion that are associated with the lower chakras and that are less conducive to clairvoyant reading. Energy can be redistributed through a simple visualization of opening and closing your chakras and moving your energy upward or downward.

Begin by creating a reading screen in front of your sixth chakra, or third eye, located slightly above and between your eyebrows, in the center of your head. Then visualize your first chakra, which is located at the base of your spine. You can imagine that it looks like the lens of a camera that opens and closes. Look to see how open it is. Is it open 100 percent, 75 percent, 50 percent, or is it totally closed? If you are having trouble determining how open it is, you can visualize that there is a gauge or a meter with numbers on it, and then ask the percentage of how open it is to appear on the gauge.

Now it is time to close your first chakra down so that it is only about half open. On your reading screen, imagine that the opening of your first chakra is getting smaller and smaller until it is only half open. You can give your gauge a grounding cord and imagine that any foreign energy in your first chakra is effortlessly falling down the cord into the center of the planet. Look at your gauge and watch as the arrow goes to 50 percent. As you close down your first chakra, notice how it feels. Are you experiencing any bodily sensations? Do you feel any emotions or pain being released? Do you feel more relaxed or nervous? Realize that as you close down your first chakra, your own vital energy is naturally rising up to your higher chakras.

Next, create a clear glass rose on your reading screen that represents your own energy in your first chakra. Look to see what color it is. Now watch that color as it rises up your chakras until it gets to your crown chakra. Once the color reaches your crown chakra, imagine that your crown chakra is opening up like a lotus, and visualize it growing brighter and brighter.

You can then repeat this process with your second and third chakras. Again, start off imagining that these chakras are growing smaller and smaller, so that any excess energy is squeezed outward and upward to your third eye (sixth chakra) and crown chakra (seventh chakra). See these spinning energy centers expand and grow brighter as you remind yourself that you are now activating the energy in these higher chakras, which will further stimulate your clairvoyance and make it easier to remain centered, balanced, and calm.

Turning Down Your Analyzer

One of the most challenging things about doing clairvoyant readings is that you need your analytical mind to at least lead you to the doorway of your clairvoyance in terms of helping you formulate questions that will elicit a clairvoyant response. However, once you have posed a question with the use of your logical/analytical mind, you must abandon that part of yourself momentarily so that extrasensory information can come to you.

Consciously turning down your analytical/logical mind is a very simple but effective technique that can remarkably decrease the thoughts and general noise level of your mind. It will bring you into a deeper state of relaxation where you can enjoy the flow of your clairvoyant images rather than resist or doubt or question them. While you will still have access to your logical faculties, these will no longer dominate your intuitive processes.

First say hello to your reading screen. Check to see if it has any holes or is dusty. Give it a grounding cord and release any energy that has accumulated on it. If you don't like how it looks, then destroy it and create a new one. On your screen, place a big, old-fashioned gauge with a big arrow. This represents your analytical mind. Postulate that whatever you do to this gauge will actually affect the part of your brain that generates your analytical thoughts.

First look to see at what number your analytical mind is currently set. Next, give this gauge a really big grounding cord and ground it firmly into the center of the planet. Now very slowly start to move the arrow on the gauge down by five degrees. As you do this, look for the color of energy that can now be released from this gauge into the center of the planet. When you turn down your analytical mind, you are releasing extraneous energy that you do not need. So this exercise is giving you a healing at the same time that it's helping prepare you to use your clairvoyance.

Notice how you are feeling. Let any emotions or fears that come up be released down your own grounding cord. You may want to increase the size of your grounding cord. Now slowly continue to move the gauge down further and further until it is at the 10 percent mark. You really only need 10 percent of your analytical mind to be operating at this point. Continue to release any fearful thoughts that suggest you may lose control or not be able to think anymore. Send these thoughts and emotions down your grounding cord. The nature of your logical mind is that it wants to be in control of every aspect of your life, even when its presence will only interfere with your goals.

Turning Up Your Clairvoyance

This is a warm-up exercise that will help you begin to flex your visualization "muscles" and stimulate/clear your sixth chakra. It also serves as a signal to your mind that you are preparing to enter into an altered state of consciousness, in much the same way that a hypnotic suggestion works.

Begin by visualizing your reading screen. Imagine that there is a big eye on it. This is your third eye, which corresponds to your sixth chakra and your clairvoyance. Notice how big the eye is and how open it is. Notice all of its details. What color(s) is it? Does it have eyelashes? Is there makeup on the lids? Is it clear or is it bloodshot? Is it an alert eye or is it a sleepy eye? Is it a happy eye or is it crying? Give your third eye a grounding cord and ask any foreign energies to release out of it. Drain out any energy that may be getting in the way of your clairvoyance. This energy could be in the form of atheism, competition, self-doubt, past-life or childhood trauma, etc.

While atheism and competition are not necessarily bad things in everyday life, when they are in your clairvoyant "space," they are deadly. Imagine that you are sitting quietly, trying your hardest to concentrate, to notice the most delicate of changes occurring behind your fluttering eyelids, completely unsure of yourself and what you are about to experience. Or maybe you are a more experienced psychic, brimming with confidence and excitement about this grand opportunity to do another reading, but then someone approaches you, perhaps a stranger, but most likely someone you adore: a parent, your wife, a client, etc. They snuggle up close, slide up on your lap, fling their arms around your neck, snuggle up against your ear, stare passionately into your eyes and holler at the top of their lungs: "Who do you think you are, you stupid idiot? Why would you of all people be able to do this? You will never be good enough. You won't see a thing. You don't have what it takes!" (This is competition.) Or: "There is no such thing as this psychic crap, you imbecile! You've never seen any of this before, so why do you think you could now? It's not real. None of it is real!" (Atheism, skepticism.) While this is a silly scenario, do you think this might just have a wee bit of an impact on your concentration, confidence level, or enthusiasm for doing a reading?

Now imagine that this charming individual is not physically present, but their energy, their thoughtforms, their emotions are. They might as well be right in your face because their energy is going to have the same impact as if they were there, only it will work you over on an unconscious level. So you won't see it coming and you won't know why it is you just got distracted, why you are so frustrated, or why it is you fell asleep or got up from that chair and decided it was time to wash the dishes. All you'll know is that suddenly the last thing you want to do is the very thing you most wanted to do five minutes ago: experience your clairvoyance. This is why we do exercises like this one, and so many of the others throughout this book.

Getting back to the exercise, you have just drained any foreign energies from your third eye on your reading screen. Next, see a color for the energy as it drains out and then look at the eye to see if any of its attributes have changed. If your third eye does not look very open, then you can imagine that it is opening as wide as you can possibly open it. See this third eye getting bigger and bigger until it fills up your entire reading screen and still it grows bigger and bigger.

If you'd like, you can connect your third eye up to God by visualizing God as a golden ball of light and seeing a cord connecting the eye to the ball of light, and then filling up your eye with God's light. Talk to your third eye and tell it that you are going to need its help in a big way. Thank it in advance for working for you. Promise it that you will do everything you can to honor whatever it wants to show you by trusting that its images are relevant to the reading and by sharing the images with the readee.

If you'd like, you can also put up a gauge that represents your clairvoyance and visualize that the arrow on the gauge us going up to 100 percent open. Then pick a color that represents your own enthusiasm and amusement. Fill your third eye with this color. To increase the energy of fun and amusement in your readings, dress up your eye in a funny way. Give it long, curly, silly eyelashes or see it doing funny tricks with its eyebrow. Remember, laughter and amusement are the highest vibration of energy, and problems, worries, doubts, etc., cannot exist in the energy of amusement. Sometimes you need to make an extra effort to create amusement when you are not feeling particularly amused, but remember, laughter is infectious.

The Psychic is In: Preparing to Read

This next technique is also optional but can be quite useful. When I first began reading out of a metaphysical bookstore in Sedona, I often had very little time to meditate or prepare myself before beginning a reading. I was still settling into the idea of charging money for readings and was nervous about the responsibility that seemed to go with that. I found it necessary to come up with a visualization tool that would help me get into my clairvoyant reading space quickly and confidently, and here is the technique I developed.

First, imagine you are entering a room. It looks just like the room where you are going to do your reading. However, under the rug or the floor boards is a trap door. You open up the trap door and see a staircase. You follow the staircase down several flights until you reach a door with the sign "Clairvoyant Reading Chamber." You open the door and see a coat rack. You take off your coat and your hat in preparation to read. You then put on a special hat that says "Clairvoyance." You find some slippers. These are your favorite clairvoyant reading slippers, which you wear only when doing readings. Next, imagine that you sit down in your favorite clairvoyant reading chair. You might even take a swig out of a glass bottle that is labeled "Clairvoyant Reading Potion." This potion enhances your abilities. Yum, it's so delicious! You are now ready to begin your readings.

This exercise is very simple. You can make the decor of the clairvoyant reading chamber as basic or as elaborate as you'd like. Often, if I only have a minute or less before I'm supposed to start my reading, I will just visualize that I am entering the room, hanging up my coat, and putting on my clairvoyant reading hat. This serves as a sign to my unconscious that I am ready to begin the reading.

Saying a Prayer

I cannot teach you how to pray in words.
God listens not to your words save when He Himself utters
them through your lips.
And I cannot teach you the prayer of the seas and the forests and the mountains.
But you who are born of the mountains and the forests and the seas
can find their prayer in your heart.
—Kahlil Gibran, The Prophet, 1923

I always say a prayer before doing a reading. I say it out loud so that I, my readee, and any other being in the room can hear the prayer. Prayer helps set the intention of the reading and it sends a clear message to any spirits, entities, or negative influences in the room or around any of the participants that any interference on their part will not be tolerated. It's like a mission statement, a declaration, a contract. Physicists will tell you that nature abhors a vacuum. Space is not empty. It is filled by whatever is closest to it and strongest. If you have competing sounds in a room, the loudest sound will be heard the most. The strongest smell will be experienced, and the brightest light will outshine the weaker lights and overpower the darkness.

It's the same with energy and prayer. If you sit down for a reading, or at work, or when getting into bed, and state: "I now bring peace here," or "Please, God, bring peace here," then you strengthen this intention, this desire, by focusing on a symbol that represents this intention, such as a peace symbol, a dove, Jesus, a star of David, or your favorite soothing color. You are invoking peace to be there with you in that space, and anything that is not peace will not be able to exist in that same space.

So prayer serves as an invitation for some energies to participate and for others to excuse themselves immediately. The readee needs to know what energies you are invoking or dismissing since some of those energies are a part of them. Many clients understand the power of prayer and will be grateful, if not relieved, that you are making a point to pray during their reading. Of course there are some people who are uncomfortable with prayer because they don't understand what it is or have negative connotations associated with it (for example, they think that only fanatics pray).

As a clairvoyant reader, you are also a spiritual teacher and you can demonstrate to these people that prayer in this instance really has nothing to do with religion or fanaticism, but is more about evoking a desired outcome of energy, such as peace, love, joy, etc. When I pray, I do mention the word God; however, when I first started out as a clairvoyant reader I referred to God as "the Supreme Being" or as "the universe." I used to be a lot more concerned about offending people than I am now. I feel that if anyone is offended by the mention of the word God, that is their problem, not mine. Even if someone is an atheist, they should still be able to appreciate that God symbolizes something positive and helpful.

Visualization for Prayer

During a prayer, I will visualize a color that represents God. For me, this is usually a bright sparkly golden color. I will imagine that I am encompassing myself and the readee inside this color so that we are totally immersed in it. Since this is the color and energy of God, we are inside God and protected by the attributes we feel God possesses. This bubble not only helps us maintain a connection with God, it also keeps out any energies that are antithetical to the qualities normally ascribed to God. It reminds us that the reading is taking place between me, as a reader, and the readee, and that no one else with or without a body is invited to participate unless otherwise noted. At this time it is also helpful to ground the room again, which you should have done when you first reviewed your tools at the start of the reading (see chapter 7).

Tuning In to the Readee

In the last chapter, you learned how to clairvoyantly read yourself. In terms of the basic clairvoyant reading technique, the only difference between reading yourself and someone else is that when reading someone else, it is first necessary to tune in to that person's frequency, vibration, spirit, energy, etc., in order to establish a direct line of communication.

This is similar to what happens when you want to talk to someone on the telephone. There are millions of people out there connected into the same telephone system. In order to speak to a particular person, you need to dial their personal phone number. In the same way, if you desire to talk to a particular person face to face, you need to take steps to initiate the conversation. First, one of you will have to approach the other and get that person's attention, either through verbal communication, such as yelling, "Hey, how's it going?" or through nonverbal communication, such as touching the person's shoulder and looking into their eyes. Once this happens, you are communicating.

In the same manner, if you desire to perform a clairvoyant reading on a particular person, you must do something to establish a connection with that person. The first step is very simple; it requires you to merely have the intention to read that person. The next step is tuning in to that person's individual vibration as a spirit. Oftentimes clients will have lots of different people and energies around them. If you proceed with the basic reading technique without first tuning in to your specific client, you may end up reading the wrong person!

Next, create a new reading screen (see chapter 13). Set your crown chakra to a neutral gold color. You can do this by visualizing your crown chakra as a spinning disk or as an open golden lotus flower.

Then create a viewing receptacle/rose out in front of your reading screen. Create and destroy a couple of these, and then ask your readee to say their name. Ask the readee to say the name they were born with three times, and then their current name three times, and then any other names they have gone by, such as nicknames or names from previous marriages. While the readee says these names, invite their energy to come into the viewing receptacle. Then look for a color that represents their energy.

Once you see a color, take that receptacle and put it over your crown chakra, and ask your crown chakra to match that color. Once your crown chakra has matched the readee's color, adjust the color of your crown chakra so it becomes a bit darker or lighter than that of the readee. This is to remind yourself that you are separate from your readee.

Troubleshooting

I see different colors with the readee's different names.

The reason I ask clients to say every name they have ever gone by is because people identify with certain names. Names contain so much energy and hold a lot of information. Often I have found that when a person says their birth name, it is a very different color and vibration than their married name. If you find that different colors are coming up with each name, you can go with the name they are currently using or whichever name they like the best, since this name will be more in present time. You will sometimes need to use your intuition to determine whether a color is really the appropriate one. If all else fails, have them repeat their first name several times and go with the color of their first name. You could also combine two colors and match your crown chakra to both of these. Most of the time, however, you can just use the first color that comes to you when the readee says all their names.

I am not clearly seeing a color.

Create and destroy a few roses and then ask the readee to repeat all their names. Really listen to the sound of their voice. Ask the vibration you hear to go into your newly created viewing receptacle/rose. Postulate that it is the readee's higher self or a part of their very soul that is going into that receptacle. If you still do not get a color, then just postulate that you are matching your crown chakra to theirs.

I clearly see a color, but then it changes and I see another color.

If you see one color, but then it changes to another color, I recommend putting a grounding cord on your viewing receptacle and postulating that you are grounding out any foreign energies. Look at the colors coming out of the rose and look at the color remaining in the rose. Whatever color remains in the viewing receptacle/rose is the correct color to use. If there is still more than one color, choose the one that appears the most vibrant, or combine the two to make a third color, or swirl the two together. As the reading progresses, you can repeat the tuning in process and you will most likely discover that one of the colors has clearly become the dominant one. This is because as you clairvoyantly read a person, you tune in to that person's spirit/energy and their spirit will naturally move in closer to their body. The more present the readee's spirit is in their body, the easier it will be to see the color at which their spirit is vibrating.

I don't like the color I see and feel a strong resistance to matching that color to my crown chakra.

There are a few reasons you may feel resistance to a particular color. One might be because you have matching pictures with the readee that keep you in resistance to the energy that the color represents. Try creating and destroying some roses around your crown chakra. Postulate that you are clearing any of your own matching pictures. Have the readee repeat their name and try matching your crown chakra to this color, whether it is the original color or a new color.

Another reason you may resist matching your crown chakra to your readee's is because the color represents a very low vibration (such as judgment, pain, or anger) that your body does not want to match. If the color looks and feels very unattractive to you, put it into a rose, ground the rose, and see if the color changes. The color may not really represent your readee's spirit, but rather foreign energy affecting your readee. If all else fails, put up a rose that represents your readee's next step, i.e., the next higher vibration they are really seeking to move into. Match your crown chakra to this vibration rather than the one your readee is currently in.

My body becomes very uncomfortable as I tune in to the readee.

It's important to frequently check in with your body to make sure you are running your own energy rather than your readee's energy. It's common for a clairvoyant reader to totally match their body to that of their client or other readers in the room. If your body goes into pain or discomfort, it could mean that you are releasing matching pictures, but it could also mean that you matched your body to the level of pain and discomfort that the readee feels.

If you are reading a person of the opposite sex and you match the energy in your body to theirs, you could be adversely affected. You may feel overly sluggish or nervous, bored, angry, etc. The point of the tuning in process is merely to match a part of your crown chakra to the readee's vibration; it doesn't at all mean matching the energy of your body to theirs. Revisiting your psychic tools of creating a protection/separation rose and running your earth and cosmic energies, as well as imagining that you are bringing your own energy back into your body while the readee is bringing in their own energy (see these as two different colors), will help you separate your respective energies. You may also need to open your eyes for a moment and physically look at the difference between your body and your readee's body to prove to yourself that they are not the same.

Sending Your Readee a Hello

Once you are tuned in to your readee, send them a visual "hello." This hello can be any welcoming, friendly object, such as a bouquet of flowers or a balloon with a smiley face on it. In your imagination, postulate that this object will go to wherever the readee's spirit is, and then watch to see where the object lands. You can aim for their crown chakra and see if it goes there or somewhere else. See if they accept your hello, give you one back, return yours unopened, etc. If they don't accept it, you can try again or ask another viewing receptacle to show you the reason for this rejection. If they still don't accept your hello, there is a good chance there will be resistance to accepting your communication during the reading as well.

If you become aware of the resistance, it might help to talk to your readee about it in gentle terms. You could say that you notice some energy around them that does not want them to make changes and that might try to block them from hearing what you are going to say. Sometimes merely talking about resistance or interfering energy causes that energy to release. You can help your readee release this resistance by giving them a grounding cord and watching to see whether the energy releases. Once it releases, send them another hello and see what happens this time. If you still don't get a warm response, nothing is lost. The purpose of this exercise is not to change your readee to make them like you more, but rather to first acknowledge their spirit, and second to understand how open the readee is to you and your communication. Being aware of a readee's resistance will prevent you from falling into the deadly trap of blaming yourself for a difficult reading.

Listening to the Readee's Questions

Some readers prefer to have their clients state any questions or issues they would like addressed prior to the commencement of the tuning in process. However, I have found it useful to tune in first and then have the readee voice their questions, because as they ask their questions, I actually use their voice as another means to connect with their individual blueprint. This makes it easier to read the client rather than any other energies in the room. Furthermore, as the readee states their questions, I imagine that their question is not just going to me, but is really a call to God and the universe and their higher self to provide the readee with answers. These answers may come through me in the form of clairvoyant images that I can share with the readee, or the answers could be delivered directly to the readee via their own insights and experiences. This process of focusing intently on my readee's voice helps me concentrate and at the same time brings me into a deeper state of relaxation.

Should the Readee Ask Questions
at the Start of the Reading?

The answer to this question is complex. All of the clairvoyant training schools in the United States offer student readings to the public. These readings are structured readings that follow a particular template or format (see chapter 16) and often run anywhere from one-and-a-half to two hours. Some schools do not permit the readees to ask questions until the last ten or fifteen minutes of the reading. There are a few reasons for this.

First, for the purpose of clairvoyant training, it is often helpful for a student to have no information or predetermined notions about the readee and to have no restrictions about what they can or can't see or talk about. A readee's question acts as a focal point, drawing the readers attention to this one point, which could eliminate countless other points. New students can easily get stuck in answering a readee's question when that question may not really be what the readee is truly longing or needing to know. Clairvoyants see all kinds of things, including spirits and energy blockages, that many people are not conscious of, but that may be playing an enormous role in a person's life. A clairvoyant student will be more likely to spontaneously see and talk about these energies if they are not limited by questions. More experienced readers are often aware of this problem and can allow readers to ask questions while keeping an open mind and allowing themselves to access and talk about information that may not have anything to do with a readee's question.

Often in my readings, when a client asks a question that seems rather shallow or unrelated to herself (for example, "Will my great niece finish college?") I will quickly attempt to answer the question ("Yes, I see a tall girl with red hair wearing a graduation hat and drinking champagne"), but then I will silently pose this question to myself: "Why is my client asking this seemingly unimportant question?"

The answer I get might be in the form of images that show my readee stealing her niece's graduation hat when she is looking in the other direction, and then trying to take some steps, but then her feet get all twisted up. When I ask this image to show me what it means, maybe then I'll get another image, this one of a man dressed in an army uniform towering above her, handing her a mop. The readee might then affirm that her father was in the army and he didn't feel girls needed to go to school.

I may then become aware of the depression this woman has been feeling. I'll see her standing in front of a mirror and her clothes are too tight. She looks so exhausted that she can barely walk. I will talk to her then about how she has been stifling her need to learn, to experience life, how she has ignored her desire to go to school or to get a more challenging job. She may think that the reason she doesn't make any changes is because of her depression, but it's actually her father's energy and programming that she bought forty years ago that told her to forget those dreams and remain a housewife. Her depression is just a symptom of ignoring her inner voice. So, as this example illustrates, this readee's question about her niece actually turns out to be the starting point that will let me get to the real issues. Her question in this case is almost a symbol, a key that I can use to help illuminate the real question.

A beginning clairvoyant student who is not yet adept at working with questions might just answer the question about the niece, saying, "Yes, she will graduate," and go no further. Another student might attempt to look at the niece's future but instead pick up information about the readee's unhappiness and desire to go to school herself (because this is really what her spirit needs to know). This is fine. I'd much prefer that a reader get to the real issues. However, if a reader has a particular question swimming around in their head, they may become confused and discouraged to the point that they cannot seem to get a direct answer to the question. Some of the staff at one of the clairvoyant schools I attended would not even permit the question about the niece to be addressed. Instead they would tell the readee, "This reading is for you, so ask us a question about yourself, one that really matters." This would sometimes alienate and invalidate the readee, who would not understand what was wrong with this question.

Some clients need to get warmed up and form a bond of trust with a reader before they feel comfortable discussing personal issues, and so by asking seemingly unimportant questions or questions about people other than themselves, they can determine whether or not you are truly psychic and whether they can feel safe with you. Many people will hide their true questions in more benign questions. I feel that it really is not the readee's responsibility to ask the right question (although it helps!), but rather it is the clairvoyant who needs to learn how to work with the readee's question (or lack of questions) so that the readee will receive the communication they really need to know. This is similar to the relationship between a psychotherapist and a patient. The patient may come in with initial complaints, issues, or problems, but it is really up to the therapist to decipher and redefine the true issues. If patients could do this themselves all the time, they would not be in need of professional help. The same could be said of the relationship between a clairvoyant reader and the readee.

I know that some of my clairvoyant teachers would disagree with the above statements. One of my teachers, who is very brilliant and successful and one of the most talented healers I know, has every readee fill out a questionnaire about themselves that includes information about their family background, current activities, and present issues and concerns. This questionnaire lets clients know that if they want the best answers, they are responsible for making sure they ask the right questions. This helps my teacher get right to the heart of the client's issues without wasting time having to use his clairvoyance to uncover facts that the readee is already aware of. This makes things a lot easier on himself. He's not at all interested or willing to play the game of "prove it." At the same time, I know that despite what he says, he will still get to the true issues of a client even if they don't ask the right questions. He is really only interested in working with clairvoyant students or people who are aware of their spirituality and are truly working on themselves, and if they don't want to fill out the questionnaire, he has no interest in reading them.

This approach is certainly a valid one. However, as I already explained, for the purposes of clairvoyant development and neutrality, I believe that beginning students should have as little information as possible about their client so they can prove to themselves (and themselves only) that whatever information they are receiving is coming from their clairvoyance rather than from their logical mind. After you've been reading for thirty years (actually a lot less), you can use any approach you like!

Most people do have some questions and they may feel frustrated with the reading if they are never given the opportunity to ask them. If clients are told upfront that they can ask questions later in the reading, they will relax, knowing that eventually they will get the answers they are looking for. Often, most of their questions will be answered during the course of the reading, so by the time they are given the opportunity to ask questions, they may not have any more. If you are using a predetermined template, it is always a good idea to at least give the readee the option to ask one or two questions at the end of the reading.

Some clairvoyant training schools that offer student readings permit readees to ask questions only at the end of the reading, while others let them ask questions at the beginning. Personally, I have found that the readings where I ask my questions upfront feel more satisfying to me as a readee in that I immediately feel relieved and confident that my concerns are going to be addressed. It also seems, with this format, that readers tend to focus on topics that are of more interest to me. However, the overall quality of a reading does not seem to vary greatly with either approach.

In professional readings, many times a readee will not have any questions or will want to wait to see what you come up with before asking their questions. For the sake of your training, the more people you can read, the more opportunities you will have to experiment with your own format and ordering of events, and you will find what works best for you.

You Are a Detective

It's important to understand that clairvoyance works by giving you clues in the form of images. Every time you see a clue, you must ask this clue to show you another clue. Don't expect the entire answer to be revealed in a single thoughtform. You may occasionally get thoughts or auditory messages and that's great, but even so, you will always want to back up any nonvisual information with further clairvoyant investigation. Images rarely lie, while auditory messages are less reliable because they may come from a source other than yourself or the readee (clairvoyant images can occasionally come from other beings, but this happens far less frequently—see chapter 24). Also know that you are often not going to know the meaning of your images. The moment you realize you are trying to interpret the images with your logical thoughts, stop, turn down your analyzer, create and destroy a few roses on your reading screen, and tell yourself that you are just going to look for further visual clues.

As we discussed in previous chapters, there will be many times when you will never know what your clairvoyant images mean because they are symbols that have significance for your readee only, and perhaps your readee doesn't wish for you to know the details of their life. That's okay, because it's not your business to know everything about the person you are reading. The important thing is to wait for an image to appear or for a change to happen with your viewing receptacle/rose, and to communicate exactly what you are looking at. This is your job and you don't have to do anything beyond this.

Also keep in mind you are not responsible for what you see. When you get into making interpretations with your logical mind, then you become responsible because these interpretations may or may not be accurate. After performing a few readings, you will be better able to determine when your knowingness is giving you revealing insights and when your logical mind is drawing conclusions. Leave it up to your readees to draw their own logical conclusions. If you feel they have no idea what you are seeing or talking about, ask the mysterious image to explain itself with another image. There will be plenty of images that never really make sense, and that is all right. It is human nature to want to understand everything. As a clairvoyant, your job is not to have all the answers, but rather to sit back, observe, and describe the images on your reading screen.

Reading With a Question or Issue in Mind

The basic clairvoyant reading technique is the same whether you are performing a structured reading answering questions or merely looking to see what comes up for the readee. In chapter 16, you will learn some common formats or templates for structured readings. For the purposes of this chapter, I will illustrate how to perform a less structured reading.

Let's assume that you are already tuned in to your readee and have sent them a spiritual hello. It is time to begin the actual reading. Your readee says she is wondering about which direction to go in her life, and whether changing careers would be a good idea. These two questions are related and I suggest focusing on the most specific question first, since it may reveal information about the more general question as well.

On your reading screen, create a clear crystal image of a rose. This rose will reveal the answer to the question about the readee's career. Take a deep breath, relax your body, and just watch the rose to see what happens to it.

Look to see if there is a color coming into it. If you see a color or even sense one slightly, ask this color to show you a picture or an image. Then take another deep long breath and patiently watch the rose. You can also watch to see if the rose changes in any way. Does it open or close, shrink or get really big? Does it move, disappear, or grow brighter? Does a petal appear or disappear? Do you see more than one color in the rose? Any change, image, or minute detail you suddenly notice is the springboard for more explicit information.

When you notice one or more changes, pick one of these and make the decision to investigate it further. There are two ways to perform further investigation. The first is to just watch the clue of most interest (for example, the opening of the rose) and keep watching it to see what it does next. This is fine to do if the rose is active and changes and images seem to be appearing effortlessly.

The second method is to destroy this rose by imagining that it is exploding into a trillion pieces. Create a new rose and tell it to show you the meaning of the opening of the rose you just destroyed. Every time you destroy an object and create a new one, you are exercising your visualization muscles as well as moving energy. You are increasing your clairvoyant abilities while increasing the flow of clairvoyant energy. Any time you start to feel stuck, like you are having trouble seeing or are feeling frustrated or incompetent, destroy whatever you are looking at and create a new rose that will provide images to reveal either what you are seeing or what you are having difficulty seeing.

If you patiently watch your rose and nothing appears or you see only black, know that this nothing is really something. Destroy the rose, create a new one that represents the nothingness or blackness, and ask it to show you an image that will illuminate the situation. Continue to do this until you see something. Know that the moment you see any change to your rose, you have just used your clairvoyance! When this occurs, you can never again say or even think that you are not clairvoyant!

After you are satisfied with the information you see and communicate regarding the readee's career, put the images you have been looking at into a receptacle and blow it up. Now create a new receptacle that will reveal the sought-after information regarding the readee's path in life. Most likely you already touched upon some of these issues when discussing the readee's career, since a person's career has to do with the larger picture of their life, but you can still look at this specifically to see what else comes up. You might also choose to use part of the "life path reading template" taught in chapter 16 of this book as a guide to help you with this particular issue.

Knowingness

Sometimes information will come in on a knowing level or auditory level. It will just snap into your head, like "this person is a nurse," and it will be so clear that you will feel compelled to talk about it. When this happens, I do encourage you to talk about it. You can let your readee know how the information came in. This is not your clairvoyance but rather an ability in your crown chakra called knowingness. It is instantaneous information. Some people are more adept at this than others. I had a good friend in my clairvoyant training program who often received instant bursts of information as the readee was saying their name. The information was very straightforward and turned out to be quite accurate. My friend was more comfortable receiving information through his crown chakra than through his sixth chakra. Personally, I like to back up information delivered in the form of thoughts by asking for confirmation in the form of a clairvoyant image. Then I can be sure that it's not just my logical mind generating thoughts, or spirits giving inaccurate information, which can happen.

Communicating the Image to Your Readee

Some readers prefer to watch their viewing receptacle/rose and see the images for a while before talking about them, while others will talk about everything they see the moment they see it. I have found that students who take the latter approach tend to progress faster, because they don't have time to analyze every single thing and judge whether or not it is worthy to talk about. They censor themselves less and therefore allow the information to flow. You will find that as you talk about whatever you are seeing, more and more images will appear.

What I discovered was that the more I talked, the more images I saw. I even feared that if I didn't talk, the images wouldn't come. By talking uncensored in a stream of consciousness about every single detail, the clairvoyant information does flow more easily. After eight years of reading, I still prefer to talk simultaneously as I read, and I encourage you to do the same, no matter how insignificant or silly your images seem to be.

The only time I censor myself is if I think my words might have a very strong impact on the readee's life. If they ask me when someone in their family is going to die or if their husband is having an affair, I will watch my images and double-check them by asking for more images to confirm the first image before revealing the information (see chapter 21).

Overcoming Blocks to Communication

Energy can interfere with your readings, both by making it more dificult to access visual information or by preventing you from communicating this information to the readee. As a beginning clairvoyant student, there were plenty of times when I stopped myself from sharing valuable information. Since I was reading alongside other students, a variety of thoughts inhibiting my communication would come up. I might not say something because I felt like it wasn't my turn to speak, or that I was talking too much and the other students were getting irritated with me. Sometimes I would worry that I was saying the wrong thing, or that what I might say would upset the readee.

As a clairvoyant reader, there will be plenty of times when you will struggle with similar concerns. The important thing is to be aware of when you are seeing something but not sharing it. The moment you become aware of this, you should ask yourself why. If it is because you are afraid you are wrong or are nervous about your readee's response, I encourage you to use your psychic tools. Create and destroy some roses in front of your fifth chakra. Check to see which chakra or part of your body you are in. Reground yourself and postulate that you are getting rid of the energy that doesn't want you to communicate to your readee. Then make yourself talk about what you are seeing. If you are seeing something, there is a reason for it. Don't ever forget this.

Furthermore, every time you talk about something that you are afraid to talk about, you will become a stronger reader and a stronger person and the energies in the room that made you hesitate will have less of a hold on you. After a few years of reading, there will be very few times when you will hesitate to talk about anything you are seeing. Until then, there of course will be times when you will fail to communicate what you are seeing, and that is alright because inevitably you will later find out that you were 100 percent correct. If this happens, don't kick yourself too hard, but instead resolve to speak up in the future.

Avoid Getting Validation From the Readee

During a reading, you must not fall into the trap of trying to get validation from your clients. I cannot overemphasize this! There are several reasons why seeking validation through confirmation from your readee can be problematic.

First and foremost, your readee is not there to make you feel good. It's not fair to put that burden on them. You are there to give to them, not the other way around. You will benefit from the reading by using your tools, blowing your matching pictures, exploring, discovering, and learning—not by getting warm fuzzies from your readee.

Secondly, the feedback of your readee is often not accurate. Many people don't initially know what you are talking about. They may say, "No, you are wrong, that's not how it is," when in fact you are right on. For example, during one reading I was seeing images of the readee in which she was getting thinner and thinner. I saw her pushing away food and even vomiting into a toilet. When I said to the woman, "It appears that you have an eating disorder," she vehemently denied this. I let these images go and went on to answer one of her questions. But within a few minutes, the same images were appearing again. So once again I suggested that she was suffering from an "eating disorder," and this time she became irate. I was reading with several other student readers and I could sense that they were feeling uncomfortable and wondering why I did not just shut up, but I could not. I had enough experience under my belt to know that if these unwelcome images were continuing to intrude upon my reading screen, then there had to be a reason for this; they had to hold some significance. Suddenly after my third attempt to discuss the subject, the woman blurted out, "I don't have an eating disorder, I have a digestive disorder!"

During another reading, I clairvoyantly saw the readee wearing a white uniform and carrying a tray of medical instruments. I told her, "It looks like you are some kind of doctor's assistant." She immediately snapped, "No I'm not, you are wrong," which threw me off and shook my confidence. It wasn't until an hour later that she said, "You know, I think there was something to that image you saw, because I am actually a dental assistant." Had she not said this, I might have wondered for the rest of my life why I saw that image, except for the fact that I had already been reading long enough to know that the only reason I would be seeing images that clearly was if there was something to them. Both these examples also demonstrate the importance of describing images without drawing logical conclusions. Leave that up to your readee.

Your readees will actually respect you more if you don't seek out their confirmation because it will be clear that you are really picking up your own information rather than manipulating them into revealing things about themselves. In a reading, you tell your readees about themselves, not the other way around. Of course every person is different. Some people will be so excited when you "get something right" that they will share with you exactly what's happening in their life and how you just described it so beautifully. But a lot of other people will remain silent, which is fine. I know that validation feels great, but there are some serious drawbacks to becoming dependent on it. When I train my students, I demand the utmost discipline, including the following rules.

1. Never open your eyes during a reading, and don't look at your readee once the reading has begun. Opening your eyes will pull you out of your trance. You will become less grounded, and be pulled from a neutral reading space to a healing space. Some people have a hard time with this because they like to feel connected on a deep emotional level with people. Neutrality is key to performing an accurate reading, and the level of neutrality and accuracy decreases in direct proportion to the amount of time a reader spends looking at the readee.

2. Never ask your readee for confirmation (this is a hard one). For example, don't ask, "Do you do this kind of work?" or "Is it true that your boyfriend hits you?"

3. Keep your questions to a minimum regarding the readee's life.

4. Read with other clairvoyants whenever possible (see chapter 17).

Troubleshooting

I get images that make no sense to me, and when I ask for clarification, I continue to get more images that don't make sense.

There is a reason this is happening, and it does not have anything to do with your clairvoyant ability. More likely, it has to do either with your readee or with your own matching pictures—probably both. This is not a problem. Just keep talking about what you are seeing. It may make perfect sense to your readee. Sometimes your readee may not want you to know what you are seeing, though it makes perfect sense to them. Sometimes there are other energies that don't want you to see because this would mean that your readee would kick them out.

One thing you can do if you keep asking for more meaning but still get nowhere is to ask your readee if they know what you are talking about. If they say no (be aware that people sometimes deny it when they do know, or they don't understand until later what you were talking about), then you can pose the question to your viewing receptacle: "What is it that is blocking me from understanding my images?" However, most of the time the readee will say, "Yes, I know exactly what you are talking about." In this case, I advise against blurting out, "Then please tell me, because I don't have the foggiest idea what I'm talking about." Instead, be satisfied (to the best of your ability) that you are on the right track and continue reading with certainty and confidence.

What should I do if the readee tells me I am wrong?

Let's say you have just given the readee some clairvoyant information of a detailed nature and the readee blurts out, "No, you are wrong." You can handle this a few different ways. One is to revisit whatever you just told the readee. Put up a rose for whatever they said you were wrong about, and ask the colors and images to appear that will either help you confirm the earlier information or help you understand why there is this discrepancy. Perhaps this second set of images and the way you communicate will help the readee understand what you were saying in a different way.

I have done a surprisingly large number of relationship readings for women where I saw that the woman's partner was mistreating her or abusing her in some way. During some of these readings, when I saw an image of the man hitting the woman, the woman insisted that I was wrong. Sometimes I destroyed the roses I was reading, recreated new ones, and again watched to see how they were interacting. Again I would see some similar images, but I might get a detail that would shed light on what I was talking about. In one of these cases where a woman adamantly denied that her boyfriend was ever violent toward her, my reexamination of their relationship led to images of a purse, and the man was emptying out the contents. The woman then blurted out that her boyfriend had gone into her purse against her will because he was looking for signs that she was having an affair. A layer of her defenses suddenly came down. When I saw another violent image later of her boyfriend pulling her hair, she admitted that he had done this. Since I had gotten three different images that confirmed the initial one, I was very confident that I was right about the abuse. It was just a matter of having sufficient patience and perseverance to break through her denial.

I am not saying that you (or I) will never be wrong about things. You could misinterpret your images or occasionally let your own biases taint your reading. What I am saying is that there could be other explanations, and it's important to explore what those are before discounting the information you've received and doubting your own clairvoyance.

Empowerment Versus Problem Solving

As mentioned in other chapters, as a clairvoyant reader, your line of inner questioning will often determine the clairvoyant answers you receive. If you are looking for problems in a person's life, you will find them, just as if you are looking for what is working in their life, you will find this as well. As a clairvoyant, you can decide to read from either a space of problem solving or a space of validation. Reading from validation does not mean that you disregard the difficult issues of a person's life, but rather that you look for what empowers the person. In a similar manner, you have the choice of whether to verbally communicate about the images you are seeing in a positive, optimistic manner or in a negative, pessimistic way.

A problem is only a problem if someone labels it so. Some readees, just like some readers, are totally focused on their problems. If you start to find yourself thinking, "Wow, this poor person! What a mess her life is!" or you become overwhelmed that you can't help them, then you can be sure of two things. First, you have lost your neutrality. You need to get back into the center of your head, reground yourself, and create and destroy some viewing receptacles in front of your fourth (heart) chakra. Secondly, realize that you are in a problem-solving space. Create a rose and fill it up with the energy of problems, and then move this receptacle as far away as possible before destroying it. Then choose to read the energy of what is working well for this person. If your readee verbally objects to your clairvoyant suggestions and insists that whatever you are suggesting will not work, then create a rose and ask it to show you what is keeping the person stuck. Communicate whatever you are seeing and then let it go.

It's important to remember that you "can lead a horse to water, but you can't make him drink." Energetically, many psychics try to make their clients "drink," and these well-meaning psychics end up exhausted, depleted, sick, and overweight. It's not your responsibility to solve your readee's problems or anyone else's. You are merely there to give them insight. Remember, there is really no such thing as a problem; a problem is merely a cognitive definition of how someone is emotionally reacting to a certain situation. One person will label a certain situation a problem, while another will label it a challenge, and another will think it's funny or exciting. Problem energy is stuck energy.

Ending the Reading

The reading will be over either when you have reached the end of the predetermined time for the reading or, for a structured reading, when you have completed each predetermined step; or when it feels like you have covered all the information that needed to be addressed and you find yourself repeating the same point over and over again.

Suggested Action

I like to end every reading by giving the readee a suggestion for action they can take in order to help them reach their goals. It might be a solution to an issue previously discussed in the reading, or it may be a new piece of helpful information. Throughout the reading, it is helpful to take an action-oriented approach and to always be clairvoyantly looking for actions the readee can take, but it is especially beneficial to give some "next steps" at the end of the reading so the readee will walk away feeling empowered. Giving the person two or three simple steps or actions will help them realize that while you gave them some answers, they are really the one who has the ability to change their life. It also signals to them that the reading is wrapping up.

Technique

Simply put up a rose on your reading screen that represents a helpful action. Look to see the color. Describe the color and the images.

Say a Closing Prayer and Wish the Readee Good Luck

I always end every reading with a short and simple prayer that goes something like this: "Thank you, God, for all the help you gave us during this reading. Now I invite all of my energy to come back to me and all of (readee's name) to come back to her. May it be with the blessings of the Supreme Being that this reading be completed."

Saying a prayer of gratitude coupled with the words "the reading is completed" helps both parties (and any guides in the room) know that the reading is really over. Stating out loud that you are taking back your energy and giving the readee back their energy lets the readee know that any energy exchange that was occurring is now ending. You are reinforcing and teaching them about boundaries. In effect, you are saying, 'The reading ends here and I'm not going home with you." Following the closing prayer, you can thank the readee for the opportunity to read them. You can give them your business card and receive your payment if you have not already (see chapter 23). Physically escort the readee to the door. Now you are ready for a psychic shower.

Psychic Shower Time

At the end of a clairvoyant reading, it is imperative that you separate your energy from your readee's energy; otherwise your physical and emotional health and that of your readee could become compromised. The cleaning-out process utilizes visualization techniques that remind your body and spirit that you are in fact a separate entity from your readee, so that you don't continue to read and heal that person forever. These techniques help you call back your energy from your readee, and vice versa, and even assist you in bringing your karma and other energies into present time. They also help you work through your matching pictures and release any of your emotional energy that may have gotten stirred up during the reading.

It is best to run through the clean-out process immediately following the reading. A sign that you have not thoroughly made separations from your readee is if you continue to think about or worry about the reading or the readee. As mentioned in earlier chapters, any time you have a thought about someone or something, it is because on some level your energy is engaged with that person or thing. When you have successfully completed the cleaning-out process, you will find that you will be more in the present and will have very little need to rehash the reading. Minutes later it will seem like a distant event.

Taking a Psychic Shower

Cleaning Your Grounding Cord

First, take a clairvoyant look at your grounding cord. Has it changed in any way since you last created it? Are there any holes in it or any parts that are hard to see? Are there any colors in it that don't seem to be the ones you originally chose? Has your grounding cord matured and grown stronger and more vibrant? Make some observations about your grounding cord and then say goodbye to it. See it exploding into a trillion pieces and create a post-reading grounding cord in present time. Write your name on it with your imagination.

Cleaning Your Reading Screen

On your reading screen, create and destroy at least twenty roses as fast as you can. Start at the far left upper corner of your reading screen and work your way across and then down. Postulate that this is clearing out your sixth chakra and moving out any excess energy that accumulated on your reading screen or elsewhere in your system during the reading. Destroy your reading screen and create another one.

Clearing Out the Center of Your Head

Check to see where you are in your body. Imagine that you are sending a rose to the center of your head. Have your spirit follow directly behind the rose so that it lands in the center of your head, behind your sixth chakra. Notice where the rose and you came from. This is where you were performing the latter part of the reading. Notice the difference between how you feel sitting in the center of your head versus wherever else you just were. If you find that you are having difficulty coming back from that place, create a large yellow sticky rose and use it to clear out the center of your head. Imagine that it is inside your head sucking out grime like a vacuum cleaner. See the yellow sticky rose circulating around in there as if it were inside a washing machine or dryer. Look to see what colors have accumulated in this sticky rose. Once the rose seems full, destroy it and create another one. Repeat this process again if necessary.

Making Separations

From the center of your head, on your reading screen, create a rose that represents your readee. In the center of the rose, visualize a very strong magnet. This magnet is going to suck up any energy from your aura that really belongs to your readee. See this rose filling up with your readee's energy, growing bigger and brighter. See an image of your readee's face in the rose and say goodbye to it. Thank your readee for the lessons and experience they provided for you, and then tell them firmly that the reading is over. You can further visualize your own body and see the readee's energy and any other foreign energies related to them flowing from your body into their rose. When this rose is completely filled up, destroy it and watch as it explodes into a trillion sparks of light.

Next, create a rose that represents you. Visualize your face inside of it and label it with your name. Again, in the center of this rose place an enormous magnet. Postulate that you are calling back all of your energy that may still be with your readee or anywhere else. See your energy returning to your rose and watch as the rose gets fuller and fuller. Ground the stem of the rose deep into the planet and watch any extraneous energy drain from it. Then take that rose and place it above your head. Explode it into a million sparks of light, and watch as this light flows into your crown chakra and down to the very bottom of your toes. Watch as it fills up your feet, ankles, calves, thighs, torso, neck, head, shoulders, arms, hands, fingers, and hair, and spills out into your aura and down into your grounding cord.

Find Five Physical Differences

Next, on your reading screen, visualize your readee and yourself and notice at least five physical differences between the two of you. Make a note of these. For example, notice that you have a different hair color, different facial features, a different body size, or even a different voice. Maybe your readee has freckles, a mole, a missing tooth, bigger or smaller feet, etc. Describe these differences either in your head or out loud. Then imagine that you are taking a pen and making a list of these differences. See each item on the list and then tear it up in your mind, set it on fire, and watch it disintegrate. By noting the physical differences, you are reminding yourself that you are yourself and not your readee. If you are ever having extreme difficulty making separations, you could physically go through this exercise by using an actual paper and pen to make your list and then burning it in a real fire.

Working with Karma

Create a rose that represents the relationship between you and your readee. Visualize that there is a golden ring hovering slightly above the rose. Imagine that there is a piece missing from this ring. Postulate that you are bringing all of your karma with your readee and any of their spiritual guides or family into present time. You are essentially completing your karma with them. See the energy of this karma as it fills in the missing piece in the golden ring. When the golden ring is complete, drop it into the rose.

Ending Your Communication

Next, imagine that there is a telephone on top of the rose. You are ready to end your telepathic communication with your readee and anyone or anything in their space. Imagine that you are breaking the phone into many pieces and cutting the phone cord. Toss the phone into the rose. Take the rose and watch it as it gets smaller and smaller until it is only a tiny dot. Then imagine that you are looking at it with a magnifying glass. Imagine a bright sun shining through the glass. This sets the rose on fire, and it burns until it is merely ashes. Imagine a gust of wind blowing the ashes into the heavens.

Moving into Present Time

Now imagine a new rose. Write the current date and time on this rose. Imagine that it is sitting in your heart chakra and that it expands outward to the point that it is encompassing your entire body. Know that you—your body, spirit, and mind—are in the present and are now ready for your next adventure.

Revisit Your Intention (Optional)

On your reading screen, put up the rose that you created at the beginning of the reading that represented your intention or wish for the reading. Next to it create a rose that is labeled the "after reading rose." Notice if they look the same or are different. You can give the "after rose" a reading to see what changes might have occurred in you. Then create a new intention for the rest of the day or your future (see chapter 12).

CHAPTER 15

Relationship Readings

A relationship reading is a reading where the focus is on the relationship between your readee and another person who is not physically present during the reading (to perform a reading on a couple who are both present, see chapter 18). Eighty percent of the questions people ask me in my readings have to do with relationships. Sometimes the readee wants to know when they will meet someone special, and sometimes they want to know where their current relationship is headed or why they are having a hard time letting go of a past relationship. People want to know about their relationships with their children, parents, coworkers, husbands, wives, lovers, mistresses, bosses, enemies, teachers, etc. No matter what the nature of the relationship, the same technique can be used to clairvoyantly access information about a past, present, or future relationship.

Tuning In to the Readee and the Person in Question

Tune in to your readee using the technique outlined in the preceding chapter. On your reading screen, create a clear glass image of a rose. Invite your readee to say their present name and date of birth, and see the color of the readee's vibration/spirit flow into that rose. Match your crown chakra to that color, and then imagine that you are writing the readee's name under that rose. Move this rose to the far left side of your reading screen.

Next, create another viewing receptacle, also in the form of a rose, and ask the readee to say the person's name in question. Have your readee say the person's first and last name out loud. If the readee does not know the full name or does not want to say the name out loud (which may seem strange but happens more than you would think), then just postulate that the energy of the person in question will enter into the rose. Then look for a color in that rose. Once you see a color, write that person's name under the rose, if you know it.

Because people have so many different kinds of relationships in their lives, it is sometimes challenging to know if you are looking at the exact person in question. Oftentimes you will find, particularly as a new reader, that you are not reading the person they verbally asked about, but that you are reading another person who has played a prominent role in their life. It is for this reason that it's helpful to ask the rose representing the absent person to show you a symbol so that you and your readee will know you are tuned in to the correct person. This symbol will most likely have no meaning to you, but it will to the readee.

Reading the Relationship

On your reading screen, the two roses should stand side by side, about four inches from one another. Postulate that the way in which these roses interact will symbolize the nature of the relationship in question, and then patiently watch to see what happens to the roses. Notice any changes that occur to the individual roses or to the distance between the two. Watch how they interact. Notice if the colors change, if the size of one rose grows larger or smaller, whether the leaves fall off, whether they entwine in a passionate embrace or scatter away from one another to the far ends of your reading screen, etc. Just sit back and watch; you don't need to make anything happen. Share your observations with your readee. Then destroy these roses and create a new receptacle and ask it to show you an explanation for the most noticeable change or behavior of the roses you just observed.

Answering a Readee's Question About Someone They Know When the Question Does Not Have to Do with Their Relationship

Some of your clients will ask about everyone else in their lives except themselves, despite the fact that they are in greater need of insight and communication than those they are inquiring about. In my clairvoyant training, we were taught to pretty much ignore a readee's question about another individual (e.g., "How do you see my son's relationship with his girlfriend turning out?" "How is my father's health?") and instead say, "This is your reading, so let's focus on you." From my own experience both as a student and a professional reader, I have found that at times this approach is appropriate, while at other times it could feel patronizing and totally alienate the readee.

Recommended Approach

I suggest that as a reader, you spend a couple minutes directly addressing the readee's question about the other person, and then clairvoyantly look to see what it is that motivated the readee to ask that question in the first place. You can also look at the relationship between the readee and the person in question, even though the readee isn't asking about the relationship. This is a gentle way of bringing the focus back to the readee while allowing them to feel satisfied that their initial question has been addressed. Some people are initially very nervous about being clairvoyantly "examined" by a stranger. As they realize that you can offer helpful information in a caring and insightful manner, they will enthusiastically open up to having themselves be read.

Occasionally you may read someone who is so resistant to hearing about themselves and is so into controlling the reading on an energetic level that you realize it is pretty useless to tell them anything about themselves. In these cases I am more than happy to read other people for them. I will match my crown chakra to the person they are asking about (usually their children) and do mini readings on each person. Oftentimes it's the children (or whoever the person is) who need their mother to understand something, and I can help them by reiterating what they have been telling her for years; e.g., "I am a talented artist and will never be a doctor," "Get your own life and stop bothering me," etc.

CHAPTER 16

Navigational Tools

Using a predetermined format for a reading is especially helpful for beginning students because it allows them to control the direction of the reading; it helps them focus on the elements that will provide the most helpful information to the readee regardless of the readee's awareness of energy and other unseen forces. Beginning readers have little to no certainty or confidence and they are vulnerable to getting sidetracked by questions and concerns of the readee that might not have anything to do with the real issues affecting the readee.

Reading the Aura (60 to 70 minutes, 10 minutes per layer)

Every layer of the aura contains energy that has an effect on the physical body and mind. During a clairvoyant reading in which you merely answer the readee's questions, you are viewing information through color, images, and thoughts. Images and thoughts give you answers, but they don't reveal the underlying energy that is affecting the readee's body and mind. When you see colors, you are seeing the color of the underlying energy, which helps move the energy. However, you are still not seeing exactly where the energy is located within the person's energy field or body. During an aura reading, you can focus on one layer of the readee's body at a time. You look for the color of their energy and foreign energy, and then you ask these colors to show you information in the form of images. By seeing exactly where color/energy is located, you can move it more easily than if you merely see the color. Aura readings are an intense form of energetic healing, even though your underlying intention may be just to read the aura as a means to structure the reading.

Technique

First, take an overall look at the readee's aura. Ask the general shape and size of it to appear on your reading screen and describe what you are looking at. Then take a look at the first layer of the aura closest to the body. Create a crystal ball or rose on your reading screen and invite the color of the first layer to enter your viewing receptacle. Ask this color to show you something helpful about the readee in the form of an image or picture, and then communicate this information to your readee.

Next, look for a color in this layer of the aura that doesn't belong to your readee. Ask this color to show you images or pictures that illustrate how this foreign energy is affecting your readee. Communicate this information to your readee. Then move to the second layer of the aura. Repeat this process with all seven layers, ending with the outermost layer, which is the seventh layer.

Male/Female Aura Reading

During an aura reading, you can focus on the readee's female and male energies in each layer of the aura. This can be accomplished by creating four viewing receptacles per layer. One viewing receptacle will show you the readee's own male energy, and another one will show you their own female energy. The other two will show you foreign male and female energies that are lurking within a particular layer of the aura.

Following a male/female aura reading, I also like to perform a relationship reading (see chapter 15) on what I call the readee's inner male and inner female. This is done by creating a viewing receptacle for the readee's inner male, as well as one for their inner female, and then watching to see how these two receptacles interact with each other. Or you can create a third receptacle in between the two and ask it to show you a color and some images that represent the relationship. Your inner male and female will often manifest in the physical form of a relationship with another person, so if you are having conflicts with a boyfriend, girlfriend, or spouse, it is likely that your own female or male energies are weak, unbalanced, or in conflict or competition with one another.

Reading the Chakras (10 to 15 minutes)

The chakras contain a plethora of information. When reading them, it helps to limit the focus to a particular category of information. Many clairvoyant training programs teach students to focus on the readee's psychic abilities, which are located within the chakras.

Beginning with the first chakra, put up one gauge on your reading screen to show how open the chakra was at birth. Then create another one that shows how open the chakra is in present time. Compare the two to see whether the particular psychic ability associated with that chakra has diminished or increased. If there is a drastic difference, you can put up a viewing receptacle and ask it to show another color that represents the reason for this change. Then ask the color to show you an image that will give you insight into how this color affects the readee in general and what the readee needs to do in order to turn up or turn down the psychic ability that is associated with the chakra.

The chakras can tell you lots of other things about your readee. You can look to see how open each chakra is in terms of the readee's level of personal power/self-esteem and how this affects the health of their physical body. You can clairvoyantly investigate how the openness of each chakra influences the readee's ability to relate to others and to themselves, and you can look to see how the openness of each chakra affects the readee's ability to create and manifest goals in their life.

Answering Questions

Even when performing a structured reading, it is always a wise idea to leave at least ten to fifteen minutes at the end to address the readee's specific questions so they will feel satisfied that their direct concerns were addressed. Often, their specific concerns and questions do get addressed during the course of the reading, regardless of whether or not the reader consciously knew what these were. However, your readee will appreciate having the opportunity to ask questions, whether they are merely seeking clarification about information that was already brought up in the reading ("You said you saw a red energy in the third layer of my aura. What does the red mean?") or they are asking a question that they had been wondering about prior to the reading ("When will I meet my true love?").

Some schools allow for questions during the last ten or fifteen minutes of a reading, while other schools allow the readee to ask questions upfront, with the idea that the readers will go through the aura with the questions in mind and see where these issues are located. For more information about answering questions clairvoyantly, see chapter 14.

Formatted Daisy Drawing Reading

In this reading, you will create a transparent image of a daisy. First, take a look at the overall daisy, including the stem going into the earth. This will represent the physical health and grounding of the readee. Notice if the daisy is firmly planted into the ground, whether it stands straight or droops, whether it is firm or withered, etc. Draw a picture of this on a piece of paper and communicate what you are seeing to your readee.

Next, look at the entire bloom of the daisy, with its pistil/stamen and surrounding petals. This will represent the readee's self-esteem, sense of personal power, and communication with their inner voice. What color is it? Does this part seem to hold its head up high, or hide itself in its petals? Is it open or closed, turned toward the sun or away from it? Again, choose the appropriate color of crayon, marker, or pencil and then draw a picture of this while you communicate it to the readee.

Next, read the petals. Start with the petal on the top. This petal represents how the readee likes to have fun, what activities they enjoy and are good at, etc. Going clockwise, look at the second petal. This petal represents their education, learning potential, level of spiritual knowledge, etc. The third petal represents the readee's romantic relationships, and the fourth petal represents their family relationships. The fifth petal represents their work and career, and the sixth petal represents their finances. If there is time, you can perform a mini reading on each petal. If not, then merely look for the color of each petal and notice whether there is anything unusual about any one petal that makes it stand out from the others; e.g., it may be brighter, darker, misshapen, larger or smaller, torn, etc. Ask whatever feature that stands out to show you an image that explains the feature.

Now look at the pistil or stamen of the daisy. Notice whether the petals are fully connected into the middle or if some are pulled away. If the petals are not symmetrically connected into the pistil, then it means that the readee's various life goals (represented by each petal) are in conflict with each other. If so, look for the color that sits in between the pistil and the petal(s) and ask it to show you an image that represents the energy that is causing the readee's goals to compete with one another.

Next, look at the leaves on the stem, which represent the readee's overall strengths. If the leaves are torn or bent, then look to see what is blocking the readee from utilizing their strengths or accessing their sense of personal power.

The stem represents the readee's spiritual path and evolution. Notice if it is very long or short, or if it is broken in any parts. Clairvoyantly investigate any oddities you observe.

In this template, any rings around the stem have to do with past lives. Any bugs on the stem have to do with the readee's spirit guides (ladybugs are helpful, cockroaches are not), and any thorns have to do with challenges or limitations to be overcome. Use the clairvoyant process of investigation that, by now, you are becoming quite familiar with.

Using Mini Templates— Archetypes and Predetermined Symbols

As discussed in chapter 5, soon after I began doing clairvoyant readings, a series of images began spontaneously reappearing in my readings. These images acted as shortcuts to help me know immediately what type of subject or issue I was looking at. (When other clairvoyants read me, these same archetypal templates often spontaneously appear to them for the first time). Eventually, I learned to consciously and purposefully manipulate these images (which I call my personal archetypes) to help me navigate my way through readings. I present several of these here and offer simple suggestions for how to best utilize them in your own readings. Eventually, through clairvoyant reading practice and experience, and paying attention to symbols in your dreams and your waking experiences, you will accumulate your own personal library of symbols.

The Piano or Harp
The piano or harp represents your readee's communication with their innermost voice. This is the voice of that individual's heart and soul that knows exactly what the individual longs for and needs.

On your reading screen, visualize a piano or harp. Now, in your imagination, see your readee standing next to the piano or harp. Notice how they relate to the piano or harp physically and emotionally. How are they playing the piano? Notice whether they look peaceful or distressed, whether they play it with grace, zest, or enthusiasm or are afraid to even touch the keys or strings. Once you make your observations, ask these observations to show you a color and some accompanying images that will provide further insights into the relationship between the readee and the innermost voice of their heart.

The Window
The window represents the readee's ability to envision personal goal(s) and their potential to achieve these goals. The readee's spirit longs for these goals, but their ego may be in resistance to and unaware of them. The window often signifies a major life change or the lack of one. It will show whether a person is willing to make a necessary change or whether life circumstances are

forcing them to make the changes that they are resisting due to fear. This archetype or template deals with unconscious factors that your readee is struggling to bring into their awareness.

On your reading screen, visualize a window. Place your readee on the left side of the window and patiently watch to see how the readee interacts with the window. Notice whether the readee turns away from it or whether they earnestly look out of it. You may see any number of responses. The readee may confidently open the window and step to the other side, or may be unexpectedly blown out of the window by a gust of wind. You may find the readee standing on the opposite side of the window looking back inside or trying to get back inside. Once you make your observations, create a viewing receptacle, ask it to show you a color, and then ask the color to give you insight into your observations.

The Tree

The tree is another image that represents your readee's goals and how close your readee currently is to obtaining these goals. These goals tend to be tangible ones that the readee is conscious of and is actively pursuing and/or struggling with.

On your reading screen, visualize a simple tree. Visualize your readee standing next to the tree. If the readee has asked you a question regarding a particular goal, you can postulate that these images will interact in order to give you insight into how close the readee is to obtaining this particular goal. Or you can ask the image of the tree and your readee to show you where the readee is at with any major goal. You don't need to know the goal in order to see the readee's success with it. Eventually, if the readee wants you to understand the exact goal, it will be revealed by the clairvoyant images during the course of the reading.

Using your clairvoyance and the clairvoyant techniques we have described in previous chapters, observe how the readee interacts with the tree. Does the readee climb effortlessly to the top of the tree, or remain on the ground, jumping up and down? Is the readee stuck somewhere halfway up the tree, or crawling slowly but surely? If the readee is at the top of the tree, are they taking a nap, or looking out over the horizon with binoculars? Is the readee sweating and out of breath, or do they look like they are used to standing at the top?

The Room

The archetype of the room represents the readee's sense of personal freedom and potential within a particular structure or organization. It often demonstrates whether they will be allowed to reach goals related to the organization. This image will often appear when reading someone's career or looking at their participation and status within a company, spiritual group, organized community, etc. Many people who operate within an organization overlook the fact that their ability to achieve their personal goals is directly proportional to the support they receive from the other members of the organization. No matter how hard an individual works or how brilliant they are, they will be unable to achieve their goals if there is a lack of permissiveness or attentiveness from whoever runs the organization. Also, they may be operating within a structure that they have outgrown, that is keeping them from their true spiritual goals, or that is dominated by others who possess a lower level of "havingness." Havingness is a term that describes a person's level of permission to obtain or possess a particular thing or state of being. So, for example, even if you are the most talented salesman and are given the best leads and resources to do your job, if the person you are working for repels money because they maintain a deep-seated, unconscious belief that it's selfish to have money or that they don't deserve it, then it will be harder for you to create or hold onto the money. The archetype of the room will provide insights into these factors.

I recommend using this template in order to answer a readee's questions regarding their workplace, potential promotions, career goals, their participation within religious or community organizations, etc.

On your reading screen, visualize the readee standing in a room. Patiently watch to see what happens next.

The Mirror

The mirror is a symbol that demonstrates how your readees feel about themselves and their body. The way in which they interact with the mirror reveals their level of self-esteem and aspects of their relationship with themselves that could use some healing.

On your reading screen, visualize your readee standing in front of a mirror. Then sit back and patiently watch to see how they interact with the mirror. Does the readee give herself a big smile, or does she look displeased as she checks out her body? Does she stand there for a while, looking deep into her own eyes, or does she turn away from the mirror in disgust? If it looks like she is not happy with herself, ask a color to appear that will represent the energy that is causing this unhappiness, and then ask the color to show you an image that will help you understand the root of her feelings. You can also ask a color to appear that will show you steps the readee needs to take in order to improve her self-esteem.

Using Your Own Symbols for Navigation

Creating your own template is a simple and fun way to help yourself navigate your way through a clairvoyant reading. You can use any symbol to represent an issue in a person's life. This symbol can be any object as long as that object has meaning to you. Simply visualize the symbol on your reading screen along with an image of your readee, pose a question to the symbol and the readee, and then see how the readee interacts with the symbol.

For example, let's say your readee wants to know if a friendship with a particular man will blossom into a long-term romance. Since a wedding ring symbolizes a long-term commitment, you can visualize your readee handing a wedding ring to an image of the man, and watch to see what he does with the ring. You can then watch her response. Out of the infinite number of possible responses, the images you see will be those that reflect the subjects' actual feelings, intentions, and behavior.

CHAPTER 17

Reading with Other Clairvoyants

There are many advantages to reading with other clairvoyants, particularly when first developing your clairvoyant abilities. One of the best ways to gain certainty and confidence as a clairvoyant reader is to read with other clairvoyant students. This is because they will often see exactly what you are seeing. You may be looking at a particular image, wondering whether it's too silly or insignificant to mention, when suddenly the clairvoyant sitting next to you describes the same image you are looking at. This, of course, is extremely validating and exciting.

Reading with other clairvoyants takes some of the pressure off you. It allows you to read at a more leisurely pace. If you are having difficulty accessing information, you have the luxury of working with your tools and focusing more on yourself while the other clairvoyant(s) communicate with the readee. Another advantage is that your fellow clairvoyants can be quite a good support system both during and after the reading. They can identify energies that are affecting you and the other readers. They will be reading through their own pictures and therefore will often arrive at the same conclusions as you, but will come up with their own unique way of arriving at these conclusions. If you lose your neutrality, become ungrounded, or start to heal in an out-of-control sort of way, your fellow clairvoyants can gently point this out to you.

Reading With Two or More Clairvoyants

Both or all of the clairvoyant readers should sit together, shoulder to shoulder, in a line. Choose one person to be the lead reader before the readee arrives. Designating a leader is not essential, but is helpful for beginning students so they can feel secure in whatever role they are adopting. Usually the reader with more experience or more confidence will be the lead reader. Each person should take the time to individually run through the psychic tools. Then the lead reader can lead the other(s) through a short meditation and group prayer.

Next, the lead reader should bring his crown chakra to a neutral gold color and ask the other readers to match their crown chakras to his. They can do this by visualizing their own crown chakra and watching it turn to gold, or they can put up a clear glass neutral rose or viewing receptacle, place it over their head, and ask the receptacle to fill with the same vibration as the lead reader. The lead reader can clairvoyantly check to make sure everyone is at the same level of gold, and let the other readers know if it needs to be darker or lighter. We use gold here because it is a neutral high-vibration color. We avoid white because white is used for channeling; it is too easy for other spirits to attach themselves to this color or for our own spirits to depart through it.

The readers then should all send a hello in whatever form they choose to the spirits of all the other readers. The hello can be in the form of a rose with the word "hello" inside, or any other kind of neutral gift. Then the readee should be brought in to the room. The lead reader will sit directly across from the readee, with the other clairvoyants on either side of the lead reader. The lead reader can introduce himself and the other readers, and explain the process of the reading. Next, the lead reader can lead the other readers in a group prayer. The lead reader will be the one to tune in to the readee's vibration and set a color for the reading.

The lead reader will visualize a clear crystal viewing receptacle and then ask the readee to say her name as he watches the energy of that person's spirit go into the rose. Once the lead reader chooses a color, he should communicate that color to the other readers. The other readers should let their crown chakras match that color, again either by using a rose or by viewing their crown chakra directly. They should notice how that feels. If something feels wrong or a reader feels they are having a hard time holding that energy on their crown chakra, they can ask the lead reader to double-check the color. It may need to be adjusted.

Depending on the format of the reading, it should be determined beforehand whether everyone will read together or if the lead reader will do a certain part of the reading and the other readers will do other parts. If it is decided that all the readers will read every part, then the lead reader should still have the privilege or responsibility of being the first reader to communicate. Predetermining the role of each reader provides an organizational structure that allows the readers to read more harmoniously and confidently. At the same time, it's important to be flexible with these roles so that the clairvoyant information can flow and be expressed through whomever it needs to be. During the final clean-out stage, readers should make sure not only to make separations between themselves and the reader, but between each other as well.

Reading With a Monitor

One option for a group reading is to appoint someone to perform the role of a monitor. This person does not sit down with the other readers; instead, he stands behind the line of readers and clairvoyantly watches everything that is happening in the room with his eyes open. The monitor's job is to watch the energy of the room and how it is affecting the readers, rather than focusing on the readee. This person uses his seventh (crown) chakra and the ability of his knowingness.

The monitor takes over some of the responsibilities of the lead reader in terms of bringing the readee into the room, explaining the process, and doing the introductions. He also leads the readers through the various stages of the reading process. The monitor reminds the readers to use their tools, and offers suggestions or poses questions to the readers to help them navigate their way through the reading. The monitor acts as the conscious logical mind of the group of readers. This allows the readers to feel free to go further inward into a deeper trance where they just access the information without worrying about the process. Readings can be performed with or without a reader acting as a monitor.

CHAPTER 18

Reading Couples
and Groups

A couple's reading is one in which the clairvoyant reads the dynamics of a relationship in the presence of both partners at the same time. It is very similar to couple's counseling in which two people attend a therapy session together to work on or enhance their relationship with the assistance of a counselor.

If a couple requests to be read together, you should first determine if they are really seeking information about their relationship or if they are merely trying to avoid having to pay for two individual readings. If the couple wants you to address their relationship or joint projects and issues, I recommend reading them together. If they explain that they each have their individual issues and are not interested in hearing about the relationship itself, then I recommend reading them separately for the same reasons that you would not want a readee's companion to remain in the room during the reading, as discussed in chapter 14.

Even if a couple states that they are more interested in hearing about their combined interests and projects rather than the relationship itself, I will address these specific questions, but I will still look to see how their relationship is affecting the outcome of their creations/endeavors and how these in turn will affect their relationship. If any specific information spontaneously arises about the relationship itself, I will not hesitate to share it, because oftentimes the couple does want to hear about their relationship, but they are afraid to admit it or are worried that whatever I tell them will be too embarrassing to hear in the presence of their partner.

Reading couples can be rewarding in that it will teach you about your own relationships and about male/female energies and dynamics, but it can also be very challenging. One of the greatest challenges is being able to match information about one of the partners with the correct person. For example, you may see an image of one person doing a lot of housework while the other person sits in front of the television. Sometimes you will clearly know whom this information applies to, at other times you will think you know due to your preconceived ideas about gender roles (which you'll soon discover is a big mistake), and at other times you won't have a clue. Often, one person's energy is occupying the other person's aura or body so that at first clairvoyant glance they are virtually indistinguishable. If you are not sure whom you are talking about, you can be honest with your readees and tell them, "I'm not sure whom this applies to, but I see that one of you tends to do all the work around the house while the other one does all the relaxing. The one doing all the work is feeling resentful and the one doing all the relaxing is feeling left out of the household decisions." Most of the time the partners will know exactly whom and what it is you are referring to. If they don't, you can create a new viewing receptacle and ask for a symbol to appear in it that will demonstrate exactly which person you are referring to.

Another challenge of reading a couple has to do with maintaining a balanced perspective of both individuals and avoiding the potential to "side" with or focus on whatever individual you have the most in common with or are most sympathetic to.

As a young clairvoyant student, I performed a reading on a couple with another clairvoyant reader, Michael, who just happened to be a guy I had recently started dating. The couple sat down in front of us at a psychic fair. Michael began speaking first. He talked in totally positive terms, saying that he saw their relationship was perfect, that they were so happy together, and that everything was just peachy. This alarmed and confused the heck out of me because I was seeing images of the woman chained to a chair with tape on her mouth and crying. I knew Michael was an excellent reader, and I in no way wanted to question his clairvoyant competency since our own relationship was still on somewhat shaky ground. However, I could not ignore the images flashing across my own trustworthy screen, particularly since I felt that I had an ethical and personal responsibility to state what I was seeing. Despite my fear that I was about to totally invalidate Michael's reading ability, I shared this image with everyone. As soon as I did this, I heard a sigh from the woman who was sitting directly across from me and opened up my eyes to see what was happening with her (something I usually avoid doing since getting validation from the readee is not always conducive to the reading process and it pulls you out of your trance/ reading space). She was nodding her head and her desperate eyes pleaded with me to continue.

Further exploration of this image showed that she was feeling helpless, passive, controlled, and very stuck in the relationship. The man was startled at my comments and verbalized that I was wrong. However, the women finally turned to him and admitted that this was how she was really feeling. I realized then that the discrepancy in the assessment of the relationship had nothing to do with my or Michael's lack of competency, but rather that we were looking at two different things. I was reading the woman and her perspective of the relationship, and Michael was reading the man's perspective.

This reading taught me how clairvoyant images are not always based on an inherent truth; instead, they can be coming from the biased perspective of the readee. It also taught me how, in a couple's reading, I must purposefully focus my attention on both people and see how their unique perspectives and attitudes interact to form the dynamics of the relationship. It showed me the value of reading with another clairvoyant, and it also demonstrated to me how a couple's reading can be a powerful form of therapy that opens up or even establishes new lines of communication and honesty. Furthermore, it provided an opportunity to work through my own relationship issues and MEI pictures that actually arose during this reading in terms of trusting myself enough to speak my truth even if it meant potentially upsetting my partner or losing the relationship itself.

Reading Same-Sex Couples

One-fourth of the couples I have read have been same-sex couples, either two men or two women. These readings have taught me a lot about male/female energies and how these dynamics are played out in same-sex couples in the same way they manifest in partners of the opposite sex. When there is conflict in the relationship, it is often due to the differences between the male/female energies and qualities that are dominant within each person. One person tends to be more passive, more attached to their home, and more interested in commitment, fidelity, nurturance, and intimacy, while the other person may seek more freedom, more excitement, more independence, and more individuality (these are often the same qualities that attracted the partners to each other in the first place, and that each partner is unconsciously lacking, searching for, or exploring within themselves). There is no difference in reading couples of the same sex or of the opposite sex, other than the fact that sometimes it is a bit trickier to determine whom you are talking about when you see images that could logically apply to either person.

The Reading Technique

The couple should sit in front of you in chairs about a foot apart. Visualize your reading screen and see it growing bigger and moving away from you until it is encompassing the couple. Notice who is on the left of your screen and who is on your right. Then explode your reading screen and create a new one that is only a few inches from your sixth chakra. Imagine a viewing receptacle in the form of a clear crystal rose on the left side of your viewing screen and postulate that this rose will represent the person who was placed on the left side of your previous screen. Then create another receptacle on the right side of your reading screen and postulate that this rose will represent the person who was placed on the right side of your previous screen.

Ask each person, one at a time, to say their birthday and their current name, and watch for the color of their spirit to appear in their assigned rose. Ground each of the roses into the center of the planet, and in your imagination write each person's name under their respective rose using a crayon that matches the color of their energy. Now imagine that you are matching your crown chakra to both of the readees' crown chakras. You can see the two colors nestled side by side on top of your head, or see the two colors stacked on top of each other. Or you can swirl both colors together into one.

Technique 1
This is the same technique that you would use to read a relationship when one person is not present, as taught in chapter 15. Simply invite the two roses on your reading screen to show you how they interact together. Relax and observe any changes or activity within or between the two roses. Then create a new receptacle and ask it to show you further images that will explain these changes.

Technique 2
Imagine that there is a third viewing receptacle that represents the couple in between the two receptacles that represent the individual people. See a clear glass rose and invite the energy of the relationship to enter into it. Underneath this rose, imagine that you are drawing the word "relationship." This rose represents the actual relationship, which is a separate entity from the

individuals you are reading but is, of course, influenced by their individual traits. Give this rose a reading. This technique is helpful because on an energetic level it sends the picture to the people that they are not their relationship, but rather that their relationship is a separate entity that deserves attention but is not any more or any less important than their individual selves.

CHAPTER 19

Reading and Healing Children

I love reading children and teenagers. They still dwell in the magical world of imagination, and thus they believe that anything is possible. Their wide-eyed wonder and belief in miracles, in the unseen, in extrasensory perception, has not yet been poisoned by the atheism, skepticism, and pessimism of their parents, teachers, or other adults. Even children as young as seven or eight seem to approach a reading with great reverence and awe, as if they somehow know that they are participating in a sacred experience that touches upon the divine. Many children sit on the edge of their chair, afraid to breathe or even bat an eyelash for fear of missing a single word. Much like their adult counterparts, they are there to receive hope, validation, and direction. They want to know that they will be somebody important in the world and that they will be happy. Unlike so many adults, they still believe this is possible.

A clairvoyant reading is an experience that these young people will re-live over and over again in their minds, and describe time and again to their friends. While the exact words and sequence of events of the reading will become cloudy or distorted over time, many of the clairvoyant images that are relayed to them will forever be inscribed in their memories and imagination.

When a child or teenager comes to me for a reading, I view this as a unique opportunity to bring inspiration and hope to a young life, while teaching that child, through example, about their own psychic abilities and potential. For a clairvoyant reader, an opportunity to read a younger person is a special gift and a challenging responsibility. Children can so easily be programmed and their enthusiasm so severely crushed by negative input. Also, they have selective hearing; they are prone to misinterpret words and fill in the blanks with their own hopes and fears. Children and young teenagers don't yet know how to discriminate between information that is really relevant to them and information that is not. If a psychic tells them one thing that seems to be true, they will likely believe that every other word from the psychic's mouth is a proven fact. Furthermore, children and particularly teenagers often don't know how to responsibly handle the information they receive during a reading. They may use it as a weapon against their parents or others.

In this chapter, I offer suggestions on how to approach a clairvoyant reading and communicate clairvoyant information to children of varying ages. These suggestions will help you empower and inspire the children you read, while minimizing the possibility of detrimentally programming or upsetting them during the reading. I also offer specific techniques and age-appropriate reading formats that I have personally developed to help you navigate your way through a reading.

General Pointers

Always focus on the positive.
When reading children, focus on their strengths, their successes, and their positive relationships with others. Look at their dreams and how they can best achieve these. Acknowledge problems and challenges that the child is struggling with, but help them redefine these problems as opportunities for growth. Help them see how their strengths will get them through difficult periods in their lives.

Be honest, but don't feel compelled to tell everything
As clairvoyant readers, I feel that we must be honest with our clients, no matter what their age. We should never make anything up just to make someone feel good. Luckily there is no reason to do this, because there is always a bright side to anything. That being said, when reading children, I feel that it is all right to sugarcoat potentially upsetting information so that the child can deal with the situation at their own pace.

For example, if you see that the child's grandmother is dying, rather than stating, "Your grandmother is going to die very soon," you can clairvoyantly ask the grandmother's spirit if she has any messages for the child, e.g., "I see your grandmother loves you very much and will always be by your side, even after she has gone to heaven. She loves taking walks with you and how you laugh at her funny faces." Or, "You are a very strong and brave boy and know how to take care of yourself. Someday your grandmother may have to leave and go to heaven, but she wants you to know that you will be fine no matter what. She loves your stories and knows you will be a great writer someday. She knows that you will always have lots of friends near you."

When looking into a child's future, let them know that you are merely looking at one or two of several different possibilities.
Many kids have a fantasy about what they want to be when they grow up. They want you to tell them what you see for their future, but if you see something different than this fantasy, they become very upset. Looking at your own life, you probably can see where you have worked in many different jobs and held many different roles, and the same will be true for these children when they reach adulthood. If the child is upset by your answer, ask them to tell you what they want to be when they grow up and then clairvoyantly look to see if this is a transitory dream or if it is one they will ultimately pursue. There is no reason to take away their fantasy, even if it looks very unlikely. You can say, "Well, I see clairvoyantly in your future that you will be really good at working with computers, and lots of people are going to depend on your help and pay you a lot of money for it, but that doesn't mean you can't also be a famous baseball player if that's what you really want."

Always counterbalance a negative statement with a positive one, and always give the child proactive steps to take to change their future if it looks bleak or difficult.
Instead of saying to an eight-year-old, "It looks like you will become an alcoholic and end up in jail by the time you are twenty," you can say, "I see you are vulnerable to the problems that drinking alcohol can cause. If you want to have a happy life and enjoy your freedom, then you should stay far away from alcohol. I see you are a very strong runner, and if you stay away from alcohol, you have a good chance of becoming a very successful athlete." Again, only say what you honestly see.

Tell the child about their personality characteristics that will help and those that could present challenges throughout their life.
For example, "I see you are a great speaker and are very funny. You will always have lots of friends because you know how to make them laugh. I also see you don't like people to tell you what to do and you have a strong stubborn streak. This could cause problems at school and at your work unless you learn to give in during arguments that aren't that important to you."

Give the child hope that a current problem they are dealing with will eventually be resolved or will lessen with time.
Look to see how time will heal their wounds. For example, perhaps when you sit down to read a child you see an image of the child standing over a motionless dog. The child drops to his knees and hugs the dog, crying, trying to get it to stand up. It's clear that the child has recently experienced the death of a favorite pet or will soon experience this (be aware that you may see the pet as a dog because you had a dog yourself as a kid, or you prefer dogs, when in reality the child's pet might be a cat). In this scenario, I would verbally ask the child if he had recently experienced any kind of loss of something or someone he loved and if he has been feeling sad, or if something unusual had recently happened with a pet. If the child says yes, then you can clairvoyantly look into the present to see what might make the child feel better, or into the future to see the soonest point in time when the child will be happy again. Maybe you will see the child hitting a home run at a baseball game, or getting a new pet, or going to Disney World. If the child doesn't seem to know what you are talking about, you might say something like, "I see that at some point in your life something difficult might happen that will make you feel sad for a while. But then I see you looking happy again." Or you may just decide not to say anything and go on to the next topic because the child really isn't ready to talk about or deal with this subject, and you don't want to make him apprehensive about a future even he can't control. Most of the time, however, you will be picking up on the past or present rather than the future.

Take advantage of this opportunity to see how the child is already using their psychic and healing abilities and which ones will help the child in their life.
There is a reason why the child or teenager has come to a clairvoyant reader as opposed to another kind of reader, so tell them something about their own clairvoyance, how they can develop it, and how they can overcome any obstacles to accessing this and any other ability. You can also look to see whether the child is tuned in to their own inner voice, higher self, etc., and clairvoyantly give the child some tips about how to connect with their own spirit. You may see a specific technique for the child to practice, or you may see that they would benefit from going to Sunday school at their family church. Remember, this is not you spouting advice, it is you giving a reading to see what that particular child needs. This may be the only opportunity

the child has for a very long time to receive communication on the level that you can give, so make full use of your time together. You are one of the child's spiritual mentors, even if you only spend five minutes together.

Always address a child with the same level of respect as an adult.

Use simple words the child can understand, but don't talk down to them in a condescending manner. Many children are hidden within the shadows of their parents and long to be seen as the sovereign spirits that they are. As clairvoyant readers, this is one of the most important gifts we can offer them.

You must respect the child's confidentiality, but don't expect them to do the same.

Let the child know upfront that you will not repeat whatever is said during the reading, even to their parents, but that they should feel free to share the information with anyone. Children need to know that they can trust you and that there will not be any negative repercussions from being honest or allowing a clairvoyant reader to see into their lives and feelings. On the other hand, it's important that you don't ask them to keep secrets from their parents, because the conflict between not wanting to disappoint you but wanting to share with the people to whom they are closest could be traumatic. Some children view a secret as something that is shameful or bad, and if they feel that there is something secret about the reading, they may feel that they have clone something wrong.

Help the child understand the dynamics between himself and his parents, but know that whatever you say about a child's or teen's parent could and likely will be used as ammunition against the parent.

When reading a child or teenager, issues concerning their relationship with their parents will frequently arise. Sometimes you will see information about the parents that the parents will not appreciate. This is the information that the child will bring up later at the first sign of conflict with their parents. This is a sticky situation. Children are obviously dependent, physically and emotionally, on their parents, and yet even the most nurturing, best intentioned parents may not have a clue as to what their child's spiritual destiny entails or how to provide the proper experiences or education that will help their child move along on their own unique spiritual path. So many parents are consumed with fears, judgments, and limitations that the more they love their children, the more they suffocate and poison the children with their own doubts and lack of faith in the ultimate perfection of God's plan and the universe.

As a clairvoyant reader, you can see the child's spirit and tune in to the blueprint of their spiritual path, and often you will see where there is a clash between the child's desires and needs and those of their parents. On rare occasions, you may read a child who is being physically or sexually abused by a parent, in which case I recommend that you talk to the child about this and see if they are open to you speaking to the other parent or another family member, and possibly calling the police or child protective services.

However, most of the time, struggles at home have more to do with differences in personalities, desires, and goals between well-intentioned parents and their children. Most parents think that because they are the parents, they have the right to make all the decisions for the children. They want to control their children, and when the child asserts her own will or attempts to control the situation, the parent labels the child as being "bad" or "naughty" or even as having attention deficit disorder.

A child may come to you for a reading because she desperately needs to know that she is alright, that all the labels that are being placed upon her, all the crazy-making around her, has much more to do with the dysfunction, blindness, or self-centeredness of her parents than the flaws within herself. A child also needs to know how he can best cope with his parents until he is old enough to physically take care of himself. When you give him honest and clear communication about who he is, you will empower that child in a way that he has never been empowered before. Many parents don't want their child to be empowered because this could lead the child to become even more disobedient and outspoken.

As a clairvoyant reader, I recommend that you be honest with children about their family dynamics, and at the same help them see their parents or family members with compassion and forgiveness. Always clairvoyantly look to see how what actions and philosophies children can adopt that will help them peacefully coexist with their parents for as long as necessary, without having to sacrifice their own sense of self.

Should the parent be present during the reading?

Personally, I always prefer to read a client in privacy, whether they are an adult or child, unless the reading is going to focus on the child's relationship with their parent or I am reading a very young child who is nervous about being separated from their parent. Most children cannot clearly see themselves in the presence of their parents because even the most loving of parents are constantly projecting roles ("You are the child, I am the parent"), expectations ("As a child, you are unable to care for yourself, unable to speak for yourself, and dependent on me") and judgments ("You can never sit still, you talk too loud, you misbehave in school") onto the child. The energy behind these projections is so intrusive that the child may feel like, and therefore become, almost a totally different person when they are around their family versus when they are not.

Have you ever noticed how, as an adult, you feel different about yourself when you are around one or both of your parents? Your self-esteem and sense of independence may suddenly plummet, or you may feel generally cranky and irritated but have no idea why. This is because your parent's projections continue to persist far into adulthood, even when it is logically clear that they have nothing to do with reality.

These projections interfere with the relationship between the clairvoyant reader and the child, as well as the overall accuracy and ease of the reading itself, in that the reader will be more inclined to confuse the parent's projections with the true nature of the child. Even when the parent is not present, there is always the risk that a psychic may confuse the parent's energy, in the form of projections, thoughtforms, and emotions, with the child's energy and true characteristics, but this is much more likely to happen when the parent is present. Furthermore, both the psychic and the child may feel greater inhibitions in the presence of a parent in terms of their communication.

At times it may be appropriate, with the permission of the child, to speak to a parent after a reading and to share with them the information that you obtained clairvoyantly and communicated to the child. Some parents may be open to your communication, while others may be totally opposed to it. By the time you have completed the reading with the child, you will have a pretty good idea whether or not you and the child should even consider this possibility. If the parent and/or child insists on the parent being in the room, ask the parent to sit as far back in the room as possible.

Due to the prevalence of lawsuits and accusations of child abuse and molestation, some readers, particularly men (although women need to be concerned with this as well), will insist that another adult be present for the reading or at least within eyesight of the reading. From a legal standpoint, this is a prudent practice to adopt. It is also for this reason that I recommend avoiding physical contact with a child, with the exception of shaking their hand. When an adult shakes a child's hand, they are saying to that child, "I respect you as an equal," and this may have more of an impact than even a hug. If a child hugs you, accept the hug for just a moment and then offer them your hand.

Reading Younger Children

A few months into my clairvoyant training, while performing readings at a psychic fair, one of my teachers approached me and asked me to read a little girl who was about five years old. He was reading her mother and the girl kept interrupting them, so the mother offered to purchase a reading in order to keep her daughter occupied. Before I could protest, the little girl was seated across from me, impatiently banging her feet on the metal chair. Having no children of my own at the time nor any recent experience with them, I had no idea how to talk to a child, much less read one. I decided that I would read her like any adult. I closed my eyes, said a prayer, directed her to say her name, and asked her if she had any questions. Her response seemed very far away and I opened my eyes to discover that she had already vacated her chair and was now exploring the neighboring tarot card booth. "What's that?" she asked, picking up a deck of Rider-Waite tarot cards. She pulled out the Tower card. "This card looks scary. What's that?" she asked, pointing to the tower.

At this point I decided to abandon any idea of giving her a reading. Her mother was really just looking for a babysitter anyway. I recalled that babysitters read stories, so I decided to tell her a story about the cards.

"See this tall building?" I asked, pointing to the tower. "That is a house. And the people sticking out of the windows are kids. They are upset because one of the boys set fire to the house and it is burning down." What a charming story to tell a five-year-old! I thought to myself. But I was shocked by her response.

"Yeah, that happened to our house. My brother was playing with matches and set the grass in our backyard on fire. My mom was really mad. He always does bad things." I realized I was on to something.

"See this person on the card?" I asked her. "That is you. She looks to me like she is angry at the other people in the house."

"Yeah," the girl responded. "My mom is always too busy watching my brother to play with me. He doesn't want her to play with me. He makes me so mad."

"Well, let's see if things are going to change soon. Show me another card in the deck." She handed me the Sun card. "This looks like a happy card to I told her. "See the child's face? She's smiling. The sun is shining on her and she is having fun. She looks like she is on vacation."

The girl's face lit up. "Yeah, we are going to Disneyland for my birthday, on an airplane!"

The girl's mother later confirmed that her son had set their backyard on fire the week before and that they were going to Disneyland the following week.

Tarot Card Reading Technique (Ages 3 to 7)

My experience with that little girl taught me not only how to read a young child, but also how to utilize tarot cards to read people of any age. First, ask the child to pick a card and then start talking about the card without censoring yourself. Don't think of the experience as a reading, just tell the child and yourself that you are merely making up a story with the help of the cards. This will eliminate any feelings of pressure or responsibility. Use the images in the card as springboards for the plot and events of the story. Ask yourself what these images remind you of. As you talk, pay attention to new images or thoughts that pop into your mind and then describe and incorporate these into the story.

PART IV

Clairvoyant Healing

CHAPTER 20

What Is Clairvoyant Healing?

If you have attempted any of the techniques in this book, then you have already performed a clairvoyant healing. Whether you grounded yourself, ran your energy, or created a viewing receptacle and invited someone else's energy into it for you to read, you were engaged in healing because you were moving energy. The moment you clairvoyantly look at energy, it changes. The degree to which it changes is dependent on many factors. The most significant factor is the intention of the person receiving the reading or healing and their receptivity to change, followed by the intention of the person conducting the reading or healing. The degree to which energy can transform is also dependent on factors such as the type of healing methods employed and the experience and nature of the healer or healing guides, counterbalanced by the degree of resistance from family programming, friends, lovers, coworkers, disembodied spirits, etc.

As discussed in previous chapters, emotions, thoughts, memories, pain, information, etc., are all energy. Our physical bodies are made up of and surrounded by energy. So when energy moves, changes, transforms, or releases, transformation occurs in our bodies, minds, feelings, and ultimately our spirits. This transformation is called healing.

Basic Clairvoyant Healing Technique

There are countless techniques that can be employed to facilitate transformation and healing. Touch, sound, acupuncture, chanting, prayer, and herbs are just a few methods that have been proven to be effective sometimes for some people. Oftentimes these techniques are accompanied by visualization. It is natural for people to visualize their desires and intentions. You are hungry and for a moment you may visualize a hamburger. You hear about someone winning the lottery and you lose yourself in images of driving around in a convertible BMW, soaking in the hot tub outside your new mansion with a glass of champagne in your hand, rolling around naked in a bed full of dollar bills (don't tell me I'm the only one!). When you have the desire to heal yourself or someone else, it is natural to visualize the person getting better and/or see the illness leaving. Even if you don't realize that this desire and visualization will have any effect at all, you may be enacting powerful changes in yourself or someone else, because nothing more is really needed.

The preparations for a healing are the same as the preparations for a reading (see chapter 14). Once you have prepared yourself through grounding, running your energy, and getting into the center of your head, you will be ready to begin the healing.

Begin by visualizing the person you wish to heal. This person could be seated a couple feet across from you, or could be a million miles away on another continent. There is no such thing as space or time when it comes to performing readings and healings, so regardless of the physical distance, the results will be the same. If your healee is present, have them sit a few feet away from you in a comfortable chair. Ask them to say their current name a few times. If your healee is not physically present, then visualize that person and repeat their name and address to yourself, if you know that information. Some healers like to have a picture of their healee if they are performing a long-distance healing. Personally, I have discovered that while having a picture may help me concentrate or visualize the healee, I don't really need to have or know anything other than the readee's name. Even the name is not essential. This is because healing and reading have to do with intention.

If a woman comes to you and says her grandmother is ill, as long as you intend to heal the grandmother she was referring to, you can energetically connect with the grandmother, without knowing her name. All you need is a symbol, which in this example is the word "grandmother." If you hear about a missing child on the news but don't catch her name, you can choose to give her a healing by saying, "I now choose to heal the missing girl I heard about," and you will instantaneously be connected with that girl. Again, the value of knowing names and additional information, like the date of birth, address, and what your healee looks like, is that this information helps you, as a reader, improve your concentration, and when the readee/healee is present, stating their name out loud can help bring them back to their body if they become ungrounded or unfocused.

Whether your healee is present or far away, visualize that both of your crown chakras are turning to a bright blue or purple color. Next, give the healee a grounding cord. See their entire body grounded into the center of the planet. Then imagine that you are holding a jar of cobalt blue or glowing purple energy that looks like paint. This is neutral healing energy. First match your crown chakra to this color. Then take the energy in the jar and throw it all over your healee's body. Patiently watch to see what happens. Any area that is not healthy will light up as a different color.

You can either perform a reading on this color to understand what it represents, or you can merely watch as the color releases down the healee's grounding cord. If you wish to read the color of the unhealthy energy, first create a viewing receptacle, invite the color into the receptacle, and then perform your reading as you would any other. Destroy the receptacle when you are finished. Even if you plan to merely help release the energy, you can still create a viewing receptacle and fill it up with the color of the unhealthy energy until it grows very large. Then imagine you are sending this rose into the middle of the ocean or desert and see it exploding. Repeat this process until you feel the energy has been released.

Recharging the Readee With Their Own Healing Energy

When a person cuts their finger or bruises their knee, within a few days or weeks that injury will heal on its own, regardless of whether any care is given to that part of the body. This is because the bodies of human beings are designed to heal themselves. They possess a life-force energy that is a healing energy. Whatever energy created our body in the first place remains with us until we die, helping recreate any part of our body that may become injured or diseased. During a healing, you may be activating, complementing, or speeding up this force within your readee with the use of your visualization methods. After helping your healee release unhealthy energy, you will want to help them fill up the area of concern with their own healing energy so that it will continue to repair the damaged or diseased area and prevent the foreign energy from returning.

I recommend that you first look for the color of the healee's energy, and then ask the healee to tell you the color that they believe represents their healing energy. For those who hesitate, rephrase the question and ask them to describe their favorite color, the color that is the most soothing or comforting to them, or the color that gives them the greatest sense of peace and happiness. If the color they choose does not match the one you saw, or if it doesn't feel right to you (some people become very comfortable with foreign energies even when those energies are destructive, as in codependent relationships), then put the color into a viewing receptacle, give the receptacle a grounding cord, and look to see if the color has changed. Whatever color you see will be the correct color of the readee's healing energy.

Once you have determined the correct color, run this color through the area they just released as well as through their chakras and aura. Then ask the healee to join you in running this energy through their body. This not only empowers them, but also teaches them a handy healing technique they can independently use anytime, anywhere.

Cellular Healing

All illness begins on an energetic level before it manifests in the physical body. When an unhealthy energy invades the body, or when energy within the body becomes stuck or stagnant, it will glob onto the cells of the body first before going on to affect the glands, organs, muscles, and other parts of the body. If there are enough healthy cells already in the body, these healthy cells will fight the infected cells and eliminate the unhealthy energy from the body.

As clairvoyant healers, we can use visualization to stimulate and enhance this process by working with both the unhealthy and healthy cells of our healee's body. The healing technique discussed here is very simple, yet extremely powerful. It is particularly helpful when healing people who have been diagnosed with cellular diseases such as cancer. It can be used in conjunction with any of the other healing techniques discussed in this book. As with any type of reading or healing, it's important to first have your separation objects up, be well grounded, and have your energy running before beginning your healing.

Once you are tuned in to your readee, create your reading screen and clairvoyantly look for the unhealthiest cell in the body. Let this cell appear on your screen. Look to see what colors are in it. Give the cell a grounding cord and ground it into the center of the planet. See the unhealthy energy leaving the cell. Right beside this cell, ask the healthiest cell in the body to appear. This cell will be called the teacher cell. Patiently wait until it appears on your reading screen and then observe the size, shape, and colors in this cell. The job of this teacher cell will be to "teach," or reprogram, the unhealthy cell(s). Take this cell and lay it on top of the unhealthy cell until the unhealthy cell takes on the exact proportions and colors of the teacher cell. Continue to check in with the grounding cord of the unhealthy cell to see if any further energy or colors release from it. Know that these two cells represent all the cells in the body, so that all of the unhealthy cells are instantaneously being transformed by this one teacher cell.

Once you are fully satisfied that the previously unhealthy cell has been transformed into a healthy cell, then imagine that the teacher cell is splitting off into two teacher, or healthy, cells. See these two cells splitting off into two more cells. Continue this process until you see so many healthy teacher cells that they fill up the entire body. Command these cells to go forward on their own and seek out any final stubborn unhealthy cells that may still be lurking within the body.

Healing Your Relationships

Healing your relationship doesn't always mean that all problems will be solved or that things will work out exactly how you want them to. Performing a relationship healing could result in the termination of the relationship, if that is what is in the highest good of each party. What is guaranteed is that the communication between the parties will become more honest and peaceful and that any outside influences that may be negatively affecting the relationship will diminish or cease.

Just like individuals, relationships are vulnerable to all sorts of energies that affect the health of the relationship over time. The two people involved in the relationship are constantly bringing all sorts of thoughtforms, emotions, and energies to the relationship that can make it stronger or tear it apart. Then there is the energy and resulting influence of both individuals' families, friends, and spirit guides as well as society in general that have an effect on a relationship, regardless of whether these people are even aware on a conscious level that the relationship exists.

To perform a relationship healing, create a new reading screen after running through your meditation tools. On the screen visualize two clear glass crystal roses (or two wine glasses), which will represent the individuals in the relationship. Assign a name to each rose and write the name across the rose. Give each rose a grounding cord. See a color for each rose and notice the differences and similarities between each rose. Next, create a space between the two roses, and inside this space create another crystal rose. Write the word "communication" inside this rose. Next, conduct a quick mini reading on this communication rose. What colors do you see? Give the rose a grounding cord and command any foreign energy in this rose to exit through the grounding cord. Watch the energy release and notice the color of the releasing energy. Then do the same to the individual roses.

Once all the foreign energy has fully released, choose a vibration(s) that you would like to bring into the relationship that will positively influence the communication between the individuals. This vibration could be peace, happiness, enthusiasm, amusement, fun, love, passion, etc. Then choose a color for this vibration and see the color filling up all three roses. Watch to see if any further energy releases as you fill up the roses, and notice if there is any change with any of the roses. Then you can go a step further and visualize images in the communication rose that express the vibration or general feeling you just set in the rose. For example, if you chose peace, then you could visualize a peace sign or see the two people holding hands, watching a sunset together and looking serene and comfortable. If you chose passion, you could see the couple wildly making love to each other.

For this exercise, I recommend that you choose to see a state of mind, such as happiness, peace, love, etc., rather than get too specific about an outcome, because the outcome might be one that you think you want but that is not really in the best interest of yourself or the other person. This simple technique is so powerful that it easily creates exactly what you have visualized. On the other hand, if the outcome you choose is really what you want but not what the other person wants, it could result in the breakup of the relationship. This is because when you perform this exercise, the individual involved will subconsciously and telepathically receive the images you have just created. If the images and desires expressed in the rose are not in alignment with the other person's desires or life path, they will either break off the relationship, or life circumstances will create a rift in the relationship so both of you can go on to have the type of relationship your hearts really desire.

As a final step, create an image that represents God. You can visualize this image as a glowing star, a shining sun, a sparkling ball of light, a grandfatherly looking face, or even your dog Fred! Visualize this image as being suspended above the three roses. Choose a color that represents God's compassion, love, and all-knowingness. See the color glowing brighter and brighter until it glows brighter than any light you've ever seen. Then draw columns of this colored light from each rose to God and from rose to rose, forming the shape of a triangle with a line in the middle. See the color travel from your symbol of God down into the communication rose, filling it up completely. Then see the color travel to the individual roses on either side, and watch as these fill up. See the colored light travel back up to God. Watch this circulation for a few minutes. Know that whatever is in your best interest and the best interest of your partner will come to pass. When you have completed the healing, destroy all the images on your reading screen and commence with your usual clean-out routine.

Techniques for Handling Troublesome Entities

In your readings, you will undoubtedly encounter troublesome spirits at some point. These entities may be bothering your readee, or they may be pestering you as you attempt to read. Some of these spirits may have the highest intentions. They may wish to heal or help the readee, but are behaving in a way that is not conducive to the readee's well-being (as in the case of a loving but overbearing or controlling parent who erroneously thinks they know what is in the best interest of their child). Some spirits in this category are deceased relatives who don't realize they are dead or are not willing to let go of the readee (or vice versa). Many people erroneously assume that any spirit that has passed on is now enlightened, or at least wiser than they were before they were dead. From my readings I have discovered that some of these spirits do gain wisdom upon their passing, but many others do not. If your Uncle Fred was a jerk when he was alive, there is a strong possibility that he may still be one now that he has passed on. Even if he was a saint, if he is hanging on to you too tightly (or you to him), both of you could encounter a number of problems.

There are many types of spirits that have a strong desire to experience life as a human being on earth. They are desperately seeking parents who will bear them, and they will stop at nothing to achieve their goal. Some of these beings are in fact meant to be born, while others are not. These beings can have substantial positive and negative effects on a person's relationships, self-esteem, sex drive, desire (or desperation) for children, etc. Some beings will attempt to invade or possess an existing body instead of being born into a new one.

Another class of troublesome beings are those that lack the ability to understand and respect human life. These beings often show themselves as insects, worms, snakes, spiders, or ugly/scary faces. These beings are highly antisocial. Some seem to be human, while others are like animals or aliens. They feed off pain and fear. They can interfere with and destroy relationships, crucify a person's self-esteem, and even incite suicidal feelings and behavior.

Regardless of a being's intention, nature, or propensity for love or evil, the basic technique and approach for dealing with any spirit is the same. First, it's important to always remind yourself (and the spirit) that you always have the advantage over disembodied spirits because you have a physical body that is connected to the earth. Sometimes you may fear a spirit because you don't understand them. Other times spirits may use scare tactics to control you because fear brings you down to their vibration. If you are not scared, they ultimately have no power over you. Some spirits are like bullies: they put up a good show of being tough, but the moment they understand that you really do see them, they get scared and flee.

When you see a spirit (clairvoyantly or with your physical eyes), always first say hello to them. Let them know that you do see them. Ask them if they have a message for you. If their message is unfriendly or it scares you, you would be wise to end the communication right there. Acknowledge their presence, but don't try get them to understand you or attempt to reform them. Don't argue with them. Trying to change their nature is like trying to reason with a hungry man-eating tiger. If you try to talk sense into them, you will merely make yourself more vulnerable to their tactics.

The high vibration of amusement is your greatest weapon. When you see or sense an unpleasant, serious, or determined entity, use your great imagination to dress them up in funny clothes. Pretend that they are wearing a sparkly pink baby girl's dress with a matching frilly bonnet and sunglasses with little birdies on the ends. Throw them into a pink baby carriage, plop a bottle of milk into their homely mouth, and take them for a ride through a lovely garden while you tell them silly monster jokes and then transport them into outer space. They will often run screaming from you before you actually move them away! They won't be able to handle the vibration of amusement that you are creating. Laughter and beauty will melt them. When you raise your vibration, they won't be able to match you there and they will usually disappear.

If you are having trouble finding your amusement, there are several other tactics you can apply. On your reading screen, see this spirit connected up to God with a cord of brilliant light, and connected into the planet with a strong grounding cord. Imagine that God has giant hands and that you are gently placing the spirit into God's hands. Thank God for helping the spirit and taking this spirit away. Continue this visualization until you have a strong sense that the entity is gone.

As you do this, feel free to call in help from an ascended master, such as Buddha, Jesus, Mother Mary, Archangel Michael, or one of your spirit guides. Whether or not you consider yourself to be a Christian, the name of Christ is a powerful symbol that has been used for centuries in exorcisms (I'm Jewish and it works for me!). In the name of Christ, demand confidently, with every ounce of your being, that this spirit be banished from your kingdom. State this demand out loud.

When working with spirits, handle them in your imagination as you would handle a physical person. If an intruder were in your home, you might yell at them to leave, you might call the police, or you might shoot them, and while doing all of this you might be praying or yelling for assistance from your neighbors. In the same way, if you are performing a clairvoyant reading and discover that there is a spirit invading your aura, tell it to leave, ask God and your spirit guides to take it away, see yourself forcing the spirit to leave and go far far away, or, as a last resort, see yourself destroying the entity by shooting it, or merely taking the end of a pencil and erasing it.

PART V

PROFESSIONAL AND PERSONAL CONSIDERATIONS

CHAPTER 21

Psychic Ethics

As a clairvoyant reader, you are going to need to develop your own personal code of conduct to help you wade through a wide range of ethical dilemmas that will arise both during readings and in your relationships with people in your everyday life. The Webster's New Collegiate Dictionary defines ethics as "the principles of conduct governing an individual or group" and "the discipline dealing with what is good and bad and with moral duty and obligation." Professionals such as psychologists, doctors, social workers, and attorneys all are governed by licensing boards that have developed and actively enforce a strict code of ethics by which these professionals must abide.

In the United States, there is no governing board that regulates the behavior of professional psychics and healers (which ultimately is a good thing, given all the misperceptions the majority of people have about psychic phenomena—government regulation at this point might resemble the Salem witch trials!). Therefore, each psychic must develop their own moral code, which will determine certain choices they will have to make during the course of a reading or healing and in their everyday life.

As an undergraduate psychology student and a graduate social work student, I was required to take several classes regarding professional codes of ethics and the law for these two disciplines, which are closely related to each other as well as to psychic reading, which also involves an element of counseling. Some of the principles stuck with me and helped me understand the importance of behaving in a certain way so as to minimize the suffering of both myself and my clients in my readings. These principles have also served to strengthen my relationships with my clients and to resolve various dilemmas that involved conflicting values. Two of these principles that have been most relevant in my readings have to do with confidentiality and setting boundaries with clients. Unfortunately there have been many other issues that are unique to psychic reading for which there were no guidelines. As a result, I have had to learn through experience and, occasionally, painful mistakes how best to handle these dilemmas.

In this chapter, I will discuss my own code of ethics governing psychic readings and healing, which at the very least will initiate a dialogue or get you to start thinking about certain issues and options of how to handle them. While I do not wish to push my personal values on anyone, there is a definite possibility that these will emerge, so you can do with them as you please. I feel a discussion concerning ethics and common ethical dilemmas that arise in readings is essential both to readers who are certain they want to learn to do readings and to readers who are still sitting on the fence, because these ethical dilemmas and your resistance to or fear of dealing with them could be the very things that have stood in the way of your awareness and application of the God-given spiritual and psychic gifts that have been with you since the beginning of your existence.

Confidentiality

The American Psychological Association and Social Work code of ethics stresses the importance of confidentiality between the practitioner and their client. This agreement is vital to the client/practitioner relationship because it creates an environment in which the client can feel secure and safe enough to be totally honest. When confidentiality is breached, the client and others could not only suffer damaging consequences, but could suffer severe emotional trauma from realizing that perhaps the one person in the world they thought could be trusted, a role model whom they greatly admired, has betrayed them.

As a psychic, people are going to come to you with issues that they have hidden from others, and from themselves, for their entire lives. There are times when you will see images depicting behavior that your client is extremely embarrassed about and ashamed of. The client ultimately needed to have these issues addressed, but never consciously expected they would arise during the reading and never dreamed you would have the ability to see the details so blatantly. For example, during one reading I saw a man having sexual intercourse with a blow-up doll. While he ultimately desired help with his relationship problems, he certainly didn't expect me to see this aspect of his sexual behavior! You can imagine how devastating it would be to him if I were to share this information with someone who turned out to know him.

A few years ago, a man and his wife came for readings. I asked them if they wanted a couple's reading, but they said no and explained that they each had their own issues they were working on. I read the man first and discovered that he was thinking about having an extramarital affair. I helped him understand his feelings of guilt and responsibility that were tormenting him. By the end of the reading, he felt so relieved that I had treated him with compassion rather than judgment that he asked me if I'd like to become his mistress! Before I could say no, his wife entered the room for her reading. Talk about pressure! Did I maintain confidentiality, or did I let this poor woman know that her husband had just asked me to have sex with him and was planning on leaving her the first chance he got?

The first thing I did was ground myself and get into the center of my head. Next, I reminded myself that I was not responsible for these people's lives. They were coming to me to access information, not to hear my moral judgments. I decided that it was not my place to violate the man's confidentiality and instead gave the woman a reading, which turned out to address her issues of dependence on her husband and how she could enhance her own life so she could feel more fulfilled as an individual. The information I gave her might have potentially helped her relationship, but more likely helped her cope with the strong possibility of the marriage ending in divorce.

Some people might argue that I should have told her what had occurred with her husband because this information would have helped her make the appropriate decisions in her life. To be honest, I still wonder if that would have been the best course of action, since I know that if I were in her shoes, I'd want to know the whole truth. Had the question of her relationship or her husband's fidelity come up during her reading, my dilemma would have been easily solved, since my clairvoyant images would have given her the same information that was revealed during her husband's reading. However, the subject never came up, so perhaps it was not meant to.

This example demonstrates the confusion and difficulty of choosing the right course of action when one ethical value (confidentiality) collides with or opposes another value (telling the truth, fidelity). When it comes to maintaining confidentiality, social work and psychology codes of conduct offer some clear guidelines, which provide that confidentiality can be broken if there is a likelihood that a person's life could be in jeopardy. In fact, social workers and psychologists are actually mandated by law to report a threat of intent to harm if there is an identifiable victim. Infidelity, as emotionally damaging as it is, falls short of this requirement.

The very first reading I ever did on my own, without the assistance of another student or teacher, involved a threat of violence and demonstrated to me the particular dilemmas psychic readers are faced with as opposed to traditional counselors who access information purely through discussion or observation on a physical level.

I had been reading all day outside at a psychic fair sponsored by my clairvoyant training school. I was sunburned and thirsty and preparing to make the two-hour drive back from Sacramento to my apartment in Oakland when a teacher I didn't know approached me and asked me to read a man who had been sitting for some time in the past-life booth. I told her I had never done a reading by myself and her response was, "You'll have to do it sometime, it might as well be now. Besides, reading past lives is easy, because they are not something that the readee can affirm or deny."

I greeted the man and sat several inches across from him on a warm metal folding chair. He did not speak other than to tell me his name. I began looking at his earliest life, most of which was spent on the floor of a filthy dungeon. He was having sex with a guy who was whipping him. His next life was not much better. In fact, life after life I saw images depicting the sadomasochistic torture he endured as a sex slave. I had only intended to look at a couple lives, but I was on a roll.

Next, I saw the man as a boy standing in the kitchen with his father, who was beating the crap out of him. He was wearing fairly modern clothing. And then I saw him as an adult once again, also wearing modern clothes, but this time there was a child with him. He was beckoning for the child to get off his bicycle as he rubbed his hands over his crotch. Next, I saw another child, even younger, crying, as the man unbuttoned the child's pants. And suddenly, I knew beyond all doubt that I was reading a child molester.

At that moment, I did the only logical thing I could think of. I panicked, silently. And then I grounded myself. And then I told the man everything I had seen. I left out not one single detail and he never said a single word. When I ran out of words, we sat there in silence and I prayed for God or anyone to help me know what to do. Seconds turned into minutes, and then finally I asked the man if he wanted me to look to see what actions he should take that would help him and his situation. He did not respond. I opened my eyes for the first time since I had sat down and repeated the question. He lifted his eyes for a brief moment and I saw gratitude in them. He nodded his head yes. I closed my eyes and I created a viewing receptacle in my imagination. I then connected it up to God with a cord of golden energy and again prayed feverishly for an answer to appear in the rose, an answer that would not only help this man, but that could stop him from hurting any more children.

The first image I saw was of a little boy talking to his mother and to a police officer. It looked as if there was already an investigation going on. I then saw an image of a church. The man was walking into the church and speaking to a pastor, who had a concerned look on his face. I sensed that this man in particular would feel more comfortable with a pastor or spiritual counselor than any other kind of therapist. Next, I saw an image of this man standing before a mirror, slicing the veins in his wrists. The look of self-loathing on his face is one I will never forget. I described this vision and told him that I knew he was in pain from his own childhood abuse and the abuse he was inflicting on these children, and that his own self-hatred was something he could not bear for much longer. He had to stop the cycle of abuse in this lifetime or it would merely continue into the next. I encouraged him to immediately go to his church, whatever church he was comfortable with, and ask for guidance. I opened my eyes one last time. He stood up and walked away. He never said a word.

I sat there for several minutes, not knowing what to do. Should I go to the police? I couldn't recall his name. Should I follow him? I went up to a teacher and told her what had happened. Her response made me furious: "It's not your responsibility." On an energetic level she was right. However, on a moral level, I feel to this day that she was dead wrong.

This example illustrates a dilemma that is unique to psychics. I knew this man had done harmful things and that it was very likely he was going to continue to hurt children. But what evidence did I have? I didn't even have a statement from the man other than a nod of his head. What would the police say if I told them about my reading? What could they do?

Now, years later, I feel that if this happened again I would go to the police. Because even if they laughed at me and threw me out of the station, I would have planted a seed. And when a child's parents called with the same description of the man I had told them about, someone in that office might remember and check into things a little more thoroughly.

Today, there are many more police officers who do welcome the assistance of psychics. These officers may joke about psychics to their buddies or even to your face, and they may never admit publicly that they took you seriously, but you can be sure at the end of the day, particularly after they have made some progress based on your clairvoyant information, or even solved their case, that they are going home to their wives or husbands and saying, "You know, I can't explain it, but the strangest thing happened today..."

These examples further illustrate that as clairvoyant readers/healers and counselors, it is not our business to judge our clients, because their biggest problem, which usually is at the core of their questionable behavior, is their own self-judgment and hatred. The only way a person can heal and transform is through acceptance. This acceptance does not mean that we condone their behavior and praise the readee for cheating on their spouse or molesting children. What it does mean is that, as readers, we maintain our neutrality at all times. We navigate our way through the reading so as to help the readee understand their motivations and feelings for their behavior, and we help them find alternative ways of behaving that in the end will help them find peace and happiness in their life. The information we provide does not come from our logical minds or our code of ethics, but from neutral clairvoyant information.

What sets psychics apart from other counselors is that we know we have access to information from a higher source and we know how to access it. This higher source could be God or a person's spirit guides, their higher self, or their inner voice. This higher source has the answers that we do not. We think it is wrong for a man to cheat on his wife, but our logical minds do not know that she actually cheated on him in several past lifetimes and now the karmic scales are being balanced. Our logical minds do not know that as spirits, before they were born, this couple agreed to marry and then divorce in order to learn lessons about love, commitment, and independence.

People grow, learn, and develop as human beings and as spirits by having life experiences that involve all sorts of breaches of commitments, contracts, laws, and commandments. As clairvoyant readers and healers, the more we can put aside our judgments and neutrally look at the spiritual blueprint or path of a readee in distress, the better equipped we will be to help our clients, and the more forgiveness we will have for our own transgressions. The more forgiving and neutral we are, the more clearly they will hear us. Neutrality and forgiveness bring light into the world, while judgment brings, and is, darkness. You must decide which path you are going to choose as a reader and a healer. That decision will form the basis of your ethical code.

As a clairvoyant reader and healer, you need to know that you are not alone in your readings or healings or at any moment of your life. There is a larger force, whether you call it God or the readee's higher self, that is ever present. Whenever you encounter anything that is too difficult, too challenging, or too overwhelming for you to deal with, it is okay, because no matter how great the illusion, it is not all up to you. Any problem that is impossible for you to solve is not your problem to solve. Otherwise it wouldn't feel impossible!

As a reader, you have the ability to communicate with God, the universe, or your higher self through visions, prayer, mantra, your mind, your voice, and your heart. You can ask for help and then use your clairvoyance to receive the answer. Sometimes the answer will come and other times it won't, no matter how hard you try to force it.

As a reader, you will not always be given an answer, because your readee or healee is supposed to discover the answer on their own, through their own actions. It is important for clairvoyant readers to remember that our job is to look for answers, but also to be okay when they don't appear. We are not God, we are merely aspects of God. No matter how good a clairvoyant we are, we are not all-knowing, we are not all-powerful. We are human beings doing the best we can. Out of the purest of pure intentions, many psychics and healers forget this fact. You will not.

Common Dilemmas That Psychics and Healers Face

Once you know that you are not expected to have all the answers, it is easier to deal with the plethora of questions or dilemmas that can arise during a clairvoyant reading or healing. Several of these are presented here, in a question-and-answer format.

1. What do I do if I see something upsetting about my readee's future?

One of the main reasons people avoid going to psychic readers is that they are afraid to hear potentially "bad" news about their future. Many people avoid developing their own psychic abilities because they are afraid they will see and know "bad" things about the future. Clairvoyant readers do occasionally pick up information about other people that has the potential to cause an emotional reaction. The following discussion offers some helpful insights into how to cope with this information.

The future often can be changed based on present behavior.

For example, you are told that you will be make a mistake on your job and be fired. This happens because spiritually your job is no longer serving you, and you even hate your job but are afraid to leave it willingly. As a result of this news, you take steps to start your own business and you voluntarily retire. You are given early-retirement pay that you would have lost had you been fired.

Knowledge of unpleasant future events can help clients make physical and psychological preparations.

For example, you are told that your mother may not have long to live. This makes you so sad, but it motivates you to throw her a party, videotape her life story, visit her more often, and tell her you love her.

"Bad" things are teachers, blessings in disguise, or part of one's spiritual path.

For example, you are told that your body is rebelling against your workaholic behavior and that you have the beginning of a serious illness (which is true). This illness requires you to take a leave of absence and depend more on friends and family to help you. At first this is very difficult, but eventually you discover that others really care and you are not alone. You work through issues you were avoiding but that were blocking you from living your dreams. You begin writing a book and eventually become a well-known author. You also have more time to spend with your children.

You would not be receiving the information if you or someone else didn't need to hear it. What you consider to be bad, your readee may think is good and vice versa.

I don't know how many times in my own readings I have been nervous about revealing what I considered to be upsetting information, but once I did share it with the readee, they blurted out, "I knew that" or "That's what I thought, but everyone has been telling me I'm crazy." The greatest thing you can do for a readee is validate what they already know and feel, even if it's something they consider unpleasant. When everyone else in their life is trying to tell them that they are wrong, or that they shouldn't think about it, or that it will be okay when it will not, this is far more frustrating than hearing the truth. Keep in mind the following points when considering whether or not to disclose information to a readee:

- Some people need to undergo certain life experiences; they will ignore your warnings and learn from them in retrospect.
- Some people are very programmable, and a reading could affect their feelings and perceptions.
- Your reading may have been written into the script of the readee's life to alter the course of events.
- Most clairvoyant information will concern the present unless you choose to focus on the future.

Potential clients need to understand that you are there to validate and explain their current feelings and experiences.

The purpose of looking at the future is to see what action needs to be taken or altered in the present to achieve desired goals.

Your client may not be emotionally ready to hear your information now, but may need to hear it on a spiritual or intellectual level.

A sad or angry emotional response from a readee does not mean that you made a mistake.

2. What should I do if I spontaneously receive information about someone I know, when this person has not asked for a reading?

I have learned from experience that when you spontaneously receive information about a person you know in your life who has not solicited a reading from you, that it's important to look at your own motivation for desiring to share this information and to question why you are the one receiving the information, and then to clairvoyantly look to see how it might affect the person. You may be receiving the information for any number of reasons, many of which may have more to do with you than with the person.

Many beginning clairvoyant students will be so excited about their clairvoyance and will not yet have learned when it is appropriate to share information and when it's invasive or simply annoying. They may be motivated to share information by their desire to show off or prove that they are capable psychics to their friends and to themselves. Some readers who feel uncomfortable in social situations will fall out of a conversation and into a reading space as a means to escape or to feel superior to other people. I have known some clairvoyant students who, at a party or social event, would abruptly turn a casual conversation into a reading in which they brought up issues regarding my personal life that were none of their business and that I didn't care to address at that time.

Occasionally you will spontaneously receive information about someone because they are searching for an answer in their life but are unable to hear it on their own. This information could come to you in the form of clairvoyant images when you are fully conscious, during a meditation, or when you are dreaming. In this case, sharing the information with the person could be very helpful.

Any time you are not sure whether to share unsolicited information, particularly information concerning death or illness, I suggest that you clairvoyantly look to see how it will affect the person, and ask God to show you, through your clairvoyance, how to proceed.

3. What should I do if I have agreed to give someone an hour reading, but I don't feel it's going well and want to terminate it (or they do)?

Occasionally you will find it necessary to end a reading prematurely. Your clairvoyant reading is a gift, not an obligation. You should never read anyone at any time if you have a feeling that it might harm you in any way or that the person is disrespecting you or the gift you are offering them. As a clairvoyant reader, your personal health, safety, and well-being have to be your top concerns.

Likewise, there will be times when your readee will decide to terminate the reading. Some people become very anxious at the start of a reading because they are experiencing the energy that they are about to release. They will immediately attribute their uncomfortable feelings to you, which will lead them to conclude that there is something wrong with you or that they are not meant to be receiving a reading from you. Some people will walk out of the reading because they don't like what you are telling them. I've had a few people leave a reading because they felt uncomfortable getting a reading from a person younger than themselves.

When a readee voices displeasure with a psychic or the reading and terminates the reading prematurely, it is so easy for the reader, particularly a newer one, to blame themselves, lose their certainty, and obsess over what went wrong. Many readers could do a hundred brilliant readings followed by one reading where the readee voiced displeasure, and they would question whether they should be doing readings at all. The best thing you could ever do for yourself if you have a difficult, unpleasant, or disastrous reading is to jump right into another reading as soon as possible to remind yourself that you are clairvoyant, you do have something to offer other people, and that reading is fun.

Unless I end a reading out of fear for my own safety or because the readee is being rude, I will usually refer the readee to another reader. I do this for a few reasons. First of all, I like to be helpful. I know certain people will feel more comfortable with other types of readers due to age, personality, or the reading methods and approaches. Providing referrals is also a good business practice because it demonstrates to the readee that you do care about them, that you don't feel any animosity toward them, and that you are a professional.

I believe that one of my duties as a clairvoyant reader and teacher is to do what I can to reverse the misperceptions and stereotypes that the general public has regarding psychic readers. The best way for me to do this is to serve as a positive example. It's for this reason that I usually don't charge a readee if they or I terminate the reading early. I don't want to give anyone the impression that this is another case where a psychic was taking financial advantage of a client. I also don't want to engage in an ongoing battle over money, whether on the physical or spiritual plane.

Other professional readers have far different approaches. Some readers even have a policy that unless a readee gives twenty-hour hours' notice of their desire to cancel a reading, they will be charged the full price of the reading, regardless of the circumstances. This policy helps them establish and maintain personal boundaries and their own sense of self-respect. However, I have seen some of these people get into huge battles with clients who felt they should not have to pay, and it seemed like the extra energy they had to exert to get their way or resolve the dispute was not worth the money they were fighting for. I think that whatever approach will bring the greatest amount of peace to one's life is the best one to take. Some people cannot be peaceful if they feel that even a minute of their time was undervalued or uncompensated for. Others are far more peaceful when they know that everyone has left the situation feeling good.

Sexual Ethics

The licensing boards and codes of ethics that govern healthcare professionals, whether they be doctors, dentists, psychologists, psychiatrists, or social workers, strictly forbid these professionals from becoming sexually involved with clients because of the psychological and emotional trauma that the client would suffer. When a psychic or healer violates a client's sexual boundaries by making advances or exchanging sexual energies during a session, it is just as damaging as if a gynecologist asked his patient on a date or expressed his attraction for her while she lay naked, vulnerable, and exposed on the examination table.

Many of your clients, whether they be men or women, are not used to being in the presence of someone like yourself who can see them as spirit and who can validate their feelings and life circumstances. Many clients are desperate for attention and kindness. They will feel gratitude and admiration toward you and this can easily turn into feelings of attraction. Many psychics and healers don't know how to handle this admiration any better than young rock stars. They begin to see their clients as groupies. Others try so hard to be the perfect healer that they repress any feelings that they think a "spiritually advanced" person should not have, and as a result become disconnected with their sexual energy. This sexual energy then takes on a will and a life of its own.

As a clairvoyant reader or healer, it is imperative that you monitor and control your own sexual desires, behavior, and energy to make sure they are not interfering with the reading or the readee. If you are unable to do this, don't beat yourself up about it, just seriously consider avoiding reading and healing anyone whom you are sexually attracted to, which may mean all people of the opposite or same sex, depending on your sexual orientation.

When performing a reading and especially a healing, you need to be aware of what you are doing with your energy, because during this time, the walls between the physical and the spiritual will become permeable and transparent. Your client will feel your sexual energy as it penetrates her aura, she will hear your lascivious thoughts as if you were whispering them in her ear (or shouting them into a microphone), and if she is particularly perceptive, she may even see the images of your fantasies as clearly as if you had just thrust a pornographic photograph in front of her eyes. Some clients will consciously know when you are leaking sexual energy and will feel violated or slimed, while others may confuse your energy for their own. Those that do have an awareness of the situation are placed in a precarious position—they know they are being sexually slimed and energetically assaulted by the very person they are relying upon for healing and guidance. Because all of this is occurring on an energetic level, the client may not feel justified in confronting you and will likely feel, for the rest of the session, uncomfortable, trapped, and angry at themselves for remaining in this situation.

Those clients who confuse your energy for their own may actually end up forming a crush on you or becoming obsessed with you. They may even make an advance toward you and later (immediately following the session or months later) realize their mistake, at which point they will become overwhelmed with feelings of shame, remorse, and even self-hatred for letting themselves be manipulated by someone else's thoughts and feelings that really had nothing to do with them.

Even if your readee makes advances toward you, it is your responsibility as the psychic and healer to set and enforce boundaries and to help the person understand the reasons for their feelings. The readee is not acting on their own accord if it is your energy in their body that is driving them to act out sexually. Furthermore, you are the expert, the professional, the parent, so to speak. If a patient blatantly comes on to her psychiatrist and he responds by having sex with her, he could lose his license and face a serious lawsuit, because as a professional it is his responsibility to conduct himself in a way that is in the best interest of his patient, even when she is not acting in her own best interest.

As a psychic/healer, there is no governing board to punish you nor any license to take away, but there is your own conscience and the karmic laws of the universe that you cannot evade. If you desire a date with someone, then ask them out on a date. Don't offer to give them a reading or healing as a way to get closer to them or get to know them. This is the coward's way of handling romance.

If you find yourself feeling sexually aroused during a reading or healing, put up a separation object and ground yourself. Then check to see if your sexual energy is running solely through your own body or if it is also running through your readee's body. Sometimes you may be feeling their sexual energy, and if that is the case, then use your clairvoyant healing abilities to cut any cords that might be joining the two of you together, and watch as the readee's sexual energy returns to them.

If you feel extremely attracted to a client and believe that this is someone with whom you are destined to have a significant relationship, then I recommend the following:

1. Terminate a reading, and especially a healing, if you realize that you cannot control your sexual energy or realize that it's getting in the way of your neutrality. You have lost your neutrality if you become jealous when your client asks about a relationship with someone else, or if you are seeking information about her to determine whether

she is available or will be a viable partner, or if you tell her she doesn't have to pay for the reading because she is so attractive.

2. Do not express your feelings of attraction to your readee during the reading or immediately after the reading or healing.

3. If you terminate a reading before the agreed-upon time has ended due to your feelings of arousal or attraction, refund the readee's money. Explain that you are working out some personal issues and are not mentally focused enough to continue the reading.

4. Give yourself time away from the readee to explore your feelings. Once out of the readee's presence, you may feel totally different. If you still desire contact with the readee, then call her, tell her you are calling her as a potential suitor rather than as a reader or healer, and ask her out on a date. Regardless of her answer, make the determination that you will not see her on a professional level again.

5. If you are afraid to be so direct, get over it or give up. Your client should not have to be manipulated or misled just because you don't have the guts to be direct with her.

Unsolicited Astral Advances Are a Form of Rape

There are many healers, psychics, and spiritual teachers who use their spiritual knowledge and abilities to interact sexually with clients (or anyone they are attracted to, including students, teachers, friends, etc.) on the astral plane. They will consciously send their astral body over to her (or his) home, enter her bedroom, and actually have sexual intercourse with the client or student without her consent. Many of these astral travelers do not feel they are doing anything wrong because their physical bodies are not involved. However, I have read far too many people and counseled far too many friends who suffered tremendously from these unwelcome, unsolicited visitations, which are nothing less than rape. Having sex with a client on the astral plane is no different from physically having sex with a client. If you have sex with anyone, energetically or physically, without their consent, then you are violating and molesting that person and you have no right to call yourself a healer.

CHAPTER 22

The Psychic Minority

It isn't easy being psychic in a society filled with people who aren't even conscious of their own psychic/spiritual abilities. This lack of consciousness causes many of these well-meaning people to misunderstand, judge, criticize, fear, stereotype, and persecute practicing psychics as well as laypeople who have a casual interest in metaphysics. Many psychics and healers in the Western world struggle with feelings of loneliness, isolation, and alienation until they learn how to successfully coexist among a majority of people who experience their lives from a denser state of consciousness.

In this chapter, I offer some suggestions that will help you cope with the challenges of being awake in a slumbering world. It's important to understand that there are both people who will accept and understand you, and those who can't. Get out of judgment with those who can't, and seek those who can.

In the same way that there are entities that you cannot see because they vibrate at a different frequency and on a different plane or dimension of existence, there are people out there who cannot see or hear you. They may see your physical body, but beyond that they are only experiencing their own projections when they look into your eyes. Some of these people literally will not be able to hear you when you speak of clairvoyance; others will only hear jumbled words that their conscious minds won't allow them to process, no matter how intelligent they are. You can tell this is happening when the only response you get is a blank stare and a quick, almost frantic change of subject.

The best way to deal with people who can't understand you is to get out of resistance to them; that is, don't try to change them or control what they think about you. If you want them to treat you with respect, then do the same thing for them: let them be where they are. Treat them with the same compassion you would have for a child whose brain doesn't have the synapses and pathways to understand certain things. Don't try to make them see you, understand you, or like you. Don't prove yourself to them. It's like trying to prove yourself to a scared bunny rabbit who leaps away from you when you are offering a fresh carrot. If they are meant to break through the veils of consciousness from their plane of awareness to yours, it will happen in their own time.

Forgive Them, for They Know Not What They Do

Of course it will hurt if the people whom you have been closest to and dependent on all your life, such as your parents or siblings, don't seem to care about your spiritual interests or appreciate what you are trying to do with your life. It will be frustrating when a neighbor says you are doing the devil's work by reading and healing people, or when a coworker warns you that you may lose your job if you ever again mention seeing a spirit in the bathroom, or when your boss forbids you to do readings during your lunch hour on company premises. Just know that these people are speaking as much out of concern for you as they are out of ignorance and fear.

Some people are very afraid of clairvoyance because practice of their own abilities in other lifetimes resulted in violent persecution and death. When you speak of your clairvoyant abilities, experiences, or training, their MEI death pictures become stimulated (see chapter 4) and they literally feel like they might die unless they can get you to shut up!

Other people are not meant to understand clairvoyance because their spirits are striving to gain other experiences in this lifetime, and knowledge of this ability could steer them on a whole different path. In these cases, forcing your clairvoyant knowledge or spiritual convictions on these people would be interfering with their spiritual destiny. What is so right for you is not right for everybody.

There are a small number of mentally unstable people who would topple into madness if their psychic centers opened any further. Then there are those individuals who have misused their abilities and authority in past incarnations and are therefore banned by certain guardian spirits and councils from having any awareness of these abilities. I have a theory that most hardcore skeptics fall into this category. The karmic sentence they must live out to the end of their days is having tremendously strong psychic abilities but being completely cut off from their awareness of them. This causes an inexplicable anger and frustration that fuels their passion to debunk other psychics.

Teaching Through Example

I have discovered through my own experiences and those of many of my clairvoyant or spiritually oriented friends that the most effective and least painful way to impact other people's lives is through living your life honestly, with grace. As you follow your heart and your dreams, you will create an exhilarating life filled with peace and joy. Others will want to know your secret and will begin to question why they are living their lives the way mainstream society told them to, but they are not nearly as fulfilled as you are.

Teaching through example means that you don't beat people over the head with your convictions, but also that you don't hide in the proverbial closet. Many psychics, even practicing professionals, hide their abilities from their closest relatives in order to avoid judgments or uncomfortable confrontations. They live a double life and give away their power to people who don't know what to do with it. Most of these psychics are very stuck in their lives and tend to get trapped in a pattern of creating jobs and romantic relationships in which they feel victimized and disrespected, primarily because they continue to put other people's ideas and feelings ahead of their own.

One of my favorite quotations comes from A Course in Miracles and was made famous in a speech given by Nelson Mandela. Marianne Williamson paraphrased it in her enlightening book A Return to Love (pp. 190-191):

Who am I to be brilliant, gorgeous, talented, fabulous? Actually, who are you not to be? You are a child of God. Your playing small doesn't serve the world. There is nothing enlightened about shrinking so that other people won't feel insecure around you. We are all meant to shine, as children do. We were born to make manifest the glory of God that is within us and as we let our own light shine, we unconsciously give other people permission to do the same. As we are liberated from our own fear, our presence automatically liberates others.

Seek Your Spiritual Family, Forgive Your Birth Family

Understand that your family of origin may not be your spiritual family. Be grateful to your birth parents for bringing you into the world and nurturing you to the best of their abilities, and for all the lessons they have taught you. But if you don't feel that they understand or accept you, or see you in the way you long to be seen, then you would do well to seek out your true spiritual family.

Your spiritual family is a group of souls that are on the same level of consciousness as you. They usually originate from the same soul grouping as your own. You will recognize members of this family because they will automatically understand, accept, and honor you. Understanding the difference between your birth family and soul family helps you lower your expectations of your birth family and motivates you to seek out individuals who have a greater potential to love you for who you really are.

Seek and Ye Shall Find; Ask and Ye Shall Receive

Growing up in the suburbs of Chicago, I knew no one, except for me and my twin sister, who exhibited psychic abilities or had an interest in psychic phenomena. Decades later, when I began my clairvoyant training in Berkeley, California, for the first time in my life I was surrounded by hundreds of people who were exploring their own spiritual abilities. What was even more mind-boggling than the number of psychics I encountered was the fact that so many of these people existed for so long without my knowledge, despite the hundreds of metaphysically oriented books I had read since I was a child.

After a couple years, I realized it was time for me to leave California, which not only meant leaving my clairvoyant training schools and built-in support systems of classmates, teachers, and staff, it also meant abandoning all of my clairvoyant friends and acquaintances who lived within those particular communities. Since I did not yet know that there are spiritual and metaphysically oriented communities all over the world, I was forced to contemplate the possibility that I would never find another place where I belonged. The idea of once again being a lone psychic in the world was not a comforting one.

Then one of my clairvoyant friends gave me a reading and reminded me that I had the ability to create the kinds of people I wanted to be with, simply through having faith and determination that I would find them, and through visualizing my positive interactions with future friends. This reading helped me decide that my departure from this community would serve as a signal to the universe that I did in fact believe in my own ability to create that which would ultimately serve my soul.

From that point forward, wherever I have lived, I have found myself surrounded by other metaphysically minded folks within a matter of weeks if not days. For about five years, I lived in Sedona, Arizona, which has the largest population of psychics and healers of any city in the United States. During my time there, I knew so many people, including my hairstylist, my son's babysitter, my car repairman, many of my friends, and even my cleaning lady, who were not only believers or practitioners of psychic phenomena, but exhibited a depth of understanding, faith, and wisdom that one would expect only a great sage or yogi to possess.

If you wish to find people who will understand and respect you (this includes romantic partners as well!), then you must make the commitment to yourself to find and associate only with people who are on your level of consciousness (with the exception of a few family members you can't bear to let go of). You must have faith that you are not alone even before you have any hardcore evidence that this is true. As you meet more and more like-minded people and develop friendships that are truly fulfilling and joyful, you will know that you are on the right path.

While you may be in the minority in terms of the entire country, know that there are many, many people like you all over the world and in almost every major city of the United States. Sedona, Arizona and Berkeley, California are only two of the many cities with communities where psychics, healers, massage therapists, acupuncturists, channelers, yogis, etc., are the norm. Other places that are populated by psychics include Cassadaga, Florida; Salem, Massachusetts; Marin and Santa Cruz Counties, California; and Taos, New Mexico.

In just about every metropolitan area across the United States, there are communities of psychics and healers. You will only meet people of a higher consciousness when you are near or at that level yourself, whether these people are located on the other side of the globe or in the house next door.

Within most cities, there are certain locations, businesses, and activities where you are more likely to meet fellow psychics and healers. Obviously, metaphysical bookstores attract people who are metaphysically oriented. Other popular places to meet like-minded people are at yoga and meditation centers/schools and massage and acupuncture schools.

Most of these metaphysically oriented shops and centers offer classes or information about workshops where you will meet other psychics, healers, astrologers, or people who at the very least are interested in and accepting of what you do. Most of these places have public bulletin boards and offer free metaphysically oriented magazines or newspapers that list local practitioners and events.

CHAPTER 23

The Business of Spirituality

To Charge or Not to Charge

Early on in your clairvoyant training, the issue of compensation will arise. This is because most of the people you work with will recognize that you are providing a valuable service that requires you to devote your personal time and energy that could easily be spent elsewhere. Many of your clients will feel an instinctive need to balance the exchange by giving something back to you.

Ironically, you may be so excited to practice your new skills on real subjects that you may feel that you should be the one paying them! Many clairvoyant students and graduates do actually pay a fee to their schools in order to be given the opportunity to read clients in a supervised and grounded setting.

Hopefully you will always feel blessed to have the opportunity to read people, but most likely, after having gained some experience and confidence and realizing how much work some readings can be, you will feel the need to receive some form of compensation for your efforts. Obviously, psychics and healers have to eat. In societies outside the United States, such as in India or Southeast Asia, healers may not be paid with money for their services, but instead are given food and shelter and are cared for by their devotees who could number from a few to a few thousand. In the United States and Europe, the primary form of compensation is money. Many clairvoyant students and practitioners also exchange services, such as doing a reading in exchange for receiving a reading, healing, or massage.

There are pros and cons to charging for your readings and healings and these can change according to your development in these areas. As a beginning student, charging for your readings and healings can have a detrimental effect on your learning process. Money creates expectations for both the reader and the readee. When you are reading merely for the sake of learning, you will feel greater freedom to explore and experiment with your clairvoyance. You will also be more likely to give yourself greater permission during a reading to use your psychic tools and to release your own matching pictures.

When payment is involved, you may fall into the trap of feeling like you need to give your reader their money's worth, which translates into delivering the correct answers in an efficient manner. If you feel that you are reading too slowly (in that your images are taking a while to display themselves, which is common when you are first learning to read) or giving the readee unpleasant information, you may fear that the readee is going to feel cheated, disappointed, or angry. This will create performance anxiety, which will not only make it more difficult to access clairvoyant images, but will damage your ability to read in a neutral and honest manner, and could cause a tragic decline in your enjoyment of and enthusiasm for clairvoyant reading and healing.

Whether you have been reading for two hours or two decades, if you do decide to start accepting money for your readings, the above issues will arise. However, as a beginning clairvoyant student, you are more vulnerable to losing sight of what is important in a reading because you have much less certainty and confidence in yourself as a reader. With every image or slice of information that comes to you, your certainty will increase until one day you will know that you can trust the validity of your clairvoyance more than you can trust any other part of yourself or anyone else. When you get to this point, you will be able to recognize more easily the feelings of pressure and responsibility that come with money and will be better able to cope with them. The longer you have been doing readings and utilizing your psychic tools, the better you will understand how important it is to continue using your readings as a self-healing process and to always honor yourself as much as the readee, no matter who they are, how serious their issues are, or how much they are paying you.

Despite the pitfalls, there are definitely some good reasons to charge for readings, even as a newer clairvoyant reader. The most significant reason has to do with the readee's level of commitment to the reading. People who are willing to pay for readings are often more invested in the reading process and their own personal growth. Those who will only come for a reading if it is free or very cheap tend to take the reading less seriously and may be there only to play "test the psychic" or as a curious observer. I am not saying that these motivations are bad; in fact, some people's lives are transformed when they experience what a psychic can do because they become more fully aware of their own potential. However, clairvoyant readers invest so much of their time and energy in their readings that to spend time with a client who is not taking the reading seriously can be quite frustrating and even degrading.

Imagine if you spent hours painting a beautiful portrait for someone in which you painstakingly recreated every detail of their face and emotional expression. Imagine then that the person glanced at it for less than a moment and then threw it in the trash can. That is how it feels to read someone who is not respectful of you and your clairvoyant ability. Except the latter is worse because when you are reading someone, you can usually sense how they are receiving your words as you say them. If they are feeling distrust or disappointment throughout the reading, you'll feel this even if they don't say a word (which is kind of ironic—they're sitting there thinking "is she really psychic?" and meanwhile you're sitting there thinking "this person doesn't believe I'm really psychic, I'd better do a really good job." However, in order to do a really good job, they have to participate by allowing you access to all parts of themselves and showing up. If they are hiding themselves out of fear or mistrust, you are going to be blocked. While this doesn't mean you can't wedge your way in or start chiseling away their resistance, all of this can become quite a chore to say the least, as your ability to read someone else is as much a result of their willingness to be read. Charging money for readings, even a small fee such as twenty dollars, will help weed out readees who are just curious onlookers or skeptics from those who are really open to communication.

The more money you charge, the more you will attract people who seriously want your help. However, those who "seriously" want your help tend to be more "serious." They may have more urgent and difficult issues that are not as fun to look at and require more of your energy. It seems to be a basic spiritual law that you will attract what you can handle. As your certainty and neutrality increase, you will be presented with more challenging readings for which you will receive greater compensation. If you go for the big money before you really can handle it, you will only create problems for yourself in the long run. On the other hand, if you fail to honor your abilities and experience as you progress on your clairvoyant path by refusing compensation, you may become exhausted, frustrated, and unbalanced. Receiving money for readings is a way to honor your self-worth, to celebrate your abilities, and to validate the progress you've made through discipline and courageousness.

Practically speaking, charging for your readings often makes it possible for you to devote more time and energy to your readings/healings and less time to jobs that have been paying the bills but are not as fulfilling or fun.

The Incremental/Experimental Pricing Approach

I suggest that you begin your clairvoyant training by practicing on people who seem to be the most supportive and nonjudgmental. Let them know you are wishing to gain practice, and ask them not to have high expectations of you (then they will be pleasantly surprised at how much they get out of the reading). I suggest accepting tips during your first several readings if they are offered to you rather than charging a set price. Let yourself enjoy the freedom of being a clairvoyant student for as long as possible. Once you begin to feel the urge to charge, adopt an experimental approach. Start off with a small fee and notice how this feels. You may feel very satisfied with this amount or you may feel undercompensated, at which time you could raise your rate and again notice how it feels to receive this amount of money. When you increase your rate, notice whether you attract more or less clients, and pay attention to any changes in your level of enthusiasm. These will be your barometers to tell you whether your rate is appropriate for where you are in your life. Some psychics charge hundreds of dollars and have so many clients that they must turn them away, so if you raise your rate and find that suddenly you are not getting any clients at all, realize that this state of affairs has more to do with your own issues regarding money, your clairvoyant certainty, and/or your self-esteem than with the rate itself.

If you live in an area where there are several other psychics, it will be helpful to inquire how much these readers charge. Some people think that if they charge less than the going rate, they will get more clients. However, this is often not the case because potential clients may sense that the person charging less is not as talented or qualified.

My prices also reflect how busy I am, how much energy I have to devote to my readings versus other projects and people in my life, the location where I am living and practicing, my relationship to the readee, our financial situations, etc. Because clairvoyant reading is such a personal and intimate experience, you need to allow room to consider personal factors of both the reader and the readee. I offer a sliding fee scale for people who can't afford a reading and often refer clients to my graduate students who charge less. I also operate several practice groups where the students do readings for free. This brings business to other budding professionals, creates practice opportunities for my students and facilitators in training, and frees me up from feeling like I have to always be available to everyone at any time under any circumstances.

Exchanging Services

In general, exchanging clairvoyant readings is an excellent way for beginning clairvoyant students to gain practice and experience in a supportive environment and at the same time to feel as if they are receiving some form of compensation for their readings. There is value in exchanging readings with students or readers who have or are studying similar methods taught in this book or through clairvoyant training schools, as well as with psychics, channelers, and spiritual counselors who employ different methods or are versed in other traditions of psychic development. Psychics and healers are usually very open and receptive and therefore easier to read than the general population. They tend to be compassionate and caring people who will be supportive of your efforts and your learning process. You will share many matching MEI pictures, which will make the readings more intense but will provide you with greater opportunities to work through these pictures and to gain a deeper level of understanding about your own and other people's psychic abilities. Through exchanging readings with other psychics, you will learn new reading techniques and approaches. When reading psychics who are not familiar with the information in this book, you will have a chance to observe the detrimental effects of reading a person who is not as aware of how to maintain neutrality or energetic boundaries.

When doing exchanges, you will want to discuss expectations beforehand. Decide who will be the first to receive a reading, and whether the exchange will happen immediately following the first reading or at a later date and time. Unless the readings are kept to a short time limit of thirty minutes or less, I recommend that the readings or healings be scheduled for two different days in order to allow the person receiving the reading to fully relax and have time to process the information and energy redistribution that may be occurring within their body and energy field. The tone of the first reading usually sets the tone for the second reading, in terms of time and effort expended.

There are some factors to be aware of when doing exchanges with other psychics or healers. Beginning clairvoyant students are often naive in that they think that anyone with similar interests in metaphysics can be trusted. Unfortunately this is not always the case. Occasionally you may encounter another psychic or healer who is in competition with you or your abilities or your method of practice. Competition is connected to feelings of insecurity and resentment about not being where a person thinks they should be or wants to be in their life.

If you agree to an exchange and then become aware that you may be exposing yourself to unfriendly energies, do whatever is necessary to avoid doing the exchange or terminate it immediately, particularly where healing is involved. Your health and well-being are far more important than being polite or having someone like you. I have made the mistake of allowing people to heal me who, after getting to know them better, I would not even allow through my front door! Whether the healer is an energetic healer, a chiropractor, an acupuncturist, or an allopathic doctor or surgeon, it's important that you consider what kind of person they are. For that matter, do you even like them?

It amazes me that we let doctors who are complete strangers examine the most private parts of our bodies, and even cut open and remove parts of our bodies that will determine whether we live and die, but we don't even question for a moment who this person is, or whether we like them or feel that they will respect us. We have been socialized to respect the knowledge of mainstream medical professionals and to not ask these questions. We need to be careful not to make the same mistake with alternative healers.

I always opt for the honest approach to communication. If you feel uncomfortable letting someone read or touch you, or vice versa, let them know this. It will be harder for them to argue with your true feelings than with your excuses, particularly if they are psychic! If they take offense, this is not your responsibility.

If hardcore honesty is not your style, or you have to deal with this psychic/healer on a regular basis, or you fear they may seek revenge in the form of black magic or voodoo, then politely tell them you have a general rule of not receiving readings and/or healings from anyone other than your teacher; or you don't allow people of the opposite sex to heal you; or you just realized that you are at a point in your life where it's not appropriate for you to do exchanges with other readers or healers so you are changing your mind. If you have already received a reading or healing from the person but don't wish to reciprocate as agreed, you can offer them financial compensation in return in order to make a clean energetic and karmic separation.

On the other hand, if you have carried out your part of the exchange but they seem to be backing out, then gracefully let them go. When I worked at one of the New Age centers in Sedona, some of the psychics and healers there were intimidated by my level of training and certainty. They sought readings from me, but then came up with excuse after excuse to not read me. At first this felt unfair, but then I realized that they were really doing me a favor. As with any agreement, if someone is not living up to their end of the bargain, this may be because they are not capable of it, or because ultimately it would not serve either of you. If someone doesn't want to complete an exchange, allow them to gracefully bow out of it; otherwise you may become chained to them in a karmic battle for the rest of infinity!

Regardless of the lightness or darkness of the person you are reading or healing, you will always want to make sure you use your tools, keep your energy running, and clear the readee's energy from your energy field, and vice versa, at the completion of the exchange.

Embarking on Your Professional Career of Psychic Reading

Once you have decided that you are going professional (i.e., ready to charge for your services), you will want to decide whether to go into business for yourself, or work for someone else, or do a combination of both. You will also want to consider whether you wish to do in person readings, phone/internet readings, or a combination.

Determining the Proper Situation/Location for In-Person Readings

Once you have decided to take the plunge, you will need to find an appropriate location in which to receive clients. Many psychics read out of their homes, others rent office space, and still others opt to read out of metaphysical centers or bookstores. Some psychics make house calls or, in heavy tourist areas, read visiting clients in their hotel rooms. Other options for reading are through psychic hotlines, at psychic fairs, or at parties.

If you desire to work independently, reading out of your home may be appropriate if you have a particular room or area that you can devote to your readings (an office with a separate entryway from the rest of the house is ideal) and if your home life is conducive to receiving strangers without attracting a lot of notice. The advantages of reading out of your home are that you have no commute and you hopefully are comfortable there. The disadvantages include safety concerns, the time it may take to clean your place prior to the client's arrival, the effect your work will have on family members and their level of interference with the reading, and the extra energy you will have to deal with following a reading.

During a reading, both you and your client release a lot of energy. No matter where you are, you will want to ground the room and do your best to clear out the energy, but you may not always be thorough. Long after the client has physically departed the location, their emotional energy and the energy of all their spirits guides and their family members will continue to return whenever they think about you or the reading. When this energy is deposited in your home, which is your personal sanctuary, it can create problems for you and your family that will range from increasing emotional tension, to disrupting relationships, to disturbing sleep and meditation patterns. Locations away from home may also become contaminated with foreign energies, but since you will not have to spend as much personal time there, you will not be as adversely affected.

Having a Phone/Internet Based Business

Working for yourself has a lot of perks. It's easy and requires very little start-up money if you are simply offering readings via telephone or Skype.

Those of you who are re-reading this 2nd edition of You Are Psychic may notice that I've rewritten this entire chapter. That's because so much has changed in the past decade that I and so many other clairvoyant readers and mediums and healers have made the switch from only doing readings in-person to primarily offering them over the phone or via Skype or conference call. The reason for this is:

1. Readings conducted over the phone can be just as effective, if not more so, than in-person readings as there are fewer visual and emotional distractions. Clairvoyant healings can be just as effective as well, although other types of healings (hands-on healings) are of course not possible.

2. Issues related to expenses and location decrease. You may still need to find a quiet place to do your sessions where your family and roommates won't disturb you, but for many this is a lot easier than finding a separate physical space that's affordable and feels safe. (Earlier in my career, I was doing readings out of my car—definitely not something I advocate as a long-term plan but, as a short-term solution or back-up when you can't control what's going on in your home, it can work. You will want to make sure that you find an adequate location to park, a place where you won't bake or freeze and where you won't be interrupted, and one in which you'll feel safe enough to close your eyes).

3. It is safer than reading over the phone, both on a physical level and energetic level.

4. By offering phone readings, you eliminate the time and costs involved with traveling for you and your client. It also eliminates any prep time you need for a physical location. In other words, there is nothing like being able to roll out of bed, grab a cup of coffee, and help a lot of people while earning an income and doing what you love, all while

wearing your pjs. Your client saves the driving time (and gas money), and both of you can relax and integrate the experience rather than having to get in your cars and have a stressful drive home through traffic. Also, many times you and your client will be in a somewhat altered state for a while following the reading. Altered states are not conducive to driving.

Technology for Connecting With Clients

For any phone-based business, psychic or otherwise, the soundness of your communication devices is of utmost importance. I recommend having at least two different phone systems, with one serving as a back-up. Make sure you can talk hands-free and that the sound is of the highest quality on both phones. Also, you will want to look into having an unlimited long-distance calling plan so the amount of time you spend on the phone won't be an issue. I pay about $30 a month for a landline with unlimited calling within the U.S. and Canada.

It's very important to offer your clients multiple ways to be able to connect with you. Also, make sure you have the latest version of Skype and a Skype account, which is free, so that international clients can speak with you via this system without any charge to either of you. All of this will take a bit of time and research and require some additional costs, but this technology is the backbone of your business.

It's also very important to check the sound quality at the start of the call and let your client know that if they can't hear you for any reason they should interrupt you immediately. Why? Well I can't tell you how many clients I had in the first couple years I was in business for myself that sat through an entire reading only to admit they didn't hear half of it because they didn't want to be rude or bring me out of trance. I was like, "Really? It's a phone reading. If you can't hear me, then why did we even bother to do this in the first place?!" Then I realized it was my responsibility as the professional to set the rules with my clients and not just expect they will speak up. It's my responsibility to put them at ease and to let them know what is expected of them, what they can expect in our reading, and how they need to behave.

Of course, there are many very talkative and animated clients that need to be told it is preferable if they don't speak continuously or comment on every word, which can make it almost impossible to stay focused. This is why these days I tend to tell my client at the start of a reading, "If you can't hear me, feel free to interrupt at any time. If we get disconnected, please call back right away. Otherwise, you can pretty much just sit back and listen without feeling like you have to respond. At the end of the reading, any feedback you'd like to give will be appreciated but is not mandatory."

Creating Your Own Website

I can not overemphasize the importance of having a website for your business. Having a website is not just a marketing tool, it's an integral part of any business.

Whether you have your own office or storefront, or are doing readings over the phone or via email, you will absolutely need and want to have a website to promote yourself and help clients learn about you. Some business owners who are blessed with heavy foot traffic outside their shop or who live in smaller, rural towns believe a website is unnecessary (or believe it's too much of a hassle to develop one). What they don't realize is that the very same customers who may walk or drive by every single day, even several times a day, may not be inclined to just pop in the door until they research it online, read reviews and fully understand what you are offering. Many potential clients want assurances before they walk in the door that they are going to have a positive experience. They will want to check you out, in private, at their leisure, before you check them out. This is the reality of business, at least business in the United States today.

Your website will help you manifest on a creative level.

This is something that I realized early on. I found that when I spent a few hours working on my website, writing content or designing it with the addition of photos and playing with colors, I'd suddenly get several calls for readings. This was true even if the website or changes were not yet published. I also became aware that I would move into a relaxed state that sometimes bordered on euphoria (once I got over the initial learning curve that comes every time you embark on learning a new program). Not only was this highly creative process putting me into an elevated state which is great for business, it's like sending out radio waves telepathically that say, "Hey! I'm here, loving what I'm doing and offering, and so will you!"

This is one of the many reasons I feel it is so beneficial to design, build and continue to maintain a website yourself. The same is true of designing newsletters with e-newsletter builder programs (which are typically template-based and easy to use) or designing other types of promotional materials like flyers or business cards. It is the act of creating these functional promotional works of art that helps people find you on an energetic or spiritual level, and that's more important than whether or not everything on your site is absolutely perfect. As far as I'm concerned, our websites and promotional materials are always works in progress.

As you create your own website, or at least actively participate in its creation, this will help you define for yourself who you are and what you do, what to call yourself, and how to word all of the above.

Your website will inform potential clients.

Your website is how clients will learn who you are, what your background is, what your policies and procedures are, what your beliefs and values are, how much you charge, how you structure your readings, etc. It will often be the single thing that helps determine whether or not they want to work with you.

Your website will educate.

Your website can educate clients not only about the way you operate but about related subject matters. Whether you post static information about metaphysical topics that become permanent features on your site, or you frequently swap out shorter blog posts, you will be offering a benefit to anyone who comes across your site while helping them to view you as the expert you are. Oftentimes, it is within the educational portion of your website where you can insert key search terms that will help those surfing the Internet find your site.

Your website will serve as a payment portal.

Accepting payments in person is very easy these days as there are a number of credit/debit card processing companies such as Square and PayPal that provide a tiny device that you can insert into most smartphones. These do not require you to have good credit, only a checking account that is directly linked to the processing system so funds can be automatically deposited in your own bank account in real time. These systems enable you to email your client automatically with a receipt, and generate reports for record keeping.

Accepting payments online is just as simple. This encourages clients to pay ahead of time, which not only grounds their appointment but drastically decreases the likelihood of no-shows. While there are ever expanding options, PayPal currently is one of the easiest options to navigate. PayPal doesn't require good credit or any credit, and they don't care what type of business you have. All you need is a checking or savings account with a bank to link up to the account, and an email address. PayPal offers billing options so even if you don't have a website you can send someone a detailed invoice and track payments/refunds and generate reports.

While companies like this do take out a fee or percentage, based on the amount paid, I can guarantee you that any fee taken is well worth the additional funds you will receive when you enable customers to have an easy and effortless payment/registration process. PayPal allows them to pay right at the moment they are inspired to do so. I've known a few people who seriously limited their own income-earning potential simply because they were hell-bent on avoiding fees. Not only did they lose business, they seriously inconvenienced their clients. PayPal also offers a debit card option, which means when someone pays you the funds will be instantly available on your card, as opposed to having to wait 3 to 5 business days before being transferred to your bank account (as is the case with other credit card processing companies, some which may take out fewer fees).

Most website hosting companies and social media sites, even the most basic, allow for PayPal links to be easily inserted into the pages of your site without the need for understanding coding or programming. Therefore, even if you don't have an online store or shopping cart beyond a very basic single webpage, you can still have clients send payments to you online, even prior to their scheduling an appointment.

Your website will allow people to sign up for your newsletters to learn about future offerings.

Most template-based website companies offer contact and newsletter signup forms that will help you capture the names and emails of those who have visited your site, so that you can stay in touch with them. Since they are browsing your site, these are the people most likely to want to make use of your services in the future.

For those of us who are not the most organized people in the world, keeping track of clients and contacts can be a daunting task, but no more! Fortunately today, if you have your own website, there are plenty of apps that can be inserted into a widget, like a contact or e-newsletter sign up form, that allows you to collect, save and alphabetize each person's name who contacts you through your website.

Newsletter builder services enable you to easily take this list and insert it into a newsletter program so you can send out emails, newsletters or special offers and coupons to an entire list of potential clients with the click of a button. This is a great way to drum up more business or to say thank you to clients.

Your website will help you to protect yourself.

Clearly stating your policies regarding payments, refunds and expectations on your website is the ethical and professionally sound way of doing business, as well as the best way to avoid all issues. There is no reason to be vague about anything, as far as I'm concerned. While that may be a sales tactic in other fields, when it comes to operating a spiritual business, transparency is key.

If you feel you can only help someone with more than one session, as is the case with some healing or hypnotherapy work, then state that on your website. I don't see why that would be the case with clairvoyant readings, as a single reading is usually enough to give the person a lot to work on for quite a while. In fact, I discourage people from coming for readings within too short a period of time unless they have so many questions and issues that they just couldn't all be addressed during the first session. (I usually tell my clients to wait about 3 months before booking another session with me).

Do not do an entire session with a client, and then spring it on them that the only way they will be OK is if they sign up for three more sessions…with you! Not cool. If you feel clients will benefit from multiple sessions, then clearly state that on your website. If you believe that clients are going to want more than a 15-minute reading, then don't even offer 15-minute readings.

I'm not an attorney, but as far as legal protection goes, I will recommend this: Please do not state (as some attorneys would recommend) that your readings are only for entertainment purposes. This just does such a disservice to the field. My readings are not simply for entertainment, although they may be enjoyable and occasionally feel entertaining if I'm in a humorous mood. I'm not teaching the techniques in this book simply for entertainment purposes, and given that you may be seeing into the deepest reaches of someone's soul, there is no way you are being honest if you say that what you are doing is purely for entertainment. Maybe if you are simply describing what people have in envelopes, then that would be an entertaining use of your psychic abilities. I've been doing this lately, and even that I am not doing for entertainment purposes, but rather to increase my abilities and learn about what works and what doesn't work.

Also, I recommend that you clearly state on your website outright that you are not always right. Please make sure your clients are of sound mind to understand that sometimes you will be very wrong, because I don't know a single psychic who is not sometimes wrong.

A professional reader is not professional because they are never wrong, just hopefully they are less often wrong than inexperienced readers. You should clearly state, as well, that clients should never rely on psychic advice alone (which they shouldn't). Seeking the opinion of a licensed medical professional or psychological professional is highly recommended and the responsible thing to do in some cases, and that's the truth. There is never a reason for someone to only rely on psychic advice on matters that are life-threatening or have serious implications, no matter how talented the reader is or how trusted they are. No one is right 100 percent of the time. For this reason, I make it a practice to not read minors under the age of 18 without the express permission of their parents, as minors are much more impressionable and may not understand that psychics are sometimes wrong.

Do It Yourself!

For most metaphysical practitioners, creating and maintaining a website yourself, or at least in partnership with a professional, is the best way to go. Find someone who is motivated to bring you to a level of self-sufficiency and proficiency as quickly as possible and invest in this regardless of your computer skills. Today there are so many wonderful template-based website hosting companies to choose from that there is absolutely no reason you can't build a website or basic webpage by yourself in a matter of days, if not hours. If you are capable of surfing the Internet, of using the basic functions of word processing programs like Word or Pages, or are utilizing popular sites like Facebook, then you are more than capable of creating a template-based website.

If you wish to hire a graphic designer to help you design a banner or logo for your company, or the overall look and feel of your site, that can sometimes be helpful. Consulting with those who understand the use of keywords or search engine optimization can also be very helpful, so I'm not saying to completely disregard the experts.However, I am saying that you don't NEED them if you don't have the money to spare. Even if you do have the money, it's important to have a long-term perspective with your website. You are going to be changing constantly as you grow as a clairvoyant, healer and now business owner. You are going to want to have the freedom to change how you structure your readings and your time, and these changes will need to be reflected on your website. In the future, your preferences may change as far as what colors and designs appeal to you as well.

There is nothing worse than having someone else design a beautiful website for you, only to find that they are now too busy, too expensive, unavailable or unwilling to continue to help when you want to make a change to your website. I and so many other psychic practitioners add and change things on our websites weekly, even daily sometimes, so it's a great investment for you to learn how to make these changes yourself. You will save yourself a lot of frustration, time and money once you do. Plus, the more you post, the higher your site gets ranked on Google.

Your Energy Frequency and Level Is Your Greatest Marketing Tool

Again, when it comes to spiritual work, what is going to bring about the most success is your own energy level and this includes your mental, emotional and physical states. If you are miserable, all the advertising in the world is not going to make a difference when it comes to this work. Conversely, if you are well-rested, well-fed, well-exercised, balanced, happy, passionate, and well-loved, you will generate an energy that gets people's attention more than a million Twitter or Facebook posts ever will (although these can certainly help).

Sometimes, oftentimes, the best action to take when it comes to seeking clients is to go meditate, to pray with gratitude and feeling, to take a walk in the most beautiful place you can find, to go have the most wonderful evening dancing with your friends or partner, to watch an inspirational film, or to do whatever you love the most. Of course, if this is all you are doing (having fun) but no one knows who the heck you are or where to find you, then more attention is likely needed in promoting your business via your website, newsletters, social media, YouTube, etc.

The key is to balance the outside work with the inner work. The most productive work happens when you can merge what you love to do with your promotional work. When I play around with the colors and images on my website, or search through dozens of lovely templates offered through a newsletter builder program, or when I write about what matters most to me, I feel more exhilarated than I ever could have imagined. This is the time when I usually receive the most calls from clients wanting to book sessions.

Your Photo

I want to emphasize how important it is to have an up-to-date professional headshot of yourself that you are proud to show to the world. Potential clients need to know that you are someone they will feel comfortable with and can trust. You will need a terrific photo for your website and social media pages and many other opportunities that come your way. A faded, fuzzy photo will give you the appearance of being faded, fuzzy, out-of-date and even unconfident.

Also, it's important that you look happy in your photo. The photo's clarity, the quality of the lighting, and how approachable you look are really the most important things. These are much more significant than whether you look chubby or wrinkled or anything else. Choose a photo that represents you. You can't control what people think of you. If you look like a model, some people will come to you because of that and some will avoid you. If you are 100 pounds overweight, some people will come to you because of that and some people will avoid you. If you are a woman or a man, young or old, blonde or brunette, black or white, some people will come to you for those reasons and some will avoid you for those reasons.

I highly recommend getting professional headshots done, and for you ladies, think about having your hair and makeup done just before getting your photos taken. Look up photographers who do headshots for actors and/or corporate people, and contact them first before booking with them to make sure you feel comfortable with them. I had very nice photos taken when Extraordinary Psychic was first coming out, where I look absolutely miserable. This is because the photographer was a young, strapping guy and we shot them in his penthouse Hollywood studio. His walls were plastered with nude photos of the most stunning models I had ever seen. Being 40 years old and about 40 pounds overweight, I just felt completely awkward with him, no matter how hard he tried to make me feel comfortable. I would have been a lot more at ease with a woman or perhaps a guy who was used to photographing kids. If you can find a photographer you will feel relaxed with, professional headshots are the way to go. Yes, they can be expensive—typically anywhere from $150 to $600 for a photo shoot—but they really are well worth the cost.

Most people find that having professional headshots gives them a sense of confidence they didn't feel before the shoot. Plus, it's a great feeling knowing that you can easily click a file on your desktop and upload a great image of yourself any time you need one, as opposed to painstakingly searching through your files for an old photo that has terrible lighting and cuts off the top of your head.

Attracting Clients Has as Much to Do With Your Energy as it Does With Your Marketing Materials

A successful marketing campaign can help you bring in clients, but there are other forces at work that will ultimately determine your success. I know intuitive practitioners who spend thousands of dollars on full-page newspaper ads, their business cards are works of art, and they are actually very good psychics. However, they are lucky if they attract even one client a month. I know others who do no advertising at all, and they attract several clients a week. The ability to attract clients has more to do with your level of enthusiasm for reading, your Mental Emotional Image pictures surrounding both readings and money, your present energy level, the appropriateness of your reading location, the types of clients you are currently working with, and your personal life circumstances.

To Offer Recordings or Not?

Many clients like to have their readings recorded. It's up to you to decide whether or not you are comfortable with this. Personally, I like the idea of my clients being able to re-visit a reading, especially if they'd like to make sure they didn't miss anything or want to listen to it again in the future to see how things have come to pass. The one thing that concerns me is that the recording could end up in the wrong hands (or wrong ears) and that it could be used against my client or myself in some way. This has never happened, though, as far as I know.

For those of you who are just not comfortable being recorded, you may lose some business but it's much more important that you set parameters that make you feel comfortable when you work than anything else.

There are three main considerations when recording, from a technological standpoint. First, what will be easiest to operate when you are in a trance. Even remembering to hit the record button can be an issue at the start of a reading. Second, what will be the easiest method of delivery. And third, what will be the easiest for the client to access once they receive it, so you can avoid getting distress calls that they can't open the file.

There are many cell phone voice recording apps that seem to work well, although storage capacity can become an issue. I personally have found a conference call system that I utilize for both my classes and my readings to be the best for me. It automatically records and converts the recording to an mp3, then emails me when this mp3 is available to send to my client.

Any readers interested in recommendations can contact me to find out what I'm using, as I'm always adapting to newer and better products as they are developed and as I learn about them.

The Golden Rules to Maintaining a Successful Psychic Reading Business

Treat others how you'd like to be treated, never compromise your integrity or honesty, and never, ever sell out!

Not selling out means that you never put the need for money over what you intuitively know is best for yourself and for others.

This means that if you need a break from readings, then you will have to take a break or you will simply not get clients. Or you'll start to have negative experiences in your readings.

If you don't feel comfortable reading someone, or reading under the circumstances they are asking you to, then don't do it.

For psychics, it's so easy for things to get energetically messy very quickly. The more we are depleted or stressed about finances and survival, the easier it is to take on others' energies that are detrimental to our health and well-being. This is not the kind of work one can do around the clock, hour after hour, on demand. Setting boundaries with clients or potential clients, and even friends and family members who just have just "one quick question," is essential. Believe me, a question is never quick—"Just tell me what I'm supposed to be doing in my life" is not quick. "Why didn't he call?" is never quick. "Why is my white blood cell count so high?" is never quick. All of these questions are going to take time and concentration, not just to get the information but to communicate it as well, and then chat before and afterwards. Setting boundaries with others can only happen after you set and maintain firm boundaries with yourself.

Sometimes this will mean saying no to desperate callers in the night: "Oh, sorry, did I wake you? I didn't realize it was 3am. But while I have you on the phone, I just had a fight with my boyfriend and he left, ah, could you do a reading for me right now?" Or having to tell a client, "No, you can't have another reading with me, you just had two, I've told you all I can, and it's not going to do you any good until you go out and live a little and put into practice some of what we discussed." Sometimes the test is having to set limits on how many people you will work with in a day or a week. Oftentimes, it's having to tell people things that they don't want to hear that could potentially lead them to not wanting to work with you again: "No, you won't be successful until you get off your butt, stop drinking and stop being lazy," doesn't always lend itself to repeat clients.

Not selling out also means turning down generous offers from other business owners who want to make money from your efforts or reputation, even though they don't believe in psychics. There are countless "tests" a psychic reader will be put through as they embark on their professional practice, and I believe many of these come from the spiritual plane. Whether you pass the tests or not depends on your ability to accept delayed gratification, to maintain faith in the presence of uncertainty, and to always be asking yourself, are my actions leading to the greatest good? You sacrificing your health for others is not the greatest good.

What has helped me the most is always knowing that I am NOT the only psychic or healer out there. If I'm not able or available to help, then as long as I give the person in need some references and options, I'm doing my job. I can't save everyone right when they need saving. I am quite certain that sentiment is the only reason I am still here—here working as a psychic, and here as far as still being healthy and alive on this earth. In the same way, I always know that if I turn down money because it's not in my best interest to do what would be required of me in order to accept it, the money will come back, often twofold or twentyfold, in the not too distant future. I've seen this same principal work for many others. Never sell out.

Don't Ever Start Your Psychic Reading Business Expecting That It's Going to Support You Right Off the Bat, or Be the Thing That Saves You From Destitution

Coming from someone who's been working with the power of positive thinking for over 40 years, and who has written an entire book on the subject, that statement might seem hypocritical. It's not. You should stay positive. You should expect that you will do incredibly well. But you need a back-up plan in the interim because, as I write in Freeing the Genie, there is a lot more involved when it comes to manifesting and conscious creation than just thinking positively.

While this subject is too in-depth to outline in this book, the bottom line is that putting pressure on any new endeavor, while insisting that it be the thing that is going to be your sole supporter and save you from all that you need saving from, will mostly likely stop the flow and ensure that you do not get very far. If you need income, then I highly recommend finding something else in addition to starting your psychic reading business. Just do something that will have enough flexibility, and that won't be too draining, so that you can do readings as well. There is nothing spiritual about being poor or about making other people support you because you refuse to do anything except your perfect idea of a profession before you are blessed with enough business to sustain yourself. You may think you want to be a full-time psychic reader, but you may not be ready to handle all that comes with it right away. Ease into it without putting pressure on it. You can do more than one thing at once when it comes to your career choices.

Of course even if you need a job, do not just accept or stay with any job if it seriously compromises who you are, or your own health and well-being. There are always options. As a spiritual practitioner, if you are not yet bringing in enough income from your spiritual work to support yourself or your family, then there is absolutely no reason you can't go out and get a job that will allow you to have some regular income while building your business. Working during the day as a janitor or receptionist or dishwasher while you study and practice in the evening is far more honorable, if that's all you can find, than starving and crashing on other people's sofas simply because you got it into your head that you have a higher purpose and shouldn't have to do such work.

Working Through a Metaphysical Center

Many psychics choose to work out of a metaphysical bookstore or center that offers readings to the public. These places tend to operate in a few different ways.

Option 1: Renting or Leasing a Space
Some of the larger businesses rent or lease space to readers, healers, and massage therapists. These practitioners are employed as independent contractors. As long as they pay their rent, the owner gives only minimal input into how they conduct their readings or how often they show up to work.

When I first moved to Sedona, I worked out of the largest and most successful metaphysical center in the area. It consisted of a bookstore, a crystal and clothing shop, and approximately twenty rooms of varying sizes that were leased to readers. Upon my arrival, I signed a lease that required me to pay eight hundred eighty dollars every month for an eight-by-eight-foot room as well as a security deposit that would serve as my last month's rent providing I gave thirty days' notice prior to my departure. Downstairs by the front door was a bulletin board that displayed the flyer and business cards of all the practitioners renting rooms. Tourists would visit the center to explore the store or to seek out a reading and eventually choose a reader based on the flyers.

During the first six months, I earned just enough money to pay my rent at the center, my living expenses, and child care expenses (which averaged five hundred dollars per month). However, during the slow season of summer and early fall, fewer tourists came through the door and I was unable to pay these expenses, even though I was still doing several short readings a day (mostly fifteen-minute readings that brought in about twenty dollars each). When I realized I was so burnt out that I was dreading even the thought of doing another reading, I gave notice and opted to find a regular nine-to-five job in the field of social work. Some readers who had been in the business longer had more repeat customers or referrals from former clients and were more financially successful; however, in general there was a constant turnover because there were always too many readers for the amount of clients that came in. The owner did her best to advertise the center, but she was never willing to lower the rent, or the number of readers, because there was always a new reader to replace any of those who left due to lack of business.

I value my time there because it made it possible for me to do a lot of readings on a lot of different kinds of people without having to do my own advertising or marketing except for creating a flyer. At times I had a lot of fun meeting and working in close proximity to other psychics and healers with similar interests. However, there was a lot of competition to deal with. I choose to believe that the clients who are meant to work with me will find me, so I don't have to worry about other readers "stealing" my business. However, this seems to be a rare perspective among readers and healers who, despite their claims of being enlightened and well-versed in the laws of creativity, are some of the most competitive and envious people I have ever encountered. There would be days when I was very busy and no less than five or six readers would make a snide remark about my success. When I was not doing so well, they were as compassionate as anyone could be! Many of the readers seemed particularly curious and intimidated by my strong clairvoyant abilities, since none of them had any formal training in this area and most did not know how to call forth their own clairvoyance at will.

Most of the readers in Sedona use spirit guides and their abilities of clairaudience or clairsentience (knowingness) to conduct readings. Many of them are excellent readers, so I'm not criticizing them in any way, just explaining that their approach is different from the techniques I used and that are taught in this book.

Despite these pitfalls, my time at this center helped me make the transition from being a sheltered student at a clairvoyant school (where I read under supervision in a completely protected environment) to becoming a self-reliant professional. Many students never go on to make this transition due to their own fears and lack of encouragement from their clairvoyant training schools whose staff encourages students to enroll in their advanced programs or remain involved in the school as graduate readers or teachers.

Option 2: Giving a Split of Your Earnings to the Store Owner

Another common option for psychic readers is to work for a metaphysical shop or bookstore where, rather than paying rent, you split a percentage of your earnings with the owners of the store. The advantage to this arrangement is that during slow times you don't have to worry about making your rent, and the owner is more likely to be motivated to advertise or solicit business for you so you will both make money. The downside is that you make less money per reading, since the owner is likely to price the reading competitively and then take a commission (which could be anywhere from 20 to 60 percent). Even if the overall monthly amount you earn is equal to what you would earn at a business where you pay rent but make more money per reading, when you receive less per reading you may feel that you are putting out more energy than you are getting back. This may lower your enthusiasm for reading out of that establishment and decrease your motivation for showing up to work.

Psychic readers and store owners often run into conflicts with one another. Psychics tend to let their intuition and feelings direct their actions. When a reader doesn't show up for work, perhaps because her intuition told her that she needed some time to reconnect with herself, the store owner earns nothing and understandably becomes very upset. Most owners of stores that employ psychics are more concerned with the success of the business than with a reader's energetic well-being. They don't understand if you turn down a reading because you are feeling too "low on energy" or because you have a "bad feeling" about the readee. They don't understand why you may feel the need to take a half-hour to meditate after a particularly challenging reading before you are ready for your next reading. Most shop owners will also not appreciate it if you complete a reading in a half-hour because you feel your client got all the communication they needed or could handle, when the client originally told the owner that they were interested in an hour reading, which would yield more money.

Another issue that frequently arises between business owners and readers is that of who has the right to repeat business or referrals. I have encountered owners who forbade me and other readers to pass out business cards even when the client requested them, because they were afraid the client or someone referred by the client would contact me directly and the owner would miss out on a potential commission on that future reading. It seemed to me that the store owners were already getting a large percentage of the profits from my reading. So for them to expect to get a cut of any future readings I did for that person or their friends outside of the store was not only unreasonable, but impractical and invasive of the reader/readee relationship, especially because these same business owners usually refuse to provide a reader's forwarding address once they have left the business. If a reader and client are forbidden to exchange information, they could easily lose track of one another. This is an issue that many readers and business owners grapple with and should reconcile prior to acceptance of employment by either party.

Option 3: Reading at Local Businesses

Some local businesses, such as coffee shops, restaurants, or night clubs, may welcome your presence in their establishment and will ask nothing from you in return other than that you show up at a regularly scheduled time each week. Owners of these businesses feel that the presence of the reader and the opportunity to receive a reading will attract customers. The owners will not make any money directly from the readings or the reader, but rather will make money from the food or drinks that are purchased by these customers. Some of these businesses (most of which are located in areas where psychics are not as numerous or common as in Sedona) are incredibly successful, largely because they offer readings from talented and charismatic readers.

This situation is therefore financially ideal for readers, since they can earn more money per reading and have minimal expenses. The downside is that they may be placed at a booth or table in the corner of the establishment where they have no privacy or control over the noise level. Some psychics thrive under these conditions. They learn how to use the outside noises and distractions as a tool to bring them into a more focused inner state. Others soon crumble under the distractions and attention from curious onlookers.

Option 4: Reading at Parties

A fun and educational way to earn money as a psychic is to perform readings at parties, either by getting your own gigs or by working for an agency that contracts readers for parties. As the former owner of one of these agencies, Sedona Psychic Entertainment Services, and a former employee of two others, I have read at every type of party imaginable, from small intimate cocktail parties to corporate functions with over a thousand attendees.

At the majority of parties, the psychic will sit at a table and guests will line up to receive a five- to ten-minute reading, depending on the number of guests versus the number of readers and the number of hours the readers have been contracted for. At very large gatherings, psychics may be instructed to roam through the crowd, offering one- to two-minute readings. Most agencies request their readers to dress up in a gypsy-style costume for entertainment value, which usually goes over extremely well with the guests at parties and is usually fun for the readers as well.

Of course, some readers will find the idea of dressing up to emulate a stereotypical image demeaning and insulting to them and the profession. I don't even want to imagine what one of my remote viewing instructors, Lyn Buchanan, would do if he was required to sit at a table with a scarf around his head and sparkly beads around his neck reading tarot cards. The party would certainly be over at that point. So again, if you are asked to play dress-up and this doesn't feel comfortable, then it's your prerogative to try to work out a suitable alternative or decline the job.

Professional psychics can expect to make anywhere from seventy to two hundred dollars an hour for reading at parties, depending on whether they are working through an agency or are self-employed. Expectations should be discussed between the reader and the host or coordinator of the party or event prior to the event. When a psychic is working through an agency, that agency will be the one to pay the psychic and will often provide a representative of the agency to be present at the event to supervise the psychic and oversee the readings. In this case, the reader and the agency should discuss expectations prior to the event. These expectations include the amount of money the reader will receive per hour; how many hours they will be expected to read;

how overtime work will be handled (will they have the option to refuse working overtime; will they be paid extra); whether the psychic will be permitted to accept tips or should do anything to encourage tips; whether they will be seated or expected to stroll among the guests; whether they will be served food and beverages or need to bring their own snacks; whether they are expected to wear a costume; whether they are permitted to hand out their own business cards or must give out the business cards of the agency; whether they are encouraged or forbidden to socialize with guests following the readings, etc.

Reading at parties can be challenging and rewarding at the same time. It's imperative that readers stick to their time limit to ensure that all the guests receive a reading (something I still find to be extremely difficult!). The readers usually are placed in an environment that is not particularly conducive to reading in terms of noise, activity level, and amount of privacy. They must read numerous people back to back, with little time for cleaning out or meditation. The psychic must therefore exert extra energy to remain focused, grounded, and neutral, and to continue on with the readings no matter what occurs. Reading numerous people over the course of several hours can be exhausting, and it is important to continue to call back your own energy as frequently as possible (see chapter 8). This is actually an incredible opportunity for psychics to challenge themselves and to realize that they can really read under any circumstances, provided they continue to use their tools and practice the techniques taught in this book.

Most of the time, guests at parties are very excited to receive a reading. This is a great opportunity to expose people to clairvoyant readings and help them examine their stereotypes and misconceptions of what a psychic reading is all about. However, many of the guests will be quite skeptical, which always makes a reading more challenging.

Another challenge that psychics must grapple with when reading at parties is the question of how to deal with serious or difficult issues that arise during a reading that could put a damper on the guest's experience at the party. I encourage my employees to read from a space of validation (see chapters 14 and 19) so that they will look to see what is working for the person in their life and remain as positive as possible. However, there will always be instances in which a guest has been grappling with a certain issue, and during the reading they receive information that not only gives them insight into this issue, but that could potentially transform or determine the course of events of their entire life. This is information they need to receive, even though it may result in tears or even cause a premature departure from the party.

One of the most difficult things about reading at parties is the alcohol factor. As the party progresses, so do the effects of alcohol on guests and on the readers. Many readers are so clairsentient that they will actually absorb the effects of the alcohol into their aura and experience feelings of drunkenness, which could include feeling dizzy, tired, nauseous, giddy, and confused. When a person is intoxicated, they are flying somewhere outside of their body and this makes it very difficult to read them. Since there is no way to limit the guests' use of alcohol at parties, preparation can be made prior to the event to minimize alcohol-related problems by scheduling the readings during the early hours of the party.

If a reader is approached by a guest who seems to have been drinking alcohol, I suggest that the reader clairvoyantly look at the outer layer of the guest's aura, which contains some very basic information about the guest's personality or how others see this person's personality. The reader should tell the guest about these personality traits and then conclude the reading as quickly as possible. This will satisfy the guest's desire to receive a reading while preventing the reader from having to delve into deeper issues that would require more energy and time. Of course, if a guest is belligerent or so intoxicated that they are unaware of their environment, the reader has the right to refuse the guest a reading or to immediately terminate the reading at the point the reader begins to feel uncomfortable.

Reading at Psychic Fairs and Expos

Many readers earn money and gain experience and exposure by performing short readings at psychic fairs and expos. These fairs are usually organized by someone else or a group of people. The fair may be a very large one, located at a convention center, with thousands of attendees and hundreds of attractions besides the psychic readers (such as the popular Whole Life Expo, which travels around the United States), or the fair may be a small one, held in a conference room of a hotel, where the main attraction is the psychic readers.

Most clairvoyant training schools hold their own fairs, in which students, graduates, and staff perform readings and offer workshops for minimal prices. Readings can be as low as five dollars, and aura healings may be offered at no cost. The school keeps the profits while the students gain experience under the supervision and protection of their teachers. Attendees of the fair may or may not pay a small entry fee for workshops.

At most other fairs, psychics from diverse backgrounds are available to perform readings of varying lengths and at higher rates. Psychics will rent a booth for either one day or for the course of the fair. The rent will reflect the value of the booth in terms of the booth's size, its proximity to the flow of foot traffic, and whether the psychic is selling products in addition to performing readings. In rare cases, the psychic will not pay a fee for a booth upfront, but rather will share or split their earnings with the fair's organizers. Booth rates could range from twenty-five to hundreds of dollars a day, depending on the anticipated attendance of fairgoers.

Since there are only so many readings that one psychic can perform in a day, if the expense of the booth is very high, the reader will need to charge higher prices for shorter readings, or may choose to bring other readers into their booth, which may or may not be permitted by the fair's organizers. Another option is to sell related products, such as books, audio or videotapes, etc., which may increase the cost of the booth. Many psychics tend to just break even at psychic fairs, but find that it is an excellent marketing venue to network and meet clients who will come to them at a later date for longer, more lucrative readings.

Many readers have found financial success and have a wonderful time reading at medieval or Renaissance fairs, which are becoming more and more popular every year. These fairs often make a circuit around the United States and come to a rural area once a year, for a period of time that could range from a single weekend to a few months. Besides psychic readers, these fairs also employ actors, musicians, singers, dancers, artists, etc., all of who are required to dress up in period costumes and pretend that they are living in the Middle Ages. Psychic readers usually rent a booth and in exchange are able to keep their earnings. They are required to decorate their booths, and the more elaborate, attractive, or authentic their booth and wardrobe are, the more clients they will attract. Because there are so many attendees roaming around, psychics who read at Renaissance fairs often do very well financially, even if the initial rent of the booth is fairly high. The downside is that they are required to man their booths for long hours. Reading continuously every day for weeks or even months can be extremely exhausting, if not downright impossible. Many readers solve this dilemma by subleasing their booths for a day or week to other psychics.

Working for a Psychic Hotline

Obviously, from the many television ads and infomercials you have seen, there are quite a number of telephone psychic hotlines out there. Readings can be performed as effectively over the telephone as in person; however, from my own experiences and discussions with numerous psychics who have worked for or investigated these hotlines, it appears that most of the larger ones that can afford to advertise on television employ people who have little understanding of their own abilities and are more versed in how to keep callers on the line than in psychic reading.

When a person is initially employed as a reader with one of these hotlines, they are specifically told that their mission is to keep the caller on the line as long as possible. Many of these hotlines charge anywhere from three to five dollars a minute (which totals anywhere from one hundred eighty to three hundred dollars an hour). Callers often tell themselves that they will only stay on the line for a few minutes, but lose track of time because of the sales tactics employed by the "psychic readers" and because of their own desperation. Many of these callers are already facing serious difficulties in their lives, which prompted them to call the hotline in the first place, and the last thing any of these people need is to discover a three-hundred-dollar charge on their phone bill that they will either have to pay or will have to fight with their phone company to dismiss.

Occasionally a "real" psychic and/or caring person will go to work for one of these hotlines, but they usually last only for a short period of time because they realize that there is no way to maintain their integrity when working for a person or company that is cheating and deceiving its clients.

I was once invited to audition for the same company that produces the omnipresent "Miss Cleo" infomercials. In these commercials, Miss Cleo conducts several readings for callers who are delighted and amazed at her psychic abilities. She encourages people to call her on the hotline and gives the distinct impression that she is the person who will answer the phone, even though in reality she does not work the hotline. There are currently legal actions being taken against this company and Miss Cleo due to this misrepresentation. During the initial audition I attended, I was informed that this company was searching for authentic readers to perform readings in similar infomercials in which they encourage viewers to call them directly on the hotline. However, we were told that we would not actually be required to work on the hotline once we were chosen for the commercials.

Although there was the potential to earn a lot of money, I realized that it would be a huge personal mistake for me to represent a company whose practices I find to be not only unethical but downright criminal, and I happily dropped out of the audition process soon after it began. However, there were a lot of authentic psychics in Sedona who did pursue this "opportunity." A few of them justified their participation by explaining that their presence on the infomercial would spread "light" and positive energy to the millions of viewers who watched these commercials, and therefore they would be serving humanity by counterbalancing the darkness of the greed of the company that hired them. It continues to amaze me how so many self-proclaimed "light workers" can so easily delude themselves about their own motivations when it comes to the promise of money and fame!

Telephone hotlines do exist that are run by people who practice the utmost integrity. Most of these are privately owned by individuals who are in touch with their own spiritual abilities. The Berkeley Psychic Institute runs its own hotline in which student readers and graduates hone their long-distance reading skills by volunteering or earning a small hourly wage for reading over the hotline. Callers receive authentic and reasonably priced readings in which the readers do not benefit any more from a one-minute reading than a two-hour reading. For some psychics, working over a hotline offers them an ideal work situation, because often they can work independently from the safety and privacy of their own home, and they can avoid the costs of commuting and enjoy a flexible working schedule.

Many psychics who would never work for a psychic telephone hotline do offer readings over the phone in addition to reading clients face to face, and are able to reap the same benefits. They charge the same predetermined fee for reading over the phone that they would in person. Some of these readers have their own credit card processing machines so they can accept payment by credit card over the phone at the time of the reading. Obtaining the capacity to process credit card payments can initially be quite expensive and requires good credit. Many psychic readers opt for payment by personal check or money order. They usually request that first-time clients send them a check or money order prior to the reading, while occasionally permitting repeat clients to send their payment following the reading.

CHAPTER 24

Finding and Choosing
a Psychic Reader

How to Find a Psychic Reader

There are many ways to find a psychic reader. If you are looking for an in-person reading in your area, I suggest going to a metaphysical bookstore, which will usually have a bulletin board advertising local psychic readers and healers, or will offer free local magazines and newspapers that have many advertisements for readers. In most areas other than the San Francisco Bay area, the majority of psychic readers use their abilities of clairaudience or transmediumship rather than clairvoyance. This is not a problem, since many of them will be able to give you excellent readings; however, if you are interested in experiencing a clairvoyant reading, then you will need to find someone who specifically states that they receive information in the form of images or pictures. Some people erroneously use the term clairvoyance to cover any psychic ability, so even if someone says they are clairvoyant, you should inquire further and ask them whether they see information, hear it, or feel it.

Finding a Clairvoyant Reader
Through a Clairvoyant Training School

Due to the number of clairvoyant training schools in the San Francisco Bay area, there are hundreds of clairvoyant readers there. You can locate many of these schools through the Internet. The curriculum of all these schools is based on the original teachings of Lewis Bostwick, the founder of the Berkeley Psychic Institute, and are run by either his former students or their students. However, they are not affiliated with one another, and there is quite a bit of competition between particular schools. All schools offer the option of receiving a reading from students, graduates, or staff.

Student readings tend to be very inexpensive and quite in-depth. Students obviously read a little more slowly due to lack of experience and confidence, but oftentimes they can offer information that is just as helpful as that of professional readers. The downside to receiving a student reading is that sometimes the readers are overly vigilant about protecting themselves and maintaining their boundaries to the point that they become paranoid and make the mistake of blaming the readee for "getting in their space." They try so hard to read from a neutral place in their sixth chakra that they close their heart chakras down too far. While I have always had very positive experiences receiving readings from students, I know some people who have left a reading feeling insulted or alienated.

Also, sometimes these schools don't give the readee the opportunity to ask all of their questions. The schools usually de-emphasize a connection with a particular reader or psychic, so while the owners may offer professional readings, if you sign up for a student or graduate reading you will have no idea beforehand who that person will be. I never really saw that as a problem as I have always been pleasantly surprised by the readings I received, but I do know some people really like to have a say in who reads them before arriving. In fact, I was just thinking about re-taking an online class from one clairvoyant school that costs $600, and when I asked who exactly would be teaching the class (hoping it would be the owner of the school) I received an email stating, "One of our staff will be teaching the class." I was like, really? Well, I kind of figured that. Thanks, but I'd like a little more assurance that my teacher knows a bit more than I do about the subject matter.

Graduate readings at these schools cost about twice as much as student readings but are still remarkably cheap, while professional-level readings from experienced graduates or staff are on par with the fees of most practicing professional psychics within the United States. Some of the directors and staff of these schools are some of the most talented clairvoyants in the world, even though they have their own neuroses, personality quirks, etc., that may or may not complement or clash with your own! All of these readers offer readings in person or over the telephone. And of course these days there is no shortage of clairvoyant readers with websites of their own.

Take a Proactive Approach

Whether you receive a reading from your local neighborhood psychic or from a clairvoyant reader associated with a clairvoyant training school or via the Internet, I very much encourage you to take a proactive approach when choosing a psychic reader. Find out how much they charge prior to the commencement of your reading, what methods they use, where they received their training, how experienced they are, and whether they will address the issues you are concerned with. Every reader has their own particular talents and weaknesses and it's perfectly fine to ask questions about their competence in particular areas.

It is not appropriate to ask them to prove to you prior to the reading that they are really psychic, or to expect them to spend more than five to ten minutes at the most discussing their reading approach. It's also not appropriate to ask them a question that you want addressed in the reading, prior to the reading, such as, "I know my reading isn't until tomorrow, but could you just tell me really quickly whether my boyfriend is going to leave me? It will just take a minute." Know that it never just takes a minute!

Discuss Expectations Prior to the Reading

Prior to a reading, you should make sure that the reader knows the length of the reading you desire. Also, find out how both of you will know when the time has expired. I know some psychics who will tell a readee that they charge one hundred dollars per hour. The readee will assume that they are getting an hour-long reading, and then two-and-a-half hours later they are told they owe two hundred fifty dollars. During a reading, time goes by very quickly, and both the reader and the readee can easily lose track of it. If a reader goes over the predetermined length of time and doesn't ask you if you would like to extend the reading, then you as a client should not be expected to pay extra. But you always want to make sure this is the case. For myself, I no longer charge per time frame, as I hate to feel in a rush and half an hour is never enough. I simply let people know my readings are usually around an hour long. If I go over the hour, which I do most of the time, it's my choice and that means they pay nothing more.

Look Out for Psychic Scammers!

Beware of anyone who tells you that they can only help you if you give them more money than the price of the reading session. There are plenty of psychic scams out there where a psychic will tell you that there is a curse on you, or you are in need of some kind of healing, and that the only way you will recover is if you pay them a large amount of money that they will supposedly use to purchase materials that will break the curse or reverse your ailments.

If anyone asks for substantially more money than your original session or their usual posted rates (many readers do offer a first-time discount), this should raise suspicions. Beware of anyone who tells you that you are cursed and the only way the curse can be removed is by paying them a lot of money. Also beware of any psychic that is offering you ongoing readings for free. Unless you are sick and clearly desperately in need of help, few professional psychics have the time or energy to continuously offer free readings, so there may be some ulterior agenda.

Occasionally, a reader may see that you are dealing with a lot of issues or health problems and will recommend additional sessions for healing, either from themselves or someone else. Some serious health problems do often take more than one healing session to sort out, and many readers offer reading packages. Some practitioners and healing schools offer healing packages in which you can purchase a combination of healing sessions in advance for a discounted rate. The advantage to receiving a healing package is that not only are you being healed during each session, but a lot of the healing also occurs between sessions due to the strength of your intention and level of commitment invested in your healing process. If a psychic/healer suggests that you return for additional healing, the cost of these sessions should be approximately the same price as your original reading or healing.

Buyer Beware...

Beware of anyone who tells you that only they can help or save you. No matter what your situation is, this is just not true. Also beware of any reader that encourages you to get readings from them on a frequent basis (I feel that more than twice a month is too frequent and encourages dependency—I tell my clients to wait anywhere from two to six months before returning to me), or who befriends you, or offers to do things for you, and then later hands you a bill.

Do Not Idolize a Psychic Reader or Healer, No Matter How Talented They Are

A particular talent or ability is nothing more than that; it doesn't say anything about the individual as a whole who possesses that talent. Psychics are often just as messed up and self-obsessed as anyone else, and if you place them on a pedestal above yourself, at some point they will fall, taking you with them. The expression "The bigger they are, the harder they fall" comes to mind.

There are some people out there who can do miraculous things. They can levitate, manifest objects out of thin air, or read every single thought in your mind. Some of these people are enlightened yogis, while others are thieves, con artists, or rapists. It's a lie that God only bestows special gifts and talents on those who deserve them or will use them in responsible ways. If a psychic ever treats you in a manner that feels disrespectful, condescending, hurtful, or abusive, by all means communicate your feelings to them and, if necessary, terminate communication with that person immediately. When you idolize someone, you give them your power. Whatever qualities you are able to admire in someone else are qualities that you possess within yourself. You, your birth, your life, your existence, your love—are miraculous.

Finding a Clairvoyant Healer

When considering a healer, find out what methods the healer will employ. Does the healer channel energy through you, put energy into you, take energy out of you, or use your own energy? I would be cautious of methods that involve putting energy into you, or of healers who aren't aware of the energies they are using. Find out if the healer is working with healing guides and whether these guides have been taught to respect boundaries or if they may be trying to recruit you into a particular discipline. Through questioning and observation, find out if the healer seems concerned with maintaining and respecting energetic boundaries. Determine the healer's intentions for desiring to give you a healing. Find out if sexual desire or the intention of recruiting you into a particular group or as a future paying client has anything to do with the healer's motivation to interact with you. Former clients of the healer/reader can offer insight into that healer's integrity and methodology; however, it's important to understand that their experience could be very different from your own, particularly if their level of self-esteem, their age, or their level of physical attractiveness varies from your own.

Beware of Sexual Predators

Women need to look out for male psychics and particularly healers who are sexual predators. Unfortunately, there are quite a few of these men in Sedona, Arizona, as well as in Santa Cruz, California, and every other area that attracts healers. These men tend to attract more vulnerable women who are in need of a male's attention and validation.

Most of the sexual metaphysical predators I've known actually do have healing abilities and knowledge in the healing arts, yet are as motivated by their addiction to sexual pleasure and money as by their desire to heal. Many of these men are not conscious of their motivations and how they are adversely affecting their clients. These men are dangerous energetically because they put all kinds of cords into the woman's second chakra, which will cause her to be attracted to him or even to feel as if she is in love with him.

These men are destructive on an emotional level because they intuitively know what a women is needing and desiring most and then they give this to her during her healing session, so by the end of it she feels as if this person has the power to make her feel like no one else has in a long time and she becomes desperate to see him again.

This feeling, accompanied by the second-chakra cords and his sexual energy pulsating through her body, are a dangerous combination that lead many women to give the male healer exactly what he wants in terms of sex and money. Many of these men's clients actually delude themselves into believing that this man is their soulmate because they feel both a spiritual and sexual connection with him. The sexual connection comes from his sexual energy that is circulating through her body, which she misinterprets as her own. The spiritual connection may be coming more from the energy that he is channeling during a healing than from himself, and from her perceptions of him as a spiritually aware human being. She projects God-like attributes to this healer because she experiences God through him, even though his mind is filled with thoughts of how to get into her bed or her wallet.

Some of these men actually come highly recommended by their female clients because many of these clients are unaware of the way these men are manipulating them until months or years later. I have seen the emotional and psychological devastation that these psychics, healers, and spiritual teachers can wreak, and feel that there needs to be greater awareness, discussion, and intervention at least in the metaphysical communities where these people operate.

Most of the psychics and healers I'm referring to above are not evil people. They aren't trying to hurt anyone. In fact, they are motivated by the desire to heal and help, but their own sexual needs and arousal and egos get the best of them. They are just unconscious to their own behaviors and are unaware of how to establish boundaries.

However, there are actual sexual predators who know very well what they are doing and are very good at what they do. I've had a few friends and clients report that they were introduced to a man who told them that they would either receive special powers or would be able to aid in the healing of others through having sex with him or even a group of people. I say they were introduced because the person introducing them was a friend or acquaintance who they trusted, which led them to having their usual defenses down and they were sucked into a bizarre and twisted situation that was nothing less then traumatizing.

Some of these sexual predators were, or claimed to be, leaders of churches, spiritual organizations, and even secret government organizations. It's not too different than what happens with those highly intelligent people who get sucked into financial scams. Under ordinary circumstances, they'd be extremely leery of someone making outrageous get-rich-quick claims, but when a close, trusted friend who has also been scammed (yet is still unaware of what has transpired) introduces them to the con artist, they get onboard.

Gender Issues

You may want to consider the gender of a potential reader and/or healer. I know some male readers that won't like to hear this, but there are many issues that come up for women during a reading that they may not feel comfortable discussing with a man. These could have to do with sexual abuse, reproductive issues, relationship concerns, etc. More significant is the fact that female bodies are extremely receptive to male energies; their ovaries are like sponges, ready to soak up any male attention that is directed their way. When even the most caring, considerate male healer works on a female, particularly on her female or reproductive organs, he often cannot help but leave behind some of his male energy in her body or energetic field, particularly if he becomes aroused or is not conscious of maintaining energetic boundaries. This is very similar to what happens during intercourse between a man and a woman, and helps explain why a woman can get so "attached" or become dependent on a man with whom she has been intimate.

CHAPTER 25

Clairvoyant
Training Schools

This book will teach you everything you need to know to perform a clairvoyant reading and healing on yourself or anyone else. However, there is one thing this book cannot do and that is create opportunities and experiences for you to practice your skills; you will have to create these for yourself. For some people this will be easy; others will find it more challenging.

While this book offers plenty of suggestions for overcoming many obstacles, challenges, and dilemmas that you may encounter in your readings both as a clairvoyant student and as a professional reader, it obviously cannot provide personalized emotional support to help you through your "growth periods" that will arise as a result of all the energy you are releasing and all the changes that may occur in your life as you practice these techniques. For those of you who learn better and feel more secure in a structured setting where you have direct access to teachers and to experiential opportunities that are already established for you, enrolling in a clairvoyant training program may be the greatest gift you can give yourself.

In this final chapter, I will provide some overall information about clairvoyant training schools and programs, and discuss the pros and cons of participating in these programs. I will not discuss the merits of any particular school, but instead will provide an overview so you will know what kinds of questions to ask when researching the schools, and what to expect from participation in one of their programs.

General Information

There are several clairvoyant training schools in the United States and a few in Canada that offer year-long training programs. Then there are many other schools that offer short-term workshops and classes, ranging in length from a few hours to several weeks of intensive training. The following discussion focuses on those schools that offer long-term programs.

These programs can be divided into two categories: in-person programs and distant teleseminar or webinar programs.

I'll start off with a discussion of the teleseminar programs because these are available to anyone around the globe who can speak English. Also, this is most prominent for myself since this is the format I utilize through the online school I founded, The International School of Clairvoyance.

Although it took a while to develop my program, I've found that distant training classes can be carried out in much the same way as in-person classes, provided that they are small enough that each student can get individual attention, have plenty of time to interact with the instructor and other students, have ample participation and practice opportunities, and have supervision and assessment throughout the course.

Because in-person clairvoyant classes require students to have their eyes closed and remain in a light trance state throughout, there is really no reason anyone needs to be able to see each other. In fact, there are less distractions reading someone over the phone or doing a session remotely than reading people in-person and the same is true when training, as much of the training involves direct practice. The hassles of travel are eliminated, and it may not be quite as stimulating or rewarding as connecting with others face-to-face, it's quite possible and common for students to bond closely with each other and for friendships to develop throughout the teleseminar classes.

Much depends on the instructor with telephone-based classes and the amount of emphasis they place on creating an interactive atmosphere of fun and community. This is true of both in-person and distance classes, but particularly with distance classes. When students are viewed as valuable contributors to the process (which they are) and given opportunities to bond with one another in class—through practice group participation and social media groups (established just for the class)—and when they are perceived as equals by their instructors rather than as underlings, who must remain on mute or speak only when spoken to, the class then turns into something they look forward to and miss when it's over.

There's nothing worse than having an instructor who perceives him/herself above his/her students or who is so controlling that half of the students' questions are never heard because they are placed on mute, or met with, "That's not important" or "We don't have time for that." So when researching programs, it's important to find out what the instructor's style is and what practice opportunities there will be outside of the class itself. While instructors need to set boundaries, they also need to be non-controlling so students feel like there is room for them to be different from the instructor, or to voice their own experiences and make adjustments to the curriculum or to their own approach.

When comparing programs, it's helpful to find out about the overall length of the program and the number of hours each class will be, and to find out who will be teaching the classes and who will be facilitating the practice groups. Inquiring about the teacher's openness to you participating in other classes and activities during the course of your program, or utilizing different methodologies, is also important as some schools discourage this.

My personal attitude is that students need to find a balance between the program and the rest of their lives. I encourage my students to study with as many different teachers as possible and to study as many modalities as possible. However, sometimes it is necessary to just focus on one or two methodologies at a time in order to really master them before moving on. Some students do sabotage themselves by taking on too much at once.

Some clairvoyant training programs have prerequisites. Students are required to take and pay for a certain number of short-term classes at the school before they are permitted to join the program. Some programs allow students to take their prerequisites while going through the actual clairvoyant training program. I encourage students to take a few classes before committing themselves to any program, so they can get to know the staff and form an idea of how well they will fit into the structure and personality of the school.

Some programs have a tithing requirement in which students are required to tithe or volunteer a certain number of hours of their time to the school in addition to monetary fees. Staff members try to work with the student to assign them tasks that fit with their goals and interests. Schools also have requirements in terms of how many readings a week a student must participate in or how many fairs and outside events a student must attend.

While requirements can serve students in many ways, I've found that in today's climate, where so many people are absolutely overwhelmed with work and family responsibilities, students perform best when they have options. In the 12-week programs I teach, I try to provide as many practice opportunities as possible, while not making them mandatory, so that students participate in them. I also provide flexible options so that students can take a class while knowing that there are ways to make it up, or they can take a break and continue at a later date if something comes up that requires them to travel or take care of a loved one. This is important to me, as I feel that part of clairvoyant training is to help students manage and decrease stress, not increase it through harsh demands that not everyone can meet.

So researching programs to ensure there are elements of flexibility built in is important. That being said, if you already know you are someone with a pattern of not finishing things, constantly moving from one class or program to the next without really integrating what you've learned, you may want to put yourself into a more structured situation with less flexibility and more requirements. Integration of material is essential and that only comes with practice and time. However, that doesn't mean you can't be studying more than one methodology at once. But three or four? That is too much because then you aren't going to have the time or energy to get really proficient at any of these. Ultimately, it should be up to you to find that balance and not up to your instructor. Of course, some would disagree with me completely. That's fine, it's a matter of you finding people to work with that are on the same wavelength as yourself.

Don't Let Others Place Restrictions on Your Freedom Unless That Serves Your Goals

I firmly believe that students who are interested in developing their abilities should explore a variety of methodologies and subjects. Clairvoyant reading and healing is one area. Mediumship is another. Remote viewing is another (for more about these topics, please check out my other books in this series, Extraordinary Psychic: Proven Techniques to Master Your Natural Abilities and Freeing The Genie Within: Manifesting Abundance, Creativity & Success in Your Life).

Within each one of these disciplines are multiple techniques and approaches. The more methods you use, the more tools you have at your disposal. As noted above, there is definitely something to say for studying a methodology in-depth and focusing primarily on that one for a while until it's mastered, as many students get a bit of a taste and sampling in a variety of these but then never discover what they can achieve from sticking with one methodology and training through to advanced levels.

But the bottom line when choosing a program and instructor to work with is, how open are they to allowing you the freedom to study elsewhere? Of course, some instructors have only studied one methodology and they are experts in that methodology so there is much to learn from them. They probably became as knowledgeable as they did because they stuck with one thing for so long. However, many of these experts may not even realize there are other approaches that are just as useful and, as a student, you'll just have to give them some slack if you want to learn from them. As long as you see that they are limited in their overall understanding of the intricacies of the other approaches, you will be just fine. Don't resist their teachings, just set aside what you've already learned so you can make the most of your education. Remember, a full glass can't hold more liquid so it's up to you to set aside what you already know at least long enough to refill your own glass with with the new information you are learning.

For example, some of my remote viewing instructors of the past few years, former military viewers, to date have not read my books and have no idea that there are clairvoyant methods that can be as useful, if not more so, then their own methods in certain situations. Meanwhile, there are many very accomplished clairvoyants, mediums and healers who have no idea that there are some very useful techniques for describing locations and objects that they have never even considered.

Some schools have a program that is tailored to women and their specific issues. Others are not gender-specific, but do offer additional gender-related classes that are separate from the clairvoyant program.

Some schools have certain entry dates when students can begin a program, while others allow students to begin whenever they desire. Classes may be divided into two categories: students who have been in the program for six months or less, and advanced students. New students learn from the more seasoned students as well as from teachers and staff members who oversee the readings. Some schools only teach weekend or week-long workshops.

Some clairvoyant schools have their own church in order to receive nonprofit status and to ordain students as ministers so that they can be free to practice their readings and engage in spiritual counseling without violating any laws. Some of these churches are wonderful places in which to worship, receive healings and inspiration, and to heal oneself from religious programming.

Pros

Due to the intensity of these clairvoyant training programs, you are likely to make more positive changes during your training than you have ever made in your entire life. You will very quickly access your clairvoyance and become adept at reading. You will have plenty of other students with whom to read, which will help increase your certainty with reading. You will be able to observe and learn from these students. You will have a safe physical environment in which to read. Your clients will be provided for you; you will never have to find them. You will not have to deal with money issues related to reading. You will have staff at your disposal to monitor your progress, answer questions immediately, teach you additional techniques, remind you to use your tools, give you readings and healings, etc.

Cons

Some students who have issues around authority find these schools to be overly oppressive. Some schools have strict policies about engaging in any other spiritual discipline or attending classes outside the school during the duration of the program. These policies were originally established to protect clairvoyant students who are vulnerable to outside influences that might want to interfere with their clairvoyance. However, some of the staff at these schools are competitive with the staff of another school. They fear that you might be recruited by an outside school or teacher. Some schools have rigorous yet reasonable requirements that must be followed in terms of class attendance, punctuality, preparing yourself adequately before a reading, etc. In some schools, staff may have free rein to read you at all times and give you uninvited suggestions for self-improvement. This can lead to personal growth, but can also be annoying, especially if it comes from a staff member who is motivated by their own agenda or MEI pictures.

In some ways, these schools appear to take on cultlike features, although they are certainly not cults. Students learn a certain vocabulary that most of the general public is unfamiliar with, so sometimes "outsiders" have difficulty understanding or relating to the students. Because students are reading so frequently, they are rapidly deprogramming their MEI pictures, releasing foreign energies, and breaking a lot of energetic agreements with family members who often don't understand what clairvoyance is or why anyone would invest time and money learning about it.

Many students who study clairvoyance undergo changes in terms of becoming more self-empowered, more self-sufficient, and more communicative with the inner voice of their heart and with the spirit world or with God. These changes are miracles to the students, but are disturbing to those suspicious family members who don't understand the drastic changes the student is undergoing. As a result, many students tend to minimize contact with their birth families, or in some rare cases cease contact altogether, during the duration of their training program. This is a personal choice that students seem to naturally make and has nothing to do with any mandates by the schools or staff.

Some students of these schools struggle with the fact that they often do not have a choice as to who they will read, or what role they will play in the reading (i.e., center-chair position versus monitoring a reading). The schools have the philosophy that wherever you end up is where you are ultimately meant to be. This may be true, but it can be frustrating if there is a certain position or person you want to read—or avoid!

One of my biggest complaints with many clairvoyant training schools is that they fail to encourage students to read outside the school. I learned nothing in my own clairvoyant program about reading professionally or how to handle reading on my own, except that it was supposed to be a scary and lonely thing to do. I believe the number-one reason for this is that most of the staff members at these schools do not have much experience reading independently. Those who finally venture out of the school to read usually do not return because they get used to making a certain amount of money that far surpasses what they are paid at the school (which is usually very little, if anything), and because their ideology changes to the point where they can no longer fit into the school's philosophy about how classes should be taught. Students and staff who eventually learn how to read on their own gain a substantial level of empowerment that seems to surpass that of staff members who never venture away from the security blanket of the school. These independent readers have a more balanced viewpoint of the world and gain skills and knowledge from the various readers they meet and from their own experiences that they could not have if they had remained forever at the school. In this book I have included information about reading professionally that I would have loved to have learned when I was just a student; information that would have given me far more confidence and peace of mind a lot sooner in my life.

I feel strongly that my own initial clairvoyant training, which took approximately one year, and my subsequent remote viewing training, which has spanned over the course of six years (and that I actually didn't start until after the first edition of this book was published), was worth more than any amount of money. For me, the pitfalls and challenges discussed here are nothing more than a drop in a bucket filled with miracles, fun, excitement and growth. For other people, their lifestyles, schedules, personalities, or level of personal, psychic and spiritual development make them incompatible with these schools. That's one of the reasons why I developed a distant telephone training program of my own: so students from around the globe with busy lives could receive quality training without so many of the restrictions or requirements that some of the lengthier in-person programs might place on them. Some of the other schools have recently followed suit and do now offer distant learning opportunities as well.

Summary

I couldn't sleep. I was obsessing about a relationship turned sour and wondering, as I lay still beside my four-year-old son, Manny, who had already been asleep for several hours, "Was it my fault? Am I to blame?" Suddenly Manny bolted upright in bed. With closed eyes he shouted, "Mommy, stop it! You are thinking too loud! It wasn't your fault!" He then fell backwards onto his pillow and let out an indignant snore.

Despite my years of experience as a psychic reader and teacher, after having written an entire book illustrating how clairvoyance and our other psychic abilities are as natural as our ability to breathe, hear, and speak, an incident such as this one still does not fail to startle and amaze me. While it is my hope that this book will help you recognize, nourish, develop, and really enjoy your own natural psychic abilities, I hope that you never lose your sense of awe over all the gifts that your Creator has built into your being, whether that Creator is God or your own creative soul intent on experiencing the wonders of living here on this glorious planet in the wondrous vessel known as your body. I won't even try to guess how the miracle of our beings, of our bodies, of our everyday struggles and joys, came into being. But as Descartes said, "I think, therefore I am" and if there is one thing the faithful, the faithless, the psychics, the skeptics, the conservatives, the liberals, and everyone in between can agree on, it is that we do exist. There really is nothing more remarkable and nothing more scientifically impossible to explain than this fact.

"Lakshmee!" This word exploded into my head one recent morning before I was quite awake, causing me, this time, to bolt upright.

"Lakshmee? What the heck is a Lakshmee?" I pondered this strange word for a few moments and forgot it by the time breakfast was served. The next day I was painfully combing the tangles from my hair in the shower, when again the word bombarded into my consciousness.

"Lakshmee!" I cleared my mind and again asked what Lakshmee meant. I had the thought, "It is a name." But what kind of name, and what did it have to do with me? When I finished my shower, I wrote the name on my hand with a pen so I would not forget it this time.

My friend Tony Carito from Sedona arrived for a visit that day. (I had recently moved to

Los Angeles to begin my career as a screenwriter/filmmaker.) I told him about this strange word that would not leave me alone. His response surprised and intrigued me.

"Oh, Lakshmee. Sure, that's the Hindu goddess of prosperity and abundance...Why don't we go to the bookstore and look her up?" Tony and I took a drive to the nearby town of Ojai, and stopped at the first bookstore we saw.

"We don't carry metaphysical books. Why don't you try the library down the street?" The friendly salesgirl gave us directions. We arrived at the library and I was excited to see that I was standing at the door of the Theosophical Society. This is a worldwide organization dedicated to the study of spirituality. The first books I ever read on psychic development and on psychic self-defense came from the Theosophical Society Library in Illinois, where I grew up as a child. I had always wanted to visit one of their centers, but this was my first opportunity. We strolled into the cozy dark-paneled building and approached a petite Indian woman at the reception desk. Tony spoke for us.

"We'd like to learn more about the Hindu goddess Lakshmee. Do you have any books on the subject?" With a darling accent, the woman held out her hand graciously.

"Oh yes, yes. So nice to meet you! I am her." Confused, Tony and I looked at each other. He laughed. "Yeah, I guess we'd all like to be the goddess of prosperity!"

"No, you don't understand," she said in broken English. "I am Lakshmee. My name is Lakshmee." That's when one of the other librarians walked up to her and said, "Lakshmee, you have a call on line one."

Later, as Lakshmee pulled books for us, she confirmed, "Lakshmee is the goddess of prosperity, and of fertility."

Only half-joking, I mumbled something to the effect of, "I don't know about the fertile part, but I could sure use some prosperity right now."

She turned and looked me in the eyes. "Oh, the Indian people know that prosperity does not have anything to do with money. It's what is in here," touching her heart, "and here," touching her forehead.

After reading further about Lakshmee, I wandered into the bookstore attached to the library and walked up to the "Extrasensory Perception" section. Next to one of the very books that I had read as a young teen, The Power of the Subconscious Mind, by Joseph Murphy, there was an empty space. As I had done many times at many bookstores, I visualized my own book, this book that you're reading now, filling the empty space. I allowed myself to feel happy about how many lives it would touch and, yes, how much money it would bring in so I would be free to work on my other creative projects. And at that moment, I had no doubt that this book would someday be available in this store, if not stores like this, and I understood completely what Lakshmee had been trying to tell me: It didn't matter whether I had a million dollars or just one dollar in my pocket. What mattered was that I had the certainty, the knowingness, and the faith within me to create the life I desired.

Despite my clairvoyant ability, I did not ultimately know at that moment what the future would hold, but I did know that if all the world crumbled beneath my feet tomorrow, if I suddenly lost everything and everyone dear to me in this physical world, that I would be okay. Even though I would surely have bad days where life really sucked, I would have the tools, the groundedness, the neutrality, the energy, and the ability to see, hear, and feel the boundless guidance within and around me, allowing me not merely to survive, but to prosper.

This faith comes with the practice of the techniques and principles within this book. It is the true gift. It is your gift. Behold.

Glossary

ASTRAL PROJECTION OR TRAVEL: The ability for one's spirit to leave one's body and travel on the astral plane or in other dimensions.

ASTRAL RAPE: A sexual crime committed by force or against another's will that occurs on an energetic or spiritual level.

ATHEISM: A disbelief in the spiritual, including God, psychic phenomena, or the human soul.

AURA: The energetic field surrounding every living organism that contains information about the organism and energies affecting it. The aura can be thought of as the organism's spirit that extends outward from the body.

BOSTWICK, LEWIS: Father of clairvoyant training in the United States and founder of the Berkeley Psychic Institute.

CHAKRAS: Sanskrit word for "spinning wheel," chakras are energy centers that correspond to certain parts of the human body and that regulate the body's overall functioning.

CHANNELING: A psychic ability in which a person receives and communicates information coming directly from a source outside themselves.

CLAIRAUDIENCE: A specific psychic ability in which information inaudible to the human ears is heard inside one's mind.

CLAIRSENTIENCE: A specific psychic ability in which information is received through touch or on a physical body level.

CLAIRVOYANCE: A specific psychic ability located in one's sixth chakra, or third eye, that involves accessing information in the form of images, visions, and pictures.

CLAIRVOYANT HEALING: An act in which visualization is utilized to eliminate or transmute emotional or physical pain or negative energies and to restore one to a healthier state.

CLAIRVOYANT READING: An act in which information in the form of mental images, visions, and pictures is accessed.

CODEPENDENT RELATIONSHIP: An unbalanced relationship in which one person sacrifices their own ideals or ignores their inner voice in order to maintain the relationship or get other needs met within the relationship.

CONTROL FREAK: A person who needs to understand or determine every element in life and interferes with the natural course of things, or who expends energy trying to control that which is out of their control. One who attempts to circumvent God's will.

CORE MEI PICTURES: An MEI picture that is developed early in life and that over time attracts similar clusters of thoughts and emotions that influence our perceptions and behavior. Personal transformation occurs when these pictures are destroyed or deenergized.

COSMIC ENERGY: Energy that originates from the air, sun, atmosphere, the spiritual realm, or God.

COUPLE'S READING: A clairvoyant reading in which a psychic reads the relationship or joint goals between two or more readees who are physically present.

CREATING/CREATION: To bring into being.

CROP CIRCLES: A supernatural phenomenon in which geometric patterns suddenly appear in wheat fields. These patterns range in size from a few feet in diameter to miles long. Some of these patterns appear over the course of just a few minutes' time and register as having unusual electromagnetic qualities.

DESTROY: To eliminate or alter a creation.

DISEMBODIED SPIRIT: A spirit that no longer belongs to a physical body.

EARTH ENERGY: Energy that originates from within the earth.

ENERGY: Life force; the essence of all things physical and nonphysical. Matter, atoms, thoughts, emotions, and pain consist of energy.

ENLIGHTENMENT: A state in which a person has become actualized, has accumulated a certain level of wisdom; when a person's body, mind, and spirit are fully integrated and their being holds more lightness than darkness.

ETHICAL DILEMMA: A conflict in which one must choose between two seemingly opposing values.

ETHICS: The study of rules of right and wrong in human conduct.

EXPECTATION: Having a predetermined set of ideas of how an event will unfold.

EXTRASENSORY PERCEPTION: Perceiving information through means other than the five physical senses.

FAITH: Belief or trust in an outcome before the outcome occurs.

FREE-FLOATING ANXIETY: When one person is anxious, this anxiety can be transmitted energetically to other people, who will experience the anxiety as if it were their own. These people then either have no idea why they are feeling anxious, or they may erroneously attribute this anxiety to a particular issue, thereby blowing the issue out of proportion.

GROUNDING CORD: An energetic connection securing an object or person to the earth. Other energies can be released through this cord.

GROUPTHINK: A phenomenon that occurs among groups of people in which their energies merge and they adopt each other's beliefs, thoughts, and emotions, sometimes at the expense of their individual beliefs and codes of ethics.

GROWTH PERIOD: An intense period of personal transformation during which one's beliefs, thoughts, perceptions, and self-image are altered. This can result in a temporary period of emotional or cognitive turbulence.

IMAGINATION: The act or power of creating pictures or ideas in the mind.

INCARNATION: A lifetime in a particular body.

INQUISITION: A court for finding and punishing heretics, set up by the Roman Catholic Church in the thirteenth century and lasting several centuries. These heretics included women accused of witchcraft, people displaying psychic abilities, or those practicing alternative faiths or religions.

KARMA: Spiritual award system that can include both desirable and undesirable consequences for one's prior conduct either in the present life or in prior incarnations.

KIRLIAN PHOTOGRAPHY: Heat-sensitive photography that can record information not ordinarily registered by the physical eye.

KNOWINGNESS: A psychic ability located in the crown chakra, or seventh chakra, in which a person instantaneously knows information in the form of a thought, without having to go through logical steps to gain that information.

LIBRARY OF SYMBOLS: A collection of symbolic images.

LITERAL IMAGE: An image that is what it appears to be.

MARTYR COMPLEX: A self-defeating set of beliefs and behaviors that causes a person to gain satisfaction and elevated self-esteem by sacrificing their own pleasure and needs for the sake of others.

MEDITATION: Listening to God; focusing attention inward or on a particular object.

MEI PICTURE: Mental Emotional Image picture. This is an emotionally charged thoughtform that influences one's perceptions and behavior and is located within one's body, mind, and energetic field.

MULTIPLE PERSONALITY DISORDER: A psychological dissociative disorder in which aspects of a person split off from the person's awareness and behave and respond independently from other aspects.

NAVIGATING: The science of figuring out where one is heading. Charting a course, a path, or a plan that will lead to an intended goal.

NEUTRALITY: Being neutral; maintaining a state of emotional and cognitive balance that is not invested in a particular outcome.

NONATTACHMENT: Having no emotional investment in an object or in the outcome of a situation.

OMNIPRESENT: Being everywhere all at once.

OMNISCIENT: All-knowing.

PRAYER: The act of talking to God or to a higher power.

PRECOGNITION: Knowing that something is going to happen before it happens.

PROGRAMMING: Beliefs, thoughts, ethics, information, feelings, or perceptions that are passed from one person to another that may or may not be in harmony with the recipient's own information or way of being.

PROJECTION: To see one's own qualities in someone else, often unconsciously; to assign particular attributes to another that really belong to oneself.

PSYCHIC EXPERIENCE: A supernatural experience in which information is sent or received through means other than the five senses.

PSYCHIC TOOLS: Visualization techniques that affect and influence energy that can be utilized for psychic reading and healing and to enhance the quality of one's life.

RELATIONSHIP READING: A psychic reading that focuses on issues regarding the relationship between two or more individuals.

SELF-ENERGIZATION: To call one's life force to oneself.

SEPARATION OBJECT: A mental image or visualization that defines boundaries and serves as protection.

SKEPTICISM: A closed state of mind where one doubts or questions things, sometimes to the point where these doubts obscure the truth.

SPIRIT: The essence of a person.

SPIRITUAL PATH: A course that one's spirit is destined to follow in order to gain certain life experiences while in the physical body.

SUPERNATURAL: Beyond the physical senses; beyond the natural.

SYMBOL: An object or sign that represents another object, idea, person, or quality.

SYMBOLIC IMAGE: An image that is representative of something other than itself.

TELEKINESIS: A psychic ability in which one can move or alter objects with the power of thought, emotion, or other energy, through nonphysical means.

TELEPATHY: Transferring information from one mind to another without the use of the physical senses.

THIRD EYE: The center of one's clairvoyance. The third eye corresponds with the sixth chakra and is located inside the forehead, slightly above and between the physical eyes.

TRANSFORMATION: To effect change.

TRANSMEDIUMSHIP: A spiritual ability in which a person's spirit leaves the body and accepts a foreign spirit or energy into their own. This happens both consciously and unconsciously.

UNIVERSAL SPIRIT: God.

VALIDATION: To confirm one's value.

VISUALIZATION: The act of calling forth images, visions, and pictures in one's mind.

VORTEX: A highly charged energy center or chakra within the earth that has an influence on nearby organisms.

YOGANANDA, PARAMAHANSA: An influential Indian yogi, author of *Autobiography of a Yogi,* and founder of the Self-Realization Institute.

Bibliography

Choquette, Sonia. *Your Heart's Desire: Instructions for Creating the Life You Really Want.* New York: Three Rivers Press, 1997.

Dyer, Wayne. *You'll See It When You Believe It.* New York: HarperCollins, 2001.

Gawain, Shakti. *Creative Visualization.* Revised edition. Novato, CR Nataraj Publishing/New World Library, 2002.

Judith, Anodea. *Wheels of Life.* Revised and expanded edition. Saint Paul, MN: Llewellyn Publishing, 1999.

McArthur, Bruce. *Your Life: Why It Is the Way It Is, and What You Can Do About It.* Virginia Beach: A.E.R. Press, 1993.

Murphy, Joseph. *The Power of Your Subconcious Mind.* Revised and expanded edition. Paramus, NJ: Reward Books, 2000.

Myss, Caroline, Ph.D. *Three Levels of Power and How to Use Them.* Audiocassette. Louisville, CO: Sounds True, Inc.

Myss, Caroline, Ph.D. *Why People Don't Heal and How They Can.* Audiocassette. Louisville, CO: Sounds True, Inc.

Williamson, Marianne. *A Return to Love: Reflections on the Principles of A Course in Miracles.* New York: HarperCollins, 1996.

Yogananda, Paramahansa. *Autobiography of a Yogi.* Los Angeles, CA Self-Realization Fellowship, 1946.

EXTRAORDINARY
PSYCHIC

Proven Techniques to Master
Your Psychic Abilities

DEBRA LYNNE KATZ

Living Dreams Press

livingdreamspress.com

Prologue

The gift is not being psychic. It's knowing you are.
— DEBRA LYNNE KATZ

Many people ask me what was most challenging about writing my first book, *You Are Psychic*. They expect me to say finding a publisher (which was actually quite easy) or finding the time as a single working mom to write a book. (Sleep? What's that?)

What most people don't expect is the truth: that the most difficult thing for me was getting over the ideas that were stuck in my head that clairvoyance can't or shouldn't be taught in a book available to a general audience. Along with such thoughts, I also had some pretty intense feelings of fear—fear that I was revealing secrets that some people would not be happy to have revealed. Which people? The list includes some of my former teachers, and those who ran the psychic schools that only shared such information with students who agreed to sign up and pay for in-person, twelve-to-twenty-four-month training programs. I'd also include some of the untrained professional psychics who didn't want to admit even to themselves that millions of other people could be doing exactly what they were doing—and perhaps even doing it better.

There have, of course, been other books on the market for over a century that have taught ways to enhance psychic abilities, but there wasn't anything else that provided step-by-step instructions for instant access of information through clairvoyance—a very specific psychic ability that allows people to "see" visions, images, and pictures about anything and anyone at any point in time. Furthermore, most books on psychic development did not explain how utilizing psychic abilities can enhance one's life or lead to a quickening of personal transformation and development, nor did they offer the tools for such utilization.

The main reason for the lack of available written resources was that those running the clairvoyant training schools had themselves come from a tradition in which training only occurred in person, under close supervision, and over a long period of time. These techniques are so powerful that they bring about fast—if not instantaneous—change in people, which can be emotionally tumultuous for some students. Those who ran these schools knew how effective their programs were for training psychics within a supportive environment, and they couldn't imagine doing things differently. So some, perhaps most, of their reluctance to share this information was due to genuine concern. Some of their reluctance resulted from a lack of flexibility and imagination; some of it was a product of economic interest and fear.

Fortunately, over the past five or six years just about all of the larger schools (mostly those in California) have begun adjusting themselves to the changing needs and lifestyles of overworked and underpaid Americans. Many of these schools are now offering modified programs that can be taken over one weekend per month or even online. The result is that people all over the country have greater access to clairvoyant training.

The thirteen months I spent as a clairvoyant student was certainly one of the best times of my life, and it helped form who I am today. I thought the program I went through was perfect, except for one area within the curriculum that I felt was severely lacking and that still seems to be deficient in some of the schools today: there was little to no training to help students deal with being psychic, particularly with being professional psychics, outside the security of the schools that train them. In fact, we were taught that it's cold and lonely out there in a world filled with atheists, skeptics, untrained psychics, and the ungrounded mainstream masses.

Leaving the school as a lone psychic for the big, scary world was terrifying, but it didn't take me long to discover there were lots and lots of wonderful, supportive people out there with similar interests, even if they didn't have the same kind or level of training as I did. This is why I made sure to include chapters in *You Are Psychic* such as "The Business of Spirituality," "Psychic Ethics," and "Dealing with the Mainstream" (retitled as "The Psychic Minority"), as well as to discuss other topics of concern to people seeking to incorporate their psychic skills into their work or who really wanted to live life honestly—as the psychics they truly are.

While writing *You Are Psychic*, I knew with certainty that the techniques worked when taught in class and workshop settings. However, there was no way I could know for sure how effective teaching the techniques in a *book* would be. Now, with the book having been out for three years, I have no doubt. Hundreds of readers of *You Are Psychic* have come to my workshops, called me, e-mailed me, even given *me* readings, and they never cease to amaze me with their level of clairvoyant skill. These psychics swear up and down that before reading *You Are Psychic* they had never seen a clairvoyant vision in their life nor had the slightest idea how to do a reading or healing.

All of this is not to say that such people don't still have questions, or areas in which they feel they need clarification or further guidance. In fact, that is why I decided to write *Extraordinary Psychic* and to give it the subtitle *Proven Techniques to Master Your Natural Psychic Abilities*. I felt it was time to offer additional techniques for psychic reading and healing that would help those already practicing to fine-tune their skills and overcome certain challenges that many clairvoyant students and even professional psychics struggle with. Furthermore, as I have gained more experience training psychics in various formats—from very short demonstrations to psychic "bootcamps" to a long-distance telephone training program—I've learned how to present the techniques more concisely, which appeals to certain types of personalities and learning styles.

In my personal practice as a psychic and as a teacher, I have been fine-tuning my other psychic abilities of clairaudience, telepathy, and remote viewing, and I've discovered how to help my students incorporate these abilities into their clairvoyant practice as well. In *You Are Psychic* I introduced concepts and clairvoyant techniques that can increase your ability to manifest your goals and help you to let go of that which is no longer serving you. Now, in *Extraordinary Psychic*, I offer guidance into why these concepts don't always work for everyone, or why they don't always work quickly enough and what you can do about this (besides being patient, which is the hardest thing of all and the last thing you want to hear!). In *You Are Psychic* I introduced basic energy healing and touched upon the spirit world. Here, in this book, I go into much greater detail about the beings you are most likely to encounter when removing "the veil" and how to communicate with some while eradicating others. In this book I also offer advice about how to protect yourself as a psychic and as a healer, and how to create and enforce boundaries.

I know that many of you are reading this book about exploring your psychic abilities because there are few other topics that excite you as much. Others of you are still quite undecided as to whether you want to have anything to do with being psychic, but instead are desperately seeking answers to questions about unusual and sometimes even disturbing phenomena that have been happening to you, either recently or for as long as you can remember. Still others have started to practice the techniques in *You Are Psychic* and now have some questions, or are hungry for more practical instruction.

I have written *Extraordinary Psychic* both as a sequel to *You Are Psychic* and as a training guide that can stand on its own. Whether you see yourself as ordinary or less than ordinary, I can assure you of two things: One is that by the fact of your mere existence, you are already extraordinary. Two is that as a human being you cannot help being psychic to some degree, any more than you can help breathing. Whether you know it or not, your psychic abilities are influencing you—and your thoughts and feelings and creations—at every moment of your life. If you attempt the techniques in *Extraordinary Psychic* even once or twice, you are going to see results. If you continue to practice them, you are going to realize that *you are an extraordinary psychic* after all, even if you have lived many decades thinking otherwise. This is because the gift is not *being* psychic—it's *knowing* you are.

PART I

Clairvoyant Techniques

CHAPTER 1

Introduction

What happens when you take a million ordinary citizens and
turn them into extraordinary psychics? Evolution!
—— DEBRA LYNNE KATZ

Many people would love to experience clairvoyant visions that contain useful information for themselves and others, but they haven't got the foggiest idea how to initiate or control this process. Some believe the only way to do so is to put themselves through extreme circumstances, such as fasting for long periods, banishing themselves into harsh wilderness conditions, taking hallucinogenic drugs, or paying thousands of dollars for remote viewing or lengthy and costly clairvoyant or remote-viewing training programs.

While long-term, in-depth, and in-person training is a path I fully endorse and is the path that led to the writing of this book, countless readers of my first book, *You Are Psychic*, have demonstrated that such training is not necessary to access and utilize one's clairvoyance. In fact, during a recent expo in Los Angeles at which I conducted a clairvoyant training demonstration, I taught a group of sixty-five people how to perform a clairvoyant reading in less than forty-five minutes, something even I was not sure would be possible in such a short period of time.

Out of the twelve or so volunteers I called up to the front of the room, four were "seeing" almost the exact same images within minutes. Even though the woman they were practicing on stated nothing more than her name, they each saw her standing before a microphone singing passionately. A few others saw her with suitcases and sipping drinks on a beach in what appeared to be or felt like a resort in Mexico. The woman confirmed she was leaving that night to go perform at a resort in Cancun.

The mood changed drastically as another volunteer offered herself up to be "read." Even before I finished leading them through the opening exercise, four or five of the readers had tears in their eyes, while one actually burst out in sobs. At this point they had no idea why they were having this kind of emotional reaction. However, soon a few more novice readers began receiving images and clairaudient messages indicating that this woman was grieving the death of someone close to her. She later confirmed that several of her family members had died very recently, including a parent. I wasn't surprised to discover that the reader who had the strongest initial emotional reaction had recently lost a parent herself. This is an example of clairsentience, the psychic ability of feeling others' emotions and physical sensations. This ability naturally emerges when utilizing one's clairvoyance.

What Exactly Is Clairvoyant Reading?

Clairvoyant reading is a very intensive form of meditation in which you focus on some simple visualizations, pose questions to these visualizations, and then wait patiently for the information to arrive. This information can be about anyone or anything. The only way it can work is through complete inward focus and concentration. But wait, don't let that scare you! When you know the right techniques to use, which you will soon, this intense concentration will be effortless. Why? Because when you are doing clairvoyant readings, you are not *trying* to quiet and empty a mind that by nature is addicted to being busy and noisy. Instead, your mind is so active with the techniques that the end result is you are focusing without *trying* to focus. This is particularly true when you are doing a reading on someone else, which is a lot easier than reading yourself.

When you see visions or use your clairvoyance, and you take the time to communicate the information to someone else, this is called a *reading*. When we "read" other people we can see into any aspect of their lives. The information comes from a variety of sources. Some of it comes from what I'd call a universal source of all knowingness. Very little is known about this source except that it's there to tap into it whenever we like. This source is the same one that I believe Carl Jung was referring to when he coined the term *collective unconscious*. The information contained within this source is largely or perhaps entirely of a visual nature. Because the information exists in the form of pictures and archetypal images, it can be accessed by people of every nation, regardless of their verbal language or ability to use verbal language at all. We all interact with this source every night through our dreams. It's possible even animals can tap into this source, although I don't know that for sure.

MEI Pictures/Filters/Programs

When we access information from this universal source, we cannot help but view it through own filters of perception. These filters are our own personal pictures made up of thoughtforms and feelings upon which our personalities and egos are based, and which very much determine how we approach life and all relationships, including those with others and with ourselves. In *You Are Psychic* I refer to these pictures or filters as Mental/Emotional Image pictures (MEI pictures). These filters are like minute programs running through our psyches. They are connected into particular parts of our bodies and energy fields and can even result in disease or physical pain. Sometimes they consist entirely of pain. They are like secret scripts that echo past traumatic experiences. Quite frequently these programs or scripts are written and passed on by those who raised us, or by our own selves to make sense of our past disappointments. We often carry these pictures or programs with us from other incarnations into our present one. They then act as shackles that keep us from expressing our true essence and experiencing greater freedom to be who we are or who we truly want to be in present time.

When we read other people who have something in common with us, who are strong mirrors for us, not only do we become more aware of these pictures or filters, but energetically they actually begin to shift and fall away, regardless of whether we can identify them at the time. In this way, performing a clairvoyant reading or healing on another person can be a powerful method of self-transformation because it allows us to deprogram ourselves so we are freer to be our own true selves in the present moment. This is really what all transpersonal and psychological modalities attempt to do, but clairvoyant reading can do it much faster. As a clairvoyant reader aware of this process, we can be our own therapist. Our clients are our mirrors and the impetus for change within ourselves. It's important to understand that this process occurs whether or not you think you have something in common with the person you are reading and really has nothing to do with your cognitive awareness, although the more readings you do, the more impressed you will be with the fact that you tend to read people who are in fact dealing with issues similar to those you are also dealing with in the present moment.

Other Sources of Information

Apart from the universal source of knowingness, during a clairvoyant reading other sources of psychic information can be accessed to obtain information. These include telepathic communication from other living people, as well as deceased individuals and beings we call *spirit guides*, which behave as if their job is to help out with such matters. (As I will discuss in chapter 13, I've never had an entity actually hand me a business card that identifies him literally as a "spirit guide," but this term does correctly embody the intentions of a variety of beings available to assist us.) Sometimes as the clairvoyant, it will be you who is the source of the information as your spirit travels to a particular location to observe a lost object or incident that has occurred or that will occur at a specific point in time.

Readings can be done by letting the information come to you or by you going to the information, and you will be learning both these methods in the next few chapters. Much of the time when you seek information about a person, particularly one who has solicited your assistance and is sitting beside you or is talking to you on the telephone, you will discover the bulk of the information about that person's life resides in their aura, which is another word for the energy field that surrounds every living thing. An aura is a map of the body and a history book of the soul that accompanies that body. The first chapter of this historical epic begins long before the soul was thrust into this current lifetime; indeed, our auras contain information about all our incarnations—past, present, and to some extent future (see chapter 7). Often, when a person asks a question about their health or a goal, a clairvoyant's attention will be drawn to a specific location within the aura. This is particularly true with health and relationship questions.

Many times a readee will want to know why they are suffering from a particular ailment or what can be done about it. Often, in addition to receiving an answer about the readee's physical anatomy, an image will come up that indicates the person had a weakness in that area related to emotional trauma or neglect prior to the manifestation of the illness or problem. Carolyn Myss, in her book *Anatomy of the Spirit* and her excellent audiotape series *Why People Don't Heal* and *Three Levels of Power*, does a great job of explaining various ailments with their corresponding energy dynamics. My own readings with thousands of clients have led me to come up with similar connections. After practicing the techniques in the following chapters, you will likely begin to make similar observations.

Foreign Energies

Our auras also contain a plethora of foreign energies that profoundly influence our physical, mental, and emotional health. These energies are derived from sources apart from ourselves, but they merge with us when they enter our field or when we enter the fields of others. Some of these foreign sources include family members, lovers, bosses, ancestors, spirits, and an assorted cast of other characters, with or without bodies. The type and amount of these energies that dwell within our auras and body at any given time largely determine how we feel and experience ourselves (self-esteem), and the ways in which we manifest on a creative level.

These energies influence our level of personal freedom and power, which obviously has an impact on our everyday life experiences such as finances, relationships, work, and on our overall development. Many clairvoyants have observed that these foreign energies travel back and forth through things that look like cords of electricity. These cords also sometimes show up in photographs. (I am currently working on a new book, which includes a collection of such photos taken by a close friend of mine, Kazandrah Martin, who is a healer and clairvoyant in Sedona, Arizona.) Sometimes, two people's energy fields are so merged together that they look like Siamese twins. This corresponds with the degree of codependency between the two. Most often I see this with an emotionally dependent parent and a child who has allowed that parent to feed off their energy system with the hope that someday the parent will change and give them what they were missing as children.

A common image I encounter in my readings is that of my client standing in front of a mirror. Sometimes the client is smiling, sometimes frowning; there are often other faces and bodies standing around my client in the mirror. I've discovered through corresponding symbols and intuitive information that this usually indicates the client is experiencing himself or herself through another's eyes and emotions. Now this might be terrific if the other person is a happy, encouraging, self-loving person who loves the client. But what if the "other" is picky and depressed, or filled with anxiety and self-loathing? Most of the time when I describe what I am seeing, the readee knows exactly who I am talking about, and verifies that their self-esteem and feelings of self-worth have been less than positive since being involved with this other person, or since this person began having problems in their own life.

I have personally encountered dramatic shifts in my own self-perception and self-esteem— particularly my satisfaction with my body and even my ability to lose weight—after performing some self-healing techniques during which I released from my aura the foreign energy of someone I was dating. Some of these techniques are presented in chapter 3 and chapters 15 through 17. It doesn't matter how much you love your partner or your children or your clients. Their thoughts, feelings, and pain often do not serve you when they are in your body. It is like running the wrong fuel through your engine. It will clog things up, slow you down, burn you out, and even cause your immune system to break down.

If you feel as if you are living a life that is not your own or if your job and the people around you don't make you feel good, most likely you are running other people's programs and energy through your body, which has caused you to make the choices that have led you to your current situation. As soon as you clear these out and get back in touch with your own life force, vibration, energy, path, whatever you want to call it, your life will begin to reshape itself to fit who you really are right now, in the present moment. This is what giving and receiving clairvoyant readings and healings can do for you.

Seeing Is Not Just Seeing

After twelve years of experience as a clairvoyant reader and healer, I am thrilled to be discovering the extent of quality research that confirms many of my own personal observations and experiences. Some of the books that do a fantastic job describing this research are *Mind-Reach* by Russell Targ and Harold E. Puthoff; Dean Radin's *The Conscious Universe* and *Entangled Minds*; and Lynne McTaggart's *The Field* and *The Intention Experiment*. All these authors note that quantum physicists, in their early research, discovered that particles—the building blocks of atoms, made up of electric charges, magnetic charges, and light—changed as they were being observed, even when researchers were doing nothing more than looking at them. Long before I ever heard about the above-mentioned research, I would often be looking at someone's aura or some kind of energy, and I would notice that it immediately began shifting, even before I communicated what I was seeing to the readee. After alerting the readee to the energy I was seeing, I would many times see an even greater shift in that energy.

In *The Intention Experiment*, McTaggart makes a distinction between *attention* and *intention*. Attention is focusing on something without intent; intention is focus with a desired outcome. Likewise, *clairvoyant reading* is putting your attention on the target or object, while *clairvoyant healing* is reading with the intention to initiate a change. This intention can be general—as when you approach a reading with the attitude that you are going to do your best to see and offer the most accurate information in order to help your readee achieve maximum health and happiness. Or your intention may be specific, in that it might address a particular issue—for example, your readee suffers from headaches or depression, and your intention is to free them of these ailments. For myself and most psychics I know personally, we naturally bring this general goal to our work with every client, so we can't say that we are ever just merely observing without any intent behind it. But there are definitely different degrees of intent and, as McTaggart explains, intention is not just desire; it's a definitive commitment to achieve results. From my own observations, there seems to be a proportional connection between the strength of the desire and the impact of the healing, particularly when the one being healed has the same commitment to their own healing as the one doing the healing. (You'd be surprised how often the healer is more invested in the outcome than the person being healed!)

For example, I might do a clairvoyant reading for a client and discover that she currently has cancer. As I look at the cancer cells, their location, and the underlying energy and issues that seem to be related to the cancer, I will often begin to see a shift happen in the energy field. For some reason I tend to see cancer as white, and there are times when I am just merely looking at the white color that it begins to move and dissipate. Sometimes when the movement occurs, the readee actually begins to experience a sensation. Yet it is when I actually decide to actively heal the person of their cancer, by imagining and willing or demanding that the white release out of the affected area and go down a grounding cord, that I observe the greatest changes and the client experiences the most profound physical shifts or has the greatest emotional release. This release occurs whether or not the client had any idea that I was actually performing a healing.

Quite often when reading a person, an image will spontaneously come to me that I can then work with when I am ready to perform a clairvoyant healing on them. For example, I might see a black streak cutting across my client's heart, so I will use my imagination and visualize that black color releasing from the heart. Or I might see an image of the client's heart as if it were feeble and gasping for breath. In this case I would ask the heart to show me the color of whatever has been causing the weakness in it. The color doesn't really mean anything to me other than giving me something to hold on to—to work with or manipulate. If the color seems to represent something that is not healthy, I can visualize it releasing. If it is something pleasant, such as a vibration of joy or creativity or passion, I may choose to visualize it washing away any other colors as if it were clean water swirling inside a washing machine. I may also choose to visualize this color as if it were completely filling up the client's body and aura, or a particular area in need of this energy. I may share this color with the client or ask them to describe their favorite color or one that makes them happy, in order to see if it corresponds with the one I am seeing. Then I will give the client an assignment to work with this color in their own meditation space as a self-healing empowerment exercise.

This is how a basic clairvoyant healing is done. We set the intention to make a strong difference and utilize visualizations to achieve this purpose. In a pure clairvoyant *reading*, we are just observing—with kindness, but we are not intentionally changing what we are seeing, even though such a change may in fact be the end result. Remember: it's as simple as shining a light exactly on the area that needs illumination, and the readee's spirit will see the spot that they could not quite reach before on their own, and a shift will take place.

Sometimes this spiritual communication in the form of a clairvoyant reading is all the person needs; other times the reading is just one thing in a cumulative series of events. At other times, intentional healing is necessary, and even then it may not have immediate and complete results but rather move the client one small step on their journey to health. If the client is not at all open to growth or change due to fear or a compulsive need to control something that they cannot control (which is almost always due to fear anyway), then the reading and healing may have no effect other than to really piss the client off!

I once received a letter from a woman who stated that her boyfriend was very abusive, was currently serving a prison term for attempted murder, and was addicted to methamphetamine. This man told the woman who wrote me that he never wanted to see her again. She asked me what I could do to help him (translation: change him) so that she could get back together with him. I told her, "Absolutely nothing," but I added that I might be able to figure out why she was settling for someone like him and to help her emotionally let go of this very destructive attachment in her life. I wasn't surprised when I never heard back from her. *Her problem wasn't with him. It was with herself.*

Healer, Heal Thyself

One of the most important things to understand about clairvoyant reading is that it's not just the readee who is being influenced by the clairvoyant's attention and intentions. The clairvoyant is very much affected as well. This is where we may have to part ways with the quantum physicists—not because they aren't being influenced by the particles they are observing, but because most of them would never even think to consider this as a possibility, and I can't imagine that the particles themselves would have enough strength to elicit the same effect that one person's energy field can have on another. This is why we need more of these very smart physicists to study larger particles— i.e., people!

During a clairvoyant reading, the readers will also be experiencing their own clairsentience— the ability to feel others' emotions and physical sensations as one's own, including pain, exhaustion, and sexual arousal. As I mentioned, during a reading the clairvoyant will be encountering and working through their own issues and matching pictures with the client, which will be stimulated and brought to the surface for the purpose of healing. When psychics are unaware of these matching pictures, it's easy to get stuck and fall into resistance of them, which usually translates into resisting the person they are reading, or feeling fear about doing the reading at all. If psychics are aware of how the process works, there are techniques they can utilize to allow them to use this process to their advantage. In this respect, clairvoyant reading can be a tool for paradigm shifts, emotional release, and overall rapid and significant growth. However, with rapid growth comes change—and as you know, change can sometimes be more than a bit distressing.

In clairvoyant circles this process is called a *growth period*. In other spiritual disciplines it's called a *dark night of the soul*. This is because the soul suddenly becomes aware that it was operating from false premises, such as fantasies or fears, or other people's ideas, dreams, and limitations. These premises may have been exactly the ones the spirit needed in order to learn certain lessons or achieve certain goals in life up until this point, but they no longer serve the spirit. When this occurs, sometimes our previous belief structure—in which our identity was enmeshed and into which we grounded in order to be secure—collapses. The only way we can really feel better is to adopt a new belief system that fits us better in the present time.

Sometimes, however, there is a gap in time before we can form that new belief system or ground into it. While there is much to learn and experience in that gap, our ego may actually feel as if it is dying or has died and has nothing to hang on to; this can be downright terrifying. Actually, it isn't being in that gap that's a problem, but instead it's the lack of understanding that unnerves us and tricks us into wondering if we are going nuts. This is because during such a growth period we really are losing touch with "reality." Yet that can be a good thing, if the "reality" we were previously in touch with was not really real.

When we are in this limbo, in this gap of not knowing any longer what to believe, and when we can recognize this state for what it is, and actually celebrate it, we will be in an extremely powerful place because the possibilities for what we can create and where we can go will be astounding. Unfortunately, most people don't really get this until after they've come out on the other end and can look back at the experience from a safe distance and not only say, "Wow, that was intense. I don't want to go through that again!" but also appreciate it as a defining point in their personal and/or spiritual development. This period is often followed up with extreme changes in a person's life, which can include ending relationships and giving up jobs, material items, and ways of behaving that were no longer productive in order to make way for a whole new bundle of opportunities often associated with greater creativity and peace.

It is my most sincere hope that this book will help you use clairvoyant reading to initiate this growth process in yourself, and that you will remember to congratulate yourself for the changes you are making if and when life as you know it begins to feel a bit topsy-turvy. I promise that such a feeling won't last long—although I guess *long* is a subjective word!

The process of psychic development and reading (which is also a form of remote viewing—see chapters 10 and 11) that I will focus on in this book can be merely a set of mental exercises you can utilize to call upon any kind of information through extrasensory perception, or it can be a spiritual discipline and practice that yield deep and lasting results for self-development. If you practice the techniques just a few times, you will most likely discover that they yield immediate results. The longer and deeper you practice, the greater fruits they will bear—as is true in the other spiritual disciplines, whether yoga, martial arts, or even any of the creative arts such as painting, music, writing, dance, and so on. With all of these, it takes courage, faith, determination, focus, and patience to get past both the inner resistance and outer resistance that are in operation every moment, even right this moment as you decide whether to read one more word of this book or abandon it and turn on the TV instead. One of the reasons I have written this book is to help people get past this resistance. *Resistance* here is defined as anything that would keep you separate—physically, mentally, or emotionally—from your abilities, your own inner voice, or your affinity for yourself. The root of resistance is fear (see also chapter 20).

The tricky thing about resistance is sometimes, even often, people confuse it with a "gut feeling." The expression "Listen to your gut" always makes me cringe because most of the information connected with our guts (which correspond to the third chakra) has to do with issues of power and control, and sometimes plain old-fashioned gas or menstrual cramps! Control is a mechanism that attempts to avoid and protect us from fear. But when we realize we cannot control what we fear, this part of our body will send signals that scream out "Danger! Danger!" and secrete all kinds of toxins and acids that cause indigestion, ulcers, or even cancers.

I am in no way disputing the power of intuition; rather, I am suggesting that intuition doesn't really come from your "gut." Instead, it stimulates the fear sensation or reaction in your gut, which is probably why people think it's their gut that is the voice of intuition. *Intuition* is a term used to describe a wide variety of psychic abilities and sensations, and I believe intuition originates more in the upper chakras or energy centers of the body than in the lower ones.

Fortunately, we have our clairvoyance, the ability to see information in the form of pictures and images. When we know how to work with our clairvoyance, which you will after reading this book, we have a way to obtain more detailed, accurate, and objective information so that we can make better decisions, such as whether or not we really shouldn't get on that plane, or if we just need to ground ourselves, take a nap, a yoga class, or an Alka-Seltzer.

If you don't know for certain that you are psychic, if you have never had a clairvoyant vision as far as you recall, if you have had one but don't know how to control it, or if you know beyond all doubt you are clairvoyant but are not using your clairvoyance in the ways or to the degree you suspect you could, *there is a reason for that!* You are "stuck" in a reality that says these things are not real, possible, or safe, at least not for you. However, I can guarantee you that this "reality" is anything but real! It is an illusion. Up until now there was something else at play—a force within you, or outside yourself in the form of a person, people, the entire society perhaps—blocking your awareness, preventing you from having the knowledge and access to the knowledge. I can be as certain of that as I am certain that *you are psychic. You are clairvoyant. You are clairsentient. You are clairaudient. You are a medium!*

Overcoming years of unconscious resistance to your own psychic abilities can be more than just challenging, particularly when you are surrounded by others who continue to be stuck in this very same resistance. Developing your abilities within a structured and supportive group setting is the easiest way to achieve your goal. However, it may not be practical for you right now in terms of time and family commitments, your other goals, your location, or your finances. Therefore, it is my sincerest desire and intent to give you everything you might possibly need that is in my power to give you, in order to help you help yourself as you move up, down, along, in circles, sometimes backward, but mostly forward along the never-ending path of your clairvoyant development.

I am going to give you the tools and pass along the lessons you need to pull yourself out of any potholes, to create bridges from one signpost to the next, and to slay any trolls, demons, or hollow-eyed aliens that are threatening to huff and puff and blow your house down. It will of course be up to you to make good use of these tools.

CHAPTER 2

What Is an Extraordinary Psychic?

God doesn't look at how much we do, but with how much love we do it.
— MOTHER TERESA

Most of society thinks that an extraordinary psychic is someone with special psychic powers. What people don't understand is that it's not about *having* the powers as much as it is about what we do with them. There are many people with tremendous psychic abilities who don't have the courage, self-esteem, focus, sincerity, perseverance, or communication skills to utilize their abilities consciously and effectively.

Courage, Perseverance, and Self-Discipline

The best psychics and healers are the most courageous ones. They don't let anyone or anything, particularly their own emotions, get in the way of them seeing and speaking the truth, even when this truth is the last thing they think anyone wants to hear. Usually, that which we are most afraid of seeing and reporting is the very thing our client needs to and longs to hear the most, because it is reflective of the truth of their current experience, regardless of whether we as the messengers judge it to be pleasant or unpleasant, desirable or undesirable.

Courage does not mean lack of fear. It means facing the fear, working through it, not letting it get in your way. Those who don't have enough courage give up as soon as they see an image they don't understand, or they give up before the image comes—which means they give up within five minutes since something almost always comes within five minutes of reading someone else when using the techniques taught in this book! You will learn how to recognize these images so that when you stumble you can forge head at full speed or get back on track as quickly as possible. By utilizing the basic preparatory techniques offered in chapter 4, you will be able to gain control over your emotions, both by recognizing when you are allowing them to impact you and by learning how to work with them.

Control vs. Receptivity — Balance

Using your clairvoyance involves a balance of intention (control) and receptivity (passivity). The toughest part is being passive, which requires you to let go of your will, ego, and need to control. It can be very scary to be in a position in which you are waiting for the information to come—not knowing if it will ever arrive, what form it's going to show up in, whether you will be accurate, or if the person you are reading is going to like you, agree with you, or criticize you. Many people just don't want to put themselves through this uncertainty. That's why they will never know how psychic they really are.

Practice

The only way to build your muscles, whether your biceps or your clairvoyant "muscles," is by exercising them. The more you practice, the faster and easier the information will flow. One reason for this is that after a while, you will begin to build up a library of symbols and experiences you will be able to interpret right away. Clairvoyant reading is a lot like learning a new language or musical instrument, only much easier than both. One of the purposes of this book is to encourage you to continue to practice and to help you with whatever challenges may arise in the course of your practice. Just like real life, every time you take a step or reach a goal, a whole new set of challenges you may never have faced emerges. If you have some idea what to look out for before you encounter them, you will be better able to face these challenges, and to conquer them and persevere.

I have recently been corresponding with a reader of my book *You Are Psychic* who has just completed her hundredth clairvoyant session on her own. She's been reading everyone from her neighbors to strangers she meets in online chat rooms. Yes, she gets a lot of positive feedback from these volunteers. Most of them tell her how accurate and helpful she is. But that doesn't really impress me. "Why?" you may ask, surprised. Because I expect that. I know if people utilize these techniques, they will soon receive the same kind of feedback that she gets. What *does* awe the hell out of me is her self-initiative, ingenuity (it's not that easy to find that many volunteers), and raw courage.

I've been working with several other students in my long-distance training program who also take it upon themselves to find lots of people to practice on in between our sessions. Sometimes these people are quite challenging in terms of their personalities and issues. Yet even when they've had a trying experience, these students jump right back in with both feet to the next reading to regain their confidence. These are examples of extraordinary psychics!

Holding Nothing Back

As a teacher, I have come to realize over the last several years that there is nothing more exhilarating than taking a student who has never had a clairvoyant image in their life, or no idea how to control such an image, and within one or two days or sessions seeing that student be blown away by the detail and information I've just coaxed from their not-soconfident lips. This is why I can teach the same material over and over again: once I have helped students to jump-start their clairvoyance with a few simple techniques (as I will do with you), there are a billion possibilities for what will happen next. It is like watching a thriller over and over that starts fairly similarly but has a drastically different middle and end each time. So in this book, as in *You Are Psychic*, I will hold nothing back. I don't want you to be merely as good a clairvoyant as I am; I want you to be much better. Since my own opinion of myself as a psychic is pretty darn high, that means you are going to be nearing Mt. Everest in no time!

I absolutely refuse to believe in the idea of scarcity when it comes to clients, students, or any opportunities, so if your newfound skills lead you to work with the same clients I do, then all the more power to you! We need more psychics, not fewer. In fact, as the veil is lifting; as our entire population seems to be evolving into something quite different from where we were technologically, spiritually, and psychologically even a decade ago; and as we face greater economic and global challenges than ever before, we are going to need more and more trained clairvoyants to help everyone deal with these changes and their emerging, out-of-control psychic abilities. I hope this message gets out there to those psychics who are at home sulking about their lack of clientele, something that has far more to do with resentful attitudes, self-esteem, and depleted energy levels.

The Extraordinary Psychic Creed

As extraordinary *psychics* we do not fear words, particularly not the word psychic. We neither run from it nor try to cover it up; rather, we reclaim it! We serve as shining examples of who psychics really are and what we can really do. Furthermore, we do not waste our time or energy on the hapless army of self-proclaimed "professional," anythingbut-scientific skeptics who will not even accept the now-definitive and significant findings of thousands of well-designed and repeated studies that have utilized stringent protocols to prove the existence of ESP, psychic energy, and the power of healing through intention. (Most of the standard psi research far exceeds that for any other kind of research, including studies performed on pharmaceuticals approved by the FDA.) Furthermore, as *extraordinary* psychics we do not resist or resent others' versions of reality (even those of the skeptics). Instead, we seek to understand them, and expand them through a commitment to understanding and expanding our own beliefs.

As extraordinary psychics we seek to demolish stereotypes that psychics are supposed to look or behave in some ridiculous way. There is no reason psychics have to wear crystal-studded purple muumuus, change our names to those of rocks or other celestial objects, or wander around like wide-eyed flower children on LSD—any more than computer programmers need to be geeky-looking guys with glasses and pocket protectors. These stereotypes have really made it much harder for those who wish to maintain a professional image to allow themselves their own abilities and to respect their psychic brothers and sisters.

We Can Be Happy and Abundant as Psychics!

Many psychics (as well as other spiritually-oriented people) end up being doormats or denying themselves the necessities or joys of life because they think that is what they are supposed to do.

A book containing Mother Teresa's most intimate letters, entitled *Come Be My Light*, was recently published. From this book it was clear Mother Teresa suffered from intense emotional pain throughout her more-than-extraordinary career. Upon the book's release there was a frenzy of attention in the mainstream American media, even suggestions of a "scandal" because Mother Teresa, while maintaining a public image of faith, had questioned whether or not God had abandoned her.

What some people don't understand is that faith moves up and down an ever-changing continuum ranging from serious doubt to conviction, and back to doubt as new challenges are encountered along the path. Faith is about trusting when you don't yet have all the evidence, and constantly reexamining your beliefs as new experiences are had and new information discovered. What I find most incredulous in the insinuation of "scandal" is why for an instant anyone in their right mind would or did suppose that Mother Teresa was a joyous and carefree person. Sure, she put on a brave smile for those who needed to see it, but how could anyone, while honoring their vows of poverty and chastity, and while encountering thousands of desperate, suffering people falling apart from leprosy and the worst diseases imaginable in the bowels of hell, not get depressed from time to time? Perhaps we wanted to believe she was happy so we wouldn't feel guilty about leaving the dirty work to her.

Still, I have to wonder: was it God denying her every human pleasure, even the most basic of comforts, or was it her own belief system about God, and the pictures she held about how best to honor her relationship with her creator, that made her life so difficult and led her into periods of despair? Was this self-denial truly necessary in order to carry out her accomplishments of establishing hundreds of much-needed hospitals and schools around the world? If she had treated herself better, would these never have been created? Or might she have had even more energy to do more good deeds?

These are the same questions we need to ask ourselves as psychics and healers. Why is there a perception that people in every other profession can make a living, even grow prosperous from their work, but not us? Why? Because of the idea of "the gift." God has given us this gift and we must now take advantage of it, right? Well, what about the gift of an awesome voice? Why are singers making millions? And what about smart people like doctors? Aren't they gifted with intelligence and the ability to sit through long, boring classes without falling asleep? Why should they make so much money? Oh well, they go through years of training, whereas psychic abilities just happen to us and don't require any sacrifice, right? *Wrong!*

As extraordinary psychics we need to be able to fess up to the fact that our very desire to be spiritual or even to deny ourselves pleasure or comfort could be as ego-based as a desire to rule the world for our own gluttonous advancement. We need to be real! Any attempts at appearing spiritual are symptoms of the ego. Now, if you want to light candles or incense to get you in the mood, to remind you of your spirit or God, or to honor a spirit that has passed on, that is spiritual. If you want to light candles because psychics are supposed to have candles and other smelly things lying around that impress clients, that is your choice. Just call it what it is: a marketing tactic rather than an act of spirituality.

Eyes Wide Open

As extraordinary psychics we are also not going to deny the existence of things we wish were not there, such as evil, but instead we will learn how to excise these things from our personal lives. If you hadn't noticed, we live in a world where people are not always nice to each other. Sometimes they are downright cruel. Violence is everywhere. Evil exists, no matter how many of us wish it didn't. Because these harsher forces are out there, there are times we need to be able to stand up to them, when being all nice and loving is not the correct response.

As I learned the hard way, spirituality does not occur in a vacuum of *Leave It to Beaver*ish "everything's love and light" (see chapters 12 through 14). Perhaps most important, we are not going to allow ourselves to become trapped in our own definitions, stereotypes, or fantasies of ourselves as psychics and spiritual seekers. There are some very amazing, well-intentioned healers, psychics, and spiritual leaders out there who are very screwed-up people. These same healers may be instrumental in transforming your life and may later help you to mess it up in a big way. At the same time you might encounter some very evil, selfish people who could not care less about healing, but who serve as the catalyst for you to get in touch with yourself on a very profound level. Being spiritual means paying attention to spirit. Nothing more, nothing less.

Rewards of Clairvoyant Reading

- You can see just about anything at any time.
- You can learn about yourself and anyone else.
- You can know a truth from a lie.
- You can see a situation for how it is rather than how you wish it to be.
- You can use clairvoyance to help others.
- You can use clairvoyance in conjunction with just about any other therapeutic practice.
- You can use clairvoyance to heal yourself or anyone else of pain and illness.
- You can use clairvoyance for dreams and inspiration.
- You can use clairvoyance for manifesting goals and creating abundance.
- You can use clairvoyance to help you communicate with the deceased and with spirit guides.
- Your communication with your heart, your Higher Self, God, and your guides will increase.
- You can speed up your natural transformation process.
- You can be a psychic spy.
- You can save a lot of time by diagnosing any problem, from another's health-related concern to an issue with your car.
- You will work through your fears and resistance to your own abilities.
- You will understand how you are already being psychic all the time.
- You will have more freedom in your life in general.
- You will become a more conscious, more enlightened person.
- You will learn new coping skills for dealing with troublesome entities, psychic parasites, and other troublesome beings both in bodies and out.
- You will learn how to attract and heal relationships and get over a broken heart easier.

- You will gain a better understanding of the relationship between you and the organizations you are associated with.
- You will learn how to be in the now.
- You will become better equipped to make the best choices for yourself, including whether to accept a certain job, rent or buy a particular house, or date or marry a particular person.
- You will prepare yourself for a smoother transition in death.
- You will be able to see information about past incarnations and integrate this information to help you in the present.
- You will increase your overall self-confidence.
- You will never have a reason to be bored again, since you will have round-the-clock entertainment, even when you are alone.

CHAPTER 3

Preparing Yourself to Do Readings and Healings

We are what we repeatedly do.
— ARISTOTLE

Preparation Techniques— Psychic Tools Revisited

The following visualizations can be used to prepare yourself for your clairvoyant readings. They are powerful, transformative meditation tools in themselves that can be done ten minutes before a clairvoyant reading or performed at a completely different time, for any length of time. The longer you do them, the more you will feel their effects and the more you will benefit from them, so I highly encourage you to try utilizing them so you can experience their effects, even if only once a month for at least an hour each time. Don't let lack of time or discipline keep you from practicing them even for short periods of time.

Please keep in mind that once you are adept at using these visualizations on yourself, you can then begin applying them to other people seeking your help, as these visualizations are very powerful tools for healing. Also know that it doesn't matter if these are brand-new to you or if you have done them, or variations of them, one million times.

They have a cumulative effect, so every time you do them they will assist you with maximizing your energy flow, centering yourself, reconnecting with your body and the earth, and they will help you release any energies you've taken on from other people or your environment. When you first begin practicing them, it may seem as if all you are doing is fooling around in the playground of your imagination, but what you will soon discover if you "play" consistently and diligently is that your imagination is the control panel for directing, creating, and releasing energy of all kinds that affect your thoughts, emotions, health, relationships, and your ability to manifest your goals. Energy is as real as your physical body.

Optimal Environment

It is best when you are starting to practice that you find a quiet place where you won't be disturbed. Turn off all music, your television set, your computer, and your phone. It's best to not even have a TV on in another room since you may pick up images from it when first getting started, but don't sweat it if that's the only thing that's going to keep the family busy while you are stealing a few precious moments for yourself!

If you hear noises around you, notice the distance between where you are and where the noises are, and tell your subconscious mind that the noise will bring you deeper into yourself and into a state of relaxation. Believe me: you can do any of these exercises anywhere, any time. However, the quieter it is, the easier it will be for you to focus, relax, and have fun.

Close Your Eyes

When you close your eyes, you are turning inward to a place of connection with yourself. It is pretty amazing how little time we spend inside ourselves when we are not sleeping or consciously meditating. When I was filming the DVD presentation of *You Are Psychic* with the help of my brother Brad, who was producing the DVD, he found himself following along with the instructions for grounding and running energy. He had never once meditated in his thirty-four years of existence. Afterward he could barely contain his excitement, but also he was dismayed that he could have lived his entire life without even considering that there is a whole playground right inside his very own head in which he can do tons of fun things he had never even considered. If you think about it, other than sleeping, when is it even socially acceptable to close your eyes and go within? Try closing your eyes at work or when you're with friends, and they will accuse you of sleeping or being rude, or they'll think you're nuts! I wonder what this says about our society as a whole, since closing your eyes forces you to concentrate and connect with yourself. This apparently is not the American way.

We are going to change that here. You can see visions with your eyes open, but then you have to strain and work a lot harder to ignore all the outside stimuli. Some people don't like to close their eyes because it makes them nervous. They are afraid they will miss something, or that they won't be able to control or be prepared for something with their eyes closed. Every once in a while I get students in a class who are so resistant to keeping their eyes closed at first that they almost have to experience a panic attack before they can let themselves relax.

Other people are just so used to looking at someone when they talk that they go through lots of guilt-related inner turmoil before they start to realize that they can really be of more service when they close their eyes, since doing so allows them to "see" more clearly without the distracting visual cues from their client. When we can witness every glimmer of hope, disdain, fear, sadness, or glee in the eyes or face of our client, we begin to filter out any information that might elicit an unhappy reaction, which affects how honestly we can communicate and ultimately doesn't serve anyone.

Optimal Reading/Meditation Position

Although you can use your clairvoyance or meditate in any position, sitting in an upright position in a chair or on a sofa that fully supports your back, with your legs bent at the knees and your feet touching the floor, maximizes the energy flow and release. I don't know why, but the energy flow and release is much stronger in this position than when sitting in the crossed-leg lotus position, which seems to inhibit the flow through the legs when done for a period of time. Energy can flow well when you are lying down, but in this position it's too easy to drift off to sleep. I suspect the energy flow is also maximized when standing up straight; however, most people cannot perform a reading in that position without losing their balance or getting tired.

Grounding

Grounding provides a vehicle through which your body can focus and release its excess electrical energy. Grounding works best with your feet touching the ground outside, but you can most certainly do this exercise inside any structure as well. There are a variety of ways to ground. Grounding yourself from the first chakra strengthens your natural connection with the earth, and makes it feel safer for your spirit to be inside your body. However, by strengthening this grounding you may become the most grounded thing in the room.

Electricity always seeks grounding to complete its circuit; it seeks the shortest possible route to the source with the least amount of resistance. In order to protect our homes and ourselves from being electrocuted by lightning, every electrical box has a ground stake about six feet long that has been hammered into the earth. The stake is made out of steel and is coated with copper. It channels any extraneous electricity, such as lightning, into the earth rather than into your electrical outlets, where it would seek you as the source to ground through.

When we visualize ourselves with a grounding cord, we are essentially creating a grounding stake so that extraneous foreign energies will go into our cords instead of into the rest of our body. When we extend that visualization to include the building we are in, then the various foreign energies that are already in that space will have someplace to go besides into us or our newly created grounding cords. Since gravity works with our grounding cords to form a vacuum effect, by grounding the building we are essentially giving it its own vacuum hose, thereby lessening the possibility of our own getting congested or clogged.

Grounding the Room

Sit in a comfortable position with your feet touching the floor, palms resting on your thighs and turned upward toward the ceiling. Ground the room by imagining a huge metallic beam running from the center of the ceiling deep into the core of the planet, which you can visualize as containing various metals such as iron, copper, silver, and gold. The beam can be half the width of the entire room or match its entire diameter. You can also see beams running from each individual corner of the room downward into the earth. You can also visualize these beams surrounding the outside of the house. If you feel the space really needs a healing, you can call forth the cosmic energies, which you can visualize as an intense colored light pouring down through the beams into the earth. Imagine they are washing away whatever needs to be released, such as emotional energy from yourself or other people who have occupied the room.

Grounding Yourself

Visualize any strong object that will connect your body at the base of your spine to the core of the earth to form a grounding cord. Some of my favorite objects are a redwood tree trunk, a cruise ship anchor, a heavy column made from pure gold, a crystal, or a stone that looks similar to those that form Stonehenge. It is best to see this object being at least as wide your hips. Some people just have a heck of a time seeing their grounding as anything stronger than a thread or a wobbly vine. This is because they are ungrounded or thinly anchored into their bodies. Don't worry if this describes you, because with time your grounding, and therefore the visualization of your cord, will grow stronger.

Next imagine that your grounding cord has a hollow, slippery center, and then give your grounding cord two directives. First tell it that it is going to absorb anything that comes your way that you wouldn't really want to stick to you, and then tell it that it is going to operate as the vehicle by which you will spontaneously release any pain, emotions, or thoughts that no longer serve you. Let your attention run between the points at which the cord meets the base of your spine, at the first chakra and the ground.

You can also imagine that the gravitational pull is increasing to draw out any toxins from your body. Visualize a gravity gauge and see the number rising up. You might also imagine that your grounding cord is like a straw, and the earth is like a mouth that is sucking out the energies you are now expelling. If you are sitting in a lotus or cross-legged position on the floor or sofa, you can maximize your grounding and energy release by imagining that you are drawing a line from your first chakra to one knee, to the next knee and then back to the first chakra, to form a triangle shape. Then visualize your grounding cord as if it were a triangular tube running deep into the earth.

Grounding Your Aura

Our auras hold on to the energy of pain. Many times I will feel pain in a person's aura before they report experiencing it in their body. (By running my hands through it, I can feel the pain in my hands.) Conversely, I will feel pain in a certain part of a readee's aura that corresponds to a part of their body where they felt pain a few days before but are no longer experiencing it.

Our auras or energy fields are stretchy. They expand or contract as easily as we can extend our arms to hug another or bring another close to us in a gesture of protection. During readings and healings, it helps to know where your energy field ends and begins so that you can have control over the reading experience. If your aura is encompassing your readee, or theirs is encompassing you, you both are going to experience each other's emotions. Now you might think, "Cool, then I will know how they are feeling." While this may be true, you may get very confused about which are their emotions and which are your own, and then become the effect of these before you can consciously realize what is happening. By bringing your aura closer to you and setting boundaries between yourself and the other person, you will be in a better position to observe and remain calm and composed during a reading.

This is an excellent technique to do while having a difficult or heated conversation with someone.

You can ground your aura first by visualizing that you are drawing it in around you about two or three feet (for some of you who are feeling ill or are naturally introverted, this might require you to imagine you are expanding it outward from its natural position). Next, imagine that you are tucking the bottom part of your aura into your grounding cord at the point where it runs below your feet right into the ground. Then demand that your aura release anything that is no longer serving you right into and down your grounding cord. If it doesn't feel like your aura wants to be grounded, I suggest giving yourself a larger grounding cord, giving your aura its own grounding cord, or pretending that you are sewing, nailing, stapling, gluing, or tacking your aura into the cord. Then see a turbocharged level on the side and imagine you are pressing down. As you press down, you will release whatever energy in your aura that didn't want it to ground.

Create a Separation Object

A *separation object* is that which creates an energetic boundary between you and everyone else. It is helpful to use one when encountering a highly emotional person and when performing a reading or healing. First, visualize an object that can rotate around the outermost edge of your grounding cord. You can see this as any object, but make it strong so you know it's absorbent. You can then give it its own grounding cord to strengthen it. I like to use images of smiley faces or bright cartoon flowers—really anything that is lighthearted or that makes me happy. I do this to dispel any resistance to whatever it might be that my separation object is helping to separate me from.

You can program your separation object with the command that any foreign energies directed into your field or body will instead go right into it. You can also remind yourself that everything on the side of the object facing you is you and belongs to you, and everything on the outside is something or someone else. It's a great idea to check in with this every once in a while when doing readings. Afterward, you can visualize it on your screen and look for the colors and read the ensuing energies that entered your separation object so you can get an idea of what was happening around you. You can then destroy this used one and create a new, fresh separation object.

Running Energy

When our bodies are in an optimal state of health, we have the right amount of life force energy moving through each body part and system. When we are in pain or feeling depleted and depressed, there is a problem with the flow, either due to a blockage or to an inadequate distribution of energy in a part of our body or energy field. Fortunately, we can often remove blockages, increase the flow, or bring in a type of energy that will return us or someone we are working with to an optimal state of health.

There are many ways to work with energy. Energy can most easily be visualized as a colored, active, moving substance. You can see it as colored light, water, fire—anything fluid and moving. You can decide what you wish to achieve, what type of energy or vibration you'd like to have more of in your body, and then assign it a color. Once you know the clairvoyant technique, you can use this to find the appropriate color. Until then you can just choose colors that feel good to you. Stay away from those that don't feel comfortable. You may naturally associate certain colors with vibrations based on past experiences or books you have read that assign a particular meaning to a color that stuck with you. The important thing is that you like the colors you work with, and they feel more like you than anyone else you know.

Running energy is like giving ourselves a shower. It also allows us to replenish ourselves, much like filling up a gas tank. Below are some simple but very effective ways to run energy.

Cosmic Energy

Simplest: imagine that the cosmos, or heavens, or the hands of God are opening up, and see torrents of colored light or water pouring down onto your head. Imagine the top of your head (your crown chakra) is opening up like a lotus, rose, or tulip to welcome in this flow. Inhale this breath down to your toes and even let some of it run down your grounding cord. You can imagine that this energy is as neutral as water, or you can assign it a quality you want to have in your life, such as more joy, peace, passion, creativity, and so on.

Cosmic Energy and Energizing the Chakras

The chakras are energy centers within our body and aura that correspond with a certain part of the body. They have a variety of functions that impact our level of power, consciousness, and our overall mental, emotional, and physical health. Again, imagine that the cosmos, heavens, or the hands of God are opening up, and see torrents of colored light or water pouring down onto your head. Imagine the top of your head (your crown chakra) is opening up like a lotus or rose or tulip to welcome in this flow of colored sparkling light. See it circulating in your crown chakra, take a breath, and draw it down into your sixth chakra, where your third eye is located, which also corresponds to the center of your forehead.

As you take a few breaths, see this color swirling through the energy center that you can visualize as a swirling disk. As you do this you may get a clear image of the chakra, and by all means use that image instead if you prefer it. Next inhale and draw the colored light or water down into your fifth chakra, your throat chakra. See it swirling in there like colored soap suds coursing through a washing machine. Continue drawing the color downward and have it swirl around in the heart chakra, then the solar plexus, third chakra, then the second chakra, which corresponds to the reproductive and sexual centers, and then the first chakra at the base of the spine. Once you have reached the first chakra, you can focus more on your breath. As you inhale, imagine you are capturing and pulling down more of the cosmic energy into your head and continue directing it downward every time you inhale. Imagine that as you exhale, you are blowing on your chakras like a pinwheel and making them spin even more.

Earth Energy

Our feet are the exit and entry points for a tremendous amount of energy. As I will be describing in the chapter on healing, one of my favorite healers in the Philippines used to do exorcisms during which he would hold on to someone's toe and extract the pain and negative forces through the feet. If someone is electrocuted, since the energy seeks grounding it exists through the feet. When we are psychically attacked, many times it starts with our feet. Some people who have suddenly come down with a strange illness that could not be properly diagnosed reported feeling strange sensations through the feet right before their health declined.

Earth energy can help us increase our connection to the earth. When we walk, run, or do physical activities outside in nature, we spontaneously increase the flow up through our feet. We can increase this flow easily through visualization.

How to Run Earth Energy

We have little energy centers in our feet. Imagine you are opening these centers by seeing them as spinning disks getting bigger and bigger. Practice imagining them growing large to the point that it would seem uncomfortable and then closing them until they are almost completely shut. See them opening and closing, opening and closing, until it feels as if you are really doing this. It is kind of similar to the feeling of opening your eyes or your mouth really wide and then closing it. We can easily exercise our energy muscles through visualization. Finally, have your feet chakras remain fixed at a comfortable degree of openness that will enable the optimal amount of energy to flow through your feet.

Next, imagine that earth energy is rising from a very deep and clean place, deep within the earth. See this energy as an earthy color that enters your feet. Watch as it swirls around through the little chakras in your feet and flows through every toe, each heel, and up your ankles. See it flow up your calves and legs, let it swish around in your knees, then raise it up through your thighs, really let it wash out every part of your thighs, including the muscles and fat (if you have either one!) From your thighs, direct the nurturing, vibrant earth energy into your first chakra at the base of your spine and then let it circulate in there and flush back down your grounding cord. Visualize this for at least five minutes. Ask yourself if this color feels good to you. If not, choose another one originating from a different spot deep within the ground. Choose a color that feels good to you. After a few minutes you might try to imagine the flow increasing in volume and strength.

Combining Earth and Cosmic Energies

Draw the cosmic energy downward from a clean spot in the heavens into your crown chakra, down your spine where it can circulate in your first chakra. At the same time, see the earth energy rise up from the earth into your feet and up through your legs. It will also be spinning through your first chakra before it falls back down your grounding cord. Imagine the cosmic and earth energies are meeting in that first chakra to form a combined color. Let this combined color be 80 percent cosmic energy and 20 percent earth. Then see it rising back up through the core and front part of your body as if it were a powerful geyser, shooting straight out through the top of your head, spinning the chakras with its force.

Once it exits through your head, you can imagine it shooting higher and higher in the air, and then falling back down around the entire circumference of your body and back down through your aura, cleaning that out. If your aura is grounded, the energy will then wash right back down your grounding cord. Continue to visualize this for several minutes. If you do this for thirty minutes or an hour every day, you will completely transform your entire energy field and begin to feel very different.

Adding Breath Work to Your Cosmic Energy

As you inhale, draw the breath down to your first chakra. As you exhale, let your breath carry the light upward and release out of your head, with a little of it flowing down your arms and out your hands, creating pools of light from your head.

Clearing Out Your Head and Sixth Chakra
With Light and Breath

This next exercise has most recently been a favorite exercise for myself and many of my students, and it has an immediate relaxation and centering effect.

Just sit back in your seat and relax. Close your eyes and go inward. Become aware of your natural breathing; there's no need to change it. Become aware of the point at which the air meets your nostrils. As you inhale through your nose, notice if you can actually feel the air entering that very specific part of your nose. Keep your attention here for a minute or two. Next, imagine that the air is a colored light of health of whatever vibration you'd like. As you inhale, see this color going right up your nose and circulating through your sinuses. Imagine with each inhale that you are drawing it upward and as you exhale, the breath is making the air circulate through your head, spinning your sixth and seventh chakras.

Do this for a few minutes until your entire head is filled with dancing, breath-filled light. After you do this for a minute or two you can add the exhalation breath. Imagine that as you exhale you are drawing the colored light downward from your head, down through the throat and into the lungs where it can circulate and fill up and clean out the lungs and the nearby heart. Then continue to draw it down through the core of the body, down through the lower chakras and right down through the grounding cord into the earth. Let the light and breath also wash down your arms, with some of it releasing out of your hand chakras.

After a few more minutes, you can see this all happen in single breaths; as you inhale it comes in through your nose and up to the top of your head, and as you exhale the air in the form of the colored light goes straight down through you into the center of the earth. However, as your exhales bring the air and light downward, practice remaining centered in your head, so it's as if the air and breath and light are being sent below you.

Calling Back Your Own Energy

Often we travel out of our bodies to retrieve information. While the bulk of our energy remains in our bodies, much of it is sent to other people and projects and places. Some parts of ourselves are stuck in the past while other parts are out searching for answers and security in the future. Some parts are being held hostage by others, but this usually can only happen if we think we need them or we owe them something out of guilt or past agreements. Much of our illness, our exhaustion, our hunger, and our cravings related to addictions are due to us being low on our own spiritual energy. Fortunately, we can retrieve our energy with the aid of the following visualizations.

Simple method: Imagine you are putting out a call to all parts of yourself, any of your energy that is currently part of yourself. Ask yourself what color or colors these parts of yourself are. Watch as they come back to you. Let this color pour into you and fill you up where you are most deficient. As these parts come back, you can visualize your grounding cord and ask that if any foreign or pain energy was keeping your own energy out, or you were holding this foreign energy inside because you didn't have enough energy of your own, that it will release.

Classic Golden Sun Method

Imagine a large golden sun above your head. Imagine that you are writing your name across it, which gives the signal to yourself and anyone else that this is your very own sun. Imagine there is a very large magnet at its core, the strongest magnet in the universe. This magnet is designed to attract only your energy that is outside of your body at the moment.

Start to call back all your energy from anyone, any place, anything it could possibly be engaged with. You will probably intuitively know where some of it is, but you might spontaneously get some thoughts or images of people that you are surprised about. When I have done this exercise or had my students do it, we have been shocked to see faces of people we hadn't thought about in twenty years. Just because a relationship ended decades ago doesn't mean it's not still continuing on some nonphysical level. Sometimes we need to consciously end that connection so we are free to create new and rewarding relationships in the present moment on the physical level.

Just keep calling back your energy into your golden sun until the sun swells up from being so full. Once it is as full as it will or can get, imagine the sun bursts open and all that energy pours right down into the crown of your head, all the way down to your feet, and then back up, like orange juice pouring into a glass and spilling over. Let it spurt out the top of your head and go like a fountain out and down your aura, eventually running back down your grounding cord.

You can also see the energy flowing down your shoulders and arms, with a little bit of it splashing out of your palms in little fountains of light that also seep into your now-glowing aura. You can see the cells of your body expanding with the swirling light. Your cells and entire being will get so full of this light that the light will shine through every pore of your body, forming a million pinpoints of light emanating outward, engulfing your entire energy field in one huge glimmering disco-like ball. Then see this ball of light growing even brighter and bigger, stretching upward and out in all directions like a frenzied fire.

Remember to breathe as you do this, and say prayers of gratitude for your brilliant life and the healthy body that you've been gifted with. (Say these prayers anyway, even if you don't really believe you are that healthy—because you will be soon enough!)

CHAPTER 4

Basic Training:
The Clairvoyant Techniques

*Dignity consists not in possessing honors, but in the
consciousness that we deserve them.*
— ARISTOTLE

Before practicing the techniques in this chapter, I strongly recommend at least running through the preparatory techniques in the preceding chapter. They will help to clear your mind and your energy field so as to optimize your viewing pleasure! They also serve as powerful self-healing and meditation tools.

In this chapter we will mainly focus on your clairvoyant ability. However, please be aware that your other abilities of telepathy, clairaudience, and clairsentience will also be activated, and will provide you with information through your inner senses of hearing and feeling as well. We will address your clairaudient abilities in greater detail in chapter 6. In this chapter you will learn how to perform a clairvoyant reading on yourself and others through the use of three alternatives for working with your viewing receptacle, which is the most essential component of your clairvoyant technique.

The first option involves starting off with an image of a single viewing receptacle. The second technique is almost identical to the first, except we will use two viewing receptacles and watch the relationship between the two. This is an excellent technique to utilize when you are seeking information about a relationship or desiring to heal one. The third technique is also similar to the first, but involves using a symbol and dropping it into the receptacle.

The techniques summarized in this chapter are ideal for picking up extrasensory information about a person and every aspect of that person's life, including their relationships. (Some of these techniques were first presented in *You Are Psychic*, which provides more detailed explanations of their benefits.) This chapter focuses primarily on "reading" people. To learn how to access

230

information about remote objects, locations, and unknown targets utilizing these techniques and others, please see chapters 10 and 11.

The following three techniques are intended primarily for doing readings from inside your body, centered in the area of your sixth chakra. Much of the information you will be drawing from will be coming from either a universal source of information accessed directly by your own clairvoyance, or will be projected and communicated on telepathic levels to you by the person you are reading. Occasionally some information will come from other spirits, either ones connected to you or to the person you are reading.

Usually, spirit communication comes in the form of telepathic thoughts of clairaudient hearing. Sometimes a spirit can toss you a picture (this usually has an almost intrusive quality to it), but this is far less common. In chapters 12 through 17, I discuss working with spirits and the various situations and challenges that can arise. For now you don't need to be concerned about the source of your images; it won't have that much bearing on your learning process.

The following three techniques work well for reading people. They also can be used to see into and obtain information about past or future events. There are times when you might have an easier time accessing certain kinds of information by having a part of your spirit or attention travel outside of your body to a particular location, such as when you are searching for a missing object or person or to view a very specific event (see chapter 11). However, many people do successfully access this type of information from the techniques presented below, which I recommend becoming familiar with first.

Basic Reading Technique

This technique is for in-your-body readings of yourself or other people.

Center Yourself

Since your clairvoyance is centered at the point of your sixth chakra that also corresponds to your pineal gland, this is where you will center yourself. It's also where you can observe the emotions you are feelings without being a slave to them or controlled by them. This is very important!

As spirits we can be centered or focused in any part of our body. When we are centered up behind our sixth chakra, we are less emotional. Our clairvoyance becomes activated and we are literally above our emotions. This doesn't mean we won't feel any emotions at all. To the contrary, our emotions will often reflect what the readee is feeling or experiencing; however, when we are centered in this part of ourselves, we will not have to become a victim to our emotions. We can have our emotions and know we are having them. It's the difference between being a spectator to a tornado—merely feeling some of the wind and turbulence—and getting swept away in the tornado. When we read, we are sometimes looking at other people's tornadoes. We can only help our readees if we remain neutral and a bit removed.

Familiarize Yourself with This Place

Come up or down or from wherever you are into the center of your head. You can actually place your fingers on your forehead, slightly above and in between your two eyes, to remind you of where this is. Close your eyes and imagine you are centered smack-dab in the center of your head, so that if there were a window or eye right there you'd be looking out at your fingertip. Once you have a concept of this, you can relax your hand back down to your lap.

Create a Seat

Create a comfortable chair, which will be like a director's seat or driver's seat. Have fun designing it. Imagine you are sitting in the chair. Then see yourself standing up and running circles around it. Then run in circles in the other direction. As you run, imagine you are taking your hands and running them alongside the inside of your head. Jump on top of the chair. Use it like a springboard or trampoline and do flips forward and backward off of it. Fly around the center of your head if you like, and then come back and sit in the chair. Imagine you are sitting in the driver's seat of a car, at the controls of an airplane, or at the helm of a ship on the sea or in outer space. Know that you are in charge. See yourself wearing the appropriate cap or uniform if you'd like. Have fun with this!

Open Your Third Eye

Next, while imagining that you are sitting inside your head and really centered there, also imagine that you are looking out of your forehead. Imagine that you press on the control panel in front of you and focus all your attention on the inside of your forehead. Imagine there is actually a third eye painted on your forehead and now, under your command, this eye is opening up so you can see beyond it. One of my favorite visualizations is of the viewing deck in *Star Trek*. On that TV series, on the other side of the viewing screen there was either a lovely view of outer space or the image of some planetary leader telling the crew they were about to face imminent attack if they didn't turn around immediately.

So watch as either an eye or a window opens up on your forehead, and imagine that you are now looking out of your forehead. I like to start off with a gesture of opening these parts, because that sends the symbolic and hypnotic suggestion that we are now creating a change in ourselves, opening up something not previously open. Even if you think your abilities are wide open already, by doing this visualization immediately before a reading you are sending the signal to yourself that you are now, at this specific time, allowing yourself to be more clairvoyant than you normally are in your everyday life.

Reading Screen

From the center of your head, you are now looking out the eye or window of your forehead. Focus about six to eight inches out in front of this point and visualize a reading screen. Take notice of the screen's appearance and attributes. You can see this as any shape or size. I invite you to try different images every time you do this in order to see what is most comfortable. Some popular images used by students are that of a television screen, a computer monitor, an IMAX theater screen, a black or white board, parchment paper, and the like.

Where Are You in Relation to Your Screen?

From the inside of your head, imagine that you are taking a tape measure and measuring the distance between where you are in your head and where the screen is. Just get a feel for how many inches or feet away your screen is. For the purposes of this exercise, we are reading from within our bodies; if your screen is too far away, this likely indicates your spirit or a part of you is very far from your body. If you feel as if the screen is miles away, then destroy that screen, recheck yourself to see if you are in fact centered in your head, and then create a screen closer to you.

Turn On Your Screen

Imagine there is a lamp or lights attached to the top of the screen. Imagine you are flipping the switch to these lights. Notice how nicely the lights illuminate the screen. Let this be another symbol or hypnotic suggestion to yourself that your clairvoyance is turning on strong to illuminate whatever is about to appear on your screen.

Ground Your Screen

Next go ahead and give your reading screen its own grounding cord, running from the base of the screen deep into the earth. Notice if anything happens to the screen or if it changes in any way. It may or may not.

Optional: Practice your preparatory techniques on your screen.

There are two ways you can perform these visualizations. The first way is to imagine them as if they were really happening to your actual body. The second is to visualize them on the reading screen you will be creating in a little while. There is value to both. Most people spontaneously visualize these techniques happening directly to their bodies. Even after students have grown adept at creating and utilizing a screen during readings with others, they still tend to spontaneously ground themselves or run energy by visualizing it happening directly to their body. Doing so is easier and it tends to make it all feel more real. However, I do encourage you to practice these techniques both ways once you have taken the time to visualize your screen and see what that is like. It's great to go back and forth.

The value of seeing your body and your aura with your grounding cord or energy running through your body on the screen is that you can sometimes be more precise with having a sense of the colors and energies you are bringing in or releasing. Reading yourself and particularly others really requires you to use the screen constantly and consistently, and therefore using it to work with the preparatory techniques and/or in your meditation sessions is great practice. If you haven't yet started practicing any of the techniques, don't worry if you don't quite understand the difference; you will know what I am talking about soon enough. Usually, right before a reading, regardless of whether or not I have meditated first (which I highly recommend), I will, by seeing them on my screen first, run through the above-mentioned meditation tools of grounding, running one of my energies, tuning in to my aura, and establishing a separation object. It's a great warm-up routine.

Clairvoyant Technique #1: Creating a Single Viewing Receptacle

Once you have created your reading screen, create a clear, transparent image of an object that has the ability to hold something else. This is what I refer to as a *viewing receptacle*. This receptacle can be in the shape of a rose, a tulip, a crystal ball, a chalice—really any object that could possibly contain other objects.

I like using a rose the best because roses have so many layers and attributes that will change and take on various forms during a reading.

A rose is harder to visualize than a ball, but ultimately the complexity can provide a richer tool to work with. Once you visualize this on your screen in as much detail as possible, go ahead and destroy it until it no longer exists. You can blow it up, set it on fire, shoot it, erase it, see it getting smaller and smaller until it dissipates, or you can fling it off your screen and watch it fly off somewhere and evaporate.

Sometimes it helps to first roll the rose up into a little ball. Sometimes after you destroy it, you will have a sense that there are still pieces remaining. You can take these and roll them up into a ball and repeat the process until all the pieces have disappeared. This is a step you should never skip because these contain energy that can impact you if you just leave them there. If you feel like you don't want to get rid of them because it took you a while to create them, or it seems too rude or hostile to destroy them, or whatever resistance to this comes up, know that this same resistance could very well be affecting you in your own personal life when it comes to letting go of things.

Invite the Information into Your Reading Receptacle
After creating and destroying a few roses, which will help exercise your clairvoyant muscles and move any energy off your screen, create a brand-new receptacle. Now you are reading to invite in the energy of the person you are going to read.

Read Yourself
Take a really good look at the clear, transparent receptacle or rose you have put up on your screen. Notice its size and shape. If you are interested in learning something about yourself, you can pose a question to it and then just observe it. If you want to know something about someone else in your life who is not present, you can say their name a few times to the receptacle, even write their name underneath it with an imaginary pen and then watch the rose.

The first thing to look for is a color or colors. Just sit back, be very patient, and ask the rose to show you a color that represents the person or information you are seeking. You can watch to see if the rose changes in the slightest way from when you first began to visualize it, or if it demonstrates some sort of movement or does something you did not expect. While you are doing this, an image or picture might arise as well. Whether you can barely notice a minute glimpse of a color or whether you see something in such bold Technicolor that it makes you jump in your seat, be assured that you are on the right track.

Please be aware that if you are reading yourself or someone who is not present, it is going to be a lot harder for you to stay focused. One thing that will really help in this case is to utilize some kind of voice recording device that you can speak into as you do the reading. This will keep you on task. If you find it hard to read yourself first, try practicing on someone else.

Observe Your Viewing Receptacle
The key here is to relax, observe, and have no expectations. Never underestimate the importance of anything that comes up for you, and please do not disregard something just because it looks or sounds ridiculous and you have absolutely no idea what it means. Doing that is the biggest mistake people make. The critical and analytical part of you is going to want to judge everything you see as good/bad, right/wrong, important/insignificant, impressive/dumb, normal/weird—and this is the part of yourself you have to completely ignore. Everything you notice is happening for a reason. You are a detective, an explorer, a researcher. You should not leave any stone unturned—that stone may just turn out to be the most precious of gems. All we need is the first clue, and then we have something to work with, to sink our psychic teeth into. Again, that clue can be a simple color or a very clear image.

If you are not noticing a single thing after a minute or two, I suggest destroying your viewing receptacle and checking to see if you are still centered behind your third eye. Then destroy your current reading screen and create a new one; put up a brand-new receptacle and repeat the above process by stating the name of the person you are interested in learning about, or the question you are desiring information about. You may want to ask your question in a different way. (Please see chapter 5 for a description of questions that will elicit the most helpful information.)

Once You Have Your Clue, Pose a Question or Command

Once you have the first clue—such as a color, a change in your receptacle, or an image—then you have a couple of options. One is to pose a question to that attribute, such as "What do you represent?" or "What do you want to show me?" The other is to give it a command, "Hi there, show me a clue to understand you better" or "You will now reveal more information I can understand." Then all you have to do is sit back and watch the attribute of the receptacle again as a whole, and wait and see what happens next.

Another option is to destroy that receptacle, create a new one, and ask it to show you the meaning or a clue about what you just viewed in the first receptacle. I recommend doing this when you don't feel that anything else is happening from looking at the same one. Remember that when you create and destroy any image, you are moving and releasing energy and stimulating your clairvoyance, so don't be afraid or lazy when it comes to recreating your viewing receptacle over and over. At the same time, you must be patient. Sometimes it takes several minutes before you start to notice anything.

From the above description you will start to see that once you have noticed anything, regardless of whether or not it makes sense, you are 90 percent of the way home because you now have something to focus your attention on that is related to the subject of your inquiry.

Reading Another Person Who Is Present

When you are doing a reading for another person who is present, you will use the same techniques as discussed above. The only difference will be in establishing the initial connection and then disconnecting at the end.

Preparing to Read Someone Else

Start off by asking the person you are reading (whom I will refer to as your *readee*) to sit across you at a comfortable distance, usually a few feet away. You can inform the readee that you will have your eyes closed for most if not all of the reading, but that they should keep their eyes open and remain as alert as possible. If the readee matches you in a meditative state, they may be more prone to leave their body and then it will be harder to read them.

Make sure you give yourself time to run through the preparatory visualizations before you begin the reading. This will help keep you secure, energized, and focused, and will also give your clairvoyance a warm-up and jump-start. Some people need more prep time than others, particularly when starting out and particularly if the analytical part of their mind tends to be in overdrive. So it's best to spend time meditating, ideally about thirty minutes before you invite the readee to sit down in front of you. If you don't meditate, you will still be able to do the reading, but just be aware that the information may not flow as easily, it may take you longer to be able to focus, or you may struggle with more self-doubt.

The more readings you do, the more your brain waves will naturally switch over at the beginning of the reading and the less premeditation time you will need. I am at the point after twelve years of consistent reading that the moment I dial the phone to call my client, or I close my eyes as someone sits down before me, I can feel my brain pass into a deeper state, and it becomes difficult for me to just have a normal conversation. Instead, I pretty much need to go right into the reading.

Create a Reading Bubble or Circle

Once you are ready, you can say a prayer if you'd like. You can then visualize a bubble of energy in any color you like surrounding yourself and your readee. You can give the command that any spirits or energies not needed right at that moment, or not serving either one of you, will have to wait outside the circle. Notice if you get a sense of any other colors in your bubble. You can imagine these floating outside the bubble or that you are blowing them away with your exhalations.

Greet the Readee's Spirit

During a clairvoyant reading, we are getting in touch with the essence of a person. We are reading their spirit along with their personality and body. When you put your attention on your readee's spirit, your readee will spontaneously become more in touch with that part of themselves. You can do this simply by imagining that you are sending them a note that says "Hello, spirit" or a present in the form of a bouquet of flowers. You can even ask yourself, "What would this person really like to have?" and then see what comes to you, and send over a symbol that represents that. Then watch to see where this gift you are sending to them goes and whether or not it seems they are receiving it. Wherever it goes is where they are centered. It may therefore go to a certain location within their body or somewhere outside their body. If it seems as if they aren't receiving this gift, then repeat the process. If they still don't appear to receive it, this may be an indication that they will have a hard time receiving the rest of your communication or that it may just take a while for them to get comfortable with the process. Regardless, continue on with the reading for as long as the readee has verbally asked you for one. This process of greeting the readee's spirit is a good one to repeat during the reading if you feel that you need to establish a stronger connection in order to stimulate the flow of images coming to you.

Establish a Connection

There are a couple techniques you can use to establish a stronger connection with your readee, so you can ensure you are reading your readee and not someone or something else.

Option 1—Traditional Color Method: First, you imagine a clear, transparent receptacle such as a lotus flower, to represent the crown chakra. You can see this either on your reading screen or you can imagine it is floating directly above your readee's head. Have the readee state their current name and date of birth a few times, and invite the main color their spirit is vibrating at to come into the flower.

Sit back and wait until you get a sense of a color. If you see many colors, you can give this flower a grounding cord by using the image of its stem to go into the earth. Ask that all extraneous energies and their corresponding colors release, leaving the one energy that represents them right now in present time. If you are not satisfied with this process, you can destroy the lotus flower and create a brand-new one, repeating the process of having the readee say their name.

When your readee says their name, listen to their voice and postulate that the tone and quality of the voice will come into your receptacle and translate itself into visual information such as a color. Once you notice a color, you can match your crown chakra to it by simply visualizing your crown chakra vibrating at this same color, but a notch or two brighter. When you are finished with the reading, you will want to make sure you remove this color from your crown chakra. You can do so by seeing it return to a neutral gold color and then either looking at it to see what color it wants to turn to, or assigning it a color that matches a vibration that seems to represent you or that makes you feel good.

Option 2—Musical Bridge Connection: I developed this method as an alternative to the first, since I was sometimes seeing too many colors and finding it very confusing to decide which one to use.

Visualize a bridge forming between your crown chakra and that of the readee. Imagine that the readee's crown chakra is vibrating at a certain musical note or tone. Then imagine this tone is running down the bridge to your crown chakra, and you are going to tune it to theirs just as if you'd match a note on one string of a guitar to the same note on another string.

When they are in harmony, the two crown chakras and the bridge should be seen as one united color, or you can see a rainbow-type stream and imagine these are vibrating at a faster and faster frequency. Make sure when the reading is over that you call back your energy from this bridge, release any of the readee's energy that might have come through it, let your own crown chakra go back to its original tone, and then completely destroy the bridge in your imagination.

Wrapping Up Your Reading

The best way to end your reading is to create a new receptacle and ask it to show you a next step or action the readee can take that will help them achieve a goal. This is not about you giving advice, but really asking for the answer to come clairvoyantly. Providing the readee with actions that they can take will empower them and remind them that *they* are in charge of their destiny, not you.

A Final Message from Their Guides

You can also ask for the readee's guides to provide a message about the next step to take. Put out an image of a rose, and imagine you are pointing at it. Ask the readee's most helpful guide to put their message inside the rose. You can then watch the rose and imagine you are listening to it as well. Many times, particularly when there is an established time frame during which you are going to complete the reading, you will find that the information about the readee's next step just spontaneously arrives.

Clairvoyant Technique #2

In Clairvoyant Technique #1, we performed the reading using one viewing receptacle, as I've discussed so far throughout this chapter. Clairvoyant Technique #2 is virtually the same, but we will utilize two receptacles, or roses, and look at the relationships between the two. Whether you use roses or another object for your viewing receptacle, it's important to begin using the same image for both receptacles so you can compare the changes within these as the energy/information enters and then transforms them into more complex symbols and images.

I really enjoy working with two roses because it gives me even more to look at. I can focus my attention on one at a time, or step back and watch to see how the two interact with each other. I can also look at what might stand in between them by putting out a third rose in the middle and labeling it as a communication receptacle. This is the best technique for reading relationships of any kind.

Label Your Receptacles

It is important for you to know which receptacle represents which person or thing. So visualize the first one and consciously decide if it should go to the right or left of your reading screen. Then, in your imagination, write the name of the person or thing underneath it or above it. You can say the name of the person as well to that particular receptacle, or if you are reading someone you can ask them to say the corresponding name a few times and you can invite the person's energy whose name it is to show itself in that receptacle.

Then visualize the next receptacle and put that on the opposite side of the screen and repeat the process with either you or your readee stating the second person's name. If you are reading a couple and both people are present with you, you can have one person say their name, and observe the receptacle until you see a color. Then create the second receptacle, invite the second person to say their name, and look for a color.

If both people are not present, have the one person who *is* present say both people's names, one at a time. Tell your receptacle that it is going to show you the nature of the absent person, not as the one saying the names thinks of them, but as the absent person actually is.

As is usually the case whenever one person talks about someone else who is not there, we need to understand that we are going to tend to be more sympathetic to the person who is present, at least at that moment. It helps to keep this in the back of your mind because if all is not perfect in paradise, it's going to be natural to assume that it's the absent person's fault, when in actuality our complaining readee may be the real problem. This fact will usually emerge during the reading, but it helps to go into the reading being conscious of your natural biases, which will favor the person you are speaking to—and who might be paying you for the reading!

Clairvoyant Technique #3

This technique works with reading relationships between people, or between a person and anything they are wondering about. This could include their own clairvoyant or healing ability, their finances, their future, a particular person, any creative project, and so forth.

Instructions

Once you are looking out at your reading screen and have created your connection with whomever you are reading, create a clear, transparent, neutral 3-D receptacle or viewing object such as a rose. Take a good look at this so you have a starting point to work with. Let this rose represent yourself or the person you are reading.

Next, above the rose, create a symbol of something that represents the person's goal again, whether that be more money (perhaps a dollar sign or gold bar), a relationship (you can visualize a wedding ring), a child (visualize a baby), stronger clairvoyant abilities (visualize a third eye), and so on.

Then simply drop the symbol into the rose and notice what happens to the rose once it is filled up with the symbol. You'll be amazed at what comes up!

This is analogous to giving a pill to the client to see how the client responds. In fact, you can do this exercise around medication or a course of treatment if a person is sick and wondering how best to proceed. We can also ask, "Is this food / exercise / therapy / man / job / project good for me (or the client)?"—and then drop it into the viewing receptacle and watch what happens.

I really enjoy this exercise because it's always interesting to see what comes up. Does the rose accept it or spit it out? How does the rose change? Does it look better or worse? If you would like information about the future, then visualize a calendar. Rip out a page with a particular month on it and drop it into the receptacle. You can also do this with a map of a place you are considering moving to, and see what happens.

Examples of How to Work
With the Three Techniques

Below I present some common questions asked by readees as well as examples of how to work with the receptacle. I use the words *rose* and *viewing receptacle* interchangeably.

Question: *"How is my job going?"*
1. Look at one rose that represents the readee's job.
2. Look at one rose for the readee, one rose for their job. Instruct the two roses to show you the nature of their relationship.
3. Look at one rose for the readee, and above this visualize a symbol representing their job. Drop the symbol into the rose and notice what happens to the rose.

Question: *"What is wrong with my marriage?"*
1. Look at one rose for the marriage.
2. Visualize a rose for each person in the relationship. How do the roses interact?
3. Visualize a rose for each person in the relationship. In the middle put up a third rose to represent the communication.

Question: *"Have I hired the right attorney for my lawsuit?"*
1. Look at one rose for the readee, one rose for the attorney.
2. Look at one rose for the attorney, one rose for the lawsuit.

Question: *"I am considering investing in a few business ventures. Which is the best?"*
Or, *"I am dating a few guys. Which one is the best?"*
Or, *"I have a few job offers. Which one is the best?"*
Or, *"I have a few places in mind to move to. Which place is the best?"*
Option 1: Look at a single rose for each venture. Do one at a time; after you are done with one, destroy it and then look at a rose for the next.
Option 2: Put up one rose for the readee and one rose for the venture (or guy, job offer, or location). Watch what happens between the two roses. Once you are satisfied with what you get, destroy all these images and start over with the next person or thing the readee is considering.
Option 3: See three viewing receptacles. Label each one with the thing it represents. Ask for the strongest possibility to stand out among the rest, and look at all three and see what happens.

**Question: "I would like to know if I am on
my spiritual path."**

1. Look at one rose for the readee, one rose for their spiritual path. How do they interact?
2. Look at one rose for the readee. Put up a symbol representing their spiritual path. Watch how the two interact.
3. Look at one rose for the readee. Put up a symbol representing their spiritual path. Drop the symbol into the rose and notice what happens with the rose.
4. Put up a rose that represents the readee's spirituality. See what comes up.
5. Put up one rose for the readee's spirit, one rose for their body.
6. Put up one rose for the part of the readee that is asking the question, one rose for the part of themselves with which they desire to be in touch.

Viewing Receptacles Are Just a Tool to Get You Started

In order to be able to effectively do clairvoyant readings in any situation, we need to understand how to navigate our way and guide ourselves through the reading. As you have seen, we are not just waiting for inspiration to drop from the heavens and hit us over the head, any more than we'd consider sitting down on a sofa and hoping the TV will turn on by itself.

Our reading screen is like a TV that we position at a comfortable distance in front of us. When we visualize a transparent 3-D rose or another object on our screen, and invite the information we are seeking to come into it by saying the name of the readee, it is similar to consciously selecting a TV channel or a specific radio station. We still won't know exactly what program is going to come on, or what the story line or the identity of the characters will be, but we do know we can expect something to appear with as much certainty as if we were to press the on button of a TV.

Asking specific questions is like tuning in to a particular television show. We may understand we are about to view a show that has to do with detectives or romance or animals, and we may even know who some of the characters are and what they are like because we watched it last week, but we still don't know the story line or how the characters might surprise us, nor do we know how the show will ultimately turn out until the images show up on our screen.

Reading screens and viewing receptacles are tools you can always use to access your clairvoyance and that you can return to when you get stuck, when the information stops flowing, or when you aren't sure how to proceed. Once you get started and the information *is* flowing, you will find that you don't need to be focusing on the receptacle/ roses on your screen. Some of you may not even want to use a screen, but just the receptacle or vice versa. Often the images will flow freely, mixed in with a knowledge of what the images mean, and you may realize that for several minutes you haven't needed to use your screen or a rose or receptacle, or even consciously pose a question.

Many psychics use tarot cards, tea leaves, or crystal balls in the same manner as the screen and viewing receptacle. Even remote viewers use a technique called an *anagram* to get started. In fact, it can be quite fun to use any of the above as the visualization for your viewing receptacle. You can play around by starting off with the image of a blank tarot card or a tea leaf, crystal ball, or geometric pattern, and see how those work for you.

The advantage to the techniques taught in this book is that they allow you to be self-reliant.

You don't need anything other than yourself. If you lose any part of yourself, you will always know how to bring it back!

CHAPTER 5

Navigational Techniques:
Asking the Right Questions

He who asks is a fool for five minutes, but he who
does not ask remains a fool forever.
— CHINESE PROVERB

One of my strengths as a clairvoyant teacher is helping beginning students learn how to navigate their way through a reading by giving them questions to pose to their reading screens and reading receptacles. Eventually, students begin to ask these same questions without my prompting, and that is when I know they are ready to begin reading on their own or with less supervision. Some people are naturally talented at framing questions or guiding themselves during a reading. Such students often are already experienced counselors, therapists, or interviewers who tend to be more psychologically oriented.

Not every question is created equally and not every question will elicit the response you would like. If you are not "getting anything," if you don't feel as if you are getting clear enough answers, or if you just aren't sure how else to proceed, then you need to create a new, clear viewing receptacle or rose, and pose a new question to it.

From the list below you will notice that two types of questions are generally missing. The first category includes yes or no questions. Yes or no questions usually lead to a dead end. They are overly simplistic and devoid of insight. When a psychic merely reports "yes" or "no," what are you supposed to do with that? It gives you almost no insight into the dynamics of the situation. You are left with a feeling like "Okay, now what?" Also, it's far too easy for our own minds or the plethora of spirits around us to play tricks on us.

The other types of questions to avoid are those that include the word *should*. "Shoulds" are judgments, human constructs of the mind. There really is no such thing as "should" in the realm of spirit. Instead, it's much more fruitful to ask questions that help determine the best course of action that will elicit the most desirable effect.

Below you will find an assortment of questions to ask in a variety of situations. Remember, I am not talking about posing these questions out loud to your client; rather, these questions are to be posed to the viewing receptacle you have created on your reading screen. Sometimes you won't need to pose a question at all. Instead, just put out a receptacle, invite the client's energy into it, and begin to talk about whatever comes. You may find after studying and practicing these questions and possibly referring back to them from time to time that they will become ingrained in your mind so you will never for an instant be stuck asking, "Okay, what next?" In fact, the more you use them, the more the answers will arrive when they are needed—even without you having to consciously voice or pose these questions.

Remember that it's always helpful to frame the question within a particular time frame. Past, present, and future are fine, but when it comes to the future you could be more specific, such as posing questions like "How do things look in three, six, nine, or twelve months, or year to year?"

Questions About Relationships When Someone Has a Particular Person in Mind

- What is the nature of the relationship in the present?
- What are the dynamics of the relationship in the present?
- Can you give me a symbol of the relationship?
- Can you give me a symbol of X to know I am looking at the right person?
- Why is X behaving as he/she is right now?
- Let me see the communication and what might be influencing it.
- How does X feel about Y or Y feel about X?
- Is X going to do what Y wants or vice versa?
- What is in my client's best interest or the best interest of both people at the present time?
- What is the spiritual agreement between X and Y?
- Why have X and Y come together?
- Have X and Y had any other incarnations together?
- Let me see a symbol to know if the changes will occur.
- Why is the relationship not working out?
- If the relationship is not going to happen, why did they feel so strongly about it?
- Why are they having such a hard time letting go?
- How were they so easily misled?
- Is X having an affair or being honest?

Questions About Creating the Ideal Relationship

I don't like to leave people hanging with no hope. So if you see that a specific relationship is not going to pan out as expected, I suggest you pose the following questions:

- How does the readee's relationship space look in general?

- What will the readee's next relationship be like?
- How will the readee meet their next partner?
- What will the readee's next partner be like?
- What does the readee need to do to heal their relationshipsin general?
- What does the readee need to do in order to create theideal relationship?
- Why has this person been caught in a pattern?
- What actions or next steps does this person need to take?
- What does the ideal person look like for the readee?
- What is standing in between the readee and manifesting the relationship they desire?
- Look at a rose for the relationship pattern. Look at the rose for the person's relationship in the present or their future. Compare the two roses. What looks different?

Relationship to Oneself

For me the most important relationship we can have is the one with ourself. Therefore this is the most important relationship to look at during a clairvoyant reading. This relationship encompasses self-love, one's spiritual path, one's purpose in life, and so forth. When someone asks me for a spiritual reading or life path reading, or tells me to "just look and see what comes up," the techniques offered below are those that I usually use to begin accessing the information the readee seeks.

- Look at one rose for the readee and one rose for their heart.
- Look at one rose for the readee and one rose for theirspiritual path.
- Put up a rose for readee and drop a symbol of heart of pathin their rose.
- Put up a rose for them, another for their inner voice. Seethe relationship.
- Put up one rose for their god of the heart space and look at it.
- Put up an image of the readee and have them look in themirror; see what happens.
- See a rose for the readee and put in it something they want—e.g., to develop their spirituality—and see what happens.
- See a path and put the readee on the path and then tell themto show you something as they walk down the path.
- See one rose for their inner child and one rose for their parent; see what happens.
- Put up a rose for the past life that most resonates with the readee's current life.
- Put up a rose that represents the readee's clairvoyance.
- Put up a rose that represents the readee's healing abilities.
- Look at a rose/receptacle for each of the readee's chakras.
- Look at a rose for the readee's clairaudience and spirit guides.

Career and Finance Questions

Questions regarding one's career aspirations or changes are very common. When a client asks you to tell them about their career, you will need to decide whether or not to do the reading "blind"—with no prior knowledge of what they do for a living or are considering doing—or if you want to ask the readee for some background information so you can get more quickly to the heart of the answer they seek.

For years I never asked for this information unless the readee offered it. I enjoyed the challenge of seeing what I got, even though it was more stressful. However, over the years I have become a little less patient. Now I will often ask readees for background just to save time, since they already know what they do (although they get a kick out of me seeing it anyway). They may be curious about other information or have some challenging issues that we'd be better off spending our time on. Also, if I already know what the readee does, I will be less inclined to misinterpret whatever information comes as information about the future when it really pertains to the present (something I do quite frequently).

Options

- Put up a clear transparent 3-D rose on your reading screen that represents the readee's present career. Look for a color. Or look for it to change or move or for a new image to appear. Ask the rose to show you whatever your client needs to know the most about their job space.
- Put up one rose for the readee and another one for their job and see what happens when the two come together.

Ask the following questions:

- Is this the right job for the readee?
- What is the right job for the readee?
- What kind of work would be most fulfilling for the readee?
- How will my readee start earning income?
- What job would better serve this person?
- What fulfilling job will the readee have in the future?
- If this person could be doing any job, what would it be?
- What energy is keeping this person from knowing theirideal job?
- What energy is keeping this person stuck in their current job?
- What does this person need to know in order to get unstuck?
- Compare two roses, one representing the readee's workspaceand the other representing the readee. Do the colors androses match?
- How can this person be happier in their work?
- Put out a rose for the readee's finances in general; see howit looks.
- Put out a rose for a particular financial investment.
- Put out a rose for a person who could help the readee withtheir finances.
- What is in the way of the readee earning more money?
- Put up a rose for their creative or manifestation space.

Of course this list is not exhaustive, and you most certainly don't need to memorize it before practicing or doing a reading. These questions are just here to guide you when you are stuck or need some inspiration. From the number of questions or suggestions on this list, you will see that it's really possible to read someone for hours, if not indefinitely—although I am not suggesting you do that!

Formatted Reading

A formatted reading is one that provides a visual structure to follow. I offer a few examples of these in *You Are Psychic*. I have recently begun using a new type of formatted reading that is working really well for the students in my one-on-one training program.

If you are reading someone else, establish the reading color (see chapter 4) and then ask your readee to repeat their name. As they do, visualize a diamond-shaped figure on your screen or out in front of you. Visualize a circle or a transparent rose at each point, and designate each point as one of the following: the physical body, the spiritual body, the emotional body, and the mental body. In your imagination, write the name of the body above the corresponding point. If you have a hard time remembering which point is which, you can draw it on a piece of paper first. I like to put the spiritual body at the top point, the physical body at the bottom, the emotional body to the left, and the mental body to the right, but I don't think the order matters at all. Sometimes this will change depending on the person you are reading, and might provide additional insight into what they are giving priority to in their life.

There are a few things you are looking for in this structure. The first and perhaps most important is to look at the lines in between the point. Are the lines connected to each point? Are they even? Are they smooth or jagged? Is it easier to see one part of the triangle (e.g., the top half or right side) as opposed to another part? It's helpful to look for a color for each point, and to notice if the colors are equally as bright, or if the circles/roses at the points seem bigger, smaller, clearer, or stand out in any way from the others. You can even look for a color for the center of the diamond and see what that represents, perhaps the person as a whole.

Take a look at these overall elements first, and then you can choose which aspect stands out that you'd like to address before the others. Then go through the process you've already learned by focusing your attention on the part that stands out, and asking it to show you what it represents. If nothing comes to you, you can try this: pose the question about the aspect in question to a new viewing receptacle/rose. Example questions might be "Why is the line broken between the spiritual and the emotional body?" and "Why is the point at the emotional body large but the one with the mental body small?" Notice what happens to the receptacle and then ask whatever happens to show you more information in the form of another image and/or on a knowingness level. After addressing these aspects, you can take one point (as a circle or a rose) at a time and focus your attention to see what emerges.

Lately I've been having my students use this type of reading without the readee asking any questions or giving any information about themselves, and then once the student has covered all aspects of the diamond shape, I invite the volunteer they are practicing on to ask whatever questions they've been wondering about. What we usually discover is that the person's questions were mostly answered in the first part prior to the student asking them. We also find that the energy shifts (it usually feels heavier) when the person asks questions, because the questions are often coming from the mind only and are about solving problems—which are defined as such by itself, as opposed to looking at the bigger picture that takes the person's whole being into account. Still, there is value in answering their questions, as doing so tends to quiet the demands of the logical mind.

CHAPTER 6

Psychic Hearing

*A wise old owl sat on an oak / The more he saw, the less
he spoke / The less he spoke, the more he heard /
Why aren't we like that wise old bird?*
— UNKNOWN

Clairaudience and Telepathy

Clairaudience is the ability to access information through a combination of inner hearing and thought. *Telepathy* is a type of clairaudience and is the sending and receiving of thoughts from one person or spirit to another. During a clairvoyant reading, these abilities will spontaneously emerge, but there are definitely things we can do to develop and direct these abilities. In order to give you a taste of what psychic hearing is like, I recommend doing the following exercise.

Exercise to Understand Clairaudience

Close your eyes and turn your attention inward. Silently say "I love you" ten times to yourself, inside your own head. Listen to yourself saying these words. Then do this again, but this time do it as if you were shouting "I love you," again only inside your mind. Now do this again as if you were singing the words. Do it one more time with some kind of foreign accent.

You will most surely notice that you can hear yourself forming these words and that the volume, tone, pitches, and cadence will have varied even though you were not physically saying the words. This is exactly what telepathic or clairaudience messages sound like. The only difference is that in this exercise you were intentionally forming these thoughts. When they come in on a psychic level they will arrive unexpectedly, as if they were news to you. This is analogous to the relationship between visualization and clairvoyance. When you visualize, you are directing your mind to conjure up a certain image. When you are being clairvoyant, your visualizations begin to act outside the boundaries of what you intended or expected.

Telepathy Coming From Another Person

Clairaudient messages come from a variety of sources. They often come directly from the person you are reading or focusing on. Sometimes you may hear a voice that sounds just like that of your client or someone you are sitting close to that includes an "I" statement, such as "I can't stand this anymore" or "I want this more than anything." When this happens you will often have a very clear sense it's your readee speaking to you just as if your readee were addressing you with words.

Sometimes a message will come in from a spirit guide, a deceased relative, or some kind of entity that has a vested interest in the readee. The message might just spontaneously enter your mind, or you might request an answer to a particular or general question such as "Please tell me what my client needs to hear the most," "Why has this person really come to me today?" or "What the hell did that image just mean?!" Once you ask the questions, be as still and as silent as possible and put all your attention on your ears. The more the messages come in words or a tone unlike those you typically use, the more certain you can be the message is coming from a source outside yourself, particularly when the information surprises you.

You need to be aware that some spirits will lie to you. I haven't experienced this so much during a clairvoyant reading (except for a few occasions when the language was abusive, which sent up a red flag right away), but I have been relaxing at home when I have heard a message such as "Linda is dead." I was very worried when that happened, so I called my good friend Linda who advised me she was very much alive but had been engaged in a psychic battle of sorts with beings who seemed to be projecting death or suicide thoughts at her. If you wish to seek a message during a reading, it's helpful for this reason to direct your questions to a particular source, such as the readee's Higher Self, the spirit guide who is most loving or most knowledgeable in a specific subject, or a particular deity you feel connected with. If you get a very strong message, you can always use your clairvoyance to help you "see" its source.

Early on in my clairvoyant training, I realized I couldn't always trust the auditory messages I heard, so I got into the habit of backing up any clairaudient messages with my clairvoyant images. I have this little game I play with myself even now in which I only rely on messages as a last resort, as if to do otherwise would somehow be cheating. I think I do this because if all I have to do is listen and repeat word for word what I am getting, it is much easier than taking the time to focus, receive, and interpret the clairvoyant information and, as I've noted already, also somewhat less reliable.

Clairvoyant images almost always come from the reader and the readee. On rare occasions, an entity may throw a picture at a clairvoyant. I say "throw a picture" because that's how it feels, like an intrusion. It has a different quality than most other images or visions, and is usually unrelated to the topic or has sexual or violent connotations. If you've ever been falling asleep or meditating and, out of the blue, saw a demonic face or a sex picture flash before your eyes, this is what you were very possibly experiencing.

Although they are definitely subject to misinterpretation, clairvoyant images don't lie, whereas spirits are a lot less dependable unless you have an established connection with a particular one. In my experience, there is a depth of information that comes from clairvoyant symbols that clairaudient messages often do not match. As indicated elsewhere in this book, when you see information you can alter it, so clairvoyance automatically paves the way for healing to occur in a way that sharing verbal messages does not. Still, there are many times when I draw a blank with my clairvoyance, usually because I am either feeling pressured for time or concerned my readee doesn't understand me, and then I am extremely grateful for the messages that come soon after I request them. Many times I will not understand the message but my readee will.

Most of the famous psychics you have heard of and/or observed, from Sylvia Browne to John Edward to James Van Praagh, rely heavily on their clairaudience and the information they receive either from their own guides or the deceased relatives of their clients (particularly Edward and Van Praagh). This is why these psychics are also considered mediums. Receiving auditory messages works well for them, and enables them to access and communicate information very quickly. Compare the difference between looking at a picture and describing it in your own words to someone else, and repeating word for word what someone else is telling you. Describing the picture takes a lot longer. Therefore these psychics do very well on radio and TV programs, where their messages need to be delivered in short fifteen-second sound bites.

I have great respect for these psychics, although I do think, at least in the media, that there is far too much focus on communications with the deceased. This focus has contributed to a false impression that the only thing psychics do is communicate with the dead. High-profile psychics face grueling challenges that require more talent than just their psychic abilities, because they often work/perform in front of enormous groups, and along with receiving messages they need to very quickly figure out exactly whom the messages are for, all the while being bombarded with massive amounts of telepathic interference from the audience ("Pick me, pick me!") and the gallery of entities that desire to be heard as well.

Most of these psychics are self-taught or have been doing readings since they were very young. Therefore, they don't know the exact steps that anyone can utilize to perform a reading, although from their most recent books and appearances, I am noticing a trend in which many such psychics seem to be shifting their focus to teaching as opposed to merely demonstrating their own talents. I don't know if this is a sign of their own personal development or a sign of the times or both, but it's one I appreciate because it sends the message that these talented psychics are examples of what is possible for others, too.

Channeling

Clairaudience is a mild form of channeling. I am still not certain if it's possible to hear the messages from spirits if they are completely outside your body and aura and disconnected physically from you, or if they do have to be at least partially connected or corded into you in order for you to hear them. Channeling is the spiritual ability to bring another spirit into one's body. Spirits can plug into any part of a living person's body or energy field. Healing spirits often just plug into a healer's hand chakras. Spirits that wish to speak through a person will usually plug into the telepathic channels that are located on the back of the head behind the ears, and behind the neck and throat (fifth) chakra.

When I've attended channeling sessions, it's usually been difficult for me to be there because my own telepathic channels were being em-pathetically activated, and the pressure or pain on them was intense. I think the same spirits being channeled through the hosts were attempting to come through me, and I was not in agreement with this at all. In fact, as I write at this very moment I can feel someone or something trying to plug in. There are really millions of spirits out there that would love nothing better than to communicate with someone— really anyone who will listen! Some of these spirits also plug into the back of the head, behind the sixth chakra and also into one's crown chakras. Even when a spirit is plugged into just one or a few areas of the body, the body can be readily influenced by that spirit's emotions and thoughts. When the spirit is plugged into the throat chakra, the person's voice may be drastically altered, but usually their appearance will remain the same.

In full-body channeling, a large portion of the channeler's spirit leaves their body to make room for another spirit to completely move into their body and energy field. When the spirits have exchanged places, the channeler often takes on the physical appearance, mannerisms, and voice of the entity being channeled. The spirit that owns the body will frequently be unaware of what is being stated or will not retain a memory of what was said. Two of the best known full-body channelers are J. Z. Knight, who channels Ramtha and authored *The White Book*, and the late Jane Roberts, who channeled a group of beings known as Seth and wrote books such as *The Nature of Personal Reality* and *Seth Speaks*.

Some mediums will channel just about any being that wants to come through them at any given time, while others are committed to a single entity or a collective group of beings. It is pretty interesting to see a female medium channeling a male spirit. Sometimes I wonder if this doesn't feel just a little bit strange to the woman's husband, particularly when the session is over and it's time to go to bed!

We are all constantly channeling to varying degrees at every moment, whether we are channeling our parents' judgments or channeling dirty jokes from entities that we picked up the night before at the local bar. Some people attend schools and workshops to learn how to minimize the risks of channeling and how to recognize when they are spontaneously channeling in their everyday life, so they can avoid being affected by energies that don't always have their best interests in mind. I believe that many of the mentally ill homeless people you see talking to themselves on the streets are frequently channeling multitudes of beings at any given time. These beings like to talk and don't care whether or not anyone is listening. I also think that when people say things such as "I don't know why I just did that," "I know I did it, but it's not me," or "I haven't been myself lately," that they are being more accurate than they even know.

Some spirits are very adept at working with channelers. They intuitively understand how to effectively plug into a body, and to speak in a voice and use language that can be readily understood. Others have no clue as to how to achieve a proper connection. Until they are taught by the channeler or another clairvoyant who can see them, they will plug into the wrong body part or communicate in the wrong language. Just as with other types of spirit guides, channeling guides range from being ignorant and unconscious to being fully enlightened ascended masters.

When channeling you want to be very careful about whom you invite in; otherwise you may end up with a very unruly houseguest who doesn't know when to leave. For this reason I don't recommend channeling without proper instruction and supervision by an experienced teacher. Channeled spirits tend to have a specialty. Some are healers, other are teachers, still others are charismatic entertainers, and some are just vagabond souls seeking further experiences for themselves. Full-body channeling is very hard on the body. People who engage in this type of practice are vulnerable to illness and a shortened life span and sometimes might begin to incur karma based on the spirits' actions. This is what happens when a person goes on a rampage, committing an act of violence and then having no memory of it the next morning. People who have been drinking or using drugs are obviously more vulnerable to this phenomenon.

If you have a strong interest in channeling, I recommend checking out the Aesclepion Healing Center in Marin County, California, or the Southern California Psychic Institute in the Los Angeles area. The Berkeley Psychic Institute also has a transmedium program.

Although I never intend to channel other entities when I perform clairvoyant readings, occasionally a spirit will plug into my throat chakra, particularly when I am reading a client's deceased relative who was pushy or domineering when he or she (usually he) was alive. On a few occasions, this spirit's male voice has come through my own so strongly that I found myself talking like that spirit. My voice still sounded like my voice, but I felt compelled to speak in a manner that was definitely not my own, as if I were reading for a character unlike myself in a play. Some of the words I was using were not part of my everyday vocabulary and my readees immediately told me that I sounded just like their father or grandfather who had recently passed away. I also realized that I was speaking more emphatically and expressively than I usually do. On one occasion, I sounded like a hell-and-brimstone preacher, getting all riled up when deep inside I really was very detached from whatever I was saying.

I must admit that these experiences were rather entertaining. However, after these readings I had a more difficult time making separations from the spirits than I usually do, and it took me a few days before I seemed completely back to myself. Sometimes channeling a spirit you've just met is a lot like dancing with a guy at a bar that you're not really into; it's hard to get rid of him for the rest of the night!

It seems as though some people are just pre-wired for channeling while others do have to work at it. Those who are naturals at it often do it throughout their day, usually with little awareness. These people are called *transmediums*. The *trans* prefix indicates that transmediums can channel other spirits, and they also tend to run their own energy through other people's bodies.

The biggest challenge anyone who wishes to channel faces involves trust and fear issues. The faith healers in the Philippines channel some of the most bad-ass spirits imaginable. This is what allows them to perform the psychic surgery and other feats most people consider to be impossible or miracles. Accepting some of these beings into your body is kind of like trying to stuff an elephant into a jar or filling up a bicycle tire with a truckload of helium. It is very intense, and many of these healers cope with this by turning to alcohol or other addictive behaviors despite their unfailing spiritual and religious convictions. One of the biggest lessons I've learned are the two are in no way mutually exclusive!

One of the most striking characteristics I noticed with the healers who were performing extraordinary feats was that they all had the ability to completely surrender to the spirit working through them. I tried this a few times and had some interesting experiences, but I was very aware of the amount of fear and caution I had blocking me from completely letting go in order to let these beings take over to do their job. Years later, my desire to experience this is no longer there, particularly after recognizing my ego's involvement in that desire. For now, I am content being just me...at least this minute!

I am not going to include instruction in full-blown channeling in terms of inviting other entities to enter your body, since this is not my area of expertise and I believe that it should be done under the guidance of an experienced teacher and in person. However, in chapter 16 you can learn how to work with a healing guide that will plug into your hand or arm channels. Below I will give you some suggestions about how to develop your clairaudience, which could include telepathy from your readee or from spirits that remain outside your body. I also offer advice about what to do if it seems these spirits are getting a little too frisky or too close for comfort.

How to Work With Clairaudience

I suggest following the clairvoyant techniques first, and then incorporating the skill of clairaudience once you have practiced your clairvoyance a few times. That is not to say you won't naturally be receiving information on a psychic hearing level or that you shouldn't use it sooner, but since clairvoyance for some people is a little trickier, it's worked well for me and most of my students to get the visual flowing first and to use clairaudience to fill in the blanks. You can fall back on clairaudience when you are feeling stuck in understanding the meaning of your images, when you want further communication, or when you just feel ready to incorporate this skill into your repertoire. Some of you will have already experienced your clairaudience often enough at times when you were meditating, falling asleep, or relaxed—and for you it will most likely come easily and quite frequently when you are purposefully doing readings.

Telepathy
A good time to start calling forth your telepathy during a reading is when you see an image of your client or of a person or animal, and you wish to understand something about them or their intentions, desires, or actions. You can address these images with any question you are wondering about just as you would in "real life," but perhaps with even more boldness and candor. For example, you can say something to the image such as, "Hey, [*name*], how do you truly feel about this situation?" or "Hi, what do you need more than anything right now?"

Once you pose a question to these images (see chapter 5 for a list of helpful questions), the most important thing to do is to be still and silent inside yourself and wait for a response. Give the images time. Not every one of them will have an immediate response, although you won't usually have to wait more than a minute or two. Put your attention on your inner ears; you can even imagine your ears are becoming larger in order to take in the auditory information. Just wait, as if you were waiting for someone on the other end of the phone to pick up and start telling you something you've been waiting to hear, or as if you were waiting for a teacher who stands before you at a podium to start a lecture. Remind yourself (or pretend) that there is no difference between hearing with your outer ears and your inner ears, just as seeing with your inner eyes is as easy as seeing with your outer eyes. Part of the reason this doesn't seem as natural to most of us is because we just don't expect it to be as natural.

Troubleshooting: If you don't get a response, you can try rephrasing your question, or you can go back to the visual technique using the viewing receptacle method and then later on in the reading attempt to do this exercise again with another image. This is particularly good to do if you have a sense that you are looking at a spirit that spontaneously pops up or is one that your readee asked you to look at. Nevertheless, don't shy away from using your clairvoyance with spirits, as doing so will help you to see them as they used to look if they once had bodies.

Remember also that you can always address your client's Higher Self or spirits by sending them a hello in the form of a note, some flowers, or a little gift. Wait for them to respond, or you can imagine you are shaking their hands and asking them to tell you how they feel about something, particularly when the client is struggling with a tough decision. When a client has posed a question such as "Tell me what I should do," it is a great opportunity to put it back on the deepest, most intimate part of the client by asking that deep part to tell you what its greatest longing is.

Future self: Ask the client's future self a question.

A fun technique to use is to ask your client's future self to appear before you. You can call forth that future self at a specific date or point in time, or you can ask the future self to tell you the date they have traveled from along with whatever information you are seeking. If the future self doesn't seem to be in very good shape, you could even, before sending them back to the future, do a healing on them as you would for a person or spirit in the present time.

Instant Knowing

Instant knowing is different from clairaudience. Instant knowing will sometimes precede a clairvoyant image or follow it. It requires less interpretation than the other two abilities, and it's more subtle although it seems to be quite accurate. Sometimes it's almost as if you can feel it land within your mind, and you would barely notice it if it weren't for the fact that the information is not anything you could have otherwise known. It doesn't come in as a message; it's just somehow there.

This ability, I believe, is often at play in our everyday lives. Have you ever not been able to remember a name or fact and then suddenly the information was there, so clear it made you contemplate the nature of memory itself? That is quite similar to the experience of instant knowing.

How to Develop and Work with Knowingness

Follow the instructions for working with your clairaudience. However, instead of asking for the information to come through your ears, imagine that there is a special place in your mind you are going to. Be as quiet as possible. Instruct your mind that it will receive an answer effortlessly, and then just wait. This is going to be much easier after you've already been using your clairvoyance during a session and after meditating for a while.

Many people's minds are so cluttered and busy that it's hard for them to hear clairaudient messages or notice intuitive or divinely inspired thoughts. That is one reason why people tend to spontaneously begin experiencing their psychic abilities when they start meditating or increase their meditation time. Because clairvoyant reading causes you to maintain extreme inner focus and concentration, it is the most powerful form of meditation I've experienced. Therefore, usually by the second or third reading you do on someone else, you will spontaneously experience your instant knowingness. There isn't much you need to do to get it to happen, except perhaps visualize your crown chakra opening prior to or during the reading and also asking for your instant knowingness to work for you. Of course, when some bit of information does come to you in this way, seemingly landing in your head without warning, by all means express this information, regardless of whether it is accompanied by any visual pictures. You will most certainly find that it is quite accurate. I had a good friend when I was undergoing my own training who rarely ever saw pictures, but who received crystal-clear information on a knowing level quite often.

Again, this will often spontaneously happen as you are utilizing the clairvoyant techniques presented in chapter 4. Usually it starts to happen for most people by their third reading, sometimes sooner and sometimes later. You don't need to really understand what it is or what it's like before you experience it. It would happen even if I didn't mention it at all. When it does, you will understand what I am talking about.

Music in Your Head

Quite frequently, when a song is playing over and over in your head, particularly when it's one you think you didn't just hear a few minutes or hours before, it's very possible that the lyrics that are being repeated have a strong message for you. In fact, the way to get the song to stop playing in your mind is to listen to the lyrics and think about what they might mean for you right now. As soon as you do this, you will often find the music just miraculously stops, even if it's been bugging you for hours. This is because there is something out there that is using this method to get your attention.

On numerous occasions I have heard songs during readings, dreams, and in my everyday life that all ended up having strong significance. In fact, not too long ago I did an audition for a psychic TV show. The producer wanted to test me, so she showed me an envelope with a picture of something in it and asked me to tell her what the picture was. I was feeling nervous and didn't get much of a visual image, but then I heard the lyrics to "We Are Family," the song about sisters most famously performed by Sister Sledge. The producer ripped open the envelope and inside was a photograph of two twin girls. The producer told me the photo was of her and her sister.

Sometimes I feel as though I'm in the movie *Groundhog Day*. It doesn't matter that I have verification just about every day that I am psychic. Every time something like this happens, I'm still as amazed as if it were the very first time.

CHAPTER 7

The Future

The best way to predict the future is to invent it.
— ALAN KAY

Many people initially go to a psychic because they are curious about their future. They want to know if that screenplay will sell, when they might start their own business, if they will meet Prince Charming, if their husband or wife will ever snap out it, if they will be financially secure in their old age, or how, if, and when they will find a way to pay next month's rent. However, what people usually don't realize is that most of the information that actually appears or is accessible during a clairvoyant reading tends to be about the present or past. One of the main reasons for this is that much of the future seems dependent on one's actions, thoughts, and feelings in the present. Another reason is that our physical bodies are always in the present and can't be anywhere else. Since the person asking the question about their future is asking it in the present, we as clairvoyants naturally go to where they are, in the present, unless we consciously direct ourselves to another specific point in time.

None of this is to say that we won't ever spontaneously tune in to the future. Sometimes we will. Sometimes we will know this is what we are doing, sometimes not. Sometimes we will think we are reading the future when we are actually viewing an event that has already occurred.

Various researchers have discovered that, when given a vast array of information to view and describe, psychics and remote viewers are more likely to tune in to what is referred to as *peak emotional events*. We are all obviously having experiences around the clock, twenty-four hours a day. There is no way a psychic would have the time, the need, or the interest to tap into every action, behavior, feeling, or thought, so we are more likely to find the moment of drama when emotions were most heavily invested.

When you recall your past, you are not recalling everything you did at every second. You tend to recall your happiest moments, your worst moments, and the moments when something out of the ordinary happened to you. Actually, you aren't just recalling the moments as they happened; you are recalling your feelings and perceptions of a moment, and all the subsequent thoughts and feelings of that moment.

Your thoughts about the future really are no different from your memories of the past. You are projecting ideas and feelings onto something called the future, but the quality of these are no different from memories and not necessarily any less "real." Psychics and remote viewers tend to tune in to the most dramatic, emotionally charged events and memories of a person's life, particularly those of interest to the psychic. Sometimes we can see events in the future, but again it gets confusing. Are we seeing the actual event, or are we seeing a future memory of it? The two are not the same.

The Anxiety Factor

Many people want to know about the future because they are feeling anxious. What they forget is that even though they are thinking about the future, the anxiety is with them right now. As they allow their thoughts to fixate on unpleasant future possibilities, they become even more stressed out. For these people, the answer is ultimately not about knowing what the future will bring, for what if it is going to bring some challenges they think they'd rather avoid? Instead, the answer is to help them (or ourselves) to identify and release the anxiety they are currently experiencing. (Grounding, running your energy, and doing clairvoyant readings are excellent prescriptions for this.)

Because many people use their thoughts about the future to heal their present pain, discontent, and anxiety, they will often send their creative energy into the future and then have difficulty taking steps in the present because they don't have enough of their own life force left in their body. If you find yourself obsessing about the future, or being so goal-oriented that you realize you have not been enjoying yourself for a long period of time in the present, it is likely that a part of you is out there and may need to be retrieved, which can be done through awareness and can be initiated with the simple visualization offered at the end of this chapter.

The Future and Decision Making

A large percentage of people who come for readings ask about the future because they believe such knowledge will help them make the best decisions to achieve their goals and avoid failure. For example, they may wish to know how a particular investment will pay off in the future in order to help them decide whether or not to invest at all. They may wonder how a job prospect will work out so they can decide whether or not it's worth their time to even go through the lengthy application process.

As I noted, people may want to know whether or not the person they are in a relationship with is going to ever change so they can decide if they should end things or hang in there a while longer. This is where things get confusing to our little minds, which can really only comprehend events in terms of linear causation and effect. People are essentially attempting to change their futures by knowing them, and adjusting their behavior accordingly.

This leads us into an area that is as controversial as it is mind-boggling. I think—no, let me rephrase that—I *know* there are many people who could be helped by treating themselves to the gift of a quality clairvoyant reading but who fear they might receive "bad news" about their future. In the same way, there are a multitude of people out there avoiding development and awareness of their own psychic abilities due to the same fear. Many people even question the ethics of accessing information about the future. These same issues arise in the ongoing theoretical debate about time and time machines and the question "If you travel to the future or the past, will you irrevocably change the course of events that were really supposed to have happened?"

This debate seems to beg the question "What events were really supposed to have happened: the ones that would have occurred had the time travel (or psychic intervention) not taken place, or the ones that occurred once the time traveler influenced events or the psychic information was acted upon?" From here we can ask, "Is there really any particular set of events that are ever really *supposed* to happen?" Which leads us into questions about who is making these decisions. Is it God, our Higher Selves, some little green men in shiny space suits? To try to answer these questions is like driving on an endless network of highways that all connect and twist and wind together in your brain, but all lead you in one big fat circle to nowhere. These are interesting questions, but they really distract us from forward movement.

From my own experiences as a clairvoyant, psychic teacher, and recipient of many awesome readings, it is clear to me that yes, there are definitely times when people do alter their behavior based on a reading. Sometimes this is the most valuable thing a reading can do, particularly when those behaviors are self-destructive ones that lead to unproductive thoughts and unpleasant feelings and consequences. However, it's important to understand that most of the time, when a person is given information about the future, they will *not* change their behavior. The course they were headed on remains the same. They still marry that guy or invest that money. The difference is they have more consciousness as they experience events that had been accurately predicted, and they are better able to understand what is happening to them or why it's happening as they begin to heal from it once it has all come to pass.

The fact that many times people don't act on advice about the future makes me wonder if there is a built-in, set plan. Another possibility is that at the instant you began the reading you already began altering the readee's future, and therefore the future you are looking at is different from the one that would have been viewable had you not viewed it. Or perhaps the particular future you are seeing is there precisely because you are seeing it!

Some clients really do take into consideration the information they get during the reading, and then they are able to expand their vision of what is possible for themselves. For example, I might see a client in a leadership/supervisory position, when they have always been a clerk working for someone else. The client hadn't even considered this type of job. As a result of the reading, the client decides to stop applying for secretarial jobs and instead applies for management positions.

In one reading I did last year with a client named Katie, who lived in Florida, I looked into the future and had a sense she was going to be living on the west coast. I also saw her approaching some executives with her portfolio, and one of them seemed to be smiling and shaking hands with her. I had the sense Katie would be offered a position almost equivalent to his. This seemed rather far-fetched to her at that moment, as she was not even thirty years old and had no supervisory experience. However, just about one year later she called me for another reading. She advised me that she had in fact moved to Los Angeles, where she had been thinking of moving for a very long time, and that she had met a man at a bar who turned out to be the CEO of an advertising firm. He offered her a position starting at $90,000 a year.

However, a few weeks later, the company merged with another and they had to give the position to an executive with the other company. (I had not seen this far into the future in the previous reading.) In the second reading, which focused on her losing the position, I got the sense that Katie had raised her energy enough to manifest that opportunity, but she wasn't really ready on a number of levels to handle the demands that would be required of her. Her self-esteem was not high enough yet, and she really needed to do some general old-fashioned growing up before she was ready to take on a position such as this.

Basically, she needed to have patience and once again let the natural course of time work its magic.

While I rarely have anyone tell me I am wrong about what I see regarding their past or their present, I find it most amusing that more than a few times someone has told me I was wrong about what I was seeing for their future. (Let me clarify: they told me this before the "future" happened!) This is because they can't possibly imagine themselves having that kind of opportunity or doing what I see them doing. Why? The person asking about the future is not there yet. In order to be there they will need to raise their self-esteem, open their heart, and change their way of thinking (which might require an entire mental overhaul or paradigm shift), and most important, raise the frequency at which their energy vibrates. The helpful thing here is that I've planted a seed, shown them an outline of a new door, and perhaps even slipped a tiny wedge into the door of new possibilities so they can begin to open it wider when they are ready. As a psychic, a healer, and a person trying to remain sane, I need to allow them to grow at their own pace, even when that pace is much slower than I'd prefer.

Don't forget: reading the future, and then seeing if you were right, can be fun!

Reading the Future

Pinpointing the exact point in time of an event can be quite challenging. In fact, earlier in my training there were times I thought I was getting information about the future only to discover I was describing events that had already taken place. Now that I am more aware that this might be the case, rather than ever assuming I am accessing information about the future, I instead will consciously focus my attention on a specific point in the future and request information about a certain topic.

Future Reading Option One (General)
Visualize your reading screen. Then place a clear crystal rose on it. Underneath it, label it "the future." Instruct it to show you some future events. Look for a color first, then ask the color to show you what it represents. If you are not getting a sense of when these events will occur, once you start to describe them you can ask your rose to show you a symbol that will help your readee understand when they are going to happen or recognize when they're about to happen. Some of the symbols that come up might have to do with the weather. For example, if you see the readee shoveling snow it is likely the event is going to happen in the winter. If you see a graduation cap, this may indicate the event will occur sometime around or after a graduation.

Sometimes you may not get colors, but your rose might do something that gives you some indication—for example, it may grow very large and open up, or it might shrivel and fall over on its side. This will at least give you some indication whether or not the specific events you or your readee are wondering about will turn out as hoped. This is one reason why utilizing an image of a rose can be helpful when performing clairvoyant readings.

Future Reading Option Two (Specific)

Visualize your reading screen. Put out a clear transparent rose on it. Underneath it you can imagine you are writing the date in the future about which you'd like information. This could be a specific day, as in the case of your readee requesting information about the outcome of their immigration interview, court date, or wedding. More often, however, you may just wish to choose a certain period of time in the future, such as three, six, or nine months, or one year, three years, or ten years. Remember that the future encompasses millions of seconds, events, and feelings, so you are just going to tune in to a few events at most that the person perhaps needs to hear about now.

You can ask to see anything about the future, or you can pose any specific question to the rose about a particular point in time. For example, you can ask the rose to show you information about the readee's relationship three months from now or you can ask the rose to show you if the readee will have a relationship in three months. If it doesn't look as if they will, you can look ahead six months or a year and ask for images to appear if the readee will be alone or with someone else.

If you are seeing events that you know are not pleasing the readee, you can put out a new viewing receptacle and ask it to show you information regarding the reason the readee is not creating what they want, or what they think they want!

Is It Good or Bad to Know the Future?

Most psychics don't want to see "bad things" any more than their clients want to hear them. For this reason, most psychics don't pick these up unless there is a warning message there. This doesn't mean you shouldn't look at the future; on the contrary, you can be confident that if you look into the future you will see the things that your readee can deal with. It also doesn't mean that your readee is going to react favorably to whatever you are getting about the future. The readee may not like it at all in the moment, may deny that it's possible, or even tell you that you are most certainly wrong, but most of the time it's information that will be helpful for them at a later date. They will either be able to prepare themselves for that which you've predicted or you will help them understand it, or enable them to make changes to either avoid it altogether or lessen its impact when it arrives.

Personally, there are times when I find it very helpful to be able to tune in to future events and other times when it ruins the experience of being in the present moment. My son is an actor, and sometimes I tune in to see whether or not he is going to get a callback or a certain role. Even when I see he is going to be declined, I still drive the hour or more to Hollywood in rush-hour traffic and have him do the audition, just in case he is going to meet a contact who will pay off down the line, to give him the experience, and to appease his agent and manager who don't have as much confidence in my abilities as I do! But knowing it's not going to be fruitful takes away the fun of believing there is a chance. It is kind of like gambling with the certainty that you aren't going to win.

CHAPTER 8

Common Questions About
The Techniques

When you ask for patience, God doesn't just give you patience, he gives you the
opportunity to be patient. When you ask for
courage, he doesn't give you courage; he gives you
the opportunity to be courageous.
— FROM THE FILM *evan almighty*, WRITTEN BY STEVE OEDEKERK

Since the publication of *You Are Psychic*, I have received hundreds of emails from readers. In this chapter I answer some of the questions about reading techniques that are most commonly asked by these readers and by students in my most recent workshops and classes. In the next chapter I will address a variety of topics about readings in general.

Question: I am confused about using the reading screen and the viewing receptacle together. Do I really need these? Sometimes I see images before I visualize either one.

Answer: The tools presented in this book and expanded on in *You Are Psychic* are offered as a way to help you focus and initiate the flow of visual information. Once you get started, as long as the images are flowing, there is really no need to use these visualizations solely for the purpose of accessing information. However, they will be your saviors when you get stuck, confused, or are not sure how to proceed in the reading.

The screen corresponds with your sixth chakra, and it's helpful to clean it off frequently by grounding it and dusting it off, or by destroying it and creating another one. It gives you a place to focus and even acts as a hypnotic trigger that tells your unconscious mind that it has full permission to be psychic. The receptacle, particularly that of a rose, is enormously helpful because it's complex enough so that the energy/information will interact with each part of the

260

rose and alter them so you will have lots of aspects to explore. If you just used your screen, you would sometimes get images, but the rose gives you even more to work with.

I've had some students who only wanted to use the rose. They really didn't like to use the screen at all and I told them this was fine, until I realized that there was a very specific reason why these students resisted the screen. It turned out that they weren't used to being centered in their bodies at all. By reading without being centered, they would get disoriented, have trouble seeing and communicating the pictures because they were flashing before them too quickly, or they were zooming too far out of their bodies and having trouble getting back in. At this point the screen became very useful.

That being said, these are still only tools. Some students become so focused on these tools that they forget the important thing is the end result. If you are getting images and pertinent information, who cares whether or not you are seeing a rose or your screen first? The value of using the receptacles/roses, however, is that when you are done with whatever it is you've just looked at, you now have a container in which you can deposit that energy. If you do become emotional, you can ask yourself, "Where am I in relation to my screen?" By centering yourself in your head and noticing the distance between you and your screen out in front of your forehead, you will regain your neutrality. The receptacle also provides you with an immediate vehicle to be used in clairvoyant healing (see part 3 of this book). The screen can be used on its own like an x-ray machine when you wish to look at a person's physical body or aura.

Question: I've never been very visual. The images I get are not that clear. I don't see the whole thing. I can't see very much, I just kind of know it's there. I know you say everyone is clairvoyant but maybe I'm not.

Answer: Many people are visualizing without realizing they are doing so. They believe their images are supposed to look a certain way, or they are so accustomed to their mind's images that they don't realize visualization can be that easy. And so they overlook these images.

Do the following exercise right now: Imagine a blue circle. Imagine you are taking a yellow sparkly marker and drawing a circle around it clockwise. Then draw a circle around it counterclockwise. Then imagine you are taking a pair of scissors and cutting the blue circle down the middle. Take the two parts and imagine you are rolling them into a ball. Throw the ball away or even pop it into your mouth. Imagine it tastes like a sour blueberry!

Now, if you did any part of that, you are visualizing! One of the biggest difficulties students have is with their expectations. They think that everything they are supposed to see is going to appear in vivid Technicolor images that remain there as long as they'd like them to. That might happen occasionally, but it is certainly not always the case. As you do a reading, you will likely have your images come in a variety of ways. Some of them will be vivid, others you will barely see. Some will flash before you like a shooting star, just leaving a whiff of an impression or thought (these are often surprisingly informative). Some images will disappear right away, some will reappear, some you will have trouble letting go of, some will be stationary, some will move. Sometimes you will be able to intentionally visualize something like a rose very clearly; other times you will barely be able to muster a faint outline. The thing is to accept and be thankful that you are getting anything.

Clairvoyant students who are pessimistic or perfectionistic often get frustrated with themselves because they become stuck on an expectation of how images are supposed to appear, or they will get stuck on the two out of twenty things they couldn't interpret or figure out. These are often the same people who go out to eat at a terrific restaurant and complain, without mentioning the food was excellent, that the waitress forgot to bring them their ketchup; who will point out the one spot you missed when cleaning the entire house; or who will beat themselves up because they got an A-minus on a test instead of an A.

Question: Sometimes when I am doing readings, the person I am reading gets upset with something I said or will argue with me, thinking I said something was bad when I didn't see it that way at all. How can I avoid this?

Answer: Avoid the words *good* and *bad!*

I have begun to realize that some people will categorize everything I tell them during a reading into two categories: "good" and "bad." They do this categorization on a constant basis, and it is the predominant way such people process information. Essentially, they are placing a value judgment on every word they hear, regardless of whether I intended it to be interpreted or categorized in that way.

For example, someone might ask me, "Why am I getting lots of headaches?" I might answer, "There is some red energy on your head. When I ask where the energy is coming from, I see an image of your father." So right here, we have the word *headaches*. To certain readees that of course is bad because no one likes headaches. Readees might continue in their heads, "Red energy? Not sure, but if it's associated with a headache, it must be bad, too. Hmmm, an image of my father? Okay, well my father abandoned me and was a jerk. Okay, he's bad too, I got it." But what if he wasn't a jerk in the readee's eyes? If the father gets placed in the "good" category, then suddenly there is a big problem for them. How can the "good" thing be causing the "bad" thing?!

Here's another example. A client has lost her job. She's terrified. Okay, so losing her job and the security she thought she had is "bad." This is just terrible, right? She rushes to me, insists on an immediate reading. I look and see that she may not find another job for quite a while. Oh no, that's not just bad, it's horrible! Right? To her, in this moment of sheer terror, it is. But I see in the reading that she was really exhausted, hated her job, and needed a long break. She really does have the personal resources in the form of skills, knowledge, and contacts to find work when she is ready. So I am seeing that this job loss is a blessing in disguise. Now I have helped her to see "bad" as "good," except that in her moment of panic she may not feel as happy as I do that she is finally unstuck and her life is moving along. Whether she herself can make this switch in her mind will determine the extent of her continued suffering.

Clients are not the only ones who fall into this trap. In fact, many psychics trip themselves up because they are doing this throughout their readings. The moment they see or hear something that they believe will be interpreted as "bad," they panic. This leads to them withholding information and overextending their healing energy to try and ensure their client won't feel bad. That tends to backfire; the readee wants information, not sympathy, and often the withheld information is the very thing the client needed to hear the most.

Most of us are familiar with the statement in the Bible, "Judge not, lest ye be judged." I think most people interpret this as: don't think badly of others' actions because we might be judged for our own. I suspect, however, that an even broader interpretation would be helpful: don't judge at all. Stop the constant assessment, rip up the checklist that runs through your mind: "That behavior made him a nice guy, okay, that made him a jerk; that action means we should be together; him doing that might be questionable; that behavior means she's a good mom, her doing that means she's not," and on and on. This logic is what creates pain. It gets in the way of being in the present moment. Many of us keep a running tally in our heads with our spouses or loved ones, and it very much gets in the way of us enjoying our relationships.

Question: I have been amazed with how easily I can see images, even during my first couple of readings. But there sure are times when I don't get anything at all, just black. What should I do?

Answer: Any time you are not getting anything, what you want to do is remind yourself that nothing is in fact something you can look at. Put up a new viewing receptacle that represents this nothing you are getting, and ask it to show you what the nothing represents, or why you are getting nothing. You will be surprised by what happens next!

If you find yourself getting distracted, you can always reset the reading color again by putting out a brand-new reading receptacle and asking the readee to repeat their name a few times. Check to see if your crown chakra color is matched with the reading color. You may not be getting much because the readee has zoomed out of their body. If they are not present, if their attention is somewhere else in la-la land, this is where you will end up as well. You can also ask them to pose a question to you as you look at a new receptacle. Doing this also helps bring them back to you and may elicit more information. Every question you pose to your reading receptacle acts like a button, key, or lever that releases bits of information from the universal source. Sometimes by asking your readee to pose a more specific question, or repeat or rephrase their questions, the information will begin to flow. If they are going to pose a question themselves, all you need to do is watch your viewing receptacle and see what happens to it, what color or image appears as their voice enters the receptacle.

Sometimes it helps to recheck your grounding, make sure your energy is running, or just create and destroy several neutral objects on your reading screen or in front of a particular chakra. Every time you do this it's as if you were exercising a muscle and clearing away stuck energies. I also highly recommend that you place your finger on your forehead at the location of your third eye, and double-or triple-check to make sure you are aligned back behind it in the center of your head. Remind yourself to sit in that captain's chair where the controls are located. Imagine that if you were up there looking down you'd be above your heart, so therefore you are actually able to stand above, in safety, and away from being overcome by the energy of your heart, where emotions whirl around like tidal waves, tornadoes, or blizzards.

Sometimes if you are really feeling stuck or lost in the reading, it may be necessary to ask the readee for some background information, particularly if you are feeling really compelled to do so. Recently I did a reading in which I was under a tight time frame and was not getting any clear images at all. I was hearing messages, but they made no sense to me. It felt as though I was stabbing at something blindly and erratically in the dark. I wanted to challenge myself to see if I could get more without having to ask for background information, but that wasn't going well so finally I asked—and suddenly all the messages I was getting made perfect sense and now I knew exactly what questions I needed to pose to my viewing receptacles. Sometimes our logical minds just need something to grab onto. Other times, too much information can taint the results.

Question: The images I get only last for a second and are gone. Then I get another one, but I never seem to know what any of this means.

Answer: I just had a student at one of my psychic workshops who had this problem. After spending just a few minutes alone with her and her partner, I realized that *she* was the problem. What was immediately apparent to me was that she was rushing the process. She'd see a flash of something for less than ten seconds, and then open her eyes and start trying to interpret what it meant. (She later complained that as soon as she started talking, she'd lose her concentration.) By listening to her speak, I could tell her interpretations were a creation of her logical mind as opposed to being intuitively, divinely inspired. I could tell this because of the language she used, such as "Well, it might mean this" or "It's possible it could mean this" or "Maybe it's because..." This is different from the language of "I am getting this" or "I am seeing this" or "I just got a flash that it means this."

Often, through a student's language, I can tell what they are experiencing in their imagination. Some of my savvier students quickly pick up on the terms I am looking for and will use these inappropriately, in an unconscious attempt to make it seem as though they are being clairvoyant when they aren't. It is not that they don't have the ability; rather, they don't have the necessary patience. Clairvoyance involves reading pictures and describing visual information. It is describing attributes such as colors, sizes, and objects, as well as describing actions and movement. If a student says to their readee, "I see you are wealthy or are going to be happy," a red flag goes up for me right away. How do you "see" wealth? How do you "see" happiness? These are concepts, interpretations.

The red flag is not there because I doubt what the student is getting, but because I know that the value of the information is in describing the pictures themselves, not in the interpretation—which is the weakest aspect of the reading and the most likely to be incorrect. So, in the example above I would want to ask the student to describe how the information came to them that made them say, "You are wealthy." They may say, "Well, first I saw the readee driving a expensive-looking car" or "I saw the readee holding a wallet with a lot of money spilling out." These images are much richer (no pun intended)! They might imply the readee is wealthy or is going to be wealthy, but they can also mean a host of other things. We are not as concerned with the meaning at this point as we are about getting the details of the pictures.

Question: I'm not comfortable with closing my eyes as you suggest. It's easier for me to just have them open, and then I just talk and words flow from my mouth.

Answer: People who aren't comfortable closing their eyes, except when going to sleep, often have certain control issues or are afraid to connect with their feelings. While you most certainly can do readings with your eyes open, it would be good for you to explore what happens when you do them with your eyes closed. During one psychic workshop I taught, a man just would not close his eyes. He had been doing healing work for a few years and insisted this just wasn't his style. During our practice together, he was giving the readee some information that was more complex than merely describing pictures, and I really couldn't tell if it was inspired or coming from his logical mind. Since the point of the exercise was to experience one's own clairvoyance, rather than merely be psychic, I had to be really firm with him. I told him that the point of him being in the class for the weekend, which had cost him six hundred dollars, was not to do things as he had always done them, but to learn something new. In his case, it was not to prove to himself or others that he had psychic talent, which he knew he did, but to experiment and discover this new specific skill of clairvoyance.

He agreed that I had a point but stated he just had not ever been clairvoyant. I had to again remind him that this was why he was taking the class, to learn a new skill. If he just allowed himself to relax, I could lead him to a place where he'd never been before. I also emphasized that if he wanted to gain a new skill, he just might have to allow himself to feel uncomfortable for a while.

It's amazing how many people will run from the first feeling of any discomfort. Any time we are stretching ourselves, we will feel uncomfortable. Try lifting a weight. If you don't feel it, it's not working. Try having a baby! Imagine where we'd be if women decided they should do away with childbirth because it's uncomfortable! My student finally did let go of his resistance, closed his eyes, and began to really concentrate. Within minutes he was stunned at how clearly his visions came. By the end of the reading, he stood up, dazed, and stated he had never had any reason to concentrate as deeply as he just had, and that he couldn't believe how vivid his images were. He then excused himself from class early to go take a walk alone, so he could process what he had just experienced.

Question: I have only done a few readings so far, but I am getting confused because sometimes I get images that seem really dumb or make no sense. I don't say anything and then it turns out the images mean something, but other times I have no clue as to what they mean. How do I know when to mention something I am not sure about or when to just let it go?

Answer: The answer to this is quite simple. It's my personal philosophy that you should always talk about every single detail you are getting, particularly before you've done your first twenty readings. Your logical brain should not be filtering out and evaluating whatever you see. This will absolutely impede the entire process and will mean that you end up overlooking a lot of very rich and important information.

While your logical mind is there to help you pose questions and decide what to do next when the information stops flowing easily, it should not be allowed to make any judgments about or censor the images. Of course you can't completely stop it from doing this, but once you become aware of any thoughts like "This is too dumb/weird/ confusing" or "The readee won't like this," you need to be stronger than these thoughts and describe exactly what you are seeing. This is where the creed of the extraordinary psychic really needs to be applied. Self-discipline, courage, and neutrality are going to be essential.

When I am privately training students, this is what they rely on me for the most—to pull out of them what they are too afraid to mention. Of course there will be times when you do allow the censoring to take over. That's all right, because usually by the end of the reading you will find yourself sharing the information or see that the images reassert themselves later on, either as the same image or in a different form. Any time an image reappears more than once, you can be particularly sure there is significance there. But certainly don't wait for it to reappear before you mention it.

Talking can stimulate the flow of images. This is why it can be really helpful to give a moment-to-moment account of what you are experiencing as opposed to being silent until you feel that you have the entire picture. On the other hand, sometimes you will find that the flow of information stops as you talk, and then you may need to refocus on your viewing receptacle in order to get it going again. If this is the case, there is nothing wrong with telling the readee that you are going to take a minute or two and watch the images before you describe them. The thing to remember is that this reading is not about you. It is more important that your readee understands what you are saying as opposed to you having a clear picture of the entire story of their life.

Offering the information on a micro-level rather than a macro-level is very important. Describe attributes and details as opposed to forcing yourself to come up with the end-all picture.

For example, if you see a man's face with a mustache, you should describe it exactly as such: "I see a man's face with a mustache." Now, as you see this image, you might just hear or get a flash or sense of the word *father*. In this case I recommend that you state exactly that: "I just got a sense of the word *father*."

There is also nothing wrong with telling your readee how you are feeling. If you are worried the readee will think you are weird because of what you're seeing, tell them, "I know this may sound strange, but this is what I'm seeing" or "This may not be what you wanted to hear, but this is what I'm getting." One way to help a readee feel better about something you think they will not be happy about is to expand your reading to include looking at the reason the readee is not happy or will not get what they think they want. This is when your logical mind becomes your friend again. In chapter 5, I offer a number of questions you can pose to your viewing receptacle that will eventually become second nature to you, so your readee doesn't ever have to be left hanging with bad news and a feeling of hopelessness or confusion.

Some experienced clairvoyants will leave out the details and give the final meaning. While this can save time, some of the richness can also get lost. Analogies and metaphors are very powerful teaching tools, which is one reason the Bible is quoted so often. Much of clairvoyant reading involves symbolic metaphors; when the clairvoyant keeps the metaphor to themselves and merely provides the interpretation of it, it is like a poet leaving out most of a poem and instead providing a bland summary of the poem's meaning. When you describe a symbol, image, or scene you are getting, readees can form their own mental images and pictures that will be lodged in their memories. This is what they will *access* in the future, as opposed to your interpretation.

For example, say you see an image of your readee with huge angel wings, but one wing is broken. You have no idea what this means, so you ask it to show you a clue or give you some insight. You see another image of your readee dragging a person along a path; the person is so heavy they can hardly walk. You are not sure what this means so you ask it to show you another clue, and now you see an image of their wrists with blood leaking out, or a man hungrily feeding from the wrists like Dracula.

From all these images—perhaps through deduction but also from a sense of knowingness— you get that this person is trying to help someone or perhaps many people, and that doing so is draining them and slowing them down in their own life.

Now, what is going to have more impact: merely stating "A man is draining you of your power," or describing the vivid imagery of the broken angel wing, the body being dragged down a path, a man drinking from veins? Which is more likely to get the readee to take notice and take action? Which is the readee more likely to remember? It's the difference between cooking and serving someone a hearty meal, and merely telling that person about the meal after you've digested it yourself!

Question: I can't always tell if an image is symbolic or literal.

Answer: This is one of the challenges of clairvoyant reading, and there is no easy answer here. This is another reason I suggest just stating exactly what you are seeing. Sometimes the readee will know if the image is symbolic or literal because the readee obviously has much more background information than you do. Other times it will be quite obvious, since what you are looking at is so unrealistic. Honesty is always the best policy, and there is nothing wrong with stating, "I am seeing this. I am not sure if it's symbolic or if it's literal, but I will tell you about it anyway."

For example, you might see an image of your readee hopping around on one leg, with crutches under her arm. This could mean she has really hurt her leg, or it may possibly symbolize that she is not fully standing on her own. When you communicate it to her, she might blurt out, "I just broke my leg last week!" Of course, another helpful thing to do that should be obvious by now is to ask the image to show you what it pertains to. You can put up a new viewing receptacle and tell it to let you know why you were looking at the last thing you saw. In the above example, even without the readee giving you any input, you may see an image of an ambulance, or suddenly feel a pain in your own leg, or have a sense of something medical that will lead you to the realization that the very first picture of the readee on crutches was in fact a literal representation of an event taking place.

There have been numerous times when I thought what I was seeing was symbolic, but instead I was actually looking at exactly what my readee was doing on the other side of the telephone—such as licking a spoon, putting curlers in her hair, or playing with a pet. I have the tendency to do this more with certain people than with others. For example, one time I saw an image of a friend of mine lying on her back in a strange position, with her head dangling over the edge, her leg in the air, and her toes close to her face. She was looking intently at one of her toes. I described this strange image to her, and she was quite embarrassed to admit that this was exactly the position she was lying in. Her toe was itching her, and she was trying to find the source of the irritation.

I don't know why I saw this image rather than anything else I could have been looking at, except that perhaps it would have captured my attention had I really been with her in her house. It may also be that her attention was more on her toe than on whatever I was "looking" at for her, and therefore this is where my own attention went. Had she not admitted to lying in this exact position looking at her toe, I would have never understood what I was looking at.

This example demonstrates a few things. One is that we have to be okay with not always knowing. Second, our attention goes where our readee's attention goes. Third, symbolic and literal images are often indistinguishable. Fourth, our confidence as psychics is quite tenuous. We could be 100 percent correct about the details we describe or our summation of the situation, and yet our readee could deny it all—either out of embarrassment, ignorance, or for any number of other reasons. This is why we need to have confidence in ourselves and not put too much emphasis on the feedback we get from others. One of the things I now ask of my clients who are receiving telephone readings is that they remain seated and do nothing but listen to me. Multitasking might be a plus in the corporate world, but it just doesn't work when receiving (or giving) a reading!

Sometimes the attributes we see in our visions or images are symbolic, which can be confusing. For example, you may see an image of a man with a mustache and have a strong feeling that this is your readee's father. However, your readee informs you that her father did not have a mustache. Now, you might be seeing the mustache for a few reasons. For one, her father may have had a mustache when she was very young, at a time when something significant occurred that is influencing her. He may have preferred to wear a mustache, but his wife didn't like it. Or it may be that he in fact never did have a mustache, but your own father did and therefore this is what your subconscious mind, or the part of your mind that generates pictures, conjured up so you would know you were talking about a father. In this case, you may likely have a matching picture with your readee, and you could both have similar issues with your fathers.

There are times during a clairvoyant reading with a new client that I will see images of someone I personally know. This person could be one of my friends or family members, or a famous person I have never met. This usually surprises me. I've found the best way to handle the situation is to explain to my client, "For some reason I am seeing this person that I know.

They look like this and they act like this, and this is how I feel about them. I might be seeing them because they have similar attributes to someone in your life."

Question: Why do I get images from movies or see fictional characters in my readings?

Answer: In clairvoyant readings, scenes from movies, or characters or actors, will often come up to serve as shortcuts that help us describe a person or situation in our readee's life. For example, in a recent reading I saw an image of Jack Nicholson, and I explained to my client that I was probably seeing Jack because there was a person who looked like him in her life or who shared similar personality traits. She knew right away who I was talking about. I did follow this up with details such as "I see this guy with crazy hair; he looks really intense, edgy, but also has a mischievous grin on his stubbly face. He seems to have a strong sexual appetite and somewhat of a temper." Again, she acknowledged I was right on about the man she was wondering about.

I do recommend telling your readee who the person reminds you of, and also sharing the details of your image. The nice thing about seeing celebrities is that they are universal symbols we can all relate to. Even on the off chance that my readee wouldn't know who Jack Nicholson is, seeing an image of him would instantly give me an idea of the characteristics of a man impacting my client's life, and I would be able to describe that man faster and more easily than if I had to see the collection of his traits individually.

Recently, I did a reading for a woman who wanted to know about her future romantic relationships. I decided I would look about one year ahead. I expected to see a man, but instead I immediately saw an image of the comedian and talk-show host Ellen DeGeneres. I tried to push this aside because it made no sense, but a minute later I saw an image of k. d. lang. Hmmm, two strong, openly lesbian women. My currently heterosexual readee wasn't exactly ready to hear that her next major relationship in about a year might very well be with another woman, but she didn't hang up on me when I gave her the news.

CHAPTER 9

General Questions

There is nothing like returning to a place that remains unchanged to find the ways in which you yourself have altered.
— NELSON MANDELA

Below are some common questions asked by readers of *You Are Psychic*, as well as by the students in my workshops and long-distance training programs.

Question: Is someone who naturally sees things without training, perhaps at a young age, a superior clairvoyant to someone who has learned these skills?

Answer: Well, *they* might think so!

What is your definition of "superior"? Are they more special because their "gift" was already turned on, and ours took longer to unwrap? A person who can see things with eyes wide open and who has done so since early childhood may be very talented, a very clear channel, even a psychic prodigy, but as I have indicated elsewhere, doing readings for people takes a lot more than being able to access information. It involves discernment, the ability to identify what comes from one's logical mind and one's inner motivations, and an ability to effectively describe our visions in a loving but honest way. This is why therapists tend to make good psychics. These skills come with experience and with maturity, along with certain innate personality traits.

I've seen firsthand what happens when someone is very psychic but does not have the integrity or wisdom to handle being psychic: their relationships suffer and they can cause a lot of problems for those around them. This includes children and teenagers who discover a desire to read others at an early age, something I don't advocate unless the child feels absolutely compelled to do so, and is very mature and has adequate guidance from a grounded adult. (I now only allow people over the age of eighteen to attend my psychic workshops.) Younger people are more inclined to project their own pictures and judgments onto others because they haven't yet developed the capacity to monitor their own thoughts, intentions, and behaviors. Their inner parent is not yet developed enough to keep them in check. (Obviously some adults have this problem as well!) Children also tend to want to show off, appear powerful or special, and use their abilities to get their own way.

Obviously, most children and teenagers are not yet emotionally equipped to deal with or understand many issues adults struggle with, which is why we don't allow them to watch adult television programs and movies. Doing readings is a lot like watching home movies, and these range from G-rated to XXX-rated! Rather than reading other people, I encourage my son to pay attention to his dreams. I let him know when he's just expressed a thought I was thinking and I encourage him to use psychic tools to calm himself down and focus, as well as to find his missing things. I teach him to meditate (most kids like to say "om" and use Tibetan bells and drums rather than just sit there visualizing). I also teach him basic hands-on aura healing by mostly doing it on him when he doesn't feel well or has been injured. However, I will not teach him or encourage him to read other people until he is an adult and really expresses an interest. To do otherwise would be to take away his innocence.

Question: You and other psychics use the term *energy* a lot. I don't really know what that means.

Answer: *Energy* is a catch-all word used to describe something that we know is there, and we know we can influence. We know it connects people, comes from people, and flows to them, through them, up and down them, and around them. We know it can vibrate at different frequencies, and it is the building block of emotion, thought, and our own physical body. It's a smaller unit than the atom or subatomic particles. It's seen by clairvoyants and occasionally by the physical eye as colors and shapes. It sometimes shows up in photographs when it wasn't visible to the physical eye.

The word *energy* is analogous to the term *life force*. People with no energy are lethargic and depressed. People with lots of it are active and creative. People with none of it are dead. When discussing the energy of humans and animals, the origin of energy is as elusive as life itself. We know people can influence energy with their thoughts, and likewise their thoughts can be influenced by energy. Is this term overused, underdefined, and used too broadly? You betcha. But I think it's the best thing we've currently got to describe this unseen substance that impacts us every moment and every millisecond of the day.

During my readings, when people are blocked from making changes and obtaining what they long for (whether good health, prosperity, love, or insight), I often see a color, a substance that is connected to someone or a whole group of people very identifiably, which seems to be in their way. This I refer to as "foreign energy." As soon as this substance is removed, the person begins feeling very different and takes steps they have wanted to take for a whole lifetime. Sometimes, however, it can take a long time to release or move on from this energy because it's familiar, and what is familiar feels comforting and safe even when it's not.

Sometimes, when someone is very enmeshed with their family of origin, I see an image of a cut-out figure from a mold of the same color and substance. When someone is so enmeshed with their family, their life force is almost indistinguishable from the others. They are the same color, but I can see their outline emerging from the rest of the mold. These people who are enmeshed with the rest of the material in the mold have a hard time knowing what they want to do in life; they feel stuck, trapped, and depressed. Why? Because they are not running their own life force through their bodies; they are running that of a group of people who may not be very happy or motivated. The more they can separate from this glob of family consciousness, the more they can breathe, think their own thoughts, and feel their own emotions— because they will then be running their own vibration and energy.

Your own personal energy is like a signature, fingerprint, or DNA that has similar characteristics to all other humans and yet is unique to every individual in various ways. I wish I could get away from these terms because they are not always clear enough and turn some people off, but I have yet to find others that work better for me.

Exercise: Energy Flow

You can feel energy flow just by holding your two hands a few inches from each other, palm facing palm, and visualizing a current—like light, lightning, or water—flowing back and forth. After a minute or so you will feel a pulsating, and have a sense of the direction of the flow. When you direct this energy outward to someone else for the purpose of alleviating their pain, you are performing a basic energetic healing. However, if you are going to do this, imagine that the energy in your hands is going to act like a hose or laser beam, to wash or burn away whatever the other person wants to release. Consciously withdraw or pull back this energy by using your imagination, rather than expecting you are giving them this energy to remain in their body indefinitely.

Question: Is it better to practice readings on people and about topics you know or don't know?

Answer: I find there is value in both.

Obviously, when you don't know someone, it's easier to tell if the information coming to you is significant or if it's coming from your own preconceived notions of the person. For this reason, when developing your skills it is important to read as many strangers or unknown targets as possible.

However, there is still great value in reading someone you do know. Many times, having the background information on a person does help you put the images coming to you into perspective, letting you go right to the heart of the matter. Practicing on supportive friends and relatives is fun and much more relaxing than reading people you don't know, and you may find it easier to get into a flow. The more relaxed you are, the more success you will have accessing your clairvoyance.

Even with your spouse or close friends, there are many areas of their lives you don't know that much about. You almost certainly don't know every single person they know, so reading their relationship with someone you've never met could be interesting for you to explore. Even if he has complained about his boss or his job in the past, it is fascinating when you receive firsthand insight into why your hubby really is so miserable at work or why that boss is such a jerk. (Watch out, though—you might learn it's not the boss who's the jerk!)

When you begin to access information that is different from what you expected or even wanted to see, you will know the information is coming from a source outside your logical mind. The most exciting thing about reading someone you personally know happens when you gain information that allows you to see and subsequently think about the other person's life from a new perspective. You are then able to release your previously held judgments about what they should or should not be doing, and whom they should or should not be doing it with. For example, you might have been judging your friend for staying at a particular job, or for refusing to break up with a lover your friend constantly complains about. But during the reading you will see and learn information that will help you to understand that the path your friend is on is the perfect one for them, even if you would not personally choose to step one foot on such a path!

In this way, your clairvoyant work will enable you to release your need to control and exert your moral judgments over others. You will learn how to let others be who they are, and you will understand how futile it really is for you to try to change them. Just be aware that clairvoyants and spiritual seekers sometimes replace one set of value judgments with another (e.g., a holier-than-thou attitude that everyone should become psychic, or meditate, and use only the same techniques the one judging uses). Like proselytizing Mormons and Jehovah's Witnesses, or overzealous born-agains, we psychics and healers can be equally pushy or narrow-minded.

Question: I recently did a reading for someone, but I felt as though I was giving advice rather than being clairvoyant. Is this okay or should I avoid giving advice during a reading?

Answer: During a reading (and in life), the more advice you are giving, the more lit up you probably are. By "lit up" I mean you are encountering your own matching pictures; you are being driven by your own feelings. Perhaps your own pain is being stimulated by encountering similar pictures in your readee, and you are not in a neutral, grounded space that will allow you to maximize your clairvoyance or your communication.

So if you find yourself offering advice instead of being psychic, what should you do? Simple: just stop! Tell the readee you need a few moments to collect yourself, and go through your basic tools of grounding and centering yourself. Check to make sure your energy is running and that you have a separation object up. When you begin to feel like it's all on you to solve someone's problem during a reading, it's an excellent indication that you yourself are having a problem and need to give yourself a good talking-to and remind yourself that you are here to be psychic, not to solve problems. It's also helpful to understand that it's not the problem that is causing your readee's suffering; it's that they have lost themselves in the problem. When you have emotional distance from what you are viewing, then your readee can have distance from what they are experiencing, which is what they are really seeking.

During a reading it is very helpful to look at where the readee is headed and what next steps they might take to get there. This is especially important after you've been looking at their "problems," which is where they are really stuck emotionally. Offering "next steps" might seem like advice, but it really is a psychic prescription, a specific course of action that comes from a source other than your logical mind. This information might correspond with your own ideas or it might contradict them. If the latter is the case, congratulations! This is a sign that you are accessing information on a psychic level. But be careful not to throw away any information that sounds familiar, because it is very possible you feel a strong match with this person and the steps intended for them may be the same ones—or quite similar to the ones— you will need as well. If you aren't sure, just tell the readee, "I don't know if these steps are intended for you or for me or for both of us, but I'd like to share them with you anyway."

You can look at someone's next steps or the best course of action for them to take by doing the following exercise:

Exercise: Looking at a Next Step

Create a viewing receptacle. Pose the question to your receptacle, "What course of action would be best for my client?" or demand that the answer appear. Look for a color first, and then tell your receptacle to show you some images. It helps to describe the color in addition to the images because then the client will be able to conjure these up at a later date to manifest what they seek, as opposed to what they are moving away from.

You can also put up a receptacle and ask it to show you the color of the client's joy or creativity. Instruct your client to run this color through their body several times a day. Sooner rather than later, this practice will bring about the life experiences that will actually allow your client to have this joy.

Exercise: Distancing Yourself From a Problem

Go inward. Ground yourself. Visualize two receptacles or roses—one for yourself, the other for the problem. Label each one: one with your name, the other with the word *problem*. Give each one of these a grounding cord. Ask for any excess emotional energy to release. Breathe as you watch and notice any colors coming out.

Next, call all your life force and any remaining energy from the receptacle with the problem and see it go into your receptacle. Let the problem energy come out of your receptacle either through the grounding cord or by going back into the "problem" receptacle. You are not calling the problem itself, but your own energy. As you do this, be aware of how the two things are different from each other: you and your problem. You are not your problem, no matter how bad it seems. Notice how this feels.

This exercise can be done in about five minutes, and you are sure to see results. As is the case with all the exercises in this book, this exercise is not only assisting you on an intellectual level but is also impacting you energetically.

This is also a great exercise to do around something you feel you desperately want or need, since a problem indicates an obstacle to what you want or think you need. Instead of labeling the second rose "problem," label it as your want or need. This doesn't mean you won't get what you want or need; on the contrary, it will help release the urgency and emotional attachment to it that are causing you distress.

Question: What if I am wrong about what I am seeing?

Answer: A better question is "What happens *when* I am wrong?" because there will be plenty of times you will be. Clairvoyants are usually wrong in their interpretations of the images, rather than about the images themselves. Most images are there for a reason. Many of the mistakes are made in confusing the symbolic for the literal, or vice versa, or in making logical assumptions about the images you are getting.

Have you ever played the board game Pictionary? One team member picks a card listing a particular object, person, place, or action, and then attempts to draw this subject. The other team members have to guess what their teammate is drawing within a certain amount of time. In a way, as a clairvoyant, this is what you are being asked to do. Your mind draws the pictures or receives the images, and you are left with the interpretation part. Sometimes in the mere description of its attributes, you reveal what it is but sometimes it takes a lot more to get at what you're seeing, particularly if you are describing a whole concept or specific person as opposed to a thing. If you see a flag and you say, "I see something that looks like a flag," then you are right on. But if the concept is the Fourth of July and someone draws a flag but also a bunch of squiggles representing fireworks that look like waves, you may think you are looking at something having to do with the ocean. The problem is that to you the squiggles did not accurately represent what the artist intended them to represent.

Imagine that a readee asks you to do a reading on her pet named Lassie. You might see an image of a dirty animal with four legs and interpret this as a dog. But it turns out Lassie is really a pig. Such a mistake is more likely to happen if you are in a hurry or if your logical mind just naturally assumes any animal named Lassie will be a dog. If having a pig as a pet is so far out of your everyday experience that it's something you've never imagined, it may be harder for you to see the image as a pig or you might be more likely to dismiss the idea.

The way to decrease your errors is to make sure you describe the image you are getting and all its details before jumping to an interpretation. Sometimes an answer or message will just land in your mind. This is different from "figuring it out." Over time, with practice, you will learn the difference between these two things. If you are not sure about the meaning of what you are getting, you can always say, "I see this, but I don't know yet what it means." Or "I see this image (describe the image), and I think this is what it means but I'm not exactly sure."

Question: I've noticed that some psychics call themselves clairvoyants, but they are really channeling or are getting information through feelings and hearing and not through visuals. Your approach is quite different from theirs.

Answer: I believe that it's important to distinguish between the different psychic abilities so that we can better understand them and recognize their unique characteristics.

Many psychics shy away from using the term *psychic* and therefore call themselves clairvoyants even though they are not really accessing their visual abilities. Of course, some of the terms overlap because most psychics don't do just one thing or use just one single ability. I consider myself to be a clairvoyant because I focus mostly on the visual, but during the course of a reading I am receiving messages from other spirits and feeling other people's emotions, and therefore I could technically be considered a medium, transmedium, or channeler in those moments. Still, I feel these skills are augmenting my primary ability of clairvoyance.

I will now attempt to define some of the more commonly used terms:

A *clairvoyant* sees visual information through pictures and images.

A *medium* channels information from a variety of spirits, some of which are deceased and some of which may be ascended beings.

A *channeler* is also a medium, someone who allows herself or himself to be used to communicate information brought in by another source.

A *full-body channeler* is a channeler who permits a foreign being to enter their body fully, so that during the reading the being is more in the channeler's body than is the channeler.

A *transmedium* permits other beings and spirits to attach themselves to him or her or sends his or her spirit and energy out to others. A transmedium is similar to a channeler; the difference is that some transmediums don't mean to do this—it just happens spontaneously, often without their awareness or conscious consent. Many mentally ill people are transmediums. I believe that many people who "talk to themselves" are not really themselves but someone else. That's how they can become so passionately engaged in their conversations!

A *remote viewer* follows certain protocols to view information about an unknown target that is at a separate location (see chapters 10 and 11).

A *medical intuitive* focuses on the physical body and its ailments. A medical intuitive may be using any of the psychic abilities.

Finally, a *psychic* can be any combination of the above. I believe it's important for psychics to be able to distinguish between the various sources of information they receive, but doing so comes with practice and experience, so there is no rush. I really encourage students to be careful with their words!

Question: You suggest that we focus ourselves in the center of our heads, behind the sixth chakra or the pineal gland. But what about the heart? Isn't that the place where most spiritual disciplines say we should be? If we deny the heart, are we not going to become uncaring, even merciless, psychics?

Answer: Our sixth chakra (also called the *ajna chakra*) is the center of our clairvoyance. It corresponds with the pineal and pituitary glands. When we are in this place, we are not denying our hearts but instead are better able to observe what is happening within our hearts.

It is the difference between standing in the middle of a severe storm or standing at a safe distance, observing or even enjoying the storm. When we center or align ourselves with a particular chakra, or focus our attention on that chakra, we are activating that chakra's energy. It is not that we are saying, "This chakra is better than any other." There are plenty of times when it is more desirable to be in the heart center, particularly when you are on a date or having sex.

The energy of the sixth chakra has to do with clarity, observation, insight, wisdom, being present-oriented, awareness, calm, consciousness, creativity, and neutrality. Outside of readings and your psychic work, this is a great place to center yourself when you become aware that you have lost your center, that your emotions are causing you to act in ways that are not really serving you or those around you, or when you really need to be able to assess a situation without getting caught up in the drama. The heart is about drama, emotions, passion. When we are doing readings, we are tuning in to all sorts of high drama, emotions, and passions that don't need any more fuel from us than they already have.

Experiment

Designate either one day or an entire week during which you will consciously center yourself in one chakra. At least once an hour, remind yourself of where you are supposed to be. Call all your energy from wherever else it is to that one spot. Hold the intention that the energy of that chakra will be activated and that you will learn its true nature. Then move to another chakra the next day or week. Notice the difference. Another thing you can do is practice reading from your different chakras and notice what happens.

I like to imagine I am centered in the chakra, and then I imagine that I am looking out of that part of my body and I play around with what I would see from that perspective. For example, if I am centered in my second chakra I will be somewhere below my belly button. If that part of my body had eyes, I'd be looking directly at the television set in my home, or face to face with my cat sitting on the desk. This helps me orient myself.

Question: You suggest using a separation object for our readings and even in our personal lives, but doesn't this get in the way of being able to receive the psychic information? It also seems as though it would get in the way of intimacy in our relationships.

Answer: In order to love someone, we must be able to have some distance from them. Otherwise we can't see them anymore.

One of my favorite exercises I do with my students is to have them pair off in teams. I instruct one student to begin telling the other one their problems—the worst problems they can think of. The one listening is instructed to do nothing else but listen. (It's funny how some people can't do this; they must start giving advice right away. These are the students who need to use the tools the most; they give advice in order to decrease their own emotional discomfort.) Then I instruct the listener to visualize a separation object at the edge of their aura (for more on separation objects, see chapter 3). Once the listener sees this, the listener is told to continue listening and focusing on what the partner is saying.

Most students acknowledge there is a huge difference after creating the separation object. Many report it's easier to just listen without feeling as though they have to solve this poor person's problems. They get less sucked in. Even the person who is talking about their problem reports that they found they no longer felt the need to discuss their problem, that it was harder to recall the severity of it or how they felt about it even moments before. Some people even say they no longer felt like talking about their problem.

A separation object is not a wall. It is a boundary. It says, "This is where I end and you begin." There is a time and a place for being smack-dab in your wide-open heart chakra and completely merged with another, but a clairvoyant reading is not one of them. Let's look at the sort of language commonly found in romance novels: "With our bodies entwined, we were as one, my breath his, his breath mine. He swallowed me up in his eyes and I was lost forever." (Hmmm, maybe I should be writing fiction instead!) Being merged with another is a romantic notion that is a wonderful experience—until your partner becomes sick, frustrated, angry, or afraid, or until your partner's mother's illness, frustration, anger, or fear enters your partner's aura and you experience the effect of this. Even if your partner's energy field is crystal-clear and filled with joy, what happens after a passionate night of oneness when morning comes and it's time to go to work or class and you are so merged together that you can't get up enough strength to peel your body away from your partner, or you manage to get to work but can think of nothing but him or her? (Not that I would know anything about that!) I am not suggesting you forgo the merging, but rather I am offering you some help for prying your energy fields apart when your bodies need to go their separate ways.

To have an understanding of what it is like to energetically merge with someone, think about the guy or girl you are totally into, then imagine you are Siamese twins, a completely unromantic notion (at least from my perspective as an identical twin). The only difference between being a Siamese twin and being energetically merged with someone is that you can usually walk away for short periods of time; however, you will most likely have a hard time thinking about anything else. This is why we will obsess about someone or have a hard time making decisions when we get into a relationship. This is why it helps to create boundaries and to call our own energy back to ourselves and send theirs back to them. You can think better, make better decisions, and really feel better on every level.

In a reading, setting your boundaries will make the difference between you seeing the whole picture or getting sucked into seeing things only from the readee's perspective, or getting entangled in their emotions. Go stand nose to nose with someone, or with your face right up to the television set or the painting in your living room. Can you see the whole person, the whole screen, the whole picture? No, of course not! This is what happens when your energy and attention merge with your readee's. This is why a separation object is important. It's not going to block the visual information, although I suppose it may cut down on some sensory information—but that's okay because that information will only tell you so much anyway.

Question: Why aren't all or more psychics successful at gambling or winning lotteries?

Answer: Using one's abilities for gambling purposes can be tricky for a number of reasons.

First of all, as I note in other chapters, clairvoyance works best when you are in a deeply relaxed state. Usually this requires one to prepare through meditation. Obviously, the frenetic environment of a casino is the last place anyone is going to be able to relax. I suspect the reason casinos are noisier than just about any other place is so that patrons have as few quiet times as possible to focus inwardly, where they might just get more in tune with their intuition. In most of the casinos in Las Vegas, there is nowhere to sit except in front of a slot machine, gaming table, bar, or restaurant. This is not due to oversight but rather to very intentional design.

Another reason using one's abilities in a casino is tricky has to do with all the competing energies. Everyone is so elevated in their desires, their need to win, and then there are the casino employees, whose jobs depend on doing whatever they can so you don't win. Another challenge is that when you are gambling, you are so attached to the outcome that most of the time your desires are going to outweigh the psychic information that comes in. I do hear lots of stories, however, of people just walking through a casino and getting a sudden feeling to go put money down somewhere and winning pretty big. Yet it usually goes downhill after that.

Russell Targ and Harold E. Puthoff, authors of the book *Mind-Reach: Scientists Look at Psychic Abilities*, believe that neurological functioning and the differences between the right and left hemispheres of the brain may account for why many psychics tend to do poorly when it comes to gambling or predicting numbers. They point out that "the two hemispheres of the brain are specialized for different cognitive functions: the left for verbal and analytic thought, the right for intuition and the understanding of patterns and possibly music and artistic abilities... the left hemisphere analyzes over time and codes memory in linguistic description, the right synthesizes over space and in images." These researchers discovered that clairvoyant subjects in remote-viewing experiments were much more accurate when it came to describing color and shape, but subjects had more difficulty reading letters or words—although they might be able to tell there was some kind of sign or other written material at a remote location.

For the past twenty years I have been frustrated by psi experiments that use ESP cards, in which a subject is asked to name which of five different cards is the target. Targ and Puthoff agree that "such tasks tempt the subject into an analytical matching task, rather than coax him into the more intuitive mode that is required. That is unfortunate for us because the simple matching task is best suited for the statistical analysis favored by the left brain-oriented scientific methods. Right-brain results are much more difficult to pin down." I wholeheartedly agree!

Personally, I find ESP cards to be downright boring. Research has shown that psychics are most likely to pick up on information that is most interesting to them, and to home in on peak emotional experiences and events. Sitting in some depressing classroom or lab, feeling pressure to prove oneself, shuffling through a deck of outdated cards with meaningless symbols is about the worst way to test someone's psychic talents. Fortunately, many modern-day psi researchers have come to the same conclusion.

That being said, there are people whose brains are developed in a way that allows them to be both excellent psychics and excellent mathematicians. If you add in an actual interest and knowledge of gambling and an understanding of the best way to overcome the above-mentioned challenges, I believe you will find yourself a psychic who will do very well when it comes to winning casino games or lotteries.

Question: I've been doing Reiki for a long time, and I know I take on other people's energy when I heal them. Is this a problem?

Answer: Healing through absorbing the pain of others is not a problem—as long as it's a conscious choice and you are willing to face the consequences.

Let me tell you a little story. Not too long ago I attended a book signing for a spiritually oriented book at a local bookstore. I arrived late, and when I arrived there was an attractive young man speaking praise about the book. He kept referring to the author as his "guru." I wondered why this man was doing the presentation instead of the author himself. Something told me to look behind me. When I did, I saw a man sitting in the back row whose appearance jolted me. The only way I can describe him is that he looked very sick in the most unusual way. His belly and his eyes seemed to protrude unnaturally, and I got a horrible feeling looking at him.

The man did not seem particularly distressed, though. He was just sitting there, and another man was massaging his shoulders, which the sick-looking man seemed grateful for. However, I got this intense icky feeling and a flash of an image that his body was literally a cesspool filled with the worst kind of energy imaginable. I was reminded of the animated film *Spirited Away*, in which a character absorbs dozens of other beings into its own body until it almost explodes. It pained me to see this poor man, yet something was so odd here that I could not stop glancing back at him. Each time I did I felt a growing panic that made me want to stand up and scream, "There is something really wrong here! Someone do something!" And I had no idea why.

I was shaken from my craziness by the realization that this very man was now being escorted to the front of the room. It was then that I realized he was in fact the author/guru who had written the book. After the presentation I turned to the pretty and cheerful young woman sitting next to me. I asked her, "Did you see that guy!? He looks really bad. I hope he's okay." I expected her to agree with me, not to say what she said next: "Oh yes, isn't he wonderful? He's really sick, he's been like that for years, but it's not a bad thing at all. That's his gift." "What!" I exclaimed. "Yes," she beamed with admiration. "He talks about it in his classes. He's here on this planet to take away suffering, and he does it by accepting it all into his body. He's taken my pain away a few times, and it never came back. He could do the same for you! Come on, I'll introduce you right now!"

Horrified, I declined, stating, "I think I'd rather release my pain somewhere else besides this man's body." I was quite shaken for a while, standing there among all those happy people. I was judging this man for making this choice that was obviously eating away his health, yet I felt such a pull to heal him that I could barely stand it. The longer I stood there watching him, wanting to heal him (by now he had another "disciple" massaging his shoulders), the worse I felt.

Finally, I realized what I was doing. I was essentially "matching" him in what he did, and I knew if I stood there much longer I would be taking away all the crap he had absorbed by downloading it into my own energy field. This is not the way I choose to heal clients, although I know I tend to do this in my personal relationships. I once ended up taking a boyfriend's Prozac for a few months while living with him, although I'd never been depressed like that, for no apparent reason, before or since.

I know I can and want to help people, but most certainly not like that. I hope you make the choice not to heal in the way this man did, as the trade-offs for most people aren't worth it. (As an aside, I think that extra weight on our bodies is often partially filled with others' emotional pain.) I know that my refusal to consciously sacrifice my own health for the sake of others might bar me from becoming a guru myself someday. Oh, well. I guess I'll be massaging my own feet!

Question: What to do if you've been healing others through absorbing their pain?

Answer: I highly recommend practicing the techniques in chapter 3, particularly grounding, and running your own energy and maintaining a separation object or creating a bubble around yourself filled with moving light, water, or energy.

Make sure you do these in your own meditation and before you do your Reiki or the healing techniques in chapters 12 through 17 of this book. When you are doing a healing session with someone, frequently visualize the place into which they are releasing the energy, whether it's into the ground or up to a divine source that can handle receiving it. Most important, make a conscious decision not to allow any other person to release their emotional energy, pain, garbage, crap, or whatever you want to call it into, onto, or around you!

Question: Do you think people's attitudes about psychics are changing?

Answer: Yes. I think attitudes about psychics are changing, and that we are also starting to witness the emergence of a whole new generation of psychics.

The old-school psychic stumbled onto their abilities either as a child or after a near-death or traumatic experience, and less frequently with the help of a teacher who intuitively knew how to bring out this talent.

"New-school psychics" is my term for the new generation of psychics. This new generation of psychics is armed with an arsenal of knowledge and trained in specific methodologies. New-school psychics include, but of course are not limited to, readers of *You Are Psychic* (and you yourself after you practice the techniques in this book), graduates of clairvoyant training schools, and veterans and students of remote-viewing programs and scientific research studies. New-school psychics have greater control of their abilities. They understand that their gifts are not as rare as the last generation of talented psychics believed them to be. Many of these new-school psychics know they can train others to do what they do if they are so inclined.

As more of these impassioned and caring psychics crawl out of the closet and bravely reclaim their identity, worth, and personal power, more and more people will begin to take notice of and accept their own abilities. This in turn creates a more permissive environment for all psychics and healers.

PART II

REMOTE VIEWING

CHAPTER 10

Remote Viewing and Clairvoyance

One of the ways advertisers sell products that have been
on the market for a while is to repackage them as new and improved.
I believe this is what remote viewers and researchers have done with extrasensory perception
and clairvoyance, although perhaps a kinder word than "sell" would be "legitimize."
— DEBRA LYNNE KATZ

Many people have asked me, "What's the difference between clairvoyant reading and remote viewing?" As far as I'm concerned, these are really two sides of the same psychic coin. They are two methods or disciplines for essentially achieving the same thing: obtaining information through extrasensory perception. Both involve viewing information from a distance that was not previously known. Both involve utilizing one's clairvoyant ability to see visions and pictures, but they also incorporate the other inner senses of hearing, feeling, and spontaneous knowing. The main difference lies in the methodology used, differences in terminology and the type of information that is sought.

Thus, a student trained and excelling in clairvoyant reading may initially do quite poorly when assigned to a remote viewing practice target, and most remote viewers wouldn't have the slightest idea how to do a face-to-face reading with someone. However, either one, with the right training and a little practice, is likely to excel very quickly in both fields. There are more and more students who are venturing into both areas, although there are still plenty of people who have absolutely no idea the other exists or no interest in the other.

One of my own instructors, former military remote viewer Lyn Buchanan, once told me the last thing he'd ever want to do is to give a reading to someone face-to-face. Yet in the military, he was most often given human targets to view at a distant because it became clear that he was particularly talented at this. He viewed Saddam Hussein on an ongoing basis. Still, viewing Saddam at a distance, compared to a frantic women face-to-face or on the telephone, who has just broken up with her boyfriend and wants to know if he's cheating or if she'll meet another man of her dreams soon so she'll be able to pay her bills, is probably just a walk in the park!

Remote viewing has traditionally focused on viewing or observing "targets" such as events, locations, and objects. In the military, as far as human subjects, it was either used to spy on them or to determine whether they were still alive or where they were hiding or being hidden. On the other hand, with the exception of occasionally looking for missing keys or a pet, clairvoyant training and reading has traditionally focused on "reading" people who request this service.

Because clairvoyant reading is so person-centered, clairvoyants frequently access and make use of information in the form of symbols. For example, a clairvoyant reader might see a bull with steam coming out of its ears and this will either be interpreted or come with a knowing that this is a symbol for a person who is both stubborn and frustrated. In a remote viewing session, if a viewer saw an image of a bull, they would expect (hope) the bull was something that was physically present and was giving them information about the location. Symbols present endless challenges and opportunities for both clairvoyants and remote viewers.

The most distinguishing characteristics of remote viewing, particularly the methodology of "Controlled Remote Viewing," are the stringent "protocols" that the remote viewer must follow in order to not have his or her session go astray from symbols, which are referred to as AOL's (analytic overlays), or other distractions.

In order to understand remote viewing today, it's absolutely necessary to understand the context from which it emerged.

A Brief History of Remote Viewing

In September 1995, the CIA publicly admitted its involvement in setting up a remote viewing program that had begun at the onset of the Cold War and had spanned at least two decades. This program was fueled by concerns that the Soviets were engaged in similar efforts to train and utilize psychic spies.

According to Russell Targ,[1] scientists at the Stanford Research Institute (SRI) had been contracted to develop and later evaluate remote-viewing programs variously referred to as Star Gate, Scangate, Phoenix, Sun Streak, Aura, and a host of other highly classified project names. The mandate of these programs was to develop stringent protocols, based on continuing psychic research, that could be taught to specially selected military personnel for the purpose of accessing information blocked from ordinary perception due to time, shielding, and distance.

Thus was born the first generation of American psychic spies, or *remote viewers*, who practice SRV, which stands for *Scientific Remote Viewing*, and CRV, which originally stood for *Coordinate Remote Viewing* and later was changed to *Controlled Remote Viewing*. Originally it was called Coordinate Remote Viewing because the early targets were actually longitude/latitude coordinates, but as the tasking of the subject matter changed, so did the name.

Two of the original scientists at SRI were Russell Targ and Harold E. Puthoff, coauthors of Mind-Reach, the first book of its kind to introduce remote viewing to the world.[2] Ed May went on to become the director in the later years.

---

1. Russell Targ and Harold E. Puthoff, *Mind-Reach: Scientists Look at Psychic Abilities,* new edition. Charlottesville, VA: Hampton Roads, 2005, preface.

2. Targ went on to write *Limitless Mind: A Guide to Remote Viewing and Transformation of Consciousness,* as well as numerous other books.

Ingo Swann was an extraordinary psychic who has been credited as the creator of CRV protocols and is often referred to as the father of remote viewing.[3] He passed away in 2013. Besides being a gifted psychic, he was also a talented artist and prolific writer.[4] I highly recommend reading his books.[5] Ingo Swann helped develop the process of remote viewing at SRI by participating in hundreds of experiments in which he was the remote viewing subject. These experiments yielded highly detailed and accurate results that led to the willingness of congress to finance the military sponsored programs. Several of the original recruits of the CIA's program have broken their silence, and have written their own books and begun their own training programs that have exploded in popularity over the past several years.

Some of these have been my own teachers.

One of the most brilliant men I've ever met is the above-mentioned Lyn Buchanan, whose very well-written book, The Seventh Sense: The Secrets of Remote Viewing as Told by a "Psychic Spy" for the U.S. Military, is one of the best on the subject. Lyn Buchanan is one of my own Controlled Remote Viewing teachers, as is his protégé, Lori Williams of Intuitive Specialists, who was one of the first civilians to start teaching these techniques. I highly recommend them both as CRV instructors.[6]

Paul Smith has written an extremely in-depth account of his experiences as a remote viewer in the military and offers intensive CRV training.[7] He is the former president of the International Remote Viewing Association (www.IRVA.com), an organization I highly recommend joining for anyone interested in remote viewing, as it's a hub for many remote viewing activities and development opportunities. I am a member myself and have spoken at their last three conferences.

David Morehouse wrote one of my all-time favorite books, *Psychic Warrior: The True Story of America's Foremost Psychic Spy and the Cover-Up of the CIA's Top-Secret Stargate Program.* David Morehouse teaches both Coordinate Remote Viewing and a much less structured methodology that brings viewers into a Theta state, called Extended Remote Viewing.

Joseph McMoneagle is the author of, among other books, *Remote Viewing Secrets* and *Mind Trek: Exploring Consciousness, Time, and Space Through Remote Viewing.* He has the reputation in the remote viewing community as being one of the most talented viewers of our time. He has aided in successfully locating over a dozen missing persons when all other attempts had failed. He is not a proponent of CRV but rather developed his own style over the years of remote viewing.

Within the remote viewing community, there is much debate as to whether the methodology of Controlled Remote Viewing is necessary. Those who ran the government-funded research

---

3. Both Ingo Swann and Rene Warcollier have been referred to as the father of remote viewing. Warcollier (April 1881–May 1962) was a French chemical engineer and parapsychologist who is credited with conducting some of the very first published remote viewing experiments. I recommend reading his book, *Mind to Mind: Studies in Consciousness* (Hampton Roads Publishing, 2001).

4. It's obvious once you start to remote view and observe other viewers' sessions that those who can remote view and sketch well have a huge advantage in terms of the data they present. If you don't consider yourself to be an artist, don't fret. Sketching is something that can be learned, and there are no shortage of art classes one can take these days, whether in person or online. I'm currently enrolled in a couple of online classes for no other reason than to improve my own remote viewing skills.

5. Ingo Swann passed away in 2013. Several of his books are out of print and can cost hundreds of dollars, but there is an effort being made by his family to bring them back. Some can be found through the www.irva.org website. Many of his writings can be found online.

6. Another of his long-time students, Teresa Frisch, started her own mentoring program and often offers free webinars through her website at www.aestheticimpact.com.

7 Pam Coronado also teachers some fun psychic detective classes online that are inexpensive and provide the opportunity for a lot of practice.

programs at SRI, such as Russell Targ and, later, Ed May (who is currently a lead researcher in a project I am viewing for), do not believe practicing CRV is necessary.

Personally, after training in the CRV methodologies myself now for almost six years, which has involved retaking numerous classes from beginning to advanced, I have to say that it has tremendously improved my sessions, even though I only really strictly follow the protocols when I am doing sessions for my CRV teachers. While I'm not always "staying in structure," there are concepts that I've learned that carry over to all of my sessions and psychic work, and that's why I continue to train in this methodology.

The fact is, when a teacher or researcher monitors a student or subject through a session, even if they don't have a formalized methodology in place, whatever process they use then becomes a methodology. So to say that no methodology is needed to yield strong results is not really accurate. Sure, anyone can attempt to tune into a "target," whether that target is a photo, a person, or something about to happen in the future, and have success. In fact, I highly recommend that everyone practice remote viewing even before they have any formal training.

Just understand that there are going to be a lot of errors, and most students without training will get discouraged and quit if they don't have help understanding why these errors occurred and how to mitigate them. A brand new student with absolutely no guidance or technique is going to have a much harder time shifting through all the challenges than someone who is guided with the aid of a more experienced person. However, that doesn't mean they won't have success. In fact, part of the problem is they may have more success than they realize because they don't understand how to interpret the data they are receiving.

Even those who stumble through the darkness without another person or system will eventually see improvement as they develop their own self-correcting process. The bottom line is that, just like in clairvoyant reading, remote viewing does require some tools and that's why I'm presenting this chapter in this book. Remote viewing and clairvoyant reading can both be thought of as martial arts like Karate, Hapkido, or Judo. Some of these may be more comprehensive, more structured, more tedious, and more time-consuming than others.

The process of Controlled Remote Viewing requires a lot of discipline and can be tedious so it's not for everyone, but I do recommend it for anyone who is absolutely determined to have their abilities up there as high as possible. Meanwhile, there are some basic concepts that come from Controlled Remote Viewing that are easy to understand and to apply, that do help one improve their session tremendously, and this is what I will be teaching you in this chapter.

For myself, I believe it's essential to train in many different techniques and methodologies, under many different instructors, because doing so can bring forth new abilities or new ways of accessing psychic information that one may not have even known were possible because that methodology was more inclined to bring out a particular skill set while repressing another.

The Second and Third Generations of Remote Viewers

In the first edition of this book, I wrote that "there continues to be a pretty strong wall up between clairvoyant training and remote viewing, and the students and practitioners of both end up missing out on having greater breakthroughs in their level of understanding and practice of the subject as a whole." I'm happy to report that while there is still vast room for improvement, I'm finding that wall is starting to crumble, as evidenced by the fact that the current president of the International Remote Viewing Association is Pam Coronado, who does psychic readings herself and who starred in the popular TV show Sensing Murder. Pam and I have taken classes together and she started learning Controlled Remote Viewing techniques later in her career, after she had established herself as a successful psychic detective.[8]

In the same way that clairvoyant training has spawned new generations of teachers, the psychic spies of the 1980s and 90s have birthed their own protégés who have gone on to create their own training institutes.[9] Some of these newer training programs (all unaffiliated with the government, as far as we know) have modified the stringent, rigid protocols of scientifically controlled remote viewing in order to accommodate some of the different needs and interests of today's students.[10]

The Hawaii Remote Viewers Guild, headed by former military viewers Glenn Wheaton and Dick Algire, a well-known news anchor in Hawaii, are also doing some very interesting projects and offer some helpful resources to budding students.[11] Glen Wheaton, a brilliant man and insanely talented remote viewer with whom I've had the pleasure of speaking on several occasions, credits another extraordinary talented but presently all but forgotten psychic named Richard Ireland as his first remote viewing teacher. Ireland was contracted for a shorter period than Swann, and by a different agency and location, to teach a select group of servicemen who inadvertently demonstrated some level of psychic potential prior to being selected for this unusual work.[12]

I've personally been working with, or I should say "playing with," Associative Remote Viewing, a system that pairs photos with various outcomes for sports betting and financial futures, so that the viewer is not directly viewing the winning outcome itself (i.e., winning team or over/ under score) but the photo instead.

The largest, most established group for this is the Applied Precognition Project, founded by Marty Rosenblatt.[13]

---

8. Pam Coronado also teachers some fun psychic detective classes online that are inexpensive and provide the opportunity for a lot of practice.

9. One of these includes the Farsight Institute founded by Dr. Courtney Brown, a professor at Emory University, who is the author of numerous books including *Remote Viewing: The Science and Theory of Non-physical Perception.*

10. Daz Smith, also a second-generation viewer, has recently published what is essentially a comprehensive CRV training manual called *CRV – Controlled Remote Viewing: Collected Manuals & Information to Help You Learn the Intuitive Art.* Jon Nobel's new book gives a nice introduction to the subject as well. This is called *Natural Remote Viewing: A Practical Guide to the Mental Martial Art of Self Discovery.* Alexis Poquiz is an analyst for APP and founder of a very active remote viewing Facebook group which just about everyone mentioned in this chapter is a member of. They would all welcome your own participation in this group.

11. The book and feature film *The Men Who Stare At Goats,* starring George Clooney, was supposedly based on interviews with Glenn and another current Hawaii resident and former army officer, Jim Channon. They insist the film is only about ten percent true, but gave their consent for it to be made because they felt it would help get the word out about remote viewing. Channon is still very much alive and kicking and, while eccentric, seems at least somewhat more sane than the film portrayed. He lives within an artist's commune that he created himself, and is about as colorful and creative in real life as is his character in the film. He is credited as the creator of the now infamous slogan, "Be all that you can be."

12. Wheaton speaks extremely highly of Ireland and feels that it's very unfortunate he's gotten little to no attention or credit for his contributions to the field of remote viewing. There are currently YouTube videos of Richard Ireland appearing on the Steve Allen show that give a sample of this man's talents that anyone interested in psychic development should watch. His son, Mark Ireland, has set up a website in his father's memory, and Ireland's book, *Your Psychic Potential,* can be found through Amazon and major bookstores.

13. Marty Rosenblatt was not a military remote viewer, but rather a nuclear physicist before retiring and turning his attention to remote viewing. While he'd never say this himself, he really is the current Associative Remote Viewing guru, as he's been working on improving and utilizing this facet of remote viewing for years and has more projects going on than anyone in the field at the moment. He's also a super sweet guy who places a lot of emphasis on encouraging people to learn how to communicate with their own unconscious, which in remote viewing is seen as the source or doorway to the information one seeks during a remote viewing session. I've been personally working with this group for years now as we strive to get our hit rates up past the 60 to 65 percent success hit rate they are currently at. His website is at www.appliedprecognitionproject.com. Samples of remote viewing sessions can also be found at www.arv4fun.com.

Differences in Techniques

Both clairvoyant reading and remote viewing are active processes. We aren't just sitting there hoping for the information to arrive; we are following specific steps. The difference is that clairvoyants are often doing these steps in their minds, while some remote viewers are trained to do their sessions with eyes open, while writing on paper.

Getting Started / Tuning In / What to Focus On

When we begin a clairvoyant reading, it helps if we have something to tune in to. This is why we ask our readees to repeat their names a few times. When the readee says his or her name, we are like radios tuning directly in to their specific frequency. Remote viewers don't have their subjects sitting three feet in front of them, or waiting patiently for them on the other end of the telephone. Often they have no idea who or what it is they are going to view.

In the methodology known as CRV or SRV, the word "target" describes the subject that the remote viewers have been assigned to observe. SRI researchers discovered that psychics were better able to accurately describe locations when they were "blind," or did not know the identity of the location. "Blind" is a word used in psychological research to describe the awareness of the person participating in the experiment. Researchers discovered that the best way to label a target so that the viewers could have something to focus on was to assign it a set of multi-digit numbers. The target numbers don't have any meaning in themselves, but have been randomly selected. However, when the military or government needed information about a specific location, sometimes the numbers given to viewers were actual longitudinal/ latitudinal coordinates. This is why initially the process they used was called "Coordinate Remote Viewing."

Formulating targets is a science and an art in itself. Research and direct practice have demonstrated that certain targets and those creating them yield better results than others. Part of the reason for this is that the person choosing the target must be very clear in his or her construction of the tasking question, even though the viewers will likely not be told what the tasking question is. For example, if the target designer writes down the tasking/target question as "View my dog at 5:00 p.m," but doesn't provide a specific date, then the psychic might see the dog at 5:00 p.m. on any other day of its life or even afterlife, depending on how interesting that day was or how sympathetic the viewer is to what was happening on a particular day.

Another possibility would be for the viewer to erroneously tune in to the target designer's other dog, if a specific name for the dog was not indicated and the target designer has another dog or once did at any time in his life. If the target designer was thinking of his girlfriend instead of his dog when he was designing or writing down the target, the psychics might just start viewing this girlfriend. Now in all these instances, the remote viewer may be demonstrating remarkably strong psychic abilities but would be missing the intended target, and therefore whatever information they have reported would be recorded as a "miss."

In clairvoyant reading, our target is often the person we are giving the reading to. When that person says their name, or verbalizes the name of another person they wish to know about, the name acts like a string of light that we can follow right to the source. Another way to look at it is that we are inviting a bit of their energy to come through this string right into our viewing receptacle where we can observe it. However, sometimes if that person has a lot of foreign energies around them, and they are more out of their body than in it, we will lock onto the strongest energy signal in or around them (for example, their husband or mother) and may begin to read that person instead. This also will happen if the readee brings someone along to the reading with them. This is why I don't usually allow others to sit in the room while the reading is going on.[14]

As we've covered in other chapters, in a clairvoyant reading the key to calling forth information is to build a specific place within your mind in which the information can be collected and then be observed—hence the reading screen and viewing receptacle. Remote viewers don't use a receptacle or rose, but many do work with a symbol called an ideogram. The difference here is that this symbol is drawn on a piece of paper by the remote viewer, rather than visualized with closed eyes.

While focusing on the target number, remote viewers are instructed to draw an ideogram, which is really just a reflexive mark that looks like a scribble, and reflects the major "gestalts," or aspects, found at the target. The key with an ideogram is to simply relax and let one's hand do what it wants without thought. The ideogram is not intended to look like the target, but it will contain shapes that can later be decoded that each represent a particular aspect. For example, when I have been assigned a target (without my knowledge) that contains water, my ideogram will have a wavy aspect to it. When a target contains a man-made object, it'll have a sharp right angle. When it contains land, it'll have a diagonal straight line. If a target contains all of these, then all these shapes will be in what is considered to be a "complex" ideogram.

Ideograms can be worked with so that the rest of the session can be organized around them. Some viewers spend years learning how to decode their ideograms, while others simply utilize theirs as a tool to focus their attention on. For those of you who are new to this concept, I suggest you start off just allowing yourself to write your target number, then let your hand do the reflexive mark, and then simply run your pen or finger over the line, or tap it, with the intention that you are going to allow the ideogram to act as sort of portal to the target.

Most of the remote viewing courses and books mentioned in the footnotes of this chapter provide detailed instruction about how to work with ideograms. When working with ideograms, I believe remote viewers are utilizing some of the same skills or forces involved in scribing or automatic writing. It's definitely a process that involves the subconscious because it completely bypasses the conscious mind, at least until the hand has made the scribble on the paper. After that, the conscious mind may kick in to decode it. So in CRV, there is a constant moving back and forth between being in an intuitive state to being in an analytical state. This has both pros and cons to it that are outside the scope of this discussion.

Body Orientation and Bilocation

Clairvoyant training has typically required students to do their readings from within their bodies, although various programs do teach out-of-body healing. Some schools even offer programs in which students are taught to rise up out of their body and hang out in the chakras above their

---

14. When I first began doing readings, I would frequently have someone tell me they wanted to know how things looked with their boyfriend, girlfriend, wife, or husband. They might say the person's name, but I would begin to describe someone else. This someone else frequently turned out to be a secret lover or person of desire that they wanted to know about even more than the person they had originally asked about, but were too embarrassed or too nervous to bring up. So now when someone wants to know about a love relationship, I often ask them if they are involved with more than one person, and then ask them to say both people's names, or I will ask them to tell me who they are most interested in hearing about first.

body in order to let another being in, though that's something we don't need or really want to do during clairvoyant reading. (I do teach you how to have a guide connect into your hand chakras later in this book. However, I suggest if you have a strong interest in channeling spirits through the rest of your chakras or body that you obtain specific and additional training for this.)

Some forms of remote viewing have incorporated the work of Robert Monroe, who founded the Monroe Institute and wrote some great books on the topic of out-of-body experiences. The Monroe Institute's programs teach people how to move into deeper states of consciousness and to achieve out-of-body and psychic experiences through the use of biofeedback machines. Their programs are typically highly rated, though tend to be expensive.

When in these altered states of consciousness, a process called "bilocation" can occur. While there are different theories about the nature of bilocation, I believe it is a separation of part of you from your body. It's what most of us would consider an extreme conscious out-of-body experience. If clairvoyant reading is analogous to sitting at home and watching images of an event on your TV, bilocation would be actually going to that location and observing it directly, except that people can bilocate to events in different time periods. So bilocation is either time and space travel, or it is similar to entering into a hologram of the event, where the hologram can feel as real as the event itself.

When doing clairvoyant readings with a person sitting in front of you, bilocation, at least the conscious experience of it, is rare. This is because very often you are connecting with your readee's energy that is right there with you. Bilocation is more likely to occur when remote viewing than when reading someone sitting in front of you, although it can happen when you are reading a person who is not physically present or when performing a long-distance healing. Therefore, I suspect that bilocation is the effect of sending your energy to remote locations away from your own body.[15]

Just like any other phenomenon, I believe bilocation may occur in degrees, so that you will not be aware of it until more of you is out of your body than present within it. Some of the most experienced remote viewers I've personally talked to about bilocation have said that they usually have a full conscious sense of bilocation (being more at the target site than in their physical body is extremely rare). Lyn Buchanan explained to me that full conscious bilocation was actually discouraged in the military to access certain information because it can distract from the task at hand. However, he did say the six or seven times it's happened to him, they were just about the most exciting things he's ever experienced.

Since most of my focus has been on performing readings while being centered within myself, most of my personal experience with bilocation has occurred while I was meditating or close to falling asleep. Upon reading about bilocation, I held the intention for about a week that I would be able to experience it. One afternoon while napping I found myself flying over a field of golden grass, near the ocean. It was quite fun and really exhilarating, because there was such a strong kinesthetic sense of movement. It reminded me of a few cherished lucid dreams I've had where I became aware I was dreaming and chose to fly. During my bilocation experiences, I was very aware of the feeling of wind somehow on my body, even though my body was snugly tucked into bed.

This experience was slightly different from the out-of-body experiences I've had, perhaps since during the out-of-body experiences I remained right in the room with my physical body.

---

15. The form of remote viewing taught in the next chapter that I have coined "Freestyle Remote Viewing" can lend itself to bilocation, as can that called Extended Remote Viewing, as taught by former remote viewer David Morehouse, author of *The Psychic Warrior.*

The problem with bilocation is that sometimes when you are finished you might feel "out of it": dizzy, ungrounded, or intensely fatigued. The psychic tools offered in chapters 3 and 4 can help bring you back fully to your body and reverse these effects. It's just important to understand, as I mentioned above, that the moment you say to yourself, "Wow, that sounds cool. I want to experience that," it is very possible you will do so to some extent.

Aesthetic Impact

Much more common in remote viewing than full bilocation is the related experience of having an "aesthetic impact" experience (AI). This should actually happen at least once, if not several times, in every session. I believe this may actually be a low-grade version of bilocation. In CRV methodology, part of the protocol is to indicate on your paper when you've had this, and if you haven't, you can force yourself to have one by merely commanding yourself to do so at a particular time.

An AI occurs when you have a sense of yourself in relation to the target. This is often in terms of dimensions, but can also be emotional, or both. Some of the following are examples from my own sessions and what I identified as AI's: "There is a structure that is bigger than me"; "I feel an object that I can almost wrap my hands around"; "I'm standing on something that is wobbly that feels very unstable"; "There is a light source that is shining in my eyes"; "I'm standing within a ring of trees and when I look up I can see the leaves waving in my face and sunlight is shining in my eyes"; "There is a dark corridor and for some reason I'm feeling very frightened about going inside."

It's been said, and I believe this is true, that once a viewer has a sense of an AI, which can happen immediately at the start of a session or not until several minutes (or pages) into one, it's likely that the information that follows will be even more accurate and detailed. That's why in Controlled Remote Viewing methodology, one important step is declaring one's AI.

Structuring/Organizing the Session Data

Some of the most important protocols of remote viewing have to do with the rules regarding the viewer's data collection process, which includes their choices of what to focus on, methods of observation, and how information is presented on the paper and summarized. This is where the differences between remote viewing and clairvoyant reading become most apparent. In my opinion, clairvoyants can very much benefit from understanding the research behind these protocols, because they have been designed to minimize the errors and pitfalls that all psychics encounter when utilizing their abilities of extrasensory perception. While I do not have room to present any sort of detailed course in remote viewing here, I will present some general concepts below that any psychic should be aware of, whether they are reading people or coordinates.

CRV distinguishes between hard and soft data. The hard data (aka low-level descriptors) are really the most important. This type of data includes observing, recording, or reporting the basic attributes of the target as opposed to providing a conclusion as to what the target is. Most of the terms in this type of data would be classified as adjectives. You are looking for colors, shapes, sizes, movements, textures, sounds, and dimensions, as well as smells, tastes, and feelings. Words like *red, small, round, smelly, fluid, sharp,* and *shiny* would be used here. This is the micro level.

Soft data (aka high-level data) are the larger concepts. These are useful but are more subject to interpretation that can be incorrect. Some of these terms could be *castle, swimming pool, dog, person,* and so on. These are all nouns. The reason the soft data have traditionally been separated into a different category in remote viewing is because the person assessing the data needed to be aware that this type of data might not be as solid. For example, the castle might not really be a castle but could be a fancy house or a miniature golf course. The swimming pool might actually be a holding tank for chemicals. The dog might not be a dog but rather a goat or a cow. The person might be a statue. Since our minds naturally seek to classify and pair one piece of information with something we are already familiar with, this is what happens when we observe anything through either our physical eyes or our psychic ones.

As a remote viewer or clairvoyant, you certainly wouldn't want to leave these nouns out of your description of what you are seeing or sensing, since much of the time they are going to be valid and important, if not absolutely 100 percent correct. It's just helpful to under-stand where your own mind might be filling in the blanks. In scientifically controlled remote viewing, you or your monitor would, for future analysis, record on paper these nouns (soft data) in a different column from the adjectives (hard data).

Another type or category of data would include your final impressions or interpretations of the whole. This category of data is the least reliable because, again, it leaves a lot of room for the remote viewer's mind to fill in the blanks. A building, a cornfield, a bunch of animals in a field—a remote viewer might assume the overall target is a farm. However, it could be a zoo, or it could be a slaughterhouse, or it could turn out to be something the remote viewer has never heard or thought of, which would make it almost impossible for the viewer to effectively label it. The same is true of a person who was actually physically present at an unfamiliar location and attempting to define what it is.

One day, after hearing a radio program about the instability of Yellowstone National Park, I decided to take a peek and see what might be causing or contributing to this instability. I immediately saw an object that looked familiar, actually several of them, but I didn't know what it was. So I wrote down that it was a large, metallic (more rusty than metallic) mechanical object that was moving up and down in a steady, consistent motion and rate. It had an oblong, almost squarish "head" to it connected to something straight. It was the "head" part that was going up and down. It was large, at least three sizes bigger than a tall man (this would be hard data). The object really reminded me of a hammer, or perhaps more accurately an anvil (soft data). But why would there be a mechanical anvil moving up and down on its own accord in the middle of the desert? It seemed as though there were several of these. I had seen these before but just could not remember what they were, and it was driving me crazy.

About three days later I was driving farther north than I usually do, and along the road I saw the same exact object. "What is that?" I asked my companion. "It's an oil drill," came the reply. I thought that was strange because I had never heard of them drilling for oil in Yellowstone. However, I began doing more research about the area and discovered that some scientists were convinced that oil drilling in other parts of the country is having an enormous impact on Yellowstone, the national park that has been called the "heart chakra of America." If the area around Yellowstone ever erupts in an earthquake or volcano, most of the United States would be adversely affected.

Obviously, when reading people, particularly ones present with you, it would not be at all practical to go through the above procedure of analysis, of separating your observations into soft and hard data. I wouldn't recommend this because one of the worst things you can do during a reading is to get too analytical. Instead, I suggest that whenever possible, you should remind yourself to look for the basic building blocks first. If you see a woman, don't just say, "I see a woman" and move on. Describe instead the attributes that make you think you are seeing a woman. If you don't get any specifics, then ask your receptacle to show you these, or one definite symbol by which your readee will be able to recognize the woman.

The difficulty here is that you might be describing the actual attributes of a real woman, or you might instead be seeing a *symbol* of a woman who represents the actual woman in question. If your aunt Emma was very mean and had black curly hair, and your readee's aunt is also very mean but has blond straight hair, the part of you that generates pictures might show you someone who looks like your aunt. This may be happening because you and your readee have a strong match, or maybe because this is the only way you'd think of mentioning a mean aunt who might have had a large impact on the readee.

However, sometimes you might see the real or literal physical attributes of the person as if they were standing in front of you, and by mentioning these your readee will known exactly who you are talking about. If you are not sure, you can always say, "This is what I am seeing. I don't know if the person really looks like this because she looks a whole lot like my mean aunt Emma who I had to live with for a year when my parents got divorced." At this point your readee might exclaim, "Wow, I lived with a mean aunt too when my parents got divorced, and I've been trying to deal with the trauma I still feel. But my aunt has blond hair."

When I am training my clairvoyant students, I have to remind them frequently to go back to the building blocks of what they are seeing. This is particularly true of the psychics I work with who have been reading with their other abilities apart from their clairvoyance. If I ask such people to look at a rose and tell me what the rose looks like—is it big or small? open or closed? Standing straight at attention or drooping?—and instead they give me a five-minute assessment of the readee's psychological issues and what they have to do to overhaul their life, then they did not do the assignment correctly, even if the rest of the class is sitting there with their mouths wide open in awe.

That's not to say that such a reading might not be right on and very helpful, but what I want to know for the sake of their clairvoyant training, and to help them overcome the possibility of filling in the blanks with their own assumptions and projections, is how that information came in. I slow them down. Focusing on the minute details requires a tremendous amount of focus, concentration, and mental energy. However, it gives us a better chance to obtain quality information, whether we are working with the literal in remote viewing or with the symbology that is an integral part of clairvoyance.

We've got the rest of our lives to increase the speed and complexity of our readings, which is sometimes desirable and sometimes not. Working closely with students one-on-one, I'm always brought back to how that which is simple can be more powerful, since the simple is usually a lot less tainted with analytical influence.

From my own experiments and research, I believe one of the greatest challenges of remote viewing is in formulating the best targets for viewers to look at. By "formulating targets," I mean determining what it is you are assigning the psychic to look at. This is why reading people is often easier. All you have to do is give a psychic the person's name, and the psychic will be locked on to that specific person. When you ask a psychic to view an event or location, you have to be specific—not about what you verbally tell them, because often all they will be given is a number to lock on to. But once they start their "mission," they could look at any aspect of the target. The problem is that since they don't know what they are looking for their minds may come up with all sorts of things they think they are supposed to be looking for and veer them off track. Oftentimes, inexperienced viewers will go to where they would most want to go if they were actually physically at a location, and this is not always where their tasker wants them to go.

For example, when I first started working with remote viewing, I gave my students a target that I assigned the number-and-letter combination 1A. I wrote the target on a piece of paper and described it as "Caleb's (my son's friend's) birthday party today at the Cliff Castle Casino." Several students immediately saw a large pastel-colored resort, which Cliff Castle Casino is. One student saw kids playing with balls, which is just what they do at the "kids' club" at that casino. Many others saw tropical decor, umbrella drinks, and a big swimming pool. (I didn't know the casino had a restaurant there with this motif so I thought these students were way off at first.) A couple of other students described a wedding. The problem was that my students were all going to parts of the casino they thought were the most interesting, which were not necessarily the parts of the casino I as the target formulator wanted or expected them to see.

This experience further confirmed for me that assigning the target is the trickiest business for researchers, something many other psi/remote viewers will also confirm. During another experiment I asked my students to look at my sister's present location. Almost all of them saw her walking through the rooms of a mountainside rustic house, opening doors and feeling bored, as though she didn't want to be working. As it turned out, my sister was en route to such a house (she was a real estate agent about to do an open house in the Santa Barbara hills) but had not yet arrived. Since the target was where she currently was at the time of the exercise (first in a coffee shop and then in her car), technically, all but one student (who saw her in her car on a winding hillside road near the water) was incorrect.

Personal Transformation and the Impact of Psychic Work

From the accounts provided by the early pioneers in clandestine remote viewing programs, it is clear that remote viewers were very much personally impacted on every imaginable level by their viewing sessions. Their belief systems, concepts of self, emotional states, and relationships underwent enormous shifts soon after they began their training. Just about every one of these viewers will tell you the person they were and the person they became within the course of a year was very different. While this was at times confusing and painful, it could also be intensely rewarding.

This transformation is very similar to what clairvoyant students experience. The difference here is that, to my knowledge, the remote viewing protocols addressed neither the spiritual development of the viewer nor the potential side effects of time and space travel. Rather, these were unanticipated by-products of the training and viewing sessions. This is not surprising given that remote viewing was developed in a lab, mostly by men, to be utilized by military or government personnel. You would think (hope) that the first thing soldiers trained for war would need would be a good amount of psychological support in order to know how to handle what they are about to deal with. But that is certainly not the case.

Instead, soldiers arc indoctrinated into a belief system that ensures they will put concepts such as patriotism and heroism over the importance of their own personal mental or physical health, which they are taught to override for the benefit of their country.

Since remote viewing was done as part of a team, the viewers had each other to commiserate with, and this likely saved many of them from going completely mad. However, some didn't fare so well. Fortunately, many of today's remote viewing programs are placing much greater emphasis on the personal well-being and development of their students. As I've already noted, since their inception, clairvoyant training programs have been emphasizing this aspect of personal growth, transformation, and self-protection.

Healing

Remote viewing has been used since its inception to collect information about people at a distance, without their consent. These people were not usually aware (or supposed to be aware) that they were being viewed. They could be probed for their physical attributes, their thoughts, their emotional mindsets, their behaviors or activities, and so forth. Remote viewing has also been used to influence or control the minds of other participants. It can be used to harm or help people. Although I doubt either our military or the Soviet military were too concerned about healing their unwitting targets, more and more remote-viewing training programs today are incorporating healing into their teachings and practices due to the interests and needs of current students.[16]

Unexpected Sightings

The remote viewers working for the government probably weren't too surprised when they encountered an enemy's combat training camps, lost airplanes, captured soldiers, minefields, submarines, or assassination plots. However, can you imagine what it was like for them when they encountered deceased spirits, demons, or aliens? In reading such entities, it becomes clear that remote viewers, regardless of how skeptical or scientific they were, encountered and continue to meet the same types of entities that clairvoyants have been seeing and communicating with for centuries. They are just a little less likely to mention these to anyone who cares to listen!

Remote-Viewing Snobbery

"How dare you call me a psychic! I have nothing to do with those embarrassing fortunetellers! I am a remote viewer!" This is still a common response you get from those trained in the early remote-viewing programs. I see this as unfortunate for a number of reasons. First, it's just outright confusing. Oh, okay, sorry, of course you aren't psychic. You just use your nonphysical senses to gather information about the past, present, or future that your logical mind has no access to. But wait a second, isn't that what being psychic is? Isn't this the same thing that clairvoyants and channelers do? Hey, come to think of it, isn't this what Jesus, Moses, and Mohammed did as well? Weren't they prophets who had visions of the future and heard voices no one else could hear? Whether these religious icons were gods, men, or both is still up for debate; however, it's clear

---

16. Lyn Buchanan developed a methodology for remote influencing/healing through the use of remote-viewing techniques. Today this is taught by his protégé, Lori Williams (www.intuitivespecialists.com), in a course entitled "Medical Applications."

that they became famous for their psychic or remote-viewing talents. Psychics? What! How dare you, you blasphemous infidel. ESP is the work of the devil! Oh, okay. Now I understand. Yeah.

One of my best friends and a talented clairvoyant of thirty years, Rachel Mai, recently pointed out to me that, like disobedient slaves who were tarred and feathered, psychics have been splattered with the most toxic of accusations and stereotypes since way before the Crusades. This has happened despite the fact (maybe because of the fact?) that they were the very people who have enacted the most change and to whom millions upon millions of people today not only pray but completely hand their lives over ("Jesus will save you"). Every time we see a cross, we are told to think, "He died for our sins." But a deeper message is, "If you rock the boat, talk directly to God, foresee the future, heal the sick, perform exorcisms, or try to get people to see the truth, then you could end up like Jesus but worse because, after all, he was the incarnation of God. You are a mere mortal, and therefore it's gonna hurt."

It's no wonder, then, that the remote viewers, who invested years laboring in dingy college laboratories, pulling themselves up the wobbly ladder of success amidst tornadoes of hardship, who have acquired every ounce of their reputation and status with their own sweat and blood on the battlefields and within their stifling office cubicles, are extremely loath to be classified as lowly, bourgeois psychics.

That the remote viewers working for the government wanted to distance themselves from the debilitating stereotypes around the word *psychic* is therefore understandable. As Joseph McMoneagle states in his book *Memoirs of a Psychic Spy*, "The ridicule and derision encountered during contact with outside personnel on a week-to-week basis is difficult to relate." The amount of cognitive dissonance that remote viewers such as McMoneagle experienced must have been absolutely exhausting.

However, years after the dissolution of these governmental programs, there are still remote viewers today who are so concerned with their reputations and with maintaining a positive public persona that they will chastise or debunk any psychic who does not adhere strictly to the remote-viewing protocols, which in my opinion are not always practical or applicable to every situation involving the use of one's psychic abilities. If I can close my eyes, focus on a simple rose, invite the target's energy into the rose, and within thirty seconds correctly identify the target or describe its attributes; if I can describe a person I've never met down to specific physical, mental, and emotional characteristics, even occasionally getting their name, then obviously the methods I employ and teach are more than adequate for what I am specifically attempting to achieve. Are these as effective as the remote-viewing protocols for viewing coordinates or distant targets? I believe they are.

The fact is that most psychics, whether clairvoyants or remote viewers, don't have our own controlled laboratories equipped with isolation chambers lined in acoustic insulation for electrical shielding and soundproofing. We don't have biofeedback brainwave recording equipment. We most certainly don't have Stanford-trained scientists standing by our sides, whispering instructions into our ears or piped in through little microphones sewn into our lapels. We don't have anyone handing us a list of pre-selected, time-tested targets when we meet with our clients. We must therefore do the best with what we have: the techniques offered throughout this book and a genuine desire and commitment to be as accurate as possible, given the circumstances and nature of what it is we are doing.

I don't think enough research, if any, has been done specifically on clairvoyant training and on utilizing one's abilities for the purpose of accessing information about a person who requests it. I believe this is the next step in psi research, one that is long overdue, and I hope to be a part of this at some point in the near future. The reason reading people has not been the focus of psi experiments is the same reason psychological research in general lags behind other types of research in funding and support. When dealing with people, there are just so many variables that are difficult to control.

In her book *The Intention Experiment,* Lynne McTaggart outlines several studies that look at the effect of one person's intentions on another. These experiments have high validity and are extremely controlled, and they have yielded statistically significant and repeatable results. Therefore, it should not be impossible to design and implement studies that look at the accuracy and impact of clairvoyant reading by one person for another.

Clairvoyants Are Not Immune to Judgements Either

I know far too many psychics who are graduates of clairvoyant training schools, and who are convinced that any psychic who has not followed their same path is an ungrounded, unbalanced, wacky New Age sickly psychic vulnerable to all the insidious energies waiting to attack at any moment. I was programmed to believe this myself until I graduated from the school I attended, moved to the Philippines and then Sedona, and then eventually to the L.A. area. I discovered that yes, there are a lot of wacky people out there, but some of these people are also extremely talented, loving, self-taught psychics who have become my very best friends! Would they benefit from my training or the training that I received? I'm sure they would. But this isn't their path, and I am sure I would have benefited from some of their experiences, which I will never have.

Divide and Conquer — It's Worked So Far, Against Us All

Both clairvoyant training programs and remote-viewing protocols are at risk for becoming antiquated if each one continues to be conducted in a spirit of elitism, possessiveness, paranoia, and an unrelenting addiction to the way it's always been rather than the way it could be better. We need not criticize each other, but rather learn from each other to further perfect our techniques and approaches. We have formidable opponents out there in the forms of ignorance, fear, and a dogmatic skepticism that continues to deny the experiences of millions and continues to ignore the undeniable results of what are now thousands of quality scientific studies that have proven psychic functioning is as much of a reality as are the turned-up noses on our faces. The only way to disarm these enemies of truth and spiritual freedom is to sever our own alliances with them. We must stop allowing our fears, egos, and economic interests to divide us. Instead, as psychics and lovers of the innate psychic talents within us, whether latent or blatant, we must stand, sit, float, fly, dream, study, practice, learn, develop, and transform together.

CHAPTER 11

Hybrid Remote Viewing: Experiments and Techniques

If you want to be incrementally better, be competitive
If you want to be exponentially better, be cooperative.
— UNKNOWN

My Own Remote Viewing Experiments: How We Can Use Our Clairvoyance to View Objects and Events

As I've noted, I was trained as a clairvoyant reader, not as a remote viewer. Therefore, all of my training centered on reading people who request information and assistance, and most of my professional practice has as well.

However, ever since I read David Morehouse's book *Psychic Warrior,* I've been utterly fascinated with anything having to do with remote viewing. I purchased a few home-study courses and vowed to follow them step by step, but then I broke those vows almost as soon as I made them, because quite frankly I was too impatient. I wanted to jump right to viewing the targets to see if I could just use the simple methods of utilizing a rose and my reading screen. What I discovered was that most of the time, that was all I needed. Occasionally, I felt as though I did need to go into a deeper state or actually do some out-of-body travel, but many times I just focused on the target number and immediately began getting images that turned out to really pertain to the actual target. During my very first attempt, I saw an image that looked like the shape of Texas. I saw people fighting and a structure that looked like an adobe castle. The target turned out to be the Alamo.

Soon after the publication of my book *You Are Psychic*, I began getting tons of e-mails (this is the best way to contact me) from readers who were unable to find clairvoyant training programs in their area. In response, I designed and implemented a long-distance clairvoyant training program so that I could at least accommodate some of these budding clairvoyants. In order to keep the training fresh, and for my own curiosity, I decided to conduct some little "experiments." These experiments involved the remote viewing of objects, and later events, with pretty awesome results! I do want to point out that, from a scientific standpoint, they were not well "controlled" and would not stand up to the rigorous standards that psi experiments must adhere to. (Note: such requirements are far more rigorous than those applied even to studies on pharmaceuticals.) However, since my goal was one of discovery and insights for me and my students, you will see that we had what I feel are some pretty interesting results.

For my very first "experiment," I placed a few objects in a shoebox and asked Masaru Kato, one of the students in my long-distance telephone training program, to leave his body at his home in Chicago and to send his spirit over to my place in California. I instructed him to focus on a brown and orange box resting on my lap and to describe its contents. I told him to visualize the box and wait and see if he got anything about the contents. (The box in this case was taking the place of a receptacle.) He wasn't very confident in his ability to do this, but as usual he pushed himself and courageously reported that he saw a shiny black ball with something floating in it. He stated it seemed like the ball had a "window in it," and inside was something displaying a message. The message was unclear but seemed to be written on a triangle. He also stated it was reflective.

Masaru was right about almost all of these characteristics, except that I didn't think the object was reflective. However, I decided to check. I opened the box to look again, and sure enough I saw my own reflection! He had no idea what this object was that he was describing and stated he felt rather foolish. I finally explained to him that this was a toy—a black, plastic, shiny fortune-telling cue ball with a triangle-shaped cube inside floating in liquid. When you shake it up, one of eight inspirational messages written across a triangle cube appears in the window, except most of the messages had worn away over time and were unreadable. At first he didn't know what I was talking about, but then he remembered he had once seen such a ball in a cartoon.

Excited about his accuracy with the details, I asked Masaru to imagine he was freely wandering around the room and to tell me what else he noticed. He stated, "I know this sounds pretty strange, but I see a dinosaur sitting in an egg that looks kind of plastic." I assured him that was not strange at all, as there was in fact a stuffed dinosaur inside a plastic egg on the shelf about five feet from me. He later saw "two Muppets, like from *Sesame Street*" sitting on the dresser. He was accurate about that as well.

The following week I repeated the same experiment with another student named Deborah Sharif, who was located even farther away, in South Carolina. Up to this point I had been encouraging her to do her readings from within her body, but this time I gave her full permission to let her spirit venture out onto the etheric highway for a visit to my home (much faster than the Los Angeles freeways!). This time I placed a souvenir inside the box. The souvenir was a snow globe that contained a miniature of the White House in water. When you shake it up, it looks like it's snowing. It didn't take her more than a minute to report a "heavy object, like a paperweight, almost like a crystal ball, with glitter or snow swirling around." She then went on to describe my own house, admitting it looked cozy but much smaller than she had anticipated (it is rather small). She also saw it looking very clean and well-organized. Fortunately, she wasn't viewing a few days earlier, before I had cleaned up my house!

Next, I walked into my living room, stood in front of a window, and asked Deborah to describe some objects on the windowsill. She wasn't really able to get anything about these objects, but instead she began describing the view from the window. She saw a scene in which a woman who she thought was me but had red hair (she didn't know I had highlighted my hair red) and a dark-haired and dark-complexioned boy (my son, who she didn't know looks nothing like me) were "laughing and laughing" along with a "stocky guy," who she thought was my boyfriend Danny. She was confused about this last point, because during a prior session she had spontaneously tuned in to him and at that time he had no facial hair. She said this time it looked like he had a goatee, which he had in fact recently sprouted. She reported she "saw" us having a great time sliding down hills outside on something that looked like a "wooden sled with wheels." I told her that this was exactly what we had been doing the past weekend, only it was a makeshift wooden go-cart.

During a recent ongoing class held at my home with a few enthusiastic students, I invited them to meditate on their own for a few minutes, while I hurried off to my bedroom where I dug out the now-familiar box that I had been using with my long-distance students the week before. At first I placed the above-mentioned snow globe with the snow swirling around the White House in the box along with a figurine of a decorative, brightly painted horse, but then I changed my mind and decided to replace these with objects I had never before experimented with. I finally decided on an action figure of a little guy riding a toy motorcycle.

Less than ten minutes later, I sat in front of three of my students with the sealed box on my lap, and two of the three described the action figure in the exact position he was sitting in. They were not able to get a grasp on a couple of other objects that I had hurriedly placed in the box, but instead saw a "paperweight-type object, like a ball with liquid in it, and something like glitter or snow floating around a white building." Another student saw a "decorative show horse." These were the exact objects that had occupied the box during prior experiments, and that I had momentarily included in the box earlier before changing my mind and removing them. While this was very interesting, I was not surprised since it is common to confuse points in time when reading people, and similar incidents have been reported by other remote viewers and experimenters using different techniques.

Although it was now after 10 p.m., my students were still raring to go, so I retreated to my bedroom again and decided on another object, this one still in its long, narrow gift box. I wrapped the box inside a large towel so as not to give away any clues about its shape, before returning to the students in the living room. I asked them to use the same techniques they usually use to read a person in order to "view" this object, now placed only a few feet from them in the towel on my lap. They all immediately reported seeing an orange/red color. One student named Sandy saw "an orange-y reddish tulip, with lines in it with a very long narrow stem that curved a bit." She stated that it seemed like it should "be in a vase."

"Close," I advised, "but it's not a tulip; it's a rose." I unwrapped the towel, exposing first the narrow box and then its single occupant: an orangeish, reddish chiseled-glass flower with a long, skinny stem that curved a bit at the bottom. It was still in the box because I had not yet found the right vase to put it in. It was at this point the students corrected me.

"Hey, that's not a rose. It's a tulip, just like Sandy saw." I looked more closely, as it had been a few weeks since Christmas, when my son had given it to me as a gift. I couldn't believe my eyes. They were right. It was indeed a tulip!

This experiment also showed me that selecting a target or objects to view, and the way they are placed, is paramount to the perceived success of the psychic. This is why rigorous controls are needed for this type of experiment. I had the knowledge of what had already been in the box, and was aware of my own indecision about what to place in there. A scientist looking at the data would automatically record the responses of the students as incorrect, since the scientist would be required to mention only what was currently in the box. In an ideal experiment, the same box would not be used unless the study sought to understand how psychics can be confused by time and space. The person running the experiment would not be the same person who selected the objects or targets, nor would they even have knowledge of what the objects or targets were, because then it would not be clear if the students were reading the experimenter's mind or really viewing the contents.

For my next informal experiment, I thought I would try to fix at least one of the above flaws by making myself blind to the target. I asked my boyfriend, Danny, to come up with any event at any time in history and to write this event on a piece of paper. I told Danny to write a description of this event, put it in an envelope, and assign it a six-digit number unrelated to the subject matter. I then went to my bedroom to go to sleep. However, as soon as my head hit the pillow, my curiosity got the best of me. I wondered if I would be able to see what the target was. I knew that if I were successful, I would no longer be blind to the target, which would then contaminate the validity of my experiment with my students, but I told myself that I would just take a quick clairvoyant peek. If I didn't get anything in one minute, I would stop.

I created a reading screen, then a transparent 3-D rose on the screen, and instructing myself to stay centered within my body and behind my sixth chakra, I invited the attributes of the event Danny was presently writing about in the other room to appear in my receptacle, then forced myself to just watch and see what happened. Within thirty seconds I saw a very clear image of the Statue of Liberty. I decided not to look any further, and I drifted off to sleep.

The next morning I couldn't find the envelope and asked Danny where it was. Right before he handed it to me, I said, "I just want to know one thing. Does it have anything to do with the Statue of Liberty?" "Yeah," he said nonchalantly, "that's it."

He handed me the sealed envelope and left the room without another word. Since he'd been quite a skeptic, and a monumental jokester, I didn't believe him. I thought again that maybe, for the sake of the experiment, I should just not open the envelope until after I worked with my students. But that thought lasted about two seconds. I tore the envelope in half, pulled out the piece of paper, and there it was: Danny had written, "The rededication and unveiling of the Statue of Liberty, New York City harbor, July 4, 1986."

Even though now I was not blind to the target, I decided to go ahead and see whether or not my student Masaru (who had done so well seeing the objects in my room during a previous session) would have success with the particular target as well. Once again we conducted our session over the telephone, with him in Chicago and me at home in California. Several times during our session he stated that he felt as though he were traveling to New York. He did not mention anything about the Statue of Liberty, but instead began describing ships— old war ships, from many different nations. He saw cannons and gunfire on the ships. He saw the scene on Iwo Jima in which the Americans won the battle and put up their flag. Since I was mostly thinking about the Statue of Liberty, I assumed Masaru must be way off.

But something told me to go ask Danny what he was thinking about when he had written out this event. Danny told me he had actually been in New York for the rededication of the Statue of Liberty, and that the harbor had been filled with every kind of ship imaginable from every war in the history of the planet. There was also a massive fireworks display, but to him the ships were the highlight of the event. Danny is a real war-movie fanatic and can identify just about every kind of boat or plane that has ever been made.

This experience reminded me of a fact that many psi researchers have pointed out: that we will "see" the things we have the most interest in. Had I actually been physically present for the Statue of Liberty's rededication, I would have likely found the statue the most interesting aspect—and that is likely why I saw the statue rather than any of the ships.

At a recent workshop, I gave this same target to a whole group of students. It was at the end of the day, and there were numerous distractions in the room. I didn't give the students the specific date of the event, so I wasn't surprised that for the most part the results were mostly inconclusive. However, one student, an attorney named George who had been performing distance healing for several years, did see the Fourth of July in the New York City harbor and did see an image of the Statue of Liberty.

From the experiences above and many others like them, I have become convinced that the clairvoyant techniques taught in this book, with perhaps a few modifications, can be effectively utilized for remote viewing of objects and events at a distance.

Combination Remote Viewing/ Clairvoyant Exercise

I suggest that you get a tape recorder and tape your session. Buy a ninety-minute tape and give yourself permission to have very long pauses on it. This is not a performance, so it doesn't have to sound good! No one else will hear the tape unless you choose to share it with them. Later, you can listen to the tape and transcribe it onto paper if you'd like.

Taping your session is of course optional. If you are going to use a tape recorder, turn it on and place it close to your mouth as soon as you begin, so you don't even have to think about it once you get started. If you don't have a tape recorder, then make sure you have paper and a pen or pencil next to you.

It helps to decide on your target before you begin. You might have something in mind that you are wondering about, such as a missing object, a specific location, or an event at some point in history, whether past or future. You can choose this for yourself, or you can ask someone to give you a target that they place in a sealed envelope and assign some number to. You can also check out the website for the Western Institute for Remote Viewing or the website for Ed Dame's company, Learn Remote Viewing. Both of these offer plenty of targets that have been selected as ideal ones for students to practice on, and as I noted above, it doesn't matter at all that you may be using different methods from these instructors.

I suggest you write down your target or target number, and hold it on your lap or under your pillow. You may sit or lie down for this exercise—just make sure you find a place where you won't be disturbed. Turn off your phone!

Slow down your breathing. Let your mind wander to a number of different times and places. For example, remember the last time you were at the beach, then immediately think of the first time you recall riding your bike, then recall your first airplane ride. Next, think of your first, last, or only kiss, then imagine what it must be like to fly on a space shuttle to the moon. The important thing here, and really the sole purpose of this exercise, is to keep your mind darting back and forth from subject to subject without allowing it to hold a thought for more than a second or two at the most. Do this for about five to ten minutes; if you start to fall asleep, sit up or go right on to the next exercise. (This exercise is actually great in and of itself if you suffer from insomnia.)

Next, imagine that there is a cord of light coming either out of your third chakra or out of your crown chakra (you can experiment to see which one works best for you). Imagine one of these cords is connected to an energy body that looks just like you but is made up of pure energy (some people refer to this as an *etheric double*). Imagine that you are transferring the bulk of your consciousness to this body. Now imagine that this body is beginning to move away from your physical body. You can turn around and look at your physical body, ground it, say something sweet to it, and tell it you will return to it soon, safe and sound, as soon as you are finished gathering information from your trip. Now imagine that your etheric body either has wings, is like a moving cloud, or is like Wonder Woman's see-through airplane. Any of these travel instantaneously through time and space. Imagine you can feel the air moving past you. Just relax.

Give your energy body with your consciousness in it the directive that it's going to go to a few places. For example, let it go up to the top of the atmosphere, then to the bottom of the ocean, then to a few different countries. Just do this quickly, making a mental note of one sensation you might feel if you actually were there or something you might see from an aerial view if you were actually flying over one of these places.

Now that you have warmed up your personal energy vehicle, give it the command that it and you are going to travel to the destination that is the target on the piece of paper resting on your body. This is the point at which you can completely relax and wait, as if you were waiting for an airplane to take off. You don't have to do anything else or think about anything else, except be aware. Give yourself as much time as you need. You are waiting for some kind of stimuli to come into your consciousness. As you start to see or experience something, just make a mental note of it or start to talk loud enough for your tape recorder to pick up your voice and describe what you are starting to notice.

If you don't feel as if anything is happening, then visualize a door, with the target numbers or your destination written across it. See the door open and imagine you are passing through it. On the other side is a tunnel that takes you directly through to your destination, regardless of whether you know what that is. Let yourself float through the door and through the tunnel.

Imagine this tunnel is dark but warm and nurturing, even soft and cushy as you pass through it. Be patient and notice where it takes you. Look for a sign of light. Once you begin to see the light or see some kind of shape, start making mental notes about what it is you are seeing. Look for colors, shapes, sizes, textures. Ask whether there is plant or animal or human life. Ask yourself if there are man-made or natural structures in this place.

Remember that just as in real life, your position, in terms of angle and proximity, will determine how well you can view whatever is there. So when you start to make observations, don't forget to tell yourself to move in closer or further away, or to go to the front or back or all around. This is very important!

Your Return Trip

Once you are ready to come back, it's important to give yourself the command that you are going to return fully, with all your energy intact. You can invite any of your energy or spirit that might have already been separated from your body before you began this exercise to join you. You can do this by assigning this energy a color and watching to see if that color comes in around you.

If you used a tunnel and door to get to your destination, come back the same way you came in. Once you reach the door, tell any energies you might have engaged with that they must stay on the other side. Make sure you close the door. Let yourself slowly reunite with your body. Imagine you are hovering above the planet, and then the city and then the street you live on, then the house in which your body sits or lies waiting for you. You can linger in a corner of the room or beside it. Using a rose or an object, you can run this from your energy body through the cord into your third chakra or head, giving it the command that it will fill up with anything you are ready to release. Check the grounding cord on your body and look for any black spots or things that look like rips or tears.

Use some cosmic energy to wash through these parts, and watch the colors release down your grounding cord. Then imagine you are floating right back into your physical body through the cord joining your energy body. Just make sure you return through the same chakra from which you left. Center and ground yourself.

You might feel sleepy and need to take a nap after this exercise, and that's fine. If you did not use a tape recorder, you may want to jot down some notes as it's likely the more time that passes, the more you will forget what you just saw. Have fun!

Alternative Bilocation Technique: Hand Focus

There is another technique I've been working on lately that seems to induce bilocation or an out-of-body experience, in which targets can be accessed on a clairvoyant level with extreme clarity.

You may try this technique while lying down. Relax your body by slowing down your breath. Put your attention on your hands. Notice how they feel. Imagine you are moving all of your consciousness into your hands, even your fingertips. Do this for a few minutes, then imagine you are stretching out your fingertips, hands, and arms further and further. Play around with this, stretching them in various directions (note that you are not really moving them physically, but postulate that you are doing so energetically).

Next, tell yourself that your hands are going to reach all the way to the target of your choice, either one you are aware of or one someone else has given to you. Once your hands have landed there, tell yourself you will either be able to touch the target, wherever it is, or your spirit will be projected through your fingertips right to the target. You can also tell yourself that as soon as your fingertips reach the target, you will be able to see through them with your psychic eyes. Notice how your hands feel now; continue to breath slowly and just wait and see what happens.

It is likely you will begin to get visual sensations in addition to bodily sensations. Just make a mental note of all you are observing. If you have a recording device, I suggest talking into it from the moment you begin putting your attention on your hands. Continue giving a play-byplay account of what you are experiencing until you are finished with the exercise. When you are ready to return, imagine you are retracting your hands and bringing them back to their normal positions. Don't be alarmed if you feel any strange vibrations in your body at any point during this exercise; I've been experiencing these in a way I never did with any other exercise. I believe this may be the same type of feeling Robert Monroe experienced and describes so eloquently in his book *Ultimate Journey*. If nothing happens with this exercise I suggest attempting it again on another night. Sometimes there is a cumulative effect, so it may take even a week of practice before you get any results.

PART III

HEALING AND WORKING WITH NONPHYSICAL ENTITIES

CHAPTER 12

Welcome to the Spirit World

Anything I've ever done that ultimately was worthwhile...
initially scared me to death.
—— BETTY BENDER

As a Psychic, You Must Deal With Your Fear

When I first began developing my psychic abilities, like many of you I was absolutely terrified by the idea of ghosts, entities, spirits, whatever you want to call them. I had absolutely no interest in communicating with any of them! I had signed up on a whim for the clairvoyant training program through a psychic training institute, after receiving a couple of readings from a teacher and some students who were able to see all kinds of things about me, my life, and even my own visualizations, all of which they could not possibly have otherwise known. I was more enthusiastic about being able to see visions and knowing things about anyone and anything than I had been about anything else in my life. It didn't occur to me that this would include seeing and communicating with spirits!

However, it only took about a week before I began seeing spirits clairvoyantly and realized that, at least in this context, they really aren't scary at all; to the contrary, it was really fun learning about them and hearing what they had to say...even when they were being kind of nasty.

During the course of my earliest readings, it became undeniably clear to me that there are beings surrounding all of us who can very much influence the person they are connected to. This influence is sometimes very positive, sometimes quite destructive. These entities are as varied and unique as any living human being. Some are very aware, intelligent, kind, creative, and communicative; others have the intelligence of a cockroach. Many have their own agendas and personalities, while just as many have no awareness of themselves at all. They exist at all points in time, including in the past and the future. Some entities love you more than you love yourself, while others will do what they can to bring you down.

Below I will offer some pros and cons to increasing your awareness of the spirit world through the use of your clairvoyance.

Pros

Spirits have more power over you when you don't see them or know they are there. When you see spirits, you can set boundaries with them. You can consciously choose whether to let them remain in your energy field or banish them. When you are unaware of them, you are at their mercy. You fear what you don't understand or know. Once you bring something into the light, it is not as scary.

Many spirits can assist you in your life. They can provide helpful information; they can heal you; they can protect you, teach you, help create and manifest for you, and comfort you. Many spirits are people you have known and loved in this lifetime or other incarnations. When you are aware of them and can clearly communicate with them, then you can more easily recover from the separation caused by their death, or heal aspects of your relationship with them that were not resolved at the time of their death. When you see spirits, your communication with them automatically increases, so you can better hear those that have helpful and important messages for you.

Cons

Spirits are drawn to people who can see them. Clairvoyants have to be careful not to get pushed out of their own auras even by their most well-intentioned but over-enthusiastic fans. Ever have someone give you a bear hug that almost suffocated you? This is what sometimes happens with some of our guides when they realize we are aware of them. Occasionally, clairvoyants and psychics inadvertently open doors to less savory visitors from the spirit world.

During readings, clairvoyants can be "slimed"—very mildly shocked and emotionally, mentally, and in rare cases physically abused by entities that are connected with their readees. This happens to every one of us in our everyday lives at some point; it's just sometimes more exaggerated when we are performing psychic readings, both due to the clairvoyant's sensitivity and to the entity's heightened efforts to prevent being seen. Spirits don't usually have to put out much effort to keep the average human being in the dark. A little pain here, a little punishment there, and most humans will abandon whatever activity they are engaged in that could break the game that the spirit is playing. On the other hand, clairvoyants can not only see the spirit, but they can see the game and break it up. Therefore spirits need to exert more effort in order to thwart the efforts of a clairvoyant.

Luckily, clairvoyants who use their psychic tools are better equipped to deal with any attack that comes their way than the average individual is. Often, all that is needed is to see and acknowledge the presence of a spirit and alert the readee to its presence. The spirit is released the moment readees say to themselves, "I no longer want to play with you."

We Live Within the World of Spirit

Wishing there were no spirits around you is a lot like wishing there were no insects. Give it up! Most humans can feel the spirits around them. We can hear their thoughts in our minds; we can feel their emotions and even their desires in our bodies. However, most people are unaware of the origin of these feelings and thoughts, and therefore attribute them and their overall influence to something else other than spirits. Likewise, we as humans are constantly affecting these spirits with our own thoughts and emotions.

One of the goals of this chapter is to help you understand how you can use your clairvoyant abilities to increase your awareness of that which is influencing you in your environment, so you can effectively communicate with the entities of your choice in a safe and effective manner. When dealing with the spirit world, I cannot overemphasize the number one rule: *You are in charge.* You call the shots. See yourself as a general, with these spirits as your own soldiers. If any of them gets out of line, you can throw them in the brig or toss them into outer space. If you are attacked by enemy forces from the dark side, you have the right and the power to obliterate them. This can be done through the power of your imagination and your words.

Now, I can already hear some of you saying, "Obliterate!?! Well, that's not very nice! That's not very spiritual!" You are half correct. It's not nice. In this book we are learning how to cure ourselves from *having* to be nice when being nice is an inappropriate, misguided, or self-destructive response. We are also relearning the definition of spirituality, a word that means nothing more and nothing less than "of or pertaining to spirit."

The fact is that not everything having to do with spirit is nice. Whether you want to admit it or not, in addition to the enlightened loving guides looking out for you, there are some nasty, conniving critters out there that want to keep you in pain and fear. Some want to lure you into self-hatred, suicide, addiction, physical violence, even suicide. Some can manipulate material objects, but so can you! And you can obviously do this *a lot* more easily than they can!

In *You Are Psychic* I provided examples of how I came to know about these beings. In this chapter and the next one, I will jump right to providing detailed instructions that will enable you to strengthen your communication with all spirits and better understand how to deal with them, including your allies and your enemies. You will learn how to recruit and train some of these who qualify as your healing guides.

You will learn how to examine and amend your contracts with them. You will learn simple psychic self-defense and aggressive combat strategies for dealing with the dark side. Do not worry: your battles will be swift and final. The key here is to disengage as quickly as possible and to always keep your sense of humor.

So it is above, so below: this tenet sets the stage for all other tenets.

Think of your interactions with spirits in the same way as those you have with humans. Some people are your best friends, and some are your worst enemies. Some are enlightened, some are completely ignorant. Some are respectful, others abusive. Some are helpful, others draining.

For Any Relationship, You Set the Boundaries, Dictate the Rules, and Enforce Them

This is true regarding physical and nonphysical communication, as well as relationships with living people and with the spirit world. If someone or something is doing something that makes you uncomfortable, it is your responsibility to speak up and tell them to stop. If they don't stop, then you need to do whatever is necessary to save yourself and ensure that they don't violate your boundaries again.

Through our words and our silences, through our actions and our lack of action, we train both the people and spirits around us how to treat us. The greatest challenge is in setting and enforcing boundaries with the very people and spirits who in the past have helped us to feel safe, secure, and loved.

All Relationships Are Based on Agreements and Contracts That Can Be Altered and Broken

When you were a child, you were dependent on your parents. They were like gods to you. Most of the time you did what they told you to do, regardless of the quality or integrity of their advice. Fast forward forty years. Do you still have to do what your parents tell you to do? Of course not! (This may be news to some.) Relationships change. Now fast forward one thousand years. The spirit that was your parent, child, or lover may still be hanging on to you, or occupying a new human body in this current lifetime, loving you or punishing you, guiding or pulling you in directions you are or are not in agreement with. Do you have to put up with this? Absolutely not, unless you don't even know this is what's going on! One of the biggest, most insidious way others control you is through guilt. Guilt is an emotion that should never dictate behavior. And yet for most people, particularly women, it's the prevailing motivational factor.

Disclaimer: You can only help those who are open to your help!

It is very possible and quite easy to remove spirits from your home or to heal others struggling with negative entities. However, this is true only if you are truly in control of the environment and only if the other person is ready to be healed. If you live in someone else's home or work for someone else who has annoying entities wrecking havoc and running wild through the environment, you are at a definite disadvantage. Your ability to defend yourself or change and improve the environment will be quite limited as long as the people in charge of the environment agree to allow things to remain as they are.

If you try to clean out the entities from a workplace run by a boss who has a symbiotic relationship with these entities, then the entities may begin to attack you (or increase the severity of an attack) through this person, by manipulating the other person into believing that you have done something wrong, that you are out to get them or show them up, or by running anger through them that will be directed at you. It is important to remember that often a person has let that entity inside them because they weren't feeling strong enough on their own; it gives them power and does their dirty work, even though they then feel like a victim because on one level *they* feel they did nothing wrong (it was the being they are unaware of) and now here you are reacting to them with anger or distrust. So if you try to separate the person and the entity (whether or not that person has any idea what you are doing), you will anger the entity and send the person into a state of panic—and the situation will most likely worsen for you. The person might even find ways to turn others against you as well. The only good part about this is usually the situation gets so unbearable that either you decide to leave or in their anger the other person tells you to do so, and then you are free to find a situation that is better suited for you. Believe me, I've learned these lessons the hard way!

Your inner and outer environments set your energy and determine the types of spirits that are in your world. Drugs and alcohol can increase the likelihood of possession by evil spirits.

In this example, I am defining your "inner environment" as your mental and emotional state and physical health. Your "outer environment" includes the type of people you hang out with and the places you hang out in. Both these environments affect each other. They can be influenced by the spirits around you and they also attract particular beings to you. If you dwell on angry, stressful, or judgmental thoughts, you will be sending out an open invitation to other people and spirits that resonate at this same vibration. If you hang out in places with angry, aggressive, depressed, and unhealthy people, you will find a plethora of low vibrational spirits feeding off this energy and exacerbating it. This is particularly true where drugs and alcohol are consumed, where dissonant and angry music is played, and where sex is being sold. I know I risk sounding puritanical, but I can assure you that the only reason I can make these above statements is because I've hung out in my fair share of these places!

Many spirits feed off and instigate addictions. They can vicariously experience the drug-related or sexual energy by attaching themselves to the living through a symbiotic or parasitic relationship. They can make it more difficult to cure someone from their addiction, whether to cocaine or to a destructive relationship, because such spirits are highly invested in making sure the addict does not stop their behavior. I believe this is why wonderful people will suddenly become monsters, particularly when alcohol is involved.

Not only are alcohol and drugs lowering inhibitions and impairing judgments, they are preparing our bodies to be vessels for anything to occupy them—and that is when people commit heinous crimes they sometimes don't recall later. The point here is that if you live in a pigpen, it doesn't matter if you shower every five minutes, you will still be perpetually dirty. Likewise, if you meditate in a house filled with resentful, depressed people, you will clear yourself off and then get all slimed again. The difference is that through meditation you may very well get enough moments of respite so that you might actually wake up and say, "What the hell am I doing here?!"—and then have enough of your own energy to get out.

Some entities are even attached to objects such as sexually explicit printed materials or items utilized in rituals and ceremonies. Be wary about bringing home used objects!

Your agreements and relationships with spirits are not limited to this lifetime or to this physical world.

Many of the spirits that are around us or attached to us in some way have followed us from other lifetimes and incarnations. Sometimes we need to get clear and be firm about ending the agreements or karma that are no longer serving us, particularly if the spirit that has followed us is stuck on something that we now have no power to fix. Some spirits want to punish us, and then we walk around feeling perpetually guilty. When you feel guilty, it's easy to find any number of reasons to justify this guilt. This is really true of any emotion. Many people think situations in their lives elicit negative emotions. However, I have seen that just as frequently, if not more often, we already had the emotions, so we just glob onto and blame whatever is right in front of us. That's when fights of the worst kind are started with loved ones.

Sometimes spirits we have karma with will work through people who are mistreating us.

Be Careful What You Wish For!

When we say we want to understand or communicate with the spirit world, it takes less than a second for spirits to hear this and respond. Even just mild curiosity will attract spirits to us. When we are feeling desperate for help or answers, we send out emotionally charged calls for assistance that attract immediate attention. Since spirit works on telepathic levels, it doesn't matter if you verbally state, "Leave me alone" but in your mind you are thinking, "I don't know if I want you to go away." Your words and your thoughts must be in alignment with each other. Otherwise, it will be a lot harder to clear out troublesome entities from your life. The difficulty here is that sometimes it is the beings that are trying to convince you that you should allow them to stay when it's not in your best interest, which makes things confusing. This is of course no different from being in a relationship with someone you wish to leave, but who is doing everything in their power to convince you otherwise.

A couple of years ago, my good friend Darrah Waters invited me to work on her documentary crew filming a reenactment of the Battle of Little Bighorn and Custer's Last Stand. We flew to Montana and camped out for a week at the site of the battle. I barely slept a single night. From the moment I lay down, the images of Indians and soldiers exploded in my mind like a marathon fireworks display. Even when I returned home, it took a good week to clear out all the faces and blood and noise from my head (through grounding, running my energy, and utilizing several of the healing techniques in this book). I also found it necessary to intentionally turn down my clairvoyance. Doing so is possible by simply visualizing a gauge that represents your sixth chakra and seeing the arrow moving downward, or visualizing that chakra as if it were closing. It can always be opened right back up by doing the reverse.

House Hauntings

I have seen many people who were being tormented by beings, either through house hauntings with poltergeist activity or through overactive clairaudient communication. In every one of these cases, although the client initially presented themselves as a frightened victim, it turned out that the client who had contacted me was to some extent enjoying the drama, battle, attention, or interactions, despite the very real fear the clients also felt.

Spirits Are Passed Down Generationally

Spirits are passed down generationally, including both those whose only desire is to help us and those who enjoy feeding off pain. If we have been abused as children, we will be more vulnerable as adults to victimization by human and nonhuman spirits alike.

When a child is abused at a very young age, or grows up with extremely controlling parents, the child is taught that they don't have control over their own bodies or a right to say no. They are then more vulnerable to becoming victimized by subsequent abusers, those with physical bodies and those from the spirit realm.

It has become absolutely clear to me that many adults who abuse children are possessed or at least strongly influenced by angry entities at the time they are doing the abuse. The beings that are instigating this abhorrent behavior often attach themselves to the children. (After twelve years of working with so many people, I don't have an ounce of doubt about this.) The children aren't really able to distinguish between the being and their parent although many of my clients, even those who don't really believe in spirits, do recall that during the abusive episodes, they had a sense their parents were being possessed in some way or acting like a completely different person. This makes it extremely difficult for the children because they love the parent when the parent is just themselves, and are absolutely horrified of the parent when the parent is leasing themselves out like a timeshare. This is why victims of child sexual abuse often need healing of a spiritual nature, in addition to psychological counseling.

Many times when children are being abused, it is too painful and frightening for them to remain in their bodies, so they vacate the premises. Obviously, anyone being mistreated is going to be angry, but it's not safe for a child to be angry at a parent who is beating the crap out of them, so they call in another being to help them with these emotions. This is one of many reasons why those who were abused often don't really remember the abuse; they weren't quite all there either.

Abusers often see themselves as victims because they weren't fully present during the abuse (due to intoxication, leaving their bodies, and channeling foreign beings), and because they choose to focus on the subsequent reactions of the victim to the abuse the abuser is denying. This lends itself to what psychologists refer to as a dissociative process. What most psychologists don't realize is that disassociation, which I define as "various parts of an individual being closed off to awareness of the other parts," is as much a spiritual, transmedium process as it is a cognitive and emotional one.

Many schizophrenic people are also major out-of-control mediums. The boundaries between their mind and the astral/spirit realm are so ill-defined that it's like living in Grand Central Station. I've always wondered why mentally ill, homeless people tend to congregate in overcrowded and chaotic urban locations as opposed to the open wilderness. I believe their outer environment mirrors what is happening to them on a psychic level, where they are bombarded by throngs of parasitic entities on a constant basis.

Spirits plug into our pain pictures. This means that they will literally attach themselves to the areas of our body and energy field where we carry emotional pain or that were the location of some kind of physical trauma. As we release this pain, the stronghold of spirits plugged into this pain is either weakened or severed. This can happen naturally or can be facilitated with the help of a healer or counselor.

As spirits in physical bodies, we are far stronger than spirits without bodies.

While some spirits can impact or manipulate physical matter, this is fairly rare and most of the time even these exploits do little more than create fear. Fear is the primary modus operandi for abusive spirits, actually those both with and without bodies. If their hosts or victims become fearful, then they can be easily manipulated. Many beings feed off this fear, which is why they seek to create it. Most people aren't aware that they are being influenced by troublesome entities. They just hear upsetting thoughts about all the bad things that could possibly happen to them or someone they know, and they fall into a perpetual cycle of anxiety. When that happens, the being that projected the thoughts or exacerbated them in the first place has a lifetime meal ticket.

The good news here is that as long as you are aware this is what is happening, then you have won 99 percent of the battle. You can do whatever you need to get yourself in the vibration of good humor or enthusiasm, and the spirits will tire of the game and go find someone else to harass.

The Haunted and the Haunter:
Which Is Which?

One of the most shocking revelations of my clairvoyant training came to me during one of my early readings as a clairvoyant student. We were reading a woman who seemed to be suffering from irrational fears that were keeping her from achieving certain goals. It soon became apparent that there was a spirit plugged into her aura that was somehow connected to these fears. One of my teachers asked me to work with the spirit to "help it take its next step."

My earlier preconceived notions of disembodied spirits (which were based more on horror movies than on my clairvoyance or any direct experience) led me to assume that this was an evil spirit that was victimizing my readee. I felt as though it was my job to save the poor woman from this big, bad spirit. However, when I clairvoyantly looked at this spirit, I was surprised to find that not only was he scrawny and timid-looking, but he was also actually wearing shackles and straining to break a chain that bound him to the readee.

In my vision, when I asked him why he appeared this way, he looked at me with pleading, frightened eyes, and began sobbing. He looked so miserable that my imagination began breaking apart the chains to free him even before I consciously realized what I was doing. I described this scenario to the readee and explained that I was in the process of conducting a healing in which I was helping the two of them make separations, and was shocked when the woman yelled at me for interfering with their relationship! She explained that if she let him go she would feel too lonely; she needed him. She ordered me to terminate the healing at once. For the first and only time in my work as a clairvoyant, I ignored her demands and continued with the healing, because I realized that I was here for him, not for her. He had brought her here. He was my true client. She had just come along for the ride. In my healing, I did my best to break the karmic agreement that had bound this being to this woman for centuries. I saw him break free and fly off toward a bright light. However, her will was very strong, and I still don't know for sure whether he managed to escape her entirely.

When you are performing clairvoyant readings and healings, it is imperative that you do all that you can to put your judgments and preconceptions on hold. Many people will come to you complaining that they are being victimized when the opposite it true, just as there will be those people who blame themselves for situations and other people's behavior that they could not possibly be responsible for. You will also encounter spirits and other energies attached to them that want you to think the client is bad, so you will be less inclined to help them. Furthermore, if you see that being victimized is a pattern in your client's life, regardless of how much they have truly suffered, it's always most helpful to see whether or how this state of victimhood is serving them, or how they believe it's serving them, because therein usually lies the greatest answer to helping them out of their situation.

CHAPTER 13

Specific Types of Entities

An idea, like a ghost, must be spoken to a little before it will explain itself.
—— CHARLES DICKENS

In this chapter I am going to discuss energy forms that have a certain level of consciousness that I have personally come into contact with. These energies include those that are commonly referred to as spirits, beings, entities, guides, ghosts, alien life forms, angels, demons, spirit councils, ascended masters, and orbs. Names are of course symbols we assign to things, so I don't want anyone to get stuck on what I am calling the entities I've encountered. When I see these entities, like anyone else I ask myself, "What is this? What do I call it?" I then look for something that has the most comparable characteristics to that which others have named.

It's not as if these things walk out to me with an outstretched hand and state, "Hi, I'm an alien" or "I'm an angel." Instead, I see them, observe them, and decide which category they seem to fit into. I am most certain that many entities will take on a particular façade in order to achieve a certain effect on the viewer, whether to ease our fears or to scare the pants off us, so it is important not to get too caught up in appearances or in labeling. Still, for simplicity's sake, in this chapter I am using the common names for these entities with the hope that my observations or experiences will add more data to the unofficial collection that has been accruing on the subject for centuries.

Spirit Guides

My definition of a *spirit guide* is an entity that desires to offer guidance in some way. Like the millions of living people who serve others, spirit guides are a diverse group of beings that exhibits an enormous spectrum of personality traits, motivations, and altruistic behaviors. Some spirit guides exist for the sole purpose of aiding humans. The extent of their love, purity, and selflessness is at a level that we cannot even comprehend. (This includes spirits in and out of physical bodies.) Some spirit guides are deceased relatives and friends. However, not all of these guides are enlightened.

One of the first eye-opening realizations I had as a clairvoyant student was that many deceased spirits who pass over to the other side remain just as ignorant, judgmental, opinionated, and messed-up as they were when they were alive. It seems as if many of the spirits that fall into this category do want to assist the living, but their methods of problem solving and communication can be dysfunctional, disruptive, and sometimes just plain silly. People who were particularly controlling, domineering, stubborn, and authoritarian when they were alive seem to hold on to these characteristics for quite a while after they die, perhaps because their staunch thinking does not permit them to accept the new reality they are in. These beings are likely to continue to pass judgment on their living relatives and to boss them around, out of the "goodness of their hearts."

As a clairvoyant reader, you will want to use discernment when receiving messages or advice from spirit guides, since the advice may be earth-shattering or it may be akin to what you'd find written on a bathroom wall (which I guess is sometimes exactly what you need to hear at a particular moment, even if it's crude!).

Deceased Relatives and Loved Ones

As a clairvoyant, once you realize you have the ability to tune in to the spirit world, it's quite normal to want to check up on someone who has just died. This is a fantastic way to gain insights into life after death and beyond. However, I advise you to be very cautious with what you do with the information or communication you receive. One of the biggest mistakes psychics make is to tread upon others' grieving processes by providing information that has come to the psychic either spontaneously or by intentionally tuning in. I am not saying this isn't sometimes welcomed. In fact, it can be the one thing that saves the grieving person from having a complete meltdown. Conversely, it can be taken as a gross intrusion into something very private that could serve to destroy your relationship.

Sometimes the grieving person thinks, "Why would my deceased relative or friend come to you and not to me?" These people obviously aren't able to understand that perhaps they are not objective enough or clear enough to receive the information at that time, particularly if they don't even believe in psychic communication with spirits or they have been programmed by their places of worship to believe this type of communication is evil. Sometimes the grieving person just isn't ready to share their feelings or memories with the over-eager psychic, particularly if they haven't been that close to the psychic before. So if you do have some information for a grieving person, I suggest you use your clairvoyance to determine whether or not they would be open to your communication. It may be a matter of timing. This is pretty much true of psychic information you've received about any topic. After making a couple of painful mistakes in my early days as a clairvoyant student (mostly due to overzealousness), I have a general rule: I don't share unless someone asks. That being said, many times people ask and I just haven't taken or don't want to take the time to look.

It seems as if there are countless paths a soul can follow upon discarding their physical body. Just as living people will have totally unique reactions, responses, and effects after undergoing similar experiences, there are limitless potential responses and effects on a spirit that experiences the death of its own body. A deceased person's personality, philosophy, and understanding of death;

their attachment to the physical body and to possessions and relationships; their vulnerability to others' feelings and thoughtforms; and the circumstances that surrounded their death all play a role in how their spirit is affected and where the spirit goes after death.

Sometimes a client will be upset because they feel they are unable to communicate or connect with the spirit of a deceased loved one, and many times I have had the sense that the reason for this is that the deceased really no longer exists as we understand existence. I have seen in my readings that some spirits pass over into a realm that is so far away from the physical plane that all that remains of them or their connection to the physical world is an echo. This echo is like an inanimate hologram of the deceased spirit's body, personality, and voice that a clairvoyant can see and describe, but there is no conscious interaction in present time. The many brief glimpses I've seen into the places spirits go after death have been only shadows, and I had to be careful not to project my own perceptions onto the experience, particularly since my readees are usually quite inclined to do this as well. Some readees will even try to corner me into agreeing with their limited perceptions and argue with me when I refuse to do so.

During these experiences I've had the feeling that my mind was only able to comprehend about 2 percent of what really was going on way out there. I hope this will change as I continue to grow as a person and as a psychic. On the other hand, when a spirit is quite present around a living person, there is usually no way for me to miss them, and information about these earthbound spirits is a lot easier to comprehend.

Our Attitudes Toward the Dead Determine Their Next Steps

A few years ago I gave a reading to a woman whose five-year-old son had died after a lengthy illness. She wanted to know that his spirit was all right. When I tuned in to his spirit I saw that he was not all right.

I saw an image of him lying in a bed, with all kinds of tubes running in and out of his body. He seemed to be in an uncomfortable, groggy state of confused unconsciousness, somewhere between a sleeping and waking state. I felt he was stuck in the trauma of his death.

His mother confirmed to me that her son had died in the hospital and that she feared he had suffered more from the treatment than from the illness itself. When I asked his soul along with God what would help to free his spirit, I was told that his mother's thoughtforms played a significant role. Her unhappy thoughts were actually pinning him down and trapping him in a repetitive reenactment of his traumatic death. She needed to visualize him being all right, at peace.

When I told the woman this information, she admitted that the only way she could ever picture her son was as he was during those final weeks in the hospital. She never pictured him happily playing with his toys or laughing; it was almost impossible for her to recall how he looked when he was healthy. I saw and told her that she must, for both of their sakes, train her mind to visualize her son in an absolutely perfect state of health and happiness whenever she thought of him. One thing that would help her was to look at photographs of her son that had been taken prior to his illness. She admitted that she had many such photos but had not looked at them since his death.

This reading continues to haunt me because, just as any other mother would, I wanted desperately to see that the spirit of this woman's son was all right. No matter what I see in my readings, emotionally I want to believe that when anyone dies they immediately go to a better place—a beautiful, wondrous place where they find peace. At the same time, I am thankful for the understanding my readings have given me regarding the power we as spirits in physical bodies hold over disembodied spirits. We are actually as much their guides as they are ours. We have the ability to free them or to hold them captive. We can affect their destinies.

There are many people who are meant to die a pain-free death but who are chained mercilessly to their failing bodies by the selfish grief of their loved ones. We need to rechannel our love for the dying into saving their spirits rather than their physical bodies. The greatest gift you can give to a dying person is to celebrate their passing and the life they have just accomplished, as the Tibetans (read *The Book of the Dead*) and many indigenous cultures do.

As a clairvoyant reader, you will be presented with plenty of situations in which your natural inclination will be to provide assurances that everything is all right when it's really not. Such statements may make your readee feel better in the moment, but ultimately no one will be served—because whatever problem is occurring will continue and ultimately your client will realize you were not being honest, which will create a whole other level of pain. When you are faced with giving upsetting information as I was in the above example, use your clairvoyance to generate feasible steps that your readee can take to alter or mend the situation. This is ultimately why your readee has come to you, whether they know it or not.

Angels

I did not start out believing in angels; I used to think Catholics and New Age enthusiasts put way too much stock in them. However, from time to time I do see angels in my meditations, as well as figures that look like angels standing behind my clients. These angels seem to have a very different vibration from other spirit guides. When I think of them I hear a single musical note, about two octaves above middle C. Their energy reminds me of the energy of certain mountainous areas where there is a lot of open space and clear skies. They seem unencumbered by the thoughtforms, emotions, and agendas that many other spirits carry. They actually seem to be less obtrusive and invasive than any other beings I have observed.

The angels I've observed seem to be prepared to help, but they won't step in until they hear a call for help. This call could come in the form of a willful silent prayer, or from the screaming heart of a person in need. I wish I could say angels make up most of the population of the spirit world; however, as most of the psychics I know will agree, they only make up a very small percentage. If you see an angel in a clairvoyant reading, say hello to the angel and ask it what its purpose is, what its favorite name is, and how the readee can better communicate with it.

Sometimes I see my clients with angel wings, and I have the sense that this client is an earthbound angel. Occasionally, I see clients with broken wings. These broken wings seem to symbolize that this soul came from a place where evil was not known and they've had an especially hard time coping in this lifetime, not just with the ugliness on Earth but with the very fact that ugliness exists at all. They are also vulnerable to being taken advantage of by others who are not coming from the same place. These souls seem to have a lot of catching up to do when it comes to managing their finances, or with successfully meeting the physical needs of a human body that they may feel quite trapped in.

Healing Guides

Another common class of spirits can be referred to as *healing guides*. These guides are spirits whose main mission and talent is to heal. They are as diverse as the healers within the living human population, with an assortment of methodologies and approaches. Some seem to work individually while others work in clusters. Just as there are surgeons, psychologists, and massage therapists, so there are healing guides who do intensive operations, those who work more on a psychological level, some who are very subtle and gentle in their touch, and some that are quite aggressive and intrusive. Some merely work in your energy field, while others dive right into your body and yank out the energy that is not working well in there.

This latter group includes those healers that I have been working with most closely for the last decade or so, the psychic surgeons. These spiritual surgeons can pull out diseased matter and foreign energies from a specific location in the body. They also fight against lower astral energies and work with students in their dreams to rid them of troublesome entities. I've had quite a few experiences during which clients and even young children, who had no idea that I or my students were using guides in our healings, have seen these spirits and describe them as looking like doctors, with surgical instruments in their hands.

For most of my life, I was pursued, chased, and haunted by any number of lower astral beings who took a variety of forms in my dreams, including those of monsters and criminals. After one week of working with these psychic surgeons and asking them to enter my dreams to assist me, I had a series of dreams in which these guides appeared and helped me to wipe out my attackers. By the next week all signs of any troublesome pursuers in my dreams had vanished. It's been well over a decade since then, and I rarely have dreams of being pursued.

Filipino Psychic Surgeons

When I lived and studied in the Philippines with actual living healers known as psychic surgeons, people with the rare ability to extract physical matter from a person's body by making an actual incision with their bare hands, I was approached by a strong-vibration group of healing spirits of the type that I also refer to as psychic surgeons. These spirits are more aggressive and intense than ones I had worked with previously.

In my own training, I learned to allow spirits to only plug into my hand chakras and to call upon them when I needed them. However, this new group of spirits would plug further into my arms, usually up to my elbows. Sometimes they are so bent on performing a healing with the use of my hands that I find myself wandering around with my arms outstretched, looking for anyone to heal! I usually know I am about to encounter a person who will need and request a healing because my hands, and sometimes my arms, begin to vibrate and twitch as if they have a life of their own. (They just started to do this as I began writing about them!)

It is important when working with any kind of healing guide or spirit guide, no matter how evolved or impressive, that you remember you are ultimately the boss of your own energy field. You call the shots and set the boundaries when it comes to your own body. These spirits are very enthusiastic, and if permitted will infiltrate your aura or chakras and set up camp indefinitely. I recommend only allowing these spirits to plug into your hand chakras until you gain more experience working with healing guides or channeling. (This is good advice to follow in regard to your spiritual teachers in bodies as well!)

Spirits have a number of ways in which they can communicate with you. Just as some of your psychic abilities are more developed than others, the same could be said of disembodied spirits and healing guides. Some communicate through clairvoyance, others communicate through mental telepathy, some communicate through telekinesis, and still others will actually attempt to speak to you on a verbal level. We will be working with the psychic surgeon guides in chapter 16.

Ascended Masters or Gods

I am certain from firsthand experience that God figures, saints, and yogis such as Jesus, Mary, Buddha, and Paramahansa Yogananda continue to exist in spirit form. (Fortunately, they don't care what religion you are!) They will often spontaneously appear to clairvoyants, healers, and even laypeople when their type of energy is needed and welcomed. They have the ability to be everywhere at the same time, so they can be available to many people at once. They have strong healing abilities. They vibrate at such a high frequency and carry such a tremendous amount of light that merely visualizing their image or stating their name is a powerful tool for protection, transformation, insight, and healing. I recommend calling upon one or more of these figures when you are faced with a challenging situation in your healings, particularly when lower astral spirits or energies are involved.

Telekinetic Guides

Another class of spirits are *telekinetic guides*. These guides have the ability to influence physical matter. They can generate sounds that range from a baby's cry to laughter to people chattering to deafening hammering noises. They can beat on drums, turn on children's electrical toys and kitchen appliances, and open and close doors and windows, and so forth. They can also create smells that range from the pleasing aroma of flowers or sage to the noxious odor of feces or spoiled milk. (I have personally experienced this entire spectrum.) These spirits range from lower astral forms (poltergeists) with the mentality or consciousness of a baby to healing spirits of a very high vibration.

Spiritual Councils

During a few readings and in several meditations in which I have practiced astral travel either consciously or inadvertently, I have clairvoyantly encountered councils. These councils seem to be a collective group of spirits that are gathered together for a specific purpose. They seem to have a leader or gatekeeper. These spirits have usually appeared to me as older, arrogant men who took themselves very seriously. They always have the same message for me: "You are not supposed to be here. Go back." They seem to be guarding certain dimensions or information.

Alien Beings

During readings and occasionally during a meditation, I've encountered the traditional-looking Gray aliens. A couple of times they appeared as a group, which reminded me of the council I've just described. There seemed to be numerous miniature Grays, only knee-high, who seemed to be controlled by larger Grays. They appear to operate on a hierarchy, which is one reason they remind me of ants, except for their eyes and the fact I don't like them any more than I like ants.

The first time I ever saw them I was doing a reading for a close friend who was also a clairvoyant student at the time. We were tracing some emotional problems he was currently having that apparently went all the way back to his birth, when suddenly I saw some unusual objects that reminded me of outdoor furniture. I then realized I had never seen furniture like this, and that somehow I was in a place I had never seen before here on Earth. As I had this realization, a gray alien face popped up in my mind, and in no uncertain terms demanded that I get out of where I was. It startled the sh— out of me that the image was actually talking to me! My clairvoyant images almost never interact with me, any more than an actor on television interacts with the viewers. But this one did. He was pushy and controlling, and I have to admit I heeded his instructions and terminated the reading. I felt the consequences of doing battle with him would not be worth the effort.

In 1997 I was traveling by jeepney to the remote terraced villages in the Mountain Province of the Philippines with my son's father, Manuel Lukingan, who was one of the only acupuncturists in the country at the time. We were visiting people who had no access to medical care. Some of them were dying. I was assisting Manuel with clairvoyant diagnosis and doing energetic work on those who could not tolerate the needles.

One early morning I was taking a cold shower, which consisted of dunking a little plastic cup into a barrel of frosty water and pouring it on my head in spastic, agonizing intervals. After a minute or so of this, I felt a pain creep up my spine and settle in the back of my neck. I knew in a way I never had before that I was about to become quite ill, and then I did, with severe flu-like symptoms. What I didn't know at the time was that I was also pregnant.

Yes, I realize that sounds silly coming from a psychic, but I just wasn't ready to admit it yet. (If it makes you feel any better, I did have a psychic dream prior to this in which my son came to me as he looks now and told me, "I am your future child, but you aren't ready to accept this yet.") Anyway, in one of the towns, which consisted of three roadside shacks posing as stores, someone handed me a dilapidated copy of one of Sylvia Browne's early books. I can't tell you how thrilled I was to find a book written in English by a fellow American psychic! Toward the end of the book, there was a healing exercise that instructs the reader to lie down and visualize a room in which the ceiling, floor, and each wall is a different color. (I still love this visualization, but now I am wary of it for reasons you will soon see.) I believe, if I recall correctly, that the next step was to imagine a table or bed in the middle of the room and to see yourself lying down on it.

Since I was feeling so sick, I decided to do this exercise before bed one evening. However, before I read the next steps, I fell into a restless sleep. Sometime after that I woke up and seemed to go right back into the vision of the multicolored room. But now someone else was there with me. It was a tall entity that was unmistakably alien. This alien seemed more feminine than masculine and had a pointed, sloped head that reminded me of the Coneheads from *Saturday Night Live*. I could only see its back or side, and it seemed to have a tray with something on it that was to be used for the healing. There was something very scientific or clinical about its attitude, even though I was pretty certain it was there to heal me. I was really torn about allowing it to work on me; I was feeling so sick, but at the same time I did not totally trust it. Finally, I decided to allow it to work on me, if only for a minute, to see how I felt as we proceeded. However, I immediately fell asleep.

The next thing I knew, I was lying there in my room, looking into the very black, slanted eyes of several gray or greenish aliens. They seemed to be staring at me, extremely close up. I was terrified! I screamed and woke up, freezing cold, only to have the sense they were still right there, only now I couldn't really see them. My screams woke Manuel up, and it took me quite a while to fall back to sleep. However, as soon as I did drift off to sleep, exactly the same thing happened again. I didn't go back to sleep after that. We packed up our few things and moved on to a warmer place. Since that time, I've only seen flashes of these guys in meditation or during readings. I know it's not very neighborly, but I really can't even stand to look at funny pictures of them.

Several years ago I gave a reading to a sweet, innocent-looking college student in Berkeley, who had a part-time job as a prostitute (well, *dominatrix* was the term she used, but only after I described a vision I received of her donned in black leather undergarments and whipping some sorry-looking sap). What disturbed me more than her occupation was that I saw her hungrily chowing down on what seemed to be psychedelic mushrooms. These seemed to be causing her a slew of problems in school and with her thought processes. When I told her that it appeared her unusual addiction to these mushrooms was keeping her from reaching her educational goals (something I was afraid to mention for fear she'd tell me I was wrong and nuts), she became quite angry and adamantly insisted that even though she was having a lot of personal problems, she would never, ever, *ever* stop eating these mushrooms! She stated this with such conviction that I almost fell off my chair!

I looked to see what was contributing to her addiction and was surprised to see what appeared to be an entity turning a switch on her back as if she were a wind-up doll. He was quite grotesque and had a bulbous, ugly white face and a big transparent head displaying an oversized brain. I somehow knew at once this was an alien being. In my vision, he had her tied up in ropes and was feeding her mushrooms. I had the eerie feeling that it was he who was speaking when she told me she would never give up her drug habit. I wondered if he wasn't somehow participating in her role as a dominatrix as well. That was one of the oddest clairvoyant experiences I've had, and really the only one in which I had such a strong sense that an entity involved in promoting someone's addiction was an alien.

A couple of years ago I had a dream that I was lying in bed embracing a tall female alien that seemed to be very sick—actually dying of something like cancer. She was mostly white but had some other colors in her as well. I seemed to be doing a healing on her by using my whole body, but I was rather uncomfortable with the whole thing. The strange thing was that her face seemed to be covered with these large rock-like jewels that were embedded in her, and I knew if the jewels came out she'd have large holes in her face. I woke up from this dream very disturbed and not feeling well.

More recently I had a very vivid dream of an alien: this one also had a head larger than felt normal for a human. His eyes were not like that of the Grays; instead, his eyes reminded me of the eyes of a fish. They were spread out so that they almost seemed to be on either side of his head. In the dream I specifically told him that I wanted more than anything else to remember this experience when I awoke. He assured me I would. He then approached my partner, Danny, who in reality is about as skeptical as you can be about aliens, and stated very clearly, "Someday you will know for sure that we exist." Danny says he's still a skeptic, but he seems to get rather perturbed when I remind him of this message (which I like to do quite often)!

Baby Beings

Baby beings are a particular group of spirits that have a strong desire to experience life as human beings on earth. They are desperately seeking parents who will bear them, and they will stop at nothing to achieve their goals. Some of these beings are in fact meant to be born. They have strong agreements with certain individuals, and it is only a matter of correct timing before the proper body is created for them to inhabit. These beings are usually conceived easily and born without much trauma.

These beings can be both of service and annoying. They can actually help create relationships, as they are able to indirectly introduce prospective parents to one another. They can also stimulate people's sex drives and help manifest anything on the physical level that will facilitate their conception and birth. These beings can convince people to say no to safe sex and cause the most conscientious women to forget to use birth control. Some of these beings are actually the leaders behind the right-to-life movement! At least a couple of them, at this very moment, are sending pain into my third eye, causing me to get sleepy all of a sudden! They are probably doing this so as not to alert the world to their presence.

(Okay, I'm back. I had to clear them out, and then I took a long nap!) Then there are those beings that, for whatever reason, are unable or not meant to inhabit a particular body or any body, no matter how much they think they want to do so. Sometimes these spirits are just too weak or uninvolved; some of them are essentially alien beings whose energy would not be compatible with that of a human body. In my readings I have seen that many miscarriages and abortions involve this latter of group of spirits.

Sometimes, when the spirit's efforts to be born are thwarted, as in the case of a miscarriage or when the targeted parents fail to meet each other or stay together, the spirit can become very frustrated, angry, fearful, or panicked. These feelings are easily transmitted to the targeted potential parents, who are usually unaware of the presence of these beings and therefore naturally attribute their feelings to a problem within themselves or their relationship (which causes the beings to become even more frantic). People who are obsessed with having babies are often being tormented by frustrated baby beings. Someone's obsession with a particular person is often also connected with the influence of a baby being.

Women who have had miscarriages or abortions are often hammered by confused beings that don't understand they will never and can never be born. I have seen this in dozens of readings with women whose past histories I knew nothing about. Sometimes these beings are literally trapped with the women's body or aura. These beings could wreak havoc on the woman's self-esteem and emotional, mental, and physical health throughout her lifetime if she is not aware of them. Most people are constantly surrounded by a multitude of baby beings, although they may only have strong agreements with one or two of these beings, agreements that may or may not pan out.

Not all baby beings are cute and cuddly. They are more like reckless toddlers with a ferocious appetite and little regard for others. Just like their potential parents, some are very capable, intelligent, loving, and evolved, while others possess none of the qualities you would want in your own offspring.

Creating, Updating, and Healing Agreements

You can create agreements with baby beings that you would like to bring into this world, as well as break strong agreements that have not come to fruition, by using the same methods you would to create or break agreements with living beings, as discussed in chapter 12.

Simple Methods for Moving Out Most Baby Beings

Many baby beings are pestering you merely because you have the ability to create a baby, or they think you do (some don't understand the meaning of menopause or infertility!). You can unwittingly pick them up from anyone, particularly members of the opposite sex who are attracted to you or to whom you are attracted. Clairvoyant readers also tend to inadvertently attract them during readings and healings. You will have little connection with most of these beings, so it will be easy to extract them from your aura with some simple visualization techniques.

You can easily perform the following healing on yourself or someone else. Ground yourself. Create and ground your reading screen. On your screen, visualize your body surrounded by your aura. Postulate that every baby being that you are not in agreement to bear as a baby is going to light up as a sparkling blue balloon. Imagine that you are collecting all these balloons and tying their strings together to make one large bundle of balloons. Say hello to these balloons and explain to them that you cannot be their mommy or daddy, and that it is time to move on. Let them know this is an order, not a suggestion.

Tie this bundle of balloons onto the railing of a special crib that is nicely decorated with fluffy down pillows and shiny quilted blankets. Ground this crib into the center of the planet with a heavy-duty grounding cord that is decorated with pictures of cute fuzzy animals. Turn on the mobile attached to the crib that plays soothing music so they will have some entertainment on their journey. You can ask the spirit/balloon that is the strongest of these beings to rise up above the others, and appoint it the task of protecting and overseeing the other spirits/balloons. Then take a giant imaginary scissors and cut the grounding cord of the crib. Watch as the crib floats upward, out the window, into the sky, past the horizon, past the atmosphere, past the stars and the universe to a place that is commonly referred to as God or heaven.

Following this exercise, it is vital that you fill up your body and aura with your own energy, particularly in any areas where the baby beings were plugged into. These areas will be more vulnerable to reinfestation from other beings who will be less able to plug in if you are adequately running enough of your own energy through these areas. Also, destroy your grounding cord in case any baby beings are hanging on to it, and create a new one. As you do the above healing, on yourself or someone else, you will likely experience sensations of pain, pressure, or temperature change as the baby beings are stimulated and released. It is advisable to repeat this healing at least once a week (this is something you can easily teach to your clients) or whenever you feel you are being affected by these beings.

Lower Astral Entities

A plethora of parasitic beings are attracted to and feed on the energies of pain, fear, hatred, and addiction. Some have almost no consciousness or self-awareness, while others are highly intelligent but lack a conscience. I have witnessed in my readings how these beings gravitate toward abuse of drugs, alcohol, violent films depicting demonic images, some heavy metal music, sadistic/masochistic sex, and physical and sexual abuse. People who engage in or subject themselves to these activities are more vulnerable to attack or infiltration of these beings, or seek out these activities due to the influence of these beings. Many people see these beings as snakes, spiders, rodents, and roaches.

In my readings I occasionally see images of snakes, spiders, and roaches nestled somewhere in the readee's aura, chakras, or physical organs, where they cause pain and disrupt the flow of energy. Sometimes these beings are sitting on eggs. Sometimes they scurry away and hide when they see me; other times they do nothing. When I utilize the technique of erasure (see chapter 14), often both my readee and I can physically feel pain as the being is eradicated.

I have witnessed, during readings and in my personal life, the surprisingly detrimental impact these beings can have on relationships. They interfere with communication, causing confusion, doubt, and mistrust. I have seen over and over again how these beings can disrupt and destroy even a strong relationship between two people who love one another. When the beings are eradicated from the relationship and energy fields of the individuals, instantaneous healing and rejuvenation of the relationship often occurs.

Demons

Demons are similar to but slightly more intelligent or aware than those beings that appear as snakes and spiders. Often in my meditations and when falling asleep at night, I have clairvoyantly seen the faces of demons. Through the years I've come to understand that these ugly, disfigured faces are projections sent by an ill-intentioned group of entities for the purpose of scaring me. On a couple occasions that I am aware of, they infiltrated a reading and tried to turn me against my readee, who was suffering from a variety of drug addictions. They did this by projecting negative, derogatory thoughts. Since I rarely have judgmental thoughts during a reading, it was easy to realize what was happening, step out of these thoughts, and find the source of them.

Demons or other nasty beings will sometimes throw sex pictures at people. I use the term *throw* because that is the sensation, as if something being thrown at you is abruptly landing in your mind. The quality of these pictures is different from other clairvoyant images. They are quite sexually graphic and rude. It's as if an angry guy who wants to throw you off balance or anger you were to throw a hardcore pornographic photo into your lap and laugh at you. This is not going to happen often. But I mention it because these pictures can be thrown at professional psychics and unsuspecting people who are unknowingly being psychic by receiving these pictures. I believe spirits are often at the heart of sexual addictions as well, and can cause us to do some pretty silly, self-comprising things.

I am also mentioning these beings here because I have learned how to destroy and eradicate destructive entities, and now their scare tactics only backfire on them by alerting me to their presence—and I hope to help you learn to do the same. These beings are sometimes connected to a living person who has ill intentions, and the beings' presence alerts me to the fact that I am about to encounter such a person, or that such a person is presently up to no good. I may not know who this person is, but they are usually revealed over the course of the next few days, at which time I am prepared and equipped to clean up any damage they have done.

Mind Eyes

There are also beings whose eyes I see only when I close my own eyes. I don't know if these eyes belong to one specific group of beings or if a variety of beings appear to me in this way. I see these eyes surprisingly clearly. They feel mean and cold. It's as if they are in my head, watching me. They appear sporadically, unexpectedly, and most often right at the beginning of a reading with other people, so they actually alert me to the fact that there is a spirit I am going to be contending with soon. Usually I will ask the being to introduce itself. If I don't get a response (I rarely do in these cases), I then tell the being in no uncertain terms to leave. If it still doesn't leave, I threaten to erase it. If it still does not leave, then I hook it up to God, give it a grounding cord, and wait to see if the eyes disappear. If they do not, then I do use the technique of erasure, at which point the eyes always disappear.

Dwarf Tree Spirits

Another group of spirits I have clairvoyantly encountered in readings, dreams, and in waking life are those I refer to as *dwarf tree spirits*. These are boxy, homely guys who stand only two to three feet tall. They dwell outside, near trees and sometimes water. They are very mischievous and even mean-spirited. I never get the feeling that they will do too much damage, but they do like to trick and toy with people for their own entertainment. This is how they have fun.

When performing readings outside or in a building that is near a wooded area, be aware that these and other kinds of nature spirits may attempt to interfere with your reading by distracting you or the readee, or by playing around with the images you see. By now you have learned enough tools to adequately deal with varmints such as these!

Walk-ins

Walk-in is a common term among psychics, referring to a spirit that has taken over a body that did not originally belong to the spirit. Most of the time there was another spirit who gave up the body, either before the new spirit arrived or at the same time. Sometimes when a baby is born, the baby's spirit is not fully connected into the body or the spirit departs or is forced out of the body during infancy or early childhood. This commonly happens when the baby or child is placed in a dangerous and traumatic situation, such as during a physical accident or in a domestic-violence situation. Often, during a near-death experience or during a severe psychotic episode, the person's spirit will actually take its next step and vacate the body. Sometimes there will be a period of time before another being moves in; at other times the transfer will happen immediately. This is one reason why many people seem significantly changed after they have recovered from a near-death experience.

Walk-ins are often fairly easy to identify because they seem to have greater difficulty operating the physical body than spirits that have been born into a body and matured with it. Many mentally ill people and street people are walk-ins who can't operate the body well enough to handle maintaining a job, paying rent, or even conversing in an intelligible manner. Some walk-ins are more adept at handling the physical body, due either to experience or to having a better body/being connection, but even they will still have difficulties dealing with other people. People who are high-functioning walk-ins often explain that they feel different from others, and have a sense that they don't really belong here. Some walk-ins seem to come from other planets or dimensions that are very different from our own. I've also suspected that some people who are obsessed with aliens and UFOs may be walk-ins from places other than Earth.

During your clairvoyant readings you may occasionally encounter a walk-in. You will begin to get some clues during the initial stages of the reading when you are attempting to tune in to the readee's spirit, although the situation may not become totally apparent until much later in the reading, when your clairvoyant images unexpectedly reveal information about the exodus of the original spirit and the entry of the one sitting in front of you.

Some people who are walk-ins tend to change their name soon after the transfer. They also tend to remember less than other people do about their past. Some people who are walk-ins realize exactly who they are and are even familiar with the term. Others don't realize this but are actually relieved when they find out, because it explains so many of their feelings and difficulties.

If you suspect that the person sitting in front of you is a walk-in, use your clairvoyance to help them understand why it is they chose to come into that particular body at that time, what their agreement was or is with the original occupant of the body, and what actions they can take to help themselves cope with life on Earth. Don't try to remove that spirit (your readee) from the body unless it is clear that the original owner is still very much present within the body and fighting with every ounce of its being to regain sole ownership of the body. Otherwise you may end up with an unconscious body on your hands!

Space Invaders

Space invader is a term I have coined to describe a walk-in that is either in the process of kicking out the original owner from their body or is cohabitating with them within their body. I have done several clairvoyant readings in which I have encountered these types of beings. These readings were particularly difficult. I had a sense something was going on, but I couldn't quite put my finger on it until the being sent an electric shock through my third chakra, at which point I suddenly became very aware that there was a very large spirit that was dominating most of my readee's body, one not at all happy that I was seeing him.

I am not sure why this being chose to shock me in this way, other than to try to scare me and chase me away. However, this kind of response always has the opposite effect on me, in that it motivates me to investigate the source of this attack. Although the shock is uncomfortable and, well, shocking, it is not really any more painful than receiving an electric shock from static electricity so it doesn't scare me in the least, even though it tends to fill up my entire solar plexus. When I become aware that another being is cohabitating within my readee's body, I will often clairvoyantly look to see what the agreement is between the two spirits. I will then gingerly address the subject, and test the waters to see if the readee has any level of awareness of the situation. I will usually ask them if they would like a healing on this situation. Sometimes they will say yes. Other times they will refuse, telling me they think they need this spirit.

In my early days as a clairvoyant student there were times when I earnestly attempted to talk the readee into removing such a spirit from their body, only to discover later that it was the invading spirit that I had been addressing all along. I would open my eyes and see this being staring angrily at me from behind the readee's eyes. On a few occasions, the readee's spirit actually vacated the readee's body and another spirit took over during the course of the reading. It became clear that the invading spirit was not at all open to any kind of communication from me, and the most prudent course of action seemed to be to end the reading and get out of there as quickly as possible!

Sometimes a readee will share their body with a number of spirits. A few years ago a very sophisticated-looking woman who owned her own business and appeared very confident sat down in front of me for a reading. I spent several minutes describing her personality characteristics, and then suddenly I began describing other characteristics that seemed to contradict the ones I had just mentioned. I felt as if I kept losing my connection with her spirit, so I frequently asked her to state her name to regain that connection. I began to realize that I was not actually reading her; I was reading instead at least two if not several spirits who seemed to be flying in and out of her body at their leisure.

In order to make sure I was still tuned in to the woman's particular vibration, I asked her to say her name one last time, but I got no response. My eyes were closed so I could not see her to determine why she was not responding. I asked her again to state her name, but she still remained silent. I asked her if she was not responding because she didn't want to repeat her name. I still got no response. I then got the eerie feeling that maybe she was not able to respond, and I asked her if this was the case. I opened up my eyes and saw a look of complete horror on her face. She began crying, and she explained that she literally could not remember her name. I performed a clairvoyant healing to move out the beings enough so her spirit could come back in, and she was once again able to say her name. She later admitted that she had been diagnosed by two therapists as having multiple personality disorder, although she had felt this was not an accurate diagnosis.

My reading later revealed that she had been severely abused as a child and had called in these spirits to help her cope with the abuse. This is a common scenario among people who suffer from possession by multiple spirits, as well as people who are diagnosed with multiple personality disorder, which I have found is always related to possession. Although this client acknowledged she had been abused, she began to get very condescending and hostile toward me and I realized she was not emotionally able to handle addressing these issues at that time.

I believe that the reason some patients diagnosed with multiple personality disorder actually test positive for physical illnesses such as diabetes or hypertension when they are exhibiting one personality, but test negative for these disorders when exhibiting another personality, is because they are actually channeling other entities. These diseases are linked as much if not more so to the spirit within the body as they are to the body itself.

Extrasensory Emotional Energy

Emotions are one form of energy. Such energy is generated from within our bodies but is very often projected outward to other people and our environment; this is the primary way people release their emotions. This release might make someone feel better, but it can make those around the person miserable and even sick. Just look at the spouse or long-term partner of an unhappy person who doesn't know how to deal with their own emotions, and you will almost certainly find someone who has or has had cancer or another equally unpleasant disease, particularly if they never really knew how to block this invasive energy.

The emotional energy generated through a heated argument or a violent or traumatic incident can linger inside a room or building for decades. Anyone, but particularly a sensitive person, will feel and experience this energy as they step into this area. Most of the time they will not understand the dynamics involved, but they may experience the emotions as their own. In this case they may feel and exhibit anger, fear, or depression more intensely than usual.

I've seen and directly experienced how this energy can impact people on a physical level by making them weaker, causing them to lose their balance, drop things, and become nauseous or dizzy. It can interfere with electrical equipment, computers, and lights. This extraneous emotional energy can also seep into furniture, clothing, and especially jewelry. Sometimes it is mistaken for an actual entity. More often than not, it's found in the same locations where other entities are having an impact on the current occupants.

CHAPTER 14

Battle Techniques

*The victorious strategist only seeks battle after the victory
has been won, whereas he who is destined to defeat first fights
and afterward looks for victory.*
— SUN TZU

Techniques for Handling Troublesome Entities

In your readings you will undoubtedly encounter troublesome entities at some point. They may appear as I have described them in this book, or they may look totally different; however, you will know what they are when you see them. Evil occasionally disguises itself behind the appearance of a loved one or loving one but can only do so for so long before its true nature betrays itself. If you ever see an image of a loved one in your readings, meditations, dreams, or waking life but something seems slightly off or makes you feel uncomfortable (e.g., a look in their eyes, the color of their hair), you can be fairly certain a being is trying to imitate that person in order to lower your defenses or trick you.

In one of my dreams several years ago, a spirit disguised itself as one of my respected teachers and told me that my boyfriend at the time was cheating on me and that I should break up with him. The teacher took my hand and asked me to follow him. I felt a level of devastation I've never before felt in a dream. However, as I walked down a corridor with this teacher, I suddenly became aware that my teacher's eyes were brown instead of their true color, blue. The moment I noticed this, the spirit could no longer maintain its disguise and its diabolical face was revealed.

On another occasion I entered my front door and saw this same friend standing in my hallway. I was confused because he didn't have a key and I had just left his house. Then I realized I was looking at an image of him that was not entirely solid, and I thought, "Oh, he must have decided to pay me an astral visit, maybe he misses me." But then I felt a cold chill wrap around me, and I saw his eyes. There was something off about his eyes, something evil. That's when I knew it was not him; it was an evil entity trying to impersonate him. I told the entity that I knew he was not who he was pretending to be and ordered him to leave at once, which he did.

It is important to remember that you always have the advantage over disembodied spirits because you have a physical body that is connected to the earth. They use scare tactics to control you because fear brings you down to their vibration. If you are not scared, they ultimately have no power over you. When you see such entities, say hello to them. Let them know that you see them. Some of them are like bullies; they put up a good show of being tough but the moment they understand that you really do see them, they get scared and flee.

These lower astral beings are antisocial; they lack the ability to empathize with and respect human life. Acknowledge their presence but don't try to reform them or get them to understand you. Don't argue with them. Trying to change their nature is like trying to reason with a hungry man eating a tiger. If you try to talk sense into them, you will merely make yourself more vulnerable to their tactics.

If a misguided entity has invaded your territory, then by all means kick it out. However, if you have inadvertently trespassed into their territory (as I did with the Grays and the spiritual council), I recommend turning back and leaving them alone. You actually don't have a right to go anywhere in the universe you please, even if you think you should have such a right.

A few years ago I performed a reading on a man who had recently been diagnosed with schizophrenia. My reading revealed that he was infested with a multitude of parasitic entities that were projecting all kinds of horrifying pictures and thoughts at his sixth chakra. This man was extremely clairvoyant, and he saw these images as clearly as if they were really there. He was also extremely clairaudient; he could hear the thoughts of spirits and living people as loudly as if they were standing inside his head. His complaints that things were crawling over and around his body and his paranoid thoughts of persecution were actually astute perceptions of the energies that were in fact attacking him, rather than the unjustified delusions his doctors naturally assumed them to be.

When I attempted to remove these beings during a healing, I clairvoyantly saw that this man did not really want these beings to go. He had some kind of fascination with them. I saw that he spent hours on the Internet researching subjects like aliens and ghosts, and that this was opening up doors that were attracting the beings to him. When I suggested that he get rid of all his books on the subject and avoid the Internet altogether, he adamantly insisted that he was not going to abandon his favorite pastime just because these beings were upsetting him; he was going to make it his mission find them and fight them until his death. It looked as though death would not be too far away for him if his combative attitude persisted.

When you choose to actively go into battle with a person or entity, you become intimately entwined with that spirit. (This is what happens when you sue someone; you end up engaging with them and perhaps suffering more than if you just took the loss and severed that unpleasant connection.) Self-protection or prevention is one thing; an offensive invasion into their territory is a whole other ballgame and some people just don't know when to back off! Whenever you think about an entity (or person), you give them your energy. I suggest that you don't talk about them or even think about them except when you spontaneously see them and need to deal with them.

The high vibration of amusement or a sense of humor is your greatest weapon.

When you see or sense an unpleasant entity, use your great imagination to dress them up in funny clothes. Pretend that they are wearing a sparkly-pink baby girl's dress with a matching frilly bonnet and sunglasses with little birdies on the ends. Throw them into a pink baby carriage, plop a bottle of milk into their homely mouths, and take them for a ride through a lovely garden while you tell them silly monster jokes. Many spirits will automatically depart because they won't be able to breathe in the vibration of amusement you are creating. If they are vibrating in fear and you are not, it's like being on two different floors of a building. You can take the elevator up just by pressing the amusement button with your thoughts and feelings.

Esther and Jerry Hicks' book *Ask and It Is Given* is an excellent resource for understanding the vibrational scale of emotions. While the authors of this book present this information in order to assist readers with manifestation, I think it's also helpful in terms of breaking free from all the entities that feed off and instigate the lower emotional vibrations of humans.

If these entities don't disappear, then there are several other tactics you can apply. But you must ensure you do your very best to apply these tactics while holding on to your sense of humor and amusement.

On your reading screen, see this spirit connected up to God with a cord of brilliant light and connected into the planet with a strong grounding cord. Imagine that God has giant hands, and you are gently placing the spirit into God's hands. Thank God for taking this spirit away.

As you do the above, feel free to call in help from an ascended master or one of your guides. Whether or not you consider yourself to be a Christian, the name of Christ is a powerful symbol that has been used for centuries in exorcisms. (I'm Jewish and it works for me!) In the name of Christ, demand confidently with every ounce of your being that this spirit is now banished from your kingdom. State this demand out loud.

You can also create a large viewing receptacle, such as a rose, a glass bubble, a boat, or a cage. Visualize the entity inside the receptacle. Send the receptacle far away, into outer space or across the globe to the bottom of the ocean, and then watch the receptacle as it explodes into a trillion specks of light that ultimately will be returned to the source of all creation.

The Power of Repetition

Religions and spiritual disciplines have long understood the power of repetition for prayer, manifestation, and protection. Just about all religions utilize repetitive words, sounds, or phrases known as mantras; others put these to music, which is called chanting. Roman Catholics utilize a beaded rosary called a chaplet that helps them say the prayers that they must repeat over and over again. Tibetan prayer wheels (called *mani wheels* by the Tibetans) are devices for spreading spiritual blessings and well-being. Rolls of thin paper, imprinted with many, many copies of the mantra (prayer) Om mani padme hum, printed in an ancient Indian script or in Tibetan script, are wound around an axle in a protective container, and spun around and around. Tibetan Buddhists believe that saying this mantra, out loud or silently to oneself, invokes the powerful benevolent attention and blessings of Chenrezig, the embodiment of compassion.

Repetition accomplishes a few things. It builds up energy in a person's psyche; that energy and the thoughtforms can then project themselves more powerfully. By repeating an intention, affirmation, or prayer over and over again, we reaffirm it, energize it, implant it. Doing so also seems to clear out whatever is opposite to that which is being repeated. Repetition can clear our minds, and it eliminates matter from space.

Make Your Own Prayer Wheel

Choose a prayer that states your intention, and repeat it over and over again. You can make your own prayer wheel by writing down your prayer over and over as many times as possible, then taking a lint brush that you can get at any store, taping the prayer to the brush, and spinning the wheel. This can be done with any prayer to evoke any desired intention and is effective with difficult entities.

One prayer that I like to say—sometimes in full, sometimes just in part—is "The light is all-powerful, powerful is the light. It shall dissolve all and anything not of the light. I am all-powerful, I am the light. God is all-powerful, God is the light. Together we generate the power of one million lights that will turn all darkness to light, darkness to light, darkness to light. So it is, so it will be, for now and forever more." (An abbreviated version is "The light is all powerful, powerful is the light.")

Remember that darkness is only the absence of light, so on the spiritual plane, as soon as you increase the light, darkness ceases to exist. As you repeat your prayer or mantra, imagine the brightest light you could ever imagine pouring from the wheel and zapping and consuming the negative entity, like a light saber from Star Wars. You can also use this technique for moving out any kind of negative energy from another person's body or aura as well as for dealing directly with entities.

Weapons of Mass Destruction

While the word *mass* may have startled you, I use it here to refer to matter! The following techniques can be utilized when extreme measures are called for. These techniques are designed to instantly weaken and ultimately eliminate the structural building blocks of an entity so that it will no longer exist. It's important to understand that the following steps must not be done on living people. Instead, these techniques are intended only for those demonic or low-vibration entities in spirit form that are attacking you, draining you, or causing you to have violent or obsessive thoughts. These can also be utilized as mini-exorcisms or to remove parasitic beings during your clairvoyant reading/healing sessions with others.

Establish Communication If Possible

Visualize your reading screen. Create a viewing receptacle. Demand that the source of whatever it is that might be causing you discomfort or unease show itself in your receptacle. Watch it and see what comes up. Look for a color. You can either see how it affects the rose you are looking at or see if you get an actual image.

Once you get something, you can communicate telepathically and ask it what it wants or why it is there. See what response you get, but it is important to understand you may not be able to trust it and you will want to use your clairvoyance to evaluate the communication. If you are working on yourself and you have determined you definitely want the spirit or entity to vacate your premises, you can first politely tell it to leave. Then demand that it *must* leave.

Imagine you are opening up a door in the receptacle or on your screen and tell the critter that it either has to leave on its own or you will destroy it. If you like, you can visualize a symbol for

God and create a tube or column of light running from the door to God; imagine that this tube or column is an elevator or a teleportation machine like the transporter in *Star Trek*.

Show the spirit the light and see if it goes or if God takes it. You can also call in some of your backup spirit guides. See these as glowing yellow figures there to help escort the critter out, up, and away. Remember to keep up your sense of humor and amusement. Tell yourself some jokes and dress up the spirit in funny clothes.

When Working With a Client

If you are reading someone else, then I suggest that you describe the spirit and your clairvoyant findings to them, asking your client if they would like you to help them get rid of the critter. If your client is confused, you can do a reading on that confusion by putting up a new receptacle on the screen and inviting the energy of confusion into it so you can take a look at it. Sometimes the confusion is the being not wanting to let go. If you have not done one already, you can also do a relationship reading at this point (as discussed in chapter 4) around the agreement between the person and this entity. Doing such a reading will help both of you decide how to proceed.

If your readee objects to you evicting the spirit, you can ask your readee if they'd be open to you moving the spirit out of their body or aura enough so they can make a clear decision, or you can refer your readee to this book, so that when they are ready they can do it themselves. Sometimes it can get confusing in your readings, because if a person has a strong entity attached to them and you are discussing that entity, the entity may be using more of your readee's body than the readee is and will therefore do whatever it can to hide by making it hard for you to clearly see them or the situation and by convincing the readee that you are the enemy.

Such a scenario only occurs in very rare cases, but I have had the experience in a few readings of spending two hours with a person only to realize in the last five minutes that I was addressing the wrong spirit in the body. I compare these experiences to what Little Red Riding Hood encountered when she arrived at her grandmother's house. She thought she was talking to her grandmother, even warning her grandmother to look out for the big bad wolf, but instead she was really just addressing the wolf dressed in her grandma's clothes.

If you feel as though there is more of the entity than the original spirit in your readee's body, it is important to remind yourself that it's not up to you to break any agreements for your readee but rather to look at these agreements and the situation, communicate them, and do what you can to bring more awareness so your readee can make the changes.

Call in reinforcements. Give them the option of going to the light. Ask God if God will take them for you.

If it still feels as though the entity isn't leaving, then proceed with the next set of instructions:

Technique #1: Rearrangement

I've been doing this technique lately and getting excellent results. The entity is made of energy. Imagine this energy has finer particles, smaller than atoms and molecules. Your imagination is strong enough to rearrange these particles and essentially reorganize or break down the current organization of this being.

Imagine you are separating the particles and then rearranging them in new places. So if a scary face is popping up, imagine the atoms, molecules, and particles are moving all around, getting jumbled. You could even see the larger elements, such as the eyes, mouth, and other features rearranging themselves to look like a funny face or a fuzzy, cute animal. You can also see these particles breaking up and splitting apart, which is essential as you rearrange this being and it is breaking down. Continue watching until all the particles have broken down and dissipated. This technique should never be performed on a living person. And the other methods should be employed before this step.

Technique #2: The Black Hole Method

Gravity is the most powerful force on the planet; it pulls matter toward the center of the planet. A black hole is thought to be an area where the force of gravity is magnified to the extent that anything coming into its realm will be sucked in at such intensity that it will implode on itself.

Keeping the above in mind, we can either visualize a black hole as a place to send the entity where it will collapse into itself, or see the entity itself as a black hole, collapsing into itself and thus imploding. For this first method, use the power of your imagination to place the entity on a spaceship. Send the spaceship into an image of a black hole and postulate that this black hole you are creating actually does possess the real qualities of a black hole. See the entity inside the spaceship implode over and over again until it disappears.

Another way to do this technique is to visualize the entity itself, or a receptacle with the entity inside, and see this imploding into itself over and over again until the entire image is gone.

Technique #3: Erasure or Duplication

The erasure method is currently taught at a variety of clairvoyant training schools throughout the United States. It was first introduced to the Western world by Lewis Bostwick in the early 1960s. A very powerful method that destroys lower astral entities, it essentially erases the entities' information so they no longer exist. I can't exactly explain the mechanics behind it, but it really seems to work and often elicits a powerful shift in a person who has been bothered by a disembodied spirit or entity. This is a great exercise to practice during your own meditations, even if there is not presently an entity you wish to get rid of.

You can replace the word *entity* in the directions below with any kind of energy you'd like to rid yourself of (such as pessimism, doubt, hate, and so on). Also, note that just performing this exercise can cause a strong shift in your own energy field that you may consciously experience.

Step 1: Once you are certain that you wish to evict an entity from your space or the space of someone seeking healing, visualize a clear transparent rose. Either see the entity inside the rose, or ask the rose to take on/fill up with the energy of the entity. Watch to see what happens to the rose; note its appearance in terms of color, shape, and size. Next, see a symbol for God above the rose and draw a column of light running down from God, straight through the rose and into the earth. This is grounding it to the light and to the earth. Tell the entity that you have placed it inside the rose and tell it that this is it's one and only opportunity to take a hike. Show it the column of light leading to God and invite it to go there. You can also ask God if God is willing to take this entity off your hands, or if this is something you have to take care of yourself. If you see the entity leaving the rose, or the entire rose moving towards God, or some other image indicating the entity is leaving, then you are done—just visualize the rose dissipating. However, if you still have a sense the entity does not want to go on its own, proceed to the next step.

Step 2: Visualize the rose containing the entity (i.e., spirit) or energy of the entity. Take a good look at it, and then right next to it, create a duplicate version of that rose. So now you will have two of the exact same roses side by side. They should appear identical. Take the second one you just created and imagine you are tossing it right into the first. Notice what happens. The goal is to have both roses disappear, which they quite often do via this process. If they don't disappear, whether both or just one still remains, repeat the process, tossing the second rose into the first until you have a strong sense they are both gone, that you can't see them anymore. If the images are changing on you while you are attempting to perform this technique, imagine that you have a bucket of something called "frozen energy." Pour the bucket over the rose and imagine that the rose absolutely has no power to move or change. Sometimes the entity will impact your visualizations or your confidence about your visualization in order to prevent you from carrying out this technique. I believe most of the time that before the entity can be absolutely destroyed, it ends up leaving on its own accord.

Alternative steps to erasure: If you don't wish to use an image of a rose, you can visualize the entity directly, or you can visualize a card, such as a tarot card, and place the entity on the card. In this case, you will be duplicating the card, and tossing the duplicate of the card into the original.

If you feel you are having trouble with this exercise, you can simply do step 1, and then imagine you are moving the rose with the entity inside off your screen and sending it to a faraway place. Then imagine that the rose with the entity inside is exploding. If there are any remaining pieces, roll these up into a ball and explode the ball. Repeat this process until all pieces seem to be gone.

CHAPTER 15

Basic Aura Healing

Of one thing I am certain, the body is not the measure
of healing—peace is the measure.
— GEORGE MELTON

What Is Clairvoyant Energy Healing?

To me, healing is merely replacing something undesirable with something desirable. It's transforming that which is out of balance into a greater state of equilibrium. Healing includes replacing pain, disease, and discomfort with a state of health. It also includes replacing mental and emotional distress with a state of peace, enthusiasm, and excitement. Healing can also mean opening a closed mind, releasing limits to expanding one's range of possibilities, transforming one's negative sense of self into a more positive sense of self, and transforming one's apathy into creativity.

It doesn't take long for an clairvoyant to realize that not only is there a mind/body/spirit connection, but they are also really all parts of the same thing. The concept of "we are all one" takes on new meaning when we see for ourselves how people are sharing the same thoughts and emotions, and how strongly one person, with or without awareness, can influence another through thought or emotion alone. Clairvoyants see firsthand how there is a very real correlation between our physical pain and our thoughts, emotions, and even our relationships with others. When you enable someone to release thoughts and emotions that are no longer serving them, this can significantly impact their physical body. Conversely, changes on the physical level can drastically impact our thoughts and feelings. Our mind/body/spirit connection is not a closed system. To the contrary, it is very much connected with the minds and spirits of everyone around us, including people we no longer have physical contact with, people we have not actually met yet, and people we may never meet.

When you as a clairvoyant even just begin to "look" at someone, doing so spontaneously effects a change in them, and that change resonates outward to all the people both of you are connected with. As noted elsewhere in this book and in *You Are Psychic*, we all carry the energy of others around with us. Their ideas, their judgments, their needs, doubts, and pain become lodged in our bodies and we experience them as our own. So releasing these can have a significant impact on our overall state of well-being, and even on the well-being of the people who have so generously shared the energies with us that we are now trying to release.

We Need to Place Less Emphasis on Cognitive Understanding

Many people think that if they can just figure out the right answer, then everything will be okay and they will broaden their spectrum of what they believe is possible for themselves. Healing can occur when one undergoes a shift in consciousness, and it can also occur through the manipulation of energy. Far too many people try to heal their emotions through thought, and this just doesn't work; it only creates an excess of unproductive mental activity that causes more suffering.

The Power of Simplicity

Because people's thoughts, bodies, problems, and lives are so incredibly complex, it's helpful for us as clairvoyants and particularly as healers to keep things as simple as possible. This is sometimes hard for students or those interested in learning about energy healing to accept. In school we are taught that the more "facts," the more details, and the more complex information we can cram and hold in our minds, the better we will be at any given profession or task.

When it comes to healing, the two most important things are that the intentions of the healer and healee are in alignment with one another, and that the healer can allow herself or himself to be both an active participant and a watchful recipient at the same time. This requires the healer to be able to get out their own way, something that is also the hardest thing for most healers. This is why healing can be particularly powerful in traditions of healing or prophecy in which the healer goes unconscious or leaves their body and allows in another spirit to do the work.

Still, that's not to say the type of healing we are learning here cannot be as powerful; it just requires us to be able to have an intention and let go of that intention at the same time. This is really what's required of us in life. We are always going to have desires and goals, and it's important for us as humans to do all we can to achieve them. At the same time, we need to let go of our emotional attachment to them. When it comes to healing or even saving lives, this is quite a challenge.

The simplest yet most effective healing technique that I've used, received, and now teach to others, is to reduce every issue to its smallest energy component. I define *effective* as achieving both the intended result and unintended consequences that ultimately bring the healee into greater balance. The technique I am about to share can often be felt by the one being healed through a variety of physical sensations, even when the healee is unaware of the healing. However, as a healer it is important not to get caught in the trap of wanting to prove to your healee or yourself that you are actually doing something by putting your energy, efforts, or attention into getting them to feel it.

Color, the Smallest Visual Component

Whether someone is dying of cancer, feeling suicidal or stuck, or suffering from obesity, alcoholism, or boredom, we can ask ourselves three questions: What is the color of the energy that forms the foundation/ basis/core of this problem? Where is it in the body or the body's energy field? Does this color need to be released or removed, and/or is there a different color (representing the desired state of being) that needs to be increased or flowing through this area? Once we know, or even just have a minute sense of these things, all we have to do to effect change is to visualize the flow and release of the colors.

Some people are just not going to believe it's this easy. Many are not going to believe that through simple visualization you can impact another person's health. If you have these beliefs, I highly recommend that you read Lynne McTaggart's book *The Intention Experiment*, in which you can learn about the hundreds of fine experiments that have been done according to the strictest protocols, which show that through mere thought, even at a distance when the receiver is unaware of the thought, thoughts can impact, and be perceived by, the receiver's mind or reflexes. Even more importantly, I also encourage you to exercise some faith, suspend your skepticism long enough for you to try these techniques, and observe the results for yourself.

Working With Color

We really are only concerned about color insofar as it gives us something to latch onto for further exploration and manipulation of energy. I recommend that you first utilize the clairvoyant reading method of conjuring up a viewing receptacle and asking it for the color of the thing you are wondering about. You may see a color quite vividly, even before you begin to imagine your receptacle. You may just get a vague sense of a shade, or you may not get anything. If the latter is the case, then you can always assign the subject a color of your choice, and alter it later in the process if you get a color later on.

Remember that the color is really just a way of visualizing invisible energy. This is the same thing that is done in imaging technology, in which an image's colors are assigned to frequency bands that are normally invisible to the human eye (such as infrared radiation or gases), in order to enhance contrasts. This helps to differentiate features or convey information. In clairvoyant healing, we work with colors so we can differentiate one energy from another. When performing readings, it gives us something tangible to work with as a foundation for further exploration.

Aura Healing

The more students I work with, the more I am learning to appreciate the simplicity and power of working with the aura to access information and healing. The beauty of doing an aura reading is that you see and describe the energies that need to be released and/or increased, and then you can switch into healing mode by facilitating the readee to do this themselves at that moment, and also give them something to do once they've gone home or hung up the phone.

How to Perform an Aura Healing

1. Get an overall picture of your readee's entire aura.

Follow the directions for how to begin a reading and establish a connection with your readee. On your screen, visualize an image of your readee as a silhouette figure; even a stick figure is fine. Ask to see the overall appearance of your readee's aura, including shape and size, and the texture and color of the energy filed around them. Just sit back and see what first impressions you get. Notice if one side of the aura looks any different from the other. You can imagine you are seeing both their front and back, and look for differences there. Feel free to communicate or investigate what you are noticing by posing further questions to the spot of interest, or by putting up a viewing receptacle and asking it to show you information about what you are looking at. If you have trouble seeing the entire aura, don't worry; that is common. Instead, just proceed to step 2 below.

2. Investigate your readee's own energy in this layer.

You will be working with the seven layers of the aura, one layer at a time. Some people like to think of these as energetic bodies and that's fine too. I realize one's aura might have more or fewer than seven layers and that these layers may not be very distinct. I've seen hundreds of Kirlian photos, and while I could see lots of colors, none of them depicted very distinctive layers at all. Honestly, I've never actually spontaneously seen distinct layers apart from when I chose to visualize them this way. However, intellectually dissecting or categorizing the aura into seven general layers does seem to yield excellent results, and that's what we are going for here. If you don't have much time, you can mentally divide the aura into three layers. (This is kind of like taking a pie and cutting it up any way you want. You could cut the entire pie into three big pieces and then taste the three and describe how they taste, or you could cut it into seven smaller pieces and then describe each of those pieces.)

I recommend starting with the first layer of the aura closest to the body since this layer will contain information most relevant to your readee's body. Put up a receptacle such as a rose on your screen and ask it to show you the color of your readee's energy in the first layer. Make a mental note of this color, or write or draw it on a piece of paper. Notice if the receptacle or rose is showing you any other attributes. Then you can ask the color or attributes to show you further information, in the form of images. If you aren't getting anything, ask your readee to say their name a few times and repeat this step. Some good questions to pose in this part of the reading are, "What does this color represent?" "Why is this color in this particular layer?" Take about five minutes or so to do this part of the reading.

3. Investigate the foreign energy in this layer.

Next put up a new rose, or revisualize the figure on your screen, putting your attention on the area just outside the body, asking it to show you a color that represents any foreign energies in this layer. Repeat the process above of investigating this color. If you see a color, some good questions to pose to it are, "What does this color represent?" "Who or what does it belong to?" "Why is this color/energy there in this particular layer of the aura?" "In what specific way does this impact the readee and their life?" "Is the readee ready to release this color/energy?" and "What would best facilitate this process?"

Spend another five minutes or so reading the foreign energy in this layer (if there is any; there may not be).

(*Optional:* Instead of, or in addition to, looking at the readee's own energy and foreign energy, you can look at the "masculine energy" and "feminine energy" in each layer.)

Before proceeding on to read the next layer, you can ask the readee if they'd like you to help them release the foreign energy and bring in more of their own. If they say yes, which 90 percent of people who are receiving aura readings typically do, then tell them that together you are each going to visualize the color representing the foreign energy release from their body. You can give them a grounding cord first. Then remind your readee of the color of the energy that seems to represent their own in this layer. You can also decide to use the color you established as the overall reading color at the beginning, or choose one that seems to represent a vibration they need more of. Then visualize this desirable color coming into the area, or increasing or circulating, and watch as it washes away the color representing the foreign energy.

You can invite your readee to do this visualization along with you, by merely instructing them to visualize the color representing their own energy (which you can share with them, or ask them what color they would choose) and by visualizing the color of the energy that isn't working for them to release. If they don't know about grounding, that's okay; don't get caught up in a teaching session, just let them know you are imagining the color leaving through a cord that connects their body to the earth and trust that they will do fine from there. (If you feel your readee really needs and is ready for these techniques, then recommend either this book or *You Are Psychic*. That's why I wrote these books, so I would not have to leave my reading/healing mode and go into teaching mode, and so you wouldn't either.)

You can of course teach these techniques yourself, but it's best to wait until you've got some practice and experience under your belt first. As a teacher, it is important for you to create boundaries for yourself so you know when you are in teaching mode and when you are in healing or reading mode. This is healthier for you, and your readee will appreciate it, too. I find it annoying when someone is supposed to give me a reading but instead it turns into a lecture, although I must admit I have quite often been guilty of this myself!

4. Repeat this process for each layer.
As noted above, you can break the aura into three main layers: the one closest to the body, the one in the middle, and the one furthest from the body.

CHAPTER 16

Advanced Healing and Psychic Surgery

Practice acquiring the consciousness of childhood. Visualize the Divine
Child within. Before falling asleep suggest to your consciousness,
"I now realize that there is within me a spiritual joy-body ever young,
ever beautiful. I have a beautiful, spiritual mind, eyes, nose, mouth,
skin—the body of the Divine Infant, which now, tonight, is perfect."
— BAIRD T. SPALDING

Supreme Being, Holy Spirit, and Ascended Master Healings

When someone is very ill, to the point at which it seems they have no life force energy left, or is so stuck because they have so much of other people's energy in their body and aura, or they have so many issues that it seems to be overwhelming (if not to them, then to me), then I perform a healing with the energy of the Supreme Being, the Creator (God), Jesus, Mother Mary, Buddha, Holy Spirit, Archangel Michael, or any other deity I or the readee feel a connection with at the time.

No matter how powerful the deity is that you are working with, if you don't acknowledge the power within yourself and your healee (particularly in your healee), then something is going to be missing in the healing. This is because it is not even so much the power of God or Jesus or Mary as it is the power of the relationship between these ascended beings and the one receiving the healing. These figures are the unexpressed potential of your healee. They are the embodiment of all that your healee is. Creation, health, love, strength, faith, perseverance, courage, power, and so forth have been expressed and emanate from these beings, but their core is made of the same stuff as your healee. By bringing the two together, your healee can begin to express these aspects, which may lie dormant or may have been forgotten within himself or herself. This expression will manifest itself either in a healed body or a transformed emotional/mental state.

This is where the concept of the Holy Spirit comes in. Most of the faith healers in the Philippines use the energy of the "Holy Spirit" in their healings. You can think of the Holy Spirit as being the energy between God and the manifestation of God.

When the Creator (a name by which you can call God or the Supreme Being, if you like) of a tree creates a tree, the force or energy that was used to create the tree is the Holy Spirit. It is the same energy that comes from our Creator and creates us. By evoking the Holy Spirit, we are evoking that which created us and the same energy within ourselves. If we were created once, we can be re-created, either back to the state of health we once had, or to a state of health we may never have had in this lifetime but that we know is possible because other human beings exhibit it. This is what we must hold on to.

One other important thing to remember: the moment we think about healing energy (sometimes even before it's a conscious thought), that energy is activated. Even at this moment, I can feel it as soon as I think about it. Perhaps that's because it's always there, just out of our awareness. It's that easy!

Visualization Technique #1: Working With the Deity of Your Choice

This technique uses visualization only. Once you have run through your psychic tools and are in the center of your head, well-grounded with your earth and cosmic energies running, you are ready to begin the healing. If your healee is present, sit directly across from them and make sure both of you are in comfortable positions. Ask your healee to say their current name and date of birth a few times.

If your healee is not present, then repeat their name, date of birth, and current address to yourself if you know them (it is not essential to know all of these, but it can help you to establish a clearer and stronger connection if you do), and visualize your healee. If you don't know what your healee looks like, you can physically put a chair across from yourself and invite the healee's energy into that chair and conduct the healing as if they were sitting a couple of feet from you.

Next, say a prayer invoking God, the Holy Spirit, or the deity of your choice. Usually, when conducting a God or Holy Spirit healing, I will imagine a very bright shimmering ball of light above the healee's head. When conducting a Jesus, Mother Mary, or Buddha healing, I will imagine the faces and bodies of these figures and see them floating above the healee. Once you have a clear image or symbol of the deity of your choice, using your imagination you can either draw a column of energy (i.e., a ball of light) from the image to your readee's crown chakra or you can pull that ball right into your healee's heart center or solar plexus.

See sparkles of the deity's light pouring into the healee's head, and down or out through every cell of their body until it is streaming from their feet and down their grounding cord. See their aura filling up as well. See the healing light fill up your healee's arms and fingers, spilling out of their spinning hand chakras. See their organs, their chakras, their brain, their eyes, and their bones becoming energized by God's light. Remind yourself as you do this that this is the creative energy that created your healee in the first place. It is all-knowing, all-loving, all-powerful, and can perform any miracle. Know that it is not you performing the healing; you are merely an observer. Know that the moment this energy touches any part of your healee, the unhealthy or foreign energy stuck in your healee's body will immediately be released or transform into God's light. Finally, ask the deity to transmit or infuse your healee with the qualities and powers that the healee is ready to accept. Look at your healee and watch to see what happens when you do this!

Technique #2: Visualization and Touch

If your healee is present you may wish to add touch to the above technique, which will intensify the effects. Touch is a very powerful aspect of healing and one that we don't have time to address in great detail in this book. Sometimes your healee will be in dire need of touch, either because they have not been touched in a long time or because their body is very ungrounded or has incurred a trauma that makes it feel unreal. Touching your healee or readee lightly on the shoulders or arms will help ground them, providing they trust you and welcome the physical contact.

During a God or Holy Spirit healing, your healee can either sit upright in a chair, with their feet resting on the floor, or they can lie on their backs on the floor, on a bed, or on a sofa.

Place your hands on the healee's head. Reground yourself, including your aura, and check to make sure that you are centered. As discussed above, choose an image that represents God or the Holy Spirit or whatever deity or figure you'd like. Let's say we are going to visualize the Holy Spirit as a glistening golden star. Draw a column of energy from the star to your own crown chakra. Then draw columns of energy from the star to your hand chakras, forming a triangle or pyramid shape. See sparkles of light pouring down through these columns—this time through your own head, down through your throat and circulating through your heart, down through your shoulders, then down through your arms and out of your hands, into the crown chakra of your healee. See this energy wash through every cell of your healee and watch as it effortlessly flows out through their feet chakras. Watch this flow of energy for a few minutes as you continuously thank God or the Holy Spirit for their assistance.

Next, you can physically move to the healee's feet. Cradle the healee's bare feet in your hands (it's okay if the healee is wearing socks, but ask them to take off their shoes prior to the start of the healing). Make sure the center of your palms, where your hand chakras are located, have contact with the center of their feet, where their feet chakras are located. You may want to visualize that your hand chakras and their feet chakras are spinning and opening wider. Many foreign energies and entities enter through the feet, even through the big toe. Gently place a finger or hand over the big toe and demand that any spirits or negative energies occupying this body drain out from the toe. In your mind, or out loud if you'd like, yell at these energies to release from the toe. Don't be surprised if your readee experiences pain here. It should subside within a minute, and you can explain that this is part of the healing. If your healee does feel pain, talk them through it and tell them it will subside within a minute or so. Encourage them to continue, and do not stop this process until the pain is gone.

Then, once again, visualize God or the Holy Spirit and draw a column of light from this deity to your own crown chakra and hand chakras. See sparkles of light rush down through these columns, down through your crown chakra and out of your hands into the feet chakras of your healee. This time see God's light as it rushes up through the healee's feet, legs, torso, chest, arms, shoulders, neck, and out the top of the healee's head. See the light cleaning out every layer of the healee's aura. See every cell growing brighter and brighter as God's healing energy transforms illness into health, darkness into light. Let this energy run for a minute or two. Then you can thank God or the deity of your choice for sharing their energy with the two of you. From time to time, tune in to yourself and notice if you feel your body going into any effort. If you feel yourself "trying" to do anything, this means you are overextending yourself. Healing is not really about *doing* anything; it's about witnessing the energy flow. You are merely acting as a channel for God's light. You are merely an observer. Nothing more, nothing less.

When you feel you have finished (this entire process shouldn't take more than ten minutes), you can ask for the light to give you a healing on any matching issues you have with the person you were working on. Just relax and notice what happens. Finally, imagine that you are disconnecting the columns of energy from God to yourself (know that you are always connected, but you don't need this much of an energy rush all the time; it could overwhelm your chakras and body). Say out loud to your healee, "With the blessings of [God, the supreme being, the Holy Spirit], my role in the healing is completed. May the deity continue to work with you for the next twenty-four hours as needed."

With healing, particularly long-distance healing, it's really important that you are clear about when you are beginning it and when you are finishing it. Otherwise your own energy can become depleted very quickly.

Clairvoyant Psychic Surgery

At times you may be conducting a reading and healing, and you will become aware of a strong foreign energy that has invaded the healee's body or aura. You might even see a color or an image of an object that seems to be stopping the flow of energy from one part of the body to the next. One very effective technique to remove this foreign energy is what I call *clairvoyant psychic surgery*.

The method of clairvoyant psychic surgery I now teach is based on experiences gained from my own personal practice as a psychic and healer. It is also very much inspired by techniques I learned during my own course of clairvoyant training with a variety of teachers in the United States, and from the hundreds of healings I observed, received, and participated in while studying with several faith healers in the Philippines in the late 1990s. Some of these healers, known as psychic surgeons, had the extraordinary ability to make an actual incision in a patient's body with their bare hands, reach into the incision, and pull out the foreign energy, which would then manifest into physical matter such as tissue, blood clots, tumors, stones, fluids, and the like. (To learn more about some of the most popular healers of the Philippines and Brazil, I recommend reading any of Jaime Licauco's books about the Filipino healers, such as *The Magicians of God* or *Jun Labo*, or *John of God: The Brazilian Healer Who's Touched the Lives of Millions* by Heather Cumming and Karen Leffler.)

One of the most extraordinary things I have ever experienced was when one of my Filipino teachers, Brother William, made an incision in a patient's chest with his bare hands and held the incision open while he instructed me to take a pair of tweezers and extract a large tumor from inside the incision. The tumor was connected to tissue, and I had to yank on it a little before it would come out. I was terrified that I would pull out the wrong thing! As soon as I removed the tumor, Brother William took his hands away and the incision immediately closed without a trace of a scar. This specific operation was observed by no fewer than twenty people.

When doubt from the multitudes of doubters around me sets in about the dozens of healings

I received myself, or the hundreds I observed by numerous healers, I always go back to this one experience, which is why I believe I had the experience.

Clairvoyant psychic surgery mimics the techniques used by these healers. In fact, I believe there is not much difference between the two, except that in clairvoyant psychic surgery, the diseased energy does not typically manifest as solid physical matter, as it does in traditional psychic surgery.

How to Perform Clairvoyant Psychic Surgery

You can actually have your healee lie down, or you can merely visualize your healee lying on a table. You can then imagine that a white sheet is covering the healee's body. Wherever healing is needed, in your mind's eye look for a dark spot to appear on the sheet. (This is also a popular diagnostic technique among the psychic surgeons of the Philippines.) Choose one area of the body that seems to be in the greatest need of help. If you feel uncertain as to what part of the body is in need of healing, or if you feel that there is a systemic problem, you can work solely with the healee's third chakra, located at their solar plexus. Simply postulate that all illness, pain, or negative energy in the body will be magnetically pulled to the third chakra, where you will soon help it to release. (This is another technique commonly used by the healers in the Philippines, and I have heard that the very popular healer John of God, in Brazil, often works with the third chakra in this way as well.)

Next, imagine that you are looking at your hands. See columns or cords of energy running from your hands to either God or the Holy Spirit (you can visualize God in any way that works for you). See sparkles of light traveling from God down through these columns/ cords and bursting out of your hand chakras. See tiny, dancing, healing flames flickering out of your palms and fingertips. Feel the heat of these flames pulsating through your hands and your arms.

Now imagine that you are taking your glowing hands and making a clean incision into the affected part of your healee's body. You can do this seated at a distance from your readee, or you can actually lay your hands on the location of the body you are working on. In your imagination, reach in and grab hold of whatever foreign matter is ready to release. You may need to gently pull on it, or it may glide out effortlessly. Observe the color and shape of whatever is coming out. If it is attached to a particular organ or chakra, you may need to imagine that you are cleaning that organ with the use of your imaginary hands. See the brilliant lights beaming through the layers of the inside of your healee's body, penetrating deep beyond the areas that need attention. Know that this light is strong enough to dissolve anything that is no longer conducive to your readee's well-being. The matter may disintegrate before you pull it out. If the foreign matter does not want to release, give that part of the body a grounding cord and watch the color of the resistance as it releases, and then try again.

Once you have pulled out the foreign matter, imagine that the healee's incision automatically closes up as if it never existed. Then take the matter you extracted and throw it into a fire pit that exists somewhere outside the room. You can also send the matter up to God. See it landing in God's hands and watch to see what happens to it. This will usually give you insight not only into what your healee is dealing with but also into the very nature of God and the Universal Laws.

As a final step, make sure you fill up your healee with the color of their own healing energy. When you are finished, you and your readee can discuss both your observations and your experiences with the healing. You can then disconnect yourself from God or the Holy Spirit, say a prayer of gratitude or words of thanks, and state out loud, "May it be with the blessings of God that this healing is completed."

Working With a Psychic Surgeon Guide

When practicing clairvoyant psychic surgery, you may find that when you go to picture God, you will see another figure in God's place. This will most likely be a healing guide or psychic surgeon. It is up to you whether you would like to work with this guide or work only with God. Psychic surgeon guides are extremely powerful guides that can be very helpful but also very domineering.

If you experience twitching in your hands or eyes, if your hands or arms begin moving without your intending them to, if you feel an overwhelming urge to go and find someone to heal, and if you hear ringing in your ears, these are signs that these guides are seeking to work with you and are plugging into your body. Pressure on the back of your neck is a sign they may be plugging into your telepathic channels. Most likely, these spirits will not approach you if on some level you are not open or ready to work with them. If you choose to work with a healing guide, I recommend undergoing the steps below.

The healers in the Philippines who can actually operate on a body with their bare hands have the ability to do so because of the powerful guides they work with. These healers not only form a connection with these guides at their hand chakras, but they actually let the guides take over their entire body—which works for them but is totally unnecessary for the type of healing we are doing. Full-body channeling is complicated and risky, and should be done only under competent supervision and after extensive training. That being said, there are some people who spontaneously do this channeling with little awareness, as they go about their everyday lives. A small minority of people are absolutely compelled to do it. I wholeheartedly believe that you will know if you are meant to do healing in this way, or meant to do any activity for that matter, by your degree of interest in it and natural inclination to do it or try it.

Meeting Your Healing Guide

This method can be used to establish a relationship with any type of healing guide. First, imagine there is an empty chair facing away from you, about eight feet from you. Invite the guide to sit down in the chair. See a light above the chair and, at the count of three, turn on the light. Tell the guide that as you turn on the light, you would like the guide to turn around and show you what it looks like. Ask it to show you both a color and its physical characteristics. Once you have an idea of what the guide looks like, say hello to it, introduce yourself, let it know why you are tuning in to it, find out what the guide would like to achieve by working with you, and ask if it has any messages for you.

Some guides have certain specialties, certain talents that they can bring to a healing. For example, they might be particularly adept at removing other entities, they may have extensive knowledge about healing cancer, or they may be very good communicators. Ask your guide to clairvoyantly show you what its specialty is. Chances are, you will share some common talents and interests.

Next, you will want to establish some simple boundaries. Tell the guide it may only plug into your hand chakras, and only for the duration of the healing. After that it will need to step outside your aura and wait until you call upon it again. If you don't set these limits, the guide might stay plugged into you indefinitely, and while the guide may be good at healing, it is not going to know any better than you how to get along in your everyday life (many of these guides have never had the experience of having a physical body), and the guide may have an agenda of its own that can interfere with your goals, desires, and overall health.

Furthermore, let the guide know the best way to communicate with you. You can tell it to communicate with you through images and pictures. It is also important to give the guide notice that if at any time you wish to do so, you can fire it and it will not be allowed to approach you again without your permission.

There are as many spirit and healing guides out there as there are people, and a lot of them are desperate to work with you. The more you interact with them, the clearer your communication with and understanding of them will be. These guides usually know when you are going to perform a healing well before you do, and sometimes the way you will know that someone is about to ask you to perform a healing is that you will feel your guides plugging into your hands or buzzing around you. If you aren't comfortable with your guide, you can always fire them and recruit a new one. The nice thing is that you won't have to pay them unemployment insurance!

Connecting With Your Guide

To actually connect with your guide, first ground yourself, then ground the guide. Then hold up your hands. Direct the guide to plug into one or both of your hands. Imagine that there is a cord of energy that runs from your hand chakras to the guide's hand chakras. The color of the cord is the same color that the guide showed you previously. As the guide plugs in, notice how your hands feel. Now ask the guide to give you a two-to five-minute healing. Ask the guide to specifically clear out any blockages in your hand chakras and any other part of your body that might be inhibiting your healing energy. Sit back, relax, and notice how you feel. Feel free to watch the healing clairvoyantly. At the end of the healing, ask your guide if it has any communication for you. If you are immediately going to conduct a healing on someone else, keep the guide plugged in and begin the healing. Otherwise, thank the guide for the healing, and let it know you will call upon it again soon. Then visualize it unplugging from your hand chakras, cut its grounding cord, hook it up to God, and see it floating away.

Technique #3: Clairvoyant Psychic Surgery With a Healing Guide

You can utilize the help of psychic-surgeon healing guides when performing clairvoyant psychic surgery. You can go through the same steps described above, but instead of merely seeing your own hands, you can see the hands of your guides working alongside or though yours. For a particularly tricky healing, you can just sit back, relax, and clairvoyantly watch your guides as they fly around the healee. You can let them make the decision about where and how to perform the healing. Occasionally you will want to clairvoyantly check the connection between your hand chakras and those of the psychic-surgeon healing guides. As your guides conduct the healing, you can help by observing and communicating which colors are being released from the healee and which colors the healee is using to fill up with. Another option is for you to take responsibility for one part of the healing, while assigning the other part to your healing guide.

Clairvoyant Psychic Surgery Using Touch, With or Without a Guide

If you would like to use touch for your healing and your healee is receptive to this, you can physically take your hands, gently lay them on the area of your healee that you wish to address, and perform the visualizations discussed on the previous page. When you get to the point of visualizing yourself (possibly with the help of healing guides) removing the unhealthy matter, you can pretend that your hands are actually pulling out the matter. Let your hands move in any way they desire, just avoid actually touching any areas of the readee's body that could make them uncomfortable (you can always wave your hands above these body parts to work in their aura).

Whether you are plugged into God or into a Filipino psychic surgeon guide, you can sit back, relax, and observe what happens as the guides or God/Holy Spirit perform the healing. It's likely you will be picking up some impressions through your clairvoyance or clairaudience or through instant knowing. This is great, and feel free to communicate this information. However, don't get too much into doing an intensive reading here because your attention really needs to be on the healing. When someone tells me they want a reading and a hands-on healing, I tell them I really need to do these separately. They will then be pleasantly surprised when I give them some psychic insights, but these will be minimal.

Remember that at the end of the healing it will be very important to clean out your hand chakras and any other part of your body that may have absorbed energy from your readee or your guides. You can either ground your hand chakras or see tiny roses circulating inside the chakras until the roses become so full with the foreign energy that they explode. If you are near a sink, it is always advisable after a reading to physically wash your hands well, and to take a shower before going to bed that evening.

CHAPTER 17

Female Healing

American women expect to find in their husbands a perfection
that English women only hope to find in their butlers.
— WILLIAM SOMERSET MAUGHAM

Soon after I moved to the Philippines I met the man who became my favorite healer, David Oligoni (aka "the Exorcist of Pangasinan"), in his little chapel adorned with a mural of a blue pyramid with an eye above it, and an assortment of village dogs sleeping in the pews. I observed and personally experienced David's exorcisms, which involved pulling evil spirits from a person's toe. David would lightly touch the healee's big toe and yell at the spirits to leave while his wife stood close by, usually laughing at the spirit or the healee. (I was never quite sure which!) Within a few seconds of this, the healee would usually experience a searing pain that might last for a minute. For me, this pain was almost unbearable.

Sometimes people would have other reactions: I watched nearby as a friend of mine almost levitated off the table. Another talent of David's was to clear people's nasal passages. He did this by taking what appeared to be a pair of tongs and jamming it up a healee's nose. A moment later David would proudly extract something that resembled a large wad of chewing gum. Some of these people later reported that David improved their breathing and alleviated their sinus problems. Another common practice was to ignite oil in a glass jar and place this jar on the healee's bare skin, creating a tight suction. This was supposed to draw out the toxins in that part of the body. Those who received this treatment reported that it didn't hurt; however, the jars did leave a blazing red ring for more than a couple of days following the procedure.

So when I visited David for my own healing in November 1997, I was more than a bit apprehensive. I was experiencing an irregular menstrual cycle and thought he might be able to help. I did not tell him why I was there and he didn't ask. However, he immediately placed his hands over my pelvic area for about ten seconds (something he had never done before), and then asked me a question that seemed quite odd at the time but that has been perhaps one of the most important questions ever asked of me. The question was "Do you enjoy being a woman?" He repeated it two more times before I responded enthusiastically, just to get him to lower his voice, "Yes, I do enjoy being a woman." "Good!" he and his wife laughed and shuffled me out the door. That was the last time I ever saw him. Less then four months later I was pregnant with my son Manny, who is now nine years old.

I wondered for quite a while about what exactly David was getting at. Almost a decade later I think I might have an inkling. I now realize that I can either enjoy what I have—what my body can do, how it can look and feel, what it can create—or I can despise these things. It's a choice. When I remember to appreciate the fact that I am having the rare opportunity to experience life in a human female body, I feel excited and overjoyed. When I feel oppressed, exhausted, vulnerable, crampy, or burdened, and I curse such feelings, I begin to feel worse and worse. The more I celebrate being a female, the more fun I have and the better I feel. Recently, a reader of *You Are Psychic* e-mailed me and directed me to her MySpace page. It turns out she is a he. She wrote at the top of her e-mail, "Being a woman is 100% priceless!"

One of the reasons many women don't enjoy their own bodies is because their bodies are filled with everyone else's energy (quite often men's energy or that of the woman's disapproving or angry mother). As women, our bodies are extremely absorbent and receptive. They are designed to receive a male's sperm and even the soul of an unborn baby. Unfortunately, our bodies do not discriminate between whose energy they take in. Even if we are far past our childbearing years, our female organs act as magnets with just about every man we encounter and from other women who are comparing themselves to us on a body level. Furthermore, many women, somewhere along the line, were taught their bodies were not truly their own, that they had to put everyone else before themselves. This unconscious belief makes many women feel resentful of their lot in life.

While the women's movement has given us many freedoms, it has given us twice as much responsibility as we had before, since now we are expected to do all we did before, plus be the breadwinners of our families. Of course, given the fact that there are trillions of dollars being made by corporations who profit solely from ensuring that women find fault with themselves, it's no wonder we are all more than a bit dissatisfied with our bodies. In fact, in most of America it's really as though there is a covert and relentless assault on our psyches and self-image from hundreds of sources each day.

In fact, we literally cannot leave our homes or turn on our television sets, computers, or radios without being assaulted from every direction with the message that we are defective, not good enough, not enough. This is in such stark contrast to the reality of the situation: that we as women possess a force within ourselves that enables us to be creators of life itself. To downplay our power or allow ourselves to be degraded by the people around us (here I am talking about a comparatively small group of people hiding behind the fortress of the "corporation") is akin to God herself allowing Satan to suck out her soul. Whether or not we are actually able or interested in bearing children, we posses a creative energy within our bodies. When this creative energy is focused—whether to create a new life or art or for the purpose of healing—it is a force of unimaginable strength and beauty. However, when this creative energy is suppressed inside ourselves or is misdirected, it can be devastating—mostly for ourselves but also for our children and others around us.

When a woman has sex with a man, or is an object of another person's sexual desire, energetic cords form between the two individuals that often make it difficult for her to focus on herself or to emotionally separate from a relationship. When a woman becomes obsessed with a man, it is often because these energies have become entwined or enmeshed. The more entrenched she becomes in his energy field, even when his motivations are purely to protect or provide for her, the more she loses herself. The more she loses herself and becomes like him, the harder it is for him to find her, the needier she becomes, and he begins to appreciate her less and less.

Not only do we as women have to contend with the plethora of foreign energies we carry around (sometimes literally as extra pounds), but many women are also dealing with their own unexpressed emotional energy that is trapped within their bodies, as a result of societal or family programming that says it's not polite or caring to express these emotions. When a woman fails to express anger or disappointment, they become toxins that often contaminate her own female organs, such as her ovaries, uterus, breasts, and so on. Many women don't realize that emotions like anger or disappointment are actually there to protect them. When expressed in a healthy manner, these emotions serve both as shields and as warning signals that not all is good in paradise. Without these she is vulnerable to sacrificing too much of herself and she can never be in her own power; she will play the eternal victim because these feelings will always manifest within someone close to her who will project them back onto her.

As mentioned above, women have the profound ability to create life. This creative process is fueled by a vital energy that is always active within a woman's body, regardless of whether she is physically able to create a child. This creative energy can be directed into any number of creative projects, work, and even relationships (that's why many times men become our creative project, something to transform). When a woman is running this energy in full force within her own body, she will feel particularly at peace and will even appear more attractive to herself and to others (hence the pregnant woman's "glow"). When this energy becomes stifled, misdirected, or ungrounded, it can cause women to become bored, depressed, hysterical, neurotic, hyperactive, and sexually dysfunctional.

Female healing is a clairvoyant technique that helps women release foreign energy and unexpressed emotional energy of their own, and to overcome the illnesses, diseases, and pain that result from these misguided energies. Female healing also helps women stimulate and redirect their female creative energies.

Female Healing Technique: Female Grounding

The first thing to do when embarking on a female healing is to give the woman healee both a regular grounding cord, as discussed in chapter 3, and a female grounding cord. A female grounding cord will ground her female organs as well as her creative energy. This is an excellent exercise to do if she is feeling overwhelmed with too many tasks, or is having a hard time approaching or conversing with a particular man. To create this cord, draw a line of energy from each of the woman's ovaries and connect it into her main grounding cord at the base of her spine, to form a triangle or pyramid shape. Then imagine that you are writing the name of your healee on her ovaries and ask the ovaries to show you the color of the healee's own female energy in the ovaries. Then ask them to show you the color of any foreign energies that are ready to release. Next, watch as these foreign energies slip down the grounding cord. You can give them a push by circulating some earth energy, or a mixture of cosmic and earth energy, in order to rinse her ovaries as well. Invite the energies of guilt, shame, and fear to light up as black spots, and watch these release.

Once you are satisfied that her ovaries contain only her energy, you can continue to ground out and rinse the healee's other female areas. You can also use a viewing receptacle such as a rose as a type of clairvoyant washcloth. See the rose circulating around in her uterus. Imagine that the rose has a sticky surface and is collecting up all the foreign and emotional energy that needs to be released. Once it is full, take a look at the colors inside and then imagine you are sending the rose out the window and over to a large open space where you can see it exploding into a million pieces. Continue the process with the woman's breasts as well. During a female healing, you can utilize other healing techniques discussed in this chapter and the next.

One of the important steps in a female healing is to help a woman ground her female creative energy. You can imagine that this energy is located around her baby-making organs. You can imagine that she looks nine months pregnant but instead of her tummy being large, it is really just a ball of female creative energy that is swelling out in front of her. See this ball of energy as swirling, pulsating, dynamic. Ask the energy to show you its true color(s). Then imagine that you are giving this vibrant ball of energy its own grounding cord. Ground it into a soft, peaceful, dark place deep within the earth. Write the woman's name on this bubble of energy and command any foreign energies that are no longer serving the woman to release from the grounding cord. If the woman has been dealing with a particular man or relationship, you can state this man's name and specifically order his energy to release as well. Next, look for energy such as competition, envy, doubt, guilt, or anything else that is keeping the healee from being in her true power—anything that is keeping her from expressing her full creative energy—and help her release these down the grounding cord as well.

Then, for the most important part of this process, visualize the woman's creative energy rising up and circulating abundantly through her entire body and aura. You can use your clairvoyance to see a color for this, or you can ask the healee which color makes her feel creative, happy, and passionate. See the flow of this energy begin to circulate and vibrate faster and faster, and as it does this, see it getting brighter or more sparkly.

Help Her Separate From Baby Beings

It is always important to help a woman to separate from any baby beings that are connected into her female energy, unless she is trying to become pregnant and feels that she wants to keep the beings near her. (See chapter 13 for a more in-depth discussion on baby beings and additional techniques for working with them.)

A simple way to locate and move these pesky spirits out is to simply imagine that you are throwing some neutral purple or cobalt-blue energy into the healee's bubble of creative energy and watch to see if any white cords appear. Then create an imaginary pair of scissors and cut the cords. Imagine that any baby beings or other spirits that were attached to these cords are now flying off into outer space. If you are concerned about their well-being, you can show them an image of God (located at a far distance from your healee) and reattach to your image of God the ends of the cord that were formerly attached to the healee, so that the beings will have a safe and comforting place to go to and will be less inclined to turn their attention to you! Chances are that your healee is going to feel physical sensations in her body as you move out these spirits.

Working With the Umbilical Cord

Finally, during a female healing I like to work with the healee's own energetic umbilical cord. While every baby's umbilical cord is physically severed at birth, many people, particularly women, remain energetically attached to their mothers throughout their entire lives. On one level this gives them a sense of comfort and security, but on another level it keeps them from ever fully coming into their own full power.

During a female reading or healing, you can clairvoyantly look in the area of the woman's belly button to see if there is an umbilical cord, and follow it to see if it is attached to anyone or anything. You might find her mother or you might find someone else. If you find a connection or sense one, then put up a viewing receptacle on your reading screen and ask the question, "How is this connection serving or not serving my client in the present moment?" If the images show you that your client is not benefiting from this connection, you can do two things. First, write the current day and time across the healee's stomach with an imaginary pen, then imagine a timeline with the current date and time in the middle of the timeline. Next, imagine that this umbilical cord is placed in the middle of the timeline. Watch to see what happens to the umbilical cord. If it does not detach, then take out your imaginary scissors and cut it close to the healee's body. Watch what happens when you cut it.

Next, tie off the end of the cord, making a strong knot. Now take the end of the cord that is still attached to the healee's mother and tie it off. Then give the mother a general grounding cord as well as a female grounding cord. Complete the healing by describing the work you just did and explaining that both your healee and her mother may feel the effects of the healing over the next several days (whether or not her mother is even aware of the healing). This technique is helpful for women whose mothers are still around as well as for those whose mothers have physically passed on.

PART IV

Understanding and Improving Your Own Life as a Psychic

CHAPTER 18

Healing the Healer Within

The important thing is this: to be able, at any moment,
to sacrifice what we are for what we could become.
— MAHARISHI MAHESH YOGI

Most of Us Are Healers

Chris was a client of mine whom I worked with every few months over the course of two years. He came to me because he wanted to make sure he was on his "spiritual path." He was a gay man in his sixties. During one reading I was surprised when I saw an image of him turn into a big piece of...*Kleenex.* Then I saw an even funnier vision of his partner picking him up and blowing his nose in him. "Hey," Chris said excitedly, "do you know what I just picked up right before you said that?" Since this was a phone reading, I obviously did not. He continued, "I was just looking at a big Kleenex box, reading the words on it, and wondering about why they named it Kleenex."

I told him I couldn't answer that question, but that I did know why in my vision he turned into a piece of Kleenex. "Your partner has been emotionally dumping on you," I told him. "He uses you to release his toxic feelings." Chris wholeheartedly agreed that this was a strong dynamic in their relationship, which at that point had lasted more than a decade, but he stated he didn't know why he allowed this dynamic to continue or how he could even change it. I told him that it wouldn't be impossible but it would be hard, because he is such a healer. "Healer?" he asked me, surprised. "You think I'm a healer? But how can I be a healer? I don't even know how to do healings!" I suggested to Chris that his problem is that he doesn't know how *not* to heal.

Except for psychopaths, most people are healers. Whether or not people choose to consciously perform healings—by working with energy, touch, herbs, or allopathic medicine—is irrelevant.

356

When we have the desire to help someone or make someone feel better, and we talk to them or extend them a helping hand, we are in a sense healing them. Some of us are absolutely driven to help others. We feel pain the moment we see someone else in pain, or the moment we assume they must be in pain, because if we were in their situation, we know we would be in pain.

The biggest challenge for any healer is having to live with the fact that others around us are in pain. The next biggest challenge is to live with the fact that many of those in pain are unwilling or unable to take the steps they need to take to get out of their situation. That situation usually includes subjecting themselves to toxic people, toxic substances, or toxic thoughts, and engaging in other self-defeating behaviors. Have you ever had a friend or family member who had the following ongoing problems?

- They refuse to leave an abusive situation.
- They refuse to let a relationship go that they are no longer in.
- They are drinking themselves to death.
- They are abusing drugs to the point that their body is falling apart.
- They weigh so much that they can hardly get out of bed.
- They weigh so little that they look like a skeleton.
- Their spouse left or died, and now they don't know how to support themselves and refuse to do anything except rely on relatives.
- They keep making bad financial decisions and are always in a state of crisis.

Doesn't just reading this list give you a knot in your stomach? Doesn't it make you sad, irritated, and frustrated to the point that you can actually feel your blood pressure go up? Why is this? It is not because the person you care about has a problem; it's because that person does not seem to have the capacity to make the changes you want them to make within the time frame you want. It might take them half a century to get to where you'd like them to be now. It's important that you give them the room they need to take the steps, or not take the steps, they need to take. This doesn't mean you abandon them, but you do need to understand that some people—lots of people, adults—want to be taken care of by others. They are afraid, and you could give them every ounce of your energy and they still would not have the courage or determination that you do. They want the easy road, the shortcuts, and therefore they will not even consider choosing the road that has led to your own awakening and healing.

Those feelings that you feel from reading the list above are toxic. They come from overextending yourself, literally. This is because you've crossed the line. You've jumped from your path to theirs, and you are fighting a fight that you cannot win because it has nothing to do with you. Essentially you are taking on their karma. You are trying to overshadow their self and will with your own, hoping to transfer your power into them. No wonder you are exhausted, frustrated, depressed, or worse!

I know it's bad writing to use clichés, but the expression "You can lead a horse to water, but you can't make him drink" is completely apropos here. Imagine if you did try to make the horse drink. He'd be spitting the water out at you and messing up your clothes; he might kick you, bite you, or trample you. He might go berserk and disturb the other horses in the barn. I suppose you could anesthetize him and give him an IV. That might save his life. But what happens when he wakes up? Will he now be ready to drink?

What happens when the horse is your husband or parent?

How do we deal with people who are not ready to change in the way we want them to change? Do we just abandon them? Do we give up? Do we avoid them? Do we remain in this agonizing situation?

I am starting to realize that the people I heal most often and lose my energy to are those who aren't willing to do the same work I am to change my life. They are scared, and they are convinced they need a greater level of security, even though some of them have a lot more security than I do with regard to long-term jobs and savings. Some of these people are actually looking at me to do the things they don't want to do themselves or don't feel they can do. It is as if on one level they are screaming out "Save me!"—but then they shoot down every way you come up with for them to be saved. This can make you absolutely crazy. It happens with some clients and, as you know, it can happen with those closest to you.

Time Does Make a Difference

As a forty-year-old psychic, now with twelve years of reading under my belt, I am finally beginning to see shifts in some of the people I've been trying to heal for years, including my own friends and family. In some cases, I am seeing glimpses of change now that I had yearned to see decades ago. Patience is the answer to just about everything.

Reasons People May Not Be Healing

1. The person is not ready to heal.
2. The person is actually benefiting from the illness or problem—e.g., getting disability, attention, or time off from work.
3. What you are defining as a problem is not one for that person.
4. You have lost your neutrality. You might be leaving some of your pain with them or making them feel worse.
5. It's the person's life lesson, destiny, or karma.
6. The person doesn't really believe they can be healed or that you can help.
7. The patterned, programming energy is really ingrained, and if you just ripped it out the person couldn't function normally; their reality would be shattered and they would feel as if they were going nuts, so they must do this at a much slower pace than you would have.
8. There are changes happening but you can't see them.
9. You are not giving the person enough time to go through the process of changing or healing.
10. You are only seeing half of the story.
11. The person's physical body has gotten to a point at which there is not enough healthy energy to regenerate.
12. The spirit is ready to depart from the body; it is preplanned. You are trying to play God.

Hold the Vision, Even When Others Can't See It

I am only beginning to understand the power of holding a vision for someone who can't yet see it themselves. Many people suffer because they are locked into a fixed idea of who they are and what they want and need. They are afraid of the unknown or can't imagine a different reality.

Sometimes, as soon as I communicate a different version of how a readee's life could or will be, they are relieved, even excited. However, sometimes they are upset, confused, frightened, and occasionally angry. They want what they want now and nothing other than that, while as a clairvoyant I can see that there is really something much better out there for them. This is true whether the person is an isolated seventy-five-year-old woman who has done nothing but watch TV for the past twenty-five years and now is facing (and resisting) moving into a retirement home where she will have new opportunities for friendships and fun activities, or a man who is being told that he won't have the woman he's obsessed with but that there will be someone else out there who is perfect for him, perhaps when he's "ripened" a bit.

When my client or someone I meet can't yet comprehend this alternate reality or future, I will focus my attention on their spirit, and postulate that I am mentally showing them this picture. I will keep sending hello to their spirit. I will sometimes advise such a client, "I understand what I am saying doesn't make sense to you right now. That's fine. File it away in the back of your mind, and when you are ready it will be there for you."

Most important, I remind myself that it's perfectly okay that this person's ego or mind is not yet ready to grasp a greater version of reality or an expanded notion of possibilities. It doesn't mean I am a bad healer or psychic. On the contrary, it means that I can see what is, rather than what others want me to see.

CHAPTER 19

Overcoming Limits to Manifesting

No one in the world was ever you before, with your particular
gifts and abilities and possibilities. It's a shame to waste
those by doing what someone else has done.
— JOSEPH CAMPBELL

Surpassing Limits

In every area of our life, including relationships, money, freedom, and success, we develop and operate from conscious and unconscious parameters around what we believe is possible or not possible for ourselves. These parameters can also be considered "limits." These limits may be quite low in one area and quite high in another. Our parameters or limits are based on many factors, including our belief system, our past experiences and memories, the emotions and programming that we've internalized from parents and society, and the energy of others in our body and aura. The "limit" is whatever line is drawn at the top of this threshold that says, "Stop. It's not possible or safe to go beyond this point."

Often, our limits are set at the same levels as those of our parents and the culture we grew up in. If we are ready on a soul level to exceed these limits, then we may encounter our parents' resistance on an energy level (if they are deceased or unaware of what we are doing) or on the physical plane, as when they try to tell us that what we are doing is not possible or is dangerous, selfish, or won't work. If we demonstrate that it *is* possible for us, then it suggests perhaps it could be possible (or could have been) for them. This knowledge could inspire them, or it could make them angry and fearful if it means letting go of excuses that they have talked themselves into believing.

One of the main ways we can help a person in a clairvoyant reading is to help them recognize, identify, understand, and move past their limits. This is the primary reason I get readings myself. However, this is also what makes clairvoyant readings quite challenging at times. You as a clairvoyant must access information about and for a person who believes this limit is absolute reality and who may be very emotionally invested in holding on to this reality. This person's entire existence may have been a self-fulfilling prophecy that demonstrates over and over again that this limit is real, and now you are about to require them to look at a whole new range of possibilities outside that limit.

When the readee is close to tearing down these walls and overcoming blocks and limitations, the clairvoyant will often be able to see the information about the situation quite easily and clearly. However, this can be confusing and difficult even for a person completely committed to their personal growth, one who has been praying for insight and change. So as a clairvoyant, you may begin to encounter their resistance, confusion, or any number of fears and energies even before you sit down with them and set the reading color. You may find yourself dreading the reading and having no idea why. You might feel nervous or overwhelmed. Or you might lose your confidence. You may find when you put up a viewing receptacle on your screen that you are unable to see anything, or that you just see black.

During a clairvoyant reading with someone who is hitting a limit or has something blocking them from achieving a goal, I will often see an image of a wall, which represents the limit. However, sometimes the readee has been doing a lot of work to break down the wall, and the moment I see and describe it, the readee's spirit is able to push down this weakened structure (in my visualization and also in reality) and is flooded with insights and a fresh perspective on a situation that may have seemed quite hopeless. This can be followed by sudden changes, new opportunities, and a huge influx of energy and movement. It is as if the wall were a dam, and the person's life force that was collecting up on the other side of it all that time is now released with tremendous gusto. Since our ability to create and manifest is dependent on how much life force we have in our bodies at any given time, people are often able to manifest really big goals, even miracles, at this juncture. I also suspect this is why occasionally the things we manifested after getting unstuck in a big way don't always last (e.g., sudden fame or fortune or an opportunity that seems unbelievable). Sometimes, the energy loses its momentum before the person has had a chance to assimilate all the changes, or the person doesn't have the self-esteem or wherewithal yet to handle the thing they were able to manifest with the excess of energy, and so they lose that physical manifestation. The good news is that even when this happens, the person doesn't lose what they have gained on the inside, which is a new awareness and an expansion of their limits or parameters, and they are able to re-create that miracle again further down the road when it is more likely to last.

Sometimes our readees come to us because they are just in the initial stages of this process of releasing limits and expanding their parameters. They are not ready to open the floodgates of consciousness completely, even if they say they are. This may be because they have conflicting desires. If they really had an awareness of their entire situation, they would have to make the changes they are afraid of or are unwilling to make. In this case, the clairvoyant has been called into their life to unlock the door and allow in just a glimmer or light. The readee will then go back to their life, and likely encounter similar patterns, but they may begin to respond to these differently than they did before.

Please be aware that we might be talking about just one aspect of the readee's life—say, their relationships, finances, or the way they operate from a need to control or in response to fear. In other areas they may be very conscious, happy people.

We all have our own walls and limits. The nice thing is that we can help each other become aware of them. Anytime there is someone in your life who seems to have a lot of limits or a really big one they can't seem to crawl over, it can be an indication that you also have some, or at least one, really big wall yourself that you are working through as well.

Matching Pictures

There is another reason why reading someone's limits or walls can be quite challenging for a clairvoyant. The psychic is being asked to look at information that they themselves have been unconscious to. They may have the same limit themselves, and now it's as if their subconscious mind is presented with a major dilemma: if the clairvoyant is absolutely not ready to see it or handle it, they may just not be able to get any images, or they will see an image but its meaning will completely elude them.

This is probably the main reason why people sometimes just can't get the answer they are seeking. The clairvoyant wants to see what is behind the wall, but if they do so they will see the very thing they have protected themselves from. If the clairvoyant is actually ready to see this, has in fact been chipping away the bricks or stones for quite a while, and has attracted or been attracted to do a reading on this person for this very reason, then the subconscious mind or another part of the clairvoyant will permit or bring forth the illuminating images, visions, and/or messages that will move them forward. Even then, the clairvoyant may have difficulty communicating what they are seeing because they are too "lit up"—there is too much emotional charge on what they are looking at because they are encountering their own limits or pictures, underneath which there may be a lot of fear or control.

If fear has been a factor, the clairvoyant will feel it now but within the context of the reading, so they will become fearful that whatever they are looking at will not be well-received, will be misconstrued, or that they may just be wrong.

Most of the time, if you as the clairvoyant work past this fear and deliver the information, the readee will accept it and benefit from it. However, occasionally the readee will respond unfavorably by insisting that you are wrong, that it's not possible for them to do what they say, or the readee will give you lots of excuses as to why they don't have the options you are seeing for them (for example, leaving an abusive relationship, applying for a management position instead of a clerical one, searching for work they might enjoy, and so on).

If this is the case, then what I usually do is look at the part of them that is resisting what I am saying as the stuck part. I will then imagine I am sending greeting notes to their spirit, or the part of them that is really receptive and wanting to move past the stuck part. I will direct my communication to that part and point out the fear. I may look to see where in their body the fear is, because usually it's the fear that is doing the talking. Sometimes I might tell the readee that there is "a lie in your space that says this is your only choice." I won't say, *you are lying* since they aren't; they completely believe themselves and their own excuses. That is the nature of being stuck. I will just clairvoyantly look to see why they are so fearful or wanting to avoid the other options, or I'll look for where the lie is located.

It is always helpful to ask your clairvoyance to show you the actual location where any emotion, energy, or issue is, because then your attention and that of the readee can go to that exact spot. Our attention is like a powerful laser that will immediately zap the spot and burn away whatever is ready to go. This is why a clairvoyant reading is also considered a healing.

Solution: Havingness Gauge

"Havingness" is a concept that indicates the degree to which we can love ourselves and permit ourselves to have our goals, dreams, and desires.

Step 1: Close your eyes and ground yourself. Visualize a crystal-clear rose out in front of you. Choose one goal or desire for yourself. This can be an object, such as a specific amount of money, or a particular quality, such as peace or more fun. Somewhere above the rose, imagine you are either writing the name of this single goal/quality or visualize a symbol for it. Next, imagine you are dropping the name of the goal or the symbol into the rose. Then be silent for a minute or two, place your attention on the rose, and wait to see what happens to it. Does it take on a color? Does the bud get bigger? Smaller? Change positions? Does it open or close? Grow brighter or shrivel?

Step 2: If you don't like how your rose looks, destroy this one and create a new one. Ground the rose by seeing its stem go deep into the earth. Next to it visualize a gauge that goes from 1 to 100. This gauge will represent how much permission you are giving yourself to fully have this thing or quality for yourself. Visualize the gauge and notice where the arrow lands. If the arrow of the gauge lands on a number lower then you'd expected, then go ahead and raise the arrow to the number you'd like it to be at. This could be 100, but it doesn't have to be. Do this very slowly, and postulate that you are going to release anything from the rose that might be in the way of allowing yourself to receive and keep this creation for yourself. Watch the rose and stem, and notice if any colors or even images release out of either one. Then take the gauge with the new number and drop this revised gauge into your rose. Notice what happens to the rose.

You may need to repeat the exercise a few times before you are happy with the results. Anything that comes up that is not to your liking can always be dropped right down the stem into the earth. It doesn't have to be a problem, and if you are feeling that there is a problem with this rose or are struggling with any feelings of effort, hopelessness, or frustration, then just see a color for this struggle or for the feelings, and release these down the stem of the rose and/or your own grounding cord.

Step 3: Finally, see an image of yourself receiving the rose into your heart. See yourself jumping around with absolute joy and enthusiasm because you have already received what you wanted. Imagine what you are doing now that you have attained your goal, and imagine yourself telling someone who is supportive of you how happy you are that you were able to manifest, receive, and have this for yourself. Thank yourself for allowing yourself to have this wonderful gift.

Note: This exercise can be intense, can bring up strong emotions, or make you sleepy. Take a nap as needed.

CHAPTER 20

Overcoming Psychic Stage Fright

*It is not work that kills men; it is worry. Work is healthy; you can hardly
put more upon a man than he can bear. Worry is rust upon the blade.
It is not the revolution that destroys the machinery, but the friction.
Fear secretes acids, but love and trust are sweet juices.*
— HENRY WARD BEECHER

Fear is one of the first things you will encounter when exploring your psychic abilities. Whether you are just taking you first baby steps on your path of psychic development, or whether you have covered millions of miles along that road as a professional psychic, you are susceptible to the many factors that may put you into resistance to doing further readings and that diminish your joy and enthusiasm for readings. Fear is an emotion that may keep you from ever attempting to consciously use or develop your abilities, and particularly from practicing readings on or for other people.

Most psychics, if not all (including the most famous), battle with this fear their whole lives, sometimes falling prey to it but then wrestling out of its tangled clutches and finding their way back to their certainty and passion, soaring, and then being sucked back into it through an endless cycle that becomes quite familiar. Others fall into the muck and never find their way out. Still others learn to identify the enemy of fear so that each time it rears its ugly head it's easier to sidestep. This is my hope for you. Every time a psychic takes a new step—whether expanding their clientele, raising their rates, or moving into the public spotlight—they must grapple with the fear all over again.

The most renowned psychics don't speak about this fear because they are in it. They fear that by talking about it, they will seem less capable, less in control, less confident. I certainly fall into this trap myself. I took out the chapter on this subject from my first book, but now I understand that it has really got to be included in any discussion about the mastery of psychic skills.

This fear results in what I call *resistance.* Resistance is a feeling and attitude, sometimes with accompanying negative thoughts, that you just don't want, or even can't do, something—in this case, clairvoyant readings. I emphasize readings instead of healings because for most people it's a lot more threatening to verbally communicate something to another person, since there is greater potential for the person to say, "You are wrong." Keep in mind that sometimes you will be completely aware of the fear and its impact on you, and at other times it will morph into excuses and justifications that seem logical at the time but really are doing you a disservice (fear of anything does this, by the way).

Sometimes you will interpret your fear as a "gut feeling" and wonder if it is not a premonition telling you to stay away from this odd fascination you have with your psychic abilities. The problem with gut feelings is that they can be right on, but at other times they are nothing but nervous butterflies or indigestion. (That's one reason to turn to your clairvoyant images, which can be a lot more informative than a simple feeling.) Sometimes you may feel nervous before a reading because the reading will in fact be a challenging one, either because the person you are reading is challenging, or their issues are, or because your own issues, pictures, or blocks are going to come to light.

Some of the most challenging readings turn out to be the ones that serve to remove the first or final brick in the wall keeping you from the life you really want to have. Would you avoid this opportunity just because it's going to be challenging? When it comes to clairvoyant readings, it's really not very common to find yourself in a situation in which you really wish you had not done the reading. (If this does happen to you, it has more to do with your choice of clients and your decisions about how you wish to work with them—for example, the frequency, the compensation, or the boundaries you've set.)

Resistance will fluctuate from person to person, from one end of the continuum to the other, and it may be so strong within someone that they are not even able to contemplate the possibility of psychic talents in themselves or others (this category includes professional skeptics). For others, resistance might hit them as they contemplate doing readings, or once they start charging money for their readings. Still others might hit their resistance after a particularly trying reading or after receiving some kind of negative feedback or response. The important thing to remember when you hit your resistance is to not let it stop you from doing another reading because, ultimately, continuing forward is the only thing that will help you to work through the resistance.

Below are some of the thoughtforms through which the fear expresses itself for both those who have not even begun to explore their own abilities and for seasoned professionals who have been doing psychic reading or healings for years. It is important to understand that these come up for even the most talented, successful psychics, so it's not a matter of just gaining a certain level of skill or confidence. As you read this list, it would be helpful to put a check mark next to any of these that may have ever crossed your mind or that might ring true for you.

- I am afraid I might not really have psychic abilities.
- I am afraid I might not see anything.
- I am afraid I might be wrong in what I see.
- I am afraid I might see something that will scare me.
- I am afraid I might see a spirit, even a bad one.
- I am afraid I might tell someone something that will upset them.
- I am afraid I might influence this person in the wrong way.
- I am afraid of what the readee might do with the information.
- I am afraid I might be messing with something I shouldn't.

- I am afraid I am dealing with an area I don't know enough about.
- I am afraid this readee will think I am a bad psychic or a bad person.
- I am afraid if I am charging money that this person will feel cheated.
- I am afraid they may not believe I am really psychic.
- I am afraid I may not be able to convince them I am psychic.
- I am afraid the person might get angry if I tell them what I see.
- I am afraid my parents or friends will think this is all ridiculous.
- I am afraid that people from my church will not understand.
- I am afraid I might get psychically attacked.
- I am afraid I might take on too much of this person's energy.
- I am afraid I will be too vulnerable right now.
- I am afraid if I get into this stuff too much I will lose my relationships with people in my life who don't believe in it or approve of it.
- I am afraid because my church says it's the work of the devil.
- I am afraid I can't explain what this is all about.
- I am afraid I am doing something I should not be, but I don't quite know why.

When we are not conscious of the above thoughtforms and fears (and even when we are), the fear can easily impact out behaviors. Some of these behaviors may be accompanied by feelings of nervousness, or even dread, particularly before you've begun your reading. These feelings are really not any different from good old-fashioned stage fright or performance anxiety. Some of the most common are as follows:

Resistant Behaviors Before a Reading

- Canceling the readings
- Failing to do anything to solicit readings, or to let people know you are available
- Rescheduling readings because you are too tired, too emotional, or too sick
- Avoiding calling back interested clients

Resistant Behaviors During a Reading

- Excessive apologizing for the things you are not seeing, as opposed to just stating what you are seeing and experiencing
- Failing to do further exploration when you see something you don't understand
- Withholding information you are seeing out of fear of disapproval or a negative response on the part of the readee
- Consciously making things up or guessing during your reading to get through it, as opposed to making yourself be patient and concentrate more
- Making emotional statements such as "How am I supposed to know?" or "I don't know"
- Failing to creatively ask your viewing receptacle the right questions to elicit a response
- Asking your readee too many questions
- Constantly asking your readee to validate or confirm too much of what you are seeing

- Refusing to look at something with the excuse that it can't be done without trying it out first
- Giving advice based on your beliefs as opposed to waiting for information to come to you
- Falling into a teaching mode as opposed to a reading mode
- Falling out of a clairvoyant mode and into a counseling mode

Resistant Behaviors After a Reading

Note that these behaviors can cycle back into the above thoughtforms and behaviors.

- Obsessing about how you should have done something differently
- Wondering if you did the right thing
- Beating yourself up for not having stated something
- Feeling like you are not a very good psychic
- Feeling like you might not want to do readings again
- Feeling fear about doing another reading
- Offering to give back the client's money even though you've just spent an hour and a half with them working your hardest
- Focusing on the one or two things you didn't see, when in fact you know you saw enough to take up more than an hour of your time

Just this last week, I found myself offering to refund a client's money, even though I had already spent close to an hour with him. I realized I was working so hard to access the information that I was sweating more than I do when I physically work out! He wanted to know if a particular woman loved him, but every image that came to me clearly indicated that this woman was absolutely enraged with him. It seemed as though things could easily lead down the path of physical violence if they hadn't already. However, every time I described what I was getting, the man replied that he did not understand me, that what I was seeing could not be correct, and please could I help him. I could feel myself going too deeply into his energy field and felt my own being compromised, and so I finally just offered to end the reading and refund his money.

At this point he decided to explain what was really going on, which was that he was married and having an affair with this young woman who had indeed told him that she intended to marry someone else and that he must never contact her ever again. (Mind you, not once did he say to me, "You were right.") I asked him why he was still pursuing her, and he said he felt she didn't know what was best for her. Since she was from a "little village in a Third World country," he said she should be satisfied with occasional visits from a lover who would give her money as opposed to wanting to be married to someone willing to commit to her. All he needed to know was whether or not she loved him. I told him I'd take one last look at her. I saw an image of her spitting in his face. In the next one it looked as if she were slitting his throat. In the next image it was as if she were stomping on his heart. I described these images exactly as I saw them. His response: "All right, fine, but you still haven't answered my question. Does she love me?" Arggggh!!

Following this reading I found myself thinking about this client a lot and I came down with a headache that didn't go away until the next day, when I decided to clear him out of my head. I did this by visualizing a sticky rose entering my head and swirling around to absorb his energy, questions, demands, and whatever might be causing the pain in my head. I then visualized the rose getting bigger and bigger and took it out of my head. As I did this I felt a pinpoint of pain increase sharply for about thirty seconds, and then all pain completely vanished. This entire process took less than five minutes.

Categories of Resistance to Readings

Those dealing with your doubts about your own clairvoyant abilities
- Feeling overly responsible for others
- Being overly concerned about others' opinions of you
- Not liking or wanting to read certain people
- Resisting your own matching pictures and issues
- Feeling the fear of others around you

Doubts About Your Own Abilities

The only way to work through your fear is to grin and bear it, and get enough readings under your belt with enough people in as many situations as possible until your confidence and certainty grow. This means you will have to have *faith*. You will have to say, "I feel afraid, but I am going to do this anyway."

It is really the same thing with any skill or ability, regardless of your natural talent. You need to encounter enough situations in order to know that you can really handle them. It means pushing past the fear. You will understand this if you do physical activities like motorcycle riding, snowboarding, surfing, or rock climbing. If you've never done these activities, you will have no idea if you can. The fear will be great. If you've tried any of these once or twice and did not fare so well, the fear will be almost unbearable. Yet if you try a few more times, particularly with the help of a supportive and skilled instructor and the right type of quality equipment, you will discover, "Wow, I can stand up on my feet at least part of the way," or "I made it out past the waves and back without drowning, and it was kind of fun!" or "Wow, I did make it up, back down, and around that cliff!"

Then after a few more attempts it becomes, "Wow, this is pretty easy!" or "I can make it down the mountain this time without having to slide down on my butt!" So little by little you advance and enjoy the activity more and more.

It is no different with clairvoyant reading. But still there are all the pitfalls, the little accidents, the growing and learning pains that torment us with messages such as, "No, I am not capable or cut out for this," particularly when we compare ourselves to others who have either been doing it a lot longer than we have or who have gained other comparable skills.

A guy (should I say *dude*?) who grew up riding skateboards and doing bike tricks, and has developed both the muscles and the experience to understand the physics of a board and how much tolerance and strength he has in a variety of situations, is going to do a lot better the first time he jumps onto a snowboard or a surfboard than someone who has had no experience with these things. In the same way, if you are a fledgling student who has never meditated or spent much time inside yourself in a disciplined and focused way (as opposed to daydreaming), it's important that you don't compare yourself to a classmate who is a master at Tai Chi or yoga and is now taking up learning clairvoyance. Your classmate is going to have a stronger advantage. This doesn't mean they will ultimately be better, however, so of course by no means should you should just give up; it's only that you may require a bit more time, practice, and definitely patience.

Don't Compare Yourself to Others!

The biggest problem I see with students is not just that they are comparing themselves to others, but that they also have an ideal in their mind about what they are supposed to be doing. Take one of my students, who, as I noted earlier in this book, has fantastic abilities and was able to see the contents of my room so clearly. I would notice during a reading that he would see something so clearly about a person, describe this characteristic, and then end his reading with statements such as, "But that's all I'm getting" or "But I'm not sure." From his language it's easy to determine that he is putting himself down for what he is not seeing as opposed to really congratulating himself for what he is seeing. Is the glass half full or half empty? Is it more important that you get one piece of vital information or that you don't see another piece of information?

I believe there are many reasons why we don't see what we want to see other than the possibility that we are just falling short as psychics. Some of these reasons include:

1. We are not meant to see the information. The readee needs to have an experience without interference.
2. We are too close; we have too many issues that are similar to the readee's issues.
3. The readee knows what we are talking about but isn't ready to let others know.
4. The readee is not yet ready to handle the information.
5. We are asking the wrong questions or are focused on the wrong thing.
6. Your own frame of reference is too limited, so you can't make sense of what you see.
7. There is no answer, or there are multiple answers.
8. You may in fact have already answered the question, but your readee doesn't realize that was the answer or doesn't want to accept it.

It is important to remember that when doing a clairvoyant or really any psychic reading or remote viewing, there are at least two if not several parts of ourselves that are resting, acting, and reacting at all times. One part is receiving, one is guiding, another part is assessing, assimilating, interpreting, judging. It is this last part that you must be wary of because this is the part that will torment and terrorize you. If you feel that this is the dominant part of you, tell it to go away and focus on the parts that get to have fun exploring new worlds.

Feeling Overly Responsible

There is a fine line between being ethical and caring, and taking responsibility for something that doesn't have anything to do with you. Many people believe they must protect others from their own emotional responses. They think they have to say or do the absolute right thing or else they are going to cause the other person harm or get a response that makes them uncomfortable. Such people are therefore either afraid to speak up at all, or they fall into manipulation tactics that include being extra nice, hiding the truth, and placing judgments on every word, image, and feeling.

Many men think that unless they have the power to do something about someone's problems, they might as well not even bother hearing about them, or they might believe that every time a woman complains about something she is asking for help. Sometimes she is, but many times she fully understands there is nothing this man can do except listen, which will make her feel better.

As a psychic, you are not responsible for what you see. In terms of what you communicate, there are some gray areas. However, I think you will be okay as long as you communicate from a place of love and respect and use your clairvoyance and other intuitive abilities to guide you with what you should or should not communicate. Except for occasions when I did unsolicited and uninvited readings (something I don't do anymore), I have always found that a certain bit of information came up precisely because the client did either want or need to know it. My errors came not from speaking up but from withholding the information. Again, I am not talking about just blurting out, "Your husband is having an affair" if you haven't been asked, or "I think you are going to die soon." (As noted elsewhere in this book, there would never, ever be a reason to say such things; instead you'd want to discuss the details of the pictures you saw that led your mind to form these conclusions.) But you might be surprised at how some students can barely mutter, "I see a dark energy cord poking out of the left side of your aura" or "I see an image of a refrigerator and it looks like you are eating a lot" or "I see some black colors around you" or "I see a spirit plugged into your heart that looks kind of sad" without following up that statement with an urgent, terrified remark such as "But it's okay, it's not a bad thing."

Your job as a psychic is not to say if something is bad or good, but rather to describe what you are observing. When I hear a student making such statements, it's a warning sign because I know they must be censoring and subsequently withholding other information that might really be quite valuable to their readee.

Being Too Concerned About What Others Think About You

My all-time favorite title for a book is *What You Think of Me Is None of My Business,* by Terry Cole-Whittaker. Being overly concerned about what others think about you is a set-up for misery, failure, and disaster. Again, this is about balance. Making a good impression is important for business, for relationships, and for your overall self-esteem. However, there is a fine line that is frequently overstepped, particularly by women, who don't just desire but have a strong need to feel as if they are accepted by everyone. The fact is that some people are going to hate you for being too beautiful, too successful, too wealthy, too famous, too talented, too psychic, even too nice or accommodating. They could hate you because you believe in them more than they believe in themselves. They could hate you simply because they want to hate you. Therefore, if you feel that you *need* (as opposed to *would like*) every one of your clients to like you or believe in you and what you do, then you are setting yourself up for failure before you even start.

Sometimes people you read will resist what you are saying, even if it is a compliment. For example, you might see that a client is much stronger than she gives herself credit for, that she is hiding, selling herself short, and that she has more power than she believes she does. If the client isn't ready to acknowledge these things in herself, if she wants to believe she is a victim who can only be helped through other people saving her, or by some miracle like winning the lottery, then she isn't going to want to hear that she is the one with the power to change her life. Ironically, your reading may be one stepping stone that ultimately brings your client closer to being ready to step into her power, but that readiness may not happen until a week, month, or decade after she has told you that you must be wrong or be talking about the wrong person. ("What, can't you see how sick I am? What kind of psychic are you?")

Not Wanting to Read Certain People

There doesn't need to be a deep-seated psychological reason for having the feeling you don't want to read someone. I don't need to tell you that some people, lots of them, are absolutely annoying! They are argumentative, stubborn, stuck, close-minded, and accusatory. They don't have any interest in taking responsibility for their life and are coming to you because they just want to hear about what is going to happen to them as opposed to how they can influence their own life.

It is no more fun to read these people than it is to speak with them. Getting any information for them psychically is like pulling teeth, or like having holes drilled in your teeth without Novocaine. Sometimes before a reading you will sense this even if you've never met or spoken to the person before. I am not saying you should want to read these people or need to. Many psychics begin reading people like this because they put themselves into places that more of the general public frequents, such as street fairs, restaurants, nightclubs, or stores. That being said, there is value in reading people you don't like. The main value is that you get to work on your own matches with them, those things in yourself you don't like, the things in yourself you are trying to avoid. If you want to adamantly argue with me on this point, it's just further proof that you may really have some similarities with this person, and that is precisely why I recommend reading them!

I need to emphasize that it's not about going head-to-head with the client in a combative stance or trying to get them to see or do things your way. It is about exploring what's up for them so you can hear yourself speaking some words of wisdom, which later on you can apply to your own life. If someone you don't like asks you to do a reading, I have no problem with you turning them down. Instead, what I am saying here is that sometimes before a reading you are going to feel nervous, a sense of dread, and it's important to understand that this may be because you are about to encounter a difficult person or reading, but the feelings don't mean you shouldn't do the reading. Only if you feel a sense of danger, a sense you are vulnerable to attack, do I suggest letting yourself be stopped.

If you are unsure whether or not you should read someone, I suggest agreeing to do only a phone session—the reading can be just as good as it would be in person, but your energy field will be less. The worst that will happen is that the client says no, they only want you in person, and you will lose a client, which in the end is probably the best thing that could have happened. That being said, one of the things I love most about readings is that sometimes I will completely misjudge or underestimate a person, and by the end of the reading, after spending an hour connecting with them on a deep level and really getting to know them beyond my first impressions, I will be in absolute awe of their strengths, talents, or all that they've overcome in their life.

Feeling Your Readee's Fears

Please don't think you are going to become psychic only once you sit down to do the reading or put up your reading screen! Many people about to receive readings are quite nervous. You may easily feel that person's unease or any of their emotions (including anger) prior to the reading, sometimes as soon as you wake up that day. Again, if you have close matching pictures and issues with that person, you will likely be more impacted by their feelings. Sometimes through running your energy and grounding yourself you can release these quite easily. At other times all it takes is a simple questioning or acknowledgement, "Are these really my feelings or am I picking them up from somewhere else?" At other times, you will just need to grin and bear it and not let it get in the way of you doing the reading. I guarantee that by the time the reading is over, you will very much understand what your prereading jitters or emotions were about, and you will feel 100 percent different.

Healing Resistance and Psychic Stage Fright

How do you get over psychic stage fright? Certainly not by avoiding the stage! Although some actors say the fear never completely subsides, they learn to use the energy of the emotion rather than let it take over. I believe it's the same for psychics, whether they are in front of an audience of five thousand on a soundstage or sitting on their bed in their pj's (my usual attire) while chatting on the phone. You've just got to push yourself! One thing I recommend if you have a really severe case of the jitters is, for a while, to read only your most supportive friends or those who are psychic themselves or have a strong interest in this area. Don't charge for your readings until you feel quite comfortable doing so.

Sometimes the resistance you are hitting is not so much related to an avoidance of reading as it is to an avoidance of your own growth.

That is not necessarily a bad thing. When it comes to growth, we need to pace ourselves. A rapid period of growth needs to be followed by assimilation and rest. If you've been doing a lot of clairvoyant or psychic readings packed into a short time, have been going through huge emotional shifts, or even life-changing events like getting married, having a baby, or enduring a major health challenge, you may just need a break from the intensity of readings and focusing on other people's issues.

What If You Really Do Have a Bad Reading?

If you do have an unpleasant reading experience, it is imperative that you perform another reading on a different person as soon as possible, even though your natural inclination will be to want to avoid ever reading again. You will understand what I am talking about as soon as you follow this advice. The only way to cancel out a bad experience is to create a good one in its place. You may do a hundred easy, fun, excellent readings that make you feel as though you are on top of the world, but when you do one that turns out badly (for example, the readee runs from the room crying, saying you are not psychic), it's human nature to get stuck on that bad experience and disregard all the others. When you bravely overcome your fears and resistance and go out to do one more (even if you swear it will be your last), you will again remember that you are a talented clairvoyant after all and be ready for your next adventures in clairvoyant reading.

Resistance to reading can come out of nowhere, even when all of your readings have been positive. It also comes in many forms, in many disguises. You may feel too tired or too busy to read. You may feel angry, like you don't want to be bothered by people's problems. You might feel afraid, as though you are not going to be able to see anything. You might feel overwhelmed or judgmental, like you don't think you are going to like the person you'll read. You may forget about scheduled readings, get the dates and times confused, show up late, get lost along the way, or fantasize about your readee not showing up. This resistance is energy that doesn't want you to perform the reading. It is either coming from you yourself (because you are going to blow some major matching pictures), from foreign energies connected to you (family or spirits that don't want you to make changes that the reading might inspire), or from energies surrounding your readee.

There is a difference between resistance to reading and your intuition or spirit advising you that it is not in your best interest to read. Telling the difference between these can be difficult and often impossible. If you have already done several readings one day and just feel you can't stomach another one, or are feeling really emotional and unbalanced, then reading may not be what you need to do.

Reading and healing does take a lot of energy. It means giving other people your time and attention, which you may need for yourself to accomplish personal goals. During the last several months that I was writing my first book, I performed very few readings because all of my personal resources needed to go to the book and to caring for my son. During the writing of this book, I have been doing a lot of private training sessions with students and readings, which is giving me material for the book, reminding me of the topics to cover, and giving me new bursts of enthusiasm for the subject. There is nothing wrong with making the decision not to read; it's just important to be aware of your reasons and not to let fear and other destructive energies get in the way of your enjoyment of reading.

CHAPTER 21

Psychics Are People, Too

If you aren't good at loving yourself, you will have a difficult time loving anyone, since you'll resent the time and energy you give another person that you aren't even giving to yourself.
— BARBARA DE ANGELIS

You Must Set Boundaries on Every Level

Due to the nature of what they do and who they are, psychics often have poorer boundaries than other people. Setting boundaries means knowing what works best for you and what feels right for you, and communicating this to your clients. Enforcing boundaries means sticking to your guns and making sure your clients' desires and needs don't encroach upon your own.

For many psychics, it's not just drawing the line and stopping others from crossing it, it's keeping yourself from leaping over it in desperation to save every man, woman, child, animal, and blade of grass that seems to be crying out for your help! Enforcing boundaries is not selfish; it's self-preservation. Many psychics fail to ever draw the line between acceptable and unacceptable behavior of their clients because they fear that if they do so they will repel or lose clients. The more in survival mode they are, the more inclined they are to sacrifice themselves.

Many of us psychics and healers are easily manipulated due to our tendency to be overly compassionate to the point that we experience others' emotions as our own, and because we have been brainwashed into believing we have to make up for the wrongs of other psychics or of society's stereotypes of psychics. Psychics carry around a collective sense of guilt, not because we personally have anything to be guilty about but because so many people don't believe we are doing what we say we are. We, particularly women, are controlled through guilt as much as through fear (if not more so), because we've been socialized to respond to feelings of guilt with actions that we believe will decrease this guilt. (Ridding oneself of guilt should never be a motivating factor for action; doing so only creates more problems in the long run.)

Too much compassion, poor boundaries, guilt, and self-doubt form the perfect cocktail of vulnerability for exploitation. Ironically, it's the handful of psychics who don't have these qualities and are acting selfishly that have been partially responsible for giving the rest of us a bad reputation. I say *partially* because the bigger problem is really that there still are so many people out there who have been brainwashed into believing ESP is nonsense or the work of the devil. If that's the case, then who are we to them, those of us who claim to be psychic?

The thing we need to remember is that it's not us who have the problem, it's them!

The Business of Spirituality Revisited

As a psychic, setting boundaries will make a huge difference in your readings in terms of accessing, processing, and communicating the information you receive, and will ultimately determine whether you are a healthy, happy person or a basket case. If you hope to do, are attempting to do, or are succeeding at doing psychic readings for a living, setting boundaries will make the difference between being a prosperous businessperson and spending your life in and out of financial crisis or worse.

In *You are Psychic* I included a chapter called "The Business of Spirituality," in order to help psychics figure out whether or not and when they are ready to shift from student or amateur reader to professional. Below I will highlight a few essential points that have helped the psychics I've been working with, whether they are brand-new students who are practicing on volunteers in Internet chat rooms or seasoned professionals who can barely peel themselves out of bed because they are so exhausted.

Rule #1: You don't have to give anyone a free reading to prove yourself!
Don't get me wrong. Doing readings for free is a great way to hone your clairvoyant skills and get practice under your belt. You really shouldn't be charging money for readings unless you feel confident enough and strongly compelled to do so. Charging for readings adds a whole new dimension of pressure to your readings. I've had one or two of my students begin charging after their first reading on their own, although most take much longer before they realize they really do have something of value to offer and need to be compensated for their time. What I *am* opposed to is offering readings or agreeing to do readings for free when you really feel you should be paid, and particularly when you are considering doing readings for free in order to prove yourself.

Once again, the twenty-four-hour psychic hotline craze that has infiltrated TV over the past decade can be blamed for people's misperceptions that asking for a free reading as proof of one's authenticity is acceptable. There are several reasons I will absolutely not do this. First of all, it is a waste of time and it never takes just a minute—not for a psychic who adequately prepares herself or himself before a reading and who does a thorough clean-out after a reading. I cannot guarantee anyone that I can get the answer to their question in exactly one or two minutes. It is often not that simple. The process just takes longer.

That's why I no longer offer readings that are less than thirty minutes in length and why unscrupulous hotlines that charge by the minute often do become very successful; the reading always takes longer than the client planned. Hotlines can afford to offer free readings for the same reason certain major department stores will accept returns without receipts or questions whereas smaller stores will not. The larger stores can afford the loss. Personally I can't afford the loss of my time, and I doubt if you can or want to either.

Furthermore, even if you are the best psychic in the world, the person "testing" you is not necessarily going to like what you have to say; they may not get it right away or ever. "No, you won't find Prince Charming or have a baby until you drop at least 150 pounds" isn't exactly going to bring back repeat business, although the person may be impressed that you were able to "see" over the phone how overweight or lethargic they really are!

In what other profession that you know of are people expected to provide their services for free? Can you imagine going to a doctor, a lawyer, an electrician, a mechanic, or a tutor, and telling them, "I don't really know if I'm going to like you, if I can trust you, or if you're what I'm looking for, so will you take time out of your busy schedule and do this for free so I can make sure first?" Can you imagine going to a restaurant and asking if you can taste any given dish before ordering because you aren't sure you're going to like it? Who is going to pay for the food you just tasted, or pay the cook who just created that meal? No one thinks of doing this because we know that whether or not we like what we are getting, these people are working. If I sit with you for an hour doing my best to receive clairvoyant messages, whether I ever receive one or not, I am working my butt off! As adults, we know that anytime we put down even a penny on an item or a service, we are taking the risk that we might not like it, that it might not meet our expectations. We know this going into every situation. If the risk doesn't seem worth it, then we have the choice not to go forward.

As a professional psychic, I can guarantee that I will do my best to use every technique I know, every skill I have, to access information with my abilities. From past experience I can say I am pretty confident that I will at least come up with some relevant, helpful, accurate information, but since I am in the position of receiving it and therefore dependent on forces outside myself to bring me this information, I can't guarantee that every time every person will walk away 100 percent satisfied. Does that mean I shouldn't be compensated for the time it takes for me to do the work I do? When you or I pay for a psychic, first and foremost we are paying for the time they are focusing on us instead of all the other things they could be doing, like playing with their kids, writing, doing the dishes, sleeping!

The public needs to be reeducated to understand that psychics and healers are professionals and individuals who are doing their best to help, but who also have families and needs of their own. I think the misperceptions and rude behavior will only change if enough of us stand firm, and politely explain why it's not acceptable to ask us to look at or solve others' problems for free, or to have to prove ourselves at any time of the day or night.

Rule #2: If you work for yourself, you set your own hours.

Certain hotlines can afford to offer readings twenty-four hours a day only because they have dozens of psychics working for them who are signed up for particular shifts. Some of these psychics or employees try to make themselves available around the clock for calls that come in at odd hours, and these are the psychics who have the most problems. It is therefore unreasonable and unhealthy for you to expect yourself to be available whenever someone is having a crisis and wants to talk to you. Some potential clients do have this expectation and, rather than you comprising your personal time and well-being to meet this unrealistic demand, it's up to you to educate them. If you lose that person as a client, you will soon attract someone else who has more respect for you and your time.

Rule #3: *Understand your own motivations for working with repeat clients.*

Nothing is wrong with working with the same people on a regular basis, as long as you feel that your work with them is about empowering them, as opposed to giving them readings on the same subject over and over again with the hope that you will eventually see what they are hoping you'll see. Ironically, you will inevitably see what they want if you keep readdressing the same topic, not because that is what is really going to happen, but because you will be merely reading their pictures of what they want to happen.

Have you ever answered a child in a certain way, only to have them ask you the same or similar questions ten more times? Kids do this because they know that if they can wear you down, catch you at a moment of weakness, you might just say yes. It is the same thing with clients who are seeking information in order to cope with their own emotions of fear or sadness. Sometimes you will spend an hour or even two hours with a client, and they have so many questions or areas of interest that you both feel it's appropriate to set up another session within the next week. However, more often and most of the time, you will find that the client would benefit by having more time before the next reading or healing in order to undergo the transformation that your session has initiated. It is ultimately about the client taking the steps and doing the work, not you, so giving them the time to do this is what will be most empowering. If you allow some time to pass, perhaps two or three months or longer, and then they come back and say things still haven't changed or they feel stuck, then you can look at why that is. Sometimes things will have changed so much that the client will have a whole new slew of questions for you to address.

I'd say that 80 percent of people (at least of the ones I read) who get readings will feel as if they got enough at the end of the first reading, so they don't feel a need to come back for another session until at least six months have passed.

Rule #4: *Use your intuition to help you choose your clients, and exercise common sense.*

Many people prefer to get a reading in person. If you work for yourself out of your home, be very cautious about whom you invite over. Phone readings work just as well as in-person readings, if not even better sometimes. Some clients don't understand that, or they will only want a reading if it's in person, but you should never compromise your safety or the safety of your family in exchange for money.

CHAPTER 22

Conclusion: The Awakening
of America

We must be prepared to make the same heroic sacrifices for the cause of peace that we make ungrudgingly for the cause of war.
— ALBERT EINSTEIN

Americans are waking up, and this process has been painful. In the past decade alone we've witnessed not just the fall of our heroes and leaders from their proverbial pedestals but the desecration of the illusion that we live in a society where our votes count, or are even counted. We have begun to question whether we are truly free or more like indentured servants, shackled to dehumanizing jobs just to pay off our student loans (but you must go to college, how else will you get a job?) or credit cards (the only way to improve your credit score), or to keep our health insurance, car insurance, homeowner's or renter's insurance, product insurance, professional insurance—and if you love your kids, you'd better not forget that life insurance! (If you are concerned about health insurance, I highly recommend Michael Moore's film *Sicko*.)

Up until recently, many Americans thought of themselves as part of a sophisticated and evolved race that had overcome its primitive, predatory urges, and yet our society is filled with ever-craftier predators who continue to figure out more and more ingenious ways to separate us from our own money, resources, and sanity. These predators are not the ones lurking in drug-infested, urban alleyways, but rather they are in corporate cubicles and offices with their Bluetooth devices ringing into ears closed off from the beating of all human hearts except their own.

Many of us metaphysically oriented people are feeling rather schizophrenic these days. We understand the profound creative potential within ourselves. We know from personal experience and years of experimentation that our thoughts and emotions can create and impact reality, and we do our best to remain positive. However, many of us find ourselves teeter-tottering between feelings of hopeful optimism and disillusioned, even angry pessimism. I, like many of you, find myself wavering between these two positions as quickly as it takes me to shift from one foot to the other. On the one hand (or foot), I am sickened by what I see on the news and around me and by personal experiences that show me how corporate, capitalist greed is sucking the very life force out of our country. I am shocked by the gas prices, the housing prices, insurance laws and costs, and the fact that it's becoming more and more difficult to even rent a place or find a job unless you have a "competitive" credit score, which is more about how much you are willing to allow yourself to go into debt than it is a reflection of how financially responsible you are.

In the past decade we have witnessed countless scandals surrounding both our Democratic and Republican leaders. In the same way, we've seen the fall of the Catholic Church, with so many of its leaders convicted of the most heinous sex crimes imaginable against children. During this same period, millions of American workers have lost their jobs to outsourcing, have lost their retirement funds in corporate scandals and mismanagement, and have lost their homes to foreclosure.

Like children abandoned on bustling streets, many of us are crying, confused, ashamed, grieving, and in shock. We're somewhere between resisting, struggling with, and accepting the fact that in the end there is no guarantee that those who led us into this mess will stand by us. We possess a growing suspicion that they might even turn against us when the shit really hits the fan. Perhaps most difficult to handle is the realization that maybe those we idolized didn't really have the answers after all, that they didn't really know what was best for us—and perhaps never even cared in the way we needed to believe they did.

What does all this have to do with developing your psychic abilities? Everything! See, when you say you want to get in touch with your own intuition or with your heart, your spirit, your Higher Self, your guides with wisdom, or a perspective greater than your own, and when you say you want to heal yourself and others, what you are saying is that you want to see things for what they really are—not what you have been told, programmed, and brainwashed into believing. Many people in the New Age community increase their awareness of spirit but want to turn a blind eye to anything that is not full of love and light. Doing this constitutes outright denial of the world we live in. Problems such as global warming, racism, institutionalized extortion, insane gas prices, and pollution don't go away when we deny their existence, but it's also true that these problems won't get solved by obsessing about them every second, which only serves to diminish our quality of life.

When you develop and use your clairvoyance, you are essentially removing the veil that's been keeping you from seeing what is. That means you can't help but notice lots of unexpected things behind that veil, partition, or wall that is now crumbling to pieces before your very eyes. I am not just talking about seeing spirit guides or auras but rather the true intentions and behaviors of those spirits in physical bodies around you, including your parents and your political and religious leaders. I don't believe it's a coincidence that more and more people are opening up and becoming aware of their psychic abilities at the very same time they are waking up from the illusions of the American dream, a dream that has kept us milling around in a fog of ethnocentrism, elitism, racism, and a most insidious type of sadomasochism.

This awakening is not just beginning now; on the contrary, it really began in the 1960s with the uprising of American youth who protested everything from the oppression of their parents' puritanical values to the Vietnam War to racism against blacks to sexism against women to anything having to do with "the Establishment" and its authority figures. That this period also corresponded with an explosion of psychedelic, mind-altering drugs is certainly no accident. People needed a method by which to make huge leaps in the way they thought about the world, and drugs both facilitated this process and eased the pain that comes with any paradigm shift.

By the end of the 1970s, however, an interesting thing happened. Most of the population was lulled back to sleep, while only a much smaller sector remained aware. Why? How? Let me ask you this: What is the biggest reason you don't meditate, pray, or exercise as much as you'd like to? What's the biggest reason you don't get or give yourself enough of the sleep, rest, or relaxation that you know helps you connect to yourself? What's the biggest obstacle standing in your way of doing that which makes your spirit soar, whether it be writing, doing your art, traveling the world, even developing your psychic abilities? Most of us will have the same answer: *money*—either the lack of it, the need for it, the quest for it, or the fear of losing it.

Ironically, when we put first in our lives our creative projects and the people and things we love, the money often flows even more abundantly. At a time when money is going to become scarcer and more difficult to come by for millions of Americans (largely because a small group of individuals owning massive conglomerate corporations and supported by our government have figured out how to charge the rest of us more and more while offering less and less), it's vital that you take the time you need to go inward. It is imperative that you put your creative projects, your spiritual goals, and the overall health of your body at the top of your list. It is essential that you join forces with other like-minded individuals pursuing their own path of consciousness, and that you wholeheartedly believe that you can still have abundance and love and happiness in the face of everything else.

Most of us sit in our living rooms watching the news, which is doing more to traumatize us than inform us, as we are force-fed an unhealthy diet of homicide, despair, and violence. However, while we sit there wondering why we are sitting there, in that moment we really are okay. We really are warm, well-fed, and safe. If we do nothing else to protect ourselves, when we feel overwhelmed we've got to remember to bring ourselves into the present moment and remind ourselves—no matter how bad things seem, how awful we are told they are—that most of us really are just fine and dandy in this moment, and in the next moment and in the next.

These little conversations with ourselves are the only things that are going to get us through the next several years without going bonkers. I am not saying to focus only on your inner work instead of going to the job that helps you pay your bills. I am saying you can do both if you see one as being equally as essential as the other. The crazier things get on the outside, the more time you will need to revitalize yourself on the inside and connect with a solid support system of like-minded people.

A part of me believes that there are evil forces behind the corporate takeover of America. I don't know if this is exactly the case, but I do know without a doubt that what evil wants is for us to get stuck in our fearful emotions and self-defeating thoughts, because those are really the only places evil can reach us. We need to be informed, but listening to endless hours of talk radio or depressing and violent TV broadcasts mostly filled with propaganda is as unhealthy for us as adults as it is for our children. It is easy to get addicted to newscasts and talk shows because they infuse our sometimes monotonous lives with a quick fix of adrenaline, and they serve to make us feel that we are not alone in our frustration. They help us to feel connected. But what are we connecting to?

There are many people who believe we are going to ascend in the year 2012, which is the end of the Mayan calendar. There are many who think World War III is about to start and we have already entered the beginning of Armageddon. I find when I am excited about my life and the money is flowing, I am inclined to believe in the first version of the future. When I am feeling bored, ignored, or defeated in my own life, I lean toward the latter, pessimistic view. I know I am not alone in my projections.

So what to do? First, we need to replace our negativity with humor and inspiration so that we can raise our vibrations and manifest the things that truly make us happy. Utilizing the psychic's tools in the first part of this book and practicing your clairvoyant readings and healings will most certainly help with this. Do whatever you have to do to secure peace in your personal life, and at the same time do whatever you can, in whatever way comes naturally to you and excites you the most, to help out as many people as you can without draining yourself. We can let ourselves sink down into hopelessness or bring ourselves to a vibration where the evil can't reach us. Remember: when you are happy, your happiness brings more happiness to others. Happy people are less likely to go around fighting, raping, and killing each other or attract others who engage in these behaviors. To a great extent, you can make yourself happy by thinking happy thoughts.

The expenses and stressors in our lives are not going to decrease any time soon, but there are ways we can cope and rise above them. Stop giving the credit-card companies your power. If you are at the top of the credit-card game and understand how to work the system, then more power to you. But if you are already losing, then just opt out. Do your best to pay off any debt you've accrued but forgive yourself and let yourself off the hook. Those people calling you every day are earning about ten dollars an hour and are drowning in as much shame and debt as you are. Save your cash and pay for things with cash. Buy only what you love or really need, and then appreciate those items for being available to you—even if it's just a roll of toilet paper!

When someone calls you demanding money you don't have, don't argue with them, bless them! Tell them you love them. They really won't know how to respond! Regardless of the state of your credit score or bank account, let go of the shame. It is vital to understand that just about everyone else around you is struggling in the same way. Most Americans are one or two paychecks away from poverty. Start a dialogue about this. Admit what you are going through.

Have you ever noticed that finances are the one topic we are still not supposed to talk about? It's okay to share the most intimate details of a sexual encounter with someone you hardly know, but telling someone what you earn, how much money you have in your bank account, or—gasp!— what your credit score really is, is just not done. Why? I'm not sure. I know my parents told me that money is a very private matter. People won't respect you if they think you don't have it.

If you do have it, people will try to take it from you. Well, I have news for you. Abuse can only happen in secrecy and in isolation. This is true on an individual level and on a national one.

Most important, remind yourself that the status quo doesn't matter. Even if your credit score is zero, you can simply imagine that you are going to find the best place to live, that you will manifest cash for a home you wish to buy, or that you will find a landlord who could not care less about credit (maybe they're aware of the game and have dropped out, too) and who will love you at first sight. Delight in the fact that you obtained these so easily and effortlessly before you even go about trying to obtain them. Do this at least a few times a day until you manifest that which now seems quite unreachable.

The clearer you are about what you want and whether or not you deserve it, the easier it will be to draw these things to you on the physical level. I am utterly convinced that it's getting easier and faster to manifest with our thoughts. This is why everything seems so intense right now. Use this to your advantage rather than to your detriment.

In Search of a New Freedom

Most Americans have been taught that democracy is the most important tenet of our country. We've been taught that democracy is what gives us our freedom, what sets us apart as leaders and heroes in the world. The most essential component of American democracy is our right to vote, to choose our own representatives. If we believe we have exercised this right, then we're taught that this means that no matter how ignorant or unethical our leaders are, we must bear the cross that it's us who have chosen them and therefore accept the consequences. This is, of course, a pretty silly idea, and it's one that I believe has led to us allowing our leaders to degrade the integrity and reputation of America. Our voting system is severely outdated and has very little to do with the interest and voice of the people anymore (particularly when we can't trust the results of our own elections or when our choice of leaders is between the not-so-bad and the worse).

Depressing? Well, yes, of course it is depressing on one level. But on another level, I find these revelations quite exhilarating. Why? Because once we get past the stages of whining, anger, and grief, we can really get to the good stuff. Once we've cut through the illusions, we get to experience the pulse of life authentically and fully. We can begin to update and introduce a new version of democracy that better encompasses the needs of people today, in the present time.

New ideas and new ways of being start with visionaries who create the future first in their mind's eyes and then are courageous enough to share these revolutionary ideas with others. That's where you come in, as an extraordinary psychic. Whether you are American or from Saudi Arabia, whether you speak English, Polish, or Bengali, you have the power to start making changes by simply turning inward and imagining a new world with new solutions where *you* are the heroes and heroines, leading to the light those who can only see the bleakness.

On a national or global scale, I cannot guarantee things are going to get better anytime soon. They may, very possibly, get worse. But regardless of the outer conditions, if you practice the techniques in this book, whether on a constant basis or when you find yourself slipping back into the muck, you will always have a way to pull yourself up and out.

You have been given gifts that keep on giving. Whether you gain the whole world or lose it all, you will always be okay, because with the information in this book, you now have all you need to create what you need when you need it.

Security is ultimately not found in a retirement fund; it's found in the skills, including your innate psychic gifts, that can never be taken from you once you are aware of them. When all else is gone, you will still have *you*. That is the true freedom.

Bibliography

Of all that is written, I love only what a person has
written with his own blood.
— FRIEDRICH NIETZSCHE

Brinkley, Dannion. *Saved By the Light.* New York: HarperTorch, 1995.

Brown, Courtney. *Remote Viewing: The Science and Theory of Nonphysical Perception.* Atlanta: Farsight Press, 2005.

Buchanan, Lyn. *The Seventh Sense: The Secrets of Remote Viewing as Told by a "Psychic Spy" for the U.S. Military.* New York: Paraview Pocket Books, 2003.

Cole-Whittaker, Terry. *What You Think of Me Is None of My Business.* New York: Jove, 1988.

Cumming, Heather, and Karen Leffler. *John of God: The Brazilian Healer Who's Touched the Lives of Millions.* New York: Atria Books/Beyond Words, 2007.

Hicks, Esther, and Jerry Hicks. *Ask and It Is Given: Learning to Manifest Your Desires.* Carlsbad, CA: Hay House, 2004.

Karma-glin-pa, and W. Y. Evans-Wentz. *The Tibetan Book of the Dead.* Oxford: Oxford University Press, 2000.

Katz, Debra Lynne. *You Are Psychic: The Art of Clairvoyant Reading and Healing.* St. Paul, MN: Llewellyn, 2004.

Knight, J. Z. *Ramtha: The White Book.* Yelm, WA: JZK Publishing, 2005.

Kolodiejchuk, Brian, and Mother Teresa. *Come Be My Light.* New York: Doubleday, 2007.

Licauco, Jaime T. *The Magicians of God: The Amazing Stories of Philippine Faith Healers.* Manila, Philippines: National Book Store, Inc., 1980.

———. *Jun Labo: A Philippine Healing Phenomenon.* Manila, Philippines: self-published, 1984.

McMoneagle, Joseph. *Memoirs of a Psychic Spy.* Charlottesville, VA: Hampton Roads, 2006.

———. *Remote Viewing Secrets: A Handbook.* Charlottesville, VA: Hampton Roads, 2000.

McMoneagle, Joseph, and Charles T. Tart. *Mind Trek: Exploring Consciousness, Time, and Space Through Remote Viewing.* Charlottesville, VA: Hampton Roads, 1997.

McTaggart, Lynne. *The Field: The Quest for the Secret Force of the Universe.* New York: Harper, 2003.

———. *The Intention Experiment: Using Your Thoughts to Change Your Life and the World.* New York: Free Press, 2007.

Morehouse, David. *Psychic Warrior: The True Story of America's Foremost Psychic Spy and the Cover-Up of the CIA's Top-Secret Stargate Program.* New York: St. Martin's, 1998.

Myss, Caroline. *Anatomy of the Spirit: The Seven Stages of Power and Healing.* New York: Three Rivers Press, 1997.

———. *Three Levels of Power and How To Use Them.* Louisville, CO: Sounds True Publishing, compact disc.

Glossary

The true poem rests between the words.
— VANNA BONTA

ANALYTIC OVERLAY: A common term used in remote viewing, it refers to the analytical response of the viewer's mind to make sense of information it receives. Often, the interpretation is wrong although it tends to be based on data that is valid. There is no formal word for this in clairvoyant training, although the tendency of psychics, particularly new students, to provide inaccurate interpretations of the data is common.

ASTRAL PROJECTION OR ASTRAL TRAVEL: The ability of one's spirit to leave one's body and travel on the astral plane, in other dimensions, and to remote locations.

ATHEISM: A lack of belief in the spiritual, including God, psychic phenomena, or the human soul.

ATTENTION: A focus on something without intent. Intention is focus with a desired outcome.

AURA: The energetic field surrounding every living organism, which contains information about the organism and energies affecting it. The aura can be thought of as the organism's spirit extending outward from the body.

BLIND: Term used in psychological research and among remote viewers to describe the lack of awareness of the person participating in the experiment regarding the purpose, target, or other elements that otherwise might influence the experiment's perceptions, observations, and results.

BOSTWICK, LEWIS: Father of clairvoyant training in the United States and founder of the Berkeley Psychic Institute.

CHAKRAS: Sanskrit word for "spinning wheels," chakras are energy centers that correspond to certain parts of the human body and that regulate the body's overall functioning.

CHANNELING: A psychic ability in which a person receives and communicates information coming directly from a source outside themselves.

CLAIRAUDIENCE: A specific psychic ability in which information inaudible to human ears is heard inside one's mind.

CLAIRSENTIENCE: A specific psychic ability in which information is received through touch or on a physical body level.

CLAIRVOYANCE: A specific psychic ability located within one's sixth chakra, or third eye, that involves accessing information in the form of images, visions, and pictures.

CLAIRVOYANT HEALING: An act in which visualization is utilized to alleviate or transmute emotional or physical pain or negative energies and restore one to a healthier state.

CLAIRVOYANT READING: An act in which information in the form of mental images, visions, and pictures is accessed.

CLAIRVOYANT TRAINING SCHOOL: A school that offers a course in clairvoyant development. The first of these included the Berkeley Psychic Institute, founded by Lewis Bostwick. Several of his original students have gone on to establish their own training programs, including the Aesclepion Healing Center, Intuitive Way, and Psychic Horizons.

CODEPENDENT RELATIONSHIP: An unbalanced relationship in which one person sacrifices their own ideals or ignores their own inner voice in order to maintain the relationship or get other needs met within the relationship.

CONSCIOUSNESS: Perceiving, apprehending, or noticing with a degree of controlled thought. It involves rational power, perception, and awareness. The "conscious" part of the human being is that portion of the human consciousness that is linked most closely to and limited by the material world.

CONTROL: A person who assists a clairvoyant during a reading by providing analytical support through the process of posing questions or structure for the clairvoyant to focus on. The control may also help the clairvoyant prepare for and debrief from the session. Controls are used in many long-term clairvoyant training programs for beginning students, and often are students themselves who are learning to work with their crown chakras.

CONTROL FREAK OR CONTROLLING PERSON: A person who needs to understand or determine every element in life and interferes with the natural course of things, and who expends energy trying to control that which is out of their control. One who intends to circumvent God's will.

COORDINATE REMOTE VIEWING (CRV): The process of remote viewing using geographic coordinates for cueing or prompting.

CORE MEI PICTURES: An MEI picture that is developed early in life and that over time attracts similar clusters of thoughts and emotions that influence our perception and behavior. Personal transformation occurs when these pictures are destroyed or deenergized.

COSMIC ENERGY: Energy that originates from the air, sun, atmosphere, the spiritual realm, or God.

COUPLE'S READING: A clairvoyant reading in which the psychic reads the relationship or joint goals between two or more readees who are physically present.

DESTROY: To eliminate or alter a creation.

DISEMBODIED SPIRIT: A spirit that no longer belongs to a physical body.

EARTH ENERGY: Energy that originates from within the earth.

ENERGY: Life force; the essence of all things physical and nonphysical. Matter, atoms, thoughts, emotions, and pain consist of energy.

ENLIGHTENMENT: A state in which a person has become actualized, has accumulated a certain level of wisdom; when a person's body, mind, and spirit are fully integrated and their being holds more lightness than darkness.

ETHICAL DILEMMA: A conflict in which one must choose between two seemingly opposing values.

ETHICS: The study of rules of right and wrong in human conduct.

EXPECTATION: Having a predetermined set of ideas of how an event will unfold.

EXTENDED REMOTE VIEWING (ERV): A hybrid method of remote viewing that incorporates relaxation and meditation with the scientific protocols of Coordinate Remote Viewing.

EXTRASENSORY PERCEPTION: Perceiving information through means other than the five physical senses.

FAITH: Belief or trust in an outcome before the outcome occurs.

GROUNDING CORD: An energetic connection securing an object or person to the earth. Others energies can be released through this cord through conscious intent and visualization.

GROWTH PERIOD: An intense period of personal transformation during which one's beliefs, thoughts, perceptions and self-image are altered. This can result in a temporary period of emotional or cognitive turbulence, corresponding with a paradigm shift.

IMAGINATION: The act or power of creating pictures or ideas in the mind.

INCARNATION: A lifetime in a particular body.

INTENTION: Focus with a desired outcome.

KARMA: Spiritual award system that can include both desirable and undesirable consequences for one's prior conduct either in the present life or in prior incarnations.

KIRLIAN PHOTOGRAPHY: Heat-sensitive photography that can record information not ordinarily registered by the physical eye.

KNOWINGNESS: A psychic ability located in the crown chakra, or seventh chakra, in which a person instantaneously knows information in the form of a thought, without having to go through logical steps to gain that information.

LIBRARY OF SYMBOLS: A collection of symbolic images.

LITERAL IMAGE: An image that is what it appears to be.

MEDICAL INTUITIVE: A psychic who focuses primarily on the physical body and its ailments, in order to determine the cause, cure, and connection between an illness or disorder of the body and the mind and spirit of that being. Some psychics specialize as medical intuitives while others will act as medical intuitives in addition to focusing on other areas of a person's life as well.

MEDITATION: Turning inward and focusing within oneself or an outside object for the purpose of clearing one's mind and/or achieving a certain state of mind, which often includes relaxation and acceptance. Meditation is a technique for improving your life, healing yourself, and getting through difficult situations.

MEI PICTURE: Mental Emotional Image picture. This is an emotionally charged thoughtform that influences one's perceptions and behavior and is located within one's body, mind, and energetic field.

MONITOR: A person who oversees and assists a remote viewer during a remote-viewing session by providing analytical support to the viewer. The monitor provides the target and records relevant session information, providing feedback when appropriate.

MULTIPLE PERSONALITY DISORDER: A psychological dissociative disorder in which aspects of a person have split off from the person's awareness and behave and respond independently of other aspects.

NAVIGATING: The science of figuring out where one is heading. Charting a course, a path, or a plan that will lead to an intended goal. neutrality: Being neutral; maintaining a state of emotional and cognitive balance that is not invested in a particular outcome. nonattachment: Having no emotional investment in an object or in the outcome of a situation. omnipresent: Being everywhere all at once. omniscient: All-knowing. A quality of God. prayer: The act of talking to God or to a higher power. precognition: Knowing that something is going to happen before it happens.

PROGRAMMING: Beliefs, thoughts, ethics, information, feelings, or perceptions that are passed from one person to another that may or may not be in harmony with the recipient's own information or way of being.

PROJECTION: Seeing one's own qualities in someone else, often unconsciously; assigning particular attributes to another that really belong to oneself.

PSYCHIC EXPERIENCE: A supernatural experience in which information is sent or received through means other than the five senses.

PSYCHIC TOOLS: Visualization techniques that affect and influence energy that can be utilized for psychic reading and healing and to enhance the quality of one's life.

RELATIONSHIP READING: A psychic reading that focuses on issues regarding the relationship between two or more individuals.

REMOTE VIEWER: A person who employs their mental faculties to perceive and obtain information to which they would have no other access and about which they have no previous knowledge. This information can concern people, places, events, or objects separated from the remote viewer by distance, time, or other obstacles.

REMOTE VIEWING: The act of accessing information through one's psychic abilities about a distant location, object, or person.

SELF-ENERGIZATION: Calling one's life force to oneself.

SEPARATION OBJECT: A mental image or visualization that defines boundaries and serves as protection.

SKEPTICISM: A closed state of mind in which one doubts or questions things, sometimes to the point that these doubts obscure the truth.

SPIRIT: The essence of a person.

SPIRITUAL PATH: A course that one's spirit is destined to follow in order to gain certain life experiences while in the physical body.

STANFORD RESEARCH INSTITUTE (SRI): A research laboratory in California that spearheaded the research and formulated protocols that were utilized in clandestine remote-viewing programs in the United States.

STAR GATE, SUN STREAK, GRILL FLAME, CENTER LANE, INSCOM, AND SCANATE: Some of the names of remote-viewing programs financed and administered from the 1970s until at least the 1990s by the Defense Intelligence Agency and the Central Intelligence Agency of the United States government. (There may still be programs that we are unaware of!)

SUBCONSCIOUS: Existing in the mind but not immediately available to consciousness; affecting thought, feeling, and behavior without entering awareness. The mental activities just below the threshold of consciousness.

SUPERNATURAL: Beyond the physical sense; beyond the natural.

SYMBOL: An object or sign that represents another object, idea, person, or quality.

SYMBOLIC IMAGE: An image that is representative of something other than itself.

TARGET: A subject that remote viewers have been assigned to observe.

TARGET NUMBERS: Randomly selected numbers assigned to a target used in a remote-viewing session. These numbers enable viewers to remain "blind" or unaware of the item about which they are attempting to access information, in order to keep their own logical assumptions from tainting the information. The numbers have no significance in themselves.

TELEKINESIS: A psychic ability in which one can move or alter objects with the power of thought, emotion, or other energy, through nonphysical means.

TELEPATHY: Transferring information from one mind to another without the use of the physical senses.

THIRD EYE: The center of one's clairvoyance. The third eye corresponds with the sixth chakra and is located inside the forehead, slightly above and between the physical eyes.

TRANSFORMATION: Effecting change.

TRANSMEDIUMSHIP: A spiritual ability in which a person's spirit leaves the body and accepts a foreign spirit or energy into their own. This happens both consciously and without awareness.

VALIDATION: Confirming one's value.

VISUALIZATION: The act of calling forth images, visions, pictures, and colors in one's mind through conscious intent.

DEBRA LYNNE KATZ

Freeing the Genie Within

Manifesting Abundance, Creativity
& Success in Your Life

Living Dreams Press
www.livingdreamspress.com

Introduction

Travelers, it is late. Life's sun is going to set.
During these brief days that you have strength,
be quick and spare no effort of your wings.
—RUMI

In the 1990's I was working as a clairvoyant reader at a New Age bookstore in Sedona, Arizona. My rent was paid and my baby's tummy full, but my bank account and wallet were empty. It was past lunchtime, and I was hungry and well on my way to feeling sorry for myself. Then I looked towards the sacred crimson peaks that had made this landscape famous for its powerful vortexes of energy, and I remembered that I, like all humans, actually possess an inner vortex of energy. All the knowledge needed to manifest something grand and mountainous was in my psyche. Or, something as simple and desirable as lunch! so I decided to do a little experiment. I closed the door to my office, sat down in my favorite chair, and declared that I was not going to get up until I had manifested something to eat. Not just anything, but something I really loved, like Chinese food.

Next came the doubts. How long might I really have to sit here? What would the baby sitter say if I told her I wasn't going to be able to pick up Manny until next week, or next year? But I pushed aside these pesky thoughts and got busy. First, in order to psych myself up for success, I reminded myself of all the things I had created over the last couple of decades. These included trips and cars, furniture and spiritual teachers, friends, jobs, and more peace and joy than I had ever thought possible in my younger years. Next, I conjured up a feeling of gratitude for where I was in the present moment. I reminded myself that I wouldn't be sitting here in this room, doing the work I loved, in one of the most stunning and mystical places on earth if it wasn't for my ability to create what I needed, when I really needed it. Now I was ready for the core technique: I visualized myself being handed a hearty plate of steaming food that tasted and smelled so good that it dribbled down from my lips because my smile was so big.

I had barely settled into my meditation when there was a knock at my door. It was Scottie, whose office was down the hall. She was a busy woman who rarely had time to chat with a newcomer like myself, but this time she said, "Hey, you've probably already eaten, but I was just wondering if you might like to join me for lunch as my guest?"

Hmmm, that was a hard one!

"There's only one catch," she warned. "I'm really craving some Chinese food. Is that okay with you?"

When I arrived back at my office after this fulfilling lunch, I found a box of warm cookies outside my door that a clairvoyant reading client had baked for me. A few minutes later, a handsome man came to see me for a session. He was a famous radio sports announcer. After our session, he invited me to join him for dinner at L'Auberge, the only French restaurant in Sedona—and part of a very expensive resort. Before that night, the only time I had ever set foot in their plush lobby was when I'd applied for a job, for which I'd been turned down (which was fine with me; I'm not a very good waitress.) That night we had a fantastic dinner (despite the fact that he showed up in a bright yellow pinstriped suit.) I can't recall what I ate—heck, I probably couldn't even pronounce it—but I sure remember the champagne! The bill came to over two hundred and fifty dollars, but the sports announcer refused to let me pay a penny, which was good—because I still didn't have a penny.

That's what an inner genie will do for you when you remember to release her from her bottle. And feed her.

Embracing the Genie Within

There is a force within each of us as powerful as creation itself. Perhaps it *is* creation itself. It is that which manifested our bodies and all that we experience here on this crazy place we call Earth. This creative force has the ability to draw to us whatever we really, truly need and desire. Some people may call this force "God," "Hashem," "Allah," "Buddha" or "Christ," but I like to call it "the genie within." Like the genie of countless stories, it is bottled up inside, waiting to be freed, and then in gratitude, to serve us with undying devotion. When our genies are awakened from their slumber, there is nothing they won't and can't do for us. Our genies are our allies and our creative muses. Like Peter Pan's Tinker Bell, the more we believe in them, the stronger their powers grow. When we clap our hands for them, giving them encouragement and honoring them with physical action, their life force grows. Conversely, the more we ignore our genies (or faery guardians!) the dimmer their light becomes—until we lose all sense of them. This is when we feel disconnected, alone, hopeless, and broken.

The good news is that our genies never truly leave us. They are always working hard on our behalf around the clock; it's just that they require attention. The clearer the requests or commands we give our genies, the better the results. The question of course is: how can we give them clear directives when we ourselves are not always clear? After working with hundreds of self-proclaimed "confused" people, I could write a whole book about that challenge—in fact, you are reading it now!

The Problem With Wishing

If you think back to any story involving a genie, you will recall that there was always some limit to the wishes the genie was willing or able to grant. Either the wishes were restricted to the number three, or there were some unfavorable stipulations attached. The protagonist, who was perhaps a wannabe prince, a clumsy knight, or a battered fisherman, just about always messed up this opportunity of a lifetime by wishing for something much smaller and less helpful to him than we as observers would have chosen for him—or for ourselves. Other times he was indeed granted his wish but instead of it bringing him happiness, it only served to complicate things.

One of the most frustrating things about these stories is that the wisher rarely just wishes for an unlimited stockpile of wishes, which is certainly what you or I would have done if we were lucky enough to be in his shoes, right? Hmmm . . . maybe, maybe not. Did it ever occur to you that you might actually be in his shoes right now? Not just in terms of your wishing power, but in the way your own wishes may be mis-guided or limited?

An interesting thing about these fairy-tale protagonists is that they are always the underdog. They seem to have lots of wishes, but not a whole lot of power, self-confidence, or focused concentration. I suspect that if instead of making three wishes, they had made three *intentions*, three *determinations*, or three *proclamations*, they would have fared better. After all, these words project a much greater sense of strength than the word "wish," which holds an inherent feeling of ungrounded dreaminess, of longing and waiting and hoping. I wonder, have you been doing more wishing or more proclaiming lately? Beggars beg, fairy-tale prince wannabes wish, but kings, queens, and presidents proclaim!

Of course for some of the unlikely heroes in our favorite stories, whether fictional or our own, it isn't so much about what is being wished for or how the wish is being wished, but rather whether the wisher/ dreamer/ hoper feels worthy of receiving the wish. Perhaps in these all too familiar tales, it isn't the genie that needs to be freed from the tiny bottle, but rather the one who wishes.

What to Wish For?

Whether you are seeking greater peace, love, or all the riches in the world, I believe it boils down to this: if you would like to be king or queen, is wishing for the jeweled crown or the fancy title *really* the wisest wish? A servant who is handed a crown will never be a queen, or remain one for very long, if she doesn't transform her *identity* from servant to empress. This means she must not only believe herself already to be a ruler, but she must also really know how to carry out the duties and responsibilities of one in a queen-like fashion.

This doesn't rule out the possibility that she might end up queen (or president of the United States, the CEO of a company, or the head of a rock band) before she is ready. She may be given jewels or fancy gowns, a throne or a teak desk, and a nice bed to sleep in, and perhaps even some nice young courtiers to consort with, which may be more than enough for some! But, she will quickly be deposed by her adversaries, competitors, and even her closest advisors (perhaps including those suitors) if they prove to be more king or queen material than she is. Wouldn't that servant better serve herself with a wish—no, scratch that, with a proclamation—that she will soon manifest in herself queen-like qualities that others will subsequently recognize and reward?

Such a process may, of course, take more time than she—or you—are hoping. But the cool thing is that in the end, you will enjoy your new and improved identity, whether or not you achieve the official title. Importantly, perhaps by then you won't even want or need it, but will be led down a path that is even more fulfilling than you could have dreamed. And if you do end up in a castle, the White House, or Wall Street, you will be able to spend your time enjoying your reign from your throne, as opposed to wallowing in the moat because the job was way too much for you and your little star-studded crown to handle.

The Problem With Butterflies

I have a love-hate relationship with butterflies. Their transformation from a rather drab, slow, worm-like thing to a brilliant, colorful being that can fly elevates them to a magical, even enviable status in the eyes of us humans, who are still very much confined to the ground. They are a symbol of change, of hope, of the creative power brewing within the cocoons of our own hearts and souls that whispers promises of flight from what we are to what we long to become.

That's all fine. However, the problem is this: butterflies are insects and I, like many of you, don't like insects. There is always the chance one will land in our hair or spew a bunch of maggotty eggs on our hamburgers. There is always the danger we will swat it or accidentally smash it, and incur a karmic debt as its executioner. However, the main problem I have with butterflies is that they just make this whole transformation thing look so darn easy—at least to the casual observer who really doesn't get to see what's going on inside the silent, steady cocoon. Now if the cocoon swayed violently from side to side, emitting little butterfly screams rivaling the frightened clamoring of our minds when we're going through a similar period of growth, then we'd have something in common with these beady-eyed guys. But instead it appears as if they just weave themselves a cozy little sleeping bag, take a nice long siesta, and *voilà*—there they are in all their winged glory: no sweat, no tears, no three hundred dollar telephone or psychiatric bill. That's just not fair!

Caterpillar Soup

I am fortunate to belong to a spiritually oriented screenwriters group, of which Lyena Strelkoff is a member. Lyena is the creator and star of a one-woman show called "Caterpillar Soup." Her story begins on the day she had the best and last orgasm of her life. On this day, after making love to her new boyfriend, she had the urge to go frolic in the forest. She was feeling playful and climbed to the top of a tree, never suspecting that the limb she sat on was rotten underneath. The limb cracked, tumbled to the ground, and took her with it. Like the limb, Lyena's back snapped in half, and in one instant out of the millions of instants of her life, she became paralyzed from the waist down.

Lyena, who had been a dancer and an extremely independent, self-reliant woman, recalls the initial pain and difficulty of not being able to walk, bathe, or even use the bathroom on her own. However, the inner turmoil she experienced was even more challenging than coping with her physical disabilities. Without warning, all the former notions of who she was, what she was capable of, and what made her a worthwhile human being were ripped away. The fall from the tree didn't just take away her legs—it stole her identity. She no longer knew how to think or feel about herself. To make matters worse, anyone who even looked at her was quick to place a label on her, from complete strangers to the medical personnel who couldn't understand why she did something as "silly" as climbing a tree.

Lyena refers to her life after the accident as "caterpillar soup." She knew she still had some pieces of her old self left, but they were stewing in a murky, unfamiliar substance that did not look or feel the same from one day to the next. However, over time, by staying aware, curious, and hopeful, her spirit began to sprout wings of creativity she never knew she had. She feels her life is now more exciting and fulfilling than ever before. Part of this is because her loving boyfriend became her devoted husband and her partner in every sense of the word. Where she cannot go in her chair, he carries her.

During one of our meetings, Lyena discussed her plans to turn her successful one-woman show into a film. She shared that when she was falling from the tree, she did not feel any fear. She loved that tree, and as the branch cracked beneath her, she recalls having the thought, "There is nothing I can do to stop falling. I am just going to be present and observe the feeling of flight through the air." She said she felt only curiosity and peace during the fall, which seemed much longer than it must have taken. I suspect if the rest of us adopted Lyena's attitude as we find ourselves letting go of the limbs that can no longer support us, we might be able to achieve that state of grace she now enjoys. She feels she has traded her legs for wings.

The Choice

Recently there has been a lot of talk about spiritual alchemy, the power of the mind, and the law of attraction. The main tenet of these concepts is that we can manifest our desires through thought alone. I believe that is true for some people, but not for all. It is only true for those of you who are willing to enter into the hot and murky soup of uncertainty, and remain there long enough until it turns you into something far more complex and tastier than you were before. It is only true if you are willing to let go of parts of yourself that may not have really been you in the first place. Otherwise, you may be destined to remain a caterpillar.

Don't get me wrong: being a caterpillar is not necessarily a bad thing to be. You can still ascribe to have plenty of tasty leaves to eat and other fascinating caterpillars to hang out with. It's just that you'll end up moving much more slowly through life, with less freedom and perhaps more frustration.

This is a choice we all have to make.

CHAPTER 2

Amendments to
the Law of Attraction

Don't worry about losing. If it is right, it happens.
The main thing is not to hurry. Nothing good gets away.
—JOHN STEINBECK

If you haven't already noticed, just about everyone is reading (or writing!) a book about the law of attraction. I define the *law of attraction* simply as "the force," or "invisible power, by which a body (your body) draws anything to itself while resisting separation from that same thing."

The emerging popularity of this subject is very exciting because I believe it reflects the current state in the evolution of mass consciousness—that mold from which we sprang, or out of which we crawled, and that we constantly reshape through our thoughts and actions. I use the word "mold" because on several occasions in my work with clients struggling with feelings of depression and frustration, I had a vision of a plaster mold. In my vision, I'd see the part of my client still merged with the mold, while another part had already broken free. The part that had broken free was aware that there was more to life—more possibilities, more joy—than the client had previously believed, but the client was having trouble moving forward due to the part still in bondage. When I looked to see what the mold was made of, it consisted of the rules and beliefs of the client's parents and grandparents and of religious and political leaders, sometimes going back for generations, that had set the parameters for who my client had permission to be. This put a cap on what my client could achieve.

If you are over the age of thirty, you've likely heard the expression "When they made him, they threw away the mold." This expression means that the subject is unique and special from what came before or will come after. Perhaps this expression was so popular because up until the first half of the last century, more people did seem to closely resemble their forefathers in thought and behavior. The molds were recycled over and over, so the "apple never fell too far from the tree" and there were more "chips off the old block" than there were new blocks. These are expressions our parents and grandparents bantered about mercilessly, as if they were the witty poets who invented them. Meanwhile, we the recipients found these clichés to be as irritating as a needle ripping its way across a vinyl record—not suspecting that, like our favorite 45s, these expressions were about to become obsolete.

These clichés are far less common today, not only because we got so sick of them, but also because we have been undergoing a process of individuation that is allowing us to move farther from the tree, from the mold, and from the block, so we can truly wake up to who we all really are—as opposed to who we were told we were supposed to be. This does not mean we love the people who raised us any less. It does mean that we can listen to them a little less, follow their lead a little less, and expect from them a little less, because now we can see them for who they are, as opposed to who we idealized them to be. (Gasp! There, I said it! And as of yet, no guillotine has chopped off my insubordinate head . . . although my pencil just broke!)

Many people think it's the part of the self that is still stuck in the mold or cocoon or the primordial soup that's in pain, but I believe that it's the part that's half-freed that is the one suffering. This is where a majority of us are today. The other part that's still there trapped inside the mold doesn't know that it's there; rather, it's comfortable or even hanging on for dear life to all those familiar folk inside who don't want to let us go either. So it's the half-emancipated part that is desperately searching for how to extract its remaining leg or arm or eyeball. This is the part of you that brought your body to this book and the part of me that wrote it. Welcome! I knew we'd meet sooner or later! Now let's see what we can do to emancipate ourselves completely. Hmmm, when I wrote the word *completely*, I felt some *butterflies* in my stomach! How about you?!

Why I Wrote This Book

When I was nineteen years old, I visited a psychic for the first time, in Murphysboro, Illinois. She told me three things I've never forgotten. The first news flash was that someday I'd be doing readings like she did. Of course, I thought this was complete hogwash, since I had no idea how to control any of my abilities and didn't even know it was possible to learn to do psychic readings. The second thing she told me was that sometimes when I arrived at a new place I would be overwhelmed by all the energy, so I should always first go to the bathroom and ground myself before attempting to talk to anyone. (So what if it looked like I had a bladder-control problem?!) Her third bit of wisdom was the most important. She told me that the one thing I needed to do more than anything in all of life was to get my little buns (well, they were little in those days) to the bookstore and buy Joseph Murphy's book, *The Power of Your Subconscious Mind*.

I wondered at first if maybe this psychic was a relative of Joseph Murphy or was going to make a commission somehow. However, when I saw that the book actually cost a lot less than the multitude of others there, I purchased it, read it, and re-read it three more times by the end of the week. Thus began a journey that has infused the last twenty-two years of my life with an unrelenting passion for this subject. It actually only took me a few months of direct application of Murphy's techniques to become convinced that my thoughts, both conscious and unconscious, did in fact influence my reality. However, my newfound spiritual practice was at times riddled with frustration, as it was obvious that success was not always instant or imminent. Therefore, I began a quest early on in my adulthood to understand why is it that these concepts, particularly the law of attraction, seemed to work sometimes but not always, and for some people but not for others.

As the years progressed, I continued to utilize the playground of my own life, and later that of my clients and students, as a real-life laboratory to explore these questions, the answers to which I will share with you on the following pages.

How This Book Differs From Others Like It

I, like many of you, am tickled magenta that this subject has reached mainstream consciousness. Every time one person gains awareness of their potential, it increases our own. As individuals living within a society, we are like woven threads of a material; the fabric being our reality that dictates what is possible. Every time we change a thread, the fabric itself is altered. If you change enough threads of a worn, tired, faded-gray tapestry, it becomes a blazing, brilliant flag, waving with possibility and hope.

Popular films and best sellers like the *The Secret* could not be enjoying the astounding success they are today if the path had not been paved by countless other trailblazers, including Joseph Murphy, Wayne Dyer, Jerry and Esther Hicks, Sonia Choquette, Jane Roberts, and the early spiritualists such as Edgar Cayce, Madame Blavatsky, Baird T. Spalding, and Paramahansa Yogananda (founder of the Self-Realization Fellowship and author of *Autobiography of a Yogi*). Millions of eyeballs are popping open all around the world thanks to these visionaries. However, I do feel that now is the time to move beyond the basics and to delve into some areas that have been either overlooked altogether or under-emphasized in the previous writings. Let me emphasize: this is in no way due to any weakness on the part of the above-mentioned authors whom I hold in the highest esteem. Rather, these works have led to an awakening of massive numbers of people who are now ready for new or enhanced information.

Missing Pieces of the Alchemic Puzzle That Will be Addressed in This Book

Aggravated alchemists

Spiritual alchemy refers to the transformation of one form of matter or experience into another, by utilizing one's full range of spiritual abilities. Many folks on the path of conscious creating are seeing radical results in some areas of their lives, but are feeling stuck or unsuccessful in other particular areas. Like a physician or shaman who cannot cure someone, a psychic who draws a blank, or a teacher who doesn't have an answer, many spiritual alchemists, whether experienced practitioners or ordinary people who understand the basic concepts, are beating themselves up for not being good enough manifesters.

This feeling of not meeting their own unrealistic expectations is therefore causing them more emotional pain and mental turmoil than whatever problem they were originally struggling with.

Energy

As humans we are energetic beings. The characteristics of the energy within and around all of our bodies directly influences our ability to bring our creations to fruition.

Our past creations are now haunting, even stalking, us!

We need to take steps to let these go so that we have room and permission to welcome in that which serves us in the present moment.

There is a need to protect and heal your creations!

Just as our own thoughts and emotions are energies that magnetize and attract objects of desire to us, other people's thoughts (their goals and desires) and emotions (their anger, concern, or jealousy) can and most certainly do influence our ability to create. It's important that you understand my objective in pointing this out; it's not that I want you to see yourself as a victim, but rather I want you to see yourself as the *master of your own universe*.

Improving self-esteem

The way we perceive and feel about ourselves is a vital ingredient (perhaps the most important ingredient) in any alchemic recipe, yet it is consistently overlooked. In this book I will be addressing many factors and energies that influence our capacity for self-love, including societal ones such as capitalism, consumerism, and corporate greed.

Expansion

As our manifestation abilities increase, our creations are growing stronger and faster; this process is creating as much stress as it is opportunity.

Personal vs. global

How can we be positive about ourselves and our world when we seem to be surrounded by oceans of negativity and suffering? Many of us feel as though we are suffering from manic-depressive disorder. One second we are feeling like masters of our own universe, meditating on the peaceful beauty of the oneness of it all. The next, we are spewing out a list as long as our grocery receipt about the unfortunate, unjust state of the world, as the pimply bagger trembles behind the five-dollar loaf of generic white bread that triggered our unseemly outburst to begin with. (Not that I'm ever negative, but can you believe these #*!@ prices?!)

Note to Advanced Practitioners and Those With Short Attention Spans!

If any of you are thinking, "Oh, no, here we go again . . . if I hear, 'All you need to do is think positively and everything will be okay' one more time, I am going to puke!" you are not alone. If you have been lamenting, "I am the poster child for the law of attraction! I teach it myself! I've been saying my prayers, my affirmations, my mantras, my Hail Marys, Hail Joes, and Hail Bobs, but I still don't have the relationship I want, or the money, or that whopper of an opportunity I've been seeking, so what the hell is wrong with me?!" then you have probably experienced the law of attraction, at least in small enough doses to know there is something to it. Otherwise, you'd be questioning the law itself, instead of yourself. So for you, I will be brief and then help flesh out why you may still be having problems.

The Law of Attraction Revisited

The main tenets of the law of attraction, found in some form in just about all the literature on the subject, are as follows:

Your thoughts and feelings magnetize situations, objects, and people to you.

Positivity breeds positivity, negativity attracts negativity.

By raising your vibrational frequency, you attract things more quickly to yourself.

Your underlying, unconscious feelings and programming can influence your manifestations.

Okay, there, I said it was going to be brief. (My editor will be impressed!) Now here are some of the topics that we will expand on in subsequent chapters. I think of these as amendments, important reminders, or new takes on classic concepts. They seek to answer the questions, "Why am I having to wait so long for my wish to be granted?" "Why am I encountering this obstacle in my life?" and "Why doesn't the law of attraction work for me all of the time?"

Your spirit/body connection needs to be in alignment.

You need to be anchored into your body.

Your energy as a spirit needs to be consolidated.

You need to be running your own energy in your body.

You must release your resistance to your obstacles.

You may need to forgive yourself and have more patience.

Do not rely on your creative projects to rescue you!

Your obstacles may actually be there to propel you forward.

Your obstacles may be there to propel you in a different, better direction.

Your obstacles might be your wake-up call or even your 911 call.

Your obstacles may be forcing you to know your own strength.

Your obstacles may be giving you the experience you need to accomplish your goals.

You must rise above your own limitations by increasing your "havingness." (I will discuss havingness in more detail in chapter 10, but here's a quick definition: havingness is the extent to which a person can allow himself or herself to have abundance.)

Different parts of yourself may be in conflict with each other, wanting different things.

Your masculine (action/logic) and feminine (intuition/receptivity) energies may be out of whack.

You may have several goals that are contradicting each other.

Your fears may be blocking you.

Your self-esteem is your greatest ally or enemy Your past intentions may be interfering with your present ones.

Your boredom might be creating problems in your life.

You may need to raise your energy vibration Your expectations may be too grounded in fantasy.

You may be too lazy! Are you seeking the easy way out or coasting through life?

Your own time impositions may be getting in your way.

Your body or current life situation may be too out of sync with your intentions.

Your neediness may be creating an energy field you can't rise above.

Your inability to let go may be the culprit.

You may be wishing for the wrong thing—confusing the means with the end.

You may be trying to manifest something for which you are not yet ready.

Your ability to manifest may be severely impacted when in relationship with others with conflicting goals (e.g., within your marriage) or within an entire society.

Someone else may be intentionally blocking you or their energy may be interfering with your own.

You may be hitting the limits of the organization you work for or belong to.

You may be stuck in a group or societal agreement that is keeping you weighed down.

You may be waiting for permission or approval from others.

You may be trying to create, as part of a couple, with someone who has different needs and intentions.

Your need for approval may be getting in your way.

Faith

Before I gave up my lucrative job as a federal probation officer and moved to the Philippines to study with the faith healers there, I remember wondering what the word "faith" really meant. It was a word that I found annoying, since it is used as frequently and passionately by religious fanatics as are the words "dude" and "beer" by most teenage boys. What I came to realize is that faith is a word you can't really get your mind around until you've put it into practice because it's the only thing you've got left.

I was going to start this paragraph by writing, "I don't expect you to accept anything I say with faith alone," but I realized that's not true. I am not asking for "blind faith." If I were, we wouldn't need to move beyond this chapter. Instead, I am asking for the kind of faith that requires you to have an inquisitive "let's try it and then wait and see" approach. If these concepts and techniques are new to you, you are going to have to have enough faith to risk taking time out of your insanely hectic schedule of working and worrying so you can practice them. What I am going to give you are the exact tools you need so that you can prove to yourself that there is in fact a genie who is standing by ready to serve you. No worries: you won't need a credit card! But she does have a few requirements if you are going to get the most out of your relationship with her. Some of these requirements include the following:

Patience!

The will to look honestly at yourself and those you love.

The will to allow yourself to experience and accept all of your own feelings.

The will to give up control in certain areas.

The will to take more control in other areas.

The will to let go of old thoughts and patterns.

The will to be disciplined in your thoughts and actions.

The will to put your spiritual development at the top of your to-do list.

The will to stop making excuses.

The will to stop asking others permission to be yourself.

Did I mention patience?

If you know you have trouble with any of the above, congratulations! You are a human being, after all! The good news is that you can actually utilize the techniques in this book to increase the qualities in yourself that are currently lacking or in need of improvement. Rather than asking immediately for prosperity, you might want to focus first on manifesting courage or self-discipline or even the ability to manage your time better so that you can read and practice the exercises. For those of you who are great multi-taskers, there isn't any reason why you can't work on all these things at once!

CHAPTER 3

Overcoming Resistance to Obstacles

All the adversity I've had in my life, all my troubles and obstacles,
have strengthened me... You may not realize it when it happens, but a
kick in the teeth may be the best thing in the world for you.
—WALT DISNEY

$$S = I + E + P - R$$

Here is a handy formula for you: The **S**trength of your manifestations equals your clarity of **I**ntention, plus the intensity of the **E**motional and **P**hysical energy behind that intention, *minus* the amount of **R**esistance.

As human beings, we are massive electrical currents. Like all electrical currents, we are always seeking to complete ourselves by finding *ground* in one form or another. When we have a goal (e.g., creating a relationship), it is as if we send out a portion of ourselves that is also an electrical current that can sometimes feel as if it is stronger or even bigger than the whole of us. I believe these currents feel so huge because they are emanating from our very souls. Your soul is infinitely larger and more powerful than your mind, even though most people are only or mostly aware of the mind, which is therefore the part of themselves they identify with. Alice Bailey, in *A Treatise on White Magic*, suggests that the closer we are to realizing a goal, the more intensely we desire it, and our souls have already done 90 percent of the work necessary before the desire ever enters our conscious mind. I believe she is correct.

The mind is merely the vehicle that translates the electrical current into thoughts, words, and pictures, which we then fashion into goals or desires. When this current moves to our heart center, emotion is added to it. This emotion is first felt as enthusiasm and excitement, which should serve as an impetus to move us forward in pursuing the goal. However, for reasons I will discuss throughout this book, we often ignore or fight against these impulses of the mind and the heart. Sometimes we do listen to them, but the enthusiasm turns to frustration or anger when the current or goal fails to reach completion. In either case, the original electrical current, now fueled or altered by negative emotion, rises up from the heart to the mind, where it is labeled as an "obstacle" or a "problem"—causing even more emotional upset. Thus a negative and unnecessary feedback loop is established until the current finds ground in the realization of the goal. I write "unnecessary" because the problem is not that the goal isn't being realized, it's that it isn't being realized fast enough as far as the mind/ego is concerned.

My goal, therefore, is to help you remain in a state of excitement over your goals by encouraging you to pursue them with absolute expectancy and patience, knowing that at the point you experience intense desire or intense pain about not having that which you desire, you are not encountering a problem, but rather a sign that the desire is close to becoming realized.

Stop Resisting!

It's often the resistance to our obstacles and our defining them as "problems" or claiming they "shouldn't be happening to us" that stops our own life force from flowing freely, which ends up causing us more distress than the problem itself. We try to ground through objects, people, and even projects to keep ourselves feeling safe. When we start even to consider letting go of these people or things, we encounter fear—even when we know this letting go is what we need to do. What or whom do *you* "ground through"?

Obstacles help propel us forward at a greater force and speed, providing we don't fall into the common trap of *resisting the resistance,* which will have the opposite effect and will slow or weigh us down even more. An obstacle is therefore not necessarily something that is in our way, but rather something that we perceive to be in our way. I know you already realize this, but it helps to be reminded: many obstacles, particularly the real stubborn ones, are like guardian angels. They are sent from another, wiser part of yourself to protect you or to bring you to an even better place than you could have imagined while you were in the state you were in when the obstacle popped up. On the other hand, obstacles are sometimes more a reflection of our own stubbornness or laziness than anything else.

Have you ever noticed that the more stubborn someone is, the unhappier that person tends to be, particularly when compared with someone whose mind and personality are more flexible? Most self-described stubborn people believe this trait is as unyielding as their skin color or gender. They are extremely stubborn about letting go of their stubbornness! This is unfortunate, both for them and for those in relationship with them. As much as some of you aren't going to like this, I am going to say it anyway: "stubbornness" is really a sign of egotism and immaturity. The need to be right, whether about one's life ambitions or any topic under debate, is a self-destructive psychological defense mechanism. A person who has a need to be right is likely to be a lonely person indeed.

What Does it Mean to Resist the Resistance?

To your ego or to the analytical mind that is so desperately convinced it knows exactly what it must have and how it must have it, an obstacle is often perceived as an enemy in need of immediate and absolute annihilation. Yet this perception is the true obstacle. When you are feeling frustrated, your frustration often results more from your belief that you are not getting what you want than it does from the problems arising directly from not having what you want. One part of you is feeling like it *should* be somewhere other than where it is, or it's worried that it will end up being somewhere other than where it presently is, and it is this discord that quite often creates the crisis.

Just Let Go of It!

Right now I'd like you to ask yourself a question: in this very moment, how much resistance are you in? Place your hand on your heart, and ask yourself this question: how much of you and your life force are caught up in trying to fix something you perceive to be a problem, in your way, or just not right? It doesn't matter whether you are in resistance to another person or in resistance to a situation (for example, war in the Middle East, the state of your kitchen, the price of gas, your financial status, or your very own apathy, weariness, or confusion). It doesn't matter how justified you are, or feel you are, to be resisting this thing, or if you could point to millions of other people who might respond just like you. Instead, just ask yourself: how much of you is pushing or fighting against something that seems to be standing in between your peace of mind and having what you want? You might even close your eyes for a moment and visualize a gauge with an arrow. Ask the gauge to show you how much resistance you are sitting in right now, how much resistance you have to any or all of the things you would identify as obstacles.

Ground Out the Resistance

A *grounding cord* is a powerful visualization tool for releasing resistance of any kind. I welcome you to imagine you are connected securely to the earth through the force of gravity. You can even visualize that, like a tree, you have a trunk running from the base of your spine deep into the planet. Imagine that any resistance you have been feeling, carrying, and sitting in is releasing down this trunk. Allow any thoughts or feelings that say, "It shouldn't be this way," "There is something wrong," "I am not going to change my mind," "But you don't understand, my problems are really, really horrible!" to slide gently down the trunk, aided by the all-powerful force of gravity. I recommend that you perform this meditation for five minutes or longer, and then notice how you feel.

You Are Fine in This Moment

As you continue reading about obstacles, I encourage you to check in with yourself from time to time in this way and give yourself permission to release through your grounding cord, particularly when you come across a familiar scenario. I also encourage you to remind yourself, as I frequently remind myself, that right now, in *this* very moment, as you read this book, no matter what difficulties, dramas, or even tragedies are occurring in your life, you are just fine. You are fine even if you are reading this from the tattered seat of your dusty car, uncertain as to where you are going to sleep tonight. You are fine even if you are clinging to a bookshelf in a bookstore, where you've dragged yourself in search of the tiniest morsel of inspiration, unsure of whether you can even afford to buy this book. You are fine even if your home is going into foreclosure next week or if your spouse is going to leave you or if you are going to leave your spouse. In this very moment, as you read these words, you, *you as a spirit*, are really okay. (If you are really not OK you would not be reading a book at this moment.)

If you don't *feel* okay, then let that feeling drop gently down your grounding cord, and breathe. Breathe it out of you and into the self-replenishing earth. Trust, even tell yourself, that by the end of this book, even by the end of this chapter, your life will undoubtedly, undeniably begin to yield unexpected and positive results through means that are taken care of for you. (For more grounding techniques and explanations, please check out my first two books!)

Technique: Transform Every Worry Into a Happy Ending

If I could give you only one simple technique, it would be this one: as soon as you notice you are worrying, ask yourself what it is you are most worried about. What are you most fearful will happen? Once you are conscious of this fear, don't dwell on it but instead imagine the opposite outcome. For example, let's say you are worried about paying your upcoming rent. You are fearful your landlord will be angry, perhaps even evict you. Okay, stop. That's enough! Now take just a minute and visualize yourself smiling as you count out your rent in hundred-dollar bills. See yourself handing the money to your landlord and pocketing several other hundred-dollar bills as well. Imagine you are telling your friends, "Wow, that was silly for me to worry because the money flowed to me so easily, and now my landlord really loves me!" See your landlord hugging you (or buying a one-way ticket to Tahiti). Say some prayers of gratitude and conjure up feelings of relief and joy over your ability to manifest.

Doing this exercise will not only help you to create the money, but it will also provide relief from your anxiety. When you worry about lack of money, you are often suffering more from anxiety than from lack of money. Remember to utilize all your senses when using your imagination in this way: see it, think about it, feel it, and appreciate it. It doesn't matter if you can visualize in full high-definition Technicolor or if you can barely muster a cartoonish outline that fades away as soon as you create your images. Both will change your state of mind and magnetize the desired outcome to you.

CHAPTER 4

Why Is It Taking So Long?

The universe is full of magical things patiently waiting
for our wits to grow sharper.
—EDEN PHILLPOTTS

Many of our goals take much longer than we are willing to let them take. Most of us want what we want now. The idea of having to wait months if not years for success can feel devastating. However, the more our survival is dependent on that which we wish to attract, the more of an urgency we will feel and the more pressure we will put on it and ourselves. We will be prone to slip into a fantasy world where we will avoid making the proper wishes or taking the proper action.

It is one thing to believe that you can manifest what you need. It's something else entirely to believe that the *one single thing* you've designated as your savior will be what actually comes to your rescue in the nick of time. This is true whether your savior is in the form of a book deal, a private investor, or Prince Charming himself. If these are what you are hoping for, what you may end up with is a couple of burly tattooed trolls with a tow truck instead, demanding that you hand over the SUV, refrigerator, or Snookums, the miniature toy poodle you bought on credit.

While I never had any possessions repossessed, I can't tell you how many times I convinced myself that I just needed to sell my screenplay or finish my book or my television pilot or start a psychic reading business right away to save me from the wrath of my landlord. My first book, *You Are Psychic* , was accepted for publication within six months after I submitted it. However, my first royalty payment didn't come for another three whole years! And that initial payment was far from the thousands I expected; rather, it was enough to fill my tank with gas. I probably wouldn't have even gotten that royalty if my own father had not pre-ordered a few books directly from my publisher! I am still not immune to this propensity.

In order to finish this book, I needed to wipe my calendar clear of clients and students so

I could really focus. I felt this would work out financially since I was told my advance would be mailed to me early in the month. However, when it did not arrive, I began to stress. I was relying on it to pay my rent for October. When weeks passed and it still wasn't here, I began sending frantic emails to my editor, which seemed a little strange since I am writing a book about manifesting. When I didn't hear from her (I found out she was out of town), I became even more agitated until finally I realized what I was doing and told myself, "Okay, I am going to let this go. I release my attachment to my advance and instead open the gates of possibility so that rent can pour in some other unexpected way." Not surprisingly, the day I made this decision/ proclamation, money began pouring in from unexpected sources. I still had two weeks before my rent was due, but now I had everything I needed, even though the thing I was depending on originally had not arrived.

Something that helped me the most when I was down and out in Sedona (as so many other spiritual seekers are there) was meeting the legendary chanter/musician Krishna Das. While in town for the weekend, he agreed to come to my modest apartment to be interviewed for my television show, *The Psychic Explorer*. I explained to him that there were so many people in Sedona who were doing everything possible to devote themselves to their spiritual and creative work, but were having trouble surviving. I asked him if he had any advice. From the desperation he heard in my voice, I'm sure he must have known this question was more for me than anyone else. His answer was simple: "If you need money, get a job. If you're not making it with your spiritual work, do something else until you are. There is nothing spiritual about being broke."

This response from Krishna Das seemed to imprint itself deep into my brain. I've realized that it's not that we can't make a living from our spiritual or creative work—I'm finally doing just that—but that there are many factors involved, as I will discuss below. *There is no need to put pressure on the thing you love or feel compelled to do by insisting that it must be the thing that instantly supports you.* In fact, the quickest way to dry up your creative juices is to put demands on your creative projects. Yet there is also no reason why you have to wait to do the things you love until you can do them full-time, or even receive any compensation for them. You can do that which you love to do and also do other kinds of work at the same time, right now! If a full-time career zaps too much of your time and energy, you can switch to a different position or a job that requires less of an energetic commitment.

Or you can find ways to incorporate your spiritual work into your mainstream job. For example, if you want to be a filmmaker, you might be able to get your employer to agree to let you make a promotional video or a documentary of a team-building retreat. If you are an energy healer, yoga teacher, or massage therapist caught in between your corporate job and your dream of owning your own business, perhaps you can begin by offering your services at the office, during lunch. If that sounds too far-fetched (it may not be for very long!), you could go get a couple of part-time jobs, which are usually less demanding. There is no reason why you have to abandon your ultimate dream. At the same time, there is no reason why your ultimate dream has to work out perfectly right now.

Many times it's not an either/or scenario. When you are ready, you can begin supplementing your work with money earned from writing, acting, boxing, healing, bungee jumping, singing, race-car driving, or anything else you love to do. As these things take off, you will naturally move toward doing them more, and pulling your energy out of work that is no longer paying off for you on a personal level.

It's quite common to experience feelings of desperation when you've left behind your old life and identity for a new one. You may be fearful that if you don't get what you want immediately, then whoever was judging you for your choices might say, "There, I told you so; you're an idiot after all." If this is the case, then just laugh at that person and your ego, and give yourself the same advice you'd give a child who is crying because he or she wants to be in second grade instead of kindergarten: be patient!

Why We Sometimes Manifest Goals That Are Later Taken From Us

You must really be capable of the opportunity you wish for!

Over a year ago I did a clairvoyant reading for a woman in her early twenties. Right away I saw a vision that told me she had outgrown her current job. I saw her visiting the offices of some executives with a portfolio under her arm, and I told her that, as unlikely as it seemed, one man looked to be offering her a management position way above the one she had now. I also saw her moving to the West Coast.

I didn't give her or the reading much more thought until she contacted me almost one year to the day later. She explained that everything I had seen had actually come to pass. However, a couple of weeks after she was offered the job (which would have paid her ninety thousand dollars per year), the company merged with another company, and someone from that other company was offered her job instead. My client was offered a position with less status and less pay that was similar to her last job, just a step above. She wanted to know why, at least on a spiritual level, this fantastic opportunity that she had manifested through the power of intention, good fortune, and action had been stripped away.

What I saw was that she really wasn't ready for it. She would have been in a position of supervising an entire department, and it seemed as if she hadn't quite had enough life experience that would help her be successful or cope with the pressures and responsibilities that came with this high paycheck. She admitted she had suspected the same thing, and that the woman who had been chosen from the other company had quite a bit more experience than she did. When she asked what she could do to prepare herself as quickly as possible, I got a very clear answer: "Live. Grow up." This was something she couldn't *make* happen.

I've seen many times that no matter how well-versed we are in the law of attraction, we are not going to be able to manifest a particular job, an amount of money, or a joyful relationship until we have developed the skills necessary to handle it. Especially when it comes to relationships! Being a wife or even a girlfriend is a job in itself. No matter how perfect a relationship is, there are going to be conflicts and a battle of wills—and if we don't know how to negotiate our way through these battles, the relationship is going to suffer, if not collapse. The same thing is true if you want to be in business for yourself. Until you can handle all that comes with it, you are not going to manifest a full schedule of clients. All this does not mean you shouldn't set your goals high, or give it your best effort, or avoid getting into a relationship or a new position. Go for the gold. Doing so may be the only way you can get to where you really want to be.

Obstacles Are Often Unconscious Choices

Remember the saying "What doesn't break me makes me stronger?" Obstacles actually require us to expend extra energy. They can help us to increase our determination and the definition of what is truly important to us. For example, let's say the man you love and want to marry just got a job overseas. However, you really don't have much of an interest in leaving your own job or community. Now you seem to be caught in a terrible dilemma. What should you do? Most people would become very stressed out over this choice. However, I've discovered through my own personal experience and countless readings with people in this exact situation that most of the time, it's not about doing the "right" thing; it's about making a strong choice that will increase your commitment to a particular goal.

By choosing to give up your present life and join this man overseas, you make a strong commitment to him and your own goal of putting love and a relationship above all else. Provided that his commitment is as strong as yours is, you will most likely be successful. On the other hand, if you choose to remain where you are, perhaps to enhance your own career or because it is in the interest of your children, you are declaring to the universe, "This is what is truly important to me." This choice may very well yield greater success in your career, not just because that's where you are going to be putting your attention and time but also because there was an enormous buildup of emotional and mental energy before making the choice. This energy has now magnetized your choice, which means it will be attracting further desired experiences to you related to your choice. You are now also further along in your understanding of yourself, who you are, and what matters most. The problem occurs for people when they think that they want both things equally. However, the fact is that whatever someone ends up doing, even with a mind that complains and objects the whole way, is actually that person's true choice.

Excuses as Obstacles

I recently did a reading on a woman who very much wanted to write a book, but was convinced she didn't have time to write it, since she runs her own business and is a single mom. I asked her why she doesn't write in the evenings after her kids go to bed. She said she was too tired. I asked her why she doesn't go to sleep early and wake up early. She said she wasn't a morning person, and the kids get up early anyway. I asked her why she doesn't get up every night at midnight, write from midnight to 3:00 am, and then go back to sleep. She then asked me why I was asking her so many stupid questions!

I suggested that perhaps she really didn't want to write a book. I told her I'd had to make those sorts of adjustments to write my first two books—and if it was possible for me, then why not for her? Was it easy? Of course not! But by making those adjustments, it eventually became possible for me to work for myself, so now I can choose to write whenever I like. So I told her that she should say, "I want to write a book, but I haven't found the discipline to do it yet" or perhaps, "Writing a book would be nice, but sleeping through the night is more important to me." These are statements no one can argue with, because they are her truth.

People who are always making excuses do so because they think their own desires and preferences are not valid enough. They use their excuses as a shield against others' disapproval or disagreement. An excuse is a type of lie. Those who utilize them are usually very transparent. They don't realize that with the excuse, they relinquish their true power. They also have to expend extra energy defending themselves from people who call their bluff.

How many people out there are using their disabilities and illnesses as excuses for letting themselves off the hook from doing jobs they hate, from giving too much of their time and energy to others, or even from having to relate to their partners on more intimate levels? I believe these excuses are why many people get sick and why they stay sick. All we have to do is look at the people with only one leg or with no legs at all who have completed marathons and triathlons to understand how nothing is impossible if we want it badly enough. The important point here is: *there is no shame in not wanting it enough.* I have far more respect for a person who says, "I don't want anything more in life than to drink beer and watch football" than I have for someone who gives me a hundred excuses for why they aren't doing more than that.

Lack of Patience is Often the Real Obstacle!

A new client came to me recently for a psychic reading, whom I'll call Janie. She explained that she was having problems at work, but she did not give me any details about these problems. The first image that came to me was of her running a race. Janie looked quite happy until a man came up beside her, then passed her. As soon as he passed her, she halted. I addressed Janie in my imagination (the vehicle through which one's psychic abilities work) and asked why she was stopping. She told me, "What's the use, he's obviously faster than me!" She then collapsed on the ground. I next asked the image to show me what would happen if she pulled herself up and continued on anyway. I saw after a short while the other runner grew tired and slowed down, and there Janie was, crossing the finish line.

She later revealed to me that she used to be on a track team but quit because she felt she wasn't the best on her team, so what was the use? Janie also acknowledged this was a lifelong pattern that was affecting her at work. She had been passed over for a couple of promotions and was therefore thinking perhaps she wasn't in the right place, even though she really liked it there. I felt that her answer was not to run away, or to wallow in rejection, or to get angry at her boss or the people being promoted, but to keep doing her best: eventually she would be recognized and rewarded.

Halfway Home

A few months ago I met with a man named Ben who seemed to be contemplating suicide. He said he was tired of trying so hard all the time to "make it" without getting anywhere. His question for me, as a psychic, was whether or not he would go to hell if he killed himself. As you can imagine, my first thought was, "Oh my God, how am I going to save him?" But as I discuss in my book *You Are Psychic: The Art of Clairvoyant Reading and Healing*, the job of a psychic is not to judge or join the client in his or her trauma, and it's certainly not to preach one's own viewpoint. (Thank God the same is not true for an author!) Instead, the job of a psychic is to be as neutral as possible in order to receive the clearest, most untainted information possible. The first image I got was very clear: I saw my client hiking up an enormous mountain, looking worn out. His positioning on the mountain was what stood out: he was a little more than halfway up but still had a lot farther to go.

I was reminded of times before my son was born, when I had silently implored, "Is this all there is?" If so, then just let me go, God, because I think I've now experienced and learned all I possibly can." I was able to share with Ben what I have since realized: that these periods of boredom, apathy, and even depression mark the end of one phase or level of awareness followed by periods of intense change and growth, and the introduction of brand-new creative endeavors.

This information seemed to give Ben encouragement, and we ended the session with his promise that he would give life another chance. Less than a month later he was unexpectedly offered a job in Hawaii, and the last I heard he was engaged to a wonderful woman he met through this new job.

Obstacles Can Bump You Into a Brand-New Direction

Several years ago during a clairvoyant reading, a client asked me to look at his business. He didn't give me any other details, and as is my usual practice, I didn't ask. Instead, I relied on my clairvoyance. The first image that came to me was of James sitting in the driver's seat of a little toy bumper car. His car was surrounded by other bumper cars. It seemed like every time he hit another car, he was bounced backward or sideways and was facing a new direction. In this vision James was furious, and responded by turning his car around back in the original direction, where he'd crash into yet another bumper car or into a rubbery wall off of which he'd continue to ricochet. This vision was as comical as it was perplexing.

When I asked the vision to show me what it meant, I clearly heard the word "obstacles." The cars then turned into large hands that lifted my client up and placed him on a road that looked like a rainbow. The answer here was that if he would only choose to follow the direction he was pushed in, things would work out. If he resisted it, he would not get out of the perpetual traffic jam.

James thought these images were funny and poignant because he had recently opened a used-car business. However, he confirmed to me that his business was not going well and that he felt that at every turn he was facing one obstacle after another—which was why he had come to me, wondering what he was doing wrong. What he was doing wrong was fighting the obstacles instead of asking himself what they were trying to tell him. Ultimately, they were telling him he was in way over his head, that he had not done the adequate planning he needed to start this business, and that it was not even one he really wanted to be in but rather what seemed like his only option after inheriting the business from his brother-in-law, who had structured it poorly himself.

Obstacles Pop Up When We Ignore Our Intuition

How is our intuition supposed to speak to us if we refuse to listen? You might ask, "God supposedly appeared to Jesus and Moses, so why doesn't God just show up in my bedroom one night and speak directly to *me*?" Well, is your mind really quiet enough to hear God's voice, or the voice of your Higher Self or Soul? Are you disciplined enough to accept and respond to these voices when they may be suggesting you do exactly the opposite of what your more vociferous and obstinate ego or fears are pressing you to do? When we ignore our feminine side (intuition), it then needs to speak to us by getting our attention through our masculine (outer, physical) world.

The more we ignore the messages, the more aggressive these obstacles become. When we are completely ignoring or resisting them, their wake-up calls will turn louder and more violent, until we might actually encounter real physical harm such as accidents or illnesses. Of course illnesses can come about for any number of reasons. When they do happen, it can't hurt to ask yourself whether or not they are part of a larger message or direction that life is trying to point you in. However, the last thing you'd want to do is judge or blame yourself or anyone else for an illness. It's unfortunate that doing so has become a prevailing attitude within many New Age communities.

Competition With Spirit

I wholeheartedly believe that we are *aspects, reflections,* and *co-creators* with God/Spirit, whoever or whatever God/Spirit is, but that many people forget the "co-creation" part. They want what they want when they want it, regardless of any divine plan. From my clairvoyant readings, I am beginning to believe that some people have divine plans, directives, and missions they are here to carry out, while others do not—except perhaps to live, experience life, and die. Some people convince themselves that what they are seeking is their divine plan. Sometimes it is, sometimes it's not. I believe that it's pretty obvious it's not their divine plan when the thing they are seeking is eluding them, if not running from them screaming (as in the case of a thwarted relationship). As adults, we are all from time to time—more often than not—a bunch of babies, screaming inwardly or outwardly because we are not getting our way fast enough.

Many people say they go to psychics because they want to know the truth. But this assertion is not true. What many want is their version of the truth confirmed. When this doesn't happen, these people blame the psychic or get very upset. Usually, the only time during a reading that people will argue with me or tell me I'm wrong is when I'm viewing their future, and I glimpse a future they don't want. Hmmm, what's that about?! The funny thing is that they often have this reaction when I tell them I see them doing something positive and creative!

One woman told me flat-out that I was wrong when I told her I saw she would be teaching a class in her living room. She insisted she would never teach again. We laughed about this less than two months later when she began teaching a class—in her living room. Ironically, I ended up enrolling in it and she turned out to be one of the best teachers I've had. This class actually helped her pay her rent and get caught up on bills that were months behind. When she said she didn't want to teach again, what she meant was she didn't want to teach under the same circumstances as in the past. Until I offered an alternative possibility, she could not imagine anything else.

Spirit or Ego?

Quite often, the line between the yearnings of our spirit and the yearnings of our controlling ego is rather vague. I don't even know if these are two absolutely separate things, as many people propose. We tend to think they are, and judge our egos, but what is the part of ourselves doing this judging if not the ego? What is the part doing the accepting? Is the part accepting better than the part judging? If so, what part is determining that accepting is better than judging? Is that not the ego? I don't think there is anything wrong with the fact that we want what we want. But when we absolutely insist on getting *it in a very specific way* when everything in our lives is indicating it's not ours to have, or at least not yet, then we are the main ingredient in a recipe for disaster.

For example, how many people have rejected the suitors yearning to be with them as they pursued the one guy or gal who didn't want them? When we desire to be in relationship we may fixate on one person and insist no one else in the world could ever make us happy, when the reality is if we spent a whole day or month or year with that person we might find he/she isn't who we thought they were at all. There are over 7 billion people in the world, yet how many of those suffering from unrequited love insist there is no one else for them except the one person they are obsessing over, who most of the time they don't even know well.

I used to work at a New Age bookstore where an older man from Australia worked as a healer. He was quite outgoing, and radiated what I would call a "guru" persona, which was partly due to a very strong love of his healing work harnessed by a hard-hitting, salesman-like approach. He guaranteed that anyone who worked with him on an ongoing basis would ascend, or at least become enlightened. (In my opinion, anyone making claims such as this should be avoided.)

He asked me if I wanted to do an exchange with him. I felt a little hesitant about this as I didn't completely trust him, but he was rather insistent and I ignored my feelings and agreed to do a reading for him. He wanted me to look at his finances and see how soon they would be improving. The images that came to me told me they were not going to improve anytime close to soon. Before telling him this, I asked the images to show me why this was. It seemed as if at one point he'd had lots of money, and it didn't look like he had been very generous with it. The message also came to me in several different ways that despite his age and self-appointed status as a spiritual leader, he was still quite a young soul, learning the meaning of humility and faith.

While I didn't dare tell him about the young soul part, I gently explained the rest. He exploded with rage! At the top of his lungs, he yelled that he had already been living in survival mode for the past three years, and he knew beyond all doubt his life was not supposed to be like this, that he had already learned all his lessons. I told him I would continue on with the reading and see if perhaps the information I was getting was wrong (thank God I knew how to ground and center myself). However, the same visions came to me again and again, confirming what I had already told him. Again he threw what looked very much like a temper tantrum. I got the strange feeling that he wasn't arguing with me at all, but rather with himself, and with his God. I don't know exactly what his definition of being enlightened was, but if this was a display of it, I don't think I'd want to go there!

Stubborn People Manifest Stubborn Obstacles!

The more stubborn you are, the more you will get stuck. When you get stuck, you will really be stuck. People with strong personalities are often strong alchemists who really have to look out for and listen to their own feelings, because their feelings will start manifesting for them in very extreme and powerful ways. I had a student like this. Whenever I did readings on her, I was awestruck by the amount of energy her body generated. She had been overweight her entire life, and I really think that was partially the reason for all this energy: her body was a mega-energy machine. She had pretty strong ideas about what she wanted for herself and fear about what might happen if she didn't get what she wanted. The problem was this: as soon as she felt unhappy about a situation, her being said, "I want out of here!" even though her brain was saying, "You have to stay here in this miserable, abusive situation." She would therefore begin to manifest situations (i.e., drama) that forced her out, such as accidents that left her disabled and unable to do her work, or people who would become angry at her and end up firing her.

Whenever I did a reading for her, I would see that these situations were projections from herself trying to push her in a direction that would make her happier. Had she just allowed herself to be in the flow of wisdom and grace, she wouldn't have gone through such trauma and drama before getting to where she truly needed to be. Once she could own her constant problems as her own manifestations, she was able to feel less of a victim, although it took her about a decade to really get this.

CHAPTER 5

What Do You Really Want?

*In light of knowledge attained, the happy achievement seems almost
a matter of course, and any intelligent student can grasp it without too much trouble. But
the years of anxious searching in the dark, with their intense longing, their alterations of
confidence and exhaustion, and the final emergence into the light—only those who have
experienced it can understand that.*
—ALBERT EINSTEIN

Don't Confuse the Means With the Ends!

One of the criticisms of the recent law of attraction mania is that there is too much focus on money and prosperity. While I think that some of this judgment, if not most of it, is coming from people who themselves are not financially well off or are suffering from being trapped beneath a ceiling of their own limitations, it is important to understand that money is just one of the many things that we can attract into our lives, and that money is never the be-all and end-all.

When we have a need or desire for more money, it is very important that we be clear about what we hope to achieve by accumulating this additional money. Many people want to be rich, because they think wealth will free them from a boring job, free up their time, make it possible for them to travel, or allow them to be more creative or drive a nice car. Money may help with these things, or it may not. Many people say they want to travel and actually do possess the money to do so, but they either don't make the time or they can't figure out where to go or whom to go with. If you want more than anything to travel and you really are able and willing to allow yourself to have this goal, you will have an easier time manifesting a trip even if at this moment you don't have a dollar, as opposed to someone who has millions but is struggling with something inside themselves that won't allow them this time off.

Many people want to have plenty of money so they can feel secure and ward off feelings of fear. While money can make it easier to do these things, it may not be the answer. A fearful, anxious person is not going to become happier through having money any more than a person who feels undeserving and bad about themselves will suddenly have higher self-esteem because of a large bank account. Fearful people may in fact accumulate money because they are more likely to do everything possible to have a stable income; however, such people will sacrifice their own happiness by putting up with things not in their best interest. The person who feels undeserving may be able to manifest money but won't be able to hold on to it for very long.

One of the most important things you can do for yourself when seeking more money, or seeking to manifest a certain goal, is to ask yourself what steps you can begin to take *today*, regardless of your situation. Many use lack of money as an excuse for not taking care of themselves: going to the dentist, the doctor, eating healthily, etc. It's a very convenient excuse, but as long as you hold it, you are not going to have money or the things you really crave.

~ EXERCISE ~
Understanding Your True Goals

1. Separate a piece of paper into seven rows. In the first row, write your most pressing goal or wish. Then ask yourself, "What end will this goal achieve or why do you desire this?" Write the answer in the second row. In the third row, rewrite the goal to include the reason you want to achieve what you just wrote in row number 1.
2. Look at your answer and redetermine what it is you really need or want. You can record this response in the fourth row and label it your final goal. In the fifth row, you can include specific details about the reworked goal; and in the sixth row, restate your wish as an intention. In the seventh row, state how this will make you feel and make a declaration that you have already manifested your goal. You can include emotions along with your intentions, too. Here's an example:

1. Goal/wish	Money.
2. What will this achieve? Why do I desire this?	Money will make it possible for me to buy a new car.
3. Reason I want to achieve what I just wrote in row 2	I want a new car so I will have a reliable, comfortable, fun way to get around.
4. Rewrite goal as the final goal	What I really want is a car.
5. Specific details of this goal	The car will be safe, run perfectly, have air conditioning, and be in a color that makes me happy.
6. Restate your wish as an intention	I intend to manifest a great car with all the features I would love.

| 7. State both the emotion you feel and the certainty you have already manifested your goal | I feel so very joyful, excited, relaxed, and at ease knowing this car has already manifested for me, so now I am just waiting for it to arrive. |

From this exercise, you will be able to reword and formulate your goals so that they best suit what you are really seeking. There is nothing wrong with desiring money for the sake of having money. However, if the thing you really need right then, which most of your life force is going to—consciously or unconsciously—is something other than money, you may be limiting the way it comes to you by focusing on money or obtaining credit rather than the thing itself. In the example above, it is a dependable, affordable, and attractive car. A car can be given to you, it can be loaned to you, or you can come across an amazing bargain (as I did with my Mercedes-Benz). All these things can happen for reasons you never imagined, while you were trying to figure out how on earth you were going to manifest it.

By focusing on the *end* result as opposed to the *particular way* in which it comes to you, you open up many more creative possibilities for yourself and bypass the limits your logical mind normally encounters.

Relationships

Let's look at another common goal: relationships.

1. Goal/wish	To have Brad Pitt as my boyfriend.
2. What will this achieve? Why do I desire this?	If I have Brad Pitt, I'll have a really cute, sexy guy to have fun with, who will take me to exotic, exciting places.
3. Reason I want to achieve what I just wrote in row 2	I don't want to be lonely anymore. I want excitement, fun, and romance, but also a guy who is there for me every night and every day, whom I can trust and depend on.
4. Rewrite goal as the final goal	I want a man described as above so I'll get to experience what a commited, loving relationship is about while also being more happy in my life.
5. Specific details of this goal	He will be sexy, fun-loving, caring, handsome, and exciting, and also stable and committed. He will love me with all his heart and be completely available.
6. Restate your wish as an intention	I intend to manifest a great relationship with a man I love and who loves me, who is completely available in every sense of the word.
7. State both the emotion you feel and the certainty you have already manifested your goal	I feel so very joyful, excited, relaxed, and at ease knowing this relationship has already manifested for me—and now I am just waiting for it to arrive.

From the example above, you can see that who you are wishing for is not necessarily Brad Pitt, as you may have initially listed in the first row, but instead a relationship with a person who will bring the qualities to your life that you believe Brad Pitt embodies. The fact is, the actor Brad Pitt is committed to another woman. He is therefore not available right now in the way you need him to be. If you are seeking a man who will be there when you come home, then Brad isn't who you want.

Not to say Brad Pitt wouldn't be interested in you; maybe he would. I dreamed about a date with him recently (please don't tell my boyfriend!) He was actually very polite, and he even bought me champagne when all I could ask for was a beer. However, the idea of him comparing me to Angelina kind of put a damper on things, even though she wasn't around. I also dated Tom Cruise in a dream last week. He was nice, but I hurt his feelings when I left without saying goodbye, which I did because I didn't realize he'd care. Hmmm, do you think I need to work on my self-esteem, too?

The example above actually includes two wishes, which is fine but does complicate things. The fact is you might be wishing for a relationship and more fun and excitement. Or, what you might really be seeking is fun, excitement and fame, but you erroneously believe that the only way you can have these experiences is with a relationship. In this case you might break these goals into two, so you can show yourself that the two don't have to be paired together. That way, if it takes longer to manifest the relationship, you won't have to put off having the fun and excitement you seek or vice versa.

I've seen in my work with so many clients that the reason they weren't manifesting any relationship was because they wanted to hold out for "the one." These people were getting discouraged because of large gaps in between significant relationships, and they wondered what was wrong with themselves. What usually came up was that they had made a strong agreement that they would not accept anything less than "the one," who had to have a hundred and one very specific traits: six foot tall, broad shoulders, an advanced degree, wealthy, wanting children, not having kids of his own, etc. These dreamers experienced a longer gap in-between significant relationships compared to others who felt a need to fill that space with any solid, fun or productive relationship. It helps to understand that most of the time we are getting exactly what the strongest part of ourselves most desires. Sometimes, deep down, we fear relationships and those who seems to crave one the most actually are avoiding them the most. They are therefore very successfully manifesting break-ups and heart ache.

When Your Soul Mate Dumps You

Far too many people, particularly women, refuse to exchange their fairy-tale fantasies for a realistic picture of a situation. They are so focused on the feelings a person elicits within them, or so stuck on the idea that this person is the only one who can save them from the rest of their lives that they refuse to accept the facts of the present moment: which includes quite often that the object of their desire is not available or not interested in them, or both. Many women have relationships with their fantasy of a man rather than the man who actually exists. Or, they are in love with the feelings of lust and longing, and don't even know the "object" of their desire. They will give every ounce of their energy to this man or woman, when he/she may have never given them anything more than a smile, a compliment, or a healing session.

The New Age concept of the soul mate has exacerbated this problem. In the past, to give up Prince Charming meant to risk being lonely or broke. Today the stakes are higher: to give up the one you or the psychic on the boardwalk has identified as your "soul mate" or "twin flame" suggests you might very well be damned to loneliness for the rest of this life, if not for all of eternity! Never mind if the guy won't return your calls, refuses to ask you on a date, or is married with six kids and hasn't given any indication he's ever going to leave his wife.

I am not downplaying the possibility that we have attachments to people based on past-life agreements. I am saying that you can create the relationship you think you want, but you can't have every person you think you want, even when your feelings for them are intense or you had a close connection to them in the past. Most relationship problems stem from the discrepancy between what *is* and what people hoped or expected things to be. By re-orienting yourself to what is and what it is you really want, it becomes easier to let go of the person you never even had in the first place. For that matter, what people often really want is the feeling of attraction: falling fanatically in love, especially with unobtainable people, creates a numinous suffering that leads us into awareness of our own souls: it expands the heart. Many men and woman become addicted to this feeling, which is their own Self being reflected back in the eyes of the other. This is the myth of Narcissus, the God who mistook his own reflection in a pond for that of his beloved, and drowned trying to get closer to it. Once again, someone who complains they aren't having the relationship they want may indeed be manifesting the fantasy their Soul revels in. The problem isn't they aren't good at manifesting, but rather, they are excellent at manifesting the very thing their logical mind is complaining about.

Security

Let's look at one more common goal and dilemma for many people:

1. Goal/wish	Financial security. I want security, but the only way to have security is to have a nine-to-five job with a good pension plan for the next twenty years. However, I'm tired, I hate my job, and I want to be free.
2. What will this achieve? Why do I desire this?	It will ensure I have money for the rest of my life so I can live well. It will ensure I don't have to feel stressed out about money or ever be without it.
3. Reason I want to achieve what I just wrote in row 2	I don't want to ever be without money because that state is too stressful and scary. The thought of not being able to pay my rent or becoming homeless is just too awful. But so is the idea that I may have to work jobs I hate for the next twenty years.
4. Rewrite goal as the final goal	I always want to have a great place to live, to not feel stressed but instead confident I am always okay, and I want to do the things I love and feel excited about.
5. Specific details of this goal	I always want to have a great place to live, to not feel stressed but instead confident I am always okay, and I want to do the things I love and feel excited about.

6. Restate your wish as an intention	I will always be able to live in a fantastic home, and I will live a joyful life. I intend to manifest multiple ways to always be able to live in a place that feels safe, peaceful, and happy to me, and at the same time I will be happy on a daily, even minute-to-minute basis, always doing what I love.
7. State both the emotion you feel and the certainty you have already manifested your goal	I feel very joyful, excited, relaxed, and at ease knowing that I will always be able to live in a fantastic place, and I will always do what I love to do the most on a minute-to-minute basis.

You will notice in this example that I left things very wide open. I didn't say, "I always want to find a way to pay my rent," because the fact is that maybe someday I will own a house or maybe someone will give me a house to live in rent-free. I didn't say, "I will have a great job," because maybe someday very soon I won't have a job but will instead work for myself, or perhaps I won't have to work at all. In fact, the word "work" can have so many negative connotations that I might choose to leave it out of my goals entirely and instead replace it with the word *create*.

I wrote, "I will always do what I love." This opens up a myriad of possibilities. Perhaps what you will eventually discover is that you'd love to sail around the world, or adopt a child, or work in an orphanage in Bangladesh, or become a psychic or an architect or the Vice President of our nation! We want to leave a lot of possibilities open for ourselves, but at the same time get very specific about the qualities, emotions, and end result of whatever experiences come our way.

Body, Weight Loss, and Exercise: You Must be Willing to Do Whatever it Takes

When I use the phrase "absolutely everything," I'm including both physical action and the inner work of the spirit/mind. If you have not yet achieved your picture of success, ask yourself the following questions:

Am I doing absolutely everything in my power to develop my talents?

Am I doing absolutely everything in my power to meet the right people?

Am I doing absolutely everything I can do to make this goal happen?

Am I willing to do all the steps to get to my ultimate goal?

Are there conditions attached to what I am willing to do for this?

How can I volunteer my time or make contributions in this area, so that I can meet people, learn, and help others?

Am I in the best shape physically to achieve this goal?

Am I living in the best place to achieve my goal?

Have I let go or detached enough energetically, psychologically, and physically from all those people who might want to stop me from achieving my goal?

If you can't answer yes to all of these questions, then there is a part of you that doesn't want this thing as much as you think you do. Instead, the desire to sleep more, have an easier time, to have others take care of you, and to be comfortable may be stronger than this goal is for you. Once you have this awareness, you are no longer powerless, because now you know you are really getting what you want. This then makes it easier to make a new choice when you are motivated to do so.

For a long time I thought I wanted to lose weight and eat healthier. But what I really wanted more was to eat junk food, steak and potatoes, and chocolate. I wanted to eat out at restaurants and sit down to meals with my family where we all ate the same delicious food. I discovered these were the things I wanted more than losing weight because these were the things I was choosing to do. At the same time, another part of me felt powerless and not in control of my own body, and that didn't feel good.

Eventually I decided I wanted to get in shape and lose weight more than I wanted free grazing time in the kitchen. As I will discuss in chapter 17, this decision corresponded with the arrival of the perfect opportunity to help me achieve this goal. What helped me the most was to shout out a proclamation every time I was offered or came across something not on my diet. What I yell out is, "I am stronger than this french fry!" This provides endless amusement for my son, who just can't wait to see whether or not his mom is actually stronger than a french fry or a hamburger or a Snickers bar. Most of the time I am, but sometimes, well, come on, it's just one tiny little bite!

The other thing I do when I come across something that violates my diet is to take a few seconds to make a conscious choice. I will remind myself that I can eat this now, or I can fit into whatever I choose to wear in four months. I can drink this now, or I can prepare myself for the television pilot that I am sure will manifest by the time I'm at my goal weight. Which would I prefer? If I forget to do this evaluation and start chomping away, I will actually spit out the food and then do the evaluation. Taking a few extra seconds to make these choices is really working in conjunction with the diet and exercise program I am following. And it only took about a month and eight pounds to slip away before I got a call for a TV pilot! This practice can be done in many areas in which you may be facing two courses of action that seem to contradict each other.

CHAPTER 6

Creative Energy and the Clairvoyant Technique

To see a world in a grain of sand and a heaven in a wild flower, hold infinity in the palm of your hand. and eternity in an hour.
—WILLIAM BLAKE

The powers of creation and destruction exist within every human. It's my personal belief that it is our own spirit-souls that manifest themselves through the creation of the physical body. In other words, you are the creator of your body and much of the world you live in. Before birth, throughout your life, and after death, you have the ability to mold your body and your immediate surroundings into just about any form that you can first imagine.

In an instant, at every instant, we have the power to reshape, even destroy, our sculpted artistic creations, which include our own body, mind, and personality, or any material object on this planet. In this analogy, we are constantly mixing our own little lumps of clay with those of everyone around us. Sometimes in this process, our portions become indefinable, even lost; sometimes they grow larger and more stunning than we ever expected. Perhaps ultimately, we join back up with that original massive lump of clay in the sky we call God or heaven.

Acknowledging Our Small Creations First

At every waking or sleeping moment we cannot help but create or manifest something. This something starts with a thought, a wish, or a desire that may be conscious or unconscious. A conscious desire would be: *I am thirsty, I want something to drink.* We then pull our little buns out of bed, stumble to the refrigerator, and within a minute or two are guzzling down a refreshing glass of chocolate milk (soy or rice milk for you vegans out there).

"So what? I got myself a glass of milk!" you might say. "I did not produce the carton of chocolate milk, I did not milk the cow—heck, my wife did the shopping, so I didn't even buy it." But the fact remains: one moment it wasn't in your life or your tummy, and through the simple process of wishing, thinking, and taking a series of simple actions to fulfill that desire—you suddenly have this something that wasn't yours before: a glass of chocolate milk.

Take a good look around you. What do you see? A TV set, a window, the view behind the window, your cell phone on the end table, your cat, your husband, and your husband who is now drinking your glass of milk and switching the channel on your TV since you took your attention off of it for half a second. These are all your beautiful, wondrous creations that would not be in your life had you not invited them in through your expectations, your choices, your thoughts, and your actions. Did others have a hand in forming or bringing these creations to you? Of course they did! But that doesn't negate the fact that every single thing you can sense—from the nail polish on your toes to the birds chirping outside your window—is part of your experience because of your wishes and choices.

The point here is that you have already exercised your creative power a million times over. Therefore, manifesting anything consciously, no matter how large you deem it to be, is not that far-fetched. Every time we contemplate and appreciate our past successes with manifesting, it becomes easier to utilize the law of attraction.

The Classic Clairvoyant Manifestation Technique

The following exercises involve the use of visualization, clairvoyance, and healing for the purpose of manifesting. They address the fact that everything we manifest on the physical plane begins as energy, which is then directed by thought and emotion, and channeled into a picture that reproduces itself on the physical plane. Sometimes this energy is contaminated or too weak, and therefore it either cannot manifest into the physical or it manifests as an inferior and ultimately less desirable form. When this happens, most people try to make changes on the physical plane rather than starting with, or going back to, the original blueprint.

Most people aren't aware of energy dynamics. They aren't aware of the original energy blueprint or that they were the original architects of the blueprint. They therefore don't realize that they are always free to destroy it and start over, or make adjustments to it that will then be reflected within their creations that show up in their lives. An example of this would be someone who has been thinking about how much he or she needs a car. When the car shows up, it has some major flaws. In this example, the person who is not aware of energy will just put up with the car until the car falls apart, or will spend time and money to fix up the car or to go search for the right car.

What such people don't realize is that instead of taking physical action, they may be better served by turning inward to their personal drawing or drafting boards and modifying or completely revamping their blueprint, which could potentially deliver a better car to their doorstep within minutes.

The following techniques utilize visualization, clairvoyance, and healing. Visualization is using the power of intention to conjure up images and colors in your imagination. This is where you give your mind the command to imagine something. Clairvoyance is a psychic ability that allows you to receive information in the form of images and colors. It is passive or receptive so that you command your mind to wait and see what shows up, and quite often what shows up is not what you expected. Healing is manipulating the images you've created through visualization, or received through your clairvoyance, in order to achieve a state of health or a desired outcome. When these three modalities are used together, just about anything can be achieved.

These techniques are similar to those that have been utilized by thousands of psychics and alchemists for decades. Because they work so well, these techniques are currently taught in numerous clairvoyance training schools throughout North America.

~ EXERCISE ~
Creating and Clearing an Energetic Blueprint

1. See a clear, transparent rose out in front of you. Let this rose represent yourself. Make a wish and put it into this rose by visualizing a symbol for your wish (e.g., a diamond, a man, a check for $100,000) and dropping this symbol into the rose. Notice if the rose turns any colors or changes in any way once you put the symbol inside the rose. If you don't spontaneously see a color, then assign it one that makes you feel happy.
2. Next, inside the rose, visualize a little scene with you receiving the symbol and feeling overjoyed that you have received it. See yourself taking some celebratory actions as a result of having received it. See yourself benefiting from this thing you have now allowed yourself to receive.
3. Next, let the stem of the rose form a grounding cord that plants the rose firmly into the earth. Ask for a color to appear that represents any resistance to you having this goal, whether coming from yourself or from someone else. This color may emerge within the color you saw or chose in step 1. Let the force of gravity suck out any of the colors that appeared when you invited the resistance to show itself. Once you feel that the rose contains only your own energy, see this color of your own energy growing brighter and stronger until it's sparkling brilliantly from the rose in all directions. Cut the stem and let the rose either rise up into the hands of God or out into the universe to begin manifesting for you.

~ EXERCISE ~
Birthing Your Desired Symbol

Hold your hands over your womb. Visualize a crystal flower in your womb, or where your womb would be if you were a woman and had a womb. Within the crystal flower, place a symbol for the thing you desire to birth. Once you have that image, conjure up some emotions with the help of thoughts of appreciation and future memories of what a terrific time you are having. Then invite the creative energy within your womb to begin circulating through the flower with its symbols, energizing it. See a color for that energy beaming out from the flower inside your womb, which will further activate that part of your body. Once you feel as if you've accomplished this, then let the flower come out of your womb and imagine you are now holding it in your hands. Imagine it is sprouting wings and flying away to begin to manifest for you.

Healing Your Creative Energy

Within your body exists a wellspring of creative energy. This energy seems to coalesce within the area of the reproductive organs. When people are attracted to each other, it's often this part of the body that becomes activated. This is also where people tend to cord energetically into each other. For example, if a man becomes sexually aroused by thinking about a particular woman, some of his sexual energy will travel over to the woman, who will receive it within her reproductive centers. The man's sexual energy may then actually stimulate her own, even if the man and woman are standing in different rooms.

The same process occurs with emotions. If someone is angry or sad and thinking about another person, then those thoughts become conductors through which the emotion can flow right to that other person. When that other person receives the emotions, he or she will not usually understand where they came from. Unfortunately, since most people don't understand how this process works, they believe any emotion they are feeling must come from their own self.

Ironically, most people seek to heal their own emotions (or sexual arousal) by searching for an outside source that will seemingly give them justification for experiencing whatever they are feeling, so they will then blame whoever is in their immediate environment. For example, let's say my sister is having a really bad day and she starts thinking that maybe she should talk to me to feel better, but for whatever reason doesn't even get around to calling me. I might suddenly start feeling anxious and cranky. Then, if I don't know or even suspect that I've begun channeling her emotions, I might start asking myself whether I have a chemical imbalance. Or my son might walk into the room and throw his towel on the floor, and I will decide that his behavior must be the source of my crankiness. I will therefore reprimand him more harshly than I usually would. In this way, we pass on our emotions to others like viruses, both through energy exchanges and through direct action. Those who are closest to us, those whom we love the most, are the ones who frequently suffer the most. This is particularly true when an energetic connection has previously been established, through sexual activity or through the birth process.

Types of Energy Problems

Many of the problems people have with manifesting their wishes and goals have to do with the level and quality of creative energy that is stored within their own body. If you think of this energy as a fuel source for your body, as gasoline is for a car, it's easier to understand how things can sometimes go wrong. With a car:

> There may not be enough fuel The car may be leaking fuel
> You may have put in too much fuel
> You may not be using the best fuel for the car—it could be too strong or too weak
> You may be driving the car in a way that is not maximizing the fuel in the car
> Someone else might be driving your car
> You might be trying to run the fuel through the wrong parts of the car

The good news is that, unlike the fuel in your car, your creative fuel won't cost you a penny once you allow yourself to have it! Most importantly, it's never too late to get it back.

Do you have leakage?
Many people leak out their creative/sexual energy all over the place. Where does it go when it leaks? Most often it goes directly to someone whom the person desires or who desires the person. People with this type of leakage problem often struggle with boundary issues. They may also

struggle with promiscuity, infidelity, or commitment. This problem is often related to "trying to run the fuel through the wrong parts."

Much of the way we run or fail to run our creative energy is patterned after the way our parents ran their energy or put a clamp on our own. Many young people never have the slightest idea that they have a creative bone in their body, because such creativity was something their own parents either stifled or ignored in themselves. Teenagers often believe that a sexual or romantic object is the only interesting place into which to channel their creative energy. This is a setup for disaster, because the blossoming adults confuse the power of their creative energy with the power of the object of their desire, and more and more energy goes into pursuing this object. This can set young adults up for a lifetime of unfulfilling relationships, as they desperately search to find the creative energy they have transferred from themselves to their fantasy of the other person—which is also one reason a person can become really obsessed with another.

What such people don't realize is that the excitement, passion, exhilaration, health, joy, and peace that they are seeking is available to them not through another person, but from fully embracing their own creative life force. If this possibly describes or resonates with you to any extent, I highly recommend doing the following exercise. You can do this exercise either by sitting with your eyes closed, or by sitting or standing in front of a mirror, wearing comfortable clothes that make you happy.

~ EXERCISE ~
Filling the Womb

Put your hands over your womb. If you are a man, you can imagine you have a womb. (Don't worry, this will be our little secret!)

Declare that you are now calling all your creative life-force energy back to you.

Visualize your womb filling up and getting bigger and bigger as you bring the energy back, so that you resemble a pregnant person.

Ask your womb to show you the color of your creative life-force energy. Let this energy redistribute itself wherever it would like to flow throughout your body. If you lack creative energy do the exercise above, and then add the following steps:

1. See a gauge with an arrow that can move from 1 to 100, and imagine that the number at which it is set represents how much permission you have to run your own creative life-force energy.

2. If the gauge is at any less than 90, imagine you are lifting the arrow until it gets to the number you'd like.

3. Imagine you are placing this gauge in your womb.

4. Now invite the creative energy to begin brewing, as if the few cells that contain it are now being activated and tons of this energy is exploding from the cells, filling up this entire part of your body and then expanding to every other cell in your body.

5. Let this energy expand from the cells throughout every system in your body, from the circulatory system to the sympathetic and parasympathetic nervous systems. Let it wash through your bones and muscles and face and hands and legs and out the top of your head, forming a beautiful fountain that then washes through your aura, the energy field surrounding your body. Make sure you let this creative energy wash through your heart and down your shoulders, down through your underarms, through your forearms and

wrists, bubbling out your hands like fountains. In your imagination, flush your entire lymphatic system with this cleansing energy color.

If you have too much creative energy

Sometimes you can have so much creative energy running through your body that it becomes almost too much to bear. In such a case, you will either get sidetracked from whatever you're trying to achieve or you'll begin to create more than you can handle at one time. For example, you may begin to take on far too many projects or overcommit yourself to too many people. Moreover, too much creative energy running through your body will tend to push your spirit out. When you are too far out of your body, you may begin to experience symptoms such as restlessness, nervousness, feeling overwhelmed, spaciness, and having trouble sleeping or focusing on any one thing for very long. In the next chapter I will discuss this issue in more detail.

If you have too much sexual energy

When creative energy is channeled primarily through the sexual organs and/or objects of sexual attraction, it can be extremely distracting and uncomfortable—and cause people to make choices that are not in the best interest of themselves or others. Sometimes it makes them act out sexually in inappropriate ways. People who run too much sexual energy for too long might end up with health problems in this area, in the way that a device running on a battery that's too charged or too strong might burn out some of the other electrical components. I believe that our creative energy is made of the same stuff as our sexual energy; it's just that our sexual energy runs primarily through the sexual organs.

Sometimes when we are feeling completely out of control about a particular person or relationship, it is because this person is energetically corded into our sexual organs. We feel out of control because this person's energy doesn't belong to us, but we don't know that, so we are perplexed about why we can't stop it. (The same can be said about another person's emotions, such as anger or grief.) When this happens, we experience the other person's vibrational frequency as our own, so that in the case of sexual energy it may actually feel as intense as if we were having physical contact. This energy exchange can happen with those we desire, and even those we'd prefer to avoid! Tantra practitioners utilize this exchange consciously to enhance their sexual experiences, whereas the rest of the population benefits and suffers without much awareness.

This exchange is often also accompanied by thoughts that have been sent by the other person, usually unconsciously but sometimes on purpose. The problem here is many people will then follow the will of the one sending the energy, which can get in the way of their own good judgment. Once this energy connection is broken, interest in the other person or willingness to be with that person often disappears and is replaced by feelings of self-condemnation and thoughts that go something like, "Oh my God, how could I have ever considered sleeping with that jerk for even a second?" Many people then blame this "error in judgment" on alcohol.

~ EXERCISE ~
Grounding Your Reproductive Organs

The solution to running too much energy or someone else's energy through your own body? Ground your ovaries or testicles! This might sound funny, but it really works!

Sit down in a chair with your feet touching the ground. Put your hands over your ovaries if you are a woman. If you are a man, place your hands over your testicles. In your imagination, see a very strong column of energy running from your ovaries or testicles straight down, deep into the earth. Invite the force of gravity to extract any excess or foreign energy your body can't handle. You can really do this anytime during the day, not just when you are sitting alone; you can even do it while you are conversing with someone else!

CHAPTER 7

Healing the Body Connection

*Enlighten the people generally, and tyranny and oppression
of body and mind will vanish like evil spirits at the dawn of day.*
—THOMAS JEFFERSON

From the thousands of readings I've done, I've observed that people who tend to be more prosperous than the rest of us have three things going for them:

1. They are fully integrated/connected/anchored into their body.
2. The life-force energy that runs through their body is vibrant and compact.
3. Their auras appear larger than the auras of less prosperous people.

The good news is there are simple exercises you can do to obtain these qualities, which you will find at the end of this chapter. Fortunately, all of these qualities can be enhanced through intention and visualization.

Integration of Body and Spirit

I went for a while being broke after my son was born. During this particularly bumpy time, I sought out readings from several clairvoyant friends. I always asked the psychic/clairvoyant/ channeler of the week to "look" and see when my millions would be coming in; no fewer than three of these people, all of whom resided in different states and did not know each other, told me the problem was that there was more of me outside of my body than in it. They each saw a similar vision of me floating out among the clouds, in a dreamy state. They could see I was diligently sending out intentions through visualizations and affirmations, yet somehow I wasn't

430

materializing what I wanted because not enough of me was on the material plane and because I was too spread out all over the place.

Since that time I've done readings for quite a few clients who also struggle with being "spread too thin" or disconnected from their body. It's not just that they are doing too many things at once, or that their attention is shifting from one thing to the next without clear focus. It's as if a part of them, their spirit, is either too diffused, or too far away from the body. The opposite of this would be those who appear as consolidated beams of light.

Symptoms: Are you having trouble meeting your own basic survival needs? If so, do you find yourself feeling confused, exhausted, and unable to focus on any one thing? Do you feel detached, with an unreal or dreamy feeling? Do you find you are always thinking about the past or planning/trying to figure out the future? Does a part of you long to be free from the trials and tribulations of the physical body? Do you feel as though it's not fair that your own survival needs even have to be an issue? Have you experienced illness, or have you been in pain or undergone a shocking or traumatic experience lately that has impacted you? Do you feel that you know what you don't want but not what you *do* want, aside from some nebulous idea of wealth so you never have to think about money again?

To Be In or Out of the Body; That Is the Question

If you've been spending more time out of your body than in it, or if you are depleted or too dispersed all over the place, you may need to make adjustments to get yourself back into balance. This doesn't have to be a long, arduous task. Sometimes the answer is just to get more sleep and give your body more of what it wants, such as exercise and healthy, nutritious food.

Clearing out your house of everything that is no longer making you happy can also help your body/spirit connection. People tend to leave or stay away from their body when there is too much pain within it, or their physical circumstances are unpleasant. So, alleviating these issues can help draw you back in.

It is important to understand that there are valid reasons for leaving your body. We do it every night when we're sleeping. We obviously need sleep, quite often more than we get. In fact, researchers who attempt to go without sleep for even a few days begin showing signs of psychosis. When you sleep, your spirit is often very busy working out problems, healing the body, and downloading information. The same is true when you leave your body during waking states. Highly artistic people usually spend a lot of time out of the body. However, the artists who make money from their art are those who can come back in and connect deeply with the body when doing so is called for.

~ EXERCISE ~
Discover Where You Are in Relation to Your Body

Collect yourself up into your solar plexus. See yourself as a ball of energy. Notice or choose a color that represents you as spirit. Imagine you are rising up to your heart, then throat, then head, then above your head. Go up to the ceiling and land on a light fixture there.

If there is none, imagine you are hanging out in the corner of the room. From this position, imagine you are looking back at your body, but don't return to it yet. Instead, visualize a tape measure and imagine you are measuring the distance between where you are on the ceiling and where your body is.

Next, imagine you are moving up above the ceiling onto the roof. Once again, get out your trusty little tape measure and measure the distance from the roof to your body. Now go up to the nearest cloud and take a measurement, then continue on to the farthest cloud, then to the edge of the atmosphere, then to a distant planet of your choice. Once on that planet, measure the distance from there to your body.

Next, create a gift for your body such as a bouquet of flowers or a sparkling jewel, and send it back down to your body so that this mental gift will land right inside the top of your head and down to your heart. See if you can actually keep your focus from the farthest away point as you acknowledge your body down below. Now follow this gift all the way back down, passing or resting at the places you stopped at on your way up and out. When you get back to your body, enter it through your crown and move to your heart. Notice how it feels in there.

Place your hand on your heart to make sure you are really there—behind your hand, inside your body. Now, move back up to your sixth chakra, behind your third eye. Imagine you can open that eye and look out. Next, form a connection with a very heavy cord between the base of your spine and the earth. Open your eyes and look around. Things might look a little different now. Observe the objects in the room as though it's the first time you've really looked at them. Remind yourself you are now going to be completely, 100 percent present with yourself.

The Strength and Size of Your Energy Field

Some people seem to have very strong, hearty spirits. Clairvoyantly, their spirits look larger than others. These people seem to be able to manifest money more easily than those whose spirits appear smaller, or whose life force, which I see as light, is dimmer. These latter folks appear small or dim, and they tend to suffer from exhaustion, depression, and a variety of illnesses.

Other people actually seem to have an overabundance of life-force energy. These folks usually can't sit still for very long and are likely to be diagnosed with "attention deficit disorder" early on in life. Depending on their level of physical activity, they will often struggle with weight problems. If you think about the most hyper child you've seen, quite often that child has three problems on an energy level. First, their spirit is often too big for their little body to handle. Second, they are often running too much of someone else's energy through their body (e.g., their parents' emotions), which makes them act like mini versions of the Incredible Hulk. The third problem is that these kids are often completely ungrounded, having one foot, so to speak, in the body, and the other zooming out all over creation. Stick that kid in a classroom or his bedroom and leave him to his own devices, and the room will soon look like a bomb shelter attacked from the inside, with the adult no longer in charge and looking like a survivor of a nuclear attack.

Many of these children/spirits eventually grow into their body or learn to cope with it. They learn to ground, focus, and channel their excess energy into productive means. Others end up using drugs, prescription or illicit, in order to deal with the discrepancy of having too much or not enough of their own energy in their body. If you look at people like Oprah Winfrey, Tom Cruise, Elton John, Hillary Clinton, or Barack Obama, you will see people who have managed to harness their own power and achieve what others would never even dare for themselves. If adults are not able to find firm grounding or focus, their excess energy/ power may over-energize their emotional body, which will propel them from one personal crisis to another, like an out-of-control steam engine barreling down diverging tracks.

~ EXERCISE ~
Stress Relief 101—Consolidating All the "You"s

This is a terrific meditation when you are feeling overwhelmed! I developed it when I thought I was about to have a nervous breakdown, when I saw hundreds of "me"s all over the place, attached to one body that had no idea which direction to go in first.

Get out some paper and take no more than a few minutes to write down your to-do list for the next six months. This list should include everything you are responsible for on a daily basis as well as special projects. If there's too much, you can write down categories instead, such as "Respond to emails," "Call everyone back," "Clean the house," and so on, mixed in with some individual tasks.

Next, put this list aside and go into a meditative space. Close your eyes. Ask yourself, "If my anxiety were located at a certain point in my body, where would that be?" Then postulate that point is where you are going to center yourself for the rest of the exercise. Next, imagine that you are looking at a screen out in front of you, spanning 360 degrees around your head. Allow yourself to see a version of yourself engaging in each one of these tasks. You will most likely see several copies of yourself, all doing things. Make a mental note of where they are on your screen—e.g., you taking out the trash might be to the left, you giving a presentation might be to the right; then, if you have three kids, there might be three of you driving the kids to soccer practice.

Now, say hello to your own physical body and yourself inside your body, which is the real you. Visualize all of the "you"s collecting up into one single you directly in front of your body, and bring this consolidated you into your body. Then take a magnet and run it through the spaces all the "you"s were in, collecting up the energy of all those people and tasks. Once all this space is clean, bless the magnet, hand the magnet over to God or send it out into the universe, and ask that these things be taken care of without you having to do them all yourself—unless doing them all yourself is in your own highest good. Check behind you to see if you left out any "you"s.

Remember: if you ever have the feeling you are the only one who can do what you think needs to be done, you are most likely very wrong! It may just be that help has not shown up yet, because you were afraid to let it show up.

~ EXERCISE ~
Calling Back Your Energy as Light

Close your eyes and turn inward. Imagine that you are a pinpoint of light within the center of your mind or your heart. Notice or choose a color for yourself as this point of light. Imagine that you as the light are a magnet, and what it's attracting is all of your own energy.

Imagine you are pulling all of yourself out of wherever you've been, from projects, people, the past, and the future. See the color coming out of these things and going to you. As it comes to you, you as the pinpoint are now getting bigger and bigger until you are a huge ball of light that is like an entire sun shining through the atmosphere of the planet of your body. Continue to call back yourself and your life force to your center until you are the enormous, shimmering being you were meant to become.

~ EXERCISE ~
Strengthen and Enlarge Your
Energy Field With Breath

Close your eyes and turn inward. Visualize your head stretching up as high as it will go, and then your feet stretching down for miles. See every part of your body expanding until you are as large as an entire city. Now see your body filling from the solar plexus with light. Let this light be plentiful and enough for your entire body.

Breathe. Play with your breath. With every inhalation of your breath, draw in more light. With every exhalation, see yourself growing even bigger in every direction. Now bring your body back to its regular dimensions, but let the light part of it stay out there.

~ EXERCISE ~
Everyday Play

Every time you look in the mirror, imagine that you can see your spirit shining through your body. See it as much larger than your body. Play with this image throughout your day. Even if you are at the office, imagine you are so big that you become the largest thing in the room. Walk down the street imagining your spirit to be as tall as the tallest building. Feel how powerful you are as this immense energy source. Imagine that you are so big and bright that as you pass by people, they instantly shield their eyes or gasp in awe at the sight of you.

~ EXERCISE ~
Go Back to the Basics: Get Those Buns Moving!

When you move your body, you move energy and manufacture more of it. Here's a little secret that yogis figured out a long time ago: the pairing of physical and spiritual exercises (e.g., meditation, visualization) can do more for your health, mind, emotional state, appearance, and manifestation powers than either of these by themselves. Our bodies weren't meant to just sit still for long periods of time. Doing the meditations in this book while you exercise is extremely powerful! Don't exclude one in favor of the other. If you suffer from exhaustion, exercising your body—gently, at first—may just be the thing you need more than anything else. Such exercise might require you to drag your body out of the house kicking and screaming all the way down to the gym, the pool, the track, the park, the backyard, the skating rink, the yoga or karate studio, or wherever it can move freely. Start with your favorite (or your least unfavorable). You can do it!

CHAPTER 8

You Can Have it All

Not what we have, but what we enjoy, constitutes our abundance.
—JOHN PETIT-SENN

Faulty Assumptions

Many people think they have to sacrifice one goal for another. This is just not true! Our goals seem to compete with each other not because of the goals themselves, but because of faulty assumptions about the goals or because of some limitation within ourselves. If we need a job and want to be happy but are convinced jobs can only bring us misery, then we will either create a miserable job or remain unemployed, which may bring us more stress than joy.

I have a client who watched his father work two jobs until he died of cancer. This client sincerely believes jobs are evil and has never been able to hold one for very long. Instead, he has chosen to work for himself. Yet his self-employment has required him to work much longer hours than he would have with a nine-to-five job. He has no organizational or money-management skills, and it's clear he has had to undergo much more stress than he would if he were working for someone else. His life has turned out like his father's, full of stress! This is because his father's problems had nothing to do with holding a job; they had to do with his own workaholic tendencies and poor coping skills that he passed down to his son. When we completely close ourselves to a particular option in search of freedom, we are really doing the opposite: restricting our freedom.

Competing Goals and Competing Parts

A frequent image that appears to me when doing clairvoyant readings is that of my client's feet going in two different directions. You can imagine how far that person would get if this were really the case! This image suggests there are oppositional forces within the client striving for different things, which is causing the client conflict or getting the client nowhere, fast. For example, one part might long for excitement, change, and a new start, while another part is demanding stability and security.

We all have these different parts to ourselves, and they have been categorized and labeled so many different things over the years. Some of these labels include: the inner child/parent/adult; the ego/id/superego; mind/body/spirit; devil/angel on the shoulder; the north/east/west/south parts of ourselves; the shadow/light self. It really doesn't matter what we call these parts of ourselves (although some people get pretty attached to these labels). Rather, the names merely serve to help us distinguish between the different parts.

What is most important is understanding that each part or aspect has its own needs and wants. These parts take turns playing the dominant role. The part that is dominant is usually that which is in the most pain or fear, and therefore the one that is heard the loudest or has the most influence on our manifestations at any given time. When we can accept and recognize these different parts of ourselves, we begin to learn how to work with them and eventually choose which part will win the role of leadership. This is called "being conscious."

Some people are unable to observe and assess themselves. They actually become the part that is in the most fear. When we become this part, we are filled with the pain of that part and we lose perspective of the larger picture of our lives and ourselves. This is called "being unconscious." In his book, *A New Earth*, Eckhart Tolle labels this the "pain body."

Some people are aware of these parts—but rather than befriend them, they exile them. The problem is that these parts never comply, they just go further undercover and part of what Carl Jung called our "shadow." This happens frequently with spiritually oriented people who are trying to become a picture of perfection (aka "ascend"). Unfortunately, trying to suppress or ignore these parts is about as effective as throwing a blanket over a monkey and pretending it's not there. We can't escape from our shadow selves any more than we can escape from, well, our shadows!

To Move or Not to Move

People often struggle with the question of whether or not to relocate to a new area. This struggle has to do with the various parts of themselves (and others). For simplicity's sake, let's say you are single, feeling a bit lonely and like you really need a change. You haven't been very fulfilled lately, and it seems as though your current city or town has a dead feeling to it. You'd like to move somewhere with more opportunities for employment, and where you can meet some interesting, spiritually oriented people.

Let's say you've actually been considering moving for a few years. However, another part of you is comfortable with your routine. It likes the familiarity of your current location. Sure, life is boring, but it's easy, and this part of you doesn't want the upset, the risks, the turmoil. You could call this part of you "the one that is in fear," and then disregard this fear because we've been taught that fear is bad. However, this isn't really going to help, any more than it helps to tell a terrified child who thinks he's just seen a ghost under his bed not to be afraid. The fact is, there are going to be new things to contend with if you move. Ghosts can be real or imaginary.

If you just try to ignore the fear and the fear is quite strong, then you will fail to find the right place to live, or you will manifest circumstances in life that will make it even more difficult to move. However, if you are conscious of this fear, you can befriend it and become its counselor. You can come to a compromise, promising it that if you do move, you are going to find a place where it will end up feeling safer than ever before.

Solution: Talking to Your Fear

Once you become aware of a part of yourself that is fearful and perhaps blocking the other part or parts of you that long for a change, begin a dialog with that fear. I advise you to get out a sheet of paper and divide it into half. On one half of the paper, invite the fear to write down all of its concerns all at once. Then you can go back through the list, and on the other half of the paper, write down the opposites of these concerns, which will be the most pleasant outcomes imaginable. Hold on to a vision of each desired outcome in your mind's eye before moving on to the next concern.

Repeat the process until all of your concerns have been addressed. Ground yourself. Next, cut the paper in two and tear up into tiny pieces the half with your fears, which you can burn or flush down the toilet. Take the half of the paper with the desired outcomes and hang it over your bed or refrigerator, looking often at your desired outcomes. Wait and see what gifts arrive in your life!

Our Contradictory Desires Can Sometimes Really Get the Best of Us!

I recently attended a training in San Diego that utilized some pretty forceful energies for healing and transformation. My friend RayNelle Williams, a powerful and enthusiastic healer, decided to go, too, and we made plans to share a hotel room. RayNelle had asked me to carpool with her, as San Diego is about 160 miles from our area, but I had some reservations about not having my own car with me. I struggled for two weeks with the decision of whether to go with her or drive myself. I finally told RayNelle I'd drive alone, but the morning of our trip I called her at 9:00 to tell her I'd changed my mind. However, she informed me she was already a third of the way there, and that she planned to get to the hotel by 3:00 pm, so she could relax. I was disappointed, but I thought, "Well, it's my own darn fault."

Once I got on the road I hit terrible traffic. I filled up the gas tank and stopped at an outlet mall to pass some time, but when I got back on the freeway the traffic was even worse. I noticed I was still seventy miles from San Diego; I couldn't imagine driving the rest of the way, bored and alone in the awful traffic.

Suddenly my Mercedes slowed down and then completely stopped in the far-left lane of the freeway. I floored the gas pedal, but it didn't move. The engine continued to purr as it usually did, and not a single warning light came on. I gave the car gas, yelling at it, "You can't stop here on the freeway!" which prompted the car to move enough so I could inch over to the next lane and then the next, until I finally made it to the shoulder, at which point the car completely stopped again.

I thought of calling RayNelle for help, but I noticed it was already 3:30, and I thought, "She must already be at the hotel, probably in the hot tub by now; I couldn't ask her to come all this way and get me." So I shut off the engine and waited. When I turned on the engine again, the car started back up and this time moved full speed ahead.

Reluctant to risk repeating this scenario, I drove to a strip mall next to the freeway and had another thought of calling RayNelle. "Oh, what the heck, I'll just tell her I'm going to be pretty late," I decided. However, when I called her, she wasn't at the hotel. It turned out RayNelle was only four miles ahead of me on the same freeway, and so she doubled back and picked me up. We soon realized that if she was four miles ahead in this traffic at the time I called her, she must have been practically in the same spot I was when my car came to a complete stop. It is very possible that if I had looked around, she might have been right next to me. I had my car towed home (thank you, AAA!). Meanwhile, RayNelle and I had a terrific drive together to San Diego.

Some people might say this story is a coincidence; I say it was the work of my inner genie in combination with RayNelle's. Since she and I were already engaging in some strong energetic fields associated with the workshop, our desires were even more magnified. Fortunately, I set the intention a long time ago that if my car ever broke down, it would always be an easy, even pleasant experience getting my car and myself to where we needed to go. I suggest you set the same intention. (Yes, we can postulate that our cars will never break down, and they are more likely not to, but it happens.)

~ EXERCISE ~
Synchronizing Your Goals

Go inward, take a few deep breaths, and center yourself behind your third eye. Visualize a triangle or pyramid. Give this triangle or pyramid a grounding cord that runs deep into the earth. Imagine that you are drawing a circle or bubble at each point. (You can also see this as a rose or other three-dimensional object.) Inside each bubble, write the name of a goal. The goal could be related to money, work, spirituality, relationships, school, and so on. It could also encompass qualities such as peace, joy, passion, and amusement. Once you have done this visualization, you can imagine you are dropping the name of one of your goals into one of the bubbles (it doesn't matter which one).

Next, ask for a color to appear that represents each goal and allow it to appear or fill up the corresponding bubble. Once you have three colors, move your attention to the sides of the triangle that connect the three goal bubbles. Notice whether or not each side is in alignment, or straight or unbroken, or if one is harder to see or damaged in any way. This will be indicative of trouble between your goals.

Next, "heal your triangle." Imagine that the sides of the triangle are columns of light connecting each goal. What you want to do here is to clear out the columns (which represent the relationships between each one) and create a unifying energy field between each one. To do this, imagine that you have a very sticky ball that will easily suck up any unwanted energy or resistance. Begin to circulate this ball through the lines of the triangle and through each bubble as well. Imagine that this ball is acting as a vacuum cleaner.

Run this through the triangle several times. Then you can choose a unifying color, and see this color running through each side of the triangle and each bubble until the entire triangle is glowing with this color. Know as you do this that you are aligning and activating your goals.

Then simply go about your life for the next few days and observe what happens. You may be surprised that certain conflicts disappear, that your confusion lifts, or that previously challenging decisions become quite obvious.

CHAPTER 9

Freeing Yourself From
Past Creations

If someone you love hurts you, cry a river, build a bridge, and get over it.
—UNKNOWN

The Power to Destroy

When attempting to manifest any desire, you must make sure you are prepared for it to come in. This means you need to have enough time, space, and energy for it. By taking physical action to prepare for it, you are demonstrating a commitment to your goal, and sending out a stronger signal than if you merely thought about it. Often what is required is to let go of that which no longer serves you.

If you'd like to have a baby, then cutting back on your work hours, relocating from a studio apartment to a place with an extra bedroom, and perhaps even purchasing some books on child rearing would all be good ideas. If you'd like to manifest a job or business that is really important to you, it may be easier to do so by extracting yourself from your current one. If you'd like to create a healthy new relationship, you need to let go of energetic attachments to former ones. Doing so may require you to clean your home of belongings that you shared, and will definitely require that you let go of your emotional and energetic attachments to your ex. I understand this is easier said than done! However, I have done readings on many people who were having trouble manifesting a new relationship, and an energetic attachment to an ex was usually a very large part of the problem, even if the two people had been separated for years.

"Destroy" is another word for letting go. Many people don't like this word, because they think it's too violent. Destroying doesn't have to be a bad word, however. It is the natural cycle of life: deciduous trees destroy their own leaves in the autumn so that after the rest and rejuvenation of winter, fresh ones can sprout in the spring. Destroying can actually be quite fun and liberating. What is wrong with destroying an inanimate object that has no feelings? We have so many connotations attached to our belongings. We have a particularly hard time letting go of that which was difficult to acquire in the first place, or which was more expensive, or which was given to us by a person who we believe would be offended if we just gave the thing up. These are all beliefs that can be shed as simply as leaves.

What need to be examined to do this are the feelings of guilt and anxiety that arise when we look at letting go or doing what we please with any given object or relationship. When they go unexamined, these things tend to inhibit our choices and behavior. In general, I believe some boys and men have an easier time with letting go than women do. They like to build things and then break them, while girls are conditioned by our mothers to stand by in horror, fearing someone is going to get hurt, or a mess will be made, or too much time and good materials will be wasted. Part of this might be due to the fact that, as women, most of us are taught not to feel too keen about building the things or fixing them in the first place. Our parents direct our natural female energy to go toward making everyone and everything copacetic and safe. Now, that being said, please understand I am not at all suggesting that multitudes of men don't also have a hard time letting go: all you have to do is look at the toys or tools in the garage to see we are not so different after all.

Most people don't see letting go or the ability to destroy as a skill or asset, but think about it: if you can't get rid of the things you don't need, there won't be room for your new creations. Or you will be afraid to create new things out of fear you might have to put up with them for the rest of your life, whether or not you are enjoying them. We've probably all known a pack rat, or at least seen one on *Oprah* or *Dr. Phil*.

These people have collected so much junk in their homes, there is hardly any room for themselves. They can barely function, if at all.

Some people who are seriously mentally ill also have this problem. They live in clutter, garbage, and filth. This is because these people are as cluttered on the inside as they are on the outside. Others put up a good appearance on the outside, but on the inside they are stuffed too full with the energy of everyone they've ever known. They cannot possibly be present with anyone they meet, because a part of them is engaged in a million conversations and judgments and pain pictures. If any of this is describing you, then you need to improve your ability to destroy.

~ EXERCISE ~
Target Practice

Close your eyes, take a few deep breaths. Visualize an object that you like: this could be a flower, a piece of fruit, a letter, a number, even SpongeBob SquarePants. Observe its color, shape, size, and texture. Then say goodbye to it and destroy it. Imagine you are putting a bomb under it, and watch it explode or disintegrate. Then if there are any remaining pieces, roll these up into a ball and repeat this exercise until they are gone. Once you are done, either re-create the same object or choose a new object to create and destroy.

~ EXERCISE ~
Destroy Something for Real

First, ground yourself. Then go find a few objects in your house that no longer bring you joy. Now get a hammer and smash them to pieces. Notice what emotions come up for you here. Now find ways to get rid of the pieces: throw them in the trash, burn them if it's safe to do so, bury them, turn them into art.

~ EXERCISE ~
Clean Out Your House!

Your next task also involves physical action. Go ahead and get rid of whatever you can part with. Go clean out your closets and drawers. Notice what comes up for you as you do this. Items to target: anything you haven't worn or used in the last two years. Knickknacks that you never really liked in the first place or that have more than a coating of dust on them. Books or class notes you will never have a reason to read, and any bills that aren't current. Try donating some of these things and throwing some away, and stay conscious during the process of how it feels to part with your things.

When you encounter indecision, memories, or anxiety, don't let your feelings or emotions stop you from taking action—just be aware of them. Notice that the harder it was to obtain these things, the harder it is to let them go. Notice if you have a harder time letting go of items that were gifts versus those that you purchased yourself. Notice if you've been keeping things you didn't need or even like because you were concerned about how someone else might feel if you gave them up. Notice if these things have been creating more stress for you—and more work, time, or energy than if you'd never had them in the first place.

Regardless of how expensive it was, how hard it was to obtain, whom it was from, where you got it, or where it's going, if it's taking up space in your dwelling, your garage, or your mind, then why on earth should you remain shackled to it? If you are worried you might change your mind in the future, then let go of this worry and trust that you will be able to find what you need again or something better the next time around. Trust in your ability to create and re-create.

Suggestions for Letting Go

Invite your friends over to help you choose what you will let go of. Have a yard sale and make arrangements prior to the sale for where you will bring the remaining items that don't sell. Host a destroying party! Build a big bonfire (call the fire department first to ensure this is permissible in your area) and invite all your friends to bring either objects they want to burn in the fire or symbols of objects/relationships/situations they are seeking to release. Make this a gourmet potluck party, so after you are done destroying you can have a gluttonous celebration. A soak in a hot tub at the end of the night will seal the deal on the new you.

Are Your Past Creations Now Haunting You?

A few years ago I began to notice something rather odd. Some of the things I had been attempting to manifest three to six years ago, into which I had put huge amounts of energy, were beginning to show up in my life. Rather than being happy about this, however, it was proving to be quite annoying! These relationships or things were no longer in alignment with who I was. I didn't want these things or people anymore, but they were hell-bent on having me! Their presence or manifestation was making it difficult for me to move forward. I found that the same amount of effort and struggle I had put into them years before was now being required in order to get rid of them.

I've seen this happen with other conscious creators as well. When it does happen, it's important to understand how we are not obligated to accept these things or people; we can send them back.

~ EXERCISE ~
Bringing Your Creations Into Present Time

Go inward. Ground and center yourself behind your third eye. Visualize a timeline out in front of you, running from left to right. This timeline can have negative numbers representing the past and positive numbers representing the future, with the zero directly in front of you.

First, focus on yourself at the zero point. Remind yourself that your body is always in the present moment; it cannot exist in the past or future, only your mind can. Then begin to align your mind with the zero point. Your body is in the present, but your spirit might be trapped somewhere else. Call your energy back from the future or from the past to the zero point.

Next, create a clear, transparent rose and place it at the zero point. Inside it see a symbol representing that which you wish to create. Call all of your energy into this rose with the symbol. Let the rose show you the color of joy that will emanate from you when this symbol manifests into physical reality. Then see the rose growing bigger and bigger until it covers the entire timeline.

~ EXERCISE ~
Ending Past-Time Agreements

You can do this exercise on paper or in your imagination. If you are married and desiring a divorce, you can make a photocopy of your original marriage agreement and use that, or you can write up a list of the terms of what you believe made up the original agreement. These would not only include the official language (*to have and to hold, in sickness and in health*) but also what seemed to be the unspoken agreements or terms. If you never had an official agreement, or this relationship is between yourself and a sibling or friend, you can just write up a list of what you contributed in the relationship and what the other person contributed.

Take a good look at this agreement, and then you can either rewrite it if you'd like to re-create the relationship on different terms, or just tear it up into little pieces if you are completely ready to let go. Ground yourself as you do this, and visualize any cords running between the two of you cut or falling away as you break the agreement. (Refer to chapter 3 if you need a reminder of how to ground yourself.) Then burn the original agreement. Just watch out: this seemingly innocuous exercise can have enormous effects that will register with the person (or people) with whom you are ending your agreements.

The Past Does Not Dictate the Future (Unless You Let it)!

You may have heard that phrase before, but it bears repeating. I'd even recommend using it as a mantra if you feel fear or anxiety about getting back into a new relationship after ending a traumatic one, or going back into a certain line of work that didn't appeal to you when you were in it years ago.

It is absolutely essential that you realize you can re-create your life over and over again in new ways. Just because you've had jobs in the past where you were surrounded by rude, uncaring, envious people does not mean your next job will be like that. Just because someone cheated on you before doesn't mean your new love will behave in the same way. Just because your business failed or you went bankrupt ten years ago does not mean your new business is doomed as well, or that you should avoid starting a new one.

As long as we are learning from our past experiences, as long as we are conscious of what led us into unpleasant situations and what helped us get out of them, we will be less likely to re-create the same situation.

In many of the readings I've done, I've seen people really forget to update their self-image in the workplace. You now know so much more than you did when you began your job. Even if you've just had a career change, you are so much wiser than you were when you first entered the workplace. You are deserving of an easier day, of more assistance, of more respect, of more freedom and time to take care of yourself. If your job, boss, and co-workers are not reflecting this back to you, then as long as you are in this particular environment, you are not believing in the facts about what you deserve and you are not standing up for yourself. The idea that you must be a workhorse and just "take it" in order to get a paycheck may very well have been part of your past or your parents' truth, but it does not have to be yours. There are alternatives, even for the likes of you!

If you know what I'm talking about here, and you decide to change jobs or careers but again find yourself right back in a similar situation, this is evidence that you have some inner work to do. Usually, as we move from a place of endurance to a place of respecting and expecting better for ourselves in present time, we find ourselves having a bit more of what we wish for in each job or position, until finally we wake up one day to discover we are looking forward to going to work, that we love our bosses, and that our bosses love us. Often this is because we have become our own boss!

~ EXERCISE ~
Healing Your Past Creations

Relax and go inward. Instruct yourself to allow the most unpleasant memories of your last job or relationship to come up. This might be a bit painful, but spend just a minute or so letting each memory come up. Don't dwell for more than twenty seconds on each one. Then visualize a garbage can or pit with huge flames shooting out of it. Imagine you are dropping all those memories right into the flames and they are being burned up. Once they are all gone, the flames will extinguish themselves. You can then imagine you are taking the remaining ash and burying it deep in the center of the earth, or dumping it in the middle of the sea, where the ashes will disintegrate and the tiniest pieces will be eaten by colorful fish.

Once you have done the above, imagine yourself at work or in a relationship having the opposite of what you had before. If you had a rude, demanding boss, see a sweet, angelic-looking manager handing you more awards of achievement than you can find space for on your wall. If you had a boyfriend who rarely called or was miserable all the time, see a new man who's all smiles, who can't stop hugging you and is the warmest, happiest person in the world. Visualize these people often, and even have conversations with them as you are cleaning your house or driving to work. Make them your imaginary friends, pretend they are your imaginary soul mates. Listen to them as they speak back to you with encouragement and grace. The more fun you have with this exercise, the more easily you will manifest their counterparts on the physical plane. Most importantly, do not just expect that there will be positive change. *Demand* it. Scream out loud to the universe that it will be there for you and you there for it.

~ EXERCISE ~
Mantra

Repeat one hundred times, at least three times a day: *I am worthy of absolute respect by right of my presence as a living, breathing being, and I will remain true to myself even in the presence of those who have not yet learned this fact.*

CHAPTER 10

Havingness vs. Limits —
How High Can You Go?

When one door of happiness closes, another opens; but often
we look so long at the closed door that we do not see the
one which has been opened for us.
—HELEN KELLER

In every area of our lives, including relationships, money, and freedom, we develop and operate from conscious and unconscious parameters beliefs about what is possible or not possible for ourselves. These parameters can also be considered "limits." These limits may be quite low in one area and quite high in another. Our limits are part of a belief system of which we are only partially conscious. They have been influenced by our past experiences and those of our older relatives. These limits are sometimes other people's projections in the form of judgment, doubt, and blame. The "limit" is whatever line is drawn at the top of this threshold that says, "Stop! It's not possible or safe to go beyond this point." These limits are intricately connected to our self-esteem.

Our limits of what we can allow ourselves to have are often set at the same levels as our parents' limits. If we are ready on a soul level to exceed these limits, then we may encounter our parents' resistance on an energy level (if our parents are deceased or unaware of what we are doing) or on the physical level, as when they try to tell us that what we are doing is not possible or is dangerous or is selfish or why it just won't work. If we demonstrate that it is possible for us, then they can no longer hold on to the belief that it was or is truly impossible for them. Many people go to great lengths to protect themselves from this truth. So your success could be very threatening to your parents. Or it can inspire them, which it often will.

One of the first things a clairvoyant might see when reading a person who is coming up against these limits is an image of a wall or a ceiling. Then the clairvoyant's task is to see what

446

the wall or ceiling represents, what is needed to break it down, how strong or high it really is, and what is on the other side. By getting a glimpse of what is on the other side, the clairvoyant sees the life the client is longing to have.

How Much is Enough?

The term *havingness* can be defined as the extent to which people allow themselves to have something good and important. This term emerged from spiritualists and clairvoyants who noticed that a person's ability to manifest good things in his or her life is intricately linked with how much that person feels he or she deserves these things, as well as the underlying belief systems about how much of something it is really possible to have.

Most of the time, lower havingness shows itself in the extent of what we can have, rather than whether or not we can have it. Someone may feel that he can have a relationship but not one that completely fulfills him. Someone may feel that she can have a high paying job but not one that she can enjoy. Someone else might believe that adults are not supposed to have too much fun, laugh too much, or change much once they reach a certain age. I remember hearing my father saying more than once, "Most of life is about struggle. You can only hope to have a few scattered moments of happiness, but the majority of life is boring and mundane."

Even at an early age I knew he was speaking from a place of depression and a limited belief system, and this was not a universal truth, even if there were and are numerous others who believe the same thing.

I think some of these limits come from a real need to stay in balance. For example, most people can't eat everything they desire without feeling sick or gaining too much weight. We know what happens when we totally overdo it. We do need boundaries and standards in order to function as healthy human beings. However, we begin to have problems and experience the "stuckness" when these boundaries or standards become so solidified that they rule us rather than the other way around. This happens when we lose awareness of them, or when we never had awareness of them to begin with. Fortunately, the moment we become aware of these limits, they begin to shift.

Allow Yourself to Have Even More Than You Already Have

Last year I attended a workshop held by Michael J. Tamura, the author of *You Are the Answer: Discovering and Fulfilling Your Soul's Purpose*. It was co-led by his wife, Raphaelle, a woman who has mastered the art of being loving and compassionate while speaking her mind. The workshop was pricey, but I justified the cost by telling myself this would be a great opportunity to visit with some friends I hadn't seen in a number of years who live in the area.

Around the third day of the workshop, I began feeling a bit stressed out about the long drive back home and how I would squeeze in time to see my friends. I went up to Raphaelle and advised her that I was not going to be there for the final morning, since I felt I needed to start heading back. She told me outright she thought this was a terrible idea.

"I think you're hitting a limit of how much you can allow yourself to have; how much you are allowing yourself to get from this workshop," she advised me.

"But I've already gotten so much from it!" I countered, which was true. One of the reasons I was fine or almost fine with leaving was because I really felt that I had already gotten my money's worth. If I left now, I could fit in meetings with a few friends.

"Yes, you have already gotten a lot," Raphaelle responded. "But there's the limit. Why can't you allow yourself to have even more? Why can't you find a way to stay and then see your friends, and have your return trip be stress-free, even fun? You're a creative person. I'm sure you can do this."

Raphaelle had her mind made up even if I didn't. I told her I'd think about it, and crawled back to my seat with my tail between my legs, not sure if what she was saying was true or if she just didn't understand my predicament. However, half out of guilt, half out of a fear she might be right, I decided to stay. The next day we did some of the most powerful meditations I had done in the past ten years. I also received an awesome healing from my instructor. These things propelled me into a higher vibrational state than I had consciously experienced in years, and I made some major changes in my life after that.

At the end of the workshop I called the friend of mine I was most excited to see. It turned out she was visiting another mutual friend in a town directly on my way home. I arrived there just in time to have a wonderful dinner with both of them. The rest of my ride was relaxing, and easier than I had ever imagined. I didn't even get sleepy, which I usually do. This experience confirmed for me what "havingness" really means. It means having more than we think we can have or than we allow ourselves to have. This experience also reminded me to strive always for more, just in case there is more to be had even when I think I am getting something terrific. This doesn't negate being appreciative for every tiny thing I do have, but just reminds me to be open to the possibility of even more: more love, more wonder, more passion, more abundance. I've discovered that just when we think we've found all there is to find, there is even more for the taking, or having.

The ability to have more absolutely requires one to ask for more—more from oneself, more from others, and more from the universe/God/whatever guiding force is out there. Many people find that once they do manage to manifest more than they had before, it's easy to stop there. If paying your rent or mortgage was an issue, once you have that under control there may not seem to be as much incentive to continue to manifest money or put as much energy into that goal. But wouldn't it be nice to be able to pay rent and take a vacation when you want one, or have enough money to take a class or workshop whenever you come across one that piques your interest?

I was thinking just this morning about how much I love so many of my clairvoyant students, particularly the ones I work with individually. I began thinking, "How is it possible that there are really this many wonderful, talented people in my life that have as much passion for these subjects as I do?" It was really so hard for me to believe, even though there's no denying they are present in my life! I think I just went for so many years without meeting lots of people like this, that it still seems surreal. Then I thought aloud, "Well, I'm likely to meet and be surrounded by a whole lot more of these beautiful souls. What on earth will that be like! Can I really let myself have that?"

Manifesting Without Limits

The following technique is one of the most powerful you can use for manifesting any goal. It doesn't matter how much you want something or how many hours you spend visualizing it and affirming it. If you can't really let yourself have it, for whatever reason, you aren't ever going to see it. This exercise will both let you know how much of something you can have, and will let you release or get rid of the limits I've discussed. This technique has been taught to me by several different teachers, and I've modified it slightly based on my own personal preferences.

~ EXERCISE ~
Creating and Working With a Havingness Gauge

Close your eyes and ground yourself. Visualize an enormous movie theater-type screen in front of you. Imagine there is a huge transparent bubble out in front of you. Write the name of the thing you'd like to have for yourself above the bubble. Drop your named request (e.g., more love, more romance, more money, more fun) into the bubble and ask for the bubble to fill up with the energy of that which you'd like to create. Inside the bubble, see an image of yourself receiving this thing or quality, and experiencing it. See yourself looking gleeful, and then feel as much happiness as you can muster. Come on, you can still pretend, even if you think you're all grown up! After you've basked in the joy of your success, give this bubble a very strong and heavy grounding cord.

Next to the bubble, visualize an enormous gauge. You can see this gauge however you'd like. Many people like to see it going from 1 to 100, but you don't have to restrict yourself to that. Ask yourself how much "havingness" you currently have for the thing or vibration you'd like to manifest for yourself. Watch the gauge and notice where the arrow goes. Make a mental note of what happens.

If the gauge is at any less than 100, or even if it's at 100 or exceeds your top setting, imagine you are taking one of your fingers, or pressing a lever, and increasing the number on the gauge to the highest level you are comfortable with at this moment. As you raise the gauge, refocus on your bubble's grounding cord and tell it to release whatever energy has been getting in the way of you having this goal for yourself. You may want to imagine you are fastening or securing the gauge at this higher setting with some kind of apparatus that holds it in place, like a rubber band. Next, return your attention back to your bubble beside the gauge and watch to see what new colors come out and down the grounding cord. You might see some images of symbols or even people you know.

Once you feel your bubble is clear, drop the gauge with its new setting into your bubble and watch what happens to it. Then fill it with the brightest light you can imagine. This is the light of spirit, where everything is possible and there are no limits. Watch this light for as long as you'd like. Then you can either cut the cord and let it float off into the universe to start manifesting for you, or see it going up to the light or to the hands of God.

Don't be concerned if, when doing this exercise, you start to get spacey, forget what you are doing, or feel some kind of pain. There is a lot of unconsciousness involved in our permission to have, and what this exercise is doing is reprogramming your unconscious mind. In fact, in the past when I tried to write about this exercise, I got so incredibly exhausted that I had to go lie down; that's because I was working through my own limits: it will get better and better each time you try.

You don't need to use only a bubble for this exercise. Sometimes working with more intricate objects can be even more powerful. For example, you can use an image of a flower instead of a bubble, and then watch what happens to the flower as you work with the energy. You can also use any geometric shape of your choice, like a circle or triangle, and then watch how it transforms after working with the gauge.

Your Ability to Give and Receive Must Be in Balance

People often restrict themselves in the way a goal can manifest. For example, some may only allow themselves to have or receive money if they've earned it themselves. Others not only have to earn the money themselves, but also believe earning it can or will only come from very hard work. This places quite a limit on their prosperity, since there are only so many hours in one day that a person can work. These people often look at others who aren't working as hard or who don't have to work at all for their money with a mixture of envy or resentment, tinged with an underlying feeling of hopelessness.

Many people really hold the picture, through their thoughts and accompanying emotions, that there is something wrong with accepting gifts, charity, or even emotional support. Some people have an exaggerated sense of fairness. They believe that whatever they receive must be equally reciprocated, and vice versa, so they will neither ask for nor accept help unless they feel they have something of equal value to give in return.

A man from Texas I once dated is one of the most extreme examples that I have ever encountered of someone who cannot receive. One day a bunch of his friends threw a birthday party for him at a ritzy restaurant. Each of the individual's tabs was no less than eighty dollars, but this wouldn't have made a dent in most of their designer wallets. However, my friend excused himself during the dinner and went and paid the entire bill, which totaled close to two thousand dollars, before his friends could have a chance to pay themselves. When his friends found out what he had done, many of them were visibly distressed. A couple of them were outright furious. They had looked at this occasion as an opportunity to treat him to dinner, something he apparently rarely allowed (although he had confided to me more than once that he feared many women were out to get his money). What had been a really fun event ended on a sour note. And the story doesn't end there.

We arrived back at his place, and it took quite a while to carry in all the beautifully wrapped gifts his friends had surprised him with. When he turned off the lights and climbed into bed, I couldn't believe he could possibly even think about sleeping before opening his gifts, but that's exactly what he did! I was up at the crack of dawn as if it were Christmas. However, he slept in. Before work he made time for breakfast, emails, and a scan of the morning paper, but he insisted his presents were going to have to wait. (Arggghh!)

Days, then weeks, then a month went by, and the presents were still sitting there in the corner of the living room, the ribbons' shine dimmed with the dust of time. Now, when *I* looked at them, my curiosity as to what was inside the boxes had turned almost to a desperation to understand why someone wouldn't want to open a bunch of presents. My pleading with him to open his gifts became such a point of contention between us that I knew if I kept pressing the issue, it would be the end of our relationship.

One day I stopped in to say hi on my way to an interview in his neighborhood, and I asked him if I could borrow an umbrella. He was absorbed in his reading and mumbled something about the hall closet. I wasn't sure which closet he was referring to, so I opened the one nearest to me and had one of the biggest shocks of my life. The large closet was jam-packed, from the floor to the very top shelf, with unopened, dusty, wrapped presents. Hundreds of them. By the looks of it, these gifts must have been piling up in that closet for years.

I looked over at my friend and felt such sadness. Some of it was for all those people who had gone out of their way to get him something they thought he'd enjoy, but most of it was for him and the inner starvation his very soul must surely suffer from.

Sometime later he revealed to me that, throughout his childhood, his father, who was an oil-company executive, would not allow him to keep gifts that other people had given him during holidays and on his birthday.

While this is obviously an extreme example, think back to your own life. How many times has someone offered to pay for lunch, or done something to make your life a little easier, and you either outright refused or engaged in a silly back-and-forth argument until you were satisfied that you had objected long enough to retain your dignity and honor? In many cultures, this silliness is expected.

We All Are Deserving of Help

Like a welfare office, we all maintain a list of the types of people who we feel deserve extra help. Those on our lists include the helpless, such as the very young, the old, and the ill or abused. Women used to be in this category but with the "success" of the women's movement, they were bumped right off of it. Anyone else who needs help is instead handed judgment. This could include our own children, who may have grown older than the maximum age requirement of the list.

People can find themselves in a temporary position where they cannot take care of themselves and must rely on the charity of others, because an aspect of their soul is helping them learn how to receive. Their body and overall happiness may have been sacrificed because of an unconscious desire or need to be absolutely self-sufficient at all times. Such people hold not only themselves to this standard, but also everyone else around them. Those who aren't aware of this end up feeling overwhelmed and unsupported, because such people tend to attract others who rely on them instead of nurture them.

We Never Truly See the Whole Picture

I think we all need to be very careful about making our own assumptions about who really is in need. We must stop judging those who we think shouldn't be in that position. Even when we live with someone, we do not necessarily understand all of what that person is going through, what pressures that person is dealing with, or what he or she is trying to, or is meant to, achieve.

My siblings who do not yet have children of their own sometimes get irritated with me because I ask more of them than they do of me right now. About once a month, when my significant other is not available, I will ask them to watch my son for a day or even a few days when I have to go out of town to teach. Of course Manny is thrilled to spend time with his aunts and uncles. However, this means that my siblings have to adjust their schedules or drive out of their way to get him or meet me somewhere. Sometimes (okay, usually most of the time) I am doing so many things at once that I arrive late, miss some family functions, or decide to leave these functions early. Then my siblings get mad at me.

Being psychic, I can tell the exact moment when they're holding a complaint session on my behalf, which is usually confirmed later. I am not sure if it's the offense itself of being tardy or absent, or the fact that I don't profusely express guilt and remorse that bothers them more. I no longer believe in allowing myself to be punished by negative emotions for upsetting others, and so I push aside the guilt. I feel that if a family member is upset that I have to leave her party early to go home and do something that will pay my bills, then she has other options than to choose to get angry at me. She can send me supportive thoughts of love, or she can offer to help pay my bills!

I sometimes find myself defending my behavior and attitude by reminding myself I have worked long and hard to allow myself to ask for help when I need it. I tell myself my siblings are benefiting because they get the pleasure of hanging out with my son. Also, this doesn't come close to the energy, time, and effort I am expending in helping others. My siblings don't make this connection, so to them I am just thinking of myself, which I understand. They actually have no idea what I am doing on an energy level for them, but that's okay, too. Sometimes I do tell them that if they just offered to help more, they wouldn't feel as though I was always asking.

Now, if you are as perceptive as I think you are, you are going to notice that I am using the fact that I help a lot of people to justify asking for help myself. You will recall that I said I've learned how to push aside guilt, but the truth is that we can only push aside what is still there. So somewhere within me, I must believe that I am only worthy of receiving help if I am helping others: lots of others, probably way too many of them.

In the past I didn't ask for help at all, so I certainly have made progress, but if I really, truly believed I was worthy of receiving for no other reason than that I exist, then my current situation would look much different. In this case I would probably have people sending me presents or checks and knocking on my door saying, "Wow! I know you are doing so much. Can I come over and cook for you, clean your house, or take Manny out for an afternoon so you can finish the third book you've written while running your own business, before you pull out every hair in that throbbing, exhausted, matted head of yours?!"

Hmmm, excuse me for a minute, I need to go check my havingness gauge!

Can You Receive in Health as Well as in Sickness?

My father had liver cancer a few years ago. While my other relatives have pitied him, I've watched how he has been receiving more attention, more comfort, and more communication than he ever has in his life, not only from his extended family but also from countless medical professionals and complete strangers. He has also stopped working for the first time in about forty-five years.

While it is very unfortunate he had to go through pain (caused by his treatment, as opposed to the cancer itself), he seems to be happier than I've seen him in a long time, perhaps ever. This is obviously not the experience of everyone who becomes ill, but I've seen plenty of times how illness can serve our other goals. It gives us the long-needed break we weren't allowing ourselves to have. It forces us into a position where we have to allow others to help us. It forces us to give up our need for control. Of course, the more resistant we are to being in these more vulnerable positions, the more we will kick and scream and suffer.

The ideal is to get our needs met for love and relaxation and vacation or retirement without getting sick, which we can do by learning to become conscious of our deep-seeded needs and learn to ask for help.

Martyrs: Gotta Love 'em!

There are also people who will never allow themselves to be in a position of perceived weakness. They feel it is shameful or beneath them to ask for help or love directly, and yet they are absolutely desperate for help and love. So they ask for help in a million other ways, by complaining or "silently" suffering so loudly you can't help but cut your veins and let them drink. However, when you offer them help, they will either refuse it or ignore the advice that would alleviate the suffering.

This is actually one of the strongest forms of manipulation and abuse one person can inflict on another. These people don't want to help themselves; they want you to sympathize with them and agree with the impossibility of their predicament of the month. We have all known people like this. Just look at the person in your office who has never taken a day off in twenty years, and returns the day after surgery for carpal tunnel syndrome because "someone has to type all these reports."

We Need to Be Able to Accept Lots of Help to Be Successful!

There is a reason the Bible mentions so many times the acts of giving and receiving. These are abilities that really impact the quality of our lives every moment of our day. Our permission for both giving and receiving is very much determined by the norms and customs of the society we live in. When we don't allow ourselves to give or receive unconditionally, we are putting up a wall in our heart. We push away people who want to express their love through giving. When we give from our heart without expectations, whether that gift is a compliment, a kiss, a look of approval, a bouquet of flowers, or $500,000, we are affirming our aliveness and our natural abundance.

If you look at the richest, most materially successful people in the world, you will find individuals who have received an enormous amount of help from others. This help came from gifts, inheritances, loans, donations, and/or the dedicated commitment of employees, family, and friends. There is not a single politician in North America who could have won his or her position without an enormous amount of assistance and support. There is not a single actor who has won an Oscar, or a single musician who has won a Grammy, who wasn't backed up by the support, creative talent, and genius of dozens if not hundreds of people. A "break" (as in the expression "the actor's big break") is always an opportunity given to us by someone else. In all epic stories and fairy-tales, the hero or heroine receives help from friends, allies and magical helpers who may be human, animal or mythical creature. Without this assistance, the monster or villain cannot be defeated, the treasure discovered, the curse lifted, the maiden's love won, or the holy grail found.

~ EXERCISE ~
Receiving Gauge

Repeat the exercise earlier in this chapter for creating a havingness gauge, but this time label your gauge as a receiving gauge. Let your bubble represent not only money but also the ability to receive love, nurturing, sexual gratification, attention, guidance, and so on. Your bubble could also represent receptivity as a whole in order to cover all these areas.

~ EXERCISE ~
Direct Practice

1. Make it your goal that you are going to allow yourself to receive ten things this month without saying anything other than "Thank you." That which you receive could include a compliment, help, a gift, or charity.
2. Do something for someone else once a day for an entire month. Ask and expect nothing in return, but if the other person later reciprocates, then generously accept.
3. Find five things you can delegate to other people, and then do just that.

~ EXERCISE ~
Discover Your Feelings About Giving

Divide a sheet of paper into two columns. In the first column, make a list of everything you've done for other people in the last month or two. Next, with as little analyzing as possible, very quickly write down how you feel about what you did. You can simply write words such as "positive," "good," "happy," "resentful," "guilty," and so on. Many people give with underlying agendas, strings attached, or ideas of how the other person is supposed to respond.

If you find that you felt anything less than joy in giving, that is a sign you may be giving too much of yourself, or that you may be giving from a place of fear rather than love.

No Strings Attached

Many years ago I gave five dollars to a disheveled beggar who was perched outside a convenience store, mumbling to himself. I then followed him into the store to get a snack for myself and was shocked and angered to see him buying beer and cigarettes. I turned to him and scolded him, "I gave you that money for food, not for beer!" His response was, "But I already ate!"

As I exited the store he was back in his spot, and another woman was handing him money. Probably appearing as crazed as the mumbling beggar did, I lunged for the cash as it was exchanging hands, trying to save the woman from making the same grievous "mistake" I had just made.

Startled, the woman turned to me and asked what was wrong. Out of breath, I gasped, "He's just going to use your money on beer and cigarettes," and I explained what I had observed.

To my surprise, the woman scolded me outright. "Look at him. He's got to be miserable. If beer and cigarettes make his life a little easier, then I am honored to have brought him some joy. What he does with a gift is just none of my business, or yours."

I will never know that woman's name, but she was one of my most important teachers.

CHAPTER 11

Manifesting Space, Money, Relationships and Creative Projects

The surest defense against evil is extreme individualism,
originality of thinking, whimsicality, even—if you will—eccentricity.
That is, something that can't be feigned, faked, imitated;
something even a seasoned impostor couldn't be happy with.
—JOSEPH BRODSKY

Making it Real to the Body

One of the greatest difficulties people have with creating and holding on to positive mental pictures is that these pictures often seem to be in such stark contrast to their present-time experience. Many of us have learned that it's not enough to repeat empty words. We must feel them. However, just try repeating "I am infinitely abundant and overflowing with absolute prosperity" as you share a sixty-three-cent can of Friskies chicken in gravy with your cat: you are likely to end up wallowing in a pool of tears rather than in a fit of ecstasy. Maintaining a positive attitude as your cardboard box collapses on your head is going to be a challenge, no matter how uplifting the words you repeat!

Your physical body has its own needs apart from the desires of your mind and spirit, and it has its own memories. The body stores feelings of pleasure and pain. Your physical body records traumas, even apart from your mind and spirit. This is why one of the most effective therapies used to heal childhood trauma and abuse involves creating new memories through touch and other sensory input like sound and smell. People often require healing on a body level through modalities such as massage, yoga, or tai chi, in addition to talking about or visualizing away their problems.

In terms of manifesting, it is often helpful to place your physical body in situations where it can experience that which you are trying to manifest as real, in present time. Since you do not yet have the thing you are attempting to manifest, you have to be creative and put yourself in situations that will trick the body into believing it actually has that which you desire.

Below I will offer suggestions for manifesting particular goals, such as more space, peace, relationships, and creative projects.

Space

We'll start with this one, because it is often necessary we have enough of this for ourselves before we can manifest other things. By space I mean enough physical distance between yourself and others, so you can think your own thoughts and have time to yourself. Before we can have space on the outside, we need to have it on the inside. Most people erroneously believe that in order to have space on the inside, they must have it on the outside, meaning they think they need to live in a house big enough that they can close the door and no one will bother them. In fact, it's often the other way around.

A few years ago my boyfriend and I made the decision to live temporarily in his motor home while we searched for a new place to live. Doing so would allow us to save money quickly. He was a bit wary of the idea, but I thought it would be a grand adventure. We did have some good times there, but it got old pretty fast.

During one particularly difficult week, I was feeling more stress than I had in years and knew what I needed more than anything was to find a quiet place to meditate. But where? I drove around town for over an hour, but every place was more hectic than the last. Every park was filled with screaming kids, leering landscapers, and clamoring construction workers. I drove to three different churches in town, thinking surely one of them would provide a respite for contemplative solitude. One was locked, the other was filled with cheerleading squads, and the last one was overrun with rancorous Boy Scouts.

I realized I was really close to my local post office, so I decided I might as well go and check my post office box. I squealed into the crowded parking lot and waited ten minutes before a space opened up. I went inside. No mail, of course. Not even a damn bill! I returned to my car defeated and drained, started it up, but realized there was nowhere I wanted to go. Out of complete irritation I yelled, "Fine, then I'll just do it here!" The window was open, and a few heads turned to see if I intended to do anything interesting.

At first, sitting there in the frenetic parking lot was more than distracting, since car after car squealed to a halt just feet behind me, some even honking, with hopes I was about to relinquish my spot. However, within a few minutes I completely forgot where I was. At some point I went into a very deep trance, bordering on sleep, and when I woke up about an hour later, I was surprised to discover that despite it being 4:00 in the afternoon, the busiest time of day here, there were now only a couple of cars left in the parking lot. I felt refreshed now and headed back to the motor home.

I found a note taped to the squeaky door, stating that my family members had gone out for a movie and dinner, and would not be back for several hours. I sat down and meditated for another forty-five minutes or so, then read a book and took a delicious nap. By the time they returned home, I was happy to see them again. We moved a few days later to a much bigger place.

The truth that I am continuously shown is that our outer lives really do mirror our inner lives. If you have no space in your house, then you probably have little space for yourself in your aura. It's probably jam-packed with other people's ideas, feelings, considerations, opinions, and wishes. As we clear these out on the inside of us, it will be reflected on the outside of us. This change can literally happen overnight.

~ EXERCISE ~
Own Your Space for Yourself

While you can do this exercise anywhere, including in your car, I suggest that you start off doing it in the place where you intend to spend the night.

First, see a huge cord of energy running from the base of your spine to deep within the center of the planet.

Next, imagine there is a giant rose filled with flaming light in the center of your room. See the light expand so it fits around the entire building. Now, visualize any excess energies releasing down the stem. Then see a stem shooting downward, connecting the blazing bud with the earth. See the stem grow bigger and bigger until it is the size of your room. You can increase the size of the rose and the stem to fit around the entire building. As you do this, know you are really taking charge of this space, making it roomier and safer for yourself.

Please note that if you live with other people and they unconsciously react to the effects of this exercise by becoming angry or even throwing you out, then chances are you did not belong there to begin with, and they are doing you a really big favor! Do not underestimate the power of these visualizations, or the ability of others to sense a shift in the field around them as a result. Even though most people won't have the slightest inkling of what's happening, they will feel a difference, and they may experience and react to the shift in various ways.

~ EXERCISE ~
Finding Peace When You Don't Feel Peaceful

If you are not feeling very peaceful, I recommend you head outside and take at least a forty-five-minute walk where you can appreciate the beauty of nature. Take along your iPod and listen to the songs that inspire you the most, unless it's the sounds of nature that most inspire you. Find a ranch or someplace else where you can hang out with animals. Horses and cows are excellent for this, because they are always in the present moment. As you walk, use all of your senses to notice the enchanting things around you. Notice how the sunlight glimmers on the leaves of the trees, the color of the sky, and the feel of the ground beneath your feet. Doing this exercise will help get you into present time and run the energy of appreciation, which is very strong and helps you to attract other things you will appreciate as well. Once you are feeling peaceful, you are ready to begin saying your affirmations (e.g., "I am now filled with overwhelming peace, joy, appreciation," and so on).

~ EXERCISE ~
Crowning Yourself With Peace

You can also choose a color that represents peace or the state of being you choose, and imagine your crown is turning to this color. Then imagine that the color is flowing downward. See it fill up your head, throat, heart, stomach, sexual organs, and corresponding areas. See it flowing downward through the legs to the feet and out your grounding cord. See it flowing down your shoulders and fountaining out of your hands like colored pools of light. Imagine that you are so filled with the color of peace that it seeps from every pore of your skin, filling up the energy field around you.

~ EXERCISE ~
Manifesting a Great Place to Live

The key here is to find a place in a neighborhood or on a piece of land where you would love to live, and physically go there. Once you are actually there, pretend you live there and admire the building and the grounds. Stand in the doorway if possible, and pretend you are greeting guests who can't believe what a fantastic place you managed to find: "Yes, I know this place is awesome. Can you believe it, me, little ol' me, now lives here? It was so easy to find and was so affordable!"

Repeat this several times to different people, whether real or imaginary. (So what if they really believe you or think you are nuts—you probably are.) Remain there as long as possible. If you can stay overnight there, all the better.

Manifesting Relationships by Making Them More Real

Many children of divorce aren't sure if it's even possible to manifest a healthy relationship. It's therefore important for them, and perhaps for you, too, even if you aren't a child of divorce, to believe that such a relationship is possible. A good way to do this is to place yourself in close proximity to couples who are in seemingly healthy and happy relationships. Invite yourself over to such a couple's house for dinner and talk to them about their relationship. It's normal to feel envious or sad if they seem really happy. However, you can turn any of these feelings into resolve: if it's possible for them, then it is also possible for you. (It doesn't matter if they really are absolutely healthy or happy, as long as you think they are!)

If you don't know a couple who fit this description, then read books about healthy couples or watch films depicting such couples. These are somewhat hard to come by but do exist. One of my favorite movies depicting a wacky but happily married couple is *Meet the Fockers*, starring Dustin Hoffman and Barbra Streisand.

Treat Yourself Like You'd Like to Be Treated

You may have heard a version of this saying before but it bears repeating, because it does work very well. In fact, it may be one of the most important phrases in this book. Spend at least part of every day pampering yourself and treating yourself exactly as you'd want to be treated in a relationship. Take yourself out to places you like, compliment yourself every time you look in a mirror, and do activities you want to do, not just ones you think you should do or must do. Lavish presents on yourself. The most important thing is to give yourself, your soul, and your body the attention it craves from someone else.

A fantastic thing you can do for yourself is to take a class or join some kind of specialized organization where you will find people who have similar interests as you.

After you do the above, take time to visualize and play around with the emotions you might feel if someone else was taking care of you and loving you like you take care of and love yourself. Many people make the mistake of thinking they can't love themselves until someone else loves them. These people are usually alone for a very long time, because if you don't love yourself you won't be able to handle the love of someone else. You won't feel worthy, and will end up pushing the love away or not recognizing it for what it is in the first place. I know it's a cliché, but fake it till you make it is the best advice I can give you. If you don't feel like you love yourself, pretend you do!

Additional suggestions for making a future relationship real to your body:

Surround yourself with people who adore you! Ask them to tell you why you are so wonderful.

Cut out the picture of a person, even a celebrity, whom you admire, and tape it to the front of a chair. Pretend this person is complimenting you. If this won't make you laugh at yourself, nothing will! Remember: laughter raises your vibration, which then attracts others who are at this higher frequency.

Draw or paint a picture of the characteristics of the person you wish to be, and hang this picture over your bed or put it under your pillow or on the pillow next to you. For that matter, you can go buy a doll (don't worry, it doesn't have to be a blow-up one!) and pretend it's your future mate. Talk to it, say words of gratitude to it, and then fall asleep hugging it. (I said hugging it! Come on, clean up that mind of yours!)

Please note: I am not suggesting that you visualize yourself with the exact person you think you want to be with. If there is someone you have in mind, that person may or may not be able to fulfill your needs. Instead, visualize yourself with an imaginary person who has the characteristics that are important to you.

Money

Many people make the mistake of thinking that the only way they can have money is to earn it. Yet often they are already feeling overwhelmed, or having difficulty figuring out how in their line of work they will ever make more than they are already earning. It is therefore often helpful to open yourself up to the idea that a windfall of money could come to you, regardless of your actions. Below I explain in more detail about the ability to have and receive money. For now it's just important to keep in mind that when you visualize money flowing to you, see it coming from sources other than, or in addition to, that which comes from your own hard labor.

~ EXERCISE ~
Creating Wealth

In order to prepare ourselves for wealth, we often need to trick ourselves into believing we already have it or are worthy of it. One way to do this is to immerse yourself in an environment where you can begin to imagine that you are compatible with the energy of wealth and to experience real physical sensations while you are visiting this environment. Here are just a few suggestions:

Take a friend along with you who gets what you are doing. Get dressed up and spend the day visiting expensive boutique shops and trying on the most expensive clothes. It doesn't matter whether or not you actually make a purchase.

My friend Christie did this with me because it worked so well for her in the days when she used to have to work for a living. At first it was difficult. I felt like I had a sign on my forehead blaring, "She really doesn't belong here! She can't afford a single thing here! Call the fashion police!" My inclination to look at the price tags and yell out, "What! One thousand dollars for these cheesy shoes?" probably didn't help much either. However, after visiting several high-end stores and making some purchases (such as a hair tie and a crystal-studded toothpick thingy), I became much more comfortable. I still can't bring myself to spend more than a couple hundred dollars on a dress, but now I can shop in places other than Target or WalMart—if I choose.

Get dressed up in a nice outfit and go mansion shopping in a posh neighborhood. Just make sure you wash your car first. On second thought, maybe you should rent a car for the day.

On your next trip, whether you are going on vacation or just to the grocery store, rent a sporty convertible. (Don't forget your sunglasses—even if they're the cheap kind!) This will do wonders for your mood (well, at least until you get the bill—but really, you will probably find it worth it. If you don't, then maybe you will stop feeling depressed about driving your old clunker).

On a tight budget? Visit a trendy restaurant and split an appetizer with a friend. Or if this is not your style and you think it would just make you feel depressed, go to the local diner and treat yourself to the grand-slam triple whammy value meal breakfast. No matter what it consists of, it will be more filling than your customary bowl of corn flakes waiting for you at home, and it shouldn't cost more than seven or eight bucks.

Every few months, go to a major department store and actually buy yourself an outfit you love, regardless of the price.

Take a day off from work for no good reason other than to meet your friends for lunch and go see a movie. Declare that someday soon you will be able to do this every day if you so choose. (This worked well for me!)

Get yourself a full-body massage every other month, and as you do, imagine you are being pampered in this way every day. (Believe me, massage therapists work their little hineys off; they deserve every dollar and a lot more!) If a massage is just not in your budget at the moment, stop in to a massage school and inquire about a student massage. You might be able to get one for twenty dollars or less.

Instead of ramen noodles, buy yourself a steak and veggies or a nice cut of fish, and cook yourself a full meal. Make sure you sit down at the dinner table with a candle. Give yourself a nice bath afterward. Your body will appreciate a full, hearty meal and will reward you with the ability to manifest even more money to purchase extravagant luxuries—like food!

Write yourself a check for a thousand, even a million, dollars, and hang it on the wall of your bedroom. I did this for my son when he was six, and within three years he had starred in three national commercials and had earned over twenty thousand dollars in residuals from less than four days of work. Not exactly a million (yet!), but we aren't complaining.

Take out all the five-hundred-dollar bills from your Monopoly game and carry them around in your wallet as if they were real. (Just don't hand them out!)

These are just a few things you can do that will send signals to yourself that you are abundant, that you deserve to be pampered, and that you might just be on your way up in the world. Believe me: it is possible to feel like a queen from time to time, even when your wallet indicates you have less than the neighborhood bag lady.

The cool thing is after a while, your ability to manifest anything in your life will become easier, so you will be able to spend less time doing these silly exercises, although you will always have them to fall back on.

Manifesting a Creative Project That Sells

Whether you wish to write and publish a book, make and sell a film, get a record deal, become a successful actor, or do and sell your art, you first need to get it out of your head that it's impossible, unlikely, far-fetched, or unrealistic to accomplish these things. The fact is, there are lots and lots of people who make a living by promoting, producing, publishing, and distributing works of art, and by representing artists. They are out there, desperately searching for people like you right now! The things you need are as follows:

1. Talent or a quality product.
2. Confidence in the quality of your work.
3. An understanding of the market your work will do well in.
4. An ability to tell people why what you are offering is unique and valuable. If you don't know, then your goal/wish should be to figure this out. The journey of discovering this will bring you further than you could imagine.
5. The initiative to put yourself in the best possible place to achieve your goal. For example, if you want to be a television or film actor, the best place for you to go is Hollywood. If you say, "Hollywood? I'd never go there!" that's fine. But just know you may be cutting yourself off from many opportunities that will help your goal.
6. The expectation, even if everyone else thinks there's just a one-in-a-million chance for the opportunity, that you are the one in a million who will get this opportunity.
7. An understanding that fame and fortune may be just one new idea away, and that just by adjusting or altering the way you do things in a very minor way, you can increase your income tremendously. For example, for years I had been teaching groups of people in weekend workshops, but one day I got the idea to offer training to individuals over the telephone. Within two months I had four new students, which paid my rent for the next several months. The cool thing was I had so much fun teaching in this way that I fell in love with my work all over again. All of this came about from having a sudden idea, taking thirty minutes to make some changes on my website, and sending out one email blast.

~ EXERCISE ~
Goal / Action / Evaluation

Write down a goal at the top of a piece of paper. Then write down every possible thing you can think of to do that would make it more likely your goal will be successful. Your list might include going to school or getting more training, moving to a new location, contacting certain people, or changing the way you meet or connect with clients. Don't leave anything out, small or large.

Now go back and ask yourself, what on this list would I not be willing to do or am I avoiding or afraid to try or doubtful will work? Circle that thing, and look at it good and hard. That may be just the thing you do need to do. Then look at your list again, and circle all the things on it you can begin to do today, right now.

~ EXERCISE ~
Visit Your Creations in Their
Future Physical Locations

One of my favorite things to do when I was writing my first two books was to go to bookstores, to the section where I thought my books would most likely be someday, and to visualize my books on the shelf. I would actually move around the books already there (only those that had several copies) and make space for my books. Then I'd take about five minutes and see my books there with my name on them.

Now, years later, I go back to some of these same stores, and I make a point of visiting my books on the shelf, exactly where I used to stand! Every time I pass by a bookstore, my son starts to groan and pulls me away: "Come on, Mom, why do we have to go look at your dumb books again, you have a hundred copies at home!" But I explain that by viewing the books where I had previously merely visualized them to be, it strengthens my own power of manifestation.

In the past year I've started to place my books face out on a higher shelf. Or I will put them beside books by a couple of my favorite authors and take their picture there with my cell phone camera. When I am feeling very bold, I will move a copy of each of my books to the best sellers section! Coincidentally (wink wink), I was recently informed that Barnes & Noble has designated my second book for a special display, meaning it's now appearing on shelves higher up, face out. Hmmm, I wonder where you'll find this book!

I welcome you to play around with this concept. If you are an artist, visit museums and galleries and visualize your artwork hanging on the walls. Feel how happy you are that your work is being displayed there. If you are a filmmaker, screenwriter, or actor, go to the movie theater and visualize your film appearing on the big screen. See your name in the credits and pretend you hear other people speaking excitedly about it, giving it great reviews.

~ EXERCISE ~
Play With Time Travel

As you stand in the place your creation is most likely to be displayed, pretend that you are yourself in the future, coming back to admire that which you created in the past. Allow you as your future self to speak words of encouragement to your past self.

Then switch over to being the past version of yourself. Send words of gratitude to your future self for sending back the encouragement to you in time. Allow yourself to receive these words and be comforted by them.

Go back and forth in time in your imagination between your past, present, and future selves, enjoying a dialog between them. Take turns being each one. This may be confusing at first but it will get easier. I really believe that these different parts do help each other out, although I can't explain the physics behind this process.

CHAPTER 12

Balancing Masculine and Feminine Energies

*A relationship is different from a partnership: a relationship is
two people relating to each other's issues; a partnership is about two
people working together under a conscious intentional agreement—
to achieve a common goal.*

—VIKI KING

*God turns you from one feeling to another and teaches you by means of opposites, so that you
will have two wings to fly—not one.*

—RUMI

We sometimes have difficulties manifesting goals because what can be thought of as our male (yang) and female (yin) energies are severely out of balance. Our female energy is that which allows us to focus inward. It's the part of us that creates through intention, thought, and emotion. When we meditate, pray, or repeat affirmations, we are utilizing and activating our female energy. This is the part of us that is actively passive. We send out an intention and then wait to receive it. We let the intention work for us. As clairvoyants or meditation practitioners, this is the part of ourselves that must sit in silence and wait for the information or inspiration to come in. You could also see the feminine as the spirit. Please note that receptivity is not about just sitting around doing nothing and hoping for a miracle. It has to do with establishing a clear intention based on one's intuition, and remaining alert, aware, focused, and ready for action.

The male energy or aspect of our self is that which is actually compelled to take physical action. It is the part that makes phone calls, sends emails, scans the want ads for jobs or homes or whatever it is we seek—oh yes, and takes out the garbage, if it remembers.

When these energies are well integrated and balanced within an individual, that person's life will run more smoothly, with less stress and drama. Such a person may enjoy greater harmony with romantic relationships. Through my clairvoyant readings, I have observed that many people run into problems with relationships when their own masculine or feminine energies are out of balance. This is true in both heterosexual and homosexual relationships.

Too Much Masculine Energy

People who over-identify with the masculine, action-oriented self tend to be too controlling and put out more effort than is needed to accomplish a task. Such people are caught in a cycle of too much doing and not enough being. Often this obsessive "doing" is fueled by anxiety. As long as they are busy they feel they are accomplishing something. Through their busy-ness, they can avoid having to feel their feelings. This is usually at the root of most obsessive behavior and is a common trait of workaholics. Sometimes too much action is a symptom of a lack of faith. Some people believe the only way they will be able to create any kind of opportunity is through their own actions.

These people are fearful that if they don't cover every base, some opportunity might slip by. They must apply for every job in the newspaper, or visit every apartment for rent in a fifty-mile radius. Those caught in this cycle usually come to a clairvoyant out of frustration if not pure exhaustion. They know what they are doing is not working, but they don't know what else to do. They are terrified of missing an opportunity by not being in the right place at the right time. They suffer from a lack of faith.

A common image that comes to me when I am dealing with people like this is someone running on a treadmill or in circles. My usual prescription for such people is to stop all this activity and take a break. Sometimes I see they need to do some meditations, visualizations, or affirmations, but many times all it seems they need is to get lots of sleep, or even to take away their attention from the thing they want by watching TV or having fun.

You'd think people would be happy to hear that all they have to do is go home, relax, watch a movie, or go dancing, but someone with an overabundance of masculine energy won't believe this. What they don't understand is that in the course of having fun, we raise our energetic vibration, and that is what will allow goals and new opportunities, frequently wondrous ones, to flow right into our lives. Fun is a much higher vibration than stress. An hour of fun can equal if not surpass the benefits of three months of job or apartment or soul-mate searching! If this is hard for you to believe, it may be the very thing you need the most.

Not Enough Masculine Energy

On the other hand, I've observed my share of couch potatoes, including spiritual practitioners, who have no problem sitting in a lotus position for hours, diligently saying their mantras and affirmations but barely mustering enough energy to leave the house or ask someone on a date. The prescription for these homebodies is to get out, network, and engage in activities that are going to get their physical energy flowing. (Hello, all you silly people of the techno generation: staring into the eyes of your beloved's picture on Facebook or Instagram is not the same as staring into his or her eyes across the dinner table—although it may be less expensive!)

This message is particularly important for those of you who don't want to take any action until you are positive you know exactly what you want to do. Merely walking or driving around will sometimes give you the answer that was eluding you when you were stuck trying to figure it out in your head. Sometimes you actually do need to put your body in the right place at the right time.

Listening to Your Inner Female

Women throughout history have suffered because of the decisions men have made for them. Since men have traditionally been the ones who made the decisions for the entire household; a woman had to accept and then deal with the consequences of men's actions, no matter how stupid they were.

As women, it's not so much men who are oppressing us anymore as it is our very own masculine energies standing over us like the Gestapo. When the feminine within us cries out, "I don't feel like going to the office today!" or "What I really need more than anything is just to sit here and space-out, daydream, or meditate," it's our masculine part that resists and warns, "You'd better shut up or you're going to get us both into trouble." A woman who listens to her intuition is in direct opposition to the masculine part of herself and to all the other men and women who have a matching set of step-by-step instructions, rule books, and laws imprinted into their brains about the most beneficial way to get ahead in life and stay there.

So when the feminine rebels and yells, "If you don't listen to me, I'm going to get sick or we're going to have an accident," the masculine will still counter, "But there isn't time, it's not practical, it's not responsible, it's not according to the schedule! But okay, fine, have it your way, just take an extra five minutes for lunch. You can make it up by coming in early tomorrow." So then what do you do? Like a good little girl or woman or man you listen to this tyrant, maybe even take a pill or a drink to shut him out or to help you forget just how tired and miserable you really are in this trap.

Sometimes when your inner female is not heard, the only thing she can do is rebel. She does this by getting sick, or by creating so much drama and noise that the person with the controlling masculine energy is forced into responding either by honoring her, abandoning her, or destroying her. This is true whether the one with the masculine energy is another person, or whether it's the most dominant part of oneself.

Many Women Still Want a Man to Do Their Work for Them

Many women are really lacking in their masculine aspect so they seek out men who will compensate for this imbalance. (This happens with a large portion of gay men as well.)

Last month I met with three clients during the course of a twenty-four-hour period who had the same issues holding them back. One was a client of mine from the Pacific Northwest, whom I'll call Betsy. She has been separated from her husband, a successful and domineering divorce attorney, for over three years. She has been having an affair with another man, whom she referred to as her "boyfriend," for almost a decade. (You do the math.) When we began working together, she complained that her boyfriend was unwilling to spend as much time with her as she desired. It seemed he felt justified in leaving town for weeks at a time without her, with the excuse that even though she no longer lived with her husband, she was still officially married. I didn't quite buy this excuse, but I knew the only way she'd know his true intentions was to become free herself, which she needed to do anyway.

Betsy felt very "stuck" in her life on many levels. When I asked her why she didn't get divorced, she blamed her husband. She said over the past two years, every time she asked him to meet to discuss the divorce, he put it off. I asked her what her attorney thought, and she said she hadn't yet selected one, that she hadn't really been sure she needed one even though she was positive she wanted a divorce. (Okay, let me repeat: her husband is a divorce attorney, a controlling man who doesn't want to get divorced. That makes sense, let's just wait for him to draw up the deal himself!)

When we got to the bottom of things, it turned out Betsy's husband has still been fully supporting her during the past three years, with the hope she'd come back to him. While she was aware of how guilty she felt for leaving her husband, she didn't want to admit, at least to me, that money was a factor. She was waiting and relying on the very man who didn't want to let her go to set her free, and to do it in a way that would ensure she was taken care of for the rest of her life. While I can't argue that it would be nice to have income flowing in without having to work for it, I also felt that for her, needing to generate the income would be a motivating factor that would lead to positive results.

I've seen this in more than just a few friends who live off inheritances, trust-fund accounts, or alimony; these friends just don't have the same motivating factors the rest of us do to take certain steps. The need for money can be quite a powerful incentive to get off your butt and do something worthwhile! At the same time, we don't want to get dependent on the need for money to motivate us, because this sets up a vicious cycle of manifesting the need for money as opposed to eliminating that need.

In Betsy's case, she really wanted to move on with her life, but she was continuing to let her guilt, financial dependency, and the desire for someone to make things easier for her stop her in her tracks. I am not saying there sometimes isn't an easy way out, but I am noting that in many cases such women are being presented with an opportunity to be courageous, to have faith in themselves, and to accept the consequences of their actions as adults instead of as little girls.

Furthermore, by refusing to be with their husbands fully or to let the relationship go, they are keeping themselves and their husbands in an excruciating purgatory that is far more painful than it would be if they took the difficult road of going through with their divorces on their own. So many people allow their guilt to be their judge and executioner. I am not saying their husbands were perfect little angels here; but when it comes to moving forward in your life, discussions about who is right or wrong or who is the bad guy do absolutely nothing except keep you stuck. It doesn't matter who is to blame. What matters is what steps are you taking now to create the life you long for.

Please understand that I am not advocating for divorce or for leaving one's marriage. What I am saying is we really have to understand our own motivations for giving away our power. If you are truly unhappy and not willing to continue to try to make things work, it makes no sense to rely on the very person you are attempting to leave to do for you what you can't do for yourself. And of course this can be complicated by being in a relationship with someone who has encouraged you to be dependent on him or her, by convincing you to give up your own resources for the sake of the relationship or family.

Obsession

When your feminine/masculine energies are out of balance, it's very easy to become fixated on, dependent on, or obsessed with someone who is polarized in the opposite end of the spectrum of the masculine/ feminine dichotomy. If that seems to describe you or your current situation, I recommend doing the exercises below.

~ EXERCISE ~
Journey to Meet Your Inner Male/Female

The following exercises were taught to me by one of the most awesome healers I know: Kazandrah Martin, who lives in Sedona. She healed herself of a brain tumor within a month after leaving a dysfunctional relationship.

Lie down, close your eyes, relax. Take some deep breaths. Imagine you are walking down a winding path in a peaceful forest. Visualize the foliage alongside the path. Notice how bright the sun is and how warm or cold it is; you can even visualize your feet walking.

When it feels like you have found the right spot, look around for a big stone and a flowering tree. Behind the stone you will find your inner male. Behind the tree you will find your inner female. Go to the one you feel most comfortable with first. Then sit down on the stone, or next to the tree, and relax. Wait until your inner male or female shows up. Say hello to him or her. Observe what he or she looks like. Ask this aspect how he or she feels.

Then invite this aspect to cross over to the other side of the path to meet his or her counterpart. Just sit back and watch what happens. You goal here is to observe how the two greet each other, what their appearances are like, and how they communicate.

If things don't look that great, then you can always step in. Do a little couples counseling with them. Get them to talk. Show them each a mental picture of how you'd like them to be together and individually. If your inner female or male looks weary or sickly, go ahead and hug him or her in your imagination. Promise him or her you will do everything to help with the necessary healing. Offer the assurance of your continued love. I recommend doing an energy healing on your inner female or male by following the next exercise as well. Leave them both there in the forest to begin healing their relationship, or to continue as they were if it looked really positive.

~ EXERCISE ~
Healing/Balancing the Male and Female Within

Close your eyes. Center yourself in a quiet place in your mind, slightly above and between your eyes. Imagine there is a third eye or window opening up in your forehead, and visualize a reading screen out about six inches from your head. A reading screen can look like a simple rectangle, a television screen, or a computer monitor. It gives you a place to focus your attention as you work with smaller symbols.

Once you've created a reading screen, visualize two identical, transparent roses or lotus flowers—one to the far left and one to the far right. Observe them for a moment in their starting positions. Then label one as representing your inner male, the other as your inner female. You can place the label below the flower or drop it into its own bud. Next, simply relax and observe what happens to the flowers. Notice the color, shape, and size of each one. Then ask each one to show you a personification of the energy. Just sit back and observe the flowers. Notice if either one changes. Ask them to show you the nature of their relationship. Again, just sit back and see what happens.

If you notice anything that doesn't seem optimal about their relationship, you can ask each one what he or she needs from the other. You can address them directly and invite them to respond with a verbal or auditory message and/or a visual sign. You can also invite each one to do a healing on the other. Or you can do a clairvoyant healing on both of them by visualizing a rose in the middle that represents their communication.

To do this, simply ground the communication rose by giving it a stem and seeing the stem sink deep down into the earth. Next, ask for the color of their improved communication to appear first, and then ask that any oppositional energies show themselves in the form of darker colors within the center rose. As these colors emerge, gently but firmly command them to release down the grounding cord. You can facilitate this release by pushing these colors down the cord with your imagination and will. You can also ask your inner male and female to do the healing on the communication rose. Notice how they do this and what happens.

Results

The cool thing about all the exercises in this book is that when you release foreign energy from your body, your aura, and/or your surroundings, and then draw in your own energy or vibrations of health or peace or joy, changes occur both within yourself and in other people around you. Your feminine and masculine energies can rebalance themselves even if you aren't aware you are working directly with them. You may suddenly see things in a whole new light. Options will bloom where before they were about as hard to find as a cold can of soda in the Sahara desert. You may suddenly find the courage, strength, or incentive to speak about something or to take steps you had been avoiding. You may now find more time for meditation or work on your creative projects, or you might discover a whole new appreciation for yourself. At the same time, you will often notice that other people in your life will begin to act differently as well. There might be an initial confrontation or drastic change in the relationship dynamics, but usually this will quickly lead to improved relations, or perhaps the dissolution of the relationship for the betterment of both parties.

CHAPTER 13

How to Become a God

In truth everything and everyone / Is a shadow of the Beloved /
And our seeking is His seeking / And our words are His words...
We search for Him here and there / While looking right at Him /
Sitting by His side, we ask: "O Beloved, where is the Beloved?
—RUMI

One of the most powerful ways to awaken your inner genie is through the act of infusing yourself with the concept of God. You'll notice that I frame this as the "concept of God" as opposed to just stating "God." (Replace "concept of God" and "God" with your own special name for the divine: "Goddess," "Jesus," "Hashem," "Allah," "Buddha," etc.")

I do this for a few reasons. First, the "concept of God" is obviously not God in actuality, just as the "concept of an ocean" is not an "ocean" itself or our perception of the world is not the world itself. Even the most educated marine biologist does not know every creature in, or understand every aspect of, the ocean; it is too vast to know. At the time I'm writing this, everyone in my life and in the media has been talking about the state of the economy: worrying about it, thinking about it, and allowing it to influence them. But the economy is not physical—so what is it? For that matter, what is the world? And in the same vein, what is God? Since God is something so much larger than ourselves, we will never be able to come close to "figuring out" who or what God is. Fortunately, we don't need to.

In this chapter I am going to teach you how to infuse yourself with the energy of the divine, so you can access the infinite creative abilities ascribed to God. One day during a meditation, I asked how I could manifest a new place to live, and that is when the techniques in this chapter came to me. Not only have these techniques given me a stronger sense of power, but they have also eliminated my anxiety; within three days of that meditation, I had signed the lease for my new dream home.

Please understand, I am not trying to convert you. If I found that infusing oneself with the concept/energy of a banana worked just as well, I'd be talking bananas here. The problem with the word "God" is that it is a symbol that has been contaminated by all the other symbols we associate with it. Just tune in to your feelings as you repeat the word to yourself: "God, God, God." What does that word elicit for you? For many it will be nice, warm, fuzzy feelings, but for others these feelings will be tinged with or overpowered by confusion, distaste, and distress. This reaction is not to the energy of God, but to our "pictures" around the word God. Some of these pictures are painful.

Many people feel betrayed because God did not step in to save a loved one from death, or did not protect them from abusers during childhood. Sometimes God was forced down their throats by adults who used the name of God to control them. Many religious fanatics wouldn't recognize the energy of God if their life depended on it. That's why a lot of them end up dead before their time, as in the case of young suicide bombers. The important thing to remember is that these memories and thoughts laden with disappointment, judgment, and pain are a completely separate thing from the energy of God. Since I don't want to program you myself, I am not even going to try to describe what my experience of the energy of God is like. Instead, I will merely describe one of the easiest ways to access this energy. Then you can decide whether or not there is something to it.

I mention all this because in order to benefit from the technique I will introduce in a little bit, it's necessary first to let go of your preconceptions, confusion, or repulsion to the idea of God.

Overcoming Resistance to the God Symbol

I think a clue to understanding the power of the God symbol lies in one of the definitions of the word "law." A law is a rule that describes but does not explain a pattern in nature, and predicts what will happen under specific conditions. So if we think of God as a law, let's call that law "the law of God"—and then we might define this law as, "When a person infuses themselves with the concept, energy, idea, or symbol of God, that person's life will restructure itself to form a pattern of greater harmony." Notice here the law isn't at all attempting to explain how or why this all works, only that when one activity is carried out it will have a certain effect.

The nice thing about this is we can stop trying to figure out something that our puny brains will never be able to understand, and instead get right down to taking care of business—the business of drawing our wishes to us and seeing our needs fulfilled, so that our lives become far more pleasurable and easier to navigate.

Trying to Understand Keeps Us Stuck!

Our minds are like moths, constantly fluttering around trying to find the light even when the light is coming from a source that will burn them the moment they land. As babies we are taught words paired together as contradictions. Two of the first words an English speaking child learns are "yes" and "no." Then come "good" and "bad," and "boy" and "girl." Yet this is a function and perception of our minds, not of things as they really are. We as humans are programmed early on to categorize, label, and judge. It is through these lenses that we view our world, our lives, each other, and ourselves.

Our minds are like an insane filing clerk who must find the correct file immediately and then check and recheck to make sure the information is placed in the correct folder. Luckily, the filing cabinet is not really that big, since everything could potentially fall into the categories of bad or good, at least within our own system. Things begin to get shaken up when we compare our filing systems to those of others in our lives, and discover that for them, the same information (e.g., ideas and opinions about communism, a particular song or movie, your husband) has been placed in the opposite folders.

Then we become like two frightened and confused filing clerks with obsessive-compulsive disorder, battling it out on top of the Xerox machine that keeps spitting out the same blank piece of paper.

When it comes to the idea of God, our inner filing clerks insist they know exactly which file this idea goes in and will slap or kill you if you try to tell them otherwise; or else they are confused, jumping from folder to folder and unable to find the right one.

Have you ever wondered what would happen if you lit a match to all those files and fired the clerk? I think I know. You'd experience silence, peace, nothingness. At least for a few moments, until the unfamiliar silence startled you and you ran back to find the clerk in hopes of a possible reconciliation. After all, it took you a long time to accumulate these files. Some of them are even entertaining. What's there to do without them?

When we meditate or play a musical instrument, we are sometimes able to step out of the filing room and achieve short periods of this silence. Another way—easier for some, harder for others—is simply to become aware of our inner clerks and files and move away from them. This means we become aware that all these attempts to categorize, judge, figure out, blame, accuse, dissect, theorize, assume, label, solve, and analyze are tricks of the mind and may be futile. They may not be bringing us even one step closer to really understanding or knowing anything—whether that "anything" is God, the truth, our spouse, or the best course of action to take. Instead, our insistence on duality may be keeping us from experiencing life fully.

The next time you find yourself judging or comparing two things, ask yourself what you are hoping or needing to find. Why must anything be considered better than something else? The only reason we need to make others wrong is so we can feel "right" or justify our own actions. There is absolutely no other reason. Can we be right without ever making a comparison or judgment? Yes and no. The idea of being right is itself a fallacy. It does not exist; rather, it's a symptom and need manufactured by the ego. The more judgmental and analytical people are, the more insecure and judgmental they are of themselves, and the weaker they and their ability to manifest becomes. However, what we can do is be who we are. Whether that is right or wrong in someone else's mind or our own mind is not the question and is insignificant. In this respect, Descartes couldn't have been further off base when he said, "I think, therefore I am."

What I'd like you to do right now is let go of the need to have God explained, and instead allow yourself to fully experience the power of God as a "pattern in nature," one that permits us to predict what will happen under specific conditions. The conditions will be as follows:

~ EXERCISE ~
God as a Magic Symbol

1. Create a grounding cord: Visualize your first chakra, which you can see as a spinning disk corresponding to the cervix or inner pelvic region. Visualize a column of blazing energy running from this energy center all the way down to the center of the earth.

2. Next, ask yourself this question: "What do I picture when I think of God?" Warning! Don't try to judge and alter this perception before it comes in. What we are really looking for here is your unconscious picture of God. So ask yourself: when I usually think of God, what does she or he look like? Do you see an old man with a beard? A scrawny man who resembles George Burns, smoking a cigar? Perhaps a goofy guy making funny faces who reminds you of Jim Carrey in the film *Bruce Almighty*? Or do you see a cross or a star or a column of light? Do you see God above you? Do you see a light in your heart?

Now, out in front of you, form a screen like a television set, movie screen, computer monitor, or a blank sheet of paper (if you've read my other books, I refer to this as a *reading* screen). On the screen, let your most common image of God appear.

3. Next, postulate that you yourself are God. So go ahead and now replace your vision of God that you just conjured up in step 2 with a vision of yourself. See yourself as if you were looking at yourself in a mirror.

4. Continue seeing yourself as God by putting your attention back on your body. Center yourself within your heart. Say, "Hello, God" to your own heart, and continue to hold a picture of yourself as you are right now.

5. Begin contemplating the abilities that God or you as God might have. These could include power, the ability to create anything immediately, omniscience, omnipresence, and an endless capacity for love, peace, joy, and so on. So if you previously visualized God as a ball of light or an old bearded man, now replace these images with your own smiling face.

6. Imagine that you are opening up a photo album. On the first page is a blank picture. Under it there is a label that reads "God." Place an image of your face as the single image in the photo. Then write your name over the word God so that the names coexist in the same place. Meditate on this picture for as long as possible. Then turn the page. You will notice that every page has your picture with a label containing your name and God's name simultaneously.

7. The key here is to meditate on the image of yourself as God—not like God, or a part of God, but *as* God! Then begin saying to yourself, in your mind, the mantra, "I am God, I am God, we are the same." After you do this a hundred times or close to it, begin repeating this mantra out loud. Start off saying it quietly, then let the volume increase, until you are yelling it as loudly as possible. If you are fearful someone might hear you, then go find an isolated spot where you can yell this out as loudly as possible for at least a minute. You can bring the volume down until it's barely audible, then move it back into your head. While you do this, keep seeing yourself as God.

8. Here comes the activation part. Visualize yourself as God emanating the light of God. The light of God will beam through you. The light is the bigger part of the God-self that created you in the first place and that gives you your energy and the God power. It's like you are the God lamp and this is the battery. You can also think of this light as a breath moving through God's body. This breath is God's breath and your own breath. So as your breath, you are breathing God's light through your God body. This has a powerful impact and also helps cover all the bases, so your mind doesn't go into confusion about being God when it might not feel as powerful as it should. It's the light beaming through you and breathing through you as God that fully activates your God powers.

9. Begin, or continue if you've already started, to visualize the brightest, most blinding light you can envision emanating from the core of you within your body. See it streaming

outward in all directions, beaming out like light through stained glass from your center, through all parts of your body, past your body, and as far out as you can imagine it. Just when you can't imagine it getting any brighter, amp it up another few notches in your imagination. You can use the visualization that your body is the glass and the God-light beams through you as the glass, shining out far, in all directions, gloriously and triumphantly for all the world and people of the world to see. (Perhaps this is why so many churches have such large stained-glass windows.) Be God, breathing God's breath and beaming God's light through every cell and every pore of your body. This is the activation. You can see this happening directly to your body and you can view this all on your screen. Let your attention go back and forth from you, centered in your body, to the mirror image of your body on the screen.

10. The final step is to remind yourself that you and God are a pair, a combination that will set you and your inner genie free. This symbol is a key, a code, like that on your garage, front gate, or even your voicemail. Once you punch in the password, these devices open with no effort. Postulate that God as a universal symbol, energized by the masses who worship this symbol, will unlock the powers of creation, creativity, and manifestation within you. You may find that if you do this exercise before any of the others in this book, your results may be even more magnified. You are now completely primed for success.

Homework Assignment

For at least one week, do this exercise at least once a day, preferably in the morning. It would be great to conjure it up as you go about your day, all week long. Notice what happens to your day and your life. I guarantee you will see results. But look out—initially, you may begin to release a lot of negative emotions, so don't be surprised if you go through a period of emotional intensity. This will give way to that which you seek.

CHAPTER 14

Removing People's Influence From Our Creations

You have enemies? Good. That means you've stood up
for something, sometime in your life.
—WINSTON CHURCHILL

Energetic Influences From Individuals

If our own thoughts and feelings are energies that can attract our desires to us, then others' thoughts and feelings are also powerful magnets that can and do impact us as well. I am certain that the way we feel about ourselves, the risks we are willing or not willing to take, many of the decisions we make or don't make, and many of the actions we take or don't take are impacted by others' thoughts and feelings, whether or not we are aware of it. Many times others' opinions of us or their fears for us are lodged within our auric fields. These impact us physically, emotionally, cognitively, and spiritually.

People can transmit negative thoughts and emotions from thousands of miles away, and we often pick up on these thoughts and emotions, mistaking them for our own. In this way, we are all being naturally psychic all the time. As I am sure you know, most of the time it's not that these people are trying to keep us from moving forward or achieving our goals; sometimes, most of the time, it's out of their love and concern for us that they project their fears onto us. Their fears then become our own or exacerbate our own. This keeps us trapped in a cycle of apathy, confusion, or exhaustion. Then there are, of course, people who flow in (and hopefully out of) our lives who do have opposing agendas and very much want to stop us from reaching our goals.

Whether these projected fears are coming from someone who loves us or someone who hates us makes little difference. Both kinds of projections can interfere with the law of attraction and our ability to manifest. The closer we are to people (typically such people include parents, siblings close to our age, or someone we've had sexual intercourse with) on an emotional and physical level, the more we are impacted by their thoughts, both positive and negative. Also, the more people we have projecting emotionally charged thoughts toward us, the stronger the impact. This of course can work two ways. When people are sending us thoughts of love, light, and healing, we may receive a powerful healing and overcome all sorts of ailments. When they are sending angry, hurtful thoughts, it can really wear us down. One of the main reasons people suffer from confusion is because they have too much of other people's energy circulating through their heads. It's hard to hear your inner voice when there are so many people yelling at you from within.

How to Tell if You Are Being Impacted by Others' Energies

So how do we know if we are being blocked by resistance in the form of other energies, or if we are being blocked by ourselves, perhaps by something hidden deep in our subconscious? I've seen far too many psychics and healers caught up in the blame game of feeling like they are being psychically attacked or thwarted, when in actuality the culprit was really their own emotional pain, fear, or low self-esteem. I've also seen many psychology students or professionals who were so fixated on unraveling the mysteries of their own unconscious processes that they wasted a lot of time trying to fix themselves when there was nothing to fix, but rather something that needed to be released. It's kind of like walking around with an axe in your head and wondering why your years of therapy or medication aren't taking away the pain!

One of the most helpful things a clairvoyant reader can do is look to see what exactly is getting in the way of one's ability to manifest or successfully apply the law of attraction, and essentially discover if there is an axe in a client's head. If there is, the clairvoyant discovers how best to remove it, how it got there in the first place, how it might be impairing the person, and perhaps traces it back to who put it there and why they were able to get it past the client's natural defenses. However, visiting a clairvoyant is not essential either for the diagnosis of any of our problems or for the treatment. There are some signs you can be aware of that frequently indicate there is a foreign energy that is inhibiting the magnetism of your mind:

1. First, ask yourself if you are aware of anyone or anything in particular that is blatantly standing in the way of you and your wishes and goals. What do you find? Perhaps a parent, spouse, or boss telling you they will not let you do what you'd like to do, why it won't work, or how you might get hurt or hurt them? Next, ask yourself if, when you have any discouraging thoughts about going ahead with your dreams, you tend to hear the doubts as if they were spoken in the voice of someone you know, or if you find yourself having conversations with a particular person in your head explaining, defending, or making your case. Ask yourself, who is the first person that comes to mind whenever you think about doing something you've been longing to do? Does thinking about this person motivate you to pursue your dreams or to shove them under the rug?

2. Another sign that you may be picking up on others' energy occurs when you are initially very excited about what you are creating, about the steps you are taking to move toward your goals, but suddenly all the air is let out of your balloon. You feel discouraged, and you may even cancel your plans or turn down the opportunities you've been waiting for.

You have no idea what has brought on this sudden change of heart. Of course you might just be encountering your own fears, so this needs to be considered in correlation with the rest of the signs.

3. Just as you are about to take a step or get what you want, people suddenly pop up with problems they expect you to deal with. The more it seems like you are their only hope, the more you can be sure this is a sign of energetic resistance standing in between you and your ability to manifest.

4. You plan to spend time doing manifesting meditations, but then something happens. You fall asleep, get distracted, or get an offer to do something more pressing—like scrub the kitchen floor or watch a rerun of *Jeopardy*. Notice who shows up to give you something else to do.

5. You find yourself experiencing an extreme emotion that overtakes you, and that you can't shake no matter what you do. You find yourself behaving in ways you normally wouldn't; for example, you find yourself throwing objects or becoming violent, but only when you are around one particular person.

Why Would Others, Consciously or Unconsciously, Not Want Us to Manifest?

They are afraid we will leave them. They believe that as long as we are dependent on their money, on their encouragement when we feel down, or on our lack of options, we will stay with them and not find someone "better."

Competition. They don't want us to have what they don't think they can have. They are envious. They are satisfied by feeling superior.

Limits. Many of our loved ones are thoroughly convinced only certain things are possible. If we exceed the limits they set for themselves and ourselves, then this undermines their entire version of reality, and makes it more difficult for them to maintain their excuses as to why they are not taking steps to empower themselves in their own lives. Anytime we begin to exceed the limits of those who raised us, or even the society we come from, we are prone to hit resistance.

Agendas. Other people may not want us to manifest because they have a plan for us they want us to follow. They want to be in control.

The Spirit World

You may not believe in them, but I have no doubt whatsoever that we are constantly receiving information from spirits and nonphysical entities. These beings can have a profound impact on our thoughts, emotions, and self-esteem, thereby influencing our creations. It's not a matter of whether they are positive or negative, as much as it is that many of them have their own agendas, while some just can't help being a pain in the ass, as that's their nature. In this respect, they are not really any different from spirits with bodies—i.e., people.

There are some abusive spirits out there that spew curses and other disparaging words, emotions, and energetic frequencies at people. Some people can actually hear this communication as voices that they recognize as coming from a source outside themselves, while others hear it as their own voice. Those belonging to the first group might fear they are going insane, which might be what the troublesome entity is striving for. Those who hear it as their own voice will likely suffer from depression and low self-esteem. Both groups of people may be vulnerable to suicidal ideation. I am convinced that some spirits actually try to lead people down the road of killing themselves or others. Thankfully, there are spirits on the opposite end of this spectrum giving us encouragement and seeking to protect us from these invisible bullies.

From the plethora of experiences I've had as a clairvoyant, I've found that spirits can be found along a spectrum of light and darkness. Light by its very nature moves in an outward direction. It spreads and illuminates whatever is near. Darkness absorbs. The darker something is, the more it sucks in the light. Notice I am not calling one or the other "bad" or "good"; I am merely describing their qualities as I experience them. Spirits that are all light therefore have an energizing effect. Spirits that are mostly or all dark have a draining effect. This is true whether the spirit has a body, as a living human being does, or whether it dwells only in spirit form.

Spirits with less light attach themselves to living humans of a similar caliber, and then together they act like a black hole, creating chaos, drama, and pain in order to receive attention from others. What we give attention to, we give our energy to, so the more someone demands our attention, the more that person is feeding off of our energy fields. Parents who fit this description often do this to their children from the time they are born. This establishes a vicious cycle in the child's life, setting the child up as a caretaker and one who will be vulnerable to enslavement by other dark beings later in life. Often children of these types of parents are sickly, and blame themselves for problems at home.

I know this isn't the most pleasant topic to discuss, but I feel it's essential to do so. When we don't have enough of our energy, not only are we vulnerable to illness but we also have an extremely hard time manifesting. Awareness gives us the power to recognize the energy dynamics that may be keeping us stuck and to extract these people from our lives, or us from theirs. The good news is that most entities on the darker end of the continuum need a human host to work through, which means they are not just going to start bugging you for no apparent reason.

Occasionally they will attach themselves to a certain location, as in house hauntings, but even then it seems as though most poltergeist activity centers around a particular person who is either having emotional problems, running strong sexual energies that may be misguided, abusing drugs and/or alcohol, or has a fascination with these types of beings.

For more information on protecting yourself from troublesome entities, you can read my second book, *Extraordinary Psychic: Proven Techniques to Master Your Natural Psychic Abilities*. There is also a classic book by Dion Fortune called *Psychic Self-Defense* that I highly recommend. The following exercises will assist in helping you to protect and clear your creations from interference from disembodied spirits and humans alike.

~ EXERCISE ~
Maximize Attraction/Minimize Resistance

1. Close your eyes. Take some deep, slow breaths. Bring your attention to the center of your head. Imagine you are looking out your third eye. Visualize a gigantic, clear, transparent rose. Tell this rose it is going to represent the thing you'd like to create for yourself. You can imagine that you are writing the name of this thing beneath the rose. Ask the rose to show you the color of that which you are going to create. You can also drop some symbols inside the rose that represent it (for example, a relationship, money, a car, a trip,

and so on) and watch to see what happens next. Give the rose a stem, and see the stem automatically burrow downward into the earth to secure itself.

2. Next, ask for any colors to appear that represent energy that is not in agreement for you to have this creation. Once you see the colors, visualize them releasing down the stem into the earth. Notice if the main color of your rose changes as you do this. Focus all your attention on the rose. If your mind wanders, just bring it back to the rose as soon as you notice you've drifted off. You might have to redirect your attention a couple of times before completing this exercise. The more foreign energies involved, the more distracted you will be.

3. Bring your attention back to the color that represents what you are creating. The important thing here is you don't want to focus too much on the energy coming out; instead, focus on the color that represents what you are creating. See the color circulating, growing brighter, bolder, more sparkly and vibrant as it pushes out the oppositional energy. You can watch this rose grow bigger and bigger, and then you can see yourself in this rose, receiving what you want and feeling so happy that you are receiving it. It's very important to feel the emotions of happiness, gratitude, and excitement in conjunction with visualizations and affirmations.

4. Once you are satisfied that you have created the rose and released the resistance, you can cut the stem and let the rose float off into the universe to do its work. You can also imagine that the hands of God or your creator or another deity of your choice are above you. As you cut the rose, imagine that your wondrous creation is landing right into your deity's hands.

One of my personal favorite deities is the Hindu goddess Lakshmi. She is the goddess of prosperity and beauty. She appears as a beautiful Indian deity with several hands that hold jewels or gold bars, and she is often surrounded by peacocks. You can visualize her and ask her to bless your creation. She spontaneously appears to me from time to time. Another Hindu deity that has appeared to me, even before I knew who he was, is Ganesh. Ganesh looks like a man with a big elephant head. He represents the eliminator of obstacles. If you encounter a lot of resistance or are not convinced that the opposing energy is releasing down the grounding cord of your rose, you can ask Ganesh to step in and give the rose, and you, a healing. Jesus and Mother Mary are energies that are always there to help you. Just visualize them out in front of you, imagine you are showing them your rose with your creation, and ask them to bless it for you. Then observe what happens next.

Lakshmi and Ganesh appeared to me before I had the foggiest idea who they were. As I discuss in my book *You Are Psychic*, Jesus and Mary have spontaneously appeared during the course of my work with clients. On some of these occasions, other psychics who were present or in different parts of the building observed these figures at the exact same time I was experiencing them.

~ EXERCISE ~
Discover How Certain People Impact Your Creations

Once you are in a quiet place in your mind, centered behind your third eye, imagine you are looking out of your third eye onto a screen that resembles a computer monitor, blackboard, whiteboard, movie screen, or piece of white paper. On one side of the screen, visualize a clear, transparent rose. Ask it to fill up with the energy of the thing you are hoping to attract. Look at the color, shape, and size of the rose, and any other qualities about the leaves or the stem that may show themselves. Next to this, on the other side of your screen, put up an image of your mother, father, or spouse. You can see them as figures of people or visualize another transparent rose and invite that person's energy to come into it and show itself as a color.

Next, move the person or the receptacle filled with the person's energy close up to the rose representing your creation, and watch what happens when that person comes into contact with your creation. You might even introduce them to your manifestation by saying, "Dad, I'd like you to meet the boyfriend I am creating" or "Mom, I'd like you to meet the thousands of dollars I am manifesting" or "Honey, what do you think of this new job that will be in my life any day now?" Then, just sit back and watch what happens with your rose. First, look to see if it changes colors in any way.

The color is the beginning step that will give you something to focus your attention on. Once you notice a change in the rose, you can ask it to give you more detailed information through additional images or even messages. You may notice quite a bit of change to your rose, or you may notice nothing at all. If you are not pleased with what you see, move on to the next exercise, and understand that this may be telling you it's better not to discuss your manifestation with the person in question until you've actually attracted your manifestation fully into your life.

Sometimes we think someone is supportive of what we are trying to do. That person may in fact be supportive, but his or her unconscious doubts or fears could still be influencing us. It's important not to judge someone who seems to be inadvertently influencing you or to view this behavior as an attack, because such a judgment will only slow you down even more. At some point in your life, your energy has impacted others around you in the same way.

Remember the expression "What you resist, persists"? Try to be as neutral or as understanding as possible about another's influence and at the same time do what you need to do to clear that influence. This may involve working further with the energy, or it may require some action. When you live or work with someone on a daily basis, you are both living within each other's fields, and sometimes it isn't possible to clear energy from yourself or your creations until you have physically separated yourself from the other person's sphere of influence. I will discuss this more in the next chapter.

Here's the good news: If you noticed your rose being influenced in any way, that means you were using your clairvoyant ability to access this information. Congratulations! You just performed a clairvoyant reading without even realizing it.

~ EXERCISE ~
Shielding Your Manifestation

If it looks like your manifestation is vulnerable to other people's energies that are close to you or were at one time, or you suspect your manifestation might be vulnerable, then you can put up a shield that is programmed either to protect your manifestation from a specific person or from any number of people. Here's how to do it:

Visualize a clear, transparent rose and invite the energy of the thing you are wishing to manifest into that rose. Sit back, relax, and ask for a color to show itself that represents the rose. If you don't see a color, you can just assign it one. Next, choose a symbol for the thing you desire and visualize this symbol in your rose as well. In your imagination, see a stem running from the rose into the ground.

Next to this, at least a few inches away, place a symbol of the person, people, or spirit that you feel might interfere with your creation. Imagine that you are securing a mirror to the outside of the rose that represents your manifestation. See this mirror facing the people who might be impacting your creations, so that any of their interfering energy will immediately bounce back to them. You can also choose a color for their energy, and watch it float back to them or down your grounding cord just in case their energy has already entered your manifestation.

Another thing you can do is imagine you are holding a spray bottle of a substance called "exterminator protection fluid." Note that this substance will automatically repel the attention or energy of anyone who comes near your creation on an energy level. Imagine that you are lavishly spraying this fluid on your rose containing that which you wish to manifest, much as an exterminator would do to eradicate and prevent the infestation of any little critters in your backyard or house. See a color coming out of the spray bottle and watch the color completely saturate your receptacle and form a protective layer. You can also imagine you are looking at an expiration date on this bottle, which will establish for your subconscious how long this will work. The expiration date could be any number of years from now.

CHAPTER 15

Manifesting For Others

*Only time can heal your broken heart, just as only time
can heal his broken arms and legs.*
—MISS PIGGY

*Don't try to maintain a relationship, just try to maintain
yourself in a relationship.*
—UNKNOWN

Manifesting as a Couple vs. as a Single Person

I have learned the hard way that we can co-create *with* others but not *for* them. Also, I've learned that most conflicts that arise within relationships have to do with one's level of "havingness." Anyone who has transitioned from being a single person to one with a live-in partner will know what I'm talking about. Not only do you have the obvious challenges of dealing with different habits, preferences, needs, and desires, but you may be dealing with someone whose style of manifesting is completely different from yours. Of course, you may have attracted a partner who was also well-versed in the laws of attraction, perhaps even more so than you. In hooking up with this partner, creating will most likely be even easier than before. If that's the boat you are in, congratulations! The power the two of you have together is tremendous. There is very little you cannot co-create together.

However, if your partner only knows how to create from effort, stress, compulsive action, or stubborn attachment to a specific outcome, you are going to have your hands full. (Believe me, you are not alone!) In this case, you will need to be extra strong. If your partner has less faith, is less open to receiving, and has much lower expectations and personal limits than you do, then you have some extra challenges ahead. If this is the case, and you love your partner enough for other reasons to want to remain with him or her, then you are going to need to decide what it is you want to create, whether for yourself or for you both as a couple. Then you are going to have to go at it on your own until what you desire has manifested for you, which it will, as long as you don't allow yourself to get distracted.

All this is not to say your partner won't be helpful or back you up or enjoy what you create once the bulk of the preparation work is done. *The key here is to make sure you don't lower your expectations of what you can have for yourself, and that you don't wait for your partner to do for you what you really need to do yourself.* If you are feeling frustrated or inhibited as a couple, ask yourself whether you are waiting for your partner to do the inner and outer work you could be doing right now on your own.

As challenging as it may be, it is quite possible for you to live with someone and manifest your desires even when these desires are in seeming conflict with, or in opposition to, your partner's. What I suggest is to focus solely on the things you wish to manifest and then see your partner at home looking very happy and content. Visualize your partner in the state you'd ultimately like him or her to be in.

Finding a Place to Live

If you believe that you can, should, and will live in a really nice home, while your partner is thinking about a studio apartment with wallpaper made up of pages from *Sports Illustrated*, I suggest you do the exercises for manifesting in this book on your own, and then take whatever action you need to further bring yourself to your goals. In the case of house or apartment hunting, you may actually need and want to be the one to do the bulk of the footwork. Find the perfect scenario for yourself and then once it's all set up and ready to go, spring it on your partner. The worst thing you can do is insist your partner go from place to place with you, because it will only stress out your partner, and he or she will whine, complain, and try to convince you that you are out of your mind with your pie-in-the-sky ideals.

This is where many people, particularly women, go wrong. As you have already no doubt noticed, many men don't like to shop unless they have a lot of extra cash in their pockets, or unless shopping involves something they will soon put in their stomach, tool box, or computer. This is true of bigger purchases like homes as well, particularly when the man involved has doubts as to whether he will be successful in obtaining the home. However, we women have this romantic notion that the man in our life should be by our sides through the whole process of manifesting our desires, in this case a home—from envisioning it to talking about it to shopping for it to moving in and decorating it.

We want our men to be involved, or at least interested and supportive, in just about everything that is important to us. Not only that, but we really want our guys to do the things that we don't want to do or are uncomfortable doing on our own, particularly when we are feeling stressed or overwhelmed. If you make the mistake of insisting a partner come along with you who has a lower ability to manifest for himself than you do, then he will either sabotage your efforts out of his own fear or he may be inclined to accept the first thing that comes along that seems adequate. (By the way, I'm using male pronouns here to simplify things; please mentally replace these with female pronouns if your partner is a woman.)

As a conscious manifester, settling for "adequate" when it comes to a place to live or a job that will take up your precious time and energy should never be an option! (Except perhaps as a transitional, short-term step towards the larger goal.) What you are seeking is the extraordinary—the thing that makes you gasp in wonder and appreciation and self-congratulation every time you see or think about it! Once you find this thing, your significant other will be happy for you. (Unless he has serious issues he has yet to deal with.) If he isn't, because he thinks it's going to cost too much and he doesn't have the faith that you do that you can manifest the cash to pay for it, then once again it is going to be on your shoulders to come up with a way to prove him wrong. Or, another perspective is to just allow him to have his opinions and own feelings (there's a novel idea!). Yes, he can be unhappy and you can still be happy. If that is not possible, consider addressing your boundary or co-dependency issues. There is a huge difference between being empathetic and wanting another to be happy, and you not being able to be happy because you are so enmeshed in the other's emotions that you have lost your independent self.

It's not fair or wise to push our partner past his limits or too far out of his comfort zone when we are refusing to do the same. This is true especially when it comes to spending our partner's hard-earned money. If we are going to insist on having the very best, we need to be able to be the ones to financially support having the best, whether that means we are paying for the extra slack ourselves, or manifesting the resources and opportunities to make this thing work. This is how we change our partner's mind, by setting an example. So if you are in a situation where your partner is the one paying all the bills, with all the cash, but has a much lower level of what he can allow himself to have, then you are in for a challenge. Such a situation may require you to manifest your own cash flow.

Don't Go Overboard!

People occasionally get so caught up in the idea that they can manifest anything that they get themselves into situations for which they are not yet ready. While I believe you can create as you go along, if you currently have no income or only a minimum-wage job, you will be putting yourself into a very stressful situation if you find a place to live that costs four thousand dollars per month! I know more than a few single people and couples who have fallen into this trap. As I've discussed in other chapters, you may not yet really have the self-esteem, the understanding, or a high enough vibration to consistently create the amount of money you'd need for that kind of mortgage. A lot of people love the idea of the law of attraction, but have not yet done the inner work necessary to make it work. That is why I've written this book!

Another problem people encounter is that they don't do enough investigation to see what they are getting themselves into. They don't do the math or read the fine print, and they end up agreeing to pay far more than they are comfortable with as a result. Remember what I wrote in chapter 2? There is a huge difference between having faith and having *blind* faith. Bad decisions come from blind faith and ignoring what *is*. My suggestion is to start on a smaller scale. It's one thing if you do have a cash flow, but if you are completely broke and you live in a crummy apartment, you can work on manifesting a nice home that costs the same, even less, or just slightly more, rather than setting your sights on a million-dollar mansion with a huge mortgage. I am not saying you should rule out the mansion completely; rather, if you are going to set your sights on manifesting it, then perhaps include the intention that it will come rent-free or mortgage free, and see what shows up.

I've known several couples who ended up living for free on the most beautiful estates as caretakers, house sitters, or pet sitters, or just because the owner liked them a lot. Sometimes our more cautious and thrifty partner may be more on target than we are. We are often attracted to people who balance us out. There is a fine line between optimism and foolish, outright delusion—particularly when you are gambling with your money or putting it into risky investments you know nothing about!

Stepping Off Our Path and On to Another Person's Journey

Sometimes we wake up to find that we have stepped off our own path, and onto someone else's. This is an image I've gotten several times when doing a relationship reading for a client or friend who was having a very difficult time. This happens quite frequently when we first fall in love or begin to co-habitate with a person. We are so "into" the other person that we merge into this person!

The more unhappy we were with our life before we met our partner, the easier it will be to relinquish our own path for our partner's path. In this scenario, you may give up your own place, activities, friends, and interests in exchange for his, and at first this will seem great. But then sometime down the road you may find that your own prosperity stops and you are more and more reliant on your partner, and you have somehow lost control of your own life. In dreams this is usually depicted by riding in a car that is out of control, with someone else in the driver's seat who is driving in a way that is not comfortable to you as you sit in the back seat. Of course, this situation is more likely to arise if your partner is naturally demanding or controlling.

The good news is that reclaiming your life can be fairly easy. The key here is to remove your attention from your partner's conflicts, issues, and dramas, and put every ounce of your energy into your own personal goals. That may seem quite overwhelming at first. It might require you to do some visualizations that help you call your energy out of your partner's field and back to your own, or to cut some of the cords between you. Making sure you get plenty of alone time will help you get reacquainted with yourself and what you really want within the relationship and outside of it. The important thing here is also to make sure you can go about doing what you need to do for yourself, while *allowing* your partner to have his feelings about what you are doing.

Stop Seeking Constant Approval and Permission From Your Partner!

One of the most important lessons I and millions of other women (and some men) are learning is that it's really, truly okay if our partner doesn't approve of everything we do, say, like, or want. *The need for that approval is what enslaves us and keeps us stuck.* I know it's not easy to have your significant other moping around the house, grumbling because he is feeling neglected, threatened, or less powerful because you are taking steps toward something that is really important to you and your own emotional, spiritual, and mental health. But your partner's feelings, in the short term, should not and cannot be your problem when those feelings are a reflection of personal insecurities—providing you have done all you can do to let your partner know he is loved.

We often seek out the approval of our partner because we are not feeling confident or motivated enough to make a decision or take action on our own.

Never Put Your Own Spiritual Growth on Hold for the Sake of Your Relationship

People who are cut off from their spirit and spiritual abilities are initially going to have a hard time understanding why it's important for their significant other to spend money and time on "frivolous" things such as attending a spiritual-development class, reading books on spiritual growth, or even meditating.

So, if you are married to or partnered with that kind of person, what do you do? Arguing or explaining won't do anything but frustrate you, because you and your mate will be speaking two different languages. Do you just throw in the towel and spend the rest of your life wishing your partner would change? I've got a better idea: you must do what you need to do for yourself, trusting that over time your partner will notice the positive impact these things have on you and on your relationship together. For example, let's say (theoretically, of course) that every once in a while you begin acting like a crazed hyena. During one of these rare hysterical moments, let's say that instead of biting your partner's head off, you excuse yourself, go into your room, close your eyes, sit still, and then come back as the sweet and wonderful person you truly are. After this happens a few times your partner is not only going to notice the benefits of meditation, but he will beg you to do more of it. Likewise, when he sees that your income has quadrupled and that you have no problems in your life except for him and all his problems, he will start to wonder if maybe there isn't something about this law of attraction thing after all. In other words, we must give our significant other a chance to give us a chance.

Energy Vampires

There are, of course, some people who are so insecure or controlling they can't bear the thought that you would go someplace without them. When you meditate (which is what you're doing when you take the time to go inward and visualize your goals), you do temporarily shut out everyone from your attention. Nothing is wrong with that! In fact, the more you connect with yourself, the better you will be in all your relationships. Do you feel guilty when you close the door to go to the bathroom by yourself? Do you feel guilty when you go to sleep at night, and the world, along with your partner, disappears? No, of course not. Then why should you feel bad about taking a break from the ones you love from time to time?

When you put your focus on your own spirit, that which is not you begins to drop off. When you took your marriage vows (assuming you're married), you agreed to love your spouse in sickness and in health. But did you agree to let your spouse suck out every drop of your blood until you were sick and in poor health? Did you agree to sell your very soul so as not to offend your spouse, or make your spouse have to rethink his or her own views about life? No, I think not! Parasitic people aren't going to like it one bit when you move away from them, because they will sense you are about to kick them out of your space and therefore they may not be able to suffocate you with their own will. If you are attached to this sort of person, you will have to work twice as hard to be disciplined when it comes to bringing yourself to do the work that will ultimately help you get yourself back.

~ EXERCISE ~
Running Your Own Energy

See yourself surrounded in a big ball of blazing light. See yourself and your cells as if they each have an opening, a little spot that is hungry for new life. Then begin to call back your energy. See this energy as one unifying color. Start to visualize this color moving out of all the places it was healing, solving, controlling, and trying to figure out. See it moving back to you, and filling up all the empty spaces in your cells. Once your cells fill up all the way, let your energy fill up every part of your body. Now see it moving from your feet to your head, and vice versa. Allow it to go wherever it feels good: just make sure you see it moving within and around you.

Manifesting Within the Organizations You Work With

From the moment you accept a position with anyone or any business, you are agreeing to participate in an energy exchange. When you accept a position, whether or not you sign an official contract, you are implementing a verbal contract that includes not only your job responsibilities but also to what extent you are agreeing to give up your freedom in exchange for a paycheck. When you agree that you will show up at the same time every day to work and that you will take your breaks at a certain time for a certain number of minutes, you are essentially agreeing to put your employer's desires over the needs of your own body. You are plucking off part of your crown and replacing it with theirs. Quite often, you are agreeing to turn down the volume on the speakers to your inner voice and agreeing to allow someone else's inner genie to rule over your own.

Most of the time, you relinquish these things knowingly, somewhat placated by the idea that you will have a small cushion of sick time and vacation days in addition to a paycheck, to lesson the harshness of your servitude. Not only do you sign away your rights to your time, but you often give up your rights to be your individual self. The only way to be safe, successful, or even last for a week in this new environment is by finding a way to fit in. So you don a mask and a suit that make you indistinguishable from everyone else in the office, and put aside those parts of you that might possibly stand out and draw too much attention or criticism. Sometimes this means hiding our sense of humor or hiding our spiritual beliefs and practices; sometimes it means hiding our sexual orientation.

It almost always means hiding our successes and projects outside of work (if we even have enough energy left over by the end of the week to engage in them), because these will threaten our bosses more than anything else. Our bosses want us to be faithful to them. When they hire us, they do so because they want to make sure we will not stray. They want to make sure we will work hard for them but not show them up. If there is the slightest chance we have more experience than they do, we will immediately be disqualified from the position and branded as "overqualified." This is another way of describing a person who cannot be trusted, because such a person knows enough not to be willing to accept the control and bullshit that a less experienced or confident person would allow. Many people even agree to give up their decency and ethics when they go to work for someone else. They do whatever their boss tells them to do, even if this means oppressing others, harassing them, or ignoring their pleas for help. Such "others" could be customers, members of the public, or fellow co-workers.

Not only do these employees do the dirty work of their employers (whether private corporations or government agencies), but they also agree to soak up all the anger, resentment, and fear that come their way as a result of the company's unbending policies. This is not at all by chance but rather carefully designed to protect those at the top. Why do we agree to participate in such a sinister process? Some of us believe it is fair because, well, at least they are giving us the chance to earn some money, right? Having a job is a privilege, isn't it? Anyway, what choice do we really have? This is what people do to survive! No wonder so many Americans are sick and depressed and addicted to drugs! Well, I have news for you: it's not the only way! You've just been brainwashed into believing this is so.

One of the problems within any hierarchal structure is that we begin to relate to each other not as human beings, but as concepts. We have our mission statements, our budgets, our policy manuals, and our labels for everyone and everything, and these are placed above any individual human need. So if someone says, "Gosh, I feel stressed—I need a day off," or "My son is having a hard time right now and really needs me with him," the general response is, "According to our policy, you aren't due to get a day off for three more months until you've proven yourself."

Most corporations and government agencies in the United States are structured in such a way that those at the top are rarely held accountable for their insensitivity. This is done by ensuring that the work is compartmentalized. Each worker is only aware of his or her own role and often stripped of any decision-making authority. If we get pulled over by a police officer for driving too fast and explain that we didn't see the sign indicating the new speed limit, the cop tells us ignorance of the law is no excuse and writes us a ticket, stating, "I'm only doing my job." If customers complain about poor quality, lack of service, or that the bank charged them three hundred dollars in overdraft fees, they are told, sometimes even by someone with a manager's title, "I value you as a customer, but I can't do anything about that. My computer won't let me."

As customers or citizens, we are purposely kept away from the people who could make decisions. Those supervisors are hiding up above in a penthouse office, securely protected behind an army of human shields in the form of worker-bees desperate for a paycheck. These people didn't realize when they were signing up as "customer care" agents that they were really agreeing to accept the wrath of angry customers desperate not just to be heard, but also to be treated fairly.

Your Havingness in an Organization is Limited by its Owners

No matter how talented, qualified, or motivated you are as an employee, no matter how well-versed you are in the law of attraction, you will rarely be able to surpass the limits set by whoever heads the organizations you work for or belong to. This applies to your place of employment as well as to the educational and spiritual organizations you are affiliated with. These limits restrict how creative, innovative, independent, and successful you can be in your job. It doesn't matter if every ounce of your being is set on maximizing profits for the company; if the owner has lower havingness than you do or is in competition with your ability to create, you will not be able to be successful in the way you personally define success.

If your havingness exceeds that of the owner or those in charge, whether in terms of how much money or clients you can bring in, there are going to be problems. This is also true if you have a greater capacity for change, if you have a greater capacity for self-love and respect, for awareness, and if you have more faith. These things will all be threatening to an employer who has less of them. Sometimes when you first interview for a job or start with a company, it will seem as if the sky is the limit. Your boss may be successful, wealthy, and wise. However, it may turn out that your boss has reached his or her own ceiling and is not willing, out of fear or weariness, to push any further.

You may have visions of taking the company into vast new arenas of possibility while the owner, director, or manager is simply focused on biding time until retirement. Sometimes you can tell where the parameters of success are set early on in the interview process by asking about the interviewer's or the company's top goals. A good question is: are they seeking to expand, or stay as they are? If you are a writer working with a publisher (or are seeking one), it's great to ask if that company is determined to send its titles to the best seller lists or is merely satisfied with having a presence in the bookstores. The key here is to understand with whom you are dealing and respect their limitations while working toward eliminating your own.

What Happens When Our Heads Rise Up Even Past the Steeple?

When we first take on a job or join an organization, we are usually fairly well-matched with those we will be working with. However, over time our growth may be out of sync with the others.

Sometimes even when we belong to a spiritual organization, such as a church, mosque, synagogue or commune, we may find ourselves squished up under a ceiling of limitations that we will only be able to tolerate for so long. This can be quite painful when we've invested a lot of our time and energy in this organization, and particularly when we recognize that it's this very organization (or the people involved) that helped us to become who we are today.

In some cases, this organization or the person running it may have even saved our lives. Quite frequently as members of a church or school, we are much like children who grow up and then surpass their parents in terms of knowledge and skills. The difficult thing is that within our families we are usually expected to grow up and fly the coop, whereas within our churches, we are expected to grow up and continue to make contributions. When we realize we've outgrown the leaders or other members, we will often attempt at first to change the power dynamics or policies in order to make things more comfortable for ourselves. In some cases, this effort will be rewarded. We may even be given a promotion or gain status as a leader.

However, perhaps more frequently we will encounter the energy of resistance from those who are still at the stages we just outgrew. In some circumstances, they may feel so threatened by us that the only way to re-establish equilibrium within the group is to exile us, as quickly as possible. It's possible that we may find ourselves as outcasts before we are really emotionally ready to leave. To be viewed as a threat to the organization by those we dearly loved or respected can feel absolutely devastating. This has happened to members of countless churches. It happens in many metaphysical circles, even and especially those with many "enlightened" seeming members. It happens as often in secular groups.

Can an Organization Suck Out Too Much of Our Life Force?

I think it's important to understand that anytime we are involved in corporate, nonprofit, religious, or spiritual organizations, we are donating some of our energy. This is true whether you are a full-time paid staff person, a volunteer, or just a member. This energy may be in the form of money, time, or parts of your spirit.

In my readings with a few people who were having severe financial problems for the first time in their lives, I got the image of their bodies being completely merged with a particular organization they were working or volunteering for. The next images that came to me reminded me of the Borg, that class of cyborgs in the *Star Trek* franchise whose minds are all linked together so they operate as a unit and are not allowed to be individuals. My clairvoyance was showing me that these organizations were like hungry machines that could only operate through the fuel they were sucking out of their members. It was a disturbing realization, to say the least! Now, this might not be a problem if the organization has lots of resources and is making great contributions to its individual members, but it appeared that in these cases, these organizations, which were of an educational and spiritual nature, were not doing financially well at all. Therefore, the flow of abundance, rather than moving from the organization to its members, was flowing in the opposite direction, sucking them dry.

Whenever we work for anyone other than ourselves, we lend our creative life-force energy to others. What we get back in return are money and benefits. But what happens when our output of creative life-force energy is greater, much greater, than what we are actually getting back? We become depleted, and we feel bored, unsatisfied, taken advantage of, tired, and sick, and our prosperity may suffer as well. Sound familiar?

The more involved we are, the more we merge energetically with the organization and its leaders and followers. This can enable us to grow, or it can stifle, repress, and weaken us. I mention this because no matter how lofty the goals, the vision, or the intentions of an organization's founders, we need to be aware that our relationship with this organization is not that much different from our relationships with individual people. Some of these are nurturing, and we nurture them and there is an equal exchange. Others appear to have our interests in mind (they had to reel us in in the first place) but are really sucking the life out of us. Sometimes we have strong agreements with these people and we really are fine with the dynamic, and then one day we wake up and discover the relationship no longer serves us in present time.

Leaving or being exiled from an organization, whether corporate or spiritual, can feel like a divorce or death, and often results in the same type of grieving period one goes through when losing a loved one. But there is always something else for us at the end of the tunnel. Quite often it's the discovery that we have what it takes to go into business for ourselves, or that we are the true masters we sought out when we joined the organization in the first place.

Look Out for Multilevel Marketing Schemes

There's a fine line between those who believe they have the power to manifest anything quickly and compulsive gamblers. There is no reason you should take extreme risks with money you can't afford to lose just because you believe it will allow you to create more quickly.

There is an increasing trend to pair the concepts of the law of attraction with multilevel marketing schemes. In fact, several best-selling authors who have been leaders in the field of conscious creating are now marketing products for various multilevel marketing firms. What bothers me is that these "spiritual leaders" became successful by utilizing the law of attraction. Their successes really had nothing to do with the product they are selling. That is, until they used their established position of trust to convince people to buy the products! To me there is a lie in here somewhere. It creates confusion for those who are new to these concepts. They confuse the product for the methods that help to sell the product. They end up becoming cogs in a wheel of manipulation, of which they are only shown a couple of highly polished spokes. *In this way, the light is allowing itself to be used as the dark.*

I've had several friends who were involved in these schemes. A couple of them made a lot of money. Most of them sold a lot of product, irritated a lot of their friends, and in the end left the scheme feeling depleted, defeated, and confused about their ability to manifest. Those who do the best with these schemes usually already have access to a group of people who trust them and share similar spiritual ideals.

I've been to demonstrations where the presenter was in such an orgasmic frenzy over the effectiveness of a bottle of juice, you would have thought it was made from the blood of Jesus himself! This juice was not only going to free you from all pain, worry, and excess fat, but it was also going to save your soul—and you didn't need to do anything at all except drink three ounces a day, pay three hundred dollars a month, and convince all of your friends and family members to sign up as salespeople. Two weeks later I ran into one such presenter in a bathroom. She was screaming at her kid, had sores all over her face, and was popping amphetamines!

I mention this because what these pyramid schemes do is confuse boundaries between personal relationships. Those who are involved in the scheme must spend much of their energy making money for those at the top before they even see their own cut. Meanwhile, once they have expended a huge amount of life-force energy into the scheme, it becomes harder and harder to imagine quitting before seeing results. Those at the top will manipulate those below them into believing the problem isn't the product or the sales pitch, but rather their inability to correctly apply the law of attraction.

Regardless of whether or not the product does have useful qualities, those of us on the receiving end begin to wonder whether these people are talking to us because they like us or because they want to recruit us. I often think they themselves are not really sure either. A personal conversation with one of these marketers is never just a conversation, but a potential sales pitch. The more personal the conversation becomes, the easier it is to approach the subject, since the "product" has a helping component to it. In this way, the people at the top of the company pass their hungry tentacles down from person to person until the structure looks more like a skewer of bleeding hearts than a pyramid. I know these comments will upset some of my friends and readers, and I am sorry for that.

I suppose this is not that different from those unwitting people who pass around emails that share a meaningful story and then ask that the email be passed on to five other people. These emails can really mean a lot to the person receiving them. But the recipients who forward them on generally don't realize these emails contain codes that allow the original sender to gain the email addresses and other information for every person to whom the email is sent. The companies that generate these emails do this so they can market products and even scams we would never knowingly agree to promote. I have friends and family to whom I've explained this over and over, and yet they still pass on these emails to me! It just sucks up too much time and energy as far as I am concerned.

CHAPTER 16

Self-Esteem

The great prison we live in is the fear of what others think of us.
—DAVID ICKE

In order to raise our self-esteem and feel better about ourselves, we have essentially two choices. We can:

1. Change ourselves so we match our picture of how we think we're supposed to be.
2. Change our picture of how and what we're supposed to be.

Sometimes changing ourselves is appropriate, sometimes it's not. Often, it's the changing or wanting to change ourselves to match that picture of perfection that causes us so much distress.

Self-Esteem = Success, Not the Other Way Around!

From the thousands of clients and students I've worked with, I've learned that high self-esteem is one of the most essential ingredients for being able to manifest one's goals and ultimately the life one wishes to live. Self-esteem dictates how much you feel you deserve, how much you will ask for, and certainly how much you will strive for. It determines whether or not you will be able to communicate your needs, set boundaries with others, and enforce those boundaries. Success in so many endeavors—from starting your own business to excelling at a sport to developing your psychic or musical abilities—requires determination, focus, faith, confidence, skill, and communication and cooperation from others. Someone with low self-esteem is therefore going to have a hard time even starting to pursue these types of goals, much less excel at them.

To be successful in life, you must have a strong enough sense of yourself to be able stand up in a crowded room and say, "Pick me, I deserve it!" It doesn't really matter if others agree with this declaration. If you can't do this, someone else will. In case you haven't noticed, at any given time we have any number of people around us telling us why we can't achieve what we want to: because it's too hard, too expensive, will take too long, there are too many people already doing it, and blah blah blah blah blah.

Even those with nerves of steel can become discouraged by this silly chatter. (Heck, even after my third book contract, I still have occasional doubts as to whether or not I can even write.) But what about those already on shaky ground, who have been programmed with defeating messages since birth: that it's hopeless, it's not worth trying, that they are not good enough and never will be? If you don't have strong self-esteem, you aren't even going to allow yourself to consider the possibility of manifesting something that seems beyond the scope of what you've been told is possible for yourself.

When I first began teaching psychic skills, I noticed that the students in my classes who seemed to have the most difficulty accessing their psychic abilities were those whom I'd consider to have the lowest self-esteem in general. I found this fascinating. Part of it seemed to have to do with their preconceived ideas that they wouldn't do as well as everyone else. It wasn't that they weren't seeing images; it was that they doubted the validity or quality of the images they saw. It's easy to identify students with lower self-esteem right off the bat, because the first words out of their mouths are "I can't, I haven't, I don't." (Actually, they begin the majority of their sentences with these words!)

My students with lower self-esteem are harder on themselves; are constantly comparing themselves to the other students in the room (despite my instructions not to), and almost always come to the conclusion that they themselves are somehow inferior to everyone else. Quite often they aren't doing as well as the others—not because they don't have the inherent ability (usually it's clear in the first hour of class that they do), but because they give up and allow their attention to wander well before the other students do. Students suffering from lower self-esteem have even expressed concern that their lack of perceived progress or current emotional state may be inhibiting the rest of the group, which is never the case.

In my readings, a variety of common images arise for those struggling with self-love and trust. When such a client has a question about a relationship, I will sometimes see that client on hands and knees scrubbing the floor while his or her partner hovers above, pointing out the spot the client missed. This doesn't mean the client actually scrubs the floor, but you can be sure such clients expend a hundred times more energy pleasing their partner than the other way around. Another common image is that of a client looking in the mirror, but the mirror is very cloudy or cracked, or the client is breaking the mirror. Or someone else, sometimes many other people, are standing in the way of the client's ability to see his or her own image. This is pretty self-explanatory. I also will sometimes see my client sitting at a piano but barely touching the keys, or someone or several people playing the piano for my client. This means such a client is listening to others, as opposed to his or her own inner guidance.

Some Parts of Ourselves Have High Self-Esteem, Some Low

The problem with self-esteem is that it is not as clear-cut as many think it is. Some people actually have very high self-esteem in one area but very low self-esteem in another. Some people are confident in just about all areas except for one, and such people don't realize that low self-esteem is the culprit causing them to aim too low when it comes to choosing a partner or job. When I come across this situation in a reading, I will often see an image of the client with one very muscular arm and the other arm with a drooping muscle. This image is quite easy to work with, because I can first focus my attention on the strong arm to solicit information about the person's strengths, and then move to the other arm to request information about the client's area of weakness.

~ EXERCISE ~
Increasing Self-Esteem to Attract Relationships

One of the great things about both dream and clairvoyant (waking dream) images is that once you've noticed them, you can work with them to make changes and achieve desired results. Below I present meditations based on some of the symbols I've just discussed.

Option 1: Close your eyes. Ground yourself by connecting your lower body with a thick cord that shoots right down into the earth. This will keep you sturdy and help you release. Center yourself within your sixth chakra, behind your third eye, which you can imagine to be in the middle of your forehead. Pretend you are looking out of this chakra at a mirror that is about a foot in front of you. You can decorate this mirror with a border, and give it a base that connects into the earth. It is through this connection that you will be able to release whatever energy may come out of the mirror.

In the mirror, ask to see an image of yourself depicting the part of you that is strong and the part that is weak. Notice what appears. If there is any part of the image you feel is not optimal, then ask to see the color of the energy behind the part that is troublesome. Wait to see if you get a color, but if you don't, then just assign it a color and release the color down the base of the mirror. Continue to watch the image of yourself and notice if it changes now. If it doesn't, then imagine you are taking that entire image of yourself and releasing it down the base, or you can build a bonfire and toss the image of yourself (and anyone else who might pop up) into the fire. Don't worry: you aren't cremating yourself—just the former, outdated picture of yourself.

Now see yourself in the mirror exactly as you would like to see yourself. It's fine to get creative; go ahead and see yourself with huge muscles or any body feature you'd like. Make sure you see yourself with your head held high and a humongous smile on your face!

Option 2: Follow the instructions in the first paragraph of option 1.

Now, in the mirror, see an image of yourself sitting at a piano. Tell the image it is going to represent how clearly you are in communication with the innermost part of your heart, which is where your inner genie sleeps. You can start to visualize yourself playing the piano, and then see what happens next. Notice whether you actually do play or how you play, or if there is some kind of interference or if another person appears. Notice what happens to the piano.

Option 3: Follow the instructions in the first paragraph of option 1.

Look into the mirror in your imagination and visualize a pond or a very still lake. Notice the color of the water. This pond is going to represent your affinity for yourself. It's initially important to see the pond or lake as very still and peaceful (although if you can't, that's not a problem; it just reflects something going on within you). Watch this peaceful body of water for at least three minutes. If you get distracted, let whatever is distracting you flow right down your grounding cord.

Next, imagine you are approaching the pond. Look inside the pond and notice how your image appears. If you enjoy the image, then great. See yourself diving into the pond and notice whether or not the color of the pond changes. This color, if it feels good to you, will be the representation of the energy of self-affinity, and you can use it to heal yourself anytime by seeing it washing through your body from head to toe, and back up.

As you see an image of yourself gazing into the pond, if there is any part of the image you aren't happy with, then go ahead and completely drain the pond—and with it the undesirable image of yourself. Then ask the true color of your self-affinity to fill up the pond. Re-create an image of yourself in a happy, peaceful state, and visualize yourself frolicking in the colorful pond. Next put your attention on your actual physical body. You can even touch the top of your head with your hand. Then imagine taking the water from the pond and pouring it right into your physical head. Watch it flow from your head to your toes, overflowing with the color of your new self-affinity.

The Hijacking of Our Hearts by Corporate Terrorists

Americans are under siege by terrorists and extortionists who never let themselves out of our sight for a moment. The true identities of these individuals are hidden behind the fortress of the corporation. They have already succeeded in hijacking our inner genies by convincing us to wish for what is in the corporations' best interests, not our own. There are far too many of these corporate terrorists to name, but just turn on your television set and you will see one of their ads convincing you that you have or will have a problem that only they can rectify. They have only two names for us: "sucker" and "consumer."

What are these things that we need and want so badly and that they are so eager to provide? They fall into two primary categories: the need to be loved and the need to be protected.

Many of you are thinking, "What? But I don't need protection! I can take care of myself—see, I'm all grown up." Oh, but are you? Can you? What if you are in a car accident? What if you get sick? What if someone steals your identity? What if your house catches on fire? What if someone sues you? God forbid, what if the extremists attack? What if your microwave breaks or your computer catches a virus or you lose your cell phone, or your hair or your mind or your erection? What if the absolutely unspeakable happens—besides losing that erection—and you gain weight, or the faintest hint of body odor escapes from the crevices of your shaven armpits? Or, do I dare suggest it, how could you possibly stand yourself if you came down with one more wrinkle (shudder) or (whisper) another varicose vein? I mean, who will want you then? What are the odds, the remotest chances, of ever finding, keeping, or having hugs, kisses, happiness, or success if you don't purchase protection from these insidious, disgusting horrors?

How Are the Corporations So Successful?
First of all, they get lawmakers on their side to enact legislation that not only protects their right to free speech (translation: the right to bombard you every waking hour with advertising), but that also actually criminalizes you for not purchasing their services (e.g., insurance) or penalizes you (e.g., the credit report) to the point that life's necessities become more and more difficult to obtain. They speak to you from every TV set, billboard, magazine, bus, park bench, and bumper sticker. Right now, these corporations are spending more time with your teenagers than you do, because they can be everywhere at once, while you cannot be.

The scary thing is they have succeeded in getting into our minds. How did we not see it coming? Every university across the country offers a marketing program, in which the emphasis is on training students to get into our heads through "branding" and advertising. They have branded you like a cow, and now they are between you and your reflection every time you glance in the mirror or in your partner's eyes. They have intercepted the communication between your spirit and your body, so now you no longer notice that your body is exhausted or hungry or broken.

Disguising the Means as the End

Here is the typical sequence of messages that have lured us in: "So, you want to buy a house? Well, forget about ever saving enough money—what you need is credit. What you need is a good credit rating. Don't have one? Really? Why? Is there something wrong with you? Well, never mind, all you need to do is sign up for a credit card or two, make as many purchases as possible, and pay your balance in full or on time each month. What? You're not sure you'll be able to do that? You're worried that something might come up: a lost job, lack of organization, an illness in the family that will get in the way of paying on time? Well, congratulations! You're exactly the kind of person we've been targeting! What? Maybe you don't want to buy a house after all? Well, don't you know that most landlords won't rent to someone who doesn't have great credit? You don't want to be homeless, do you?"

Now we are no longer solely focused on our goal of manifesting a great place to live, nor are we even focused on manifesting enough money for a great place to live. Instead, we are trying to obtain credit cards, trying to pay off our credit card bills, trying to prevent others from stealing our credit or from accusing us of an infraction that will show up on our credit report. Then there are those hundreds of thousands of people who fared well enough in the credit game to be "blessed" with variable interest rates, which are now ballooning so high that every ounce of these people's energy is going into saving their home from foreclosure.

And that is often not even the worst of it. The worst is the shame, the humiliation, the embarrassment, and the ignorance we feel as we compare ourselves to those around us who appear to be doing better than we are.

Solutions

Okay, I think you get my point. Many of you are already becoming aware of how you are being duped. This awareness marks the first stage of reclaiming your power. The next stage is kicking these bastards out of our psyches, so we can remember who we are and what it is we really wanted in the first place. The next stage is replacing our self-loathing with love.

Advocacy

Spread the word. Get the relevant advocacy organizations on board, as well as your political representatives, who as of this writing are not yet on board. It's really hard to understand how it's a crime to deny basic rights like shelter and employment based on skin color, age, and sexual orientation, but it's all right to deny people these things based on a credit score number, a number that is largely formulated by the person's willingness to sign up for credit cards or lines of credit with huge interest rates and penalties.

If you are winning the game, then do what you can to support others who are not. Say no to more credit cards than are necessary. Evaluate people based on direct interactions with them and personal references. Understand that most people pay their rent before all other bills, and therefore strikes against them on their credit report for late payments do not reflect on their ability to be good tenants. Trust your intuition. Take an economics course. Learn the language. Educate yourself before you get suckered in even more.

One day I went to my bank, Bank of America, because an Internet company had withdrawn money from my checking account without my authorization. I didn't have enough money in that account to cover this unauthorized withdrawal, and the bank charged me an overdraft fee that then snowballed into several others because I had written small checks prior to the withdrawal, which would have been covered had the one unauthorized withdrawal not been made. So now I was looking at close to two hundred and fifty dollars in overdraft fees.

I began explaining to the woman at the bank that I was in a bind, as my car had just broken down and I needed the money that had been taken out, both by this Internet company and then the bank, in order to fix my car and get to work. Guess what the banker's response was? "Do you own your own home?"

"No," I said, "I rent. What does that have to do with my checking account?"

"Oh, it doesn't," she replied, "but I was thinking if you needed money to pay for your car repairs and you owned a home, then you could just borrow against the equity in the house and use that money for your car and other bills."

I looked at her like she was nuts. "Do you really think that would be a wise thing to do even if I did own a house with equity in it?" I asked.

"Well," she said with a sickeningly sweet smile, "you do need a way to get to work, don't you?"

For Those of You Who Are Not Faring Well

The question always boils down to this: do you keep playing, and risk losing everything because you don't have the resources to play, or do you drop out of the game? Dropping out would mean you no longer care what your credit report looks like, and you no longer answer calls from creditors unless foreclosure agents or the IRS is calling. (In such cases, you need to make some choices fast, consult with professionals, and be on top of it all. It's better to give your possessions back to the bank, or sell what you can as early as possible, instead of waiting for someone to take them away.)

If you choose not to play, then you need to believe that you will be able to manifest all you need by attracting people into your life who are willing to see you as a human being as opposed to a number or a trophy. I don't care which course of action you choose. My main concern is that you understand you are worth more than your credit score—you are worth more than that number on the scale—and that whether you are looking for a husband or a wife, a home to live in, a great job, or a contract for your creative project, there is someone out there, lots of someones , even more desperate to find you!

Recently I came across an article from the *Washington Post*, written by Alec Klein and entitled "Credit Raters' Power Leads to Abuses." The article starts out describing how Moody's

Investors Service was aggressively courting Hannover Re, one of the largest insurance companies in Germany. Hannover was already paying other companies to rate its services and didn't see why it should pay for Moody's. The following is an excerpt from the article:

> *Moody's began evaluating Hannover anyway, giving it weaker marks over successive years and publishing the results while seeking Hannover's business. Still, the insurer refused to pay. Then last year, even as other credit raters continued to give Hannover a clean bill of health, Moody's cut Hannover's debt to junk status. Shareholders worldwide, alarmed by the downgrade, dumped the insurer's stock, lowering its market value by about $175 million within hours.*
>
> *What happened to Hannover begins to explain why many corporations, municipalities, and foreign governments have grown wary of the big three credit-rating companies . . . as they have expanded into global powers without formal oversight. The rating companies are free to set their own rules and practices, which sometimes leads to abuse, according to many people inside and outside of the industry . . . In [some] cases, the credit raters have strong-armed clients by threatening to withdraw their ratings—a move that can raise a borrower's interest payments.*

I include this article excerpt here to help you understand that it's not just the little people who have been strong-armed by the system, but also small and large companies alike. If this is news to you, don't be surprised. I am writing about this here because I haven't heard a single person echo my disgust over this weapon called the credit report, which is being used not just against the American people but also against citizens and businesses throughout the world. If a rating company has the power and the audacity to alter a single number that leads to the loss of $175 million in hours for a major company, why on earth would it care about your own well-being?

The crime isn't just occurring because of these crooks; it's happening because our government has been refusing to do anything about them. These financiers are apparently above all laws, while you are paying penalties or fearful of receiving fines every time you drive your car, park your car, pay your taxes, et cetera, et cetera, et cetera.

~ EXERCISE ~
Paid in Full

See yourself paying off your creditors and having a piece of paper that reads "paid in full." You can even write a check for the full amount, tape it to your wall, and bless it whenever you happen to notice it. What this does is help you pay on an energetic level for the physical level to follow, while helping you know psychologically that you are doing your best and that everything will be easily and effortlessly manifested in the physical soon afterward.

Get out a piece of paper, and write down the following petition:

> *Dear God: Please intervene and help end my debts. Help me either to pay them in a timely, easy manner that will only positively impact my life, or have them forgiven completely. I ask that you help me release the guilt I feel and create opportunities in my life that will be lucrative and fulfilling. I ask for complete forgiveness for all of my past behavior regarding my finances, and I ask that you give me the strength, fortitude, knowledge, and understanding to make the best decisions that will help me live my life*

debt-free and guilt-free. I thank you for releasing me from these debts and burdens. I thank you for bringing abundance, prosperity, and love to anyone to whom I have ever owed money. Thank you for infusing my life with blessed forgiveness. Sincerely, [your name].

Then make a list of all the people you can possibly think of who would support you in this petition. List them as co-signers to your petition, so you can see how supported you really are. These can be real people or fictional people. Then go take a nap, a walk, or a bath, or do some other nice thing for yourself.

CHAPTER 17

The State of the World

They lend people money that doesn't exist and charge them interest... and we stand for that.
—DAVID ICKE

Boredom is the root of all evil—the despairing refusal to be oneself.
—SØREN KIERKEGAARD

The significant problems we face cannot be solved at the same level
of thinking we were at when we created them.
—ALBERT EINSTEIN

The challenge we face as conscious creators is this: on the one hand, we know that we can create our own personal realities. Many of us have even figured out how to structure much of our days so we are doing what we love, with those we love, in places that we love. Everything is just fine and dandy, until we turn on our television sets and see people being blown apart in Iraq, or losing their homes to predatory lenders. We may be feeling on top of the world until we stop for gas and discover it's gone up another fifty cents, or we run into the grocery store to buy a five-dollar loaf of white bread, or we are pulled over by the motorcycle cop who writes us a ticket for failing to wear a shoulder strap or for parking a quarter-inch too far from the curb or for picking our noses at an undesignated stop. Suddenly, we understand why some people go postal.

So how on earth do we keep our inner state of peace, when it feels like there are pressures from everywhere around us that want to take that state of peace away from us? Do we just think positively and ignore everything that's bothering us? Do we just manifest more money to pay for the ever-increasing expenses around us?

Do we just walk or drive the straight and narrow line, praying that we don't do anything wrong that will pull us into the web of the tax-collecting police state? If misfortune does come our way, do we just pay up and move on without resistance?

Do we choose to downsize, restructure, and let go, so that we have less stress, fewer expenses, and fewer people and things to deal with? Do we just tune out the world, turn off our television sets, and focus on our own personal lives?

Our Picture of the World Is Not the World

Over the course of the last nine months, I have rewritten this chapter no less than twenty times. I've finally figured out there are three reasons why. One, I have not been very neutral about the state of the world. Two, my view of the state of the world keeps changing as does the world itself. And three, whose world exactly are we talking about here?

My original goal in writing this chapter was to address the confusion plaguing most people, and particularly those on the path of conscious creation. I wanted to bring awareness to all Americans who are beating themselves up for their failure to obtain or hold on to the "American dream," in which the ideas of home ownership and the ability to pay one's bills are intricately linked. I wanted to demonstrate that one's perceived failings are not strictly due to one's own financial mismanagement, but that we have been set up for failure from the start. I wanted to demonstrate that the credit report is a dangerous tool by which the financial institutions extort money from us and lure us into financial slavery—and that we as Americans have become nothing more than pawns in a complex game, masterminded by those in a class so far removed and shielded from the rest of the players that most of us are not even aware of their existence. While the methods have been complex, the plot has been pretty simple: the puppeteers get the dough, and the rest of us get the bill or pay the price.

I was really beginning to feel like the only woman they hadn't yet gotten in *Invasion of the Body Snatchers*! I wasn't sure if I'd be able to pull out enough Americans from their pods of mind control fast enough before I myself became too weary and drifted off into sleep like the rest of them.

When I first began this chapter, I was angry and feeling victimized. I would run through my laundry list of complaints, aware that all I was doing was ranting and wasting time but unable to stop myself. I saw my deadline for the entire book approach and pass me by like a lone trucker on a desert highway, oblivious to a lost hitchhiker wandering aimlessly in circles in the harshness of the night.

Not surprisingly, my computer crashed and I lost most of this chapter. I had a full-service warranty on my computer from CompUSA, but a month after selling me the expensive service plan, they closed all their local stores (as if they didn't suspect this was going to happen when they sold me the in-store service plan). I was told my only option was to mail my precious writing tool to an address somewhere far across the country, and wait. This was highly frustrating for me, since I had also wiped my schedule clean of appointments to make more progress on this book, but I also knew it was a blessing in disguise. I needed to take a break. I realized I hadn't been running my energy.

Running Energy

Running energy is a form of meditation that helps to distance you from the pictures you are stuck in. It is like giving the inside of your body and your aura a psychic shower. It's a process by which you visualize colored light or water rushing through every part of your body. This visualization is a type of meditation that speeds up the process of letting go of the pictures that control and limit your perceptions and ultimately your creations. (I discuss running energy in greater detail in my first two books.)

After thirty refreshing minutes of running my energy, I understood what was wrong with this chapter. I realized my writing was filled with pain and feelings of rejection, guilt, and shame for not having met other people's definitions of success. Sure, I wanted to help, but I was also trying to change others' views so they would stop judging me. I knew that my angry rants weren't going to lift me or anyone else up, but rather they would create more of the same. So I went back to the basics, and I looked back to the main tenets of the law of attraction, outlined in chapter 2: your thoughts and feelings magnetize situations, objects, and people to you; positivity breeds positivity, negativity attracts negativity; by raising your vibrational frequency, you attract things more quickly to yourself; your underlying, unconscious feelings and programming can influence your manifestations.

When I read these over, it was clear that both I and most of the conscious creators I knew were forgetting to apply these tenets to whatever we deemed as the "outside world." Why was this, I wondered? Why the strong split?

It seems to me that part of the problem lies in the distinction we make between that which falls under our definition of our personal life and that which belongs to the "outside world." This distinction is based on a variety of considerations and perceptions, many of which are unconscious. They include the following:

- How many of the events revolve around us—are we the main protagonists or the viewers? How much control do we have over events and situations
- How close we are to these events in physical distance
- How much of the whole picture can we see How much the events affect our moment-to-moment enjoyment of our lives
- How obvious is it that we are impacted by events , whether we observe events firsthand or through secondary sources such as the media

When it comes to that which we define as part of our "personal lives," we are the stars and main protagonists. We see, or think we see, more of the whole picture because we experience events firsthand; they happen to us, and therefore we feel we have more control over them. They are a part of us. That which we think of as the "outside world" contains events that we mostly experience through secondary sources, usually through the media or via communications with friends and teachers who share their pictures of the world with us. Therefore we aren't as certain about our relationship to these events, and we don't feel we have the same level of understanding or control over them, because they seem to encompass so much more than our personal lives do. Because we feel we have less control, we forget that we can also apply the law of attraction to this world outside ourselves.

The News

Our choice of news programs is as limited as our choice of political representatives! We are not a truly democratic society, but rather a society that romanticizes the myths and ideals of democracy.

The media is the window that allows us to see past our little homes into other parts of the world. However, we still need to remember that we only see tiny slices of the outside world, and these slices are chosen by others with agendas that cause them to want to tell very specific stories.

If you walk into any movie rental store, you will see it is divided into sections based on topics. In the family section you will find charming cartoons about rainbows and unicorns and puppy dogs saving the day. In the horror section you will find gory tales of mutilation and bloodshed. The nice thing about renting movies is that you get to choose not only what kind of story you are going to watch, but also what type of experience you are going to participate in. The children's story may make you laugh and bring back your own fanciful dreams, or it might bore you. On the other hand, that horror movie is going to get your adrenaline going; it's going to scare you, and it's going to make you wonder what that noise was outside and whether or not you really are safe. It may even impact how well you sleep tonight or thirty years from now. Both of these have the capacity to change your pictures of the world and thus the world itself. If we scare ourselves enough, we might begin to think the world is a scary place, and our life-force may turn toward seeking protection or retaliation.

When it comes to the news projected on our television sets, we have far fewer options. The news is about whatever the producers and writers choose for us. We turn on our TV sets, open our newspapers, even sign onto our email, and there it is: what someone else has chosen. There are very few news programs that just focus on loving acts of kindness. Instead, we get the horror and the killing and the ugliness. Unlike the films we rent, the news is supposed to be real. This means there really is a bogeyman out there and he might really get you. This content is often as biased as that of any fictional horror flick, in which the choice of scenes and shots is carefully orchestrated by its creators.

Take the news coverage of the Iraq war, for instance. News programs can show us a casket of an American soldier, or they can show us a smiling Iraqi boy holding an American flag. We are flashed this image for a moment, and now we hold an idea in our minds that leads to our opinions and overall belief system about the war and the state of the world—even though the war and the world are made up of trillions upon trillions of individual flashes and images and truths. In this way, others are choosing and manipulating our pictures of reality for us based on their own positions and economic interests.

Do you ever wonder why we put up with this? What do you think people would do if the owner of their favorite video store decided that the only films she was going to make available were the horror films? Many of us would stop going to that store. Right? But what if every other store followed suit? I suspect, over time, if this were the only option for this type of entertainment, that we might eventually return to that store, telling ourselves, well, we can always close our eyes for the really icky parts. After even more time, we might actually forget that any other kind of film ever existed, or we might begin to redefine the icky parts as a normal, unavoidable aspect of life.

This might seem far-fetched, but it's not. This is actually what is starting to happen. The horror sections of these stores are expanding. Meanwhile, if you ask any agents or managers of child actors, they will tell you there are fewer and fewer projects for kids these days. Why? Because there are fewer television shows for and about kids. They've been replaced with shows like *Dexter*, the main character of which is deemed "America's most beloved serial killer"; or

Californication, about, well, need I say more?; or *Nip/Tuck*, which is about a group of plastic surgeons who molest and take advantage of the women they cut open.

Getting back to our view of the world, it is very much colored by the images and information others have chosen for us. These others are not necessarily on the same path we are on. So, now we are confused. We have these images swirling around in our heads. We begin thinking things are bad. Worse than bad. So bad that we can't even allow our children to play outside anymore.

If you grew up in a family where your parents were abusive and everyone put each other down and life was difficult, and you live in a neighborhood where everyone is killing each other and you risk your life even to go to school, how could you possibly think there was anything else other than that for you? You wouldn't. And therefore you won't strive for anything else, because what else is there to strive for? This is what is happening in our inner cities, and this is what happens in every area of our globe that is warring or poverty-stricken.

In many "developing" nations, the ambition of millions of people is to get out and go to America. Such folks are convinced that their countries and their lives there will never improve, and therefore they don't strive to make their countries better. Instead, they put all their life-force energy into getting out, and as a result their own countries further atrophy.

In America we have hope; that is what has made our country strong. However, in the past decade many of us have begun to realize that the freedoms and privileges we enjoyed have grossly eroded. Since the attacks on the World Trade Center and the Pentagon on September 11, 2001, we have been handed fear pictures and told through overt statements and covert manipulation that we must hand over our freedoms in exchange for protection. This process is no different from the one that happens to us as children, when our parents hand us pictures that say, "You are not strong enough to take care of yourself" or "You are not smart enough to become a doctor" or "You are not pretty enough to get a great man, so just settle for less." After a while we accept these pictures into our souls, and they become magnets that draw corresponding experiences.

Fortunately, most of us don't experience these pictures directly, but instead do so vicariously through our television sets. However, even from the safe distance of our living rooms we experience the emotional pain. This pain weakens the power of our inner genie by lowering her vibration, and therefore makes it much more difficult for us to manifest on a personal level. The question then is: why do we allow this process to happen?

We Still Want Someone to Take Care of Us

There is a reason why the majority of Americans have so little awareness, understanding, and perspective about topics that impact them on a minute-to-minute basis. These topics include economics, finance, history, and even parapsychology and creativity. Responsibility for this can't be placed solely on those who benefit from this ignorance. We complain about the educational system for our children, but what are we doing to educate ourselves as adults? So what if someone already handed us a diploma and told us we were done. Aren't we mature enough to pick up some books or enroll in some basic classes that teach us how to calculate a variable interest rate or understand the implications of, and differences between, prime and subprime lending?

There are some incredibly innovative and thorough authors who are attempting to provide such education. Howard Zinn has written a book called *A People's History of the United States*. Howard Bloom has written *Reinventing Capitalism: Putting Soul in the Machine*, which he calls a "radical re-perception of western civilization," as well as the earlier *Global Brain: The Evolution of Mass Mind from the Big Bang to the 21st Century.* Dean Radin's books *The Conscious Universe* and *Entangled Minds* present thousands of pages of solid research that suggests the majority of us who have intuitive and precognitive experiences are not crazy or unusual after all.

I believe most of us have a deep longing and need to feel we are being cared for by someone who seems to have more answers than we do. Researchers have clearly demonstrated that children need structure and supervision. They don't do well with parents who are overly strict, but they also don't do well with parents who are overly permissive. It's clear that most kids like to have the freedom to make their own choices—until they are confused, hungry, or overwhelmed—and then they appreciate it very much when Mommy or Daddy tells them it's time to turn out the lights. Adults are no different. We have replaced our moms and dads with our politicians, bankers, stockbrokers, and news anchors. Are these really the people we want tucking us in at night? But they are so happy to do it!

I believe that our need to be led and protected is now attracting leaders who are far too authoritarian. Our government and its enforcers are taking a far too strict approach. The police used to hand out warnings. Now they give you a three-hundred-dollar ticket and tell you to duke it out with the judge. So you are guaranteed to lose at least half a day in court regardless of whether you are "guilty" or not. Andy Griffith has turned into RoboCop!

However, I suspect that we will not be impacted by this tightening of controls unless we are already struggling with something within ourselves that mirrors this oppression. In my own case, I've just recently become aware of the relentless pressure and control I exert on myself to keep performing and achieving no matter how depleted I am (as evidenced by the fact that it's well past midnight and I'm still plugging along here). Is it any wonder that I have been bumping up against those who don't want to give me a break either? Still, this awareness didn't stop me from writing to the mayor and all the city council members of the city I was living in, Moorpark, CA, to complain after a cop wrote me a ticket for driving with my headlights off when I had only just left a lighted parking lot seconds before.

Judgment

Just as all opportunities are created by people, so are all problems. A problem is not a tangible thing. It's a situation that we are judging. It's a negative definition of a particular experience for which we lack perspective. Most of us spend our days distinguishing between whether something or someone is good or bad, right or wrong, honorable or dishonorable. We have learned to view ourselves, each other, and the state of the world through the filters of blame and judgment. This judgment creates a wedge between our own heart and mind and our spirit and body. It creates a barricade between ourselves and anyone we deem as remotely different from us in appearance, behavior, attitude, and ethics. It cuts us off from that which created us, that which can heal us, and the wellspring of creativity that is supposed to be our birthright.

When we judge someone or something, we have sidetracked ourselves from creative solutions. I am sure you've noticed how the moment a perceived injustice happens, a battle cry goes out for retribution. Nothing can happen anymore without someone else being responsible or made to pay. We try to solve our pain by finding someone, anyone, to dump the blame on, with the idea that if this other person suffers or hands over their money, our own suffering will somehow be alleviated. All of our wars and our social problems can be linked to judgment and our unconscious projections upon our enemies. We try to solve our pain by judging others, but this just creates more pain.

The Opposite of Blame Is Appreciation

While my computer was down, I spent a lot of time meditating and applying the techniques offered in this book to my goals for what I define as the "state of the world" and my perceptions of it, and some interesting things began to happen.

It's been often said, but appreciating what we have really does put things into proper perspective, because it brings us into the present moment. Eckhart Tolle reminds us and reminds us and reminds us that the present is all there is. (We really do need the reminding!) Gratitude is perhaps the highest energy you can run, after laughter and lightheartedness.

Of course, my usual response at the gas pump when the prices go up is to look around to see who else is within earshot, and then let out an exasperated, "Can you believe what they're doing to us?!" I usually get either an adamant nodding of heads, a chuckle, or a startled look that says, "Who is this weirdo?" But one morning, after visualizing the world as I desired it to be, I had a different response. It began with the thought, "Wow, I'm really fortunate in this moment even to have gas at all! I am fortunate to have a car that runs, to have a driver's license, even to know how to drive! I am blessed to have a foot that can step on the gas pedal and hands that can direct the steering wheel. I am so incredibly blessed to have gas money, even money for the cup of coffee I am about to purchase that I don't really need at all."

On that morning, for perhaps the first time in over a year, I drove away from the pump feeling lucky instead of victimized.

Are We Really Being Harmed by the Things That Upset Us the Most?

Once I began appreciating the fact that I did in fact have money for gas, even at four dollars per gallon, I wondered why it was that I was complaining about the high prices so much. I began asking myself, "In this very moment, is my life really being influenced by global warming or the national debt, or am I just getting upset over the ideas of these things?" The fact was, in this moment, on a personal level, I had more freedom in terms of my time schedule, and more clients, more love, and more prosperity than I had ever had in my life.

Now you try it. Choose anything that is getting your blood boiling about the state of the world. Let's take the price of gas, for example. Ask yourself, "Did the price of gas today really stop me from going somewhere?" Now, it may very well have impacted your decision of whether or not to take a trip. However, if you are really honest with yourself, you will most likely find that the price of gas did not make it impossible for you to do something that you truly needed to do or go somewhere you wanted to go. Perhaps like so many people, you can't afford a car in general: insurance, registration, maintenance and gas are expensive. But then there are other means of transformation: buses, trains, bicycling, car pooling, walking, taxis, Uber, etc.

For myself, I had a harder time coming up with gas money in the late 1980s, when for a while gas was under eighty cents per gallon, than I did in the summer of 2008, when it was close to five dollars per gallon. Back in the 1980s, I shared a car with my twin sister. We were teenagers and always broke, so most of the time I'd put a dollar or two of gas in our Chevy Malibu, and then she'd drive the car or vice versa; one of us was running out of gas at least once a week. Yet I haven't run out of gas since it first went up to two dollars per gallon!

The reality is that many of us are finding ways to manifest money to accommodate these higher prices, or are choosing alternatives mentioned above that encourage social interaction or getting us into better shape. Sometimes the price of gas is a convenient excuse for not having to go somewhere. It lets us off the hook. So maybe the price of gas is presenting an opportunity for Americans to do things differently, which will ultimately serve us all. Or maybe it just sucks. You don't have to choose between these possibilities; both may be true. The point here is that if we get out of resistance to what is before us—the higher prices—then we can remain or come back to a place of calmness and sanity. This is a much stronger position from which to effect change.

Oh, there's one more thing I thought I'd mention. Just a few weeks after I released all those negative feelings about the high gas prices, the price of gas started dropping; after several weeks, it had dropped in half—and it's remained there ever since! Some people say it's a matter of time before the price of gas goes back up. I say that if enough of us believe it won't (or do something to ensure it won't), then perhaps it will drop even more, or perhaps the need for gasoline will become obsolete.

Don't Fall Into the Trap of Believing in the Status Quo!

It's important for you to get this: *you can have more abundance in a recession or depression than you've ever had!*

- ☞ You can have peace, happiness, and success in a time when most people seem to be going bonkers. You can create innovative forms of income, go back to school, travel to countries with better economies. The sky—and your imagination— is the limit.
- ☞ In the midst of global warming or even a global financial conspiracy, you can enjoy the sun and the earth as the magnificent things they are. We need the sun as much as we need the plants, no matter what the manufacturers of toxic sunscreen products want us to believe.

~ EXERCISE ~
Healing the Pain of the Victim Citizen

It's time to unleash our inner genies on the level of global/world peace!
1. Sit in a chair. Relax.
2. Acknowledge your anger, frustration, or fear. After an initial minute of contemplation, bring yourself to a feeling place rather than one of thinking. Don't judge or blame yourself, just let yourself feel the emotion. Ask yourself where in your body you feel these unpleasant feelings. Put your hand over that part, and breathe. Bring your spirit, your attention, and your focus to that part. Allow yourself to be fully in that location. Immerse yourself in the feeling. Feeling is the key here. Breathe. The feeling might get really strong for a moment. Just sit there with it until it starts to intensify. Breathe through it and let it go. Hold out your hands. Imagine you are taking all your feelings—the hurt, the anger, the helplessness—and rolling them up in a big ball. At this point you might start to feel pain in or around certain body parts. Imagine you are holding this red energy ball over

wherever your body feels the pain or tightness. Hold the ball in your hands. Do the God as a Magic Symbol exercise from chapter 13. Be God for a moment and have the light of God shining through you. Hold this red ball of hurt and allow the white light of God to wash through it, dissolving it or transforming it—and then release the ball, sending it up to the heavens, into the ocean, or deep within the earth.

3. Create a symbol that represents your hope for the world. Take this symbol and hang it up on your wall. Gaze at it each day and pray to it that it helps you along your path of healing, acceptance, and right action. Draw the symbol on a piece of paper and stick it in your purse or wallet, or hang it in your car or on your mirror. Know that this is your own private symbol. It doesn't matter if everyone else around you is hopeless or talking about the end times. This symbol will help you keep a positive frame of mind. Until there is no world left at all, there is no good reason to give up the hope that things will get gloriously better. Identify one thing wrong with the world or your country right now. Then choose to do something creative to combat this: it might be your own project, or it might be jumping aboard one that someone else has begun.

Please note that every single exercise in this book can be used for manifesting the qualities and attributes that you'd like to see in the world, in your country, in your hometown, in your home, and in your personal life!

Reasons to Manifest Disaster

Within a short time of doing the above exercise, I discovered that my attitude about the state of the world was changing. The day I realized this, my computer was returned to me, seemingly better than ever. However, I found it difficult to get back to writing, because there was a much more compelling drama playing out on the television set. Hurricane Gustav was on its way, and close to three million people were evacuating from the same regions of Louisiana that had been so ravaged by flooding just three years before during Hurricane Katrina. Of course the sun was shining where I was in California, but that didn't stop me from racing from channel to channel, watching this new drama unfold. Its ending was relatively anticlimactic, as the hurricane took a detour and spared New Orleans and its people.

However, the sequel took just over a week to arrive, when Hurricane Ike came charging toward the Texas coast, prompting the National Weather Service to broadcast the most ominous warning it had ever issued, one that seemed to startle even the most seasoned news anchors. The message, in summary, was, "People living anywhere near Galveston, Texas, get out while you can. If you stay, you will be facing certain and imminent death." The warnings were correct. Galveston was pulverized, and even the city of Houston, forty-five miles inland, was severely affected, with billions of dollars in damage to skyscrapers and homes, and millions of people without electricity or water for up to several weeks.

Now, these events had nothing to do with me. I didn't even know anyone in the area, but I could hardly bring myself to do anything but watch it all come down on the tube. Why? Because I wanted to see what would happen next, and it was far more interesting than what was happening in my life at the time.

Contrast this with where I was on September 11, 2001, when airplanes crashed into the World Trade Center and the Pentagon. I had just started film school. I didn't even own a television set. I was scheduled to direct my first short film that very morning. When my sister called and left me a voicemail telling me I needed to get to a television set because something really bad was happening, I didn't consider canceling my plans for a second. Sure, I was concerned; my brother and his wife lived in Brooklyn. But I knew there was nothing I could do from Arizona. I was so excited about my film and all I was learning. When a couple of actors called to say they wouldn't be coming in that day because the events back east were just too disturbing, at first I was confused. "Do you have family there?" I asked.

"No," they said.

"Oh, well, are you going there to help out?" I asked. "No," they responded.

"Well, is there anything you can do from your living room other than feel bad and scared?"

"No," they said, "but it wouldn't feel right to be doing something as frivolous as acting on a day like today, would it?" Each of the actors spoke to me with growing irritation and distress.

"Don't you love acting?" I asked them. "Wouldn't this be a better energy to run, for yourself and the country? The terrorists want us to feel afraid. Are you going to give them what they want? It's your choice."

One of them agreed, showed up, and had a great time, later landing other roles as a result of being in this little film. The other did not show up. While I had sympathy and understanding for the events of that tragic day, I actually did not see any footage of the attacks for almost six months afterward. Meanwhile, during those six months I had the most creative time of my life and made some films that since then seem to have had an uplifting effect on others. This was not the response the terrorists wanted. Ironically, it was not the response many of my fellow Americans wanted either, as evidenced by their judgment toward me.

However, on the day of the Galveston hurricane, almost exactly seven years to the day after the attacks of 9/11, I was at home, watching TV, depressed about not knowing which direction to go with this chapter, and feeling bored. I believe that most Americans are bored, even the ones who are busy 24/7.

Boredom has less to do with being busy and more to do with passion and fulfillment. In my own life, early on, I recognized that when I was feeling bored, trouble would soon find its way to my door. I believe that, deep down, a part of too many of us longs for the drama and accompanying adrenaline rush that is experienced in the midst of the massive storms and earth changes that we are either beginning to see or are prophesied to be near.

Apart from the drama, many folks long for a complete overhaul of life as they know it. Some people can't stomach the idea that life will be the same ole same ole for the next thirty, forty, or sixty years, but they lack the gumption or know-how required to make their own personal life more satisfying. Others are so disgusted and dismayed by the existing power structures within society that they long for a change that will bring them into balance or completely flip them. They see no other way except for absolute destruction.

To be successful in America, a certain skill set is required that might be quite different if all hell broke loose. There is little place in our society for men with physical strength and prowess to shine, except in the arenas of sports or war. But send the earth into a big enough tailspin, and these are exactly the guys who will be needed to protect and rebuild our communities.

If the price of gas rockets so high, or the supply runs so low, that people can no longer drive their vehicles, then the traditional nine-to-five grind of a workday will need to shift. While I do believe that the workplace, with its regimented schedule, is in the process of changing, I don't believe it's going to happen from lack of fuel, since the moment the companies who were profiting from the sale of oil are no longer profiting, they will quickly develop new fuel or transportation sources to re-seed their bank accounts. Instead, I believe this change is coming because of a shift in consciousness, which will be precipitated by enough people raising their energetic frequencies through self-healing and gaining control of their emotional states, so they realize there is another way.

Those of you from the Midwest or the East Coast surely remember wintry days as a child, when you wished for a big snowstorm so you could stay home from school. Instead of waiting for a snowstorm, why didn't you just go to your teachers and parents and say, "I really need a day off school. I'm getting bored. I want to do something else today."

Why? Because they would have looked at you like you were nuts, dumb, or both, and said, "Yeah, right. So would I."

As adults, most of us still are in the same position, petrified to take a day off unless someone else gives us permission. From our very first day on the job, we agree to relinquish our personal freedom for eight or more hours a day. We agree to ignore the needs of our body and the yearnings of our heart in exchange for seven or seventeen bucks an hour. We leave our personality, our spirit, and our true self locked away in the hot car all day where they shrivel and cry out for us. But we've rolled up the windows, turned up the stereo, and turned our backs to their muffled screams until they fade into nothing more than a nagging itch suggesting that at some point, somewhere, we left something behind that might have mattered.

So the weather or any natural disaster is a convenient excuse to let us off the hook without us having to be personally accountable. Perhaps when the Big One comes, there won't be any office to return to.

The key here is to tune in to where are we looking for sources outside ourselves to do for us what we are unwilling or feeling unable to do for ourselves. When we are pushing away our need for change, creativity, or control in our own lives, that is when our manifestations become unhealthy and dangerous.

With the storms over, I was ready to get back to this chapter. However, it seemed as if every time I went to write, no matter how much I promised myself I would not let myself get distracted, the one phone call, email, bill, or knock on the door would come that just had to be dealt with, or so it seemed.

Technology and Stress

We have obviously been in the midst of a technological revolution-evolution for the past century, one that has grown exponentially in the past two decades. Our technology has opened up many new avenues for self-expression, creativity, communication, and new ways of doing business and earning income—not just for adults, but for our children as well. In fact, the kids are faring better than the adults. They are having an easier time understanding how to work this technology, because they have developed along with it. Teens also have more time or make the time to enjoy this technology, while adults are having to learn how it all works in order to meet the survival needs of themselves and their teens (which might include weekly trips to the electronics store!).

At the same time, the attention spans of our children and teens are decreasing. They are used to constant sensory stimulation and flitting from one source of entertainment to the next; kids will wander around in circles, not sure what to do with themselves, when made to part with their technology. My own son automatically picks up a remote control whenever he passes by the television set. I used to reprimand him for this, since he does it even after we agree he has something else to do. However, now I understand it's automatic. The second something moving catches our children's attention, they are absorbed in it. We as parents complain, but how are we any different when the second our cell phone rings, a text message beeps, or an email pops up, we jump on it as if the survival of the entire universe rested solely on answering it? While our inability to focus on any one thing certainly doesn't seem like a positive, only time will tell if we aren't actually being prepared for a future that might require this skill.

Increase in Expenses

The challenge is that much of this technology zaps up our time and energy and costs money, way more money than we had to pay in the past for household expenses. In the good ole days, it used to be that we had to pay for rent or the mortgage if there was one, a phone bill, and a few utility bills. Now we pay for cable television, computers, software, printers, Internet connections, possibly websites or newsletters if we are trying to market just about anything, and cell phones in addition to land lines, because our cell phones are not always reliable.

All of that is on top of whatever costs we have for owning a car and, of course, the multitudes of types of insurance and licenses we must pay for, or the fines we incur for not having them. Whether or not our income has gone up, we obviously have a lot more to deal with. The explosion of technology has resulted in an abundance of new avenues for communication. The number of people we come into contact with, albeit virtually, has therefore drastically increased. This is true of not just acquaintances and business contacts (whom we may meet on Facebook or LinkedIn) but of our intimate relationships as well.

With a wider pool of possible mates and a lessening of the taboos on divorce, so many of us have our current significant other and our "no-longer-that-significant other," as well as their children, to support and contend with. The positive side is we never have to be lonely, because we can connect with those with similar interests in a heartbeat, and we can constantly reinvent ourselves and our lives like never before. And if we have a question about absolutely anything, all we have to do is Google it and we will have immediate answers. What could be more exciting than that? The downside is that we are handling so many more wishes and wants and needs than ever before from other people, as well as our own, and many of us feel as though we're nearing our breaking point. It's as if we have too many options, too many choices, too many questions and even answers, too many people, too many bills, too many responsibilities—heck, even too many books to read . . . or write! Meanwhile, there are still just twenty-four hours in a day and just one of each of us.

As I write this, I get an image of two feet standing on opposite shores. One shore is farther away and belongs to the world called "when life was simpler." The closer shore belongs to the world called "today." Most children live in the world of today. However, most adults over the age of forty are struggling to balance themselves between these two worlds. The trouble is, the worlds are moving farther away from each other at a faster rate. Our legs can only stretch so far before we must choose which world we are going to belong to. This is why we have the sensation of being overwhelmed, of being "stretched too thin." If we don't make a conscious choice soon, we may be pulled in half.

To choose the old world means giving up most of this cool stuff and living in places where there are others still living more simply, such as the wilderness of Alaska or the Appalachian Mountains or the beaches of Bora Bora. Ironically, these places are being threatened by those who constantly need to find new sources of energy to feed the insatiable appetite of the world of today.

To succeed in the world of today means first, we as individual citizens are going to have get out of resistance to these changes and begin to operate differently. It means we are going to have to stop comparing the two worlds. We are going to have stop judging this one and instead celebrate it for all its wonderful creations. It's your own creations as much as everyone else's that are overwhelming you. When you acknowledge that fact, you feel less victimized. You wanted abundance and now you have it!

The good news is that once the majority of us are firmly planted in today's world, either through choice or attrition, I believe much of the stress will lift. This is because right now with two feet in opposite worlds, we are still trying to operate under the antiquated way of doing business and manifesting success. Under the old paradigm, the predominant belief system was that everything must be created through our own individual sweat and tears. The masculine part of ourselves ruled, and therefore logic, direct action, competition, effort, and hard physical labor permeated our consciousness and directed our behavior. If we wanted to make it, we had to go after every single opportunity for fear that we might miss out on something and lose the chance of a lifetime.

Many of us are still caught up in that idea. We are therefore driving ourselves crazy, because instead of having a handful of customers to go visit, now there are potentially millions! Not only that, but all we have to do is to spend a few minutes online to notice there are many thousands of people with similar businesses trying to do the same thing we are, only with more resources at their disposal.

Now I know some of you are starting to sweat, but no worries! The fact of the matter is: if you've been reading this book, you don't have to worry about the competition. You've got the knowledge and tools you need to be successful if you choose to exercise them. It doesn't matter what everyone else is doing. There is an abundance of customers if you have the resources to deal with them. As we've discussed throughout this book, a large part of the solution is simply to disengage from the chaos around you by turning within, and calling upon your inner genie to do the work.

The people who can do this will thrive. The nations that can do this will be those that survive.

There Are Always More Options Than You Are Aware of!

About five years ago when my first book was coming out, my publisher made it clear I needed to have a website. I had known for a while that I needed a website if I was ever going to leave my nine-to-five job and work for myself. I had tried to hire someone a few years back, but it was a disaster. He lost interest halfway through and shared neither my vision nor my personal tastes in terms of color and design. Now I needed a website fast and I didn't know where to turn. I also didn't have extra money to spend. So I closed my eyes, went inward, said some prayers, and visualized myself admiring my lovely, informative website. That's when I saw an image of my ex-boyfriend Raul, with whom I hadn't spoken in over a year.

Not surprisingly (well, not for me), the phone rang about five minutes later. It was Raul. He told me to check my email because he was sending over a link to his new website, which was only costing him a few dollars per month. When I commented that I wished I had his technological skills, he advised me that I didn't need them, that websites now could be built with pre-designed templates that might take the average person an hour or two to become familiar with. The one he was using was only costing him a few dollars a month. Within a week my own site was up and running.

Today I have five websites hosted by three different companies, all of which I have built myself. It costs me less than three hundred dollars per year for all of them. (Of course five is too many! Now I'm working on consolidating them.) The best part of it all is that they are so easy and fun to build. Once I got over the learning curve, it wasn't much harder than learning how to use a basic word-processing program. In fact, I recently discovered that there are brand-new companies that offer website builder tools that are faster and more attractive than the ones I found just a couple of years ago. They make your site look like a scene from a major motion picture, with you as producer, director, editor, and star! The ease and beauty of these tools at my fingertips are so exciting that at times while working with them I've experienced what I can only describe as euphoria. Yes, I am a geek! But the point here is that what once seemed like a stressful burden has become one of my most fun pastimes.

There is never a reason why we can't accomplish or have something we need; it's just a matter of allowing our creative powers and intuition to open our minds to whole new approaches about which we were not previously aware. The avenues available to us for our creative expression and income flow are expanding along with the technology.

So, if you are a salesperson, ask yourself what else you can sell. If you are a teacher, ask yourself what else you can teach. If you are a teacher, ask yourself what you can sell. If you are a salesperson, ask yourself what you can teach!

When Dreams Collide

The most exciting thing for me about the entire alchemic/creative process is that it involves a merging of dreams. When we are fulfilling our own dreams, we are almost always doing so for someone else, too. There is never a lack of opportunity for this merging to occur, since so much of what we label *opportunity* is linked to other people who need us as much as we need them.

A little over a year ago I really began focusing on my desire to lose weight and get in shape. None of my clothes were fitting well, and I wasn't enjoying the extra jelly rolls around my waist, although they did seem to provide an endless source of amusement for the "boys" in my household. Since countless half-hearted attempts at dieting and exercising, either on my own or at gyms (which I disliked), had failed, I felt I really needed a personal trainer but didn't think I could afford one at the normal rates. Finally, I realized I had failed to elicit help from my inner genie in this area of my life. No wonder I was feeling stuck! I did the God as a Magic Symbol exercise in chapter 13. The results came in almost immediately.

At that time my son had already been taking classes at a martial arts studio for about six months and was doing their after-school program. When I picked him up in the afternoons, I would see a group of women working out. I started to think I should look into these classes, but they were being taught by a man with whom I didn't feel much of a connection. Still, one day I talked to him, and he advised me that he was going to be leaving but that his partner, Cindy Blackwell, would be taking over. I could take as many as five classes per week with her and pay only about eighty dollars per month. It turned out Cindy was a personal trainer who had managed a major gym for several years. She had recently decided to begin teaching classes in addition to seeing private clients. The typical class size was two to five other students (mostly middle-aged moms like myself), and the classes were completely designed around our personal needs. I had manifested a personal trainer for only a few dollars an hour, at a place that I already had to be several days a week anyway!

Cindy's Story

Meanwhile, Cindy was working very hard. When her partner left the studio, she had to take out a loan so she could purchase all his equipment from him. Now she was paying several hundred dollars per month to teach classes out of the studio. Even though I was grateful for her low prices, I worried she wasn't getting paid what she was worth. She didn't have extra money for advertising and didn't really have the skills to market herself well. However, she continued for a year to show up to class, often twice a day. Even when she knew there would be only one student, she worked her hardest to get that student into shape.

While we, Cindy's students, were obviously becoming firmer, stronger, and healthier, we weren't meeting our weight-loss goals. She often discussed nutrition, but we weren't adjusting our diets on our own and she found this as frustrating as we did. However, that all changed one day because of a new idea that came to her. The idea was that she needed to take control of her students' diets; she decided she would begin to offer a program in which she would meet with each student once a week, and help them to prepare all their food for the week. The food would be placed in individual containers so every meal would be available when needed—in the correct portion size, with the correct number of calories and the correct fat and carbohydrate count. The meals would also be selected and prepared to satisfy individual tastes. Students could choose to prepare meals just for themselves or for their entire families. This process would take Cindy anywhere from three to four hours, and she would charge one hundred dollars for this food preparation. Since she was not just doing the cooking but also teaching, her students would soon be able to do the prep work themselves and therefore would no longer have to pay her, except for an occasional refresher session.

Within a week Cindy had her first student on board, and this student lost over twelve pounds in the first month. Her weight loss was so obvious that within two months Cindy had seven other students on board. With no advertising, she tripled her income. So far I have lost twenty-four pounds, and now I'm looking, eating, and feeling better than I have in years. For a while there, I used to think I was destined to become just a dumpy old housewife! Before I met Cindy I even bought a couple of the same kind of muumuus my grandmother used to wear! (Hello! This story is for all you middle-aged women—and men—out there who have decided that after a certain age, life just goes downhill; that's not reality, *it's a big, fat delusional lie!*)

I don't have even a particle of doubt that I will meet my final weight goal within two months, and I'm ready to meet the world. Cindy is well on her way to running a lucrative business. The moral of the story: All of this was accomplished by the converging of simple ideas and the will to carry them out. All of it happened without anyone having to pay for advertising or more than they could afford.

Isn't this colliding and merging of dreams really what our capitalistic society was built on? Yet somewhere along the way the dream part got distorted. Instead, some guy somewhere (probably a scrawny guy with glasses and a pocket protrector whose dad was a CEO of a company that he loved more than his son—no offense if that describes you!) realized that he might be able to make some extra bucks if he was able to manufacture our dreams for us, and that he'd be able to make even more money if he convinced us he was the only one who could deliver them.

The Future

Many people come to me, and to psychics in general, because they think they want or need to know what the future holds. I tell them it's not the future they are worried about; it's the feeling of stress that is running through their body right now that they are trying to find a way to deal with. When we deal with that first, and see what changes we can make in our life right now to create the future we desire, the urgency to know about the future diminishes, if not entirely disappears. (Of course, it's always fun to take a peek anyway!) The solution is not to run and rerun this anxiety through your mind, but rather to release it and go do something that you enjoy, that makes you feel good about yourself and the world. This is what I suggest for you now.

There are many folks—scientists, inventors, and artists—who are creating wonderful things and doing everything possible to improve and save us and the world we live in. Either become one of these innovators or discover how to support one or more of them. If you can't make a financial contribution, then take such people out to dinner or volunteer to baby-sit their kids.

I believe the Catholic church had it right when it requested that its parishioners tithe a percentage of their income. The problem was that much of the money went into buildings instead of people. There is so much we can do for each other. Taxation is a form of tithing, but the problem is that we really don't have a say in whether we want to contribute financially or what is done with our tax dollars. Can you imagine what a difference it would make if we could actually choose which programs our tax dollars were going to fund? This might sound silly, but it wouldn't be that hard to pull off if we were given a checklist at the time we filed. Could you imagine the difference it would make in our willingness to pay and our attitudes about taxes in general? We would then be a lot closer to having the democracy we've been told we have. This would also ensure that people paid much closer attention to what their government is doing and offering to its people. The people would become part of the government, as was perhaps the original plan.

CHAPTER 18

How to Change the World

The economic catastrophe of the present time has brought about
a condition of mass terror, and the more sensitive the individual, the more he will react to this
state of mind. Fear of the future is therefore a distressing blend of instinctual memory and
anticipatory imagination, and few there are who escape this menace. Worry and anxiety are
the lot of every man and cannot and will not be offset and overcome by any lesser factor than
the soul itself.
—ALICE BAILEY

Many of us wish we could change the world, yet the world seems so big and troubled, there is just so much pain, strife, and suffering everywhere. The more we watch the news, the more the world seems to be such a mess. This continues to add onto our own stress and emotional pain levels. For those that don't watch the news, they get enough of an earful from others in their lives who do.

So then how as conscious manifesters of our own reality, and as empathic, compassionate people with a built-in desire to ease others' suffering, do we manifest for the whole world? Can we really do this on a larger, global scale? After all, if world peace were as simple as holding the image of a peaceful world in our minds, wouldn't it have already been achieved by all the prayers and meditators of the world?

Unfortunately, this is not so easy. Part of the problem is that different parties have different wants, needs, agendas, visions, approaches, plans and ways of implementing these. If everyone desired the same thing, many problems would be resolved very quickly.

Right now, at the time of this writing, people *seem* more divided than ever. Whether or not that is truly the case can only be resolved by historians. Personally, I don't think that people are more divided than at other times, it's just presently these differences are becoming more polarized, partially by design by those driving the narrative that want us to believe all issues can be neatly divided into one political party or another. As an optimist, I'd like to think that as we become conscious of this polarization and decide we aren't going to let ourselves be defined or hedged in by labels that oversimplify the issues into soundbites and slogans, we will move away from them. Still, until we solve these differences and get refocused, we are like a married couple who individually is very adept at manifesting, but together are pulling in totally opposite directions. If we keep pulling, something is going to break – either the individuals, or the relationship. The only way they are going to manage to get along and co-create is if they can find common ground, and give each other enough leeway and support to go out and create what as individual souls they need to do at that time. This will allow them at a future date to come back together with greater cohesiveness.

The World Is Not the Same as Our Perceptions of the World

Part of our challenge as humans is that our minds, through that which we call our imagination, has a capacity to move faster than the speed of light from the macro to the micro. The macro gives us a bird's eye view of the entire planet with its diminishing ozone layer to an entire region of the world at or on the brink of war, to a whole population of displaced people without a country to call home, to a region of land consumed by fire. Moving to a mid-level view we think of school shooters; inner city elementary schools filled with asbestos; the rural high school marching band program without a budget for new uniforms; our friend's messed up family she can't set boundaries with; and the essential food or toilet paper missing from the grocery store shelves. Moving to the micro level we are reminded of the water bill sitting on the counter; the car that won't start; the chip in our favorite glass or the one on someone's shoulder; the crumbs left on the counter, etc., etc., etc.

In saying our imaginations take on this dizzying journey from macro to micro, and back and forth, is not to in any way suggest that these larger issues are imaginary, or that they won't ultimately touch our own lives in more of a direct way. As of this present writing (2020) my own home, now on a river leading to the ocean in Oregon is under evacuation orders due to four fires burning nearby, with landslides blocking the narrow roads in most directions. Not a problem though – given we are presently in the middle of a world-wide pandemic with no end in sight, it's not like we were planning on going out anyway. Meanwhile my friends on the east coast are under tornado watch and relatives in Florida are in the path of a hurricane. The list goes on and on!

The way to deal with all of this, both to reduce stress levels and to figure out the first place to start and what to focus on, is to bring your viewpoint back to the micro, to your own personal space.

Ask yourself: What is the condition of myself, and my body and my immediate environment that my body is located in right now? Is my body OK, safe, comfortable, pain free? If not, what steps can I take to help it. How are things in the room I'm sitting in? Does anything need to be adjusted? How about my house? How about the yard? These are the things that we are both in control of (to some degree) and that need our attending to. You can see from this discussion we aren't even talking about anything metaphysical or energetic, but just mentally how to start figuring out what is yours. What is really under your control? Tackle that first before moving on to larger issues.

Our friend complaining about her crazy family or her tumultuous relationship with her spouse is not something within our control. We can listen to her and give her some advice. However, if she has discussed the same issues with us more than a few times and hasn't made any adjustments, then continued conversations are going to be nothing more than an energy drain for us, even if they make her feel better. Anytime we are faced with another person's problems that are out of our control (because it's not like they are going to allow us to do what we think is best for them) we are at risk of getting depleted and taking on someone else's pain. This does not solve their own long term; it just makes them feel better in the moment. Meanwhile as we do this with friend after friend, relative after relative, we start to move away from our own center, drop in mood, energy level, and wake up one day wondering why we are just not feeling so good anymore.

It is never true that others don't have a choice to make some kind of change to their situation. It is true though that in their thinking they don't realize they have choices and options. How to handle this and still keep them as a friend? Perhaps tell them you are going to be busy for a while, hand them this book and say you'll have another conversation with them after they have read it and started doing the exercises.

Watching news on TV or reading about the news on the internet can have the same effect as a friend continuously complaining about the same thing without taking actions to change their situation. There is nothing wrong with getting the news, many of us like to stay informed, and are very interested in politics and current events. However, one of the things we are seeing in recent times is that the news anchors themselves are dumping on the viewers – they are stressed and upset, and they are choosing to report on and rehash every little word (whether from Twitter, interviews or press conferences) made by our governmental leaders. This isn't to suggest they don't have a right to be upset by what was stated, or that they are incorrect when they report that injustice, dishonesty, ignorance, or foolishness has just run amuck. However, if someone in the media spotlight says something dumb or mean or insensitive and then someone else chooses to keep repeating it over and over and over, the one repeating the statement is a big part of the problem, as are those sitting there listening to them (guilty as charged!).

Often when you bring things back to the question of *what am I dealing with in the moment?* You'll find things actually are just fine for you in the moment. You have enough to eat, today. You have enough clothes, today. The flowers are still blooming, the birds are still chirping… today. You've got to start there because what's near you in the physical is the only reality in the present moment. Whatever you are stressing about, even within your own possible future, is only imagined until your body arrives there.

This was the case for me at the time I first drafted this chapter around 2007. We were in the middle of a gas shortage crisis, and there was talk everywhere about the impending doom about this. I was getting all stressed out myself until one summer evening I pulled into a gas station. While pumping the gas I was aware of how tense and upset I felt about the idea that we might run out of gas, or that the cost might get so high we wouldn't be able to afford to even drive to work. I became aware of how all tangled up I was in my thoughts about what the solution to all of this might be. That's when I had an epiphany: I looked down at my hands and saw the gas nozzle in it and I realized "I'm fine. In this very moment, I'm actually more than fine. There is plenty of gas here, and if it's not here in a few days I'll deal with it then." I went to pay and was overjoyed by the thought that unlike days in the past where my twin sister and I shared a car and we often only had a few dollars between us for the gas tank (so we were always running out of gas) now pouring $45 into the tank was not even something I barely had to think about anymore.

Now over a decade later, as I redraft this chapter once again (writing about *How to Change the World* is not easy, especially when the world keeps changing) we are actually in a situation with the current pandemic and stay home orders that there is now an overabundance of gas.

There is so much gas that our world leaders and gas company producers presently are stressing about where to store it all! Imagine, citizens too are then getting stressed over this "problem" being discussed in the news – a problem that has now for them as individuals at least brought the prices closer to what they were in the 1980s.

In fact, the prices are lower right now in 2020 than they were in 2007 when I stood in front of the pump stressing about how bad things might get. Meanwhile I've moved to Oregon where they don't let you pump your own gas per law, which means now I get to pull up at a station, stay in my car, and after the nice guy or girl pumps my gas (at no additional charge) they often give me a piece of candy.

Once one is good in their own space, one is much better equipped and prepared to move to the larger problems of the world. Still, rather than trying to figure out how to solve the entire problem, one might ask what is simply the first aspect to the problem I could take on?

The first step often will involve more research, investigations, and self-education. You may or may not possess the know-how or skills yet to do all you'd like to in this area. Any ongoing issue that you've been hearing about for years on the news is ongoing precisely because of the level of complexity involved. All controversies are controversies because there is some degree of truth on both or all sides. This means you really want to make sure you are fully informed from all angles before spending extra time and energy.

For example, if you are concerned about the condition of our oceans, you would want to start reading published research articles about this from a variety of sources. Ultimately, you may decide the way you could be most effective in this area would be getting a more formal education in marine biology, where you can hook up with other researchers and research opportunities and get the credentials, knowledge, and tools that will be most useful to achieve your goals. So you can start to take steps towards exploring where and how you might go for this degree, but meanwhile you can start educating yourself through watching videos, and you could call up organizations already devoted to these topics and ask how you might be able to volunteer right now. Others have already put a lot of thought into what is needed, and instituted actions in that direction, so let them for starters tell you what they need help with and begin there.

You can't eat an entire pie, or cake, or steak in one gulp. That would be silly to try, even if you were very hungry. In the same way, you can't tackle any problem in its entirety. It is one bite at a time. If there are many other mouths biting with you though the whole thing will be tackled in no time and all. If it's just you, with no other mouths in sight, well maybe part of your activities will be to find those as well.

Then you can use the power of intention and visualization and all the exercises in this book to help you create what you need as you go along to making a difference. This gets back to our theme that manifesting does not simply involve sitting in an armchair and visualizing yourself and the world into a new state of being. You've also, in conjunction with these activities, have got to make use of your logic, your body, and your actions. These in concert with your energy-mind tools is what will allow you to do what you are here to do.

These suggestions are not earth shattering in their depth of insight, but they should help to sort out the enormity of it all.

Once again, as has been mentioned throughout this book, a healthy dose of patience and faith is needed. It might take a very short time to put an idea into action, but it often takes a while to really see the effects, especially when trying to do things like start new organizations, businesses, social movements, etc.

The other suggestion I'd make is to decide if you are going to be a leader in whatever area you choose to turn your energies to, or support a leader. The world needs both of these. The leader role is the harder path. People are going to resist change, they are going to question you, contradict you, put you down. You have to be willing to endure all of that and be open to adversity. Some of those same people who oppose you could then turn out to be your greatest allies later –if you can learn from their criticism, keep forgiving them, and give them the same room to make mistakes that you need afforded to you.

Also, ask yourself if you are doing more conversing than acting when it comes to attempting to make a difference in the world. How much time are you spending on social media? Are your activities on social media really and truly productive? If you provide information for others about a topic important to you, do you post it and then move on to other productive activities, or do you spend more hours checking back to see the comments, and then get sucked into ongoing debates and arguments that leave you exhausted, irritated, and hopeless? If this pretty much sums up your daily existence, then try to get into the habit of posting, if you are inclined to do so, and then immediately signing off. Allow for others to have their opinions, as ignorant as they may seem. If you can just get off social media for a while altogether, you'll find you have a lot more time for productive action. Just remember, when others argue with you that doesn't mean they didn't hear you. It doesn't mean they won't start to think about something you shared, even if it's just a kernel of what you said, and eventually come up with a new way of thinking or being. Let that seed start to bud, without having to beat your point into others who probably didn't even carefully read what you wrote to begin with. You can't control what they do with your thoughts or your words –it's about expressing what you are drawn to express, deal out the cards to the best of your abilities, and then let them fall where they may.

If you are someone who prefers to remain on the sidelines, in the shadows, or just don't like to speak up, but believe in the work others are doing, then do what you can to support them. There is no reason you have to go out and do work yourself to save the ocean. But if you know a marine biologist who is doing good work, or even a college student studying this topic, then go bake them a pie or some meals to put in the freezer for when they are working late into the night; offer to babysit their kids; do an oil change on their car; pay their tuition for a semester, or just give them some cash. Send them a simple "thank you" card for their present contributions, or a vote of confidence regarding the contributions you are sure they will make in the future. This may be just the thing that keeps them going long enough to make an important discovery that eventually will save the sharks, the whales, the coral, and maybe, just maybe, the world.

Meditation – Reading and Healing Your Relationship with the World

Close your eyes. Create a reading screen within your mind's eye.

Visualize two symbols of flowers, just white or neutral color. The one on the left is you. Drop your name into it and notice how it changes, and what it looks like.

Now let the flower on the right represent the whole world. Visualize the words "whole world" and drop them into that flower. Notice what it looks like as well. What is the color of your flower? What is the color of the world's flower? Ask to see the relationship between the two. What happens?

Now continue to look at the two flowers (you may need to keep re-visualizing them, that's fine). Ask to see how much of your life force/healing energy is busy healing the world. Watch what happens. How much of the outside world's energy is impacting your flower?

If anything looks off balance (too much of the world's energy is with you or too much of your energy with the world), then do the following:

Give your flower and the world's flower a grounding cord. Do this by planting the stems into the ground. Visualize any extra energy releasing down the stems of each flower.

Then visualize the energies rebalancing so you have your own energy, the world has its own, and see a space in between. This may seem odd, as it is impossible to totally separate your energy from the world's, since you live in it, are part of it, and need it as well as it needs you, but what we are doing here is separating out that which is not needed, the excess.

You can then connect with a light the two flowers to a higher power above such as God, and see a healing light flowing through them both. Ask to see the color of the healing light that is ideal for both you and the world and your relationship in between. Run this through the flowers, in between the flowers, and down the grounding cords.

Next ask yourself what you want for yourself. Create a symbol that represents this thing and drop it into your flower. Ask what color represents the quality you'd like to experience this in and wash it through the flower. Repeat this with the flower representing the world. What wish do you have for the world as a whole? Go ahead, you have the right to your wishes. Ask your imagination to give you a symbol that represents your wish, and drop that into the world flower. Notice if anything happens or changes. Also, what color of energy would be most healing for the world right now and/or facilitate your wish? Notice what happens.

As a final step, release the flower up to God, or the source of the light, and make the statement that you are asking for continued help with your wishes, as well as with rebalancing your desire to heal the world in a way that serves you and all your goals and desires, while not consuming you.

When finished, open your eyes, stretch and now feel free to journal about your impressions and experiences during the exercise. Get out some colored pens or markers or paints and sketch your symbols and any images that came to you during the exercises that you can look back on later, or even hang on your wall when you are in need of further inspiration. While your notes can include all that you experienced during this exercise (some of this might even be precognitive information that you'd want a record of), it might be best to only put down on paper the images you'd like to see manifest for yourself and the world.

Enjoy. Peace Out.

Bibliography

Blavatsky, H. P. (Helena Petrovna). *The Secret Doctrine*. Wheaton, IL: Quest Books, 1993.

Bloom, Howard. *Global Brain: The Evolution of Mass Mind from the Big Bang to the 21st Century*. New York: Wiley, 2000.

Bloom, Howard. *Reinventing Capitalism: Putting Soul in the Machine*. (Unpublished material.) See http://www.howardbloom.net/reinventing_capitalism/ (accessed 4 February 2009). Page 309.

Byrne, Rhonda. *The Secret*. New York: Atria Books/Beyond Words, 2006.

Calaprice, Alice, ed. *The New Quotable Einstein*. Princeton, NJ: Princeton University Press, 2005.

Cayce, Edgar. *The Lost Memoirs of Edgar Cayce*. Virginia Beach, VA: A. R. E. Press, 1997.

Choquette, Sonia. *Your Heart's Desire: Instructions for Creating the Life You Really Want*. New York: Three Rivers Press, 1997.

Dash, Eric, and Andrew Ross Sorkin. "Government Seizes WaMu and Sells Some Assets." New York Times, September 26, 2008, p. A1.

Dyer, Wayne. *You'll See It When You Believe It: The Way to Your Personal Transformation*. New York: Harper Paperbacks, 2001.

Gawain, Shakti. *Living in the Light: A Guide to Personal and Planetary Transformation*. Novato, CA: New World Library, 1998.

Gilbert, Elizabeth. *Eat, Pray, Love: One Woman's Search for Everything Across Italy, India and Indonesia*. New York: Penguin, 2007.

Hicks, Esther, Jerry Hicks, and Abraham (spirit). *Ask and It Is Given: Learning to Manifest Your Desires*. Carlsbad, CA: Hay House, 2004.

Icke, David. *And the Truth Shall Set You Free*. Ryde, UK: David Icke Books, 2004.

Katz, Debra Lynne. *You Are Psychic: The Art of Clairvoyant Reading and Healing*. Santa Barbara, CA: Living Dreams Press, 2015.

Katz, Debra Lynne. *Extraordinary Psychic: Proven Techniques to Master Your Natural Psychic Abilities*. Santa Barbara, CA: Living Dreams Press, 2015

Klein, Alec. "Credit Raters' Power Leads to Abuses, Some Borrowers Say." Washington Post, November 24, 2004, p. A1.

McTaggart, Lynne. *The Intention Experiment: Using Your Thoughts to Change Your Life and the World.* New York: Free Press, 2008.

Monroe, Robert A. *Journeys Out of the Body.* New York: Doubleday, 1991.

Murphy, Joseph. *The Power of Your Subconscious Mind.* Revised and expanded edition. Paramus, NJ: Reward Books, 2000.

Radin, Dean. *The Conscious Universe: The Scientific Truth of Psychic Phenomena.* New York: HarperEdge, 1997.

Radin, Dean. *Entangled Minds: Extrasensory Experiences in a Quantum Reality.* New York: Paraview Pocket Books, 2006.

Roberts, Jane, and Seth (spirit). *The Nature of Personal Reality: Specific, Practical Techniques for Solving Everyday Problems and Enriching the Life You Know.* San Rafael, CA: New World Library, 1994.

Roberts, Jane, and Seth (spirit). *Seth Speaks: The Eternal Validity of the Soul.* San Rafael, CA: New World Library, 1994.

Roman, Sanaya, and Duane Packer. *Creating Money: Attracting Abundance*, second edition. Tiburon, CA: H J Kramer/New World Library, 2008.

Shinn, Florence Scovel. *The Wisdom of Florence Scovel Shinn.* New York: Simon & Schuster, 1989.

Spalding, Baird T. *Life and Teaching of the Masters of the Far East* (Volumes 1 and 2). Marina del Rey, CA: DeVorss, 1978.

Strelkoff, Lyena. "Caterpillar Soup," a one-woman-show script (unpublished).

Tamura, Michael J. *You Are the Answer: Discovering and Fulfilling Your Soul's Purpose.* Woodbury, MN: Llewellyn, 2007.

Toffler, Alvin. *The Third Wave.* New York: Bantam/William Morrow, 1980.

Tolle, Eckhart. *A New Earth: Awakening to Your Life's Purpose.* New York: Dutton, 2005.

Tolle, Eckhart. *The Power of Now: A Guide to Spiritual Enlightenment.* Novato, CA: New World Library, 2004.

Walker, Alice. *Possessing the Secret of Joy.* New York: Washington Square Press, 1997.

Walsch, Neale Donald. *Conversations with God: An Uncommon Dialogue.* New York: Putnam, 1996.

Woolf, Virginia. *A Room of One's Own.* New York: Harcourt, 1991.

Zinn, Howard. *A People's History of the United States.* New edition. New York: Harper Collins, 2003.

Glossary

Affirmation: A statement that declares an intention or condition for a desirable outcome. Affirmations are used on a conscious level to reprogram subconscious or limited beliefs.

Astral projection or astral travel: The ability of one's spirit to leave the body and travel on the astral plane or in other dimensions. This is also referred to as an "out-of-body experience." It can be done with or without awareness, and to various degrees. It can occur spontaneously through intention.

Atheism: A lack of belief in the spiritual, including God, psychic phenomena, or the human soul.

Aura: The energetic field surrounding every living organism, which contains information about the organism and energies affecting it. The aura can be thought of as the organism's spirit that extends outward from the body.

Awareness: Having knowledge through focused attention.

Caterpillar soup: A term created by Lyena Strelkoff that describes the uneasy period a person goes through in the process of transformation, when they have changed from one state of being but have not yet reached a state that allows them to form a new definition of themselves. This is also referred to as an intensive growth period and can lead to what mystics refer to as the dark night of the soul.

Chakras: Sanskrit word for "spinning wheels," chakras are energy centers that correspond to specific parts of the human body and that regulate the body's overall functioning.

Channeling: A psychic ability in which a person receives and communicates information coming directly from a source outside themselves.

Clairaudience: A psychic ability in which information inaudible to human ears is heard inside one's mind.

Clairsentience: A psychic ability in which information is received through touch or on a physical body level.

Clairvoyance: A psychic ability located within one's third eye, or sixth chakra, that involves accessing information in the form of visions, images, and pictures.

Clairvoyant healing: An act in which visualization is utilized to eliminate or transmute emotional or physical pain or negative energies, and restore one to a healthier state.

Clairvoyant reading: An act in which information in the form of mental images, visions, and pictures is accessed.

Conscious creation: Creating one's own existence with purpose and awareness, and by harnessing the power of one's mind and feeling.

Control freak: A person who needs to understand or determine every element in life and interferes with the natural course of things, or who expends energy trying to control that which is out of his or her control. A control freak is one who attempts to circumvent another's will through the control freak's own interpretation of it.

Cosmic energy: Energy that originates from the air, sun, atmosphere, the spiritual realm, or God.

Creating/creation: To bring into being.

Creative energy: An energy that begins in the reproductive area of the body that can create any project. The more this energy is running, the more free we are to come up with new ideas and ways of being, and the more passion for life we have.

Earth energy: Energy that originates from within the earth. It is naturally running through each of our bodies all the time, assisting us with our connection to the planet and our body.

Energy: Life force; the essence of all things physical and nonphysical. Matter, spirit, atoms, thoughts, emotions, and pain are all energy.

Enlightenment: A state in which a person has become actualized, has accumulated a certain level of wisdom; when a person's body, mind, and spirit are fully integrated and the person's being holds more lightness than darkness.

Excuse: A justification that is either untrue or disguises one's true feelings or thoughts in order to deflect responsibility from oneself.

Expectation: A predetermined set of ideas of how an event will unfold or how another person or oneself should behave.

Extrasensory perception: Perceiving information through means other than the five physical senses.

Feminine or female energy: A polarized energy that is receptive, passive, open, and intuitive. It is guided, shaped, or manipulated by the masculine aspect.

Genie within, the: A term for the creative force within oneself that can be activated, strengthened, and utilized in order to achieve one's goals and manifest one's dreams.

Grounding cord: An energetic connection securing an object or a person to the earth. Foreign energies can be released through this cord through conscious intent and visualization.

Growth period: An intense period of personal transformation during which one's beliefs, thoughts, perceptions, and self-image are altered. This can result in a temporary period of emotional or cognitive turbulence.

Havingness: The extent to which a person can allow himself or herself to have abundance.

Imagination: The act or power of creating an image or ideas in the mind.

Intention: Focus with a desired outcome.

Intuition: The act of listening and responding to one's feelings or thoughts, the cause of which cannot easily be explained by logical processes. This is a word that is often used in place of the term psychic ability, because intuition describes a common experience among the mainstream population and is therefore generally found more acceptable by those who have a resistance to the term psychic ability, even though they essentially mean the same thing.

Knowingness: A psychic ability located in the seventh, or crown, chakra, in which a person instantaneously knows information in the form of a thought, without having to go through logical steps to gain that information.

Law: A set of rules that describes but does not explain an occurrence in nature.

Law of attraction: The force, or invisible power, by which a body (your body) draws anything to itself while resisting separation from that same thing. This force is created through manipulation of one's own thoughts and emotions.

Library of symbols: A collection of symbolic images, utilized by those who work with clairvoyance or visualization in order to interpret clairvoyant information.

Limit: The point at which a person is limited within his or her imagination. The threshold of what a person allows himself or herself to have, which is dictated by the person's belief system and feelings of deservedness. The point at which a person feels he or she can or should not go any further in allowing himself or herself to experience something. Limits can easily be surpassed once the person becomes aware of the limits or has an experience that is outside the range of the limit.

Manifestation: A form in which a being manifests itself or is thought to manifest itself, especially the material or bodily form of a spirit.

Manifesting: The creative act of transforming a thought into the material plane.

Martyr complex: A self-defeating set of beliefs and behaviors that cause people to gain satisfaction and elevated self-esteem by sacrificing their own pleasure and needs for the sake of others.

Masculine or male energy: A polarized energy or quality that is goal-driven and oriented toward action and physical activity. It is focused outside itself, and is controlling, direct, forceful and attempts to direct its feminine counterpart.

Mass consciousness: A phenomenon that occurs among groups of people, in which energies merge and people adopt each other's beliefs, thoughts, and emotions—sometimes at the expense of their individual beliefs and codes of ethics.

Materialize: To appear suddenly, to bring a thought into being on the material level.

Meditation: Turning attention inward to bring one's mind to a state of stillness, where subtler energies and information can be experienced.

Neutrality: Being neutral; maintaining a state of emotional and cognitive balance that is not invested in a particular outcome.

Non-attachment: Having no emotional investment in an object or an outcome of a situation.

Obstacle: Something usually perceived to be standing in the way or inhibiting a goal or forward movement.

Omnipresent: Being everywhere all at once.

Omniscient: All knowing.

Precognition: Knowing that something is going to happen before it happens.

Proclamation: A message that is declared with certainty and unwavering confidence.

Programming: Beliefs, thoughts, ethics, information, feelings, or perceptions that are passed from one person to another and that may or may not be in harmony with the recipient's own spiritual goals, information, or way of being.

Projection: Seeing one's own qualities in someone else, often unconsciously; assigning particular attributes to another that really belong to oneself.

Psychic experience: A supernatural experience in which information is sent or received through means other than the five senses.

Psychic tools: Visualization techniques that affect and influence energy that can be utilized for intuitive reading and healing and to enhance the qualities of one's life.

Resistance: An energy or mental attitude that insists something should be other than it is. This attitude causes the one who holds it stress, anxiety, and negative thinking.

Running energy: The act of visualizing the movement of energy, in the form of light, color, or water, through one's body, aura, or surroundings in order to facilitate the release of foreign or unhealthy energies and/or to replenish oneself with a higher vibrational frequency.

Self-energization: Calling one's life force to one self.

Self-esteem: The ability and extent to which a person cherishes oneself.

Skepticism: A closed state of mind in which one doubts or questions things, sometimes to the point where these doubts obscure the truth.

Soul mate: A spirit with whom one has a deep affinity and connection, and with whom one reconnects throughout many incarnations. This spirit may currently be in the form of another person, an animal, or a nonphysical entity, and these forms may change from one incarnation to the next.

Spirit: The essence of a living being.

Spiritual alchemy: Transforming one form of matter or one experience into another by utilizing one's full range of spiritual abilities. This also includes manifesting something that exists only on the mental or spiritual plane onto the physical plane.

Spiritual path: A course that one's spirit is destined to follow in order to gain certain life experiences while in the physical body.

Spirituality: The act of acknowledging and paying attention to one's own spirit and the spirits of others.

Subconscious mind: Existing or operating in the mind beneath or beyond conscious awareness.

Supernatural: Beyond the physical senses.

Symbol: An object or sign that represents another object, idea, person, or quality.

Third eye: The center of one's clairvoyance. The third eye corresponds with the sixth chakra and is located behind the forehead, slightly above and between the physical eyes.

Transformation: To effect change. To move from one state of being to another, often denoting progress.

Unconscious: That which lies hidden from awareness of one's own mind or actions.

Validation: To confirm one's value, importance or point of view.

Vibrational frequency: The rate at which the atoms and sub particles of a being or object vibrate. The higher this frequency is, the closer it is to the frequency of light. It is within this frequency that the law of attraction can operate most efficiently. This state also facilitates a state of well-being.

Visualization: The act of calling forth images, visions, and pictures into one's mind.

THE COMPLETE CLAIRVOYANT

A TRILOGY

BY DEBRA LYNNE KATZ

3 BOOKS IN ONE!

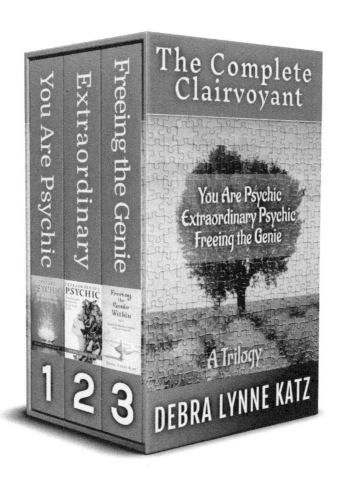

BOOK I - YOU ARE PSYCHIC:
THE ART OF CLAIROVYANT READING & HEALING

BOOK 2 - EXTRAORDINARY PSYCHIC:
PROVEN TECHNIQUES TO MASTER
YOUR NATURAL INTUITIVE ABILITIES

BOOK 3 - FREEING THE GENIE WITHIN:
MANIFESTING ABUNDANCE, CREATIVITY
& SUCCESS IN YOUR LIFE

Published by ISC Publishing House, a division of the International School of Clairvoyance.
Copywrite held by Debra Lynne Katz 2020

You Are Psychic:
The Art of Clairvoyant Reading & Healing

This first work has sold hundreds of thousand copies in the United States and worldwide, mostly through word of mouth. It has been translated into several different languages and continues to be a favorite choice as an invaluable guide offering clear and engaging instruction on developing your natural intuitive gifts of clairvoyance, clairaudience, and telepathy.

You are Psychic was one of the first books in modern times to focus almost exclusively on clairvoyance, the specific psychic ability that allows you to see, experience and manipulate energy via images, pictures, and colors. It gives you the step by step instructors and techniques so you can start to really practice on your own, or add to your present practice in new and enhanced ways.

This book is those already in the helping profession or wishing to be – it is ideal for therapists, counselors, life coaches, energy healers, massage therapists, medical doctors, as it compliments all existing practices. It is a must read for anyone thinking about moving from intuitive enthusiast to professional.

It was one of the first and most comprehensive psychic development books that discusses the business of spirituality; psychic ethics; dealing with the stressors of being psychic in the mainstream world; how to do relationship readings; and how to read with other psychics.

Just reading the book is a healing experience – you may actually feel a physical shift or experience your energy body as you read the book, and you most certainly will when you practice the exercises

It teaches you to control your abilities whenever you desire, and that teaches you to do readings on others.

It offers a clear understanding of how you are already being psychic and healing others without awareness and what you can do to reverse the effects of this unconscious use of our abilities.

This book is being used as text books in many schools that teach metaphysics, parapsychology and the spiritual arts.

In this inspirational first book, Debra Lynne Katz demonstrates how these skills can be used with clients on a professional level or in real life settings, such as you home, or workplace - even in your own relationships.

"One of the great incidental benefits of developing your innate psychic abilities is the chance to grow internally, spiritually and emotionally - When we look at the lives and energies of others, we are frequently confronted with images of our own spirit, our own opportunities for growth and enlightenment." - Debra Lynne Katz, 2004

Extraordinary Psychic: Proven Techniques to Master Your Natural Psychic Abilities

Released originally in 2008 by Llewellyn Publishing, Extraordinary Psychic is Debra's brilliant follow-up to You Are Psychic. This second book successfully details actual techniques, meditations and exercises that will allow beginners to advanced students explore their psychic abilities. It also serves by creating a framework and practice for professional psychics to fine-tune their intuitive skills.

This is a warm and practical guide offers true professional stories, and a wealth of fun exercises so that you can experience successful clairvoyant readings for yourself.

Topics such as communicating with one's guides, protecting oneself from harmful or troublesome entities, advanced techniques and concepts in healing, relationship healings, remote viewing and troubleshooting various challenges that come up when one is practicing readings are just a few topics of the many that are covered.

Professional psychic Debra Lynne Katz, author of the popular introductory guide You Are Psychic, offers clear and engaging instruction on developing your natural intuitive gifts of clairvoyance, clairsentience, clairaudience, and telepathy. She demonstrates how these skills can be used with clients on a professional level or in real-life settings, such as your home or workplace – even in your own relationships.

Become the intuitive, extraordinary psychic you truly are

Heal yourself and others

View the past, present, and future*

Manifest goals for peace, prosperity, and love

Understand the difference between clairvoyant reading and Remote Viewing

Communicate with your spirit guides and loved ones in spirit

Learn how to perform psychic readings professionally or just for fun

Freeing the Genie Within:
Manifesting Abundance, Creativity &
Success in Your Life

For anyone who has been disappointed in the many books which claim to tell you how to use "The Secret," this book has it all. The fact is, manifesting what we want in life requires a number of things, including clearing away negative thoughts and beliefs, becoming focused and clear about what we want, using visualization, having patience, letting go of the past, among others.

Freeing the Genie is not just an innovative book, but a traveling companion to help you overcome obstacles on your spiritual path. It offers numerous techniques and meditations to help you raise your frequency, get unstuck, and move forward with your goals. It helps empower readers to not only understand how powerful they really are, but to experience it. Freeing the Genie Within teaches readers how to transform energy and matter into a higher form for the purposes of personal growth and abundance. Examples of this transmutation include: Turning three dollars into $30,000; replacing an abusive relationship with a loving partnership; transmuting a chaotic, stressful life into a peaceful one; transforming negative thoughts or toxin spewing emotions into happy ones. This isn't just another "let's think positive, say a few affirmations and everything will come to you" book. Rather, this helps to answer the difficult question that many who have been on the path for years have been struggling with, which is: "Why does positive thinking work sometimes, but not others?".

To Learn more about Debra Lynne Katz and the International School of Clairvoyance
visit www.debrakatz.com.

FURTHER TRAINING OPPORTUNITIES

Interested in further instruction and practice?

Visit the International School of Clairvoyance website at

www.debrakatz.com.

APPRECIATE YOU LEAVING A REVIEW ON AMAZON!

Debra would very much appreciate it if you found this book to be useful in

any way, if you'd be willing to write a review on Amazon.

Made in the USA
Las Vegas, NV
11 January 2024

84199500R00302